MODERN CORPORATE FINANCE

THEORY AND PRACTICE

DONALD R. CHAMBERS
Lafayette College

NELSON J. LACEY
University of Massachusetts

HarperCollins*CollegePublishers*

To our families, with love

Acquisitions Editor: Kirsten D. Sandberg
Developmental Editor: Elaine Silverstein
Project Coordination and Text Design: Lachina Publishing Services, Inc.
Cover Design: Kay Petronio
Cover Illustration: Rebecca Rüegger
Production: Jeffrey Taub
Compositor: GTS Graphics
Printer and Binder: R. R. Donnelley & Sons Company
Cover Printer: The Lehigh Press, Inc.

MODERN CORPORATE FINANCE: THEORY AND PRACTICE

Library of Congress Cataloging-in-Publication Data

Chambers, Donald R.
    Modern corporate finance : theory and practice / Donald R.
Chambers, Nelson J. Lacey.
        p.   cm.
    Includes bibliographical references and index.
    ISBN 0-06-501004-3
    1. Corporations—Finance.   I. Lacey, Nelson J.   II. Title.
HG4026.C447   1993
658. 15—dc20

93-5470
CIP

93 94 95 96 9 8 7 6 5 4 3 2 1

Brief Contents

The Brief Contents above is set up to show how the supplementary material presented in Chapters 13 through 19 can be interwoven most effectively with the core material of Chapters 1 through 12. For instance, Chapter 13 on corporate ethics can be covered after Chapter 2, and Chapter 14 on cash flow estimation is a direct extension of Chapter 6.

Detailed Contents

Preface

The story of Apple Computer and its rise to success is unmatched in the industry. From the advent of the Apple I in a garage in Santa Clara, California, in 1976 to the introduction of the highly sophisticated Macintosh line, Apple has grown to become the second-largest maker of personal computers in the world. But how was Apple able to achieve this success in a highly competitive industry? The answer is that it was able to fill a significant need in the market—a user-friendly personal computer.

It is in this spirit that we introduce *Modern Corporate Finance: Theory and Practice*. Like Apple Computer, which designed a modern product from scratch, our objective is to wipe the slate clean and write a user-friendly corporate finance text. Its fresh approach to learning corporate finance, innovative chapter structure, simple pedagogy, and unique features such as Windows and Workshops work together to produce a distinctive text.

The modernist movement in finance is based on systematic methodology with an emphasis on deductive reasoning and empirical validation. While this movement has, without question, expanded the frontiers of knowledge in finance, instructors have lacked a framework from which to teach these concepts at the introductory level. To date, finance texts based on the modernist approach have been written for advanced undergraduate courses and for graduate courses. Thus, our text fills an important void in the market—a modernist book written for the introductory level of study.

THE TEXT AND ITS FEATURES

The text contains a number of distinctive features. First, it focuses on the most essential points of finance theory and reinforces these points with hands-on applications.

Second, the text's structure provides maximum flexibility and maximum assistance to instructors. For example, the content is divided into two main parts—core material and supplemental material—allowing instructors to follow their own course of pedagogy.

This contrasts with other corporate finance texts whose 25 to 30 chapters organized under eight to ten broad headings leave the instructor with the arduous task of sorting through what is relevant and what is extraneous to meeting course objectives. Third, each chapter contains two demonstration problems that take the student step-by-step to the solution, review questions, extensive problem sets, and discussion questions to be used both inside and outside the classroom.

Chapter Organization

The twelve chapters that make up the text's core material are grouped into four modules, each comprising three chapters. Module 1 introduces modern corporate finance. Modules 2 and 3 cover the firm's investment decision. Module 4 covers the firm's financing decision.

Module 1 is entitled "Foundations of Finance." Chapter 1 provides a framework from which to view the corporation and its objectives. Chapter 2 represents a new and innovative chapter that derives, through economic principles, a set of decision rules for corporate managers making decisions for shareholders. Chapter 3 highlights ownership through the corporation and introduces contracting and agency relationships.

Module 2 is concerned with "Valuation." Chapter 4 covers the basics of the time value of money for both single cash flows and annuities. Chapter 5 examines the valuation of financial securities. Chapter 6 draws an important distinction between financial assets and real assets, discusses how value can be created, and introduces the various techniques of capital budgeting.

Module 3 covers "Risk." A common theme in Chapters 7 and 8 is the separation of total risk into systematic and unsystematic components, and the use of the capital asset pricing model to "price" systematic risk. Chapter 9 introduces call options and discusses how the firm's equity can be viewed as an option on the firm's assets. The material on options sets the stage for an understanding of bankruptcy and issues of firm financing.

"Firm Financing" is the topic of Module 4. Chapter 10 discusses financing in perfect markets, while Chapter 11 discusses financing in imperfect markets. The dividend decision is the subject of Chapter 12. Taxes and bankruptcy, and their effect on the firm's capital structure and dividend decision, are highlighted throughout this module.

In addition to the four modules of core material, Chapters 13 through 19 offer a menu of special topics from which instructors can rank-order according to their own preferences. For example, for extensive coverage of capital budgeting, Chapter 14, Determining Project Cash Flows, and Chapter 15, Advanced Topics in Capital Budgeting, follow directly from Chapter 6. Chapter 13 on Corporate Ethics can be used to extend the discussion of any chapter beyond Chapter 2. Of course common threads, such as shareholder wealth maximization, the time value of money, and project risk, relate all of the text's 19 chapters. The Brief Contents suggests alternative plans for incorporating the special topics into the core material.

Windows and Workshops

A special feature of the text is the boxed material in "Windows" and "Workshops." Windows provide extra detail related to the chapter material without interrupting the flow of the chapter. They are available to be "opened" and studied at the appropriate time. Workshops present step-by-step financial problem solving. Workshops are used to embed fundamental principles in finance, such as operating leverage and financial leverage, within chapters.

ACKNOWLEDGMENTS

We'd like to thank the following professors who reviewed the manuscript as it was developed:

Eric Amel, Arizona State University
Theodore A. Andersen, University of California, Los Angeles
W. Brian Barrett, University of Miami
K. C. Chan, The Ohio State University
P. R. Chandy, University of North Texas
Jeffrey S. Christensen, Kent State University
David B. Cox, University of Denver
Robert M. Edmondson, Barton College
Thomas H. Eyssell, University of Missouri–St. Louis
Richard J. Fendler, Georgia State University
Manak C. Gupta, Temple University
Delvin D. Hawley, University of Mississippi
John A. Helmuth, Rochester Institute of Technology
Craig G. Johnson, California State University at Hayward
Steve A. Johnson, University of Texas at El Paso
Jarl G. Kallberg, New York University
Dilip D. Kare, University of North Florida
David Loy, Illinois State University
John A. MacDonald, SUNY Albany
James A. Miles, The Pennsylvania State University
Timothy W. Nohr, Oklahoma State University
Larry G. Perry, University of Arkansas

Philip R. Perry, SUNY Buffalo
Ashok J. Robin, Rochester Institute of Technology
John A. Settle, Portland State University
Gary Tallman, Northern Arizona University
Raj Varma, University of Delaware
Allen L. Webster, Bradley University
Thomas S. Zorn, University of Nebraska–Lincoln

We'd also like to thank the following people who helped us get the manuscript to publication: Paula Cousin, Pearl Klein, Lisa Pinto, Kirsten Sandberg, Elaine Silverstein, Kate Steinbacher, Nancy Tenney, and Arianne Weber.

Donald R. Chambers
Nelson J. Lacey

SUPPLEMENTS

Instructor's Manual

Created by Donald R. Chambers and Nelson J. Lacey

This teaching resource makes for a smooth transition from a more traditional to a modernist approach without sacrificing existing course notes, handouts, and practical applications. For each chapter, the guide includes the following features: one-page chapter outlines, designed to photocopy for students or to use as a basis for lectures; answers to all review and discussion questions; and detailed solutions to all problems, also designed for classroom distribution. Given the tremendous pressure to cover ethics throughout the finance curriculum, the authors provide some possible resolutions to dilemmas raised at the end of Chapter 13 on corporate ethics; the suggested outcomes are consistent with the systematic framework presented in the main text for solving such problems.

Adopters should ask their local publisher's representative about other media supplements to the HarperCollins Finance list, available on the basis of timeliness, relevance to core topics in finance, high production quality, interest to students, and added value to classroom presentations.

Testing Materials

Created by Ashok J. Robin, Rochester Institute of Technology
Available in printed and electronic formats
(WordPerfect file and TestMaster files for IBM-compatibles)

Since a test bank and its solutions can often make or break the reputation of a first edition, the test bank author has class-tested many of the items to clarify ambiguities in wording and to double-check the solutions. All of the 700 or so items are consistent with the text and the study guide in the use of terminology and problem-solving methodology. For greater flexibility, the test bank features a mix of concept and application items, including true/false and multiple choice questions, real data where possible from a variety of financial resources, and illustrations as needed.

Instructors can download the TestMaster version of the test bank into *QuizMaster,* an on-line testing program for IBM-compatibles that enables users to conduct timed or untimed exams at computer workstations. Upon completing tests, students can see their scores and view or print a diagnostic report of those topics or objectives requiring more attention. When installed on a local area network, QuizMaster allows instructors to save the scores on disk, print study diagnoses, and monitor progress of students individually or by class section, and by all sections of the course.

Given the assortment of test bank formats, instructors should contact their HarperCollins publisher's representative to find out which will best suit their testing needs.

Study Guide

Created by John A. Helmuth, Rochester Institute of Technology

The following five pages of the Preface showcase Chapter 4, "The Time Value of Money," from the study guide so that potential users can preview this superior study tool before making a purchase decision. The guide itself features a brief table of contents and a few words on studying strategies. Chapter 4 also reviews keystrokes applicable to most financial calculators. All chapters in the study guide contain three major parts that help students focus study time and exam preparation.

The first section is essentially a review of chapter content through the following elements: a paragraph giving key chapter themes; a list of learning goals under the heading "You Should Be Able To" and marked by a pointing finger; notes marked by an envelope icon; boxed key concepts, definitions, and summaries; arrowed warnings about common mistakes in solving problems; screened step-by-step examples with both time line and calculator keystroke solutions; and key equations highlighted and numbered to reinforce formulas in the main text. The second part is a brief, diagnostic self-test with both worked-out and keystroke solutions. The last section of every chapter is a practice test of completion questions, true/false items, and problems. The answers and solutions appear in detail, with both rationales and calculator steps, at the end of the chapter. Sample pages from the study guide follow on pages xx–xxiv.

Each chapter of the study guide provides a brief paragraph overview of key chapter themes and a list of learning goals marked by the pointing finger, as shown below.

CHAPTER 4

THE TIME VALUE OF MONEY

OVERVIEW

This chapter presents the time value of money. It is a **key** chapter for the rest of your course, providing important concepts that are used throughout module II and many other chapters. It is essential to master the topics in this chapter.

The central theme for the time value of money is that *a dollar today is worth more than a dollar tomorrow*. Consider why this is true. If you could choose between receiving one thousand dollars today or receiving one thousand dollars in twenty years, you would take the money today. After all, you could either consume the money now or set it aside to grow. At the current interest rate you would receive more than a thousand dollars in twenty years. Therefore, we say that a dollar today is worth more.

The central analytical techniques of the chapter are learning: (1) **compounding**, which is the process by which money grows at a compound interest rate, and (2) **discounting**, which is the process of taking a future value and finding its **present value** today. Both concepts are central to this and many other chapters in the textbook.

✉ NOTE: The problems in this chapter and later chapters are presented with **financial calculator** methods of solutions.

☞ YOU SHOULD BE ABLE TO:

- Understand the concepts of compounding and discounting.
- Calculate future values.
- Calculate effective annual interest rates.
- Calculate present values.
- Calculate the present value of annuities.
- Calculate the interest rate or the time period in a time value of money problem.

> You should view dollars at different points in time as different commodities or assets rather than as the same asset.

Why is this true? Because a dollar today is worth more than a dollar received tomorrow. The dollar today can be used immediately. The dollar in the future has an opportunity cost associated with waiting to obtain dollars through time.

Arrows warn students about common mistakes made in solving problems, and small envelope icons draw attention to important notes from the study guide author.

where **n** is the number of compound periods, **r** is the interest rate, **PV** is the present value, and **FV** is the future value.

Let's do another example: if you have a present value (PV) of $1 today, which grows at a 10% interest rate (r) annually for 25 years, what is the future value (FV_{25}) at the end of 25 years? Using equation 4.2:

$$FV_{25} = \$1 \ (1.10)^{25} = \$10.83$$

> The **Financial Calculator** Method: financial or business calculators simplify the calculations. Each brand of calculator is somewhat different in terms of the keys, though there are general similarities. This section reviews the keystrokes that are applicable to most financial calculators. Refer to your calculator's instruction manual for specifics.

The future value calculations above are comprised of 4 variables: the present value (PV), the number of future time periods (n), the interest rate (r), and the future value (FV). You need to input three of these variables to solve for the fourth variable.

Example: Re-do the problem above where $1 grows at 10% for 25 years. Solve for the future value. The keystrokes will probably be like this:

Clear the calculator and
Input: 1 and key PV
Input: 10 and key %i
Input: 25 and key n
Then key CPT (which is compute)
Then key FV
The register reads: 10.83 (rounded)

➠ WARNING: The most common mistake with a financial calculator is failing to clear the memory. Consult your calculator's manual.

✉ NOTE: Most calculators have keys PV and FV for present value and future value. The notation may differ for interest rate (r) and time period (n). Often %i is used for interest rate. Also, the order of the keystrokes can differ.

> More frequent compounding: thus far we have assumed that interest was compounded on an annual basis (once a year). However, financial markets and institutions offer interest compounded at a variety of rates: semi-annually, monthly, daily, and so forth.

Equation 4.2 is adjusted for the number of times interest is compounded within the year (m). The adjusted equation reads:

Screened step-by-step examples, with both time line and calculator keystroke solutions where appropriate, walk students through the problem-solving methods introduced by the book. Star icons call out tips for solving problems.

$$FV_n \;=\; PV\left(1 \,+\, \frac{r}{m}\right)^{mn} \tag{4:3}$$

The adjustment requires dividing the interest rate (r) by the number of compounding periods (m). Also, the number of years (n) is multiplied by the compounding periods (m). These adjustments also have to be made for your financial calculator **keystrokes**.

Example: If a present value of $100 grows at 12% for 10 years, with semi-annual compounding, find the future value.

Keystrokes: clear, input 100 Key PV, input 6 Key %i, input 20 Key n
  Then Key CPT, Key FV
The register reads: 320.71

⊠ NOTE: 6 is the input for the interest rate, since semi-annual compounding requires the interest rate (12%) to reflect the compounding periods (m=2), or 12/2. The input n is 20. The number of years (n) is multiplied by the compounding periods (m) per year, or 10 x 2.

Example: If a present value of $100 grows at 12% for 10 years, with monthly compounding, find the future value.

☆ TIP: This is the same problem as above, but the adjustments must reflect 12 compounding periods (m). Thus, input for interest will be 1 (12/12) and the input for n will be 120 (10 x 12).

Keystrokes: Clear, input 100 Key PV, input 1 Key %i, input 120 Key n
  Then Key CPT, Key FV
The register reads: 330.04

⊠ NOTE: The more frequent the compounding periods the greater the future value. There is nearly $10 additional future value in this problem with monthly compounding as compared to semi-annual compounding ($330.04 vs. $320.71). **Why?** The more frequent compounding earns more interest on interest.

Example: If we re-do the above problem with daily compounding, the future value should be even higher.

Keystrokes: Clear, input 100 Key PV, input .03287 key %i, input 3650 Key n
  Then Key CPT, Key FV
The register reads: 331.94

⊠ NOTE: The input value for %i is .03287 (or 12/365) and the input value for n is 3650 (or 365 x 10).

To reinforce notation, all key equations are highlighted and numbered in the Study Guide just as they are in the main book. Boxes capture all core concepts, definitions, and summaries.

The **effective annual** interest rate builds compounding frequency into the quoted interest rate in order to compare quoted rates each with different levels of compounding.

For example, if you have a choice of 5% compounded annually or 4.9% compounded daily, the effective annual interest rate shows the highest effective annual return. The formula for the effective annual interest rate is:

$$\textit{Effective Annual Rate} = \left(1 + \frac{r}{m}\right)^{m} - 1 \tag{4.4}$$

If we are to choose between the 5% annual and 4.9% daily, our solution is:

5% *annually*: $\left(1 + \frac{.05}{1}\right)^{1} - 1 = 0.05$ *Effective Annual Rate*

4.9% *daily*: $\left(1 + \frac{.049}{365}\right)^{365} - 1 = 0.0502$ *Effective Annual Rate*

The daily compounding in this case provides a higher effective annual rate.

✉ NOTE: Most financial calculators provide a keystroke for the effective annual rate.

Quick summary of future value concepts:

---

1. The higher the interest rate, the higher the future value.
2. The longer the time period (n), the higher the future value.
3. The more frequent the compounding period (m), the higher the future value.

Discounting is the process of taking a future value and putting it into present value terms. Finding the present value is like compounding in reverse. In this case, the future value (FV), the interest rate (%i), and the length of time (n) are known. You must solve for present value.

The present value formula is found by taking the future value equation (4.2) and placing the present value on the left side:

$$PV = \frac{FV_n}{(1 + r)^n} \tag{4.5}$$

Earlier we had an example where a present value of $1 grew for two years at 10%. We found the future value to be $1.21. Finding a present value is reversing the process.

Each chapter of the study guide provides a brief, diagnostic self-test with both worked-out and keystroke solutions. (Not shown is the chapter practice test featuring completion questions, true/false items, and problems, with detailed answers, explanations, and worked-out solutions.)

> The financial calculator method can be used to solve for the time period. We compute (CPT) for the unknown time period (n).

Example: Re-doing the above problem, we are interested in the number of years that are required for $100,000 to grow to $140,000 with an interest rate of 8.775%

Keystrokes: Clear, input 100,000 Key PV, input 140,000 Key FV, input 8.775 Key %i
Then Key CPT, Key n
The register reads: 4

SELF TEST

1. A football player receives the following contract offer: sign today and receive a $250,000 signing bonus plus a $300,000 salary paid at the end of each year for the next three years. The interest rate is 15%. What is the present value of the contract offer? Is the contract a million dollar offer?

Solution:

$$PVA = 250,000 + \sum_{i=1}^{3} \frac{300,000}{(1.15)^i}$$

$$PVA = 250,000 + 300,000\ (2.283) = \$934,967.53$$

Keystrokes: Clear, input 300,000 Key PMT, input 15 Key %i, input 3 Key n
Then Key CPT, Key PV
The register reads: 684,967.54
Add the signing bonus: $250,000 + $684,967.54 = $934,967.53

The annual salary of $300,000 is an annuity. The present value of the annuity is $684,967.54. The $250,000 signing bonus is already in present value terms since it is paid today. The sum of the annuity and the signing bonus provides a present value for the contract of $934,967.53. The contract is not a million dollar offer in present value terms.

2. What if we consider a problem that is almost an annuity? For instance, you receive $1 at the end of the month and $100 at the end of each month for the following 23 months. The interest rate is 6%. What is the present value of the 24 cash payments?

Solution:

You could discount all 224 payments separately--very tedious work. Or you could treat the

Modern Corporate Finance

Donald R. Chambers
Lafayette College

Nelson J. Lacey
University of Massachusetts at Amherst

ISBN: 0-06-501004-3

Companies in isolation of their markets and the competitive environment cannot fully evaluate their risks and opportunities. By emphasizing the economic factors and market forces that firms must consider in order to succeed, and not just accounting issues or valuation, *Modern Corporate Finance* brings the modernist perspective to corporate finance. Appropriate for both introductory MBA and undergraduate financial management courses, this text finds an appropriate balance between theories and applications. It demonstrates the usefulness of finance in corporate decision making while realistic exercises and examples make the theoretical material relevant to students. The text's modular organization further enhances its accessibility. Divided into two parts—core material (further divided into three modules) and combinable, independent chapters—the format allows for maximum flexibility in course organization. "Windows," located throughout the text, provide information on specific topics without interrupting the flow of the chapter, and "Workshops" offer valuable hands-on exercises. Other major features include a chapter on option theory (as part of the core), and a separate chapter on corporate ethics and shareholder wealth maximization.

Modular Format

To provide instructors with maximum teaching flexibility, the text is divided into **core and independent material**. This **modular format** enables instructors to organize their course to suit their individual needs. The core material is divided into three modules with three chapters each. Professors can integrate the other independent chapters as they wish. Because of its conformable table of contents, *Modern Corporate Finance* may fit more than one course at the same school.

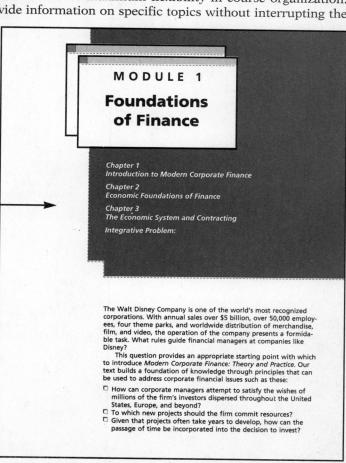

MODULE 1

Foundations of Finance

Chapter 1
Introduction to Modern Corporate Finance

Chapter 2
Economic Foundations of Finance

Chapter 3
The Economic System and Contracting

Integrative Problem:

The Walt Disney Company is one of the world's most recognized corporations. With annual sales over $5 billion, over 50,000 employees, four theme parks, and worldwide distribution of merchandise, film, and video, the operation of the company presents a formidable task. What rules guide financial managers at companies like Disney?

This question provides an appropriate starting point with which to introduce *Modern Corporate Finance: Theory and Practice*. Our text builds a foundation of knowledge through principles that can be used to address corporate financial issues such as these:

❏ How can corporate managers attempt to satisfy the wishes of millions of the firm's investors dispersed throughout the United States, Europe, and beyond?
❏ To which new projects should the firm commit resources?
❏ Given that projects often take years to develop, how can the passage of time be incorporated into the decision to invest?

Chapter Opener

Each module is further divided into three chapters.

Chapter 1

Introduction to Modern Corporate Finance

I magine that you are in the final interview for a job—your best job opportunity yet. This last appointment is with the company's president, a young entrepreneur who has driven the small company with record results. After reviewing your résumé, the president says: "I see you list finance as the focus of your studies over the past several years. I have two questions for you: First, how would you define finance? Second, since business administration is your major, what is the goal of a corporation and why?"

Defining finance and understanding the goal of the corporation provide an ideal backdrop for introducing **modern corporate finance**. Modern corporate finance is an approach that integrates financial decisions of business firms within a logical framework and teaches you to think clearly about the discipline of finance—to see the "big picture." Accordingly, this text builds a foundation for problem solving within the business enterprise.

There is a temptation to want to reduce the study of finance to a cookbook approach, developing a set of procedures and following them step by step to solve a particular problem. Our approach to modern corporate finance begins differently. It first teaches the student to understand the problem and then to organize a solution to the problem through the use of models.

For example, consider the problem of investing corporate funds. The solution is to invest if the benefits of the investment exceed the costs of the investment. The model that will be introduced to measure costs and benefits is *net present value (NPV)*. Correctly applied, the net present value model will guide corporate managers to choose projects that add value to the firm.

Once a model has been introduced, this text will then emphasize the development of practical applications. Accordingly, after each concept has been presented, techniques will be introduced to use the model to solve real-world problems.

modern corporate finance
An approach to the study of finance that integrates financial decisions of business firms within a logical framework.

Windows

Located within every chapter, **"Windows"** hold a magnifying glass up to the study of select financial concepts. They provide background and details on given topics without interrupting the flow of the text.

Window 5.1

The U.S. Treasury Bill Market

U.S. Treasury bills, or T-bills, are issued by and are obligations of the U.S. Treasury. Treasury bills fall in a class of securities known as money market securities, and are issued with maturities of 13 weeks, 26 weeks, or 52 weeks. They are offered with a minimum denomination of $10,000 and in multiples thereafter of $5,000 up to $1 million. The number or amount of T-bills issued at any one time is determined by the amount of maturing T-bills to be refunded, current monetary policy objectives, and the Treasury's short-term financing needs.

Treasury bills are sold at a discount—determined by an auction—from face value. At maturity, the T-bill is redeemed by the holder for its full face value. This means that the rate of return is determined by the difference between the amount paid for the T-bill and its value at maturity.

One peculiar aspect of Treasury bills is how their prices are quoted for trading purposes or in the newspaper. Yields are quoted on what is known as a *bank discount yield* basis, dividing the amount of discount from par value (or face value) by the security's par value:

$$\text{Bank Discount Yield} = \frac{\text{Par Value} > \text{Purchase Price}}{\text{Par Value}} \cdot \frac{360}{\text{Purchase Price}}$$

This presents a problem for investors because the technique used to determine bank discount yields is different from the standard techniques discussed in Chapter 4. Because bank discount yields understate the rate of return on T-bills, investors must convert these yields to actual or true yields:

$$\text{Actual Yield} = \frac{365 \cdot \text{Bank Discount Yield}}{360 > (\text{Bank Discount Yield} \cdot \text{Days To Maturity})}$$

Such conversion techniques are available to assist investors.

Although T-bill investors may wish to hold their securities until maturity, there is an active secondary market made by government securities dealers, who stand ready to buy and sell T-bills at their market price. Indeed, the liquidity of the T-bill market contributes to its popularity as an investment vehicle. Commercial banks, with their special liquidity needs, along with other financial institutions, state and local governments, ernment, and individual investors, are major holders of Treasury bills.

Investment returns on Treasury bills are subject to federal income tax bu exempt from state and local taxes.

Workshops

Complementing the **"Windows"** are hands-on **"Workshops."** These assignments provide students with the opportunity to explore the practical aspects of finance.

Workshop 4.1

The Present Value of a College Education

Have you ever stopped to think about the whether going to college makes financial sense?* That is, are the costs of a college education worth the projected benefits? We show in this workshop how such a question can be answered.

Let's assume that each year of college costs $25,000 in total expenses—$10,000 in added expenses (tuition, and all other college-related expenses) and $15,000 in foregone wages. We include foregone wages as a cost because if you weren't in college you would be working and receiving wages. Given that these cost projections are reasonable, and given that the college degree you seek will take four years, the total cost of obtaining your degree is estimated at $100,000.

Although the costs appear large, we have yet to consider the benefits. It might be reasonable to expect that a college degree will increase your annual wage by $10,000 throughout your work life as compared to what you would be earning if you had not gone to college. That means that if you work for 40 years (say from the age of 23 to the age of 62) the "extra" income from your college degree will total $400,000 (40 years at $10,000 per year). But adding your wages together and subtracting out the sum of the costs is an accounting approach and is not equal to their true value.

The financial question we need to answer is whether $100,000 of college costs is worth the $400,000 of increased revenues. This multiple cash flow problem must transform all cash flows to a single reference point, in this case to present values. Below are the multiple cash flows in the problem. Given an interest rate of 8 percent, we can convert future values into present values using *PVF*s. College education costs are discounted first, and then will be compared to the present value of college education benefits.

Step 1: Determine the Present Value of College Education Costs

Cash Outflow	PVF given r = 8%	Present Value of Future Cash Outflow
Year 1: >$25,000	.9259	>$25,000 * .9259 = >$23,147.50
Year 2: >$25,000	.8573	>$25,000 * .8573 = >$21,432.50
Year 3: >$25,000	.7938	>$25,000 * .7938 = >$19,845.00
Year 4: >$25,000	.7350	>$25,000 * .7350 = >$18,375.00
Total Present Value of Future Cash Outflows		>$82,800.00

(continued on next page)

Step-by-Step Demonstration Problems

These appear right before the assignment material so that students will have at least one or two worked-out examples of how to solve the problems before trying a few themselves.

DEMONSTRATION PROBLEMS

Problem 1 The following chart describes the happiness or utility that Mary derives from fruit:

Quarts of Blueberries	Total Utils from Blueberries	Quarts of Strawberries	Total Utils from Strawberries
1	50	1	20
2	80	2	30
3	105	3	35
4	120	4	38
5	132	5	39

If quarts of blueberries and quarts of strawberries each sell for $2 and if Mary has $8 to spend, how will she spend the money if these are her only choices and if she decides to spend it all?

Solution to Problem 1

Step 1: The first step is to begin with no dollars spent and to determine whether the first two dollars should be used to buy blueberries or strawberries. It is implicitly assumed that Mary does not now have any quarts of fruit and therefore no utils from either type of fruit. The chart reveals that the first quart of blueberries would provide 50 utils of happiness and that the first quart of strawberries would provide only 20 utils of happiness. Thus, to maximize utility, Mary would first purchase a quart of blueberries.

Scorecard: 1 blueberries, 0 strawberries, $6 remain.

Step 2: The second step is to compute the added happiness that another quart of blueberries would give Mary now that she already has one quart of blueberries. The chart reveals that two quarts of blueberries give her 80 utils, which is an increase of 30 utils from her current level of 50 utils. Thus the incremental or marginal utility from another quart of blueberries is 30 utils. Since this is greater than the 20 utils a quart of strawberries would provide, Mary decides to purchase another quart of blueberries.

Scorecard: 2 blueberries, 0 strawberries, $4 remain.

Step 3: The third step is identical to step 2 except that we now begin with two quarts of blueberries. A third quart of blueberries would provide a total of 105 utils, or in other words a marginal increase of 25 utils. Since this is still greater than the marginal utils provided by the first quart of strawberries, Mary will maximize her utility by purchasing still another quart of blueberries.

Scorecard: 3 blueberries, 0 strawberries, $2 remain.

Step 4: The final step is to determine what should be done with the last two dollars. A fourth quart of blueberries would provide a total of 120 utils, an increase of only 15 utils. Since this is less than the 20 utils provided by the first quart of strawberries, Mary decides to purchase a quart of strawberries with her last $2.

Scorecard: 3 blueberries, 1 strawberries, $0 remain.

Final Solution: Mary should purchase 3 quarts of blueberries and 1 quart of strawberries for a total utility of 125 utils (105 utils from blueberries and 20 utils from strawberries). ↵

Problem 2 Mary (the same person in Problem 1) has a garden with limited productive capabilities. The garden can be cultivated to raise either one quart of blueberries or four quarts of strawberries. Which alternative should Mary produce given that both alternatives require the same effort and costs? Assume that the market for fruit is well functioning and that the prices and preferences given in the first problem are applicable to this one.

Solution to Problem 2

Step 1: The first step is to recognize the importance of the assumption that the market for fruit is well functioning. What this means is that quarts of fruit can be purchased and sold at market prices with no taxes, fees, or any other sort of penalty. We can now view the productive capabilities of Mary's garden in terms of market prices. One quart of blueberries has a market value of $2. The four quarts of strawberries have a combined market value of $8. Thus, growing strawberries is the production alternative that produces the highest market value.

Step 2: The final step is to realize that $8 will provide Mary with more utility than $2. In Problem 1 we found that Mary can receive 125 utils from properly spending $8. Mary can only receive 50 utils from spending $2. It is not important that producing and consuming one quart of blueberries provides more utils (50 utils) than producing and consuming four quarts of strawberries (38 utils) since in a well-functioning market Mary can exchange the fruit that she is most capable of growing for the fruit that she most prefers to eat.

Final Solution: Mary should grow the four quarts of strawberries, sell them in the market for $8, and then spend the $8 in the manner that gives her the maximum utility. ↵

Numbered Examples

All key examples are numbered and set off for quick and easy reference in and outside the classroom.

ever, the primary business of most corporations is selling their product for more than its cost (i.e., the combined costs of the inputs necessary to make the product).

Example 2.1 ———— The primary way for a computer manufacturer to maximize shareholder wealth is to put together relatively inexpensive pieces of plastic and metal into a functioning computer that can be sold for more than it costs to make. The computer manufacturer will be successful only if other manufacturers cannot quickly undercut prices because they lack the expertise, patents, existing manufacturing ability, reputation, or the like.

Superior returns can only be consistently earned when there is a lack of competition such that others cannot duplicate the business at a lower price. Financial managers must learn to recognize where lack of competition or poorly functioning markets create inefficiencies that will enable shareholder wealth to be increased. Additionally, financial managers need to understand that in an efficient market, competition drives away the opportunities for superior returns.

There are many reasons why competition can be reduced to the point at which prices become inefficient. Perhaps there are limitations on the number of people who can produce a computer owing to patent protection or a highly sophisticated required technology. Or, possibly, the assets being traded require information that is not widely known or is extremely difficult to interpret. The assets in these markets can often sell at prices that create the opportunity for superior returns since there are a limited number of participants who have the necessary information to compete. ↵

Inefficient markets can offer opportunities for superior returns and the danger of large losses. The subsections that follow explain some of the major concepts involved in dealing with assets when there is rather limited information available to the market participants. This problem is often discussed in the context of **liquidity**, which refers to the time and cost necessary to sell an asset at its true value.

liquidity
The time and cost necessary to sell an asset at its true

Liquid Assets

A highly liquid asset can be sold at its true value very quickly. An example of a highly liquid asset is a U.S. Treasury bill. Traders in the U.S. Treasury bill market have full and immediate information regarding market value. An asset with low or poor liquidity, such as a house, usually requires considerable time before it can be sold at its true value. The time and cost required to sell a house is the time and cost

food units because he traded one food unit for five food units. Similarly, it doesn't make sense to claim that a person who trades one watermelon for five grapes has produced a profit of four pieces of fruit. The reason that such profits do not make sense is that we are comparing different commodities or assets.

⊠ Dollars to be received through time or paid out through time are different commodities that cannot simply be added together or subtracted from each other. However, there is a relation by which equivalent values can be found.

Discounting Cash Flows

If cash flows at different points in time are indeed different assets with different values, how can we make meaningful comparisons between dollars that arrive at different points in time? This is the central issue within the study of the time value of money.

The answer is that all cash flows must be changed into dollars at the same point in time. The most common solution is to take all cash flows and to convert them into the value of the cash flows in today's dollars. This is called **discounting** cash flows to the present.

discounting
The process of turning future cash flows into current cash flows.

Discounting can be accomplished by taking future dollars to the grocery store of cash depicted in Figure 4.2 and converting them into current dollars using the prices provided by the marketplace. The longer you must wait to receive future dollars, the less those future dollars are worth to you today. For instance, the marketplace might tell us that the value today of receiving $1.00 in exactly one year is $0.93. We now have a basis of comparing these two different commodities: $0.93 today is equivalent to $1.00 due in one year. The marketplace might also tell us that the value today of receiving $1.00 in exactly two years is $0.86, and that the value today of receiving $1.00 in three years is $0.79. In fact, we can envision a grocery store of cash set up to turn any future amount of money into a present value. Note that as we extend the time horizon into the more and more distant future, the value today of receiving those dollars in the more distant future becomes smaller. This is illustrated in Figure 4.3.

⊠ The longer you must wait to receive future dollars, the less those future dollars are worth to you today.

Compounding Cash Flows

It is also useful to turn current dollars into future dollars. This process is called **compounding** the cash flows. The main difference between discounting and compounding is the point of reference, which in discounting is today, while the reference point in compounding is some future point in time.

compounding
The process of turning current cash flows into future cash flows.

Highlights

For more visually oriented students, the authors have called out all key points to ponder right within the body of the text. They are marked with a small icon.

End-of-Chapter Material

Each chapter contains a wealth of high-quality **review material, self-tests, questions, and problems** that help students master the concepts they have just learned.

PROBLEMS

Complete the table given the following information:

	PV	FV	r	n	m
1.	$100	____	.10	1	1
2.	$100	____	.10	2	1
3.	$125	____	.10	1	1
4.	$175	____	.15	20	1
5.	$175	____	.155	5	1

6. What is the future value of $1,000 in two years if it is invested at an interest rate of 8%?
7. If you borrowed $10,000 today for five years at 9% interest, how much would you have to pay back?
8. If $100 is deposited in a savings account at 6% interest per year, what will the amount be in five years?
9. You deposit $500 in a three-year savings certificate at 5% interest. At the end of the second year, the bank increases the interest rate on savings certificates to 6%. What will your initial deposit of $500 be worth in three years?

Complete the table given the following information:

	PV	FV	r	n	m
10.	$100	____	.10	1	2
11.	$125	____	.10	2	2
12.	$125	____	.12	1	4
13.	$125	____	.12	1	365
14.	$125	____	.155	1	12

15. Your boss, the treasurer for a small manufacturing company, wishes to deposit $50,000 for two years until the money is needed to replace some equipment. He would like you to analyze the investment opportunities offered by two savings certificates. One certificate offers 8% interest compounded annually while the other certificate earns 7.9% interest compounded quarterly. What is the future value of the $50,000 for each alternative?
16. What is the future value of $800 if it earns an interest rate of 6.5% compounded semiannually for one year? Repeat for two years, and again for five years.
17. You expect to receive a check for $300 in three months and another check for $500 in six months from your part-time job.

Both amounts will be deposited in a savings account at 7% interest compounded quarterly. What is the future value of the total deposit nine months from today?
18. What will $1000 be worth in two years if it is compounded continuously at an interest rate of 8%?
19. You have seen an advertisement for an investment fund that offers 6% interest compounded continuously. At the moment, your savings account offers 6.5% compounded quarterly. What is the future value of $500 in one year for the fund and the savings account?

Complete the table given the following information:

	PV	FV	r	n
20.	____	$100	.10	1
21.	____	$150	.10	2
22.	____	$150	.12	1
23.	____	$150	.12	20
24.	____	$150	.155	5

25. What is the present value of $5,000 to be received in two years? The interest rate is 9%.
26. What is the present value of $1,000 to be received in one year if the interest rate is 8%? What is the difference in present value if the interest rate is 10%?
27. You would like to visit the Far East and Asia in three years. You have estimated that this trip will cost $5,000. What amount needs to be placed in a three-year 7% savings certificate today so that you will have $5,000 in three years?
28. What is the present value of a 20-year 9% zero coupon bond that has a face value of $10,000?
29. The parents of an eight-year-old child wish to deposit an amount today that will cover the child's first year in college. Tuition is estimated to be $15,000 when the child is a college freshman at age 18. If the interest rate is 10%, what amount needs to be deposited today?
30. You have just won a lottery prize and may choose between two alternatives:
    Choice A: Receive $2,000 one year from today.
    Choice B: Receive $500 today and $1,500 one year from today.
    What is the present value of each alternative, assuming an interest rate of 7%?
31. What is the present value of $25,000 discounted for 40 years at 12% interest?

Module-ending **Integrative Problems** link all three chapter concepts in an innovative way. They reinforce the practical applications of the chapter's material, making the topics more interesting and relevant for students.

Two Great Tastes

As chief financial officer you must approve or reject projects based upon the company's traditional capital budgeting method: the internal rate of return. Recently, your financial analysts calculated the cash flows that would be produced by two projects suggested by the marketing department. Half of the marketing team favored one project and half favored the other project. The cash flow analysis indicated the following cash flows for each project, one called peanut butter and the other chocolate:

		Cash Flows In:		
	Year 0	Year 1	Year 2	Year 3
Peanut butter	>$3,000	$0	$1,000	$ 0
Chocolate	$0	+$9,053	$0	$>9,053

Both projects look pathetic. The peanut butter project actually has more dollar outflows than inflows. The chocolate project doesn't begin for another year and has future inflows equal to more current outflows.

Module 2

Integrative Problem

Nevertheless, in order to evaluate the projects in terms of company policy, you compute the internal rate of return of each project. Sure enough, the internal rate of return of peanut butter is >42.265%. The internal rate of return of chocolate is 0%. Since your company requires a rate of return of 15%, you send out the bad news that both projects are rejected.

Several days later the whole marketing department runs into your office with some startling news. In a seminar on working together, they learned the value of teamwork. They suggest that the two projects be put together to form one great project. None of the revenues or expenses will change, so the combined project looks like this:

		Cash Flows in:		
	Year 0	Year 1	Year 2	Year 3
Combined project	>$3,000	+$9,053	+$1,000	>9,053

When plugged into the computer, the project produces an internal rate of return of 20%. Since

MODULE 1

Foundations of Finance

The Walt Disney Company is one of the world's most recognized corporations. With annual sales over $5 billion, over 50,000 employees, four theme parks, and worldwide distribution of merchandise, film, and video, the operation of the company presents a formidable task. What rules guide financial managers at companies like Disney?

This question provides an appropriate starting point with which to introduce *Modern Corporate Finance: Theory and Practice.* Our text builds a foundation of knowledge through principles that can be used to address corporate financial issues such as these:

☐ How can corporate managers attempt to satisfy the wishes of millions of the firm's investors dispersed throughout the United States, Europe, and beyond?
☐ To which new projects should the firm commit resources?
☐ Given that projects often take years to develop, how can the passage of time be incorporated into the decision to invest?

☐ Given that return on investment must be estimated, how can risk be incorporated into the decision to invest?
☐ Because cash inflows and cash outflows often occur in different cycles, how can the cash cycle be best managed?
☐ Can the particular mix of financial securities issued to finance projects affect the overall value of the firm?
☐ Does the set of rules change when projects are managed outside the United States?

Although these are complicated questions, the economic principles that underlie all of them are few in number and have common elements. The three chapters of Module 1 introduce these principles. Chapter 1 defines modern corporate financial management, addressing the following questions: Why study corporate finance? Who uses finance? What is the role of financial management in the corporation? What is *modern* about modern corporate finance? What is the goal or purpose of the corporation? Chapter 2 describes financial decision making through an examination of four economic principles upon which finance is built. Chapter 3 places the corporation within the financial environment, including financial institutions and governments, and discusses in detail the role of contracts in providing the linkage between people in the corporation.

Introduction to Modern Corporate Finance

Imagine that you are in the final interview for a job—your best job opportunity yet. This last appointment is with the company's president, a young entrepreneur who has driven the small company with record results. After reviewing your résumé, the president says: "I see you list finance as the focus of your studies over the past several years. I have two questions for you: First, how would you define finance? Second, since business administration is your major, what is the goal of a corporation and why?"

Defining finance and understanding the goal of the corporation provide an ideal backdrop for introducing **modern corporate finance**. Modern corporate finance is an approach that integrates financial decisions of business firms within a logical framework and teaches you to think clearly about the discipline of finance—to see the "big picture." Accordingly, this text builds a foundation for problem solving within the business enterprise.

modern corporate finance
An approach to the study of finance that integrates financial decisions of business firms within a logical framework.

There is a temptation to want to reduce the study of finance to a cookbook approach, developing a set of procedures and following them step by step to solve a particular problem. Our approach to modern corporate finance begins differently. It first teaches the student to understand the problem and then to organize a solution to the problem through the use of models.

For example, consider the problem of investing corporate funds. The solution is to invest if the benefits of the investment exceed the costs of the investment. The model that will be introduced to measure costs and benefits is *net present value (NPV)*. Correctly applied, the net present value model will guide corporate managers to choose projects that add value to the firm.

Once a model has been introduced, this text will then emphasize the development of practical applications. Accordingly, after each concept has been presented, techniques will be introduced to use the model to solve real-world problems.

Example 1.1 _____ As an overview, let's take a brief look at the types of financial decisions that confront all organizations, large or small. For a multinational firm like Toyota, this might be a decision to enter the van market currently dominated by American automobile manufacturers. Before devoting the resources needed to build factories, to hire labor to design and build the vans, and to embark on a campaign to market the vans, Toyota must weigh carefully the costs of this decision against the anticipated outcome. Similarly, the owner of a neighborhood furniture store might consider the purchase of a larger delivery truck to provide better customer service.

How do firms make these decisions? The choices can affect their fortunes for better or worse. In Toyota's case, success in van sales will enable the firm to garner a large share of the market, increasing overall profits. In the case of the furniture store, the failure to purchase the truck could mean being forced out of business by competitors who spend more on services for their customers. In both cases, financial decisions play a key role in building a competitive advantage in the marketplace. This book provides you with the means to analyze these decisions. ↵

THE MEANING OF MODERN CORPORATE FINANCE

Aristotle wrote, "Those who wish to succeed must ask the right preliminary questions." In our case, the preliminary questions relate to the meaning of the words in the title *Modern Corporate Finance*. As a vehicle for getting started in your study of finance, we examine each of the words in the title to develop some working definitions and some themes that organize the rest of the book. Thus, the starting point in this introduction is the investigation of the word "finance."

What Is Finance?

Finance is an extension of economics. However, this doesn't mean that studying finance is identical to studying economics. Economics is the foundation of finance just as physics is the foundation of engineering or even riding a bicycle. People do not need to have a thorough understanding of physics to learn to ride a bike—they just need to know a few principles. Similarly, finance relies on a few economic principles to develop powerful decision-making tools for virtually every business decision.

economics
The study of the allocation of scarce resources or, more precisely, the study of how people, acting individually or through the businesses and governments they form, make decisions regarding the production and use of scarce resources.

Let's begin with a definition of economics: **Economics** studies the interaction of people with regard to scarce resources. Concisely stated, economics is the study of the allocation of scarce resources, including how resources are produced and consumed by the participants in the economy.

Finance takes underlying economic principles and projects them into more practical tools by incorporating the passage of time as well as uncertainty or risk. We can build a definition of finance from the definition of economics. **Finance** can be defined as applied economics or, more precisely, as the economics of time and risk.

finance
Applied economics or, more precisely, the economics of time and risk.

Accordingly, the primary topics of corporate finance are how corporate financial managers make decisions today that affect outcomes occurring through time and including risk. For example, a decision to invest money today in a bagel-making machine in order to sell bagels in the future is a decision involving time. Further, there are no guarantees that bagel sales will meet projections inasmuch as competition, uncertain economic conditions, and changing tastes and preferences of consumers add risk to this investment decision.

valuation
The process of placing a value on, or determining the worth of, resources such as buildings, equipment, and ideas; the central process of finance.

An underlying theme of this text is that financial decisions are best made based on market values. **Valuation** is the process of placing a value on or determining the worth of resources, such as buildings, equipment, and ideas; market values are values determined in the marketplace. Decision making itself can be viewed as valuation. Someone who decides not to undertake a particular project has essentially placed a negative value on the idea. Conversely, people accept ideas for which they perceive there is a positive overall value.

For example, the decision to purchase a bagel-making machine may be viewed as the comparison between the value of the machine to the bagel maker and the value of the money needed to purchase the machine. Since all disciplines within business such as marketing, accounting, management, and production involve valuation and decision making, finance is core to understanding business.

The insight provided by finance is that decision making and valuation in the presence of both time and risk can be handled through the use of a few basic principles of economics—principles used by people in everyday life. This book trains you to recognize economic principles within seemingly complex problems in corporate finance, and demonstrates that solutions to problems are straightforward extensions of these principles.

Who Uses Finance?   Because everyone who makes economic decisions involving time and risk uses finance, the study of finance is often divided by the type of user. This book is about corporate finance, and therefore emphasizes the financial decisions faced by corporations and their financial managers. Since corporations comprise such a large and important portion of our economy, corporate finance is the most common type of finance course. In contrast, other finance books and courses discuss the decision making faced by households (personal finance, consumer finance, or investments), by governments (public finance), or by specialty areas such as banking or international finance.

The study of corporate finance can be characterized by three types of decisions. As shown in Figure 1.1, financial management is viewed as integrating the major tasks of raising money, called the financing decision; investing money, the investment decision; and managing cash, the working capital decision.

Example 1.2 _____ In the instance of the bagel-making machine, first, the decision to purchase the machine is an example of the investment decision. This decision would be made on the basis of the cost and the projected benefits that the machine would bring. Second, how to pay for the machine is an example of the financing decision. The sources available for payment include the savings of the individual who will own the machine, funds from individuals who become part owners of the machine, a loan from a bank, or loans from other investors. Third, how to keep the machine running throughout the year involves working capital decisions, which become important in situations where costs and benefits do not match up over time. ◀┘

What Do Financial Managers Do? At a conceptual level, financial managers gather information, analyze the information, and then

FIGURE 1.1
The Role of Financial Management

Financial management is viewed as integrating the three major tasks of raising money, called the financing decision; investing money, called the investment decision; and managing cash, called the working capital decision.

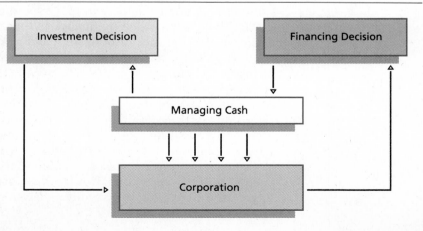

make decisions based on market values. On a practical level, the duties vary based upon the level of the manager and the area involved.

For example, the highest-level financial managers make the firm's major decisions regarding financing, investment, and working capital management. The financing and investment decisions would typically be the most important, such as where to obtain the funds and which projects to invest in.

Lower-level financial managers perform financial analyses that serve as the relevant input in making major decisions. For example, financial analysts study decisions such as which projects to recommend to top management, how best to pay the firm's bills, and where to put the firm's extra cash. Financial analysts monitor and regularly evaluate various aspects of the firm's operations, such as whether customers are creditworthy and should be allowed to purchase products on credit. Many financial managers perform these tasks for investment firms and banks as well as for traditional industrial or service corporations.

Regardless of a financial manager's level and area, the objective of the analysis is the same——to determine whether the proposed action will increase or decrease the value of the firm. The following chapters provide a foundation for performing financial tasks and for making the financial decisions that underlie virtually all aspects of business.

Defining the Corporation

corporation
A distinct legal entity defined by the contracts between individuals such as owners, creditors, workers, suppliers, consumers, those in the surrounding communities, and those in all levels of government.

The second word in the book title, "corporate," is significant because the focus of this book is on the financial decisions of businesses, specifically corporations. The term **corporation** means different things to different people. Some may think about products and services, some about employees, buildings, and factories, others about corporate slogans or logos. Indeed, it is hard to hear the name IBM without thinking of computers, Kellogg without thinking of breakfast cereal, and Ford without thinking of cars.

But a corporation is actually none of these things. While we can say that IBM makes computers, Kellogg makes cereal, and Ford makes cars, IBM, Kellogg, and Ford are really just names that define specific arrangements or contracts between people. Certainly those within the corporation produce things, but the corporation itself can only serve as a conduit between people. Viewed this way, the corporation is a legal entity—or a collection of contracts—and as such is different from some other types of business organizations.

In summary, a corporation is a collection of contracts set up by one or more persons for the purpose of engaging in economic activity. These contracts might specify labor agreements, customer agreements, or agreements between the business organizations and local governments and communities. But the corporation itself serves only as a link or connection between these various contracts.

Forms of Business Organization.

Forms of Business Organization.   In addition to the corporation, the other two general types of business organizations are the sole proprietorship and the partnership. Corporations have certain qualities that make their financial decisions more complex than those of the other two. This section will compare the contracts that define each type of business organization.

sole proprietorship
A type of business organization in which an individual, acting alone, conducts business. Because the individual does not create a formal business organization agreement, the legal rights and responsibilities of the sole proprietorship are equivalent to the rights and responsibilities of the person who owns the business.

A **sole proprietorship** exists when an individual, acting alone, conducts business. Because the individual does not create a formal business organization agreement, the legal rights and responsibilities of the sole proprietorship are equivalent to the rights and responsibilities of the person who owns the business. For example, the income of the business is taxed directly as income of the owner when he or she files a personal tax return.

Other obligations of the sole proprietorship, including repaying borrowed money, fulfilling promises such as warranties, and paying costs of lawsuits, are the same as those of the person who owns the business. Thus, the sole proprietor is personally liable for all debts incurred by the business and puts all of his or her personal wealth at risk when operating a business—an aspect known as unlimited liability.

partnership
A type of business organization formed when two or more individuals join together to conduct business. Although no formal contractual agreement is required to form a partnership, the members will often voluntarily draw up a legal agreement specifying the rights and responsibilities of each partner.

A **partnership** is formed when two or more individuals join together to conduct business. Although no formal contractual agreement is required to form a partnership, the members will often voluntarily draw up a legal agreement specifying the rights and responsibilities of each partner. These rights and responsibilities include an understanding of how funds will be raised, how profits will be divided, and how the partnership will be dissolved. For tax purposes, the income or losses of the partnership must be reported on each partner's personal income tax returns.

As with a sole proprietorship, a partnership can expose its owners to unlimited liability—the responsibility to repay all obligations of the partnership such as borrowed money, unpaid expenses, and legal costs—even if the money required extends beyond the partners' investment in the business and into their personal wealth. However, a common type of partnership is a limited partnership. It releases or protects certain partners, known as limited partners, from liability above and beyond their personal investment. The partner who sets up the limited partnership and who is not protected from unlimited liability is the general partner.

In contrast to both the sole proprietorship and the partnership, the corporation is an organization that must be formed by legal agreement. The corporation is a distinct legal entity defined by the contracts between the individuals who make up the corporation. These individuals include owners, creditors, workers, suppliers, consumers, those in the surrounding communities, and those in all levels of government.

The relationship between owners and creditors is an example of one of the contracts that constitute a corporation. In the corporate organization, the owners are protected from losing more than their investment. In other words, the owners enjoy what is termed **limited liability.**

Another important feature of the corporation is that earnings from the business are taxed at corporate rates by both the state and federal governments. The earnings are then taxed again at the personal level if and when they flow through to the corporation's owners. Generally speaking, this double taxation of corporate earnings is viewed as a disadvantage of the corporate form.

A special type of corporation known as the Sub-Chapter S corporation allows relatively small corporations to avoid the double taxation of corporate earnings by flowing all of the corporation's earnings directly to the personal tax returns of the owners (without being subjected to corporate income taxes). Other distinctions between these three general forms of business organizations are summarized in Window 1.1.

While the technical definition of a corporation includes a nexus of contracts, there are other ways to view the typical contractual relationships of a corporation. We call these the balance sheet view, the cash flow cycle view, the organizational view, and the modernist view. A discussion of each follows.

The Balance Sheet View of the Corporation.

The balance sheet view of the corporation has as its roots the financial statement with the same name. The corporation is viewed as a collection of **assets** (things owned), **debt** (things owed), and **equity** (the difference between what is owned and what is owed):

$$\text{Assets} = \text{Debt} + \text{Equity}. \tag{1.1}$$

Assets include everything that can produce value for the firm, including buildings, equipment, land, patents, inventories, and cash. Debt represents the obligations of the firm, including accounts payable, bank loans, and bonds. Another name for these obligations is liabilities, which are held by individuals known as debtholders, creditors, or bondholders. The equity of the firm is its common stock, and the people who hold equity are often called stockholders, shareholders, or equityholders. The stockholders, as owners of the equity, are the owners of the firm. Equity is sometimes referred to as a residual claim because it represents something that is left over after the claims of all debtholders have been satisfied.

Formula (1.1) of the balance sheet reduces to its simplest terms the relationship between assets, debt (liabilities), and equity. In practice, however, a balance sheet can seem complex because such a vari-

---

limited liability
Protection for the owners of a corporation against losing more than their original investment.

assets
Everything that can produce value for the firm, including buildings, equipment, land, patents, inventories, and cash.

debt
Obligations of the firm including accounts payable, bank loans, and bonds. Another name for these obligations is liabilities. Those who hold these claims are known as debtholders, creditors, or bondholders.

equity
The difference between the value of assets and value of debt. The equity of the firm is its common stock, and those who hold equity are often called stockholders, shareholders, or equityholders.

Window 1.1

Types of Business Organization

This window compares and contrasts the three major types of business organizations—the sole proprietorship, the partnership, and the corporation.

Sole proprietorships are by far the most common type of business organization. Of the over 18 million businesses in the U.S. in 1987, 13 million, or 72 percent, were organized as sole proprietorships.* Advantages of the sole proprietorship include legal simplicity, a lack of required paperwork and financial reporting, and an ability to charge any losses in the business against the proprietor's outside income to reduce taxable income.

There are, however, disadvantages to sole proprietorships. In addition to unlimited liability (the proprietor may be held personally liable for all debts incurred by the business), the reliance on a single individual limits both capital-raising ability and continuity. Sole proprietorships must usually rely on bank loans and personal savings for investment funds. This explains why sole proprietorships tend to be small businesses, accounting for less than 6 percent of total business receipts of U.S. business activity in 1987. Also, because it relies on a single individual, the sole proprietorship usually dissolves when its owner retires or dies.

Partnerships share many of the advantages and disadvantages of the sole proprietorship. They are simple to organize, require little paperwork, and enjoy tax benefits. However, they suffer from unlimited liability, limited sources for investment funds, and a lack of con-

(continued on next page)

ety of categories and formats are used. Assets, liabilities, and equity are often broken into subcategories, and these subcategories can be broken down further.

Figure 1.2 shows the balance sheet of an actual corporation, the Walt Disney Company, and we have highlighted the three major categories. Disney reports nine categories of assets that totaled just under $11 billion in 1992, five categories of liabilities that totaled just over $6 billion, and four categories of equity that totaled just under $5 billion. The categories are highlighted to reflect the formula given by assets = liabilities + equity. This allows you to see the balance sheet's big picture as portrayed by an actual company. In other words, Figure

Window 1.1 *(continued)*

tinuity. Unlike sole proprietorships, the partnership has the ability to draw from a slightly larger pool of talent and capital, but suffers from potential conflicts between the partners. Partnerships accounted for less than 9 percent of the total number of U.S. businesses in 1987, and only 4 percent of total U.S. business receipts.

The corporate organization addresses many of the disadvantages of both the sole proprietorship and the partnership. Corporate owners (shareholders) enjoy limited liability, as their losses are limited to their investment in the business. The corporation can more easily raise investment funds by issuing stock or by borrowing, in the form of debt. Also, the life of the corporation is not limited to one person or a few key people, and, finally, the corporation can benefit from professional management.

There are, however, disadvantages. Corporations require significant amounts of paperwork and regulation, and they are often subject to financial reporting requirements such that all aspects of the business must be documented and available to the public. Also, profits from the business are taxed at the corporate level by state and federal governments, and are taxed again at the personal level if and when they flow down to the corporation's owners.

As discussed in this window, there are advantages and disadvantages to each type of business organization. It is clear that the corporate form is conducive to large business operations. While comprising only 20 percent of total U.S. businesses in 1987, the corporation accounted for 90 percent of total U.S. business receipts and 76 percent of total U.S. profits.

---

*U.S. Internal Revenue Service, *Statistics of Income.*

1.2, like all other balance sheets, is simply a listing of assets, liabilities, and equity.

Formula (1.1) can be rearranged to show the balance sheet view from the perspective of the equityholders:

market values
Values that the marketplace would place on items. Market values contrast with historical values, which are the values placed on items when they were originally purchased.

$$\text{Market Value of Equity} = \text{Market Value of Assets} \tag{1.2}$$
$$- \text{Market Value of Debt}$$

Formula (1.2) places equity on the left-hand side and adds the word "market" to the formula. **Market values** are the values that the marketplace would place on items, and they contrast with historical val-

FIGURE 1.2

The Walt Disney Company's Balance Sheet (in millions)		
Year ended September 30	1992	1991
Assets		
Cash	$ 764.8	$ 886.1
Marketable securities	1,407.0	782.4
Receivables	1,298.9	1,128.2
Merchandise inventories	462.8	311.6
Film costs	760.5	596.9
Theme parks, resorts, and other property		
Attractions, buildings, and equipment	6,285.3	5,628.1
Accumulated depreciation	(1,999.6)	(1,667.8)
	4,285.7	3,960.3
Projects in progress	440.1	540.9
Land	72.9	70.4
	4,798.7	4,571.6
Other assets	1,369.0	1,151.7
	$ 10,861.7	$ 9,428.5
Liabilities		
Accounts payable and other accrued liabilities	$ 1,791.9	$ 1,433.8
Income taxes payable	381.0	296.2
Borrowings	2,222.4	2,213.8
Unearned royalty and other advances	872.8	859.5
Deferred income taxes	889.0	753.9
	$ 6,157.1	$ 5,557.2
Stockholders' Equity		
Stockholders' equity		
Common stock, $0.025 par value		
Authorized—1.200 million shares		
Issued—552.2 million shares and		
548.6 million shares	619.9	549.7
Retained earnings	4,661.9	3,950.5
Cumulative translation adjustments	86.9	35.2
	5,368.7	4,535.4
Less treasury shares, at cost	664.1	664.1
	4,704.6	3,871.3
	$ 10,861.7	$ 9,428.5

Reprinted by permission of The Walt Disney Company.

ues, which are the values placed on items when they were originally purchased. For example, the value of an individual's ownership in an automobile is equal to the market value of the auto minus the market value of the loan (the debt) against the auto:

Auto Owner's Equity Value = The Market Value of the Auto
− Market Value of the Auto Loan.

The auto owner has taken on debt (an auto loan) and has used the proceeds of the debt to buy the automobile. The person owns the auto subject to the terms of the debt, such that the person's equity or ownership in the auto must be reduced to reflect this debt obligation. If the owner does not make the loan payments, the debtholder will claim (repossess) the auto. On the other hand, if the auto is worth considerably less than the loan amount, the auto owner may find it in his or her interest to stop making payments, to declare bankruptcy, and to let the debtholder reclaim the auto.

The owners of a corporation's equity, like the owners of the auto, hold the claim to the corporation's assets, subject to the claims they have voluntarily surrendered to the debtholders in the process of borrowing money. If the value of the firm's assets is greater than the total payments promised to repay borrowed money, the stockholders will continue to make payments to the debtholders. If, however, the value of the firm's assets is less than the total payments promised on borrowed money, the stockholders will stop making promised payments by declaring bankruptcy and will thus allow the debtholders to take ownership of some or all of the firm's assets.

cash flow

Cash moving into the firm (cash inflow) or cash leaving the firm (cash outflow). Net cash flow is defined as the difference between cash inflows and outflows.

The Cash Flow Cycle View of the Corporation.   We can also view the corporation through the cash flow cycle, where **cash flow** is defined as cash moving into the firm (inflow) or cash leaving the firm (outflow). Net cash flow is defined as the difference between cash inflows and outflows. In contrast to the balance sheet, the cash flow cycle view takes the assets, liabilities, and equity of the firm and sets them in motion.

The accounting statement known as the income statement, with its revenues, expenses, and profit, is somewhat similar to the cash flow cycle with its inflows, outflows, and net cash flows. In an income statement, the activity of a firm is seen as producing revenues, causing expenses, and generating profits, where profits are defined by:

$$\text{Profits} = \text{Revenues} - \text{Expenses.} \qquad (1.3)$$

However, there are significant differences between cash flows and accounting numbers such as revenues and expenses. For example, in an income statement, an expense can be included when there is a promise to pay for something even if the money has not yet been paid. Further many cash flows such as the purchase and sale of land and buildings are only shown on an income statement to the extent that the transaction produces a profit or loss. Thus, the revenues and expenses found in the income statement can differ significantly from the cash inflows and outflows of the firm.

We illustrate the cash flow cycle with a highly simplified example in Figure 1.3. The cycle starts in the upper left-hand corner with cash,

FIGURE 1.3
The Cash Flow Cycle View of the Firm

In the cash flow cycle, cash is used in the production process, is built up through revenues when the finished product is sold, and is drawn down by expenses and taxes. Any cash remaining after all expenses have been paid belongs to the stockholders.

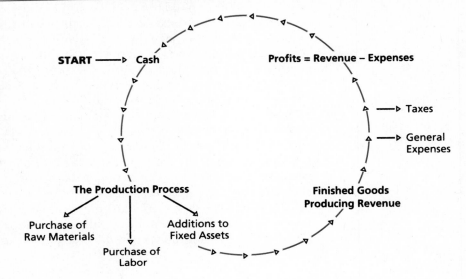

either borrowed in the form of debt or supplied as equity by the stockholders. Cash is used in the production process to purchase raw materials, to replace equipment, and to purchase labor. By following the arrows on Figure 1.3, you see that cash is built up through revenues when the finished product is sold, and is drawn down by expenses and taxes. Any cash revenue remaining after all cash expenses have been paid is a net cash flow that belongs to the stockholders.

Formula (1.3) represents a highly simplified cash flow statement. In practice, the firm's cash flow cycle is complex and can be erratic. A problem with cash flow analysis for a specific interval of time is that it can be severely affected by transactions that produce large cash inflows or outflows but have little effect on the firm's value—such as the sale of a building at its market value. Further, significant economic events such as losing a major lawsuit would not be included unless the cash were paid immediately.

The income statement attempts to correct the distortions caused by measuring cash flows over a specific interval of time. Accountants use complex rules and practices to attempt to measure and report the economically noteworthy changes in value. However, accounting procedures are far from perfect, and some people argue that accounting numbers add more distortions than they correct.

The income statement reports the components of revenues and expenses, breaking them down into sub-categories. For example, in

FIGURE 1.4

The Walt Disney Company's Income Statement (in millions)		
Year ended September 30	1992	1991
Revenues		
Theme parks and resorts	$ 3,306.9	$ 2,794.3
Filmed entertainment	3,115.2	2,593.7
Consumer products	1,081.9	724.0
Investment and interest income	141.5	183.2
	7,645.5	6,295.2
Costs and Expenses		
Theme parks and resorts	2,662.9	2,247.7
Filmed entertainment	2,606.9	2,275.6
Consumer products	798.9	494.2
General and administrative expenses	148.2	160.8
Interest expense	126.8	105.0
	6,343.7	5,283.3
Income Before Income Taxes	1,301.8	1,011.9
Income Taxes	485.1	375.3
Net Income	$ 816.7	$ 636.6

Reprinted by permission of The Walt Disney Company.

the income statement of the Walt Disney Company shown in Figure 1.4, Disney reports four categories of revenues for 1992 of approximately $7.6 billion, and five categories of expenses of approximately $6.3 billion. Profits, given in the income statement as net income, are $0.816.7 billion. This allows you to see how an actual company presents an income statement.

Thus both cash flow cycles and income statements attempt to measure a firm's economic changes occurring over a specific interval of time. Both procedures have their benefits and flaws. However, in the long run it is cash flow analysis that portrays the most accurate picture, since it is cash flow, not accounting income, from which the shareholders ultimately benefit. In other words, when the analysis includes all time periods rather than a specific interval, it is cash flow analysis that correctly measures value.

> ✕ Cash flow analysis portrays the most accurate picture since it is cash flow, not accounting income, from which shareholders ultimately benefit.

FIGURE 1.5
The Corporate Organizational Structure

The corporate organiza-
tional structure illus-
trates the separation
between the owners
(shareholders) and
management.

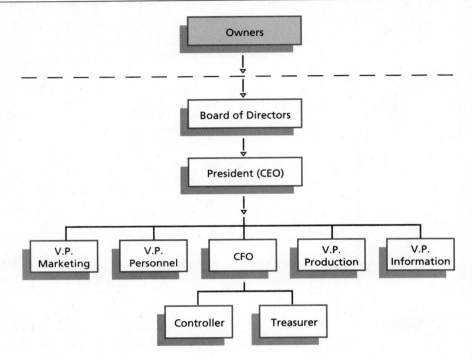

The Organizational View of the Corporation.   The corporation
can also be viewed in terms of its organization. As shown in Figure
1.5, corporate owners and managers are usually different people,
which is in contrast to sole proprietorships and partnerships, whose
owners and managers are usually the same individuals. The broken
line in Figure 1.5 illustrates the separation between owners (stockholders) and top management in the corporate form of organization.

The stockholders, as owners of the firm, have ultimate control
over decisions regarding the firm's assets. This does not necessarily
mean that the stockholders have the expertise or the desire to manage
the firm on a day-to-day basis. And even if they had the desire and
expertise, the number of stockholders is often so large that the very
notion of stockholders making every decision is impractical and perhaps logistically impossible. This is illustrated in Table 1.1, which lists
shares of stock outstanding along with other pertinent information for
the ten largest U.S. corporations in 1991.

The largest U.S. corporation in terms of market equity value is
Exxon. With over 1.2 billion shares of stock outstanding, Exxon had
a market equity value in 1991 of over $75.6 billion, had annual sales

TABLE 1.1
Ten Largest U.S. Corporations Ranked by Market Equity Value 1991

Company	Number of Shares of Stock Outstanding (in millions)	Market Value of Equity (in millions)	Annual Sales (in millions)	Number of Employees
Exxon	1,245	$75,607	$102,847	101,000
Philip Morris	896	$73,818	$ 48,064	166,000
General Motors	705	$66,105	$122,081	756,300
Merck	1,147	$64,354	$ 7,000	36,900
Coca-Cola	1,310	$53,325	$ 11,572	20,960
AT&T	1,336	$51,228	$ 63,089	317,100
IBM	572	$50,821	$ 64,792	344,553
Du Pont	674	$31,297	$ 38,151	132,578
Mobil	399	$27,035	$ 56,042	67,500
Amoco	496	$24,382	$ 25,325	54,524

Source: From *Hoover's Handbook of American Business 1993,* pp. 47, 49, 50. Copyright © 1992 by The Reference Press, Inc., Austin, Texas. Reprinted by permission. Additional data from Dun & Bradstreet, *America's Corporate Family,* Parsippany, N.J., 1992, and *Standard & Poor's Stock Guide,* Standard & Poor's Corporation, New York, N.Y.

of over $102.8 billion, and employed 101,000 people. The other nine corporations listed are recognized by most consumers. The tenth largest U.S. corporation, Amoco, had a market value of over $24 billion and 496 million shares of stock outstanding.

To overcome problems related to the diffused ownership of the typical corporation, the stockholders elect a board of directors to direct overall firm policy. The board selects a management team to participate in all major firm decisions, and the financial managers shown in Figure 1.5 are part of that management team. Window 1.2 describes the typical functions of the top financial management team.

The Modernist View of the Corporation.   A theme throughout this book is the distinction between "traditionalists" and "modernists." Although the term modern or modernist will be more formally developed in the next section, here we offer a preview of finance from the modernist perspective. Modernists view the corporation as a set of contracts with three prominent characteristics:

1. Corporations can declare bankruptcy and therefore provide a protective shield in the form of limited liability to their owners,
2. Corporations are subject to corporate income taxes, and
3. Corporations often are large enough that they require the owners (the shareholders) to hire managers to operate them. In this sense, the managers are known as agents of shareholders.

Window 1.2

The Top Financial Management Team

Almost every major decision within the firm involves the group of top managers known as the financial management team. The functions of the top management team are highlighted below.

The Vice-President of Finance (CFO, or Chief Financial Officer)

In most larger firms, the VP of Finance is also known as the chief financial officer, or CFO. The CFO formulates the major financial policies of the firm such as obtaining and investing funds. The CFO usually sits on committees of top management and is second only to the chief executive officer (CEO) in the corporate hierarchy in most corporations. The CFO is often heir apparent to the CEO or president.

The Corporate Treasurer

The treasurer manages cash within the firm. When the amount of cash held is greater than the amount currently needed, the treasurer will invest the excess cash in securities earning market rates of interest. When the amount of cash held by the firm is less than the amount of cash needed, the treasurer will borrow needed cash from sources such as banks. Thus, an important aspect of the treasurer's job is raising capital from outside sources.

The Corporate Controller

The controller prepares financial statements and manages the audits required to verify their accuracy.

Thus, when shareholders use the corporate form of business organization, their economic behavior may need to be adjusted to take into account the effects of these characteristics. In other words, bankruptcy, tax, and agency considerations may affect investment, financing, and working capital decisions. In the modernist view of the corporation, the essence of corporate finance is how these three characteristics interact with the underlying economic principles of decision making in terms of time and risk.

Now that the terms "finance" and "corporation" have been discussed in detail, we will discuss what is meant by "modern" as we define each term in modern corporate finance.

What Is Meant by *Modern?*

Finance has evolved over the past forty years from a discipline close to accounting (the traditional approach) to one dominated by economic thought and reasoning (the modernist approach). In this development, finance has adopted the rules of science in suggesting plausible reasons for observed events, proposing theories to explain the events, and using data to test those theories.

There are many parallels between the development of modern finance and modern medicine. In the Dark Ages, problem solving in medicine was unsystematic. If a person was sick, the physician might reason that since blood is an important carrier of materials throughout the body, it would be helpful to drain the bad blood and allow the body to produce new, good blood. This practice of blood letting is now known to have been the cause of numerous deaths.

Let's take a closer look at how such medical practices as blood letting could have become popular. Perhaps a physician tried blood letting on a patient who recovered (obviously not because of the blood letting but rather in spite of it) and inferred that the blood letting was helpful. Based upon this single experience, or perhaps several such experiences, the physician taught other physicians to do the same.

Modern medicine has made great strides in the careful development of knowledge using rigorous experimentation. In other words, rather than relying on a few observations, the scientific researcher performs numerous tests to separate truth from coincidence. Also, in a variety of other sciences, it is becoming clear that there is great value in the careful construction and testing of models. Once the foundation of understanding is in place, the simplified model can be used to solve real-world problems.

Because finance is not an experimental science, but one that relies on interpreting observations, it relies on models as economics does. Models simplify problems and can be used to produce tremendous insights into the behavior of people within and through corporations. Thus, using underlying economic principles, finance develops models to explain how decisions are to be made.

Models should be evaluated by the extent to which they help us understand and solve complex situations. A particular model should never be criticized as being unrealistic. This point is so important and clear that Nobel Prize Laureate Milton Friedman developed an example with which it could be illustrated. We offer Window 1.3 as an anecdote about model building.

Window 1.3

An Anecdote About Model Building

In order to understand that the reality of assumptions is not important, consider the following theory or model:

Assume that ice cubes can walk and open doors. Assume further that ice cubes are intelligent and that they prefer to be in a place that is as cold as possible. Under these assumptions, if you were to enter a house and wanted to find some ice cubes, where would you look for them?

Based upon the model's assumptions, we can deduce that the ice cubes would have moved to the freezer and that we could find the ice cubes if we looked there.

Nobel Laureate Milton Friedman points out that the model is useful because it explains or predicts something we need to know: where to find ice cubes. However, the model is very unrealistic because we all know that ice cubes cannot move or think.

The point of the anecdote is that the usefulness of a model should be based upon how well it helps us to understand a result, not on whether the assumptions are realistic. In fact, the definition of a model—an abstraction from reality—tells us that the model will have unrealistic assumptions. If a theory has no unrealistic assumptions then it is reality rather than a model.

Modern scientific knowledge is best constructed by carefully developing models and rigorously testing their ability to explain behavior. For example, using modern scientific principles, researchers have developed extremely successful models for explaining the prices of financial securities known as options (to be discussed in detail later in the book). In contrast, a careless researcher simply makes a few observations or perhaps even examines only a single case and attempts to infer knowledge.

THE GOAL OR PURPOSE OF THE CORPORATION

Having defined and described modern corporate financial management, we now discuss corporate goals. Given the definition of the corporation as a collection of contracts, defining corporate goals really doesn't make much sense. People have goals, contracts do not. The issue might be stated better from the perspective of the goal of a particular person with respect to a corporation.

The various people who contract through the corporation have potentially very different goals. For example, an employee of the firm may desire a high salary, job security, and a good working environment. A supplier of raw materials may desire bulk purchases with a long-term commitment. A debtholder may desire that the firm live up to the agreement as specified by the debt contract. A member of the community where the corporation is located may desire that the corporation control noise during nighttime hours.

In attempting to define the goal of a corporation, it is probably most useful to identify the goal of the people who organized and own the corporation. From the perspective of finance these are the stockholders. This issue will surface throughout the text, so let's explore some of the concepts.

Corporate Ownership

In a pure legal sense a corporation is owned by its stockholders, but the claim that stockholders own the corporation goes beyond that of a legality. Because the stockholders are entitled to the wealth of the corporation once the contractual claims of others have been satisfied, they are the true owners of the firm.

What is the goal of the shareholders of a corporation? Corporate finance teaches that the goal of the shareholders, and in fact the goal of the entire firm, is maximization of shareholder wealth. In other words, shareholders want the market value of their shares of stock to be as high as possible.

The principle of shareholder wealth maximization may appear to describe greedy, money-centered attitudes. However, shareholder wealth maximization in actuality means being efficient at doing whatever shareholders desire. In other words, if a manager operates a corporation in a manner that maximizes shareholder wealth, then the manager must be satisfying shareholder goals.

stakeholder view of the corporation
The view that the corporation can be influenced by—and therefore to some extent owned by—anyone who has a stake in the corporation's actions.

shareholder wealth maximization
The financial objective of the corporation. This objective states that shareholders, as owners of the corporation, desire the market value of their equity to be as high as possible.

It must be said that alternative viewpoints exist. One such alternative viewpoint is that the corporation can be influenced by—and therefore to some extent owned by—anyone who has a stake in the corporation's actions. This view, often called the **stakeholder view of the corporation,** is expanded in Window 1.4 through a discussion of Ben and Jerry's Homemade, Inc., an ice cream manufacturer founded on a business principle called "caring capitalism."

The question of ownership is an issue of legal and philosophical concepts. The argument set forth by the modern finance viewpoint is clear and persuasive: Corporations belong to the shareholders and to the shareholders belongs the right to determine the goals of the corporation. This is referred to as **shareholder wealth maximization.**

Window 1.4

The Stakeholder View As Seen Through Ben and Jerry's Homemade

The stakeholder view of the firm states that the corporation can be influenced by—and therefore to some extent owned by—anyone who has a stake in the corporation's actions. In other words, it is argued that the goal of the firm should be to benefit all stakeholders, not just the stockholders.

A firm that in some ways personifies this view is Ben and Jerry's Homemade, Inc., of Waterbury, Vermont. Although Ben and Jerry's makes ice cream, the unique aspect of the firm is their approach to business—an approach called "caring capitalism." In addition to Ben and Jerry's product mission (to make good-tasting ice cream) and their economic mission (to increase the value of their shareholder's wealth), the firm operates under a specific social mission:

> To operate the company in a way that actively recognizes the central role that business plays in the structure of society by initiating innovative ways to improve the quality of life of our employees and a broad community: local, national, and international.

One of the ways the company works toward its social mission is through the Ben and Jerry's Foundation, created to distribute 7.5 percent of pretax profits to projects that are committed to social change—for instance, to the Cristic Institute, the Welfare Rights Organization Coalition, and One Percent for Peace, Inc., an organization whose purpose is to create, promote, and fund a positive peace agenda.

The key to Ben and Jerry's Homemade is that the corporation's actions are still controlled by its owners. Many stakeholder advocates attempt to force corporations to adopt goals other than shareholder wealth maximization through government regulation.

The view of modern corporate finance is that there is nothing valuable about Ben and Jerry's social mission. This is not to say that these efforts are not worthy, rather that individuals do not need to work through a corporation to attain these goals. In other words, caring capitalism can also be performed by the shareholders of firms that maximize shareholder wealth. The maximization of shareholder wealth is a goal that will allow the firm to concentrate its efforts on their product line, leaving the firm's shareholders to satisfy their own social agenda.

Does the goal of shareholder wealth maximization mean that managers should ignore employee and community concerns or even that all that shareholders can care about is money? The answers are no! Maximizing shareholder wealth is in many cases analogous to producing products that people desire, at their lowest possible price, at high quality, and sold through convenient locations. Maximizing shareholder wealth is a goal that can result in job creation at competitive wages.

Owners Versus Managers

We have said that shareholders desire to have their wealth maximized by managers, but we must also realize that managers have their own goals. For example, managers may desire secure and lucrative jobs with travel, attractive offices, and freedom from pressures. However, some or all of these managerial goals may conflict with the shareholders' goal of having the highest possible market price for their shares.

agency relationship
A relationship in which one or more persons (the principal) contract with one or more other persons (the agent) to perform a decision-making task for them. In the case of corporate finance, the shareholders are the principals and the managers are the agents.

agency costs
Resources utilized to align managerial goals with shareholder goals.

The relationship between shareholders and managers is known as an **agency relationship.** An agency relationship exists when one or more persons (the principal) contract with one or more other persons (the agent) to perform a decision-making task for them. In the case of corporate finance, the shareholders are the principals and the managers are the agents. **Agency costs** are resources utilized to align managerial goals with shareholder goals. In other words, the competing desires of shareholders and managers create conflicts and costs. One goal of the study of modern corporate finance is to understand these costs and to try to minimize them in an attempt to maximize shareholder wealth.

SUMMARY

☐ Modern corporate finance is a two-step approach to problem solving within the business firm. The first step builds a foundation of understanding through the use of simplified models. The second step emphasizes practical applications of the model.

☐ Finance is defined as the economics of time and risk. The primary topics of corporate finance are how managers make financial decisions involving the passage of time and risk.

☐ The study of corporate finance can be characterized by three major types of decisions: the financing decision, the investment decision, and the working capital decision.

❑ The corporation is a collection of contracts organized by individuals for the purpose of engaging in economic activity. Those who normally contract through the corporation include owners (stockholders), creditors (debtholders), employees, suppliers, consumers, community residents, and the people who comprise all levels of government.

❑ Modernists view the corporation as a set of contracts with three distinguishing characteristics: (1) the corporation offers limited liability to its owners, (2) the corporation is subject to corporate income taxes, and (3) corporate owners (shareholders) hire professional managers to run the firm on a day-to-day basis. Managers are agents of the shareholders.

❑ Shareholders desire to have their wealth in the firm maximized. This goal requires managers to perform in a manner consistent with this goal.

REVIEW QUESTIONS

1. How does finance differ from economics?
2. Explain the contractual differences between corporations, partnerships, and sole proprietorships.
3. What is the role of the stockholders in the organization of a corporation?
4. List and discuss three important characteristics of the corporation.
5. Who owns a corporation, and what is its goal?
6. What is an agency relationship?

DISCUSSION QUESTIONS

1. Respond to the following statement:

   The objective of the firm—to maximize shareholder wealth—is extremely narrow-minded. This objective suggests that shareholders are more important than other groups of people who comprise the corporation. Corporate objectives should be directed to all groups, not just shareholders.

2. A U.S. senator said that a certain corporation was causing alarming levels of pollution, and that the corporation should be punished. Given our definition of the corporation, can the corporation pollute and be punished? If not, then who pollutes and who should be punished?

3. Recall Milton Friedman's ice cube example:

   Assume that ice cubes can move about (opening doors, etc.), assume that ice cubes desire to be as cold as possible, and assume that ice cubes are intelligent enough to know where it is cold. Using this theory, where would one look for ice cubes when entering a house?

a. Which of the following conclusions can be rationally deduced from the foregoing assumptions (more than one answer can be correct)?

    (1) Ice cubes can be found in the freezer.

    (2) Some ice cubes will travel to the arctic where it is cold.

    (3) Ice cubes can stay alive in boiling water.

    (4) Ice cubes can be purchased in bags from any convenience store.

b. Which two of the conclusions in part (a) could survive empirical scrutiny? In other words, which two conclusions accurately predict what we observe in the real world?

c. Which one of the conclusions in part (a) is both reasoned through deduction and can survive empirical scrutiny?

Chapter 2

Economic Foundations of Finance

What skills are necessary to become a great pool player?[1] Your first response to this question was probably not physics. However, great pool players must prove they understand physics (momentum, force, friction) better than most other people in the world. Most people do not analyze the ability of pool players in terms of physics. Rather, they assume that, through experimentation, thousands of mistakes are made until the essential principles become second nature.

Just as pool players must understand the effects of physical laws, financial managers must understand the principles of economics when making investment, financing, and working capital decisions. Unlike pool players, most financial managers cannot afford the luxury of running a firm by trial and error, particularly when their decisions determine how millions of dollars will be invested. As many managers have discovered, financial skills are best attained through an understanding of the principles of economics within simplified models, then learning how to recognize and apply these principles to complex problems of the real world.

This chapter introduces the economic principles that form the foundation for financial decision making, most of which will seem familiar because they are part of the process you use in making everyday decisions. Financial managers use economic principles to make decisions. Investments made today often promise future cash inflows, and the period of time between the development of a project and its termination must be included in any project assessment. The financial manager must also include the effect of uncertainty—whether a project will perform as expected.

---

1. Using the game of pool to illustrate the laws of physics and engineering first appeared in M. Friedman and L.J. Savage, "The Utility Analysis of Choices Involving Risk." *The Journal of Political Economy* 56, no. 4 (August 1948): 279–304.

These economic principles also help us to understand financial markets. The financial manager relies on markets to raise funds to finance investments and uses the information in financial markets to assess the value of the firm. In the models that we will build to analyze investment, financing, and working capital management decisions, we need to know about the workings of markets. Financial theories have been developed in order to explain the way markets behave, and we discuss them as part of this chapter.

ECONOMIC FOUNDATIONS

Our goal is to describe, through principles, how shareholders behave in a simplified situation. It is extremely important that our knowledge be built carefully in order to avoid mistakes. Accordingly, we first need to describe the conditions or assumptions that are essential in order for the economic principles of this chapter to hold. These conditions don't have to be true in all cases in order for the principles to be true or useful, but they allow the principles to be developed rigorously and provide a more complete understanding of the objective of shareholder wealth maximization.

Underlying Assumptions

Assumptions are the basis of models, and we start with the assumptions that underlie the economic principles of finance. First, we assume that people are rational. This means that individuals have preferences and that they act with available information and with some degree of intelligence to exercise their preferences. We know that this assumption does not hold for all people all the time, but it serves as a useful starting point. Remember: Untrue assumptions are a necessary part of model building.

Second, we assume that people have access to financial markets, and that these markets are well functioning. This means, essentially, that the law of one price holds—that the same asset can be purchased and sold by everyone at the same price. We assume that markets contain some technical properties such as the ability to trade at zero cost and the ability to divide products limitlessly, meaning that it is possible to purchase half a bond or a tenth of a share of stock.

With these assumptions, we are now ready to present our economic principles.

The First Principle: Positive Marginal Utility of Wealth

The first economic principle states that, given a choice, rational people prefer more wealth to less wealth, where wealth is defined as the sum of the values of all of the things owned. Because value can be measured through market prices, you can determine how wealthy you are by listing what you own, estimating what you could sell these things for today, and adding up the list.

positive marginal utility
An economic principle stating that, given a choice, rational people prefer more wealth to less wealth, where wealth is defined as the sum of the values of all of the things owned.

Economists call our first principle **positive marginal utility** of wealth. Utility is the measurable happiness an individual derives from consumption. For instance, most people receive utility from eating ice cream. Marginal utility is the added utility from additional consumption of a product. Because positive means greater than zero, positive marginal utility of wealth means simply that people prefer more wealth to less wealth, since in a well-functioning market, more wealth will allow greater consumption.[2]

The first principle appears trivial until it is realized that it holds not only for individual items but also for comparisons between items that trade in markets. For example, would a resident of Alaska prefer a $500 air conditioner to a $400 heater? The answer from our model is yes! As long as the market for trading goods is well functioning, prices in the market are measures of the value of each item. Thus, the resident of Alaska could trade the $500 air conditioner for the $400 heater and pocket the $100 change. Choosing the $400 heater would be a violation of our first economic principle.

In fact, the ability to trade goods at market prices is key to our first principle. Well-functioning markets allow people to exchange whatever assets they own for assets that they prefer, and allow workers to concentrate their productive efforts in areas where they have developed a comparative advantage. This concept is known as **separation**. Separation refers to the ability to make certain decisions separately from or independently from the preferences or tastes of the beneficiary.

separation
The ability to make certain decisions separately from or independently from the preferences or tastes of the beneficiary.

A farm provides a good example of separation. The farmer selects which crops to grow irrespective of what types of food the family wishes to eat. This is because the farmer knows that by maximizing the profit received from the harvest, the family can then go to the grocery store and best satisfy their individual tastes.

For the financial manager, the principles of positive marginal utility and separation provide extremely powerful implications. Because all shareholders prefer more wealth to less wealth, and because wealth is measured through market prices, the financial manager can base all decisions on the market value of the firm's stock price. This is such

---

2. To some, positive marginal utility might be equated to greed. However, most people view greed as the excessive desire for wealth in relation to other desires. Greedy people might, for example, compromise their health or family for money. Therefore, positive marginal utility is not quite the same as greed.

an important statement that it merits emphasis. Managers may know little about the thousands of a firm's shareholders, but one thing they know for certain is that shareholders desire the firm's stock price to be as high as possible.

Given a choice between alternatives, shareholders desire the financial manager to make decisions that produce the highest market value for the firm's stock. A manager who causes the firm's share price to rise has made all of the firm's shareholders better off. Conversely, a manager who causes the firm's share price to fall (e.g., rejecting something beneficial to the firm) has made all of the firm's shareholders worse off.

> ⧗ Given a choice between alternatives, shareholders desire the financial manager to make decisions that produce the highest market value for the firm's stock.

The Second Principle: Diminishing Marginal Utility of Wealth

diminishing marginal utility
An economic principle asserting that more and more units of consumption create less and less additional happiness when compared with previous units of consumption.

As we have stated, marginal utility is the added happiness derived from consuming a product. The second principle, **diminishing marginal utility**, implies that more and more units of consumption create less and less additional happiness when compared with previous units of consumption.

For example, virtually everyone would agree that it is worthwhile to purchase at least one pair of shoes, since the advantages of wearing shoes are worth the price. Many people own several pairs of footwear, since they find that the additional advantages to extra pairs of footwear exceed their costs.

Most people, however, discover an important principle when they consume—that the more individuals consume of a particular product, the less additional satisfaction they receive from each additional unit. The first pair of shoes provides a basic comfort need—an extremely high priority to most people. The second pair may also be important, but probably not as important as the first pair, and so forth.

At some point, the advantage offered by another pair of shoes no longer exceeds the disadvantages (primarily the cost) incurred when more shoes are purchased. Inasmuch as the person's preference for additional shoes approximately equals the market price of shoes, no additional shoes are purchased.

We can also express diminishing marginal utility in terms of wealth, since wealth represents potential consumption. An added $1 of wealth becomes less and less important as a person becomes wealthier and wealthier.[3] Additional wealth would mean more to a person just before winning the lottery than it would mean just afterward. Notice that many multi-million-dollar lottery winners quit their jobs.

As with our first principle, diminishing marginal utility of wealth appears trivial until it is realized that the alternatives can include other products. An interesting result of well-functioning markets and diminishing marginal utility is that the relationship between market prices of various goods reflects the preferences of virtually all the people in the economy with regard to those goods.

For example, if the market price of beef is twice the market price of chicken, then generally we will find that people prefer beef two times as much as they prefer chicken. Thus, a piece of chicken would need to be double the size of a piece of beef to be equally attractive to consumers. If this were not true, then people would be bypassing opportunities to make themselves wealthier—which violates our first principle of preferring more wealth to less. For example, if John liked chicken more than beef, he would exchange beef for chicken, making the other person happier and pocketing the change. The process would continue until the law of diminishing marginal utility forced his desire for chicken to only half of his desire for beef (or until he ran out of beef).

Common sense tells us that this principle does not work perfectly in the real world, most likely because some of the assumptions are violated. Perhaps the market for meat is not well functioning, so that the person cannot return it for exchange. Or perhaps some people may not eat any meat at all. However, most financial markets have close to ideal conditions under which our principles hold fairly well.

This explains why the most desirable products seem to cost the most. It's not a cruel conspiracy of the ruling class perpetrated on consumers— it's a result of basic economic forces. Luxury items of the past, such as salt, spices, and silk, are abundant today and are not expensive. On the other hand, some items that have been abundant, such as clean water, are becoming more and more rare and more and more expensive today.

More importantly, diminishing marginal utility is the reason that people limit the amount of risk they bear. The explanation is that risks offer opportunities for higher wealth but dangers of lower wealth.

---

3. Declining marginal utility may not hold for some people in selective circumstances. For example, a drug addict appears at times never satiated by the product—always wanting more. Without declining marginal utility, consumption of a particular product will "explode" to the exclusion of most other products. Contrary to the rule, another unit is consumed even though it appears to other people that the disadvantages outweigh the advantages.

Most people find that for a particular dollar investment, the unhappiness that would result from lost wealth is greater than the happiness that would result from added wealth. Diminishing marginal utility causes investors to take added risk only when it is compensated by higher expected return. A full explanation of this topic will be presented in Module 3, on risk.

The Third Principle: Diminishing Marginal Return

In addition to deciding where to invest, financial management must also decide when to stop investing—that is, the point at which the commitment of additional resources becomes detrimental to the firm. **Diminishing marginal return** forces a firm to limit its investment and output to some optimal level.

diminishing marginal return
An economic principle whereby, at some point, the commitment of additional resources becomes detrimental to the firm with the result that the firm is forced to limit its investment to some optimal level.

Just as added happiness diminishes with additional consumption, productive opportunities diminish with additional investment. Marginal return is the amount of additional output, expressed as a percentage, that a business can produce. Diminishing marginal return is the concept that for a given business, there is a point at which higher production becomes more and more expensive without additional facilities, employees, land, markets, and so forth. A firm will invest up to the point at which the benefits earned on the next project are just equal to the additional cost of investment. Diminishing marginal return ensures that this will occur. Once this point is reached, the disadvantages associated with producing another unit can become greater than the advantages of production.

> ⌛ A firm will invest up to the point at which the benefits earned on the next project are just equal to the additional cost of investment. Diminishing marginal return ensures that this will occur.

Models have been developed to assist financial managers in making investment decisions and finding the optimal level of investment. These tools are known as capital budgeting models and are the topic of Chapter 6.

The Fourth Principle: Conservation of Value

conservation of value
An economic principle stating that the market value of a combination of commodities must be equal to the sum of the market values of all of the commodities in the combination.

Conservation of value, a principle also known as value additivity or the law of one price, states that the market value of a combination of commodities must be equal to the sum of the market values of all the commodities in the combination. For example, suppose that the market price of apples is 25 cents and that the market price of oranges is 20 cents. At what price would two apples trade? At what price would an apple and an orange together trade? The principle of conservation

Window 2.1

Conservation of Value and the Stripping of Treasury Bonds

We observe the principle of conservation of value in the market for securities issued by the United States government. A type of U.S. government security called a Treasury bond offers investors two different kinds of payments: (1) relatively small interest payments received at specific points in time, and (2) a relatively large, one-time principal payment made at the time the security matures. For example, a ten-year Treasury bond might be purchased for $1000 and offer to the investor interest payments of $100 per year for ten years, and a principal payment of $1000 when the bond matures in ten years.

Although many investors are satisfied with receiving these payments, some may desire to receive only one payment. For example, parents of young children may wish to forego the series of interest payments in preference to a single payment in ten years to cover college tuition and expenses.

In order to satisfy the needs of all potential investors, the U.S. Treasury provides a program in which it "strips" the interest and principal payments off of some Treasury bonds and sells the payments separately to various investors who prefer to purchase only a single payment. The law of the conservation of value would suggest that the sum of the market

(continued on next page)

of value would force the answers to be 50 cents and 45 cents, respectively.

If the combinations sold for more than the answers given, say 75 cents, anyone could make an instant profit by buying the fruit individually, and forming and selling the combination. The apple and orange could be bought separately for 45 cents. If they could be sold together for 75 cents, then there would be an instant profit of 30 cents.

Since people prefer more wealth to less wealth, why would they pay 75 cents for the combination when they could create it themselves for 45 cents? The answer is they wouldn't. In the market for apples and oranges described above, we would expect the law of the conservation of value to hold exactly. In large, well-functioning markets such as the financial markets in the United States, we would expect the law to hold very closely. Thus, breaking apart financial assets does not create value, destroy value, or transfer value. Window 2.1 illustrates the

Window 2.1 *(continued)*

prices of these separate securities, known as Treasury strips, should approximate the price of the total Treasury bond from which they were stripped. This is what we observe.

The stripped Treasury bond market provides us with an opportunity to illustrate an important implication of the principle of conservation of value. Think for a moment about the U.S. Treasury's strips program. By stripping the bond, the Treasury has not created anything of value, but has simply cut up the cash flows offered by the Treasury bond. After all, is a pizza cut into twelve pieces more valuable than the same-size pizza cut into eight pieces?

Of course, investors who desire to invest in a part of the Treasury bond rather than the whole bond will compensate the Treasury for its work in stripping the bond—for example the paperwork, advertising, labor, and capital expenditures. However, the compensation will not go beyond the costs of these efforts. In this case, the advantage gained from stripping the bond (the compensation) will exactly equal the disadvantage (the cost).

This must be the case in well-functioning financial markets. If for some reason the Treasury were compensated beyond its cost, then stripping would make it better off and would make investors who purchase the separate payments worse off since they would have paid too much. These actions would surely invite private corporations to come in and make their own shareholders better off by providing similar stripping services at lower cost. The increased competition would force down the compensation to the Treasury. Similarly, if investors refused to pay to the Treasury an amount of compensation equal to the cost of stripping, neither the Treasury, nor anyone else, would supply these services.

law of conservation of value in the market for stripped Treasury bonds. From the law of conservation of value, we know that the value of the total Treasury bond is equal to the "stripped out" parts.

A Summary of the Four Economic Principles

Economic principles provide a foundation for investment, financing, and working capital decisions. The first principle of positive marginal utility of wealth states that more wealth is preferred to less wealth, where wealth is measured by market prices. Given positive marginal utility of wealth, the financial manager will always choose the alternative that produces the highest market value for the firm's stock when making decisions for shareholders.

The second principle, diminishing marginal utility of wealth, states that the more a product is consumed, the less satisfaction it will bring. Diminishing marginal utility of wealth teaches us that market

FIGURE 2.1
A Utility Function

The shape of the utility function represents positive marginal utility (always upward sloping) and diminishing marginal utility (decreasing in slope).

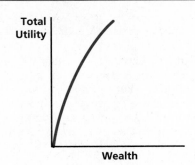

prices are accurate indicators of how people perceive value, and that risk bearing must be compensated with higher expected return.

These two principles are illustrated in Figure 2.1, which is called a utility function and demonstrates the relationship between utility and wealth. Utility is placed on the vertical axis and wealth is placed on the horizontal axis. In theory, each rational person in a well-functioning market has a utility function that links wealth and happiness, with everything else (e.g., health) held equal.

The first economic principle—positive marginal utility of wealth—is demonstrated in Figure 2.1 by a function that is always upward sloping. The second economic principle—diminishing marginal utility of wealth—is demonstrated by the way the curve decreases in its slope from left to right.

The third principle, diminishing marginal return, demonstrates that limits exist to the production of goods and services such that at some point the benefits of producing one additional unit are equal to the cost of production. This principle defines for the financial manager the level of production and the level of investment that maximize shareholder wealth.

Finally, the fourth principle, conservation of value, states that the value of two or more assets combined is equal to the sum of the values of the assets if they were separated. This principle implies that identical assets must sell for identical prices, and that in well-functioning markets, breaking apart financial assets does not create value, destroy value, or transfer value.

Next, we demonstrate how economic decisions can be simplified by way of a model. Workshop 2.1 illustrates how the principles of positive marginal utility and diminishing marginal utility can be used to model how an individual decides which products to consume and how much to consume. Workshop 2.1 provides a foundation for analyzing corporate financial problems involving decision making, which will be developed further in Modules 3 and 4.

Economic Principles and Decision Making

Most people enjoy pizza, but nobody eats pizza continuously and limitlessly. How do people make the decision of whether and how much to consume? In this workshop we demonstrate the simple utility-based economic model that explains consumption decisions. If we analyze behavior using the principles of positive marginal utility and diminishing marginal utility, we can make some predictions about the amount of pizza people will buy and even the amount of other products they will consume.

Consider Bill, who enjoys pizza and root beer. Let's suppose that the utility function given in Figure 2.1 measures the pizza-eating happiness curve for Bill. Pizza costs $1 per slice. Data used to construct Bill's utility curve are given in Table 2.1. A "util" is a fictitious unit of happiness which allows us to describe a degree of happiness with a number.

Bill derives 10 utils of happiness from eating the first slice of pizza, but less and less happiness from each successive slice. His additional happiness starts to tail off after eating the first slice, and drops from 10 utils to 1 util by the seventh slice of pizza. Notice that Table 2.1 illustrates the principles of both positive marginal utility and diminishing marginal utility. Positive marginal utility is illustrated by the fact that added consumption always results in added happiness. Diminishing marginal utility is illustrated by the fact that the added happiness decreases at higher and higher levels of consumption.

At what point should Bill stop consuming pizza? This depends on his income level and other consumption choices. If Bill has limited income, then he should stop eating pizza when he can use the next $1 to derive more happiness from another product than that offered by the next pizza slice.

An alternative consumption choice for Bill is root beer, which costs $1 per glass. Table 2.2 presents Bill's root beer drinking utility.

TABLE 2.1
Bill's Pizza-eating Utility

Slices of Pizza	Increase in Happiness	Total Happiness
1	10 utils	10 utils
2	8 utils	18 utils
3	7 utils	25 utils
4	6 utils	31 utils
5	3 utils	34 utils
6	2 utils	36 utils
7	1 utils	37 utils

(continued on next page)

Workshop 2.1 *(continued)*

TABLE 2.2
Bill's Root Beer Drinking Utility

Glasses of Root Beer	Increase in Happiness	Total Happiness
1	9 utils	9 utils
2	4 utils	13 utils
3	3 utils	16 utils
4	2 utils	18 utils
5	1 util	19 utils

Given the opportunity to decide between pizza and root beer, what should he do? With limited income and an objective of being as happy as possible, his choice becomes clear. He should first eat one slice of pizza and then switch to root beer, as the second pizza slice offers him 8 utils of happiness, while the first glass of root beer offers him 9 utils of happiness.

When should Bill stop consuming root beer? As before, the answer depends on his income level and his consumption choices. If he has a choice of pizza and root beer, and if he has a third dollar to spend, then he should switch back to pizza, as the next slice offers more happiness as compared with the next glass of root beer.

Now let's allow for trading of commodities at market prices. Bill, who often clips coupons from the newspaper, brings a coupon to the local pizza parlor entitling him to a free beverage—no purchase necessary. The pizza parlor offers as beverages root beer at $1 a glass and orange juice at $2 a glass. We know from Table 2.2 that root beer delivers happiness to Bill. Unfortunately, orange juice does not. What should Bill do?

The answer is clear if the pizza parlor allows Bill to trade commodities at market prices. He should use his coupon for orange juice, and trade back the orange juice for one slice of pizza and one glass of root beer. Of course, Bill must make consumption decisions involving many more than two products. The principles of positive marginal utility and diminishing marginal utility can be extended to incorporate any number of choices.

TIME AND RISK

The economic principles introduced above appear at first to apply only to cases of comparing two or more products at the same point in time, with no risk involved. In the real world, the financial manager must select investments that increase shareholder wealth. However, real-world investment decisions can become complicated. As we have said, benefits must be weighed against costs through time. Resources must be committed today to produce a product or service that will be brought to market in the future. Also, because benefits and costs must be estimated, there is risk that benefits will be lower than anticipated or that costs will be higher than anticipated. The timing and risk of the cash flows expected from investment will influence its value. Modern finance teaches that these simple economic principles are equally appropriate for more complicated choices involving time and risk.

Time Value and the Concept of Different Commodities

Most people would not trade a double cheeseburger for three potato chips because they view the one double cheeseburger as being more valuable than the three potato chips. Should a corporate manager invest $100,000 today in return for $125,000 in ten years? Logic might suggest yes—that $125,000 is greater than $100,000. This logic is flawed, however, because it fails to recognize that, like the comparison of double cheeseburgers and potato chips, dollars received at different points through time are actually different commodities with different values. The correct answer is found by determining if $100,000 today has a higher value than $125,000 due in ten years.

Because dollars through time are different commodities, they cannot be added to or subtracted from each other when making financial decisions. In order to analyze time value correctly we need to change the future cash flow into an equivalent value in today's dollars and then make the comparison. Just as three potato chips are not worth three times as much as one double cheeseburger, $125,000 to be received in ten years is not 25 percent more valuable than $100,000 to be received today.

Methods exist that allow precise market values to be placed on dollars that occur in different time periods. These methods (described in Module 2) help us to understand the time value of money. They also permit financial managers to use simple economic concepts to make decisions today regarding investments promising dollars to be received in the future. Once future cash flows have been transformed into present market values, separation can be applied to the decision-making process. In this context, separation refers to the idea that financial managers are satisfying all shareholders when they maximize the value of the shareholders' wealth.

Risk and the Concept of Different Commodities

Most financial decisions have some degree of risk. How can financial managers make decisions with such risks? Just as dollars through time are different commodities with different values, the promise of a risky cash flow is a different commodity compared to the promise of a safe cash flow. Said differently, an investment that promises $100 in one year with certainty might be viewed as more valuable than an investment that promises $150 in one year with uncertainty.

For example, consider a cheese manufacturer whose limited manufacturing operations can produce either American cheese or Brie but not both. Cost and sales estimates show that both are good investments, but that project Brie is expected to produce more future dollars as compared with project American cheese. Is Brie the product of choice?

The decision is not easy to make because Brie sales are uncertain, whereas sales of American cheese are virtually guaranteed. The difference in risk makes the investment in project Brie different from the investment in project American cheese. Because a safe dollar has a higher value than a risky dollar, project American cheese, while expected to produce fewer future dollars, might be the preferred choice.

Models exist to evaluate cash flows with different degrees of risk. These models, termed generally "valuation under uncertainty," comprise the material in Module 3. These tools permit financial managers to merge uncertainty with rather simple economic principles. Once again, proper use of these tools permits the concept of separation. In this instance, separation refers to the ability of financial managers to make decisions that satisfy all shareholders by maximizing the shareholders' wealth. Thus, even decisions favoring risky investments can be made on behalf of shareholders without having to worry about individual attitudes toward risk.

MARKET EFFICIENCY

This section provides a detailed look at the behavior of markets, specifically at the process by which prices are determined within markets. In Chapter 1 it was demonstrated that managers should attempt to maximize shareholder wealth by making the firm's share price as high as possible. However, in order for this decision rule to be meaningful, managers must understand how prices are determined in the market. Modern corporate finance assumes that prices observed in markets are rational measures of value, based upon all available information. We now discuss situations in which this assumption can be expected to hold such that financial managers have a meaningful understanding of how to implement the objective of share price maximization.

Many of us have encountered get-rich-quick schemes at one time or another. For instance, viewers of late-night television may be familiar with stories of how fortunes can be made trading certain commodities or real estate with relatively little effort and with a surprisingly small investment. When approached with such opportunities, most clear-thinking people understand that these advertisements are too good to be true.

Get-rich-quick schemes don't work because things of value cannot be purchased on the cheap. Said differently, the price of obtaining an asset must be (approximately) equal to the asset's value. While an occasional exception may exist in some markets, modern corporate financial management offers principles that will hold under normal circumstances.

In the broadest sense, the concept that the price of an asset is equal to its value is known as market efficiency. An **efficient market** exists when the assets in the market are traded at prices that equal their values, based upon all available information.

efficient market
A market in which assets are traded at prices that equal their values, based upon all available information.

There is growing support for the idea that most major U.S. financial markets, for example stock markets and bond markets, are rather efficient. In an efficient market it is not possible to "beat the market" consistently because prices already reflect all available information. Countless tests have been performed and published generally demonstrating that various investment strategies are unable to earn consistently superior returns and, therefore, that major markets are rather efficient.

Think for a moment about the thousands of finance professors, corporate investment analysts, and free-lance investors who are equipped with powerful computers, huge databases of price histories, and advanced statistical techniques. If markets were not reasonably efficient, wouldn't many of these people be tremendously wealthy from their own investment success?

Competition is so fierce in these markets that most people have little or no chance of consistently outperforming others by buying assets trading at prices that are too low or by selling assets trading at prices that are too high. Both buyers and sellers use available information to make decisions, so it should be of no surprise that actual prices will reflect all the information that is available. Competition eliminates prices that are both too high and too low. Did you ever notice that when gas stations are located close to each other they tend to have more similar prices than when they are far apart?

It is important that market prices be based upon available information rather than upon emotions or trends. To maximize the value of shareholders' equity financial managers must understand how the market prices the stock and respond accordingly. If market prices reflect all available information, managers will find that the only way to maximize shareholder wealth is to make decisions in which the net result of all of the implications of the decision will be positive. In other words, managers must make decisions in which all benefits will exceed all costs, since the market price will reflect all information. If markets were priced irrationally or emotionally (that is, some relevant information was ignored) the financial manager either wouldn't know what to do or could manipulate the market price by making otherwise detrimental decisions, taking advantage of the market's mistakes.

For example, if a professor assigned grades at random, students would have no incentive to perform well on exams. Similarly, financial managers must understand the process by which market prices are determined in order to make proper decisions regarding the management of the firm.

The theory of market efficiency is a solid starting point upon which to understand financial markets. For financial managers, the major implication of market efficiency is that the firm's stock price is an accurate reflection of value, and therefore that decisions should be made in such a way that all the advantages of the decision exceed all the disadvantages.

Market efficiency is discussed in Window 2.2—not from the perspective of the financial manager but instead from the perspective of the individual investor, because it is easier to understand market efficiency from the perspective of the investor. However, the role of market efficiency in this text is to provide a logical basis upon which to construct a meaningful model of how to manage a firm's finances. Regardless of the perspective, we will use the term market efficiency to describe the tendency of assets in a particular market to sell at their correct value based upon available information.

INEFFICIENT MARKETS

In a well-functioning market, rational investors will drive markets towards the concept of market efficiency through their attempts to outperform other investors. Markets that are not well functioning can be **inefficient markets**, in which assets can trade at prices that do not reflect all available information. Examples include the stocks and bonds of very small companies, real estate, equipment, cars, and other assets for which it is difficult to find numerous buyers who are already familiar with the asset.

inefficient market
A market in which assets trade at prices that do not reflect all available information.

One of the most important aspects of finance is learning how to make decisions regarding assets in inefficient markets. In fact, the objective of shareholder wealth maximization is accomplished almost entirely by applying tools that enable a financial manager to purchase and utilize assets at inefficient prices. For example, a typical manufacturer purchases land, buildings, equipment, and raw materials with the goal of selling the manufactured output at a price that exceeds the combined costs of the inputs.

In an efficient market, competition drives away superior returns found through combining assets that trade in the market. The value of a combination of assets in an efficient market is found simply as the sum of the values of the assets that form the combination. However, the primary business of most corporations is selling their prod-

Window 2.2

Market Efficiency and the Individual Investor

The idea that financial markets are efficient—that it is impossible to consistently identify prices that are too low or too high—is actually a shock to many students. Many people believe that sharp investors have the knack of identifying good buys, perhaps due to years of exposure to advertisements and other claims that seem to be based on the opposite idea. The concept of market efficiency implies that "beating the market" on a consistent basis over a long period of time cannot be done.

There is a debate among financial theorists about the efficiency of markets. To apply the definition of market efficiency to most markets, financial theorists have separated the concept of market efficiency into three forms or levels that differ by the kind of information available to market participants. These three forms are the weak form, the semi-strong form, and the strong form. Further, there are three major types of investment analysis: technical analysis, fundamental analysis, and modern portfolio theory. Each of the three levels of market efficiency relates to one of these types of investment analysis and the information they use. A description of the three levels of market efficiency along with the three major types of investment analysis are provided in Table 2.3.

An appreciation of the levels of market efficiency requires some history in investment analysis. Prior to the Great Depression (the 1930s), many people used a technique known as technical analysis to select securities. In technical analysis, information concerning past prices and trading volume is used to try to predict future movements in price. People who use charts to find good buys are often referred to as chartists, because they make graphs or charts from past data. Chartists look for patterns in past price movements in order to decide which securities to buy and sell.

For instance, a chartist might study patterns of stock price movements and conclude that stock prices tend to move in distinct waves, with the result that brief periods of price movements in one direction are often followed by reversals in the other direction. Technical analysts might chart the movements of stocks over some previous period of trading in order to identify those that are prime candidates for reversal. A key to many technical trading strategies— such as the reversal strategy—is that there is nothing special about the firm itself (its products, its management team, its competition, and so forth). The only thing that matters in predicting future stock price is its past price pattern.

Let's explore the use of technical analysis to determine whether to invest in Boeing or Sears. A chartist would begin by plotting past prices of both Boeing and Sears on a graph. The chartist would then try to predict future price movements from these patterns of prices.

(continued on next page)

Window 2.2 *(continued)*

TABLE 2.3
Market Efficiency and Investment Analysis by Type

Type of Market Efficiency	Type of Investment Analysis	Information Set
(1) Weak	Technical analysis	All publicly available past prices and trading volume.
(2) Semi-strong	Fundamental analysis	All publicly available information including financial statements, analysts' recommendations, and past prices and trading volume.
(3) Strong	Modern portfolio theory	All publicly available information. Inside information needed to beat the market.

For example, Boeing's price chart might resemble a classic buy pattern, while Sears' price chart might provide no buy or sell signal. In this case, the chartist's decision would be to invest in Boeing and not Sears.

After World War II, the most popular investment technique was fundamental analysis, which attempts to find the true value of a security using publicly available information such as financial statements. Fundamentalists look for securities whose market price differs from their true price.

For example, fundamentalists might examine a company's financial statements to identify information known as financial ratios. These ratios might relate the current profitability of the firm to its current stock price. According to these ratios, the analyst might believe that the current stock price of Boeing is too high given the firm's fundamental financial situation, and from this analysis decide not to include Boeing in the portfolio.

Finally, in the last twenty to thirty years, there has been a movement toward modern portfolio theory—which does not attempt to choose certain securities using publicly available information but rather only attempts to control risk. Modern portfolio theoreticians believe that the only way to beat the market is to have information not available to the general public. According to modern portfolio theory, investors who do not possess such information should not expect to consistently outperform other investors.

In our example of Boeing and Sears, the modern portfolio theoretician would not be concerned with charts or with the fundamental financial characteristics of either company. According to modern portfolio theory, the only concern would be to choose securities in a way that properly controls risk.

uct for more than its cost (i.e., the combined costs of the inputs necessary to make the product).

Example 2.1 ——————— The primary way for a computer manufacturer to maximize shareholder wealth is to put together relatively inexpensive pieces of plastic and metal into a functioning computer that can be sold for more than it costs to make. The computer manufacturer will be successful only if other manufacturers cannot quickly undercut prices because they lack the expertise, patents, existing manufacturing ability, reputation, or the like.

Superior returns can only be consistently earned when there is a lack of competition such that others cannot duplicate the business at a lower price. Financial managers must learn to recognize where lack of competition or poorly functioning markets create inefficiencies that will enable shareholder wealth to be increased. Additionally, financial managers need to understand that in an efficient market, competition drives away the opportunities for superior returns.

There are many reasons why competition can be reduced to the point at which prices become inefficient. Perhaps there are limitations on the number of people who can produce a computer owing to patent protection or a highly sophisticated required technology. Or, possibly, the assets being traded require information that is not widely known or is extremely difficult to interpret. The assets in these markets can often sell at prices that create the opportunity for superior returns since there are a limited number of participants who have the necessary information to compete. ↵

Inefficient markets can offer opportunities for superior returns and the danger of large losses. The subsections that follow explain some of the major concepts involved in dealing with assets when there is rather limited information available to the market participants. This problem is often discussed in the context of **liquidity**, which refers to the time and cost necessary to sell an asset at its true value.

liquidity
The time and cost necessary to sell an asset at its true value.

Liquid Assets

A highly liquid asset can be sold at its true value very quickly. An example of a highly liquid asset is a U.S. Treasury bill. Traders in the U.S. Treasury bill market have full and immediate information regarding market value. An asset with low or poor liquidity, such as a house, usually requires considerable time before it can be sold at its true value. The time and cost required to sell a house is the time and cost necessary to locate willing buyers and for them to acquire information about the property.

An asset is illiquid if it is costly for buyers to understand fully the information necessary to make a purchase decision. The seller may have to search for a specialized buyer, take time to arrange a sale, or accept a lower sales price. The discrepancies between the information known to the buyer and to the seller are known as **information asymmetries**—because the people involved have different knowledge.

information asymmetries
Discrepancies between the information held by the buyer and the seller of an asset.

To repeat, highly liquid assets like stocks may take only minutes to sell at true values, whereas low liquidity assets like a house may require months to sell at true value.

Liquidity and Corporate Finance

Liquidity has a slightly different meaning when applied to an overall corporation. A corporation is liquid if it has sufficient cash, near cash assets, and sources of credit to pay its bills and to invest in beneficial projects. An illiquid corporation does not have full ability to pay its bills or invest wisely in new projects.

Liquidity is familiar to all of us from our own experiences as a consumer. Most individuals carry cash that can be used immediately and have a checking account that allows payment on demand. Prudent consumers manage their liquidity by having enough cash on hand to meet short-term expenses and leaving the rest of the money in the bank for safety and to earn interest.

The problem of liquidity as it relates to decisions of the financial manager is similar to that of the individual. Corporations try to keep enough cash on hand to meet current needs while trying not to hold excessive amounts of liquidity—a process called working capital management. The goal of working capital management is to maximize shareholder wealth by providing an optimal level of liquidity as cost-effectively as possible.

How can the theory of working capital management be put into practice? Workshop 2.2 describes a simple cash management technique called the economic order quantity (EOQ) model as it relates to the cash balance of the firm. The EOQ model provides a useful starting point for understanding the application of the concepts of working capital management. Chapter 17 will provide more detail on working capital management and will expand the model shown in Workshop 2.2.

The bottom line in working capital management is finding the optimal level of liquidity that balances the advantages and disadvantages, and managing it efficiently.

Managing Cash: The EOQ Model

All firms need some amount of cash on hand to pay bills, meet their payroll, and to satisfy other needs. Inasmuch as the cash held reduces funds available for investment, the task of the financial manager is to keep enough cash on hand for ordinary current expenses, but to avoid waste due to excessive transactions or large cash balances. There are several techniques available to assist the financial manager in determining the optimal policy. The economic order quantity (EOQ) model is one such technique.

To demonstrate how this model can be used to optimize cash balance, consider a growing firm that spends cash steadily and must replenish its cash balance regularly to maintain its inventories, its payroll, and its advertising. The financial manager of this firm wants to achieve the needed liquidity to meet such expenses, but wants to do so as cost-effectively as possible. This means that cash balances should be as low as possible so that funds can be channeled to profitable investment opportunities.

In analyzing the situation, the financial manager realizes that there are two costs to holding cash: (1) the transactions costs of obtaining cash, and (2) the cost of lost investment earnings incurred by holding cash rather than investing those funds. The transactions costs of obtaining cash are called order costs in the EOQ model. The costs of lost earnings are called the storage costs. You may be familiar with storage costs under a different name—opportunity cost. An economist would say that the opportunity cost of holding cash is the lost earnings, but the terms used here are those that apply in the EOQ model.

To find the firm's optimal level of cash, assume that (a) the firm needs $10,000 in cash each day to meet expenses, (b) the firm's order costs are $100 because this is the fee it pays to obtain cash, and (c) the firm's storage costs are $5 for each $100 per year that must be kept as cash rather than invested elsewhere. Expressed as a percent, the cost of lost earnings is 5 percent ($5/$100).

With the EOQ model, the financial manager can strike the proper balance between order costs and storage costs such that cash is managed as efficiently as possible. Use $X to represent the amount of money that the firm needs to replenish its cash balance whenever it runs out of cash. Since the firm uses up $10,000 of cash per day, it will have to replenish its cash balance every $X/$10,000 days. For example, if $X = $100,000, then the firm must replenish its cash every 10 days. Figure 2.2 shows the change in cash balance $X through time.

(continued on next page)

Workshop 2.2 *(continued)*

FIGURE 2.2
The Firm's Cash Balance Through Time

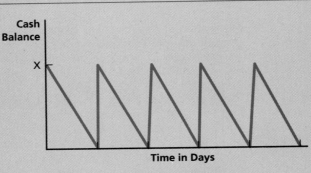

The cash balance is drawn to zero, and then gets
replenished to the EOQ, given by X.

We want to use the EOQ model to find the cash balance \$X that minimizes the sum of
the order costs and storage costs. Total costs are given by:

Total Cost = Annual Order Cost + Annual Storage Cost.

Annual order cost is found by taking the firm's annual cash need divided by the order
size (the unknown variable \$X) multiplied by the cost per order:

$$\text{Annual Order Cost} = \frac{\text{Daily Cash Need} * 365}{\text{Order Size}} * \text{Cost Per Order}. \qquad (2.1)$$

For the firm in our example, annual order costs are:

$$\text{Annual Order Cost} = \frac{\$10,000 * 365}{X} * \$100.$$

(continued on next page)

Workshop 2.2 *(continued)*

Annual storage costs are found by multiplying the average amount of cash held by the cost of holding cash:

$$\text{Annual Storage Cost} = \frac{X}{2} * \text{Cost of Lost Earnings.} \qquad (2.2)$$

For the firm in our example, annual storage costs are:

$$\text{Annual Storage Cost} = \frac{X}{2} * 5\%$$

Substituting these expressions for annual order costs and annual storage costs into the relationship for total costs we get:

$$\text{Total Cost} = \left[\frac{\$10,000 * 365}{X} * \$100 \right] + \left[\frac{X}{2} * 5\% \right].$$

Using calculus, the optimal order size can be found by:

$$\text{EOQ} = \sqrt{\frac{2(\text{Annual Cash Needs})(\text{Cost per Order})}{\text{Interest Rate}}}. \qquad (2.3)$$

In the example, the optimal order size is:

$$X = \sqrt{\frac{2(\$10,000 * 365)(\$100)}{.05}} = \$120,830.$$

Thus, the firm should order (or obtain) the amount of $120,830 in cash each time it replenishes its cash. Because the firm uses cash at a rate of $10,000 per day, it will run out of cash approximately every 12 days. The EOQ model assumes that the firm's cash balance is drawn down to approximately zero, and at that time, a new order of $120,830 arrives. This is illustrated in Figure 2.3.

(continued on next page)

Workshop 2.2 *(continued)*

FIGURE 2.3
The EOQ

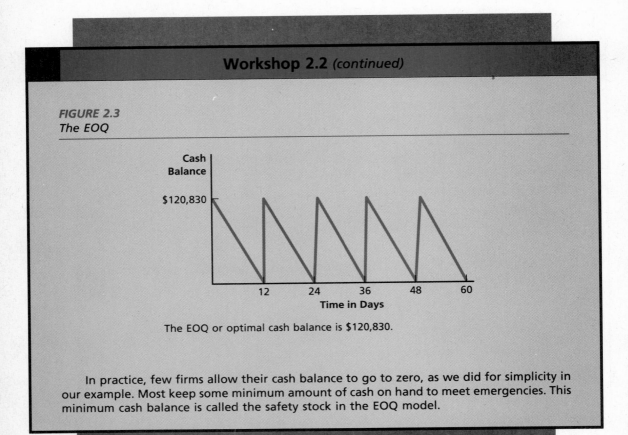

The EOQ or optimal cash balance is $120,830.

In practice, few firms allow their cash balance to go to zero, as we did for simplicity in our example. Most keep some minimum amount of cash on hand to meet emergencies. This minimum cash balance is called the safety stock in the EOQ model.

SUMMARY

- ☐ The economic principles that form the foundation of finance are positive marginal utility, diminishing marginal utility, diminishing marginal return, and the law of conservation of value.

- ☐ In well-functioning markets, market prices are not artificially determined but are the product of these basic economic principles.

- ☐ Managers need to know very little about the shareholders they represent in order to make optimal decisions for them as a group. Shareholders wish to have the market value of their claim maximized, which is known as separation. Separation holds even when decisions involve different commodities, the passage of time, or uncertainty.

◻ Cash flows through time are best viewed as different commodities that cannot be directly added to or subtracted from one another. In a similar way, promised cash flows of different risk are different commodities that cannot be directly compared.

◻ Efficient markets are markets in which prices reflect available information.

◻ The liquidity of an asset is usually related to how difficult it is for buyers to understand information concerning the asset. Liquidity and the costs of information are important aspects of corporate financial management. Working capital management is the process of providing an optimal level of liquidity in as cost-effective a manner as possible.

DEMONSTRATION PROBLEMS

Problem 1   The following chart describes the happiness or utility that Mary derives from fruit:

Quarts of Blueberries	Total Utils from Blueberries	Quarts of Strawberries	Total Utils from Strawberries
1	50	1	20
2	80	2	30
3	105	3	35
4	120	4	38
5	132	5	39

If quarts of blueberries and quarts of strawberries each sell for $2 and if Mary has $8 to spend, how will she spend the money if these are her only choices and if she decides to spend it all?

Solution to Problem 1

Step 1: The first step is to begin with no dollars spent and to determine whether the first two dollars should be used to buy blueberries or strawberries. It is implicitly assumed that Mary does not now have any quarts of fruit and therefore no utils from either type of fruit. The chart reveals that the first quart of blueberries would provide 50 utils of happiness and that the first quart of strawberries would provide only 20 utils of happiness. Thus, to maximize utility, Mary would first purchase a quart of blueberries.

Scorecard: 1 blueberries, 0 strawberries, $6 remain.

Step 2: The second step is to compute the added happiness that another quart of blueberries would give Mary now that she already has one quart of blueberries. The chart reveals that two quarts of blueberries give her 80 utils, which is an increase of 30 utils from her current level of 50 utils. Thus the incremental or marginal utility from another quart of blueberries is 30 utils. Since this is greater than the 20 utils a quart of strawberries would provide, Mary decides to purchase another quart of blueberries.

> Scorecard: 2 blueberries, 0 strawberries, $4 remain.

Step 3: The third step is identical to step 2 except that we now begin with two quarts of blueberries. A third quart of blueberries would provide a total of 105 utils, or in other words a marginal increase of 25 utils. Since this is still greater than the marginal utils provided by the first quart of strawberries, Mary will maximize her utility by purchasing still another quart of blueberries.

> Scorecard: 3 blueberries, 0 strawberries, $2 remain.

Step 4: The final step is to determine what should be done with the last two dollars. A fourth quart of blueberries would provide a total of 120 utils, an increase of only 15 utils. Since this is less than the 20 utils provided by the first quart of strawberries, Mary decides to purchase a quart of strawberries with her last $2.

> Scorecard: 3 blueberries, 1 strawberries, $0 remain.

Final Solution: Mary should purchase 3 quarts of blueberries and 1 quart of strawberries for a total utility of 125 utils (105 utils from blueberries and 20 utils from strawberries). ↵

Problem 2   Mary (the same person in Problem 1) has a garden with limited productive capabilities. The garden can be cultivated to raise either one quart of blueberries or four quarts of strawberries. Which alternative should Mary produce given that both alternatives require the same effort and costs? Assume that the market for fruit is well functioning and that the prices and preferences given in the first problem are applicable to this one.

Solution to Problem 2

Step 1: The first step is to recognize the importance of the assumption that the market for fruit is well functioning. What this means is that quarts of fruit can be purchased and sold at market prices with no taxes, fees, or any other sort of penalty. We can now view the productive capabilities of Mary's garden in terms of market prices. One quart of blueberries has a market value of $2. The four quarts of strawberries have a combined market value of $8. Thus, growing strawberries is the production alternative that produces the highest market value.

Step 2: The final step is to realize that $8 will provide Mary with more utility than $2. In Problem 1 we found that Mary can receive 125 utils from properly spending $8. Mary can only receive 50 utils from spending $2. It is not important that producing and consuming one quart of blueberries provides more utils (50 utils) than producing and consuming four quarts of strawberries (38 utils) since in a well-functioning market Mary can exchange the fruit that she is most capable of growing for the fruit that she most prefers to eat.

Final Solution: Mary should grow the four quarts of strawberries, sell them in the market for $8, and then spend the $8 in the manner that gives her the maximum utility. ↩

REVIEW QUESTIONS

1. Discuss the implication of positive marginal utility to the financial manager.
2. Discuss the implication of diminishing marginal utility to the financial manager.
3. Discuss the implication of diminishing marginal return to the financial manager.
4. Discuss the implication of the law of conservation of value to the financial manager.
5. Explain why, in well-functioning financial markets, a vegetarian might prefer $100 worth of beef to $90 worth of vegetables.
6. What is the implication of market efficiency to the financial manager?
7. What is the objective of the cash management model known as the EOQ model?
8. What does the concept of separation refer to?
9. Why is a "safe" dollar worth more than a "risky" dollar?

PROBLEMS

1. You are in a fabulous new discount store that accepts returned merchandise for exchange, with no questions asked and with a smile. In fact, if you desire they will even refund the retail price of an item. Through a local radio station you have won a free compact disc of your choice. Which of the following CDs will you select?
   a. Greatest Chants of the 11th Century $14.99
   b. Greatest Rock Hits of the 20th Century $12.99
   c. Saddest Country Hits of the 80s $11.99
   d. Most Exciting Vice-Presidential Memoirs $19.99
2. You are in a fabulous financial market where financial securities trade without transaction costs. You own one hundred shares of

a firm called Machiavellian Motors which sells for $20 per share. Suddenly, the CEO (chief executive officer) of Machiavellian Motors makes an announcement. Which of the following announcements and reactions would you prefer?

a. The firm has been bought out. The CEO says that there is nothing that can be done to prevent it and predicts that the new owners will destroy the company. The price of the stock rises to $35 per share.

b. The firm is altering its financial strategy in a move that the CEO predicts will generate huge gains in the future. The price of the stock remains at $20 per share.

c. The firm is dramatically changing its product lines in a move that the CEO predicts will save the company. The stock price falls to $19 per share.

d. The firm is fighting a takeover bid with every means at its disposal in order to protect itself from a "raider." The price of the stock falls to $18 per share.

3. Maude loves to eat cookies and ice cream at the local soda shop. Maude's utility (happiness) from these two products can be expressed as follows:

Number of Cookies	Total Utils from Cookies	Number of Scoops	Total Utils from Ice Cream
1	10	1	16
2	18	2	22
3	25.5	3	24
4	31	4	25
5	36	5	25.5
6	40	6	25.7

(Beyond six cookies and six ice-cream scoops, Maude gets pretty sick.)

a. If each cookie and each ice-cream scoop cost $1 each, what will Maude buy if she has $1? What if she has $2? How about $3 or $5 or $7?

b. If the price of ice cream rises to $2 per scoop while the price of each cookie remains at $1, what will Maude buy if she has $2? What if she has $5?

c. In general, what happens to the amount of ice cream that Maude eats as the price of ice cream rises relative to the price of cookies?

d. Fill in the blank. If the price of ice cream rises to being X times more expensive than cookies, then Maude will switch to eating cookies until the marginal utility from eating ice cream is _____ times the utility she gets from eating cookies.

e. In general, when the price of a particular item rises substantially, will people stop consuming it, consume less of it, consume the same amount, or consume more of it?

4. Farmer Ben knows that feeding a grain supplement to his cows will produce more milk according to the following schedule:

Total Pounds of Supplement Used	Total Extra Pounds of Milk
1	5
2	9
3	12
4	14
5	15
6	15.5

a. Ignoring all other issues, how many pounds of grain supplement should Farmer Ben feed the cows if the price of milk is $0.20 per pound and the price of the grain supplement is $0.50 per pound?

b. How many pounds of grain supplement should Farmer Ben feed the cows if the price of milk remains at $0.20 per pound but the price of grain supplement falls to $0.30 per pound? What if the price of grain supplement rises to $0.70 per pound?

c. Fill in the blank. In more general terms, suppose that the price of grain supplement is X times as expensive as milk. Farmer Ben should feed the grain supplement until each pound of grain supplement produces _____ more pounds of milk.

d. If a milk shortage develops, what would you expect to happen to the price of milk?

e. If the price of milk rises, what would you expect to happen to the amount of grain supplement manufactured and used? What will happen to the amount of milk produced?

f. If the price of grain supplement is exactly 3.25 times the price of milk, what do you know about every cow with regard to its ability to produce more milk using grain supplement?

5. Rank the following assets from most liquid (1) to least liquid (3).
   a. An antique car
   b. IBM Corporation common stock
   c. Modern gold coins

6. Abnormal Growths, Inc., is consuming cash at the rate of $10,000 per day. Each time they sell securities to obtain the cash it costs them $250. The interest rate is 10%. Answer the following using the EOQ model.
   a. How much cash should they obtain each time they sell securities?

    b. How many orders will be placed each year?

    c. What would be the total annual order costs?

    d. What would be the average cash balance size?

    e. What would be the annual storage cost or lost opportunity cost on the cash balance?

    f. How much money would the firm be losing each year if they replenished their cash balance daily with $10,000?

    g. How would your answer to (a) change if the interest rate fell to 5%?

7. Suppose that Firearms Are Us, Inc., has assets worth $1,000,000. They have issued several types of bonds and stocks to various investors. What must be the value of all of the firm's stocks and bonds combined?

DISCUSSION QUESTIONS

1. SportsHats Unlimited has two shareholders, Ned and Ted. Ned loves baseball, and would like the firm to produce nothing but baseball hats. Ted loves tennis, and would like the firm to produce nothing but tennis hats. The truth is that the market is flooded with both baseball and tennis hats, but not with football hats. Both Ned and Ted hate football. What should the manager of SportsHats do? Why?

2. The law of conservation of value states that the market value of a combination must equal the sum of the market values of the items in the combination. This appears to suggest that mergers don't make sense, because the market value of the firms combined is simply equal to the market values of the firms separately. How can this be true given the wave of mergers over the last ten years?

3. If you believe in market efficiency, then you believe that investors have little or no chance of consistently outperforming other investors in well-functioning markets. However, some stock investors have done what market efficiency says can't be done—they have regularly "beaten the market." Does this mean that well-functioning markets are inefficient?

4. The local toy store holds a sweepstakes in which the winner gets to choose any toy in the store absolutely free. The store has a policy of accepting any item for exchange or for a full cash refund with no questions asked. You are sure that this policy holds for sweepstakes winners as well.

    a. If you win the sweepstakes, which toy would you choose?

    b. If your best friend wins the sweepstakes and asks you to choose the toy for him or her, which toy would you choose?

    c. If your least favorite person wins the sweepstakes and asks you to choose the toy for him or her, which toy would you choose?

Chapter 3

The Economic System and Contracting

Corporations do not exist in a vacuum, but are part of a larger economic system. Financial managers making investment, financing, and working capital decisions within a corporation must have a basic knowledge of the components and interrelationships of that economic system.

For example, Disney's decision to expand into Florida and construct Disney World required the accumulation of vast amounts of land, buildings, and equipment. Who would hold legal title to the new assets? Where would various levels of the government fit in?

Financial newspapers, magazines, and television programs often discuss the economic system in a manner that makes it appear complex and confusing. Various organizations such as industrial corporations, financial firms, governments, and markets are often viewed as if they are living organisms with desires and emotions. Often, similar organizations are grouped together and discussed as if the organizations themselves behave like people. For example, we might read that the banking sector has been hurt by a poor economy and is seeking help from the government.

This chapter lays a foundation to understanding the economic system in a logical manner. Our approach provides a highly simplified and somewhat unusual description of the economic system.

Financial markets and financial institutions link people who wish to invest money with people who need money, such as those starting a new corporation or expanding an existing corporation. For example, a bank receives money from various depositors, pools the money, and lends it to a variety of users of funds. In this example, a bank serves as a financial institution that links people who wish to invest money with people who wish to borrow money.

When a bank or other financial organization serves as a link between people, this is known as intermediation, a term derived from the word "intermediary." As this chapter discusses, there are many reasons for people to desire intermediation. For example, when a bank intermediates between its depositors and persons borrowing money on a credit card, the bank provides liquidity to the depositors and convenience to the borrowers.

In practice, the interrelationships can become quite complex because more than one financial institution, such as a bank, mutual fund, or pension fund, stands between the investor and the user of the funds. For example, workers who invest in a pension program may be providing funds for a project they have never heard of and located thousands of miles away. Perhaps the pension fund used the money to purchase a certificate of deposit at a bank which, in turn, loaned the money to the government of another country which, in turn, loaned the money to one of its industrial corporations.

Our discussion of the economic system will assist your understanding of the system by demonstrating that ultimately all relationships can be viewed as extensions of the simple ownership of assets by people. Our analysis expands from the simple case of a corporation directly controlled by shareholders to a more realistic portrayal of today's economic system. Modern finance views the entire economic system as various sets of contracts between people with regard to underlying assets. The purpose of these contracts is to establish who has the rights to enjoy the benefits produced by the total assets of the world.

This chapter has three main sections describing the economic system. In the first section we discuss direct and indirect ownership of assets. People want to own assets for the value or consumption that they provide. For example, owning a house provides the owner with the benefit of shelter and is an example of direct ownership of an asset. On the other hand, owning a hundred shares of Disney's stock is an indirect form of asset ownership in which the investor hopes to benefit indirectly from the assets held inside the Disney corporation. The economic system is the vehicle through which people can acquire indirect ownership of assets. In learning about the financial markets and institutions that comprise the financial system, you will learn to view the entire economic system as linkages between people regarding assets such as land, buildings, equipment, ideas, and so forth.

Also, the first section will describe governments as sets of contracts that link people together. The government is an organization that has tremendous influence on the way a firm can conduct its business, because governments tax and regulate individuals and businesses. No financial decision should be made without analyzing the impact of taxes on the outcome. Thus, in a nutshell, the first section describes the economic system as sets of contracts.

The second section discusses the financial markets in which financial contracts are traded.

The third and final section provides a detailed look at the process of contracting. Specifically, the third section examines the contracts and conflicts between shareholders and managers. The conflicts that arise between these groups are known as agency conflicts, and the costs of these conflicts are known as agency costs.

Overall, our approach is to spend less time describing the details of tax laws and types of securities, which change through time, and more time describing underlying principles that do not. At the same time, we will review enough of the major facts about U.S. tax laws and markets to provide a common base for discussion.

ACQUIRING ASSETS IN THE FINANCIAL SYSTEM

One of the most important examples of clear thinking that finance teaches is that corporations, governments, and other organizations do not consume or produce scarce resources . . . people do! These organizations are simply conduits (connections) through which people transact or contract.

Corporations and other organizations are not people—they are sets of contracts—and they cannot invest or consume in a literal sense. Certainly people within the corporation consume, but the corporation itself can only act as a vehicle for the transactions.

Assets are produced by, owned by, consumed by, and therefore ultimately belong to people. Individuals desire to own assets because of the benefits the assets can produce. The financial system is the means through which individuals can acquire or contract for indirect ownership of assets.

For example, a 30-year-old worker may earn $35,000 per year and need only $30,000 per year to live. The worker wishes to invest the extra $5,000 for a time in the future when she might need the money more—such as retirement. She could invest the remaining $5,000 directly in assets such as land, buildings, or equipment. However, there can be many problems with direct ownership of assets. For example, she may have a difficult time finding assets that have a cost exactly equal to the amount of money that she has to spare. Or perhaps she does not have the expertise or interest in learning how to acquire, manage, and resell the assets directly.

The economic system provides an excellent alternative to direct ownership of assets by providing investors with the opportunity to own assets indirectly, such as through a bank. There are many benefits to indirect ownership: For example, the individual is able, through a convenient investment method, to produce desired cash flow at some time in the future—such as retirement—and with a controlled level of risk and liquidity. Financial markets and institutions are among the major developments that have advanced our life-styles beyond those of primitive civilizations, which offered only limited opportunities for direct ownership.

Real Versus Financial Assets

People want to own assets for the benefits they offer. There are two primary types of assets. The first, called **real assets**, directly produce or help produce scarce resources. These may be tangible real assets such as the land, buildings and equipment used in the manufacture of goods. Or they may be intangible real assets such as trademarks, patents, and human productivity.

In contrast to real assets, **financial assets** are claims on the cash flows from real assets, and they include the stocks and bonds issued by corporations to raise capital and finance investments. A share of stock represents a percentage claim on the residual value of the firm, whereas a bond is a fixed claim on the real assets of a corporation. The bondholder is promised a fixed cash flow as long as the firm stays healthy, while the stockholder is entitled to whatever cash flow remains. Window 3.1 provides a brief overview of the different types of financial assets.

Financial assets are a form of indirect real asset ownership. In other words, the benefits from a financial asset must flow from the real asset to the owner. For example, a resort hotel is a real asset because it directly provides scarce resources such as shelter and recreation. A person who owns a resort hotel would have his or her name listed on the property deed. However, instead of investing directly in a resort hotel, individuals can buy shares of stock in a company that owns such hotels, and benefit indirectly from those real assets through the stock. Among the many benefits of this indirect asset ownership is the ability to sell the financial claim to another investor without changing the legal title to the hotel. By selecting the proper financial securities, individuals can have greater liquidity and convenience than could be obtained through direct ownership of the underlying real assets.

The top portion of Figure 3.1 illustrates that people can own assets directly. When individuals own houses, cars, or books, they are taking direct control of a real asset. Sometimes the control is formally established through an ownership contract such as a car title or a deed to a property. In our example, we begin with the idea of a corner grocery store directly owned by a couple affectionately known in the neighborhood as Mom and Pop.

Years ago, when small grocery stores and other small businesses satisfied the ordinary needs of consumers, it was common for the businesses to be directly owned by a single family. (Of course it's still

real assets
Assets that directly produce or help produce scarce resources. Examples include tangible assets such as land, buildings, and equipment, or intangible assets such as trademarks, patents, and human productivity.

financial assets
Assets that represent claims on the cash flows from real assets. Examples include stocks and bonds issued by corporations to raise capital and finance investments.

Window 3.1

Types of Financial Assets

Financial securities are broadly classified as equity and debt securities. One type of equity security is common stock. When individuals purchase common stock, they are purchasing a claim on the cash flows of the corporation. In exchange for their money, they are given part ownership in the company and a right to all residual earnings, which are often distributed as dividends. Another type of equity security is preferred stock, which represents a residual claim, with priority rights, to dividends and other distributions relative to common stock. Although under no strict obligation to pay dividends to preferred stockholders, the firm cannot pay dividends to common stockholders without first paying dividends to preferred stockholders.

In contrast to equity securities, debt securities (or bonds) promise a fixed return on investment, paid at specific intervals, as well as repayment of the original amount, called the principal, at the end of the bond agreement. The returns promised to bondholders must be satisfied first, with any residual going to the equity holders. For example, if a firm has issued a bond for $1000 that pays interest at the rate of 10 percent over 10 years, this means that annual interest payments are $100 per year over the entire 10-year life of the bond. At the end of the bond agreement, the issuer repays the $1,000.

Some debt securities are backed by specific assets of the firm. For example, mortgage bonds have collateral secured by a lien on real property. In the event that the firm hasn't sufficient amounts of cash to make promised payments on its debt, holders of mortgage bonds can use the value of the property to satisfy their claims. Another type of debt securities, known as debentures, have no specific collateral behind the promises, and are backed simply by the earnings power of the firm.

common for households to take direct ownership of houses, cars, and personal property.)

In contrast, such other assets as those real assets necessary to operate a large supermarket or industrial firm are usually too large to be owned by one person and can be more conveniently owned through indirect means. In the lower portion of Figure 3.1, the financial system is performing intermediation between real assets and the people who ultimately and indirectly own them. The idea is that many of today's large supermarkets are not directly owned by a single person but are

FIGURE 3.1
Ownership of Real Assets by People

Assets can be owned directly by people, or indirectly through financial assets representing claims to real assets.

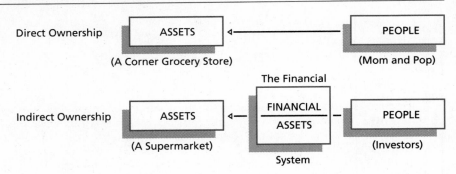

indirectly owned by many people through the financial assets (e.g., stocks and bonds) that have claim to the underlying real assets (e.g., land, buildings, equipment, inventory, and reputation).

An essential point about Figure 3.1 is that the introduction of financial assets does not change the level of total wealth: Financial assets do not produce scarce resources. Financial assets, such as stocks and bonds, do not change the people or the real assets; they only serve as a convenient way to contract for ownership. The wealth of a society is comprised entirely of real assets. Financial assets are merely contracts that people create to facilitate the ownership of real assets.

Next we move to a basic legal form through which financial assets are created: the corporation. As illustrated in Figure 3.2, indirect ownership of real assets is usually accomplished by establishment of a corporation to serve as a conduit or buffer between real assets and the people who provide the funding for the assets, and therefore ultimately own the real assets. The corporation has legal claim to the real assets and flows the benefits of this ownership through to the holders of the firm's financial securities. The owners of these securities can then trade them without having to change the contracts regarding the ownership and management of the real assets. However, all wealth ultimately flows from real assets to people and, to repeat, the introduction of corporations and securities does not by itself alter the total level of wealth.

For example, as grocery stores grew into the huge supermarkets of recent decades, it became increasingly useful for them to incorporate. The ownership of the supermarket's real assets now flows through the corporation to the owners of its stock and bonds.

Figure 3.2 recasts the indirect ownership of real assets, as illustrated in Figure 3.1, into a situation involving a single corporation that owns several supermarkets: Superstores Inc. You can see that the cor-

FIGURE 3.2
The Corporation as a Conduit Between Real Assets and People

Real assets can be indirectly owned through a corporation.

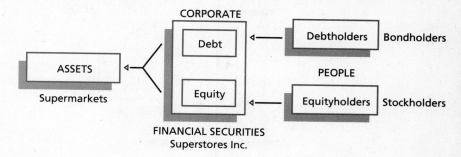

poration is simply a conduit between real assets and people—a set of papers or contracts.

We have already discussed some of the many reasons, such as convenience and liquidity, why people prefer indirect ownership of real assets. However, why do people use the corporation as the particular conduit or buffer to supply this indirect ownership? As illustrated in Figure 3.2 and discussed in Window 3.1, corporations usually offer financial securities represented by debt claims, which are fixed, and equity claims, which are residual. Generally, the bondholders, who own the debt, bear much less risk than the stockholders, who own the equity. Therefore, corporations offer investors the opportunity to invest with different levels of risk.

Asset Ownership Through Financial Intermediation

Investors can sometimes be burdened by direct ownership of corporate securities such as the stocks and bonds implied in Figure 3.2. These burdens can include an inability to sell the securities quickly at a fair price, the high costs of buying and selling securities, inappropriate risk taking, and in some cases high taxes. Investors can remove some or all of these burdens by investing in financial assets indirectly through financial intermediaries.

financial intermediaries
Financial institutions, such as banks, savings and loans, and pension funds, that serve as a conduit between people and financial assets.

Financial intermediaries, such as banks, pension funds, and insurance companies, buy large amounts of securities issued by corporations and governments and flow the benefits of these financial assets through to the individuals who invest in the financial securities. Adding financial intermediaries to our financial system as depicted in Figure 3.2 produces the more complex financial system depicted in Figure 3.3. The financial intermediary serves as a conduit between the people and the corporation's financial securities.

Because financial intermediaries pool the savings of a large number of small investors, they can provide a valuable service to investors

FIGURE 3.3
Financial Intermediaries Between People and Assets

Real assets can be indirectly owned through a financial institution.

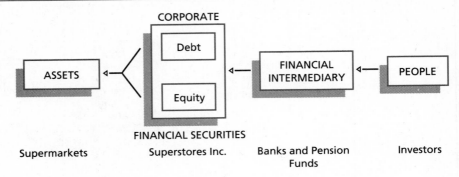

Supermarkets | Superstores Inc. | Banks and Pension Funds | Investors

by enhancing the liquidity of each investor, reducing transactions costs, increasing convenience, and assisting the investor to invest at a desired level of risk. For example, banks help provide investors with liquidity, convenience, and low-risk products. Pension funds provide investors with tax advantages. Often a corporation will find it is cost effective and convenient to borrow directly from a financial intermediary with large issues of securities such as commercial paper that individual investors could not afford to purchase alone.

As Figure 3.3 depicts, corporations and financial intermediaries serve as buffers between individual investors and real assets (the supermarkets). The corporation (Superstores Inc.) is set up to manage the real assets and sell claims to the real assets in the form of financial securities. Financial intermediaries often serve as a secondary buffer by purchasing the corporation's securities and providing individuals with services such as liquidity, convenience, and professionally managed investments. Descriptions of types of financial intermediaries and the benefits that they provide are listed in Window 3.2.

The placement of financial intermediaries in the channel between people and real assets broadens our view of the contracts that comprise our financial system. The financial intermediary establishes new contracts with the individuals who invest through financial institutions—such as individuals who set up retirement funds—and with the corporations to whom it supplies funds. These new contracts can be financial securities such as shares in a mutual fund or certificates of deposit at a bank, or they can be financial contracts such as pension accounts and insurance policies.

Although financial intermediaries are organized as corporations, they differ from nonfinancial corporations in the types of assets they own. Financial intermediaries own financial assets, whereas nonfinancial institutions such as industrials, utilities, and transportation firms own real assets. Generally, when we use the term corporation in this

Types of Financial Intermediaries

1. Commercial Banks

Commercial banks are corporations organized to accept deposits from individuals and make corporate and personal loans. Banks issue securities known as demand deposits or checking accounts to individuals and businesses, which facilitate transactions. Another popular security issued by banks is the certificate of deposit, or CD. Commercial bank liabilities consist mostly of deposits made by individuals and businesses, such as those described above. Assets consist of a variety of loans to individuals, to businesses, and state and local governments, as well as investments in U.S. government securities.

2. Savings and Loan Associations

Similar to commercial banks, savings and loans are businesses organized to accept deposits by individuals and businesses and to make loans. The major difference between the savings and loan and the commercial banks is in the character of their loans. Unlike banks, savings and loans invest heavily in real estate and mortgages.

3. Pension Funds

Pension funds are financial intermediaries that obtain funds from employer and employee contributions and invest these funds in financial assets. Pension funds are a convenient means whereby employees may invest for their retirement. Pension funds invest most of their assets in common stock and long-term bonds.

4. Insurance Companies

Insurance companies are corporations that pool payments from individuals (premiums) into funds used to offset unpredictable losses. Life insurance companies protect individuals from the financial consequences of an unexpected death, and they generally invest premiums in common stocks and long-term bonds. Property and casualty insurance companies protect individuals and businesses against unpredictable risks related to fire, theft, and negligence, and they invest premiums in stocks and short-term bonds.

5. Investment Companies

Investment companies are businesses that manage pooled portfolios for investors. Types of investment companies, known generally as mutual funds, include those with a fixed number of shares to trade, called closed-end funds, and those with an open number of shares to trade, called open-end funds. Investment companies obtain funds through individual contributions, and invest them according to the stated objective of the fund: For example, one mutual fund may invest only in government bonds and another may invest in the common stocks of over 5000 firms.

text we are referring only to nonfinancial corporations, even though technically speaking almost all financial intermediaries are incorporated.

Finally, it is common to have more than one financial intermediary and perhaps even more than one corporation serve as a buffer between an investor and the underlying real assets. This occurs when one corporation owns securities in another corporation or when one financial intermediary invests in the securities of another financial intermediary. In fact, it is typical for a corporation to invest money in a financial intermediary, such as putting excess cash in a bank account. Nevertheless, our view of the financial system remains conceptually the same. All corporations and financial intermediaries simply serve as sets of contracts joining real assets and the people who ultimately own them and therefore benefit from them.

Real Asset Ownership and Governments

Thus far we have tried to simplify the economic system by viewing corporations and financial intermediaries as sets of contracts or conduits through which people own real assets. Next, we will show that even governments can fit into this framework, beginning with the observation that governments, like corporations and financial intermediaries, are sets of contracts. Accordingly, governments cannot ultimately own or consume real assets—only individuals can. Sometimes we might think about a government as a collection of people or a major participant in the economy, but clear thinking reveals that governments are a system of contracts between people.

On the other hand, government programs and regulations influence people. Since this is a finance text we will concentrate on government's influence on the economic lives of its citizens. However, governments also influence citizens through noneconomic means such as civil regulations.

The economic role of government is best viewed through its influence on the ownership of real assets by people. Through taxation, federal, state, and local governments directly alter the asset ownership channels we observed in Figures 3.2 and 3.3. In addition, government regulations, such as environmental protection and food and drug laws, may indirectly alter the behavior of businesses and individuals and change both cash flows and the benefits that accrue from real assets. For example, pollution control devices may divert some of the cash flows derived from the real assets of the corporation to the purchase of equipment to reduce sulfur dioxide emissions, lowering the residual value of the shareholders' claims.

In the case of the United States, the contractual relationships of government are rather clearly set forth in documents such as the Con-

FIGURE 3.4
Governments as Conduits Between Real Assets and People

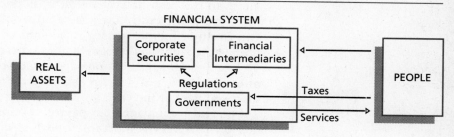

stitution, whereas in other societies the contract might be far less formal and not written down. For example, a military dictatorship might offer the following contract to its citizens: "Do as we say and we will be less likely to silence you."

Although governments differ, and some people might question whether a military dictatorship is legally a contract, virtually all governments have one thing in common: their ability to tax. Taxes are a claim by one set of people, known as recipients of governmental services, against another set of people, known as taxpayers, on the basis of the contracts that comprise the government. Of course, we are all participants to various degrees as both recipients and taxpayers. Figure 3.4 illustrates the role of governments as indirect owners of real assets.

We can view the relationship of governments to other organizations in the financial system and to the individuals who own the assets as a set of contracts, extending still further our view of a nexus of contracts. As in the case of corporations and financial intermediaries, governments do not produce or consume wealth but rather simply serve as sets of contracts between people with regard to the society's true wealth—its real assets.

An interesting aspect of Figure 3.4 is that taxes are the vehicle by which the ownership of cash flows from assets is transferred from direct ownership by people to ownership through the government. Since governments are only sets of contracts and cannot ultimately own assets, we can view taxes as transferring a portion of direct ownership by people to indirect ownership by society through governments.

This seems to run contrary to the traditional view of most governments in market economies. People certainly recognize that government ownership of assets occurs in communist countries, but they generally feel that in market economies the government does not own or control assets.

Example 3.1 —————— Consider a profitable firm whose assets produce cash flow to its shareholders. Legally, a shareholder owns the firm and has a claim to the cash flow of the firm. Economically, the value of the firm is the cash flow generated from the firm's output. Thus, in an economic sense, ownership of an asset refers to who has the right to the benefits of ownership—in this case, who has the right to the money produced by the asset. In the United States, about 40 percent (depending on the state in which you live) of the cash flow from output is claimed in the form of real estate, income, payroll, excise, and sales taxes. Taxation is a very important aspect of corporate financial management, and is the subject of our next section. ↵

Taxation

When the government imposes taxes on individuals and corporations, it causes the cash flows from the assets to be transferred from the tax-payer to the various recipients of government spending. The effect of taxes must be factored into all financial decisions, whether corporate or personal. For example, if you want to save money from a summer job to buy a car, you cannot simply add up your weekly salary and assume that you will have that amount to pay for the car. The federal government will require the deduction of income taxes and social security taxes, and your state and local governments may levy taxes on your income as well. Thus, you must deduct these taxes from your salary to determine how much you can spend for the car.

Let's also look at that summer job through the eyes of finance. A summer job may be viewed as a transaction in which a worker trades his or her time and energy, often called human capital, for money which in turn will be traded for real assets. Taxation may be viewed as the process of claiming partial ownership of the worker's time and energy on behalf of the recipients of government spending. If aggregate tax rates are about 40 percent, this can mean that government has a claim to approximately 40 percent of an employee's time, energy, and other assets. Note, however, that the worker also receives many benefits from government spending, such as highways, police protection, social security benefits, military protection, and so forth. Thus, governments are contracts through which people influence asset ownership.

Taxation exerts a powerful and often complex effect on most financial decisions, and the taxes that have the greatest such influence are the corporate and personal income taxes. Corporate and personal tax rates are legislated by Congress and can change over time. In fact, the U.S. Congress changes the tax laws on average every two years. Representative tax rates at the time of this writing are shown in Workshop

3.1. Note that tax rates graduate such that the five income steps are taxed at progressively higher rates. This is the reason that the average individual or corporate tax rate, defined as total taxes paid divided by taxable income, is less than the marginal tax rate, defined as the tax rate applied on the last dollar of income.

Governments serve as a conduit into which money flows in the form of taxation and out of which money flows in the form of spending. When taxation and spending levels temporarily do not match, the government can borrow to meet a deficit or invest to handle a surplus. In addition to these fiscal activities, the government can directly regulate economic activity.

Governments and Money

Money acts as another set of contracts between people regarding real assets. One individual will accept money in exchange for an asset knowing that this money can be exchanged for another more desirable asset. As a medium or tool of exchange, money greatly facilitates transactions in the economy, and is an accepted commodity by which people measure and exchange wealth.

Although coins containing precious metals such as gold and silver have value in and by themselves, the only value to most modern currencies such as the U.S. dollar is the value that people assign to it by their willingness to exchange it for valuable commodities. The value that people attach to money can fluctuate like other goods according to supply and demand. When the value of money drops, we observe that the price of virtually everything measured by money rises. We call this inflation.

inflation
An economic climate characterized by a decline in the value of money.

Inflation can be viewed as a decline in the value of money. For example, stating that inflation was 10 percent last year means that the value of money dropped by 10 percent. Conversely, deflation is the case (and a rarer one) when the value of money rises. We observe and measure the change in the value of money by observing the change in the exchange rate between money and other goods. In other words, we observe how prices change.

For example, one measure of the change in the value of money would be the exchange rate between money and automobiles. Another would be the exchange rate between money and haircuts. However, more useful measures utilize a variety of goods that most people use. One such collective indicator, compiled by the Bureau of Labor Statistics, is known as the consumer price index, or CPI. The rate of change in the value of money as measured by the change in the CPI is given in Table 3.1.

The CPI measures changes in the value of money through time. A rise in the index means that inflation is rising and the value of money

Workshop 3.1

Determining Personal and Corporate Income Taxes

This workshop will assist you in determining the amount of federal tax an individual must pay on earned income. Individuals earn income from salaries and wages, interest and dividends, rent, royalties, and gains on capital assets. The federal government does allow the individual to reduce taxable earned income through deductions, which include mortgage interest payments, state and local income taxes paid, and charitable contributions. Rather than itemizing these deductions, some taxpayers elect to take a standard deduction, or a fixed sum to be deducted from total earned income in every year. Individuals will usually elect to itemize deductions if they pay interest on a mortgage, and they will usually elect to take the standard deduction if they have no mortgage.

Taxable income is defined as total earned income less deductions. The tax rate that applies to taxable income changes depending on the amount of taxable income. The tax system is progressive, taxing higher amounts of income at higher tax rates. For example, married individuals filing a 1993 joint return (husband and wife filing one return) would find five different tax rates for five brackets of taxable income.

Married Filing Joint Return—1993

Taxable Income	Tax Rate
$ 0–$22,500	15%
$ 22,500–$55,000	28%
$ 55,000–$140,000	31%
$140,000–$250,000	36%
$250,000 and above	39.6%

A married individual with taxable income of $100,000 who filed a joint return would be taxed

First	$22,500 at 15%	$ 3,375
Next	$32,500 at 28%	9,100
Next	$45,000 at 31%	13,950
		$26,425

(continued on next page)

Workshop 3.1 (continued)

Just as individuals pay federal income tax based on income level, corporations, as legal entities, are also subject to federal income tax on their income. Like the individual tax system, the corporate tax system is progressive—tax rates rise with the level of taxable income. However, as shown for the year 1993, the tax brackets are such that almost all profitable corporations paid tax at the marginal rate of 34 percent:

Corporate Income Tax Rates—1993

Taxable Income	Tax Rate
$ 0–$50,000	15%
$50,000–$75,000	25%
$75,000–$10,000,000	34%
$10,000,000 and above	35%

For example, a corporation with taxable income of $1,000,000 would be taxed $328,250, determined as follows:

First	$ 50,000 at 15%	$ 7,500
Next	$ 25,000 at 25%	6,250
Next	$925,000 at 34%	314,500
		$328,250

Note that the highest corporate tax rate is greater than the highest individual tax rate. This provides an incentive for the formation of a Sub-Chapter S Corporation, described in Chapter 1, which allows corporate earnings to flow directly to the personal tax returns of the owners. For example, a professional prizefighter would save on taxes by setting up a corporation and having prize money flow to the corporation instead of to himself.

is falling. The more rapid the increase in the CPI, the more rapid the decrease in the value of money. Comparing the CPI in 1991 with the CPI in 1980 tells us that money has lost approximately 40 percent of its value in the decade of the 1980s. Comparing the CPI in 1991 with the CPI in 1970 tells us that money has lost approximately 70 percent of its value over the 20-year period. The same amount of dollars that could purchase the basket of commodities in 1970 could buy only 30 percent of the basket in 1991.

TABLE 3.1
Changes in the Consumer Price Index*

Year	Value of the Index
1970	38.8
1975	53.8
1980	82.4
1982–84	100.0
1985	107.6
1990	130.7
1991	136.2

For example, the price of the market basket of goods was 7.6 percent higher in 1985 than it was in 1982 to 1984, and 36.2 percent higher in 1991 than in 1982 to 1984.

*Bureau of Labor Statistics. The index represents a fixed market basket of goods and services available to the average urban wage earner. The market basket of goods is updated every few years. The major groups of commodities in the basket include food, shelter, energy, apparel, transportation, medical care, and entertainment.

The value of money changes in response to the same factors that cause other values to change: shifts in supply and demand. The supply of money is controlled by the federal government, and the government's printing of money and control over credit in the financial system are known as monetary activity. The demand for money is based upon factors such as the level of economic activity, new technologies, and people's attitudes toward the benefits of money. When the government causes the supply of money to grow at a pace that would otherwise outrun the demand, the price of money will fall and inflation results.

Summary of Real Asset Ownership

All economic value must ultimately come from real assets and belong to individuals. As we have stated, the entire financial system of corporations, financial intermediaries, and governments can be viewed as sets of contracts through which the ownership of real assets flows.

Corporations are sets of contracts between people and are part of the financial system. Our main interest is with regard to nonfinancial corporations and their relationships to individual investors—the people in our discussion known as stockholders and bondholders.

As we focus on the decisions facing the financial manager—investment alternatives, financing for those investments, and working capital management—we will discuss some of the contracts between the corporation and the other individuals in the financial system in more detail.

MARKETS

A market is a conduit for exchange, and when the market serves as a conduit for financial securities such as stocks and bonds it is known as a financial market. This is our interest in this book, because it is in financial markets where the financial manager issues securities to obtain financing and trades securities for working capital management. Further, the financial manager can use financial markets as a valuable tool in gathering information for the investment decision. In this section, we describe the most important exchanges financial managers make in financial markets.

Corporations can raise funds by issuing securities. Securities issued by corporations and sold to investors for the first time are called **primary securities**, and the market in which primary securities are sold is called the *primary market*. Often investors who purchase securities wish to exchange these securities for cash or other securities, and markets exist to make such trades. Existing financial securities that are traded or exchanged are **secondary securities,** and this occurs in the *secondary market*. Note that the quotes in the financial pages of the newspaper list secondary market trades.

One benefit of having a secondary market is that it increases the liquidity of financial securities. Investors know that they can trade these securities with other buyers and sellers. Secondary markets for financial securities are usually dealer markets or auction markets. Both dealer markets and auction markets are ideal for trading of financial securities as these markets work best when handling numerous small trades.

In a **dealer market**, dealers buy and sell certain types of securities using their own inventory. In other words, the dealer buys and holds securities when there is a seller but no buyer, and sells off the securities when there is a buyer but no seller. The dealer earns a commission equal to the difference between the price the buyer pays (the asked price) and the price the seller receives (the bid price). Dealer quotes from around the country are linked together through an automatic quotation system known as NASDAQ (National Association of Securities Dealers Automatic Quotations), which allows for an inexpensive and quick search for the best bid and asked prices.

primary securities
Financial securities issued by corporations and sold to investors for the first time. The market where primary securities are sold is called the primary market.

secondary securities
Financial securities already in existence and traded among investors. Trading in existing financial securities occurs in the secondary market.

dealer markets
A market where individuals, known as dealers, buy and sell using their own inventory. The dealer earns a commission equal to the difference between the price the buyer pays and the price the seller receives.

Example 3.2 _____ Consider a dealer who holds an inventory of shares in a stock known as Imex. The NASDAQ quotation system lists Imex currently trading at bid $12.00, asked $12.50. This means that the dealer is willing to buy Imex at $12.00 per share, and sell Imex for $12.50 per share, thereby earning a commission of 50 cents for each share traded, the difference between the bid and asked price. ↵

Nearly all bonds, in addition to some stocks, trade in dealer markets. Although many corporate bonds are listed on auction markets, only a small fraction of the volume is traded on these organized exchanges. Since most bond trading occurs among financial institutions like insurance companies, pension funds, and mutual funds, it is much easier to negotiate such transactions through the dealer market.

auction markets
Markets conducted at centralized locations. In auction markets, an auctioneer records bid and asked prices and notifies the two parties when trades match.

Dealers may be spread out across the country. In contrast, **auction markets** are conducted at centralized locations. In auction markets, an auctioneer records bid and asked prices and notifies the two parties when trades match. In other words, rather than buying securities from sellers, holding them, and waiting for a buyer, the auctioneer serves as a matchmaker for buyers and sellers willing to transact at the same price.

The firm operating the auction charges a fee on each transaction, known as a transactions cost or commission, as payment for providing the service. With the auction process, because all trades occur at the same place, buyers and sellers can be assured that they are receiving the best price available.

For common stock trading, the central location is known as a stock exchange. Stock exchanges may be either national or regional. The New York Stock Exchange (NYSE) and the American Stock Exchange (AMEX) are national exchanges. There are four registered U.S. regional stock exchanges: the Boston, Philadelphia, Midwest, and Pacific exchanges.

Most of the trading on exchanges is done by stockbrokers who represent their clients, although there are some private traders, known as floor traders and specialists, who trade on their own accounts. The exchanges are equipped with elaborate telecommunications systems that allow quotations of all transactions to be transmitted almost instantaneously to the offices of member brokers.

The New York Stock Exchange is the largest organized auction exchange in the United States. It accounts for between 80 and 85 percent of the dollar volume of trading on organized exchanges in this country. More than 2000 common and preferred stocks, representing over 1500 companies, are listed for trading. In addition, more than 2000 bond issues are listed; however, trading in bonds in this as well as other organized exchanges is light.

direct trading markets
Markets where sellers and buyers trade directly among themselves.

Although most financial securities trade in dealer or broker markets, other assets are traded in different types of secondary markets. **Direct trading markets** are markets where sellers and buyers trade directly among themselves. Sellers and buyers search for each other—perhaps by advertising or simply by word of mouth. Financial securities are rarely traded in direct trading markets; because they are traded in relatively small amounts, the transactions costs of getting buyers and sellers together directly would be too high to be economically feasible.

brokered trading market
A market in which the buyer and seller employ an agent, called a broker, who matches them for a fee.

A final type of secondary market is a brokered trading market. In a **brokered trading market**, the buyer and seller employ an agent called a broker to facilitate the trade. The broker matches a buyer with a seller for a fee, offering this specialized service at a cost that is usually lower than the cost buyers and sellers would face in direct trading markets. In some markets, such as real estate, this arrangement works rather well. The broker acts to reduce the cost of trading and can pass some of those savings to both parties.

CONTRACTING

As we have said, modern finance views the entire financial system as sets of contracts between people with ultimate regard to real assets. In fact, all economic activity can be viewed in the context of explicit or implicit contracts. This section will take a detailed look at the simplest case of how people contract with regard to economic activity.

Contracts between stockholders, bondholders, employees, governments, and other groups of people within the corporation are often spelled out in legal agreements. For example, a bond is a contract specifying the asset (if any) backing the bond, the payment schedule for the bond, and the firm's obligations if promised payments cannot be met. In contrast, other contracts are more flexible, and often unstated. For example, stockholders who have received dividends in the past have no stated guarantee that these dividends will continue in the future.

The process of creating contracts can be analyzed utilizing agency theory. As discussed in Chapter 1, agency theory investigates how one person, called the principal, contracts with another person, called the agent, in a situation involving decision making. For example, in a corporation, shareholders—the principals—form contracts with managers—the agents—to make decisions on behalf of the shareholders regarding the management of the firm. In this section we demonstrate some of the costs of the principal–agent relationship and ways that principals can minimize these costs.

The Principal–Agent Relationship

This section examines the principal–agent relationship existing between shareholders and managers. As in all relationships, there exists a potential conflict between what the principals desire and what the agents want to do. The goal of agency theory is to find the contract between a principal (shareholder) and an agent (management) that maximizes shareholder wealth.

Principals want the agents to make decisions that most satisfy the principals. Specifically, shareholders want the stock price maximized.

Managers clearly have other goals, such as job security, high wages, and a pleasant life style. Conflicts can arise when managers make decisions that are not aligned with the objectives of the shareholders.

Types of Agency Costs.   There are two types of agency costs: (1) the costs of trying to get the agents to do what the principals want, and (2) the lost opportunities caused by conflicts too expensive to resolve.

To demonstrate these costs, assume that shareholders—the principals—in a certain firm believe that it is in their best interest if managers—the agents—do not take home office supplies for personal use. To prevent theft of office supplies, shareholders might incur costs such as inventory lists, identification tags, and security guards. These are examples of the first type of agency cost listed above—the cost of trying to get managers to do what the principals want.

However, typically it would not be worthwhile to take inventories of small office supplies, such as pencils. Although the personal use of office supplies is considered by shareholders to be theft, these items will not be monitored and pencils will be wasted. The wastes involved with the disappearance of these small items are examples of the second type of agency cost—the cost of unresolved conflicts.

For simplicity, we view agency theory as seeking to minimize the total costs attributable to the inherent conflicts of an agency relationship. An optimal contract between a principal and agent resolves only those conflicts that can be solved in a cost-effective manner.

Agency Relationships and Compensation Plans

The primary tool that principals use to minimize agency costs is the compensation plan. The **compensation plan** is the contract between the principal and agent stating how the agent will be paid.

compensation plan
The contract between the principal and agent stating how the agent will be paid.

Agency theory teaches shareholders how to contract with agents using compensation plans that minimize agency costs. Typical compensation plans are salary and bonus agreements. One problem with traditional compensation plans is that they do not adequately interrelate the desires of the managers with the desires of the shareholders when bonuses are minor or when they are based upon imperfect measures of performance, such as accounting profits. The result can be poor performance on behalf of the shareholders rather than shareholder wealth maximization.

One way in which shareholders can maximize their wealth is to select management carefully and to compensate them with a well-designed compensation plan, such as a salary combined with a significant bonus based upon stock performance. Example 3.3 clarifies these concepts.

Example 3.3 _____

George is an executive at MBI who works in a big office at the firm's headquarters. He is a valued employee at MBI, but like most employees he favors his own interests and goals over those of the corporation. George loves to golf, and he has two alternatives at the office: (1) work, or (2) practice golf-putting. On balance, George would rather putt than work.

MBI shareholders want George to work, and they believe that the firm will benefit from having George work rather than putt, according to the following schedule:

Number of Hours Worked Per Day	Total Daily Dollar Benefit to MBI
0	$0
1	$70
2	$130
3	$180
4	$220
5	$250
6	$270
7	$280
8	$281

MBI shareholders are considering one of three alternative employment contracts to offer George for the upcoming year:

Alternative #1: Pay George $25 per hour regardless of whether he works or not.

Alternative #2: Pay George $25 to work and pay a guard $10 per hour to watch him work.

Alternative #3: Pay George $10 per hour regardless of whether he works or not and an additional $15 for each hour worked if his output is determined by the shareholders to be satisfactory, which would preclude the need for the guard to watch him work.

George and the firm together must agree upon how many hours per day he will be employed (i.e., go to work), but George alone must decide whether to actually work or practice putting during this time.

Alternative #1 is unsatisfactory because the firm will pay George $200 per day and will receive no value whatsoever. George will choose to go to work 8 hours each day at a wage of $25 per hour. George, acting in a manner based upon his own perceived interests and goals, will not work but will become a great putter.

TABLE 3.2
Compensation Plan #2: Hire the Guard

Total Hours Worked per Day	Daily Benefit to MBI	Daily Wages to George	Daily Wages to the Guard	Net Benefit to MBI
1	$ 70	$ 25	$10	$35
2	$130	$ 50	$20	$60
3	$180	$ 75	$30	$75
4	$220	$100	$40	$80
5	$250	$125	$50	$75
6	$270	$150	$60	$60
7	$280	$175	$70	$35
8	$281	$200	$80	$ 1

As shown in Table 3.2, Alternative #2 produces a benefit for the firm no matter how many hours George works.[1] For example, the gain is $80 per day if George and the guard are hired for 4 hours per day ($220 benefit to MBI's shareholders less $100 of wages to George less $40 of wages to the guard) and $1 per day if George and the guard are hired for 8 hours per day ($281 benefit to MBI's shareholders less $200 of wages to George less $80 of wages to the guard). According to the benefit schedule in Table 3.2, under Alternative #2 MBI would benefit most if George and the guard worked 4 hours per day.

Alternative #3 builds in a bonus incentive. George knows he will make $10 per hour whether he works or not, but he will receive an additional $15 per hour for satisfactory performance. Now let's assume that George will spend all his hours working if he is given the bonus. For example, if George works 4 hours per day the gain to MBI is $120 ($220 benefit to MBI's shareholders less a total of $100 wages to George), and if George works 8 hours per day the gain to MBI is $81 ($281 benefit to MBI's shareholders less a total of $200 wages to George). The benefit schedule as it relates to Alternative #3 is provided in Table 3.3. According to this benefit schedule, under Alternative #3, MBI would benefit most if George worked 5 hours per day.

You can see that the bonus plan has replaced the need for a guard as a proper incentive for George to work and not putt.

---

1. The example does not consider any resentment George might feel by having a guard watch over him. Resentment, in the form of a loss of commitment on the part of the employee or in employees leaving the firm, must be considered in an actual compensation plan.

TABLE 3.3
Compensation Plan #3: The Bonus Incentive

Total Hours Worked per Day	Daily Benefit to MBI	Fixed Daily Wages	Bonus Wages	Net Benefit to MBI
1	$ 70	$10	$ 15	$ 45
2	$130	$20	$ 30	$ 80
3	$180	$30	$ 45	$105
4	$220	$40	$ 60	$120
5	$250	$50	$ 75	$125
6	$270	$60	$ 90	$120
7	$280	$70	$105	$105
8	$281	$80	$120	$ 81

The firm would choose to allow George to work 5 hours per day, or one more hour than that chosen under Alternative #2. Compared with Alternative #2, the optimal number of hours worked provides an additional wage to George of $25 ($125 versus $100) and provides an additional $45 net benefit to MBI ($125 versus $80).

Of course this simplistic example fails to incorporate many real-world complexities of bonus plans. For example, bonuses can be costly to implement, and George may learn how to cheat and receive bonuses even when the shareholders don't receive the goals they really desired. However, judging from compensation plans that corporations choose to adopt, bonus plans appear to have advantages that outweigh the disadvantages.

The compensation plan of choice will be the plan that minimizes the total costs of conflicts, or that minimizes agency costs. In this example, the plan that minimizes agency costs is the plan that maximizes the benefit to the firm's shareholders. ↵

SUMMARY

☐ Corporate finance occurs within an economic system. The economic system comprises corporations, financial intermediaries, government, and markets that serve as conduits between people and real assets.

☐ Corporations are conduits between real assets and people via financial assets because they issue financial securities and purchase real assets.

☐ The existence of financial intermediaries and markets, also part of the financial system, makes it easier and more cost effective for people to own and trade their financial assets, which ultimately represent claims on real assets.

☐ Governments are also sets of contracts between people with regard to real asset ownership. Taxes are a claim by recipients of government services against taxpayers on the basis of contracts that comprise the government.

☐ The relationship between stockholders and managers is our example of the contracts formed in the financial system. This relationship is known as an agency relationship. Often, the objective of shareholders is to minimize the total costs—called agency costs—of the inherent conflicts. Compensation plans are a tool for minimizing agency costs.

DEMONSTRATION PROBLEMS

Problem 1 Fran wonders which income tax would be greater: the income tax paid by a married couple with $200,000 of taxable income or the income tax paid by a corporation with $200,000 of taxable income. Use the tax rates in Workshop 3.1 to find the solution.

Solution to Problem 1

Step 1: In order to compute the taxes for a married couple with $200,000 of taxable income, we must sum the amounts paid under the various rates shown in Workshop 3.1. Workshop 3.1 shows that taxes of 15% must be paid on the first $22,500 of income, 28% on the next $32,500 of income, 31% on the next $85,000 of income, and for Fran 36% on the final $60,000 of income. These amounts are summed as follows:

First $22,500 at 15% tax rate:	$3,375
Next $32,500 at 28% tax rate:	$9,100
Next $85,000 at 31% tax rate:	$26,350
Last $60,000 at 36% tax rate:	$21,600
For a total of:	$60,425

Step 2: In order to compute the taxes for a corporation with $200,000 of taxable income, we must follow a very similar procedure using the rates also found in Workshop 3.1.

First $50,000 at 15% tax rate:	$7,500
Next $25,000 at 25% tax rate:	$6,250
Last $125,000 at 34% tax rate:	$42,500
For a total of:	$56,250

Final Solution: The married couple would pay a higher tax ($60,425) than the corporation ($56,250). ↵

Problem 2   Marjorie is a trusted employee whose productivity declines as she becomes tired each day. After careful observation of her work performance, the following chart was prepared:

Daily Number of Hours Worked by Marjorie	Total Number of Work Units Completed
1	100
2	190
3	270
4	340
5	400
6	450
7	480
8	500

Marjorie's total cost to the firm is $11 per hour. Each work unit completed is worth $0.21 to the firm. Ignoring all other possibilities and considerations, for how many hours should the firm hire Marjorie per day?

Solution to Problem 2

Step 1: Since Marjorie's productivity begins high and then tails off, begin by assuming that Marjorie is being hired for zero hours each day and then examine whether it is worthwhile to add hours. This is accomplished by first computing the total value of Marjorie's output at each work level as the product of the number of work units completed and the value to the firm of each work unit ($0.21):

Daily Number of Hours Worked by Marjorie	Total Number of Work Units Completed	Total Value of Completed Work
1	100	$ 21.00
2	190	$ 39.90
3	270	$ 56.70
4	340	$ 71.40
5	400	$ 84.00
6	450	$ 94.50
7	480	$100.80
8	500	$105.00

Step 2: Next, compute the incremental, additional, or marginal value of the completed work for each hour of labor. This is found by subtracting the value of the labor before the extra hour of work from the value of the labor after the next hour of work. For example, the first hour of work created a total value of $21.00. Since no hours of work produce no value, the additional value produced by the first hour is $21.00. Another hour of work for a total of two hours per day would

create a daily benefit of $39.90. Subtracting the benefit of $21.00 from the first hour of work would produce an incremental benefit of $18.90. This value may also be found by multiplying the number of additional work units (90) times the value of each unit ($0.21). The process is summarized in the following chart:

Daily Number of Hours Worked by Marjorie	Total Value of Completed Work	Incremental Value of One Hour of Work
1	$ 21.00	$21.00
2	$ 39.90	$18.90
3	$ 56.70	$16.80
4	$ 71.40	$14.70
5	$ 84.00	$12.60
6	$ 94.50	$10.50
7	$100.80	$6.30
8	$105.00	$4.20

Step 3: The final step is to compare the incremental or marginal benefit from each hour of Marjorie's work with the incremental or marginal cost to each hour of work. The incremental cost is $11.00 per hour for each hour. So the solution is found by finding when Marjorie's productivity falls below $11.00 per hour. Since the fifth hour of work produces $12.60 of value and the sixth hour produces only $10.50, the correct answer is five hours.

Notice that the firm would receive a profit (the value received would exceed Marjorie's pay) no matter how many hours Marjorie worked; however, the solution of five hours produces the maximum profit. This can be checked by subtracting the total wage cost from the total benefit at each level of work:

Daily Number of Hours Worked by Marjorie	Total Value of Completed Work	Total Wage Cost	Incremental Profit
1	$ 21.00	$11.00	$10.00
2	$ 39.90	$22.00	$17.90
3	$ 56.70	$33.00	$23.70
4	$ 71.40	$44.00	$27.40
5	$ 84.00	$55.00	$29.00
6	$ 94.50	$66.00	$28.50
7	$100.80	$77.00	$23.80
8	$105.00	$88.00	$17.00

Final Solution: Hire Marjorie for five hours per day. ↵

REVIEW QUESTIONS

1. Distinguish between real assets and financial assets. Give examples of each to support your views.
2. How do equity securities differ from debt securities?
3. List the characteristics of dealer and auction markets.
4. In agency theory, explain why the shareholder is known as the principal and the manager is known as the agent.
5. Describe the two costs of a principal–agent relationship.
6. With respect to agency relationships, what is the objective of the particular compensation plan?

PROBLEMS

1. Label the following items from SAC Corporation's perspective as being real assets (R) or financial assets (F):
   a. Accounts receivable: money owed to SAC Corporation by other corporations who have purchased products on credit.
   b. SAC Corporation's administration building, which houses the finance department.
   c. SAC Corporation's corporate checking accounts.
   d. Land purchased by SAC Corporation from a local finance company.
   e. SAC Corporation's inventories of raw materials.
2. Identify the groups of people who financially gain or suffer in the following financial transactions:
   a. Bigstuff Corporation uses a technical loophole to avoid paying $2,500,000 in real estate taxes to the county government.
   b. Dangerous Products, Inc., unexpectedly loses a $20,000,000 lawsuit for punitive damages for selling faulty snow angels to the City of West Rochester. Assume that Dangerous Products, Inc., is uninsured and that the city retained the prestigious local law firm of Gopher, Thummuny & Runn.
   c. Through a technical error, Creditor Corporation permanently loses track of the fact that it is owed $1,000,000 by Debtor Corporation.
   d. U.S. Senator Barrelpork slips in a provision to a bill that passes and grants $9,000,000 to the Town Government of Herbanna for a particular project.
3. J.P. Moneybags is a wealthy, married investor with annual taxable income of $110,000 (this is his income after all deductions and exemptions have been subtracted).
   a. How much will J.P. pay in federal income taxes using the tax rates in Workshop 3.1?
   b. If J.P. has an extra $1,000 of income, how much of this will go toward federal income taxes?

   c. How would you answer questions (a) and (b) if J.P. falls on hard times and only has $10,000 per year of taxable income?

4. Cassidy Corporation is a pet products corporation with annual taxable income of $1,100,000.

   a. How much will Cassidy Corporation pay in federal income taxes using the tax rates in Workshop 3.1?

   b. If Cassidy Corporation has an extra $1,000 of income, how much of this will go toward federal income taxes?

   c. What would your answers be to questions (a) and (b) if Cassidy Corporation's business "goes to the dogs" and only has $60,000 per year of taxable income?

5. The current price of Nifty Nellie Corporation's (NNC) common stock is $20 per share. Churnem Brokerage Corporation charges a transactions cost of 2.5% of the total amount of a transaction. For example, on the purchase of 10 shares of stock for $200, the transaction cost would be $5.00.

   a. What would 200 shares of NNC's common stock cost?

   b. How much would an investor receive from selling 200 shares of NNC's common stock?

6. The bid price of Lucy Corporation common stock is $10.25 and the asked price is $10.75.

   a. How much will an investor have to pay to buy 100 shares of Lucy Corporation common stock directly from the dealer?

   b. How much would an investor receive from selling 100 shares of Lucy Corporation common stock directly to the dealer?

7. Nick has run the sports department of an old family-owned department store in Philadelphia for years. The firm's new modern computer system allows top management to compute profits for each department quickly and accurately. Nick is very talented, but management has noticed that Nick has priorities in life other than producing profits for the firm. In fact, Nick spends several hours each day reading newspapers, drinking coffee, and talking on the phone with friends.

   Currently the department earns $1,000 per day and Nick is paid $100 per day. Top management is confident that Nick could produce higher profits for the firm according to the schedule in columns 1 and 2:

(1) Additional Hours Worked Per Day	*(2)* Additional Daily Profit to the Firm	*(3)* Extra Salary Demanded by Nick
1	100	10
2	180	25
3	230	45
4	250	70
5 or more	250	(He quits)

Top management thinks that Nick could be encouraged to work harder if he were given a financial incentive. Column (3) in the table shows the amount of dollars he would need to earn to work additional hours. They do not want to lose Nick because he is so talented.

   a. How many additional hours a day should the firm try to get Nick to work?
   b. What would be the method (i.e., compensation plan) of getting Nick to work the additional hours?
   c. What do you think would happen if the firm simply demanded that Nick produce higher profits by threatening to fire him if he didn't?
   d. Do you have any other ideas of how Nick could be motivated or encouraged to produce higher profits?

8. Rockhenge Corporation has a huge number of clerical workers. Rockhenge has been able to attract and retain clerical workers for years in spite of offering a slightly lower pay rate than their competitors. An external investigation conducted by a consulting team indicated that many workers are engaging in the following practices at Rockhenge:

Taking home office supplies
Making personal long distance phone calls
Mailing personal correspondence through the company mailroom
Failing to purchase parking stickers (the company charges employees to park in the company parking lot)

The practices appear to be common to most of the employees and even appear to be sanctioned by the managers as part of a low-key management style.

   The consulting team estimates that Rockhenge loses $250,000 per year due to these practices. They recommend that for a one-time cost of $50,000 and an annual cost of $127,500, the firm could prevent all such abuses by employing auditors and other control measures. Ignoring ethical implications, should Rockhenge accept the recommendation?

DISCUSSION QUESTIONS

1. Your instructor takes a $100 bill and burns it in front of the class. Describe: (1) the net effect of this action on human wealth, (2) any wealth transfers that took place, and (3) what this teaches us about inflation and monetary policy.
2. Can a corporation treat people unfairly?
3. Are silver and gold bars financial assets or real assets? Explain.
4. What is the difference between a communist society and a capitalist society with a 100 percent tax rate on income?
5. If communism is wrong, how high do tax rates need to become before capitalism is wrong?

A Disaster of Bankruptcies

Assume a well-functioning world in which costs such as legal fees and accounting fees are nearly trivial.

Alan has $1,000,000 in a bank (Bank "A") and owes $1,100,000 to Beth. Otherwise, Alan owns and owes nothing else. Beth owes $1,200,000 to Charles but has no other debts or assets. Finally, Charles owes Bank "A" $1,100,000.

Charles has gone to court to demand that Beth pay back the $1,200,000 she owes him so that he can pay off his $1,100,000 bank loan and pocket the $100,000. Beth has in turn sued Alan for the $1,100,000 he owes her. She knows that this won't be enough to pay off Charles, but it is the best she can do. The best that Alan can do is withdraw his $1,000,000 and pay off part of his $1,100,000 debt to Beth.

You are the judge.

Alan and Beth argue that Charles is forcing them to declare bankruptcy and is destroying their lives by forcing them to liquidate all their assets, pay off all the debts that they can, and default on the rest. Charles argues that he is legally entitled to the payment he is requesting. On behalf of the public, some people have argued that several bankruptcies would destroy the economy of the community.

What is your decision?

MODULE 2

Valuation

Our opening module introduced modern corporate finance. The discussion focused upon the financial objective of the firm, principles of economic behavior, the ownership of real and financial assets, and the importance of the contract. Contracts provide linkages between the people that comprise the corporation as well as the vehicle by which corporate incentives are structured.

The lessons from Module 1 can be integrated into a single decision rule: Good investments are those whose benefits exceed costs, where costs and benefits are measured in market prices. This rule is consistent with the objective of shareholder wealth maximization as well as with the economic principles introduced in Chapter 2. The economic principles are (1) positive marginal utility—shareholders desire their wealth to be as high as possible; (2) diminishing marginal utility—decisions should be based on market prices as they represent accurate indicators of how people perceive value; and (3) diminishing marginal return—invest to the point at which the benefits of producing one additional unit are equal to the cost of production.

But how are benefits and costs measured? Said differently, if the value of the investment is defined as the difference between benefits and costs, then how is value determined? This is the theme of Module 2.

From the definition of finance, value must incorporate both time and risk. Module 2 will focus on the dimension of time, while Module 3 will focus on the dimension of risk. Chapter 4, The Time Value of Money, shows that the same amount of dollars to be received at different points through time are not the same commodity and therefore have different values. Various techniques will be presented to "pull" the value of dollars back to the present time or to "push" the value of dollars forward to some future time so that they become the same commodity and can be directly compared.

Chapter 5 uses time value of money techniques to value financial assets such as bonds and common stock, while Chapter 6 examines the valuation of real assets or projects. The net present value model will be demonstrated as the premier method for valuation.

Jack and Diane could hardly believe their eyes when they saw the Lotto Jackpot numbers come up on the television screen. For years they had played the same six numbers and never once had they come close to winning. Tonight they held a winning ticket to a million-dollar lottery payout. Diane looked at Jack and said "It's hard to imagine— us as millionaires!"

Although the couple has every reason to rejoice over their good fortune, the fact is that the lottery prize will not make them millionaires. You see, the couple will soon learn that the prize will be paid out at the rate of $50,000 a year for twenty straight years. Because the jackpot is not paid in a lump sum but is instead paid out through time, the value today of their lottery prize is far less than its marquee value of $1 million.

Exactly how much is Jack and Diane's prize worth? How can we incorporate the **time value of money** into financial decision making? These questions are the focus of this chapter.

time value of money
An economic principle stating that dollars to be received through time or paid out through time are different commodities that cannot simply be added together or subtracted from each other.

TIME VALUE

Just about every financial decision, including investment, financing, and working capital management decisions, must take into account the passage of time. It is common for corporations to invest money today but not receive a return for years. Financial managers have long recognized the importance of time value when making investment decisions.

As Jack and Diane will learn, a dollar[1] to be received in the future is not as valuable as a dollar in your hand today. In fact, dollars

---

1. Throughout the text we will often refer to cash as "dollars," although the concepts presented in this book are applicable to the currencies of any country.

received and dollars paid through time are different commodities that cannot be directly compared. For example, we offer the following proposition: Send to the authors $100 and we will return to you $1000. Is this a good trade? By the way, as part of the deal, the authors get the $100 today, and you get $1 a year in each of the next thousand years.

Although we're trading dollars, these dollars are actually different commodities. Even if you were certain that the authors would deliver the dollar per year for the next thousand years to you and your heirs, most people would not make the trade because the commodity of $100 today is more valuable than the commodity of $1 per year for the next one thousand years. In fact, under normal market conditions, the value of receiving $1 per year for 1000 years is close to $10.[2]

Dollars Through Time as Different Commodities

Why is the value of a dollar in your hand today different from the value of a dollar due in your hands in ten or twenty years? The answer is best found by viewing dollars at different points in time as different commodities or assets rather than as the same asset.

First, let's think about money. Money is simply a medium or tool of exchange. A dollar has no value other than what people will accept in exchange for it. This is very different from a doughnut, which has value to its owner even if it can't be traded. Which would you rather be stranded alone on an island with, a $100 bill or a doughnut?

Like most assets, the value of money changes through time. The value of a dollar today is obviously $1. But what about the value today of a dollar that won't be received for ten or twenty years—how much is it worth? As we will show, at ten percent interest rates, a dollar due in ten years is worth only about 40 cents today, and the value of a dollar due in twenty years is worth only about 15 cents today!

The relative value of money received through time can be understood by thinking of the relative value of any commodity. Why is a big red apple worth more than a small green wormy apple? The answers are that people prefer to eat big red apples and that big red apples are harder to grow. Thus, people are willing to pay more for them and in the long run farmers have to charge more for them since they are harder to grow. There is no logic in claiming that all apples must have equal values regardless of quality since technically speaking they are all apples.

In a similar way, there is no logic in claiming that dollars must have equal values regardless of when they are to be received since

---

2. We used an interest rate of 10 percent to arrive at $10. Different interest rates will lead to different present values, as we will discuss further in the chapter.

FIGURE 4.1
A Marketplace Where Different Commodities Sell for Different Prices

© Alan Carey/The Image Works

opportunity cost
An alternative foregone because a particular course of action is pursued.

technically speaking they are all dollars. Dollars in hand today can be put to use immediately, whereas people must wait to utilize dollars to be received in the future. Said differently, there is an **opportunity cost** associated with waiting to obtain dollars through time.

Figure 4.1 shows the familiar concept that commodities trade in a marketplace. Figure 4.2 shows a financial marketplace, a place in which investors borrow and invest—that is, trade present dollars for future dollars. Amazingly enough, $1 million due in 170 years can be purchased for about $1 today! Doesn't it just make you want to put a few bucks in the bank and get your body frozen for a few centuries?

investing
The trading of dollars today for dollars in the future.

Investing and Borrowing.   Figure 4.2 illustrates a marketplace where dollars today can be traded for dollars in the future. This is called **investing**. Investment is deferred consumption since the investor decides not to consume or spend the money today, but rather to trade the money today for a particular amount of money to be received in the future.

borrowing
The trading of dollars in the future for dollars today.

Imagine also that the market participants can trade future dollars in the form of future paychecks for dollars today. This is called **borrowing**. Borrowing is the opposite of investing. The borrower obtains

FIGURE 4.2
The New York Stock Exchange—A Financial Marketplace Where Present Dollars Can Be Traded for Future Dollars

© B. Roland/The Image Works

money today in exchange for promises to return a particular sum of money in the future.

In the case of investing, the investor may enter the financial marketplace and purchase future dollars today at a cost per dollar of less than $1. The exact cost of each future dollar will depend upon the length of time before the dollar is received and upon market conditions. For example, the investor may find that dollars next year can be purchased today for 90 cents such that $900 can be invested today and $1000 will be received in one year.

In this example, there is a temptation to say that because $900 was traded for $1000, the investor will receive a profit of $100. In fact, this is precisely the way accounting profits are defined. However, dollars to be received through time or paid out through time are different commodities that cannot simply be added together or subtracted from each other. Claiming that a $100 profit has been earned does not make economic sense. For instance, if Jack trades the family cow for five beans, it makes no sense to claim that Jack produced a profit of four food units because he traded one food unit for five food units. Similarly, it doesn't make sense to claim that a person who trades one watermelon for five grapes has produced a profit of four pieces of fruit. The reason that such profits do not make sense is that we are comparing different commodities or assets.

⌛ Dollars to be received through time or paid out through time are different commodities that cannot simply be added together or subtracted from each other. However, there is a relation by which equivalent values can be found.

Discounting Cash Flows

If cash flows at different points in time are indeed different assets with different values, how can we make meaningful comparisons between dollars that arrive at different points in time? This is the central issue within the study of the time value of money.

The answer is that all cash flows must be changed into dollars at the same point in time. The most common solution is to take all cash flows and to convert them into the value of the cash flows in today's dollars. This is called **discounting** cash flows to the present.

discounting
The process of turning future cash flows into current cash flows.

Discounting can be accomplished by taking future dollars to a financial market as depicted in Figure 4.2 and converting them into current dollars using the prices provided by the marketplace. The longer you must wait to receive future dollars, the less those future dollars are worth to you today. For instance, the marketplace might tell us that the value today of receiving $1.00 in exactly one year is $0.93. We now have a basis of comparing these two different commodities: $0.93 today is equivalent to $1.00 due in one year. The marketplace might also tell us that the value today of receiving $1.00 in exactly two years is $0.86, and that the value today of receiving $1.00 in three years is $0.79. In fact, we can envision a grocery store of cash set up to turn any future amount of money into a present value. Note that as we extend the time horizon into the more and more distant future, the value today of receiving those dollars in the more distant future becomes smaller. This is illustrated in Figure 4.3.

⌛ The longer you must wait to receive future dollars, the less those future dollars are worth to you today.

Compounding Cash Flows

It is also useful to turn current dollars into future dollars. This process is called **compounding** the cash flows. The main difference between discounting and compounding is the point of reference, which in discounting is today, while the reference point in compounding is some future point in time.

compounding
The process of turning current cash flows into future cash flows.

We can continue with the example of a financial marketplace to illustrate compounding. For instance, the marketplace might tell us that the value in exactly one year of $1.00 invested today is $1.08, and that the value in two years of $1.00 invested today is $1.17. Under these conditions, the marketplace is telling us that $1.00 today is equivalent to $1.08 in one year, and that $1.00 today is equivalent to

FIGURE 4.3
Discounting Cash Flows

The longer you have to wait to receive $1.00, the less its present value.

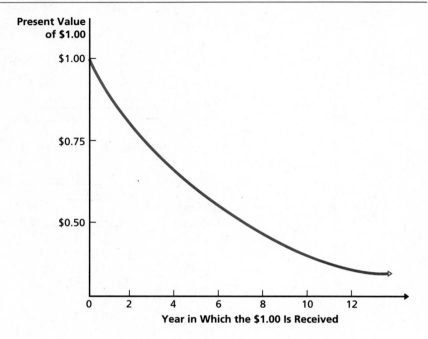

$1.17 in two years. We can utilize the financial marketplace to turn any present amount of dollars into future amounts of dollars. Note that as we extend the time horizon out into the more and more distant future, the future value of investing $1.00 today becomes larger. This is illustrated in Figure 4.4.

The line in Figure 4.4 could be illustrative of a student who borrows $25 for a date as a senior in college by charging the evening to a credit card. If unpaid, that debt might grow to $50 four years later. Four additional years later, the student is finishing an MBA. If unpaid, that $50 might now have grown to $100. If unpaid and allowed to continue to grow on the credit card, that debt could easily reach $20,000 by retirement. In essence, the student, in following this scenario, is trading $20,000 of retirement consumption for $25 of current consumption.

time lines
A way to view the process of discounting and compounding dollars through time. Discounting is the process of pulling cash flows left along the line, while compounding is the process of pushing the cash flows right along the line.

Time Lines

Time lines provide an excellent view of the process of discounting and compounding dollars or cash flows. All time value of money problems may be viewed as pulling (discounting) or pushing (compounding) cash flows along a time line. Figure 4.5 illustrates the problem of

FIGURE 4.4
Compounding Cash Flows

The longer $1.00 is invested, the higher its future value.

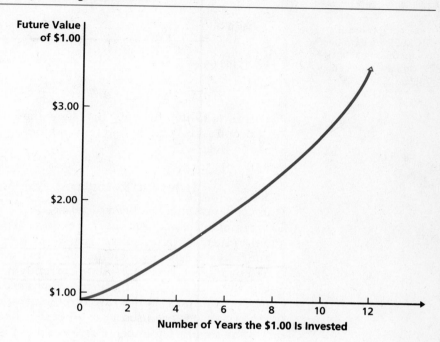

determining the present value of $100 due in five years. The process may be viewed as pulling the $100 from the right toward the left of the time line. Whenever cash flows are pulled back to the left they diminish in magnitude. Figure 4.5 illustrates that under certain market conditions, the present value of the $100 to be received in five years is $62.09.

Next, Figure 4.6 uses the concept of a time line to turn a present value into a future value. Finding a future value may be viewed as pushing forward a cash flow from left to right, causing it to increase in magnitude. Here, under certain market conditions, $100 grows to $161.05 in five years.

FIGURE 4.5
The Time Line View of Discounting

The present value of $62.09 is determined by discounting $100 to be received in five years at 10 percent interest.

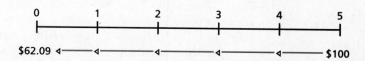

FIGURE 4.6
The Time Line View of Compounding

The future value of $161.05 is determined by compounding $100 over 5 years at 10 percent interest.

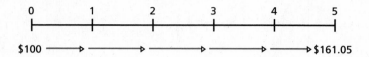

> ✗ All time value of money problems may be viewed as pulling (discounting) or pushing (compounding) cash flows along a time line.

Interest Rates and Present Value

Thus far time value has been discussed using the price of future cash flows. In many cases time value is expressed not with dollars but with interest rates. When dollars or cash flows are pushed and pulled along a time line, the rate at which the cash flows grow or diminish is determined by interest rates prevailing currently in the market. An interest rate is the rate at which these cash flows grow, in the case of future values, or diminish, in the case of present values.

Interest rates are used to express the time value of money in an easy-to-understand manner. For example, instead of a bank saying that $1.00 invested today will grow to $1.08 in one year, the bank may advertise an interest rate of 8 percent. This means that investors can expect to receive their original amount of money back plus an earned 8 percent in one year. Whether expressed as dollars or interest rates, the concept of the time value of money is the same.

A Summary of Time Value

As we have said, dollars or cash flows to be received at different points in time are different commodities that should not be added to each other or subtracted from each other. Adjusting for time value may be viewed as pushing and pulling dollars or cash flows along a time line. Moving cash flows to a single reference point in time allows for proper comparison of these different commodities, and provides for proper financial decision making.

Given an interest rate, the process of discounting and compounding can be determined with precision. The mechanics and mathematics of time value have been vastly simplified by financial calculators and computers. In fact, calculators and computers can do all the time value work for us! Now that you understand the concept of time value, learning the mechanics is a straightforward process.

THE TECHNIQUES OF DISCOUNTING AND COMPOUNDING

This text discusses and illustrates two methods with which to compute present values and future values using interest rates: (1) formulas, and (2) financial calculators or computers. For simplicity the second method will be referred to simply as the financial calculator method, although the same techniques can be demonstrated on personal computers with special software. We will illustrate each method, beginning with future values.

Future Values

Investing is delayed consumption, and waiting to consume can be considered an opportunity cost. Someone who invests gives up spending today by exchanging today's dollars for more dollars in the future. The interest rate is a convenient way of expressing the opportunity cost of waiting to consume and the rate of growth in the investment. Given any present dollar amount and any interest rate, the investor can determine the precise amount of future dollars to which the investment will grow in a given number of years.

Example 4.1 _____ Consider Ivan, who has $1,000 to invest and who takes his money to the local bank. Current market conditions allow the bank to offer Ivan an interest rate of 8 percent on his money. Ivan invests his $1,000 in the bank and informs the teller that he will return in one year to pick up his $1,080.

How did Ivan know that his $1,000 will grow to $1,080 in one year? It was because the rate at which present dollars will grow in the future was given at 8 percent, and $1,080 is 8 percent more than $1,000. Although this calculation is easy to perform, others are not. For example, how much would Ivan have in a year if he deposits $1,150 in the bank account at 8 percent? Because this is harder to do, it is necessary to solve this and other future value problems with a formula. ↵

Simple Interest: The Formula Method. Let the notation PV stand for present value, FV_1 stand for the future value in year one, and r stand for the interest rate. In the example above PV is $1,000, and r is 8 percent. The following formula solves for the FV_1:

$$FV_1 = PV\,(1 + r). \tag{4.1}$$

The right-hand side of Formula (4.1) is actually two parts put together. We could for instance write:

$$FV_1 = PV + (PV \times r).$$

The formula for future value combines the original amount, PV, with the amount of interest earned on the investment, $PV \times r$.

Using Formula (4.1), Ivan's $1,000 investment will grow to:

$$FV_1 = \$1,000(1.08) = \$1,080.$$

If Ivan deposited $1,150 in the bank account instead of $1,000, his investment would grow to:

$$FV_1 = \$1,150(1.08) = \$1,242.$$

simple interest
The dollar amount of interest received on the original investment only.

Formula (4.1) is known as the **simple interest** formula because interest is received on the original investment only. If after one year Ivan decides to spend the $80 of interest earned in the account and reinvest the $1,000 for another year at 8 percent, he will have $1,080 at the end of that year as well. The amount of simple interest earned ($80) did not change because Ivan invested $1,000 the second year, the amount equal to his original investment. As long as interest rates stay at 8 percent, Ivan can continue to remove and spend the $80 of interest earned each year and continue to turn $1,000 of present dollars into $1,080 of future dollars.

Compound Interest: The Formula Method.   Suppose that Ivan decides to delay consumption further by investing the $1,000 in a bank account earning 8 percent for two years. The difference now is that Ivan decides not to remove the $80 of interest earned in year one but instead to leave the interest in the account for the second year. What will his investment grow to in two years? At first glance the problem appears to be a trivial extension to the one above. If his investment earns $80 in interest over one year, then it might be reasoned that the investment would earn an additional $80 in year two for a total of $160 in interest over two years, and $1,160 in total.

compound interest
The dollar amount of interest earned not only on the original principal but also on interest earned over previous periods.

The amount of $1,160 will understate, however, the future value of the investment because of compound interest. **Compound interest** includes interest earned on interest. In the second year Ivan will also earn interest on the $80 earned in the first year, and his $1,000 will grow to an amount greater than $1,160. With compounding, the investment grows to a future value in the first period, and then the entire future value earns interest in the second period.

One way to solve future value problems with compounding is to use Formula (4.1) and to break the problem into two parts:

Part 1: Determine the future value at the end of the first year:

$$FV_1 = PV\,(1 + r) = \$1{,}000\,(1.08) = \$1{,}080.$$

Part 2: Determine the future value at the end of the second year starting with the result of Part 1:

$$FV_2 = FV_1\,(1 + r) = \$1{,}080\,(1.08) = \$1{,}166.40.$$

Notice that the above formulas use different subscripts for FV. The subscript refers to the future time period, such that FV_1 is the future value in year one, while FV_2 is the future value in year two. The subscripts are useful in keeping track of cash flows through time.

With compounding, the future value of $\$1{,}166.40$ in year two is $\$6.40$ greater than our first guess of $\$1{,}160$.

The two-step procedure for compounding interest can be reduced to one step by substituting the variable FV_1 in step two above with $PV(1 + r)$:

$$FV_2 = PV(1 + r)(1 + r),$$

which is equivalent to:

$$FV_2 = PV(1 + r)^2.$$

In determining the future value in year three, we can extend our example by allowing a third year's interest earned on the original investment of $\$1{,}000$:

$$FV_3 = FV_2\,(1 + r).$$

By substituting $PV(1 + r)^2$ for FV_2, we get:

$$FV_3 = PV\,(1 + r)(1 + r)(1 + r),\ \text{or}$$
$$FV_3 = PV\,(1 + r)^3.$$

Let's move directly to the general formula for determining future values with compound interest:

$$FV_n = PV(1 + r)^n, \tag{4.2}$$

where n is the number of periods interest is compounded. Formula (4.2) adds the general subscript n to the future value, and can be used to generate any future value given three pieces of information: (1) a present value, (2) an interest rate, and (3) a time period.

Returning to Example 4.1 and using Formula (4.2), we again determine that Ivan's future dollar amount after two years will be:

$$FV_2 = PV (1 + r)^2 = \$1,000 (1.08)^2 = \$1,000 (1.1664) = \$1,166.40,$$

and his future amount after three years will be:

$$FV_3 = PV(1 + r)^3 = \$1,000(1.08)^3 = \$1,000(1.2597) = \$1,259.71.$$

This solution is provided in detail in Table 4.1.

The general formula will work for any future time period. For example, if Ivan would like to invest his $1,000 toward his retirement in 30 years, and if interest rates stay constant at 8 percent, he will turn his $1,000 of present dollars into $10,062:

$$\$1,000(1.08)^{30} = \$1,000(10.062) = \$10,062.$$

Compound interest can make a significant difference in investment when the time period is long.

Financial Calculator Method.   The advantage of financial calculators is that they are quick and accurate, and most come with well-written instruction manuals that explain how to calculate future values. The most common mistake in using a financial calculator is failing to clear the memories as described in the calculator's instruction manual. We will briefly review the keystrokes applicable to most simple financial calculators.[3]

Formula (4.2) is composed of four variables; the present value (*PV*), the number of future time periods (*n*), the interest rate (*r*), and the future value itself (*FV*). Financial calculators require the input of any three of these variables to solve for the fourth.[4] For example, by entering into a calculator $1,000 for *PV*, 8 percent for *r*, and 30 for *n*, the calculator will compute the *FV* to be approximately $10,062. The keystrokes will probably be something like this: (Clear calculator) *$1,000, PV, 8, %I, 30, n, CPT, FV.*

> ✗ The most common mistake in using a financial **calculator is** failing to clear the memories as described in the **calculator's** manual.

---

3. Some financial calculators ask for different keystrokes in different order. You must refer to your calculator's reference manual if the keystrokes presented here do not apply.
4. Financial calculators have keystrokes with these variables typed on them, for instance *PV* for present value, and *FV* for future value. However, your calculator's keystrokes for the interest rate (*r*) and time period (*n*) may not match our notation. Consult your instruction manual for the proper keystrokes for all necessary inputs. It is common for the calculator to use *%I* for *r*.

TABLE 4.1
Compounding Interest over Three Years

Year	Starting Amount	(1 + r)	Ending Amount
1	$1,000.00	(1.08)	$1,080.00
2	$1,080.00	(1.08)	$1,166.40
3	$1,166.40	(1.08)	$1,259.71

Non-financial calculators with the keystroke y^x can be easily used to solve the expression $(1 + r)^n$ in the future value formula (4.2) for any value of r and n. For instance, we can use y^x key above to solve $(1.08)^{30}$. The keystrokes typically used would be: *1.08, y^x, 30, =*.

An advantage of using a financial calculator is that it can be used to solve for any one of the four variables given the other three. Thus, you are not confined to solving for the future value, but can instead solve for the interest rate or length of time given the other three variables. For example, if you wished to know how long it would take for $1,000 to grow to $10,000 if the interest rate were 8 percent, you would input these values and the calculator would solve for the answer of approximately 30 years. If you wished to know at what interest rate $1,000 would grow to $10,000 in 30 years, you would input the variables *PV*, *FV*, and *n*, and the calculator would solve for the interest rate of approximately 8 percent.

More Frequent Compounding.   We have assumed to this point that interest was compounded on an annual or once-a-year basis. For instance, when Ivan left his $1,000 in the bank account in year two, compounded interest was earned from year one. Wouldn't it be better for Ivan if the bank compounded his interest more frequently, say every six months, or every month, or even as frequently as every day? In fact, why not compound the interest every second? This must be good for the investor, because the more frequent the compounding, the greater the effect of compounding on future value.

It is common for banks and other savings institutions to compound interest more frequently than once per year. It is our job now to make the necessary adjustments to our future value formula to allow for more frequent compounding. Two adjustments need to be made to Formula (4.2). First, the interest rate, given by r, must be divided by the number of times interest is compounded within the year. For example, if interest is compounded quarterly (four times a year), then an 8 percent annual rate becomes a 2 percent quarterly rate. If interest is compounded daily, then an 8 percent annual rate becomes a .022 percent daily rate. If we let m be the number of times per year interest is compounded, then the expression $(1 + r)$ in Formula (4.2) becomes $(1 + r/m)$ in the adjusted future value formula.

Second, the expression $(1 + r/m)$, which was originally raised to the power n, must now be raised to the power n times m. Incorporating both of these changes, the adjusted future value formula becomes:

$$FV_n = PV \left[1 + \frac{r}{m} \right]^{mn} \qquad (4.3)$$

Let's return to Example 4.1 and Ivan's investment of $1,000 in a bank account earning 8 percent interest for 2 years. If Ivan's bank compounds interest once per year, m in Formula (4.3) is equal to 1, and Ivan's future value is:

$$FV_2 = \$1,000 \left[1 + \frac{.08}{1} \right]^{1*2} = \$1,166.40,$$

the same future value as before. However, if Ivan's bank were to compound interest quarterly, then m is equal to 4 and his new (and improved) future value would be:

$$FV_2 = \$1,000 \left[1 + \frac{.08}{4} \right]^{4*2} = \$1,171.66.$$

This future value is $5.26 greater than it was in the case of annual compounding. This is illustrated in Figure 4.7.

But why stop at quarterly compounding? Suppose instead that the bank compounds interest daily,[5] meaning that today's interest begins earning new interest tomorrow. For daily compounding m is equal to 365 and Ivan's new (and even more improved) future value becomes:

$$FV_2 = \$1,000 \left[1 + \frac{.08}{365} \right]^{365*2} = \$1,173.49.$$

Ivan is certainly happier with daily compounding as his future value keeps growing and growing. Is there any way to make Ivan even happier? For instance, can't we break a year into even smaller pieces—for example, 8,760 hours, 525,600 minutes, or 31,536,000 seconds? At the extreme, we can define compounding on a continuous basis, that is, over every fraction of a second!

Future value Formula (4.3) can still be used for small periods of time, but it becomes quite cumbersome. For instance, if we choose to compound every hour, then an 8 percent annual rate becomes a

---

5. Most banks compound interest daily.

FIGURE 4.7
The Benefits of More Frequent Compounding

Quarterly compounding (four times per year) makes you better off by $5.26 compared with annual compounding.

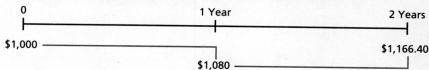

Case 1: Annual Compounding – $1,000 Invested for 2 Years at 8 Percent

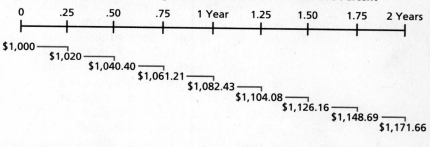

Case 2: Quarterly Compounding – $1,000 Invested for 2 Years at 8 Percent

.000009132 percent hourly rate, and the future value becomes (rounded):

$$FV_2 = \$1,000\,[1 + .000009132]^{8760*2} = \$1,173.51.$$

This rate becomes even smaller if we go inside of a hour and compound over minutes, seconds, or even over fractions of a second. Eventually we would reach a point where interest is earned continuously. For the case of continuous compounding, the value m in Formula (4.3) approaches infinity, and $[1 + r/m]^m$ approaches e^r, where e is the base for natural logarithms and is approximately equal to 2.71828.[6] Formula (4.4) allows for continuous compounding:

$$FV_n = PV[e^{rn}]. \qquad (4.4)$$

Most calculators have the keystroke e^x which allows for easy computation of Formula (4.4). Calculators without the key e^x but with the key y^x can be used to solve Formula (4.4) using 2.71828 for y.

---

6. For the technically minded reader, this footnote provides the derivation of the continuous compounding Formula (4.4). Formula (4.3), or the future value formula with non-annual compounding, is:

$$FV_n = PV\left[\,1 + \frac{r}{m}\,\right]^{mn} \qquad (a)$$

(Footnote continued on next page)

For example, if Ivan's investment earned 8 percent continuously for two years, his new future value would (rounded) be:

$$FV_2 = \$1,000(2.71828^{.08*2}) = \$1,000(2.71828)^{.16}$$
$$= \$1,000(1.1735) = \$1173.51.$$

With continuous compounding, Ivan's account grows by two cents more than it would have grown using daily compounding.

Effective Annual Interest Rates.   It is sometimes difficult for investors to choose among different investments given different stated interest rates and compounding intervals. For example, would you rather invest \$1,000 for one year to earn 7 percent compounded annually or 6.85 percent compounded daily? While you might be tempted to go with the higher stated interest rate of 7 percent, it turns out that you are slightly better off at 6.85 percent daily compounding.

To help investors make choices like the one above, we can transform all quoted interest rates, for example 7 percent annually or 6.85 percent daily, to an **effective annual interest rate**. The effective annual interest rate is given by:

effective annual interest rate
An interest rate expressed as if it were earned once per year.

This formula can be transformed into an alternative form by letting $w = m/r$:

$$FV_n = PV \left[\left\{ 1 + \frac{1}{w} \right\}^w \right]^{rn} \tag{b}$$

Formula (b) can be written more generally as:

$$FV_n = PV [f(w)]^{rn} \tag{c}$$

The function $f(w)$ can now be evaluated for different values of w. For example, when $w = 1$:

$$f(1) = [1 + (1/1)]^1 = 2.0000,$$

when $w = 12$:

$$f(12) = [1 + (1/12)]^{12} = 2.6130,$$

and when $w = 365$:

$$f(365) = [1 + (1/365)]^{365} = 2.71457.$$

We can also evaluate w at the limit of infinity:

$$\text{Limit } f(w) = 2.71828.$$
$$w \Rightarrow \infty$$

The value 2.71828 is the base number for natural logarithms and is given by the symbol e. Therefore, with continuous compounding, we obtain Formula (4.4):

$$FV_n = PV [e^{rn}].$$

$$\text{Effective Annual Rate} = \left(1 + \frac{r}{m}\right)^m - 1. \qquad (4.5)$$

Formula (4.5) builds compounding frequency into the quoted interest rate in order to compare quoted rates each with different levels of compounding. Thus, if you were faced with the choice of 7 percent compounded annually or 6.85 percent compounded daily, you would calculate the effective annual rate on each and choose the investment with the highest effective annual rate.

$$\text{Choice \#1: 7\% Annually: } \left(1 + \frac{.07}{1}\right)^1 - 1$$

$$= 0.07 \text{ Effective Annual Rate.}$$

$$\text{Choice \#2: 6.85\% Daily: } \left(1 + \frac{.0685}{365}\right)^{365} - 1$$

$$= 0.0709 \text{ Effective Annual Rate.}$$

Choice #2 with daily compounding is preferred because it has the higher effective annual rate. Many financial calculators have keys that will perform this conversion automatically.

A Quick Summary of Future Values.   It may be useful at this point to stop for a brief overview. Compounding is designed to push the cash flows toward the future into larger dollar amounts. Future values may be calculated using simple interest (with no compounding of interest), annual compounding, or even more frequent compounding. The solutions may be found by using an ordinary calculator, a financial calculator, or a computer with financial software.

Present Values

How can Jack and Diane, who have just won the $1 million lottery prize, determine what their winnings are worth today? Recall that the prize is represented by a stream of cash flows to be received in the future. Because these cash flows are different commodities, we should not simply add them together to calculate total value. The technique introduced in this section, discounting cash flows, uses the present time as a reference point and determines the value of all cash flows with respect to this reference point.

Discounting: The Formula Method.   Many of the procedures used in discounting are similar to the procedures used in compounding. For example, the four variables that are needed for compounding,

(1) PV, (2) FV, (3) r, and (4) n, are the same variables used to discount cash flows. In fact, the basic present value formula is the future value formula with PV instead of FV on the left-hand side:

$$PV = \frac{FV_n}{(1 + r)^n} \quad . \tag{4.6}$$

Formula (4.6) uses division rather than multiplication. Finding a present value is like compounding in reverse. We know the dollar amount to be received in the future, we know how long the wait will be to receive the money, and we know the interest rate that we could earn if we were to open a bank account. What we don't know is the value of those future dollars today, that is, what we would have to put into the bank account to earn those future values.

To discount a cash flow, divide the known future value by the quantity $(1 + r)^n$. As long as the interest rate is positive, PV will be less than FV. This follows from the earlier example where the value today of receiving $1.00 in one year was $0.93, and the value today of receiving $1.00 in two years was $0.86. Given a market interest rate of 8 percent, we can use the present value formula to show how we arrived at these values:

$$PV = \frac{\$1.00}{(1.08)^1} = \text{(approximately) } \$0.93, \text{ and}$$

$$PV = \frac{\$1.00}{(1.08)^2} = \text{(approximately) } \$0.86.$$

In the case of compounding, the higher the interest rate, the higher the future value. However, when discounting, the higher the interest rate, the lower the present value. If market interest rates in the above example are not 8 percent but are instead 12 percent, the present value will be lower than before:

$$PV = \frac{\$1.00}{(1.12)^1} = \$0.89, \text{ and}$$

$$PV = \frac{\$1.00}{(1.12)^2} = \$0.80.$$

Why are the present values lower for higher interest rate levels? Let's use our knowledge of compounding to answer this question. Given a choice, anyone would prefer a bank account that pays 12 percent interest over one that pays 8 percent because future value will be

FIGURE 4.8
The Present Value of a Dollar at Different Discount Rates

The higher the discount rate, the lower the present value.

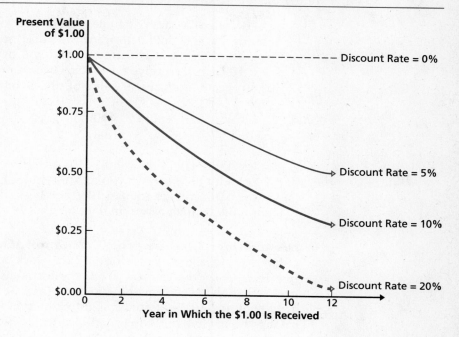

higher if invested at 12 percent. Now let's shift the problem around and think about present values. If you have to wait a year to receive a dollar, your opportunity cost of waiting for the dollar depends on what you could have done with a dollar in your hand today. One alternative is to put the dollar in a bank account now. Because your opportunity cost of waiting for the dollar is greater the higher the interest rate, higher interest rates make the present value lower.

    This is the reason the interest rate in present value calculations is sometimes known as the **discount rate**. To discount is to deduct from the value. The higher the rate of discount, the larger the deduction from the future value amount and the smaller the present value. The relationship between the discount rate and present values is shown in Figure 4.8.

discount rate
Another name for the interest rate. Because to discount is to deduct, the discount rate is used to reduce a future value to a present value.

Example 4.2 _____ Friendly Freddy's car dealership, being in need of new customers, announces the following bonus offer: a free $500 U.S. savings bond to anyone purchasing a new car within the next 30 days. Sound enticing? While the savings bond is purportedly worth $500, you must wait 10 years to receive this amount, and the bond pays to the holder an amount far less than $500 if cashed in before the 10-year period. How good a bonus is this?

Before this offer persuades you to buy your car at Friendly Freddy's, you should determine the value today of the free savings bond. While it is true the bond will pay $500, you must wait 10 years to receive full value. Given a market interest rate of 8 percent, the present value of the savings bond is:

$$PV = \frac{\$500}{(1.08)^{10}} = \$231.60,$$

or less than half of the value of the advertised bonus. Note that if Friendly Freddy gave you $231.60 in cash, you could put it in the bank and get $500 in 10 years. It's still a nice bonus, but not quite as nice as originally thought. ↵

Discounting: The Financial Calculator Method.   Financial calculators are designed to perform all the work necessary for discounting. In a sense, the calculator has the formulas built inside and can perform all the needed arithmetic. For example, suppose that Friendly Freddy's Car Agency offered a slightly different bonus scheme: a $500 savings bond that can be cashed in after 7.5 years, to any customer who buys a car within 30 days. Suppose also that the market interest rate is not 8 percent but 8.3 percent. Inputting into the financial calculator the values $500 for *FV*, 7.5 for *n*, and 8.3 for *r* will generate the *PV* of the new bonus as $274.95.

Non-financial calculators can still be of great assistance in performing present value analysis. As long as your calculator has the y^x key, your non-financial calculator can solve for the denominator in Formula (4.6) for any set of values of *r* and *n*. If, as in the case above, *r* is 8.3 percent and *n* is 7.5 years, then the present value of $500 is:

$$PV = \frac{500}{(1.083)^{7.5}} = \frac{500}{(1.8185)} = \$274.95.$$

The keystroke y^x will allow any value to be raised to any power. Most non-financial calculators have the keystroke 1/*x* which makes discounting even easier. To determine the present value, first raise one plus the interest rate to the power, and then hit the keystroke 1/*x*. Multiplying by the *FV* provides the present value.

Continuous Discounting.   Recall continuous compounding, where interest is earned every fraction of a second. We can also consider the case of continuous discounting. Formula (4.6) can be transformed to account for continuous discounting:

$$PV = \frac{FV_n}{e^{rn}},$$

(4.7)

where e is the base to the natural logarithm and is approximately equal to 2.71828. Most calculators have the keystroke e^x which allows for easy calculation of Formula (4.7). Calculators without the e^x key but with the y^x key can solve Formula (4.7) using 2.71828 for y.

For example, in Example 4.2, Friendly Freddy's Car Agency offered a $500 savings bond in 10 years. Suppose also that the market interest rate is 8 percent compounded continuously. Inputting the values $500 for FV, 10 for n, and 8 for r gives:

$$PV = \frac{\$500}{e^{.08*10}} = \frac{\$500}{e^{.8}} = \frac{\$500}{2.226} = \$224.66.$$

THE TIME VALUE FOR MORE THAN ONE CASH FLOW

Thus we have performed time value of money problems for a single or lump-sum cash flow. However, a very common situation is one in which a series of payments are either invested through time or are to be received through time—known as **multiple cash flow** problems.

multiple cash flow
More than one cash flow, as opposed to a lump-sum cash flow.

Compounding Multiple Cash Flows

Recall Example 4.1 and Ivan, the investor with $1,000 to invest in the bank today. The $1,000 came from savings Ivan accumulated while working a part-time job delivering pizza. Ivan is now completing his freshman year and plans to continue delivering pizzas through the end of his junior year. In addition to the $1,000 he has ready to invest in a bank today, Ivan will add to his investment at the end of each year over the next two years. He plans on closing the bank account when he graduates in three years. Because the pizza business is growing, Ivan estimates that the deposit a year from today will be $1,250 and the deposit two years from today will be $1,500. How much will Ivan have when he graduates if interest rates stay at 8 percent?

As shown in Table 4.2, this multiple cash flow future value problem is really three lump-sum future value problems in one. Case 1 con-

TABLE 4.2
Compounding Multiple Cash Flows

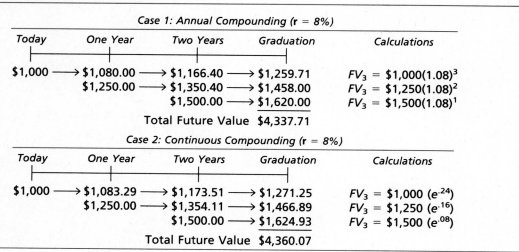

Case 1: Annual Compounding (r = 8%)

Today	One Year	Two Years	Graduation	Calculations
$1,000 →	$1,080.00 →	$1,166.40 →	$1,259.71	$FV_3 = \$1,000(1.08)^3$
	$1,250.00 →	$1,350.40 →	$1,458.00	$FV_3 = \$1,250(1.08)^2$
		$1,500.00 →	$1,620.00	$FV_3 = \$1,500(1.08)^1$
		Total Future Value	$4,337.71	

Case 2: Continuous Compounding (r = 8%)

Today	One Year	Two Years	Graduation	Calculations
$1,000 →	$1,083.29 →	$1,173.51 →	$1,271.25	$FV_3 = \$1,000\ (e^{.24})$
	$1,250.00 →	$1,354.11 →	$1,466.89	$FV_3 = \$1,250\ (e^{.16})$
		$1,500.00 →	$1,624.93	$FV_3 = \$1,500\ (e^{.08})$
		Total Future Value	$4,360.07	

siders the annual compounding of interest. We see that the first deposit of $1,000 grows to $1,259.71 in three years. The second deposit of $1,250 grows to $1,458.00 in two years. The third deposit of $1,500 grows to $1,620.00 in one year. The total future value can be found by summing the individual future values. The total future value of Ivan's investments is expected to be $4,337.71 at graduation.

Case 2 in Table 4.2 considers the continuous compounding of interest. The total future value of Ivan's investments with continuous compounding is $4,363.07, demonstrating the desirability of continuous compounding over annual compounding.

Discounting Multiple Cash Flows

Recall Example 4.2 and the bonus offered by Friendly Freddy's Car Agency: a $500 ten-year bond to any new car customer within 30 days. Now let's consider a more elaborate bonus plan. In addition to the $500 ten-year bond, Friendly Freddy's will offer an additional bond that pays $1,000 in 20 years, along with a third bond paying $2,500 in 30 years. The total bonus money is $4,000, but how much is that worth presently if interest rates are 8 percent?

Table 4.3 provides the calculations to this multiple cash flow present value problem. As the time line indicates, this is actually three present value problems in one. Receiving $500 in 10 years is worth $231.60 today, receiving $1,000 in 20 years is worth $214.55 today, and receiving $2,500 in 30 years is worth $248.43 today. The total present value of Friendly Freddy's bonus plan is $694.58.

TABLE 4.3
Discounting Multiple Cash Flows (Discount Rate = 8%)

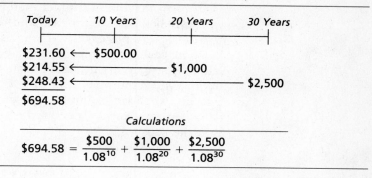

Today	10 Years	20 Years	30 Years

$231.60 ← $500.00
$214.55 ← $1,000
$248.43 ← $2,500
$694.58

Calculations

$$\$694.58 = \frac{\$500}{1.08^{10}} + \frac{\$1,000}{1.08^{20}} + \frac{\$2,500}{1.08^{30}}$$

We can use a similar procedure to calculate the present value of Jack and Diane's lottery prize. You will recall that Jack and Diane have won $50,000 per year for 20 straight years. To determine the present value of the prize, discount each of these payments to the present and add them up. These calculations are given in Table 4.4.

Given an interest rate of 8 percent, the present value of this Lotto prize is $490,907, about one-half of its stated prize value of $1 million. Notice that the present value of each of the $50,000 payments declines

TABLE 4.4
The Present Value of Jack and Diane's Lottery Prize

A Time Line View of Their Lottery Prize

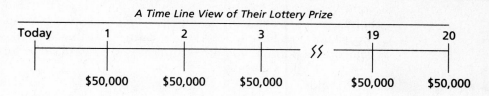

Today	1	2	3		19	20
	$50,000	$50,000	$50,000		$50,000	$50,000

Calculating the Present Value of Their Lottery Prize

Cash Inflow		$\frac{1}{(1.08)^n}$	Present Value of Future Cash Inflow		
Year 1:	$50,000	.9259	$50,000 * .9259 =	$46,296
Year 2:	$50,000	.8573	$50,000 * .8573 =	$42,867
Year 3:	$50,000	.7938	$50,000 * .7938 =	$39,692
.	.	.	.	.
.	.	.	.	.
.	.	.	.	.
Year 19:	$50,000	.2317	$50,000 * .2317 =	$11,587
Year 20:	$50,000	.2145	$50,000 * .2145 =	$10,725
		Present Value of Lottery Prize		$490,907

through time. The longer you have to wait, the less the payment is worth today.

It turns out that a simpler method exists for discounting the multiple cash flow stream for Jack and Diane's lottery prize. A special feature of the lottery's cash payments is that they are all the same. Given constant cash payments through time, procedures exist to present-value the stream in one step. Constant cash flow streams through time are known as annuities, and will be presented in the next section. But first, an expanded example of discounting is presented in Workshop 4.1, where we consider the question of whether going to college makes financial sense.

THE PRESENT VALUE OF ANNUITIES

Previous sections provided techniques for finding the present value and future value of a single or multiple cash flow. Multiple cash flows were discounted separately and added together. It was emphasized that computing present values was much like pulling and diminishing cash flows to the left along a time line, and that computing future values was much like pushing and increasing cash flows to the right along a time line.

annuities
A series of equal cash flows to be received through time.

Annuities are a special type of cash flow stream. An annuity is a stream of equal payments through time. Examples of annuities include (1) monthly payments on certain types of consumer loans such as car loans, personal loans, and mortgages, (2) the stream of coupons offered in connection with financial securities known as bonds, and (3) dividend payments offered on certain types of stock. Most annuities have finite lives, meaning that they stop at some predetermined point, while other annuities offer cash flows forever.

Example 4.3 ——————

Suppose that, soon after you graduate from college, the alumni office invites you to become a lifetime member of the alumni association. The cost of lifetime membership is $300 paid today, but the alumni association offers you the alternative of a payment plan. The payment plan requires payments of $121 due at the end of each year for three years. The payment is a three-year annuity, represented by the time line in Figure 4.9. Should you make the single payment of $300 today

FIGURE 4.9
A Time Line View of an Annuity

An annuity is an equal series of cash flows through time.

Workshop 4.1

The Present Value of a College Education

Have you ever stopped to think about whether going to college makes financial sense?* That is, are the costs of a college education worth the projected benefits? We show in this workshop how such a question can be answered.

Let's assume that each year of college costs $25,000 in total expenses—$10,000 in added expenses (tuition, and all other college-related expenses) and $15,000 in foregone wages. (We include foregone wages as a cost because if you weren't in college you would be working and receiving wages.) Given that these cost projections are reasonable, and given that the college degree you seek will take four years, the total cost of obtaining your degree is estimated at $100,000.

Although the costs appear large, we have yet to consider the benefits. It might be reasonable to expect that a college degree will increase your annual wage by $10,000 throughout your work life as compared to what you would be earning if you had not gone to college. That means that if you work for 40 years (say from the age of 23 to the age of 62) the "extra" income from your college degree will total $400,000 (40 years at $10,000 per year). But adding your wages together and subtracting out the sum of the costs is an accounting approach and is not equal to their true value.

The financial question we need to answer is whether $100,000 of college costs is worth the $400,000 of increased revenues. This multiple cash flow problem must transform all cash flows to a single reference point, in this case to present values. Below are the multiple cash flows in the problem. Given an interest rate of 8 percent, we can convert future values into present values. College education costs are discounted first, and then will be compared to the present value of college education benefits.

Step 1: Determine the Present Value of College Education Costs

Cash Outflow	$\frac{1}{(1.08)^n}$	Present Value of Future Cash Outflow
Year 1: −$25,000	.9259	−$25,000 * .9259 = −$23,147.50
Year 2: −$25,000	.8573	−$25,000 * .8573 = −$21,432.50
Year 3: −$25,000	.7938	−$25,000 * .7938 = −$19,845.00
Year 4: −$25,000	.7350	−$25,000 * .7350 = −$18,375.00
Total Present Value of Future Cash Outflows		−$82,800.00

(continued on next page)

Step 2: Determine the Present Value of College Education Benefits

Cash Inflow	$\dfrac{1}{(1.08)^n}$	Present Value of Future Cash Inflow
Year 5: +$10,000	.6806	+$10,000 * .6806 = +$6,806.00
Year 6: +$10,000	.6302	+$10,000 * .6302 = +$6,302.00
Year 7: +$10,000	.5835	+$10,000 * .5835 = +$5,835.00
Year 8: +$10,000	.5403	+$10,000 * .5403 = +$5,403.00
. .	.	. . .
. .		
Year 44: +$10,000	.0338	+$10,000 * .0338 = +$ 338.00
Total Present Value of Future Cash Inflows		$87,650.00

Step 3: Subtract Present Value of Outflows from Present Value of Inflows

Total Present Value of Future Cash Inflows	+$87,650.00
Total Present Value of Future Cash Outflows	− 82,800.00
	+$ 4,850.00

The table skips the benefits between year 8 and year 44 to save space. In terms of the benefits of a college education, the forty years of increased wages have a combined present value of $87,650. In other words, if the prospective college student went to the "grocery store of cash" he or she would be able to trade the 40 years of $10,000 benefits for $87,650 today. In terms of costs, the four years of $25,000 college payments have a present value of $82,800. The difference between the present value of benefits and costs will tell us whether or not the decision to enter college makes financial sense.

The decision makes financial sense, as the benefits exceed the cost by $4,850. The importance of the above procedure is that time value has been correctly used to make decisions involving cash flows at different points in time. In the example it was shown that the financial benefits of college slightly exceeded the financial costs of college, when time value is considered for this particular high school senior. Ignoring time value, the decision appeared obvious because the unadjusted benefits were $400,000 and the unadjusted costs were only $100,000. Although the decision did not change, the magnitude of the difference between benefits and costs has been greatly reduced when considering the time value of money.

---

*Of course there may be issues other than money involved in deciding to attend college, such as the joy and noncareer usefulness of an education. Where else in life other than as a college student can you get twenty weeks of vacation per year, ignore reality, and sleep until ten in the morning? (Let's not include being a college professor in this discussion.)

or the annuity payment plan? Assume market interest rates are 10 percent.

The present value of the single payment is of course $300. If we knew the present value of the $121 payment plan we could compare the two payment options and choose the plan with the lowest present value.

One way of determining the present value of the annuity plan is to discount each payment separately using the market interest rate of 10 percent and adding the three present values together:

$$PVA = \frac{\$121}{(1.1)^1} + \frac{\$121}{(1.1)^2} + \frac{\$121}{(1.1)^3} = \$300.91.$$

PVA stands for the present value of the three-payment annuity. The payment plan has a present value approximately equal to the single payment.

The present values can also be solved using the financial calculator. Take a minute now to verify our answer of approximately $300 for the present value of the annuity using one or both of these methods.

Because the present value of the annuity is (approximately) equal to the alternative of paying $300 today, most people would be indifferent to the choice between writing a check today for $300 or paying through the annuity plan. Note that even though the annuity plan requires $363 total dollars to be paid (3 payments of $121), the value to the alumni office of receiving $363 through time is equivalent to receiving $300.91 today, given the time value of money. ↵

Developing a Shortcut Procedure for Annuities

This section develops a shortcut for finding the present value of annuities. The key to the shortcut is that the numerator in each of the three parts of the previous formula is the same. Because the numerator is a constant, we can factor out the common amount:

$$PVA = \$121 \left[\frac{1}{(1.1)^1} + \frac{1}{(1.1)^2} + \frac{1}{(1.1)^3} \right] = \$300.91.$$

The three fractions inside the brackets are equal to:

$$[0.9091 + 0.8264 + 0.7513] = [2.4869],$$

so that the solution to our present value problem becomes:

$$PVA = \$121 \, [2.4869] = \$300.91.$$

Thus, 2.4869 is the sum of three separate present values. If we can
determine a way of calculating this sum directly, we can solve the
problem in one step. This is the annuity shortcut, and is shown next
using the formula method and the financial calculator method.[7]

The Formula Method.   The general formula for the present value of
an annuity is:

$$PVA = A \left[\frac{1}{(1 + r)^1} + \frac{1}{(1 + r)^2} + \frac{1}{(1 + r)^3} + \cdots + \frac{1}{(1 + r)^n} \right],$$

where A stands for the annuity amount, r is the market interest rate,
and n is the period when the annuity stops. An algebraic solution[8]
exists for the bracketed expression such that the PVA can be given by:

$$PVA = A \left[\frac{1}{r} - \frac{1}{r(1 + r)^n} \right]. \tag{4.8}$$

---

7. All annuities in this chapter are assumed to have cash flows that occur at the end of
each period.
8. The annuity formula can be derived by using the concept of a geometric series. First
let:

$$PVA = A/(1 + r)^1 + A/(1 + r)^2 + A/(1 + r)^3 + \cdots + A_r/(1 + r)^n.$$

Now let $j = A/(1 + r)$ and $k = 1/(1 + r)$ so that the equation above becomes:

$$PVA = j(1 + k + k^2 + k^3 + \cdots + k^{n-1}). \tag{a}$$

Multiplying both sides of the above equation by k gives:

$$PVA \cdot k = j(k + k^2 + k^3 + \cdots + k^n). \tag{b}$$

Subtracting formula (b) from formula (a) gives:

$$PVA(1 - k) = j(1 - k^n) \tag{c}$$

Substituting back for both j and k gives:

$$PVA \left[1 - \frac{1}{(1 + r)} \right] = \frac{A}{1 + r} \left[1 - \frac{1}{(1 + r)^n} \right] \tag{d}$$

Multiplying both sides by $(1 + r)$ gives:

$$PVA \cdot r = A \left[1 - \frac{1}{(1 + r)^n} \right] \tag{e}$$

Rearranging formula (e) gives the annuity Formula (4.8):

$$PVA = A \left[\frac{1}{r} - \frac{1}{r(1 + r)^n} \right].$$

Using Formula (4.8) we can solve for the present value of the alumni annuity in one step:

$$PVA = \$121\left[\frac{1}{.1} - \frac{1}{.1(1.1)^3}\right] = \$121(10 - 7.5131)$$

$$= \$121(2.4869) = \$300.91,$$

the same answer as before.

The Annuity Formula (4.8), which looks intimidating, is really quite manageable. Most calculators are equipped with the keystroke y^x, which can solve for $(1 + r)^n$ given any combination of r and n. The rest is simple arithmetic.

A final note on the formula method. Formula (4.8) for the *PVA* can be written in several different ways. However, they all give the same result. Don't be surprised if a calculator handbook or another reference has an annuity formula that doesn't look exactly like ours.

A similar development for the future value of an annuity is presented in the chapter appendix.

The Financial Calculator Method. The financial calculator method is simpler than the formula method. The present value of an annuity can be found by inputting the annuity amount A, r, and n into the financial calculator and computing PVA.[9]

The simplicity in using the financial calculator is well demonstrated in the case of annuities. For example, to determine the present value of the three-period alumni annuity, you would input the annuity amount as $A = \$121$, $r = .10$, and $n = 3$ years, and the calculator will determine the present value of the annuity to be $300.91 (usually the keystroke *CPT* and *PV*). Of course, this is not magic. The calculator has the Annuity Formula (4.8) embedded in it, and simply replaces the variables A, r, and n with those of the specific situation. Remember to clear your calculator before starting a new problem.

SOLVING FOR THE INTEREST RATE

To this point we have emphasized time value problems that determine either future values or present values. There are, however, situations where you know present and future values and the length of time but

---

9. A word of caution: All our annuity examples assume cash flows at the end of each period. To work these problems, your calculator should not be set up for beginning-of-the-year cash flows (often referred to as annuity due problems).

do not know the interest rate. We show in this section how to solve for the interest rate.

The Echo Land Development Company is planning to buy a tract of land for $118,000. Echo believes that it could sell the land three years from now for $150,000. What rate of return would an investment that turns $118,000 into $150,000 earn?

We can use the future value Formula (4.2) or present value Formula (4.6) to solve for the interest rate. In either case, we rearrange the formula to get the interest rate on the left-hand side:

$$r = (FV_n/PV)^{1/n} - 1. \tag{4.9}$$

For the Echo Land Development, the interest rate on their investment is:

$$r = (150{,}000/118{,}000)^{1/3} - 1 = (1.2712)^{1/3} - 1 = .0832,$$

so that r is 8.32 percent. This calculation can be challenging because it requires taking a value to the power 1/3; however, the keystroke y^x can be used to solve the problem easily. Taking a value to the 1/3 power is equivalent to raising a value to the power 0.333, so that 1.2712 raised to the 0.333 power is 1.0832.

Of course, the simpler method for solving for the interest rate utilizes the financial calculator. Remember that the financial calculator can solve for either PV, FV, n, or r, given any of the other three variables. By inputting $118,000 for PV, $150,000 for FV, and 3 for n, the financial calculator will solve for r equal to 8.32 percent.

SOLVING FOR THE TIME PERIOD

Finally we examine the case in which the present value, the future value, and the interest rate are known, but the time period is not known. For example, suppose your $100 can be placed in a bank account to earn 10 percent interest compounded annually. Your goal is for the bank balance to accumulate to $120. How long would the $100 need to be left in the bank until it grows to $120?

We can use the future value Formula (4.2) or present value Formula (4.6) to solve for the time period. In either case, we rearrange the formula to get the interest rate on the left-hand side:

$$(1 + r)^n = (FV_n/PV). \tag{4.10}$$

The unknown variable n appears as a power in Formula (4.10) and therefore requires that natural logarithms be used to determine a solution:

$$n * ln (1 + r) = ln (FV_n/PV).$$

where *ln* stands for the natural logarithm. In the specific problem:

$$n * ln (1.1) = ln (120/100).$$

$$n * 0.0953 = 0.1823.$$

$$n = 1.9131 \text{ years.}$$

The simpler method for solving for the time period utilizes the financial calculator. Remember that the financial calculator can solve for either *PV*, *FV*, *n*, or *r* given any of the other three variables. By inputting $100 for *PV*, $120 for *FV*, and 10 percent for *r*, the financial calculator will solve for *n* to be 1.9129.[10]

SUMMARY

☐ The time value of money is a fundamental concept in finance. Dollars received in different time periods are different commodities and, as such, cannot be directly compared with each other for the purposes of making decisions. In order to compare dollars in different periods their value must be transformed to the same period, either to the present or to some point in the future.

☐ The formula for transforming present dollars to future dollars is:

$$FV_n = PV(1 + r)^n.$$

☐ Compound interest is earned when interest is left to accumulate in an account through time. The amount of compound interest earned depends on the frequency in which interest is compounded, or by:

$$FV_n = PV\left[1 + \frac{r}{m}\right]^{mn}.$$

☐ The frequency of compounding spans the range of once per year (annual) to once every fraction of a second, or continuous compounding:

$$FV_n = PV(e^{rn}).$$

☐ Discounting determines the value today of dollars to be received in the future. When discounting, the interest rate (*r*) is often referred

---

10. Some calculators will round this number up to the nearest integer.

to as the discount rate, or the rate at which future dollar amounts are discounted back to the present:

$$PV = \frac{FV_n}{(1 + r)^n}.$$

☐ Both discounting and compounding can be done with single payment amounts or with multiple cash flows. Multiple cash flow problems can be thought of as a series of single payment problems. Thus, it is possible to determine the value in the future of a series of cash flows, as well as to determine the value today of a series of cash flows to be received in the future.

☐ An annuity is a series of equal cash flows through time. The present value of annuities can be determined in one step using the annuity shortcut formula:

$$PVA = A \left[\frac{1}{r} - \frac{1}{r(1 + r)^n} \right].$$

☐ Given the present value, the future value, and the time period (n), we can solve for the interest rate:

$$r = (FV_n/PV)^{1/n} - 1.$$

☐ Given the present value, the future value, and the interest rate, we can solve for the number of time periods it takes for the present value to grow to a future value:

$$n * ln \, (1 + r) = ln \, (FV_n/PV).$$

DEMONSTRATION PROBLEMS

Problem 1   Complete the following table:

	PV	FV	r	n	m
a	———	$100	6%	5	1
b	$100	———	5%	10	1
c	$50	$100	———	20	1
d	$50	$100	6%	———	1
e	———	$100	4%	10	4

Solution to Problem 1

The problems will be solved using both the formula method and the financial calculator method.

The formula method requires that the known values be plugged into the appropriate formula. With a little practice, using the financial calculator method is simpler. All five problems are solved by inputting the three known values and asking the calculator to solve for the fourth and missing value.

Part (a): (Finding a present value)
Using the formula method, fill in the right-hand side of Formula (4.6):

$$PV = \$100 / (1.06)^5 = \$74.726.$$

Using the financial calculator method, insert the three known values and ask the financial calculator to solve for PV. Typical keystrokes would be:

(Clear calculator) 100, *FV*, 6, *%I*, 5, *n*, *CPT*, *PV*,

which produces the same answer of $74.726 (rounded).

Part (b): (Finding a future value)
Using the formula method, fill in the right-hand side of Formula (4.2):

$$FV = \$100 * (1.05)^{10} = \$162.89.$$

Using the financial calculator method, insert the three known values and ask the financial calculator to solve for the FV. Typical keystrokes would be:

(Clear calculator) 100, *PV*, 5, *%I*, 10, *n*, *CPT*, *FV*,

which produces the same answer of $162.89 (rounded).

Part (c): (Finding an interest rate)
Using the formula method, fill in the right-hand side of Formula (4.9):

$$r = (\$100/\$50)^{1/20} - 1 = 3.53\%.$$

This is a little tricky but can be solved on most calculators using the following keystrokes: 100, /, 50, =, y^x, 0.05, =. Note that 0.05 is the decimal equivalent of 1/20.

Using the financial calculator method, insert the three known values and ask the financial calculator to solve for the %I. Typical keystrokes would be:

(Clear calculator) 50, *PV*, 100, *FV*, 20, *n*, *CPT*, *%I*, which produces the same answer of 3.53% (rounded).

Part (d): (Finding the length of time)
Using the formula method, follow the procedure at and after Formula (4.10) and solve for n:

$$n * ln\ (1 + r) = ln\ (FV/PV)$$

$$n * ln\ (1.06)\ = ln\ (2.0)$$

$$n * 0.058269 = 0.693147$$

$$n \qquad\qquad = 11.9$$

This method requires the use of a natural logarithm key. If your calculator does not have one you will have to learn the trial and error method discussed in Chapter 5, pp. 146–147.

Using the financial calculator method, insert the three known values and ask the financial calculator to solve for the n. Typical keystrokes would be:

(Clear calculator) 50, *PV*, 100, *FV*, 6, *%I*, *CPT*, *n*,

which produces the same answer of 11.9 (rounded).

Part (e): (Finding a present value with quarterly compounding)
When m, the number of compounding intervals per year, is greater than one, two adjustments must be made. The value used for the interest rate must be divided by m while the number of years must be multiplied by m in order to obtain the number of periods. Formula (4.3) shows this substitution.

Using the formula method, fill in Formula (4.3) and solve for *PV*:

$$FV_n = 100 = PV * (1.01)^{4*10}$$

$$PV = 100\,/\,1.48886$$

$$PV = \$67.165$$

The value 1.01 was found by dividing the interest rate (4%) by m (4) and adding 1. The exponent is solved using the y^x key as before.

Using the financial calculator method, the "trick" is to adjust the interest rate by dividing it by m and the number of periods by multiplying the number of years by m. Accordingly, $\%I$ is 1% (the quarterly rate), n is 40 (the number of quarters), and everything else is the same. Insert the three known values and ask the financial calculator to solve for the *PV*. Typical keystrokes would be:

(Clear calculator) 100, *FV*, 1, *%I*, 40, *n*, *CPT*, *PV*,

which produces the same answer of $67.165 (rounded).

Problem 2 Find the present value of an annuity of $100 per year to be received in years 1 though 20 using an interest rate of 4 percent. Find the future value of an annuity (see chapter appendix) of $100 per year to be received in years 1 through 20 using an interest rate of 4 percent

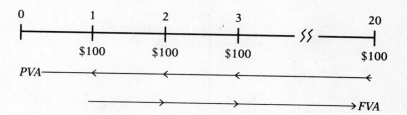

Solution to Problem 2

The present value of the annuity is solved by collapsing the 20 payments of $100 received at the end of each year into a single present value. This is accomplished by solving with Formula (4.8) where r = 4%, n = 20, and A = $100. Insertion of the variables using Formula (4.8) gives:

$$PVA = \$100 \left[\frac{1}{.04} - \frac{1}{.04(1.04)^{20}} \right] = \$100 \, [13.5903] = \$1,359.03.$$

The same answer can be found by inserting the three known values into a financial calculator and solving for the *PVA*. Typical keystrokes will be:

(Clear calculator) 100, *A*, 4, *%I*, 20, *n*, *CPT*, *PV*.

The future value of the annuity is solved by collapsing the 20 payments of $100 invested at the end of each year into a single future value. This is accomplished by solving with Formula (4.11) in the chapter appendix where r = 4%, n = 20, and A = $100. Insertion of the variables using Formula (4.11) gives:

$$FVA = \$100 \left[\frac{(1.04)^{20} - 1}{.04} \right] = \$100 \, [29.778] = \$2,977.80$$

The same answer can be found by inserting the three known values into a financial calculator and solving for the *FVA*. Typical keystrokes will be:

(Clear calculator) 100, *PMT*, 4, *%I*, 20, *n*, *CPT*, *FV*.

REVIEW QUESTIONS

1. Why is there a time value of money?
2. Explain why investment can be called deferred consumption.
3. Why are cash flows to be received through time best considered different commodities?
4. What is compound interest? How does it work?
5. Explain why dollars to be received in the future have a lower value today.

PROBLEMS

Note: Unless otherwise indicated, use annual compounding in these problems.

Complete the table given the following information:

	PV	FV	r	n	m
1.	$100	____	.10	1	1
2.	$100	____	.10	2	1
3.	$125	____	.10	1	1
4.	$175	____	.15	20	1
5.	$175	____	.155	5	1

6. What is the future value of $1,000 in two years if it is invested at an interest rate of 8%?
7. If you borrowed $10,000 today for five years at 9% interest, how much would you have to pay back?
8. If $100 is deposited in a savings account at 6% interest per year, what will the amount be in five years?
9. You deposit $500 in a three-year savings certificate at 5% interest. At the end of the second year, the bank increases the interest rate on savings certificates to 6%. What will your initial deposit of $500 be worth in three years?

Complete the table given the following information:

	PV	FV	r	n	m
10.	$100	____	.10	1	2
11.	$125	____	.10	2	2
12.	$125	____	.12	1	4
13.	$125	____	.12	1	365
14.	$125	____	.155	1	12

15. Your boss, the treasurer for a small manufacturing company, wishes to deposit $50,000 for two years until the money is needed to replace some equipment. He would like you to analyze the investment opportunities offered by two savings certificates. One certificate offers 8% interest compounded annually while the other certificate earns 7.9% interest compounded quarterly. What is the future value of the $50,000 for each alternative?

16. What is the future value of $800 if it earns an interest rate of 6.5% compounded semiannually for one year? Repeat for two years, and again for five years.

17. You expect to receive a check for $300 in three months and another check for $500 in six months from your part-time job. Both amounts will be deposited in a savings account at 7% interest compounded quarterly. What is the future value of the total deposit nine months from today?

18. What will $1000 be worth in two years if it is compounded continuously at an interest rate of 8%?

19. You have seen an advertisement for an investment fund that offers 6% interest compounded continuously. At the moment, your savings account offers 6.5% compounded quarterly. What is the future value of $500 in one year for the fund and the savings account?

Complete the table given the following information:

	PV	FV	r	n
20.	_____	$100	.10	1
21.	_____	$150	.10	2
22.	_____	$150	.12	1
23.	_____	$150	.12	20
24.	_____	$150	.155	5

25. What is the present value of $5,000 to be received in two years? The interest rate is 9%.

26. What is the present value of $1,000 to be received in one year if the interest rate is 8%? What is the difference in present value if the interest rate is 10%?

27. You would like to visit the Far East and Asia in three years. You have estimated that this trip will cost $5,000. What amount needs to be placed in a three-year 7% savings certificate today so that you will have $5,000 in three years?

28. What is the present value of a 20-year 9% zero coupon bond that has a face value of $10,000?

29. The parents of an eight-year-old child wish to deposit an amount today that will cover the child's first year in college. Tuition is esti-

mated to be $15,000 when the child is a college freshman at age 18. If the interest rate is 10%, what amount needs to be deposited today?

30. You have just won a lottery prize and may choose between two alternatives:

    Choice A: Receive $2,000 one year from today.
    Choice B: Receive $500 today and $1,500 one year from today.

    What is the present value of each alternative, assuming an interest rate of 7%?

31. What is the present value of $25,000 discounted for 40 years at 12% interest?

Complete the table given the following information:

	PV	FV	r	n
32.	$100	$110.00	_____	1
33.	$150	$169.50	_____	1
34.	$200	$213.00	_____	1

35. Your brother, who owns a small company, has asked for your help. He anticipates that he will need to spend $5,000 on computers in one year and $10,000 on other equipment in two years. What amount needs to be deposited today at 6% so these purchases can be made?

36. A scholarship service wants to set aside an amount today to cover a particular student's college costs. The student will receive $15,000 per year for four years, beginning in two years. What is the present value of the entire scholarship amount, assuming an interest rate of 8%?

Complete the table given the following information using Formula (4.8):

	PVA	A	n	r
37.	_____	$100	2	.10
38.	_____	$100	5	.10
39.	_____	$100	2	.17
40.	_____	$150	20	.10
41.	_____	$100	5	.105

42. What is the present value of 20 annual installments of $500 paid at the end of each year if the required rate of return is 9%?

43. A bank certificate offers payments of $50 per year at the end of each year for 5 straight years. Calculate the value of the security, or in other words the present value of those payments, assuming an interest rate of 10%.

44. Congratulations! You have just won a sweepstakes prize. The prize allows you to choose the method of payment.

    Choice A: Receive $10,000 today.
    Choice B: Receive $1,000 today and $1,000 at the end of each year for the next 12 years.

    Which alternative has a higher present value? Use an interest rate of 7%.

45. If a deposit of $2,000 today will grow to $2,160 in one year, what is the interest rate that is being used?

46. Your aunt, who is retiring, has asked for some investment advice. She can either take a lump-sum pension amount of $10,000 today or receive from her pension $10,800 one year from today. If she receives the payment today, she intends to invest the money herself in a one-year Treasury bill, offering 6%.
    a. What interest rate would she earn if she allows the money to grow in the pension fund?
    b. Which alternative should she choose? Explain.

47. A bank is promoting a savings certificate, which is only for new customers. The bank is promising to return $1,300 in two years if you open an account today with $1,000 for the savings certificate. What is the interest rate that you will receive each year on your deposit if you open the account?

48. How many years does it take for a deposit of $1,000 to grow to $2,000 if the money is in an account earning 8% interest compounded annually?

49. Your travel agent informs you that the agency can guarantee a trip to Australia for $2,500. You currently have $1,700 to devote to the trip. If bank accounts earn 6% interest compounded annually, how long will you have to wait to make the trip?

Complete the table given the following information and Formula (4.11):

	FVA	A	n	r
50.	———	$100	2	.10
51.	———	$100	5	.10
52.	———	$100	20	.10
53.	———	$100	2	.20
54.	———	$100	20	.20

55. A deposit of $100 is made at the end of each year for nine straight years. The required rate of return is 9%. What will the total deposit be worth nine years from today?

56. The grandmother of a newborn child will put $1,000 into a savings account at the end of each year for the child's college

expenses. If she makes 18 annual deposits at an interest rate of 11%, what will be the value of this annuity in 18 years?

57. If $100 is deposited today and in two additional installments at the end of each year for two straight years, what will it be worth in two years? The expected rate of return is 7%.

58. Deposits of $1,000 are made at the end of each year for the next five years. What will the amount grow to in five years if invested at an interest rate of 7.5%?

59. Your friend wishes to set up an annuity today that will grow to $80,000 in 15 years. The money will then be used to retire $80,000 of government loans taken out to attend medical school. If your friend deposits $2,500 at the end of each year for 15 years and earns an interest rate of 10% on the deposits, will she have enough at that time to retire the government loan?

DISCUSSION QUESTIONS

1. Respond to the following comment:
   The concept of the time value of money is a nice way to conceptualize economic decision making, but most real-world business decisions do not incorporate time value.

2. Respond to the following comment:
   Whenever you sell something for more than it costs, you have made a profit.

3. Respond to the following comment:
   I just learned that those big sweepstakes companies offer the option to grand prize winners of taking a smaller amount today instead of the larger amount that they really won. This just reaffirms my thinking that these companies will do anything to rip people off.

4. Provide a response to this statement:
   Annuities, shmuities! I think they are a big waste of time. I'm getting pretty good at single cash flow discounting, and the annuity formulas look too hard. I'll just stick to the single cash flow method.

5. The Rule of 72 states that invested money will double in value whenever the number of years multiplied by the interest rate reaches 72.
   a. Is this approximately true?
   b. Can you prove this using the single cash flow future value formula for continuous compounding?

APPENDIX

The Future Value of an Annuity

Chapter 4 developed present value techniques for multiperiod cash flows. However, techniques have been developed for future value as well as present value annuities.

To illustrate, suppose that you are to be awarded an inheritance of $5,000 to be paid in installments of $1,000 a year, with the first payment to come in one year. As part of the agreement you cannot spend the money for five years. You can, however, let the local bank accumulate the funds for you, and the bank can guarantee a 6 percent interest rate to be earned on the funds over time. How many future dollars will you have to spend in five years?

This problem can be solved by taking the future value of each cash flow separately. For example, the first $1,000 payment will be received in one year and will be invested for four years:

$$FV_4 = \$1,000 \, (1.06)^4 = \$1,262.48.$$

Table 4.5 calculates the future value of each of the next four $1,000 payments, and sums them up to get the total future value of the five payments. Note that the last payment of $1,000 comes in year five and thus is already a future value.

Because the payments represent an annuity, a shortcut procedure exists to future-value the cash flow stream in one step. The formula for the future value of an annuity is:

$$FVA = A \left[\frac{(1 + r)^n - 1}{r} \right], \tag{4.11}$$

TABLE 4.5
Determining the Future Value of the Annuity—The Long Way

	Today	Year 1	Year 2	Year 3	Year 4	Year 5	
Payment 1		$1,000 →	→	→	→	→ $1,262.48	$1,000(1.06)^4
Payment 2			$1,000 →	→	→	→ $1,191.02	$1,000(1.06)^3
Payment 3				$1,000 →	→	→ $1,123.60	$1,000(1.06)^2
Payment 4					$1,000 →	→ $1,060.00	$1,000(1.06)^1
Payment 5						$1,000.00	$1,000(1.06)^0
					Total Future Value	$5,637.10	

where *FVA* is the future value of the annuity, *A* is the annuity amount, *r* is the interest rate, and *n* is the length of the annuity. Applying this formula for the inheritance gives:

$$FVA = \$1,000 \left[\frac{(1.06)^5 - 1}{.06} \right] = \$1,000 \left[5.6371 \right] = \$5,637.10,$$

the same answer given in Table 4.5.

Remember that any calculator with the keystroke y^x can solve the bracketed expression with little effort, and thus can solve future value problems for any values of *r* and *n*. Most financial calculators can solve for the future value of the annuity by entering in the annuity amount, the interest rate, and the length of the annuity, and solving for *FVA*.

(Clear calculator) 1000, *PMT*, 6, *%I*, 5, *n*, *CPT*, *PV*.

The Valuation of Financial Securities

Megan Morrison, a financial analyst for the Gecco Insurance Company, began the workweek with an interesting assignment. Gecco was considering purchasing for $47,134,500 a bond issued by a relatively unknown cable TV company. The bond promises cash flows of $5 million per year for 30 years such that the total amount of future dollars offered by the security is $150 million (30 cash flows of $5 million each). Megan's job was to determine whether Gecco should invest in the security. Under current market conditions, interest rates are 10 percent.

Because the cash flows offered by the security are different commodities that cannot be added together, Megan is quite sure that she cannot make the decision by comparing the $150 million of total inflows with the $47,134,500 of outflow. Megan remembers from her finance class that future cash flows can be transformed into present values that can be added together. Specifically, she knows that the present value of any future amount can be determined by discounting these amounts at an appropriate discount rate. But as Megan sits down to work the calculations, she is distressed by the thought of calculating present values for each of the security's 30 cash flows. Do easier procedures exist?

As demonstrated in Chapter 4, cash flow streams of equal amounts are known as annuities, and Megan will be happy to learn that the shortcut method for valuing annuities can be used for the Gecco bond. This shortcut will prove to be a big time-saver to Megan and anyone else calculating the price of bonds as well as other types of financial securities.

This chapter will expand the techniques for determining the present value of annuities. We will show that several types of financial securities, most generally bonds and sometimes stock, fit the definition of annuities, and in addition, we will discuss how to calculate the required rate of return on a financial security.

REVIEW OF DISCOUNTING ANNUITIES

Example 5.1 ——————— Megan Morrison, the security analyst at the Gecco Insurance Company, was to determine if Gecco should purchase the bond just described. Instead of working the problem as 30 separate lump-sum amounts, Megan recognized that the bond's cash flows comprise a 30-year annuity of $5 million payments. Given a market interest rate of 10 percent, she can determine the present value of this annuity in one step:

$$PVA = A\left[\frac{1}{r} - \frac{1}{r(1 + r)^n}\right], \tag{5.1}$$

where *PVA* is the present value of the annuity, *A* is the annuity amount, *r* is the interest rate, and *n* is the length of time of the annuity. For the Gecco bond:

$$PVA = \$5\text{ M}\left[\frac{1}{.1} - \frac{1}{.1(1.1)^{30}}\right]$$

$$= \$5\text{ M}[9.4269]$$

$$= \$47.1345\text{ million.}$$

The present value of the bond's cash flows of $47.1345 million is exactly equal to the bond's price. The annuity formula allows Megan Morrison to complete her task quickly. Her report on the investment security ends: You'll get what you pay for! ↵

Special Annuities

In this section we examine three special types of annuities, which will be shown to be useful in the valuation of certain financial securities.

perpetuity
An annuity with infinite life.

Perpetuities. A **perpetuity** is an annuity with infinite life. This means that the cash flow stream of a perpetuity continues forever. The formula for the present value of a perpetuity can be derived from the Annuity Formula (5.1):

$$PVA = A\left[\frac{1}{r} - \frac{1}{r(1 + r)^n}\right].$$

Given that the perpetuity has infinite life, we can replace n in the annuity formula with infinity:

$$PVA = A\left[\frac{1}{r} - \frac{1}{r(1 + r)^{\infty}}\right].$$

The denominator in the second part of the bracketed expression explodes to infinity as long as the interest rate is greater than zero. Because any positive number divided by infinity is zero, the second part of the bracketed expression drops out, leaving the formula for the present value of the perpetuity (*PVP*):

$$PVP = A\left[\frac{1}{r}\right] = \frac{A}{r}. \tag{5.2}$$

Thus, the present value of the perpetuity is simply the annuity amount divided by the interest rate.

Example 5.2 —————— Suppose that the bond held by Gecco, Inc., delivered to the firm $5 million a year forever. The present value of this perpetual bond, given a market interest rate of 10 percent, can be determined through Formula (5.2):

$$PVP = \frac{A}{r},$$

whereby:

$$PVP = \frac{\$5 \text{ million}}{.10} = \$50 \text{ million}.$$

Compared with the 30-year annuity, the perpetual bond provides $2,865,500 more in present value:

$$\$50 \text{ million} - \$47.1345 \text{ million} = \$2.8655 \text{ million}.$$

Said differently, the present value of receiving an infinite stream of $5 million payments starting in year 31 and continuing forever is only $2.8655 million today. The reason the perpetuity's value is relatively close to the value of the 30-year annuity is that the additional payments of the perpetuity occur far into the future and thus have little value today. For example, the value of receiving $5 million in 50 years with 10 percent interest rates is less than $43,000 today; the value of receiving $5 million dollars in 100 years is only $363 today! ↵

constant growth perpetuity
A perpetuity that grows at a constant rate forever.

Constant Growth Perpetuities. A **constant growth perpetuity** is a perpetuity that grows at a constant rate forever. For example, a perpetuity that starts at $100 and grows at a constant rate of 5 percent forever would grow to $105 next year:

$$CF_1 = CF_0 (1 + g) = 100 (1.05) = \$105,$$

where g is the growth rate of the perpetuity. This perpetuity would grow to $110.25 in the second year:

$$CF_2 = CF_1 (1 + g) = 105 (1.05) = \$110.25,$$

and would continue to grow by 5 percent each year thereafter.

It would appear a difficult task to value a constant growth perpetuity. Just think about sitting down to find a present value for an uneven stream of cash flows that continue forever. However, because the growth rate is constant, we can determine its value in one step:

$$PVCGP = \frac{CF_1}{r - g}, \tag{5.3}$$

where $PVCGP$ stands for the present value of a constant growth perpetuity, CF_1 is the perpetuity's cash flow in period one, r is the interest rate, and g is the constant growth rate of the cash flows. The formula does not work when the growth rate in the perpetuity is greater than or equal to the interest rate.

Example 5.3 —————— Suppose you own land with a current rental income of $30,000 and with the expectation that the rental income would grow at the rate of 10 percent every year. The present value of this rental stream if interest rates are 15 percent would be:

$$PVCGP = \frac{\$33,000}{.15 - .10} = \frac{\$33,000}{.05} = \$660,000.$$

Note that we used $33,000 rather than $30,000 as CF_1 since the formula calls for the cash flow in period one. The current rental income is $30,000, but will grow by 10 percent to $33,000 next year. The present value of the land is $660,000. ↵

Annuities Starting Beyond Period One. Our treatment of annuities thus far has assumed that the first cash flow begins in the first period. For instance, consider again the alumni association offer (Example 4.3) in Chapter 4. You were presented with alternatives of paying for a lifetime membership with $300 today or by making three annual payments of $121 starting in year one. What if, however, the alumni association awards you a one-year free membership, and offers a three-payment option of $121 starting in year two instead of year one?

The tools we will use to value this new type of annuity are similar to those used to value annuities starting in year one. It is useful to think first about how we valued the original alumni annuity:

$$PVA = \$121 \left[\frac{1}{(1.1)^1} + \frac{1}{(1.1)^2} + \frac{1}{(1.1)^3} \right] = \$300.91.$$

We discounted the first payment back one period, the second payment back two periods, and the third payment back three periods. Because the first payment was in year one, the discounting process pulled all three cash flows back to period zero or to the present.

The new annuity is different because the first payment is made in period two, the second in period three, and the third in period four. Using the same tools as before will not pull all three cash flows back to time zero but will instead pull the cash flows back to period one. Said differently, the annuity formula values the annuity stream *one period before* the start of the annuity. If the annuity stream starts in period one, then this formula gives us the present value of the annuity. If the annuity stream starts in period two, then the formula gives us the value of the annuity at time one. If the annuity stream starts in period 20, then the formula will give the value of the annuity at time 19.

Annuities that begin beyond period one require a second step in order to compute a present value. In the first step, the annuity is valued using the same method as for an annuity that started at the end of year one. For instance, in the alumni association example where the payments begin at the end of year two, we would first compute the value of the annuity to be $300.91. But this is its value in year one—not year zero. The second step is to present-value the lump-sum amount obtained in step one back to period zero. This means converting $300.91 to a present value:

$$PV = \frac{\$300.91}{(1.10)^1} = \$273.55.$$

The process of valuing the alumni association annuity is illustrated in Figure 5.1. Given the choice of the new annuity or paying $300 today,

FIGURE 5.1
Valuing an Annuity Starting in Year Two

The three-year annuity of $121 begins in year 2 and must be discounted one additional period to get a present value.

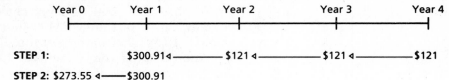

STEP 1:

STEP 2: $273.55 ◄———$300.91

you would prefer the new payment plan, because waiting an extra year to make the first payment has value.

In the above discussion we analyzed how to find the present value of an annuity whose cash flows began in year two. The mathematics of present value are so robust that we can extend this concept to finding the value of an annuity at any point in time.

The key is that these types of problems involve two steps. The first step is to collapse the annuity into a single value by applying the annuity formula. The second step is to move the value from step number one to any desired point on the time line by applying the single payment or lump-sum techniques of Chapter 4.

Example 5.4 —————— Suppose that you are analyzing how much money must be set aside to pay $10,000 per year toward each of the four years of a child's education. The money needed is shown using a time line, in which the years represent the age of the child:

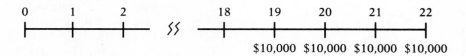

The first step is to apply the annuity formula to the four cash flows of $10,000 each. Assuming an interest rate of 8 percent, the value of the annuity in year 18 is:

$$PVA = \$10,000\left[\frac{1}{.08} - \frac{1}{.08(1.08)^4}\right]$$

$$= \$10,000\,[3.3121]$$

$$= \$33,121.$$

At this point we may move $33,121, the result of step number one, to any year that we desire. We already know that the four cash flows are equivalent to $33,121 in the child's 18th year. This tells us how large a college fund the child will need at age 18 to exactly meet the four-year cost of college. We can, however, state this value in terms of any year through present value or future value single payment or lump-sum techniques.

To find the value of the annuity at the child's birth, we pull the amount of $33,121 back 18 years to time period zero:

$$PV = \$33{,}121 / (1.08)^{18}$$

$$PV = \$33{,}121 / 3.996 = \$8{,}289.$$

To provide today for your newborn child's college education, the amount of $8,289 would need to be set aside. ↵

This two-step procedure can be used to find the value of the annuity in any year desired. For instance, instead of pulling the annuity back to the present, we could push the annuity forward in time. Suppose that you need to borrow the amount of $33,121 when you enter college to cover the cost of your four-year education. How much would you have to pay four years later when you graduate to satisfy the loan? Given an interest rate of 8 percent, this problem can be solved using future value techniques:

$$FV_{22} = \$33{,}121 * (1.08)^{4}$$

$$FV_{22} = \$33{,}121 * 1.3605 = \$45{,}061.$$

The amount of $33,121 at age 18 is equivalent to $45,061 at age 22.

To extend the example, suppose that your rich uncle gives you at age 12 a fabulous birthday present: a four-year college education. We know that the cost of the college education is $33,121 at age 18, the time you will enter college. How much would your uncle need to provide on your twelfth birthday to cover your college costs? The answer can be found by discounting or pulling $33,121 back six years to age 12:

$$\text{Value at Age 12} = \$33{,}121 / (1.08)^{6}$$

$$\text{Value at Age 12} = \$33{,}121 / 1.5869 = \$20{,}872.$$

Another item of interest is the future value of an annuity. Techniques similar to those used to determine the present value of annuities have been developed to determine the future value of annuities. Shortcut techniques for determining the future value of an annuity in one step are provided in the appendix to Chapter 4.

FINANCIAL SECURITIES

This section applies time value of money techniques to financial securities. To review, securities are financial assets rather than real assets, since they are a claim on cash flows rather than a direct claim on real assets themselves. Financial securities are issued by corporations and governments in order to raise capital and are purchased by investors in order to convert current cash into future and larger cash flows.

Most fixed payment securities offer specific terms such as the amount of payment, the length of the payment stream, and the dates of payment. Investors in these securities know exactly the amount of each payment and when it is to be received. The law of one price from Chapter 2 tells us that the present value of these known cash flow payments must be the value of the security traded in the financial markets.

The interest rate used in the present value process will reflect the market's view of the value of the promised future cash flows relative to today's dollars. This process will clearly include an assessment of the risk inherent in the cash flows promised by the security, and the risk is incorporated into the interest rate or discount rate. Procedures for adjusting the discount rate for risk are addressed in Module 3.

U.S. Treasury Bills

A **U.S. Treasury bill** (also known as a T-bill) is a promise from the United States Federal Government to pay a stated number of dollars at the end of a stated number of days. Window 5.1 provides detailed information on the institutional aspects of Treasury bill investments.

U.S. Treasury bills
Financial securities issued by the U.S. Treasury with maturities of 13 weeks, 26 weeks, or 52 weeks. They are offered with a minimum denomination of $10,000 and in multiples thereafter of $5,000 up to $1 million.

Treasury bills are purchased at a discount, which means that the investor pays a certain price today for the promise of receiving one cash flow when the security matures. The price or value of the T-bill is found by obtaining the present value of the single payment cash flow over the stated length of time until maturity. Because Treasury bill maturities are quoted in days, the maturity must be converted to years by dividing the number of days to maturity by the number of days in a year. The present value of the T-bill can be determined using the formula or financial calculator methods from Chapter 4.

Example 5.5 _____ Consider a U.S. Treasury bill offering $10,000 at maturity in 91 days, or in 0.25 years (assuming 364 days in a year to produce round numbers). Using an interest rate of 10 percent, the cash flows associated with the Treasury bill are illustrated by the time line in Figure 5.2.

The formula method requires substituting specific values for FV, r, and n into Formula (4.6) from Chapter 4:

Window 5.1

The U.S. Treasury Bill Market

U.S. Treasury bills, or T-bills, are issued by and are obligations of the U.S. Treasury. Treasury bills fall in a class of securities known as money market securities, and are issued with maturities of 13 weeks, 26 weeks, or 52 weeks. They are offered with a minimum denomination of $10,000 and in multiples thereafter of $5,000 up to $1 million. The number or amount of T-bills issued at any one time is determined by the amount of maturing T-bills to be refunded, current monetary policy objectives, and the Treasury's short-term financing needs.

Treasury bills are sold at a discount—determined by an auction—from face value. At maturity, the T-bill is redeemed by the holder for its full face value. This means that the rate of return is determined by the difference between the amount paid for the T-bill and its value at maturity.

One peculiar aspect of Treasury bills is how their prices are quoted for trading purposes and in the newspaper. Yields are quoted on what is known as a *bank discount yield* basis, dividing the amount of discount from par value (or face value) by the security's par value:

$$\text{Bank Discount Yield} = \frac{\text{Par Value} - \text{Purchase Price}}{\text{Par Value}} * \frac{360}{\text{Days to Maturity}}.$$

This presents a problem for investors because the technique used to determine bank discount yields is different from the standard techniques discussed in Chapter 4. Because bank discount yields understate the rate of return on T-bills, investors must convert these yields to actual or true yields (for example using simple interest):

$$\text{Actual Yield} = \frac{365 * \text{Bank Discount Yield}}{360 - (\text{Bank Discount Yield} * \text{Days to Maturity})}.$$

Such conversion techniques are available to assist investors.

Although T-bill investors may wish to hold their securities until maturity, there is an active secondary market made by government securities dealers, who stand ready to buy and sell T-bills at their market price. Indeed, the liquidity of the T-bill market contributes to its popularity as an investment vehicle. Commercial banks, with their special liquidity needs, along with other financial institutions, state and local governments, the U.S. Government, and individual investors, are major holders of Treasury bills.

Investment returns on Treasury bills are subject to federal income tax but are generally exempt from state and local taxes.

$$PV = \frac{\$10,000}{(1.10)^{0.25}} = \frac{\$10,000}{(1.0241)} = \$9,764.54. \quad \hookleftarrow$$

Determining the Interest Rate. In some cases the present value of the Treasury bill is known along with the future value and length of time. In this case it is possible to determine the interest rate. Returning to the T-bill examined above, suppose the Treasury bill's price of $9,764.54 was given, along with the future value of $10,000 to be received in 0.25 years. The Treasury bill's interest rate can be determined using Formula (4.9) in Chapter 4:

$$(1 + r) = [FV_n/PV]^{1/n}$$

$$(1 + r) = [\$10,000/\$9,764)^{1/0.25} = [1.02411]^4 = 1.10.$$

The interest rate to be earned on the T-bill investment is 10 percent. A financial calculator provides the answer even more simply if you input *FV*, *PV*, and *n*.

Treasury bills are one of many financial securities that offer a single cash flow. Other examples include most U.S. savings bonds, most certificates of deposit issued by banks, zero coupon bonds, and stripped Treasuries—detailed in Window 2.1. The valuation of any single cash flow security will be similar to that of the Treasury bill.

Coupon-paying Bonds

bond
A long-term fixed payment instrument issued by a corporation or government.

coupon payments
The series of cash flows offered on bonds.

par value (face value)
The lump-sum amount paid to the holder of a bond at maturity.

A **bond** is a long-term fixed payment instrument issued by a corporation or government. Bonds are generally multiperiod cash flow securities that pay to the holder a series of **coupon payments** as well as a lump-sum amount at maturity. The lump-sum amount paid to the holder at maturity is the bond's **par value** or **face value** and is usually $1,000. Bonds, unlike Treasury bills, are long-term financial securities with maturities in the range of from ten to thirty years. Window 5.2 describes some additional aspects of bonds.

The cash flow stream offered by most bonds can be broken into two portions: (1) an annuity portion made up of coupon payments, and (2) a lump-sum portion made up of the payment of the bond's par value at maturity. Accordingly, the price or present value of a bond is

FIGURE 5.2
The Cash Flows of a Treasury Bill

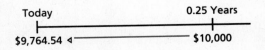

Window 5.2

Some Background on Bond Investing

Bonds are securities that offer a stream of payments, known as coupons, and a return of the bond's face value at maturity. Bonds issued by the U.S. Treasury are known as government or Treasury bonds, those issued by state and local governments are known as municipal bonds, and those issued by corporations are known as corporate bonds. The par value of most bonds is $1,000. Maturities of bonds usually range from ten to thirty years.

The bond's risk of default is dependent on the economic viability of the issuer. At one end of the default spectrum are U.S. Government bonds, considered to have zero default risk given the ability of the U.S. Government to print money and to tax. At the other end of the risk spectrum are bonds issued by private corporations experiencing financial difficulty. High default risk bonds are sometimes referred to as high yield bonds or *junk bonds*. To help investors evaluate the default risk of non–U.S. Treasury bonds, services such as Standard and Poor's and Moody's provide a rating system ranging from AAA (very low risk of default) to D (in default). States and municipalities, with the power to tax, can be expected in most cases to sustain their economic viability and thus usually have low default risk when supported by general revenue. The default risk of corporate bonds will vary from very low to very high.

The tax treatment of the bond depends upon its issuer. The interest received from U.S. Treasury bonds is fully taxable at the federal level but is generally exempt from state and local taxes. Interest payments from municipal bonds are tax exempt at the federal level and may also be tax exempt at the state and local level if the investor resides in the state in which the bond has been issued. For corporate bonds, interest payments are taxable at both the federal and state and local level. Bonds purchased for a price less than the eventual sales price or redemption price are subject to a tax on the capital gain.

---

the sum of the present value of its annuity stream plus the present value of the lump-sum par value payment at maturity.

Example 5.6 ———————— Consider the Varma Corporation which, in need of capital, issues a 15-year $1,000 par value bond with a coupon interest rate of 14 percent. A 14 percent coupon interest rate on a $1,000 par value bond translates into coupon payments of $140 paid to Varma bondholders each year for 15 years. Thus, the 15 coupon payments are a 15-period $140 annuity. The bond's payment of par value at maturity is a lump-sum cash flow of $1,000 in year 15. Combining the cash flows offered by the bond and taking their present value gives us the general bond valuation formula:

$$\text{Bond Value} = P_0 = \sum_{t=1}^{n} \frac{C}{(1+r)^t} + \frac{F_n}{(1+r)^n}, \qquad (5.4)$$

where P_0 is the present value of the bond, the Cs are the stream of constant $140 coupon payments, F_n is the bond's $1,000 face value, n is the number of periods until the bond's maturity, and r is the market interest rate assumed to be constant over the bond's maturity. The summation sign indicates that the coupon payments are made over the time span 1 through n.

The present value of the Varma bond can be determined from Formula (5.4) given $C = \$140$, $F_n = \$1,000$, $n = 15$, and some value for r, the market interest rate. Since most bonds are issued with a coupon rate that matches the market interest rate, we will assume that r is 14 percent. The present value of the bond can now be determined using either the formula or financial calculator methods. We'll illustrate both, starting with the formula method.

The general bond valuation model applied to the Varma bond is:

$$P_0 = \frac{\$140}{(1.14)^1} + \frac{\$140}{(1.14)^2} + \frac{\$140}{(1.14)^3} + \cdots + \frac{\$140}{(1.14)^{15}} + \frac{\$1,000}{(1.14)^{15}}.$$

Notice that bond valuation is really two problems in one. The present value of the coupon payments can be determined in one step as a 15-year $140 annuity:

$$PVA = \$140 \left[\frac{1}{.14} - \frac{1}{.14(1.14)^{15}} \right] = \$140[6.1422] = \$859.90.$$

The present value of the return of par value at maturity can be determined as a $1,000 lump-sum payment in year 15:

$$PV = \$1,000 \left[\frac{1}{(1.14)^{15}} \right] = \$1,000 \, [0.1401] = \$140.10.$$

The present value of the bond is the sum of $859.90 (the annuity portion) plus $140.10 (the lump-sum portion) or $1,000. Investors purchasing the Varma bond have a security whose future cash flows are equivalent in total value to receiving $1,000 today.

The financial calculator method may or may not require a two-part procedure, based upon the calculator's degree of sophistication. We will illustrate the two-part procedure that should work for most financial calculators. You should check the handbook to see if your calculator has a one-step shortcut. For the annuity portion, the values $A = \$100$, $n = 15$, and $r = 14$ percent are inputted into the calculator to compute the present value of $859.90. This value is to be stored into the calculator's memory. Next, the lump-sum present value is determined by clearing the calculator's financial memories, inputting the values $FV = \$1,000$, $n = 15$, and $r = 14$ percent, and computing the present value to be $140.10. Adding the two parts together gives $1,000, the present value of the bond. ◄┘

Bond Valuation with Semiannual Interest Payments.

The bond valuation model in Example 5.6 assumes that coupon payments are made annually. For example, if a bond was issued on July 1, 1993, with a maturity of 4 years, annual coupon payments would begin July 1, 1994, and would continue for three additional years with the last payment occurring on July 1, 1997. This, however, does not describe the coupon payment stream offered by most bonds.

Most bonds pay coupon interest twice per year, or on a semiannual basis, such that investors receive coupon payments equal to one-half the annual coupon payment every six months. A $1,000 par value bond with a 10 percent coupon rate issued on July 1, 1993, would make its first semiannual coupon payment of $50 on January 1, 1994, and continue to make semiannual payments of $50 every six months for seven additional six-month periods. The last semiannual coupon payment, to be made when the bond matures on July 1, 1997, is also the date that the bond delivers the lump-sum par value to the investor. This is illustrated in Figure 5.3.

The general bond valuation Formula (5.4) can be used to value a bond that pays coupons annually or semiannually. Prices for bonds with semiannual payments are computed by defining a period as six months instead of 12 months. For example, let's return to the fifteen-year, 14 percent coupon bond from Varma Corporation discussed above. Because the variable n in the general bond formula is the number of periods until maturity, and because we are now defining a period to be six months, the new maturity is two times the number of years, or 30 periods.

The bond analyst must be careful to make all the proper adjustments when valuing a semiannual coupon-paying bond. The size of each annuity payment is one half the size of the annual coupon

FIGURE 5.3
Bond Valuation with Semiannual Interest Payments

Semiannual coupons are received every six months and are one-half the size of annual coupon payments.

Case 1: Annual Coupon Payments

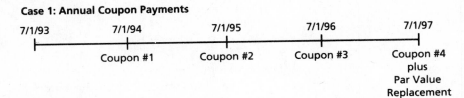

Case 2: Semiannual Coupon Payments

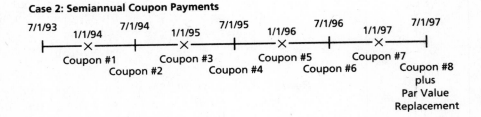

amount, and the interest rate must be adjusted so that the semiannual market interest rate, not the annual market interest rate, is used for r. Only the principal repayment of $1,000 is left unadjusted.

The cash flow stream for the Varma bond with semiannual coupons becomes:

$$P_0 = \frac{\$70}{(1.07)^1} + \frac{\$70}{(1.07)^2} + \frac{\$70}{(1.07)^3} + \cdots + \frac{\$70}{(1.07)^{30}} + \frac{\$1,000}{(1.07)^{30}}.$$

The semiannual annuity stream of $70 is one-half the size of the annual annuity stream, the 30-period length of the annuity stream is twice that of the annual stream, and the semiannual market interest rate of 7 percent is half that of the annual market interest rate.[1] With these adjustments, the present value of the Varma bond can be determined in two steps:

---

1. Technically speaking, it is not correct to take an annually compounded interest rate, such as 14 percent, and divide it by two to produce a semiannual rate. The reason is that compounding causes seven percent every six months to be more valuable than 14 percent every year. How much more valuable can be determined using Formula (4.5) for the effective annual interest rate in Chapter 4:

$$\text{Effective Annual Interest Rate} = \left[1 + \frac{r}{m}\right]^m - 1 = \left[1 + \frac{.14}{2}\right]^2 - 1 = .1449$$

$$P_0 = \$70 \underbrace{\left[\frac{1}{.07} - \frac{1}{.07(1.07)^{30}}\right]}_{\text{Step 1: } PV = \$868.63} + \underbrace{\$1,000\left[\frac{1}{(1.07)^{30}}\right]}_{\text{Step 2: } PV = \$131.37} = \$1,000.$$

Interest Rate Risk. It was no coincidence that the present value of the Varma bond, whether it pays coupons on an annual or semiannual basis, was equal to its par value of $1,000. This will be true any time the bond's coupon rate is equal to the market rate of interest, which is usually the case when a firm like Varma issues new bonds to the market.

Bonds are known as fixed payment securities because their coupon payments are locked in at issue and do not change over the life of the bond. As time moves forward, the market interest rate may change but the bond's coupon rate does not—it is fixed throughout its life. For example, the market interest rate may change from 14 percent to any level above or below 14 percent, but the Varma bond will continue to pay coupon interest at the rate of 14 percent annually.

> ⧖ Bonds are known as fixed payment securities because their coupon payments are locked in at issue and do not change over the life of the bond.

Although the cash flows of the bond don't change, the discount rate that the market uses to price the bond can change. What happens to the value of a bond as market interest rates change? The answer to this question depends on the direction of the interest rate change. If market interest rates increase, investors of Varma bonds will feel regret. Given the increase in the market rate, other firms similar to Varma will now issue their own bonds with coupon rates that match the new market rate, now higher than 14 percent. Because the 14 percent coupon rate attached to the Varma bonds stays fixed, Varma investors are stuck receiving a 14 percent coupon rate while other investors enjoy higher coupons.

The amount of regret felt by the holders of the Varma bonds will depend on the magnitude of the interest rate increase. Let's suppose that market interest rates climb to 16 percent the day after the Varma bonds are brought to the market.[2] One alternative that Varma investors have is to sell the Varma bond to another investor and to purchase

---

2. Such a sharp increase in the market rate overnight is a rare event. More realistic one-day shifts in market rates are on the order of one-tenth to one-quarter of one percent (10 to 25 basis points). We use this large increase to better make the point of interest rate risk.

newly issued 16 percent bonds. That's the good news! The bad news is that Varma investors will find that the value of their investment has fallen. The lower value reflects the fact that the Varma bond carries a lower coupon and therefore is not as valuable as new bonds being offered in the market. We can use Formula (5.4) for bond valuation to determine how much the price of the Varma bond will fall. Using semiannual coupon payments:

$$PV = \$70\left[\frac{1}{.08} - \frac{1}{.08(1.08)^{30}}\right] + \$1,000\left[\frac{1}{(1.08)^{30}}\right] = \$887.42.$$

Because of new market conditions, the old interest rate was replaced with the new market interest rate (16 percent annually, 8 percent semiannually). The price of the bond falls from $1,000 to $887.42. We say that the Varma bonds sell at a *discount*, meaning that the price of the bond is below its par value. With the lower price, new bond investors are indifferent between paying $1,000 for a 16 percent coupon bond or paying $887.42 for the Varma 14 percent coupon bond. A comparison between the cash flows of the two bonds is illustrated in Figure 5.4.

However, don't feel bad for Varma investors. Because the relationship between bond prices and market interest rates is inverse, falling market interest rates cause the price of existing bonds to rise. Suppose that interest rates fall to the extent that the day after the Varma bond is offered new bonds come to the market offering a lower coupon rate, say 12 percent. The Varma bond continues to pay the original 14 percent coupon rate. Varma investors who wish to sell their bonds before maturity will find that the price of their bond has risen in value. We can use Formula (5.4) to determine how much the price of the Varma bond will rise (assuming no time has passed so that the maturity is still 30 periods):

$$PV = \$70\left[\frac{1}{.06} - \frac{1}{.06(1.06)^{30}}\right] + \$1,000\left[\frac{1}{(1.06)^{30}}\right] = \$1,137.65.$$

FIGURE 5.4
Rising Interest Rates and Falling Bond Prices

The new bond is issued with a higher coupon interest rate. The price of the Varma bond must fall.

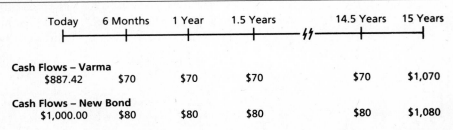

The higher price reflects the fact that the Varma bond carries a 14 percent coupon and therefore is more valuable than other newly issued bonds trading in the market. We would now say that the Varma bonds sells at a *premium*, meaning that the price of the bond is above its par value. With the change in price, new bond investors are indifferent between paying $1,000 for a 12 percent coupon bond or paying $1,137.65 for the Varma 14 percent coupon bond.

> ⊠ The relationship between bond prices and market interest rates is inverse. Rising market interest rates cause the price of existing bonds to fall, while falling market interest rates cause the price of existing bonds to rise.

Yield to Maturity

The previous section discussed how to determine a bond's price given the cash flow stream and a market interest rate. Now we show how to solve for the market interest rate given the bond's cash flow stream and price. The market interest rate, also known in this context as the bond's **yield to maturity**, is an accurate indication of the rate of return that the bond will offer until maturity under current market conditions.

yield to maturity
A measure of the average rate of return that a bond will offer under current market conditions.

Suppose you were given the opportunity to purchase the Varma bond for a price of $887.42. Paying this price today entitles you to 30 payments of $70, paid every six months, and a payment of $1,000 in 15 years. If you purchased the bond, what rate of return would the investment earn, on average, over its life?

The answer is not 14 percent (the bond's coupon rate) because the bond is selling at a discount from its par value. Given that you can purchase the bond for an amount less than $1,000 but receive $1,000 at maturity, your rate of return will be higher than the 14 percent coupon rate if you hold the bond to maturity. The question is how much higher?

Let's use Formula (5.4) to see what we know about the investment in the Varma bond:

$$\$887.42 = \$70\left[\frac{1}{r} - \frac{1}{r(1+r)^{30}}\right] + \$1,000\left[\frac{1}{(1+r)^{30}}\right].$$

As you can see, our information on the Varma bond includes everything but the market interest rate or the bond's yield to maturity. This problem looks similar to solving for the interest rate in Chapter 4. Unfortunately, things are not as simple as they were then because:

(1) we have a multiple cash flow stream and (2) the cash flow amounts are not all the same owing to the final principal repayment. No algebraic technique can be used to solve directly for r, leaving us with no choice but to use trial and error when using the formula method.

Trial and error means trying different market rates until we find the one that makes the present value of the Varma bond's cash flow stream equal to the price $887.42. For example, we can begin the search by substituting an annual rate of 20 percent (a semiannual rate of 10 percent) for r into Formula (5.4):

$$PV = \$70\left[\frac{1}{.10} - \frac{1}{.10(1.10)^{30}}\right] + \$1,000\left[\frac{1}{(1.10)^{30}}\right] = \$717.19.$$

With an interest rate of 20 percent, the bond's price of $717.19 is below our search price of $887.42. Because 20 percent is not the yield to maturity, the trial and error method asks for a new guess. Now the big question: Should the next guess be higher or lower than 20 percent? The correct answer is lower than 20 percent because a lower interest rate will produce a higher price. Remember, our goal is to get the right-hand side equal to the original left-hand side value of $887.42. Let's try 18 percent annually, or 9 percent semi-annually:

$$PV = \$70\left[\frac{1}{.09} - \frac{1}{.09(1.09)^{30}}\right] + \$1,000\left[\frac{1}{(1.09)^{30}}\right] = \$794.53.$$

An annual interest rate of 18 percent gets us closer to the search price but is still below $887.42. The trial and error process requires still another guess, and will continue to require guesses until the interest rate is found that produces our search price of $887.42. We know from a previous example that the search will end with a guess of 16 percent annually for r:

$$PV = \$70\left[\frac{1}{.08} - \frac{1}{.08(1.08)^{30}}\right] + \$1,000\left[\frac{1}{(1.08)^{30}}\right] = \$887.42.$$

We say that the bond's yield to maturity is 16 percent, meaning that if you purchase the Varma bond for $887.42 and hold it to maturity, you will earn an interest rate (a yield) of 16 percent on average per year.

Students are often surprised to learn that in our sophisticated world we are forced to rely on the method of trial and error to solve the yield to maturity. One lesson this teaches is that sometimes even the most advanced algebraic techniques cannot produce a shortcut.

We can, however, sympathize with those who dislike the trial and error process and can offer two suggestions. First, consider using a financial calculator with built-in programming capability. Many financial calculators can solve for the yield to maturity by performing the calculations of the trial and error process internally. Computer spreadsheet programs, for example Lotus 1-2-3 or Quattro Pro, offer similar capability. If you have a sophisticated financial calculator or have access to a computer spreadsheet, solving for the yield to maturity reduces to inputting the bond's cash flow stream and the price and allowing the calculator or computer to do the rest.

Our second suggestion is to use an algebraic solution that approximates the exact yield to maturity:

$$r = \left[C + \left\{ \frac{F_n - P_0}{n} \right\} \right] / \left[\frac{F_n + 2P_0}{3} \right], \tag{5.5}$$

where C is the bond's coupon payment, F_n is the bond's par value, P_0 is the current price of the bond, and n is the number of periods until maturity. We can imagine that to many readers the thought of using Formula (5.5) is worse than using the trial and error process. Putting everything in its proper place, the approximate semiannual yield to maturity for the Varma bond is:

$$r = \left[\$70 + \left\{ \frac{\$1,000 - \$887.42}{30} \right\} \right] / \left[\frac{\$1,000 + 2(\$887.42)}{3} \right] = .0797.$$

The annual yield to maturity is approximately twice the semiannual yield of 7.97 percent, or 15.95 percent. The approximation gets us close to the actual yield to maturity of 16 percent.

THE VALUATION OF COMMON STOCK

The second major category of financial securities is stock. Stockholders have claim to the cash flows of the firm only after all other claimants, such as employees, bondholders, suppliers, and governments, have had their claims satisfied. Stockholders are sometimes referred to as residual claimants because they have claim only to the residual cash flow.

dividends
The proportion of the corporation's earnings paid out to the firm's stockholders, on a per share basis.

capital gains
The dollar gains that result when a capital asset is sold for more than it cost.

Stockholders derive their common stock investment return in the form of **dividends** and capital gains. Most firms pay dividends on a regular schedule to their shareholders, but some pay no dividends. **Capital gains** occur when shares are sold at a price above their original purchasing price. For example, the price of a firm's stock will rise when demand to invest increases due to the introduction of a new product. Thus, if you buy stock for $1 a share and sell the same stock in the future for $1.50 per share, you have realized a capital gain of $0.50 per share.

Unlike bonds, which offer fixed payments according to a specified schedule, neither dividends nor capital gains are fixed obligations of the firm. Thus, the process of valuing common stock is difficult because the key cash flows from stock—dividends and capital gains—must be estimated. In most models the price of the stock is the present value of all estimated future cash flows. The more sophisticated the model, the more realistic is the attempt to estimate the cash flows, but the more difficult the estimations become.

The Discounted Cash Flow Model

An explanation of the discounted cash flow model for stocks might begin with the assumption that the common stock is purchased today, and is sold in one year. Consider Mirage, Inc., a firm that specializes in difficult-to-see processes. Claudia has come to know of this firm and believes it to be a good investment opportunity. She estimates that the stock price next year will be $20 per share, and she believes that the firm's dividend—now being paid at the rate of $2 per share—will stay at this level over the next few years. Given a discount rate of 15 percent, what price should Claudia be willing to pay for each share of Mirage's stock?

The single-period model is similar to the single cash flow present value model introduced in Chapter 4:

$$P_0 = \frac{DIV_1 + P_1}{(1 + r)^1}, \tag{5.6}$$

where P_0 is the current price or present value, DIV_1 is the dividend expected in year one, P_1 is the stock price expected in year one, and r is the discount rate applied to the investment. The value of Mirage stock given Claudia's estimates is:

$$P_0 = \frac{\$2 + \$20}{(1.15)^1} = \$19.13.$$

We would say that Mirage stock is estimated to be worth $19.13 per share. As long as other investors share these estimates, Mirage will trade in the market at approximately $19.13 per share.

Determining the Interest Rate.   As with bonds, if we know the market price along with other variables we can compute the model's interest rate. Formula (5.6) can be solved for the interest rate investors are using to present-value Mirage stock:

$$r = \frac{DIV_1}{P_0} + \frac{P_1 - P_0}{P_0}. \tag{5.7}$$

$$\underbrace{\phantom{\frac{DIV_1}{P_0}}}_{\substack{\text{Dividend} \\ \text{Yield}}} \quad \underbrace{\phantom{\frac{P_1 - P_0}{P_0}}}_{\substack{\text{Capital Gain} \\ \text{Yield}}}$$

As with the case of bonds, the interest rate has special meaning when valuing common stock. The interest rate is an estimate of the rate of return investors expect when investing in a share of stock of a certain company, and is composed of a dividend yield and capital gain yield. Given Claudia's estimates of a $2 dividend and a $20 stock price, and knowledge that the current stock price of Mirage is $19.13, we can determine the rate of return Claudia and other investors expect to receive:

$$r = \frac{\$2}{\$19.13} + \frac{\$20 - \$19.13}{\$19.13} = .105 + .045 = .15,$$

so that the rate of return investors expect on the investment in Mirage stock is 15 percent.

Extending the Holding Period.   One important feature of common stock is that it has no fixed maturity. We expect competitive firms to continue to operate far into the future. Claudia might therefore decide to invest in Mirage's stock today and continue to invest for more than one year. For instance, she might decide to invest for two years. How would she value the stock price given a two-year investment horizon?

The two-year common stock valuation model starts with the single-period formula and extends the formula to include a second year:

$$P_0 = \frac{DIV_1}{(1 + r)^1} + \frac{DIV_2 + P_2}{(1 + r)^2}.$$

The value of the common stock today is derived from estimates of the firm's dividend payment for year one and two, and an estimate of the firm's stock price in year two. If Claudia estimates that dividends will stay constant at $2 per share and that Mirage's stock price will rise to $21 in year two, the value of Mirage stock today is:

$$P_0 = \frac{\$2}{(1.15)^1} + \frac{\$2 + \$21}{(1.15)^2} = \$19.13,$$

the same as before.

The discounted cash flow model can accommodate any holding period. For example, suppose Claudia wishes to hold Mirage stock for three years. In this case, the valuation model can be written:

$$P_0 = \frac{DIV_1}{(1 + r)^1} + \frac{DIV_2}{(1 + r)^2} + \frac{DIV_3 + P_3}{(1 + r)^3}.$$

The discounted cash flow model can be extended into an n-period model, where n is defined as some period in the future:

$$P_0 = \frac{DIV_1}{(1 + r)^1} + \frac{DIV_2}{(1 + r)^2} + \frac{DIV_3}{(1 + r)^3} + \cdots + \frac{DIV_n}{(1 + r)^n} + \frac{P_n}{(1 + r)^n}.$$

Because common stock has no maturity date, n is in theory infinity if, unlike Claudia, you have no intention of selling. But substituting n with infinity in the above model makes the model simpler. As n gets large, the present value of all cash flows to be received at or near this end point becomes small. However, when n becomes infinity, the present value of P_n in the model becomes zero and can be dropped from the model:

$$P_0 = \sum_{t=1}^{\infty} \frac{DIV_t}{(1 + r)^t}. \tag{5.8}$$

Formula (5.8) states that the present value of a share of stock is equal to the discounted value of the stock's expected stream of dividends. Formula (5.8) is written in a compact way, with the dividend stream beginning in period one and continuing to infinity.

Formula (5.8) is applicable for investors with short-term time horizons as well as for investors with long-term horizons. In other words, the investor's time horizon does not matter when determining security prices. To see this, recall the single-period model from Formula (5.6). From the perspective of a one-year investor who might buy the stock next year, next year's stock price can be written:

$$P_1 = \frac{DIV_2 + P_2}{(1 + r)^1},$$

meaning that any investor intending to purchase the stock in one year and sell the stock the year after will value the stock as shown above. Substituting P_1 from above into the single-period formula (5.6) gives:

$$P_0 = \frac{DIV_1}{(1 + r)^1} + \frac{DIV_2 + P_2}{(1 + r)^2}.$$

We can continue this line of reasoning by asking for a specification of P_2 in the formula above from the perspective of another one-year investor. This would be:

$$P_2 = \frac{DIV_3 + P_3}{(1 + r)^1},$$

which when substituted for P_2 gives:

$$P_0 = \frac{DIV_1}{(1 + r)^1} + \frac{DIV_2}{(1 + r)^2} + \frac{DIV_3 + P_3}{(1 + r)^3}.$$

The process of substitution can continue until we are left with the multiperiod Formula (5.8). Thus, our single-period model is actually a multiple-period model in disguise. Although it looks like the multiperiod model is applicable only to the long-term investor, it is applicable to investors with investment horizons of any length because the value of the stock is the value of its collective dividends even if they end up being received by different people over time.

Special Discounted Cash Flow Model—No Growth in Dividends. The estimation of future dividends is a particular concern of stock valuation models. The concern can be simplified by assuming that future dividends will not deviate from the current dividend. Assuming constant dividends that continue forever greatly simplifies the multiperiod valuation model:

$$P_0 = \sum_{t=1}^{\infty} \frac{DIV}{(1 + r)^t}.$$

The only difference between the above formula and the discounted cash flow model, Formula (5.8), is the lack of subscript on the dividend variable. In other words, we assume here that $DIV = DIV_1 = DIV_2 = DIV_3 = \cdots = DIV_\infty$. The constant dividend stream is an example of a perpetuity inasmuch as the dividend continues forever. The present value of the stock according to the constant dividend model is simply the current dividend divided by the discount rate:

$$P_0 = \frac{DIV}{r}.$$

To illustrate this special case, suppose that Mirage, Inc., which currently pays a dividend of $2 per share, is expected to pay a $2 dividend each year forever. If the rate of rate of return on Mirage stock is 15 percent, the present value of Mirage is:

$$P_0 = \frac{\$2}{.15} = \$13.33.$$

The above formula is an example of how standard formulas for discounting can be used to find the prices of financial securities. The common stock of firms that pay a constant dividend, as well as preferred stock, can be valued as a perpetuity. However, this model is usually too simplistic, because most corporations change their dividend quite often. For example, growing firms can be expected to increase their dividend on a regular basis. The model accurately describes the cash flows from preferred stock, as preferred stock pays a constant dividend and is priced rather accurately using the perpetuity model.

> ✗ The common stock of firms that pay a constant dividend, as well as preferred stock, can be valued as a perpetuity.

Special Discounted Cash Flow Model—Constant Growth in Dividends.   It might be more realistic to model a growth rate in dividends through time. The constant growth in dividends model assumes that dividends grow at the same rate in each period. Common stock offering a dividend stream that grows at a constant rate can be valued as a *constant growth perpetuity:*

$$P_0 = \frac{DIV_1}{r - g}. \tag{5.9}$$

where DIV_1 is next year's dividend, r is the interest rate, and g is the constant rate of growth in the cash flow. The model can be used only in cases where r is greater than g. For example, if the $2 dividend paid currently by Mirage is expected to grow by 4 percent forever, the value of Mirage today would be:

$$P_0 = \frac{\$2.08}{.15 - .04} = \$18.91.$$

> ✗ Common stock offering a dividend stream that grows at a constant rate can be valued as a constant growth perpetuity.

Note that the numerator in the formula is the expected level of next year's dividend, assumed to be equal to this year's dividend grossed up by the growth rate. Thus, $2.08 is 4 percent higher than the current dividend of $2.00 per share.

The constant growth perpetuity formula also provides insights into the interest rate used to discount common stock. Earlier we defined r as the rate of return investors expect to earn on the common stock investment. A rearrangement of Formula (5.9) provides information on the components of that return:

$$r = \frac{DIV_1}{P_0} + g. \tag{5.10}$$

The first component is the dividend return or dividend yield, defined as next period's dividend in relation to today's investment. This is easy to estimate for most stocks, as information on the stock price and the dividends is readily available. The second component is the return derived from future growth and is much more difficult to estimate. Some analysts estimate future growth by:

$$g = \text{Plowback Ratio} * ROE, \tag{5.11}$$

plowback ratio
The percentage of the residual cash flow that is retained by the firm for growth purposes.

where the **plowback ratio** is the percentage of the shareholder's cash flow that is plowed back into or retained by the firm for growth purposes, and ROE is the historical accounting rate of return on the firm's equity. The intuition here is that the future growth rate in dividends will be based upon the amount of funds reinvested or retained for growth purposes times the rate of return the firm earns on equity. For example, the estimate of a 4 percent growth rate in dividends for Mirage stock could be derived from Formula (5.11) in the following way. First, the historical accounting rate of return on equity is estimated at, say, 12 percent, and the company has a policy of plowing back 25 percent of retained earnings to support growth:

$$g = .12 * .25 = .04.$$

Special Discounted Cash Flow Model—Nonconstant Growth in Dividends. The final special model considers the more realistic case of nonconstant growth in dividends. Of course changing growth rates in dividends bring us back to the general discounted cash flow in dividends model given by Formula (5.10). But suppose that dividends can be assumed to grow by a certain rate for a set number of years, and then change to a different rate for each year thereafter.

Example 5.7 ———— Suppose that the current $2 dividend of Mirage, Inc., is expected to grow by 10 percent for two years, and then by 5 percent forever. The following process would be used to value Mirage stock per share:

1. Determine the present value of the dividends to be paid over the first two years:

$$P_0 = \frac{\$2(1.1)}{(1.15)^1} + \frac{\$2(1.1)^2}{(1.15)^2} = \$3.74$$

```
0                    1                    2
├────────────────────┼────────────────────┤
              $2.20                 $2.42
P_0 = $3.74 ←────────┴────────←───────────┘
```

2. Determine the stock price at the end of year two from the present value of the dividends expected from year three out to infinity:

$$P_2 = \frac{D_3}{r - g} = \frac{\$2(1.1)^2(1.05)}{.15 - .05} = \frac{\$2.54}{.10} = \$25.40$$

```
0     1     2     3     4     5              ∞
├─────┼─────┼─────┼─────┼─────┼──── ʃʃ ──────┤
               $2.54 $2.67 $2.80              ∞
P_2 = $25.40 ←──┴──←──┴──←──┴──←──────────────┘
```

3. Determine the present value of the year-two stock price:

$$P_0 = \frac{\$25.40}{(1.15)^2} = \$19.21$$

```
0                    1                    2
├────────────────────┼────────────────────┤
                                     $25.40
P_0 = $19.21 ←───────────────←─────────────┘
```

4. Add the present value of the year-two stock price to the present value of the first two years' dividends:

$$P_0 = \$3.74 + \$19.21 = \$22.95. \ ↵$$

As the example demonstrates, the process of determining the value of nonconstant growth in a dividend stock is greatly simplified by using a shortcut method, in this case by recognizing the constant growth rate in dividends from year two onward. Nonconstant growth is useful because it allows for more flexibility in dividend patterns while incorporating useful shortcuts.

SUMMARY

☐ This chapter examines the valuation of financial securities. A number of cash flow models have been derived to assist in the valuation of these securities. These models include the annuity:

$$PVA = A \left[\frac{1}{r} - \frac{1}{r(1 + r)^n} \right],$$

the perpetuity, defined as an infinite set of equal cash flows through time:

$$PVP = \frac{A}{r},$$

and the constant growth perpetuity, defined as a perpetuity that grows at a constant rate through time. The present value of the perpetuity is given by:

$$PVCGP = \frac{CF_1}{r - g}.$$

☐ Treasury bills promise one cash flow and can be valued using the lump-sum technique discussed in Chapter 4:

$$PV \text{ Treasury bill} = \frac{F_n}{(1 + r)^n}.$$

☐ Bonds offer a stream of cash flows. In order to value bonds, it was shown that the stream of coupon payments paid by the bond is best valued as an annuity, while the payment of the bond's par value at maturity is best valued separately as a single cash flow or lump-sum cash flow:

$$\text{Bond Value} = P_0 = \underbrace{\sum_{t=1}^{n} \frac{C_t}{(1 + r)^t}}_{\text{Annuity}} \quad \underbrace{\frac{F_n}{(1 + r)^n}}_{\text{Lump Sum}}.$$

☐ The value of bonds already outstanding is inversely related to any changes in market interest rates. When market interest rates rise, the value of outstanding bonds falls. When market interest rates fall, the value of outstanding bonds rises. This relationship derives from the fact that bonds are fixed payment securities, and the promised cash flows from the bond do not change as market conditions change.

☐ The interest rate in the bond pricing formula is known as the yield to maturity. Yield to maturity is an estimate of the average rate of return the bond will offer given current market conditions.

☐ Common stock valuation is difficult because the stock's cash flow stream, given by dividends and capital gains, is not fixed. The general formula for valuing common stock is the discounted value of all future dividends:

$$P_0 = \sum_{t=1}^{\infty} \frac{DIV_t}{(1 + r)^t}.$$

☐ Two special stock valuation models are the zero growth in dividend model and the constant growth model. The present value for zero dividend growth relies on the perpetuity model and is especially useful for pricing preferred stock:

$$P_0 = \frac{DIV}{r},$$

while the constant growth perpetuity model is useful for pricing common stock:

$$P_0 = \frac{DIV_1}{r - g}.$$

☐ From the constant growth in dividends model comes an expression for the interest rate in common stock valuation models:

$$r = \frac{DIV_1}{P_0} + g.$$

The interest rate, or the rate of return common stock investors expect to earn, can be broken into two parts: an expected rate of return on dividends, and a return expected on the future growth of the firm.

DEMONSTRATION PROBLEMS

Problem 1 Compute the price of a 12% coupon bond with a maturity of 10 years if current interest rates are 8%. Assume that the bond's face value is $1,000 and use annual payments and compounding.

Solution to Problem 1

This typical bond problem is solved using both the formula methods and financial calculator methods. The problem involves three steps on many calculators. First the present value of the annuity stream formed by the coupon interest payments must be found. Second, the present value of the lump-sum principal payment must be found. Third, the two numbers must be added together. Some financial calculators can do this in a single step.

Step 1: The bond offers 10 annual coupon payments of $120. The $120 figure was found by multiplying the bond's face value (or par value), $1,000, by the coupon rate, 12%. The present value of this ten-year annuity can be found using the annuity method.

The formula method involves substituting $r = 8\%$, $n = 10$ and $A = \$120$ into Formula (5.1) and solving for PVA. Note that the interest rate used is a market interest rate, not the bond's coupon rate.

The financial calculator method involves substituting the three known values ($r = 8\%$, $n = 10$ and $A = \$120$) and asking the calculator to compute the PV. Typical keystrokes are:

(Clear calculator) 120, *PMT*, 8, *%I*, 10, *n*, *CPT*, *PV*.

Either method produces a present value of $805.21. This interim result should be stored in the calculator's regular memory or written down. It is present value of the coupon payments only.

Step 2: The bond's remaining cash flow, the $1,000 principal payment at year 10, can be discounted using the lump-sum techniques of Chapter 4. Formula (4.6) provides the formula with $r = 8\%$, $n = 10$, and $FV = 1,000$. The keystrokes for a typical financial calculator are:

(Clear calculator's financial memory only) 1000, *FV*, 8, *%I*, 10, *n*, *CPT*, *PV*.

Either method produces a result of $463.19, which is the present value of the principal payment only.

Step 3: Sum the answers to Steps 1 and 2. This can usually be accomplished by simply hitting a memory plus key after Step 2. If necessary, the sum may be found from writing down the answers to each step and then re-entering them into the calculator to sum them.

Some more advanced financial calculators will allow this problem to be solved in one step by inserting the four known variables ($r = 8\%$, $n = 10$, $A = 120$, and $FV = 1,000$) and computing the fifth variable, PV. Typical keystrokes would be:

(Clear calculator) 120, *PMT*, 8, *%I*, 10, *n*, 1000, *FV*, *CPT*, *PV*.

Final Solution: Either way, the final answer is $1,268.40. ↵

Problem 2   A common stock has a current dividend of $2.00, an annual growth rate of 5%, and a required rate of return of 15%. Using the growth perpetuity model, find its price.

Solution to Problem 2

The growth perpetuity model has four variables: the price (P_0), the next year's dividend (DIV_1), the required rate of return (r), and the annual growth rate (g). Most problems involving the model simply require the solution of one of the variables, usually the price, given the other three known variables. A common complication is that the current dividend, DIV_0, is supplied to the user rather than next year's dividend. Thus the first step is to transform the current dividend into the next year's dividend.

Step 1: The next year's dividend can be found from the current dividend, since dividends are assumed to grow at the rate g:

$$DIV_1 = DIV_0 * (1 + g)$$

Since we know that $DIV_0 = \$2.00$ and that $g = 5\%$, DIV_1 is:

$$DIV_1 = \$2.00 * (1.05)$$

$$DIV_1 = \$2.10$$

Step 2: The stock price can be found by inserting the known values into Formula (5.10) and solving for P_0:

$$P_0 = DIV_1 / (r - g)$$

$$P_0 = \$2.10 / (0.15 - .05)$$

$$P_0 = \$21.00$$

Final Solution: Stock price is $21.00. ↵

REVIEW QUESTIONS

1. Explain how an annuity differs from a perpetuity.
2. Why are Treasury bills called pure discount securities?
3. Explain the relationship between bond prices and changing market interest rates.
4. How does the payment of coupons on a semiannual basis change the bond valuation model?
5. What is a bond's yield to maturity? How is it estimated?

6. Why is it generally true that bond valuation is easier than common stock valuation?
7. When is the perpetuity formula useful in common stock valuation?
8. What does "r" mean in the common stock valuation model?
9. What is the biggest shortcoming of the equity value model?

PROBLEMS

1. What is the price today of a 20-year zero coupon bond if the required rate of return is 12%? The bond's face value is $1,000.
2. What is the price of a 2-year bond that pays no coupon? The required rate of return is 12%, and the security has a par value of $1,000. Comment on why the price of the 2-year bond exceeds the price of the 20-year bond in the previous problem.
3. Calculate the value of each of the following three zero coupon bonds:

   Bond A: $1,000 par value, 5-year zero coupon bond. Required return = 7%.
   Bond B: $2,000 par value, 10-year zero coupon bond. Required return = 8%.
   Bond C: $5,000 par value, 20-year zero coupon bond. Required return = 11%.

4. What is the price today of a 2-year 9% coupon bond that has a par value of $1,000 and a required rate of return of 9%?
5. A $1,000 par value bond was issued one year ago with a coupon of 8%. The bond has five more years until maturity. What is the bond's price today if the required rate of return is currently 9%?
6. You are trying to price two bonds that have the same maturity and par value but different coupon rates and different required rates of return. Both bonds mature in three years and have par values of $1,000. One bond has a coupon of 5% and a required rate of return of 7%. The other bond has a coupon of 7% and a required rate of return of 9%. What should the difference in price between these two bonds be?
7. You are concerned about the value of a bond that you own. The bond was issued five years ago with a 7% coupon and was priced at its par value of $1,000. The bond matures three years from today.
   a. What is the bond's price today, assuming a current required rate of return of 10%?
   b. Why is the current market price below the par value?
8. You have invested in a bond which pays semiannual coupon payments of $40 and has a par value of $1,000. The bond matures in

one year, and its required rate of return is 10% compounded semi-annually. Determine the bond's present value.

9. A bond paying a coupon payment of $100 is currently worth 95% of the value it had when it was issued one year ago at a par value of $1,000. The bond has three years remaining until maturity. What is the yield to maturity?

10. What is the yield to maturity for a 5-year 7.5% coupon bond priced currently at $940.65?

11. A bond with two years to maturity is priced today at $900. The bond's coupon rate is 8%, and its par value is $1,000. What is the bond's yield to maturity?

12. A bond with ten years to maturity is priced today at 105.04% for every $100 of par value. The bond's coupon rate is 9%. Determine the bond's yield to maturity.

13. A bond with an 8.5% coupon and two years until maturity is priced at $1,008.91. What is the bond's yield to maturity?

Fill in the missing information using Formula (5.9):

	P_0	DIV_1	r	g
14.	_____	$1.00	.10	.05
15.	_____	$1.00	.12	.11
16.	_____	$1.50	.09	.01
17.	_____	$1.50	.09	.08
18.	_____	$1.00	.19	.02

19. In one year, a stock is expected to pay a $2.11 dividend and be priced at $50 per share. What is the stock's price today if the required rate of return on the stock is 8%?

20. You expect a stock to pay a dividend of $1.59 and be priced at $38 in one year.
   a. What is the stock's price today, assuming a required rate of return of 7%?
   b. If the required rate of return is 6%, how would that change the stock's price today?

21. Historically, a certain stock has paid a dividend of $1.50 per year. If this pattern holds and the stock's price is expected to be priced at $100 in two years, what is its price today? The required rate of return is 7%.

22. After careful research, you estimate that each of two stocks will be worth $100 in three years. Stock A pays a dividend of $4 per year and is expected to stay at this level for the next three years. Stock B pays an annual dividend of $4 currently but it is expected to increase at a rate of 10% per year for three years. What is the price today of both Stock A and Stock B, assuming a 6.5% required rate of return?

23. You are considering buying one of two stocks, both of which are expected to be worth $100 in two years. However, Stock C pays a

dividend of $2 per year for two years, while Stock D will pay a dividend of $1 this year and $3 next year. Assuming a required rate of return of 8%, what is the difference in the price today of the two stocks?

24. What is the price today of a stock whose dividend is $3 per year forever? The stock's required rate of return is 7.5%

25. What would you be willing to pay for a stock that promises to pay a $20 annual dividend forever? The required rate of return is 8%.

26. Your uncle is interested in buying a certain stock, which he says is undervalued and should be worth $35 per share. He has asked for your help. The stock's dividend, currently at $1.10, is expected to increase at a rate of 5% per year forever. What should the stock be worth today, assuming a required rate of return of 8.5%?

27. A certain stock is priced at $30 per share today and is expected to pay a dividend of $1.50 in one year. The dividends are then expected to grow at a rate of 5% forever. What is the required rate of return on the stock?

28. You have been following two firms in the health care industry. You expect the dividend payment of both firms to grow at an annual rate of 5%. Dividend payments are $1.00 currently. Stock E is priced at $10 today, while Stock F is priced at $11.20 today. What required returns were used to price these stocks?

29. A firm provides an annual dividend that is consistently 2% of the value of its stock. The dividend is currently $.25 per share and is expected to grow at a rate of 5 percent forever. What required rate of return is being used?

DISCUSSION QUESTIONS

1. Provide a response to this statement:

   Chapter 5 stated that the present value of a perpetuity is a finite amount. That doesn't seem logical. The value of receiving some amount of money forever, even $1, should be worth an infinite amount of money.

2. Provide an intuitive explanation to someone who has not taken a finance or economics course as to why the value of bonds already outstanding is inversely related to changes in market interest rates.

3. Provide a response to this statement:

   The common stock valuation model cannot be correct. I personally know of a stock that has never in its twenty-year history paid a dividend, and yet its price is consistently above $20 per share.

4. Suppose Microsoft's stock is selling for $100 a share, and that approximately half of the firm's earnings are paid out as dividends. You own a share of Microsoft stock, and design a unique deal to a potential buyer of that share. The deal is this:

The person buying the share of Microsoft gets to hold the stock. However, every future dividend that Microsoft pays goes to you (or your family should you die). Anyone purchasing the stock must agree to this arrangement. Thus all dividends (or any other distributions) for all future generations from that share of stock belong to you or your heirs.

a. If the person who buys the stock from you cannot sell the stock to anyone else, how much would the share of Microsoft sell for under this unique arrangement?

b. If the person who buys the stock from you can resell the stock to one person, how much would the share of Microsoft sell for under this unique arrangement?

c. How much would the share of Microsoft sell for under this unique arrangement if there were no restrictions on reselling the stock?

Chapter 6

The Techniques of Capital Budgeting

Phelps Products is one of the world's leading producers of fiberglass products.[1] Founded by William J. Phelps II in 1918, the company has grown from a family-operated concern to a multinational corporation with over 10,000 employees and sales eclipsing the $1 billion mark. But all is not well at Phelps. The company has been in serious decline for five straight years, and there is now talk of major cutbacks and even the possibility of bankruptcy.

The story of the rise and fall of Phelps is an interesting one. William J. Phelps II was a chemist and inventor who, when he was only twenty years old, developed a glass now known as fiberglass. Phelps obtained a patent for his process, and found that his product quickly became popular in all types of manufacturing operations. William Phelps played a major role in building the company, and was active in all facets of its operations until his death in 1980.

In 1980 the control of the company was in the hands of his two sons. While they understood the business, they didn't seem to have the skills to lead the company. For instance, they made a decision to open a new division of specialty products in 1981 without a careful analysis of the financial details. Although they could recall their father basing new product decisions on such things as "value present," "rate internal," and "back pay," they seemed to be more interested in making decisions based upon what felt right. They believed that investment decisions should be based upon the firm's strategic plan as they tried to position their firm for the global competition of the twenty-first century.

The new division was a disaster. The sons significantly underestimated the costs of production to the point that they were actually

---

1. The story of Phelps Products is a composite of real and fictitious events. All names and circumstances have been changed.

losing money on each unit sold. They did not take into account the fact that production delays increase costs today and at the same time postpone revenues for years into the future. By 1990, it was clear that the investment in the new division was bringing the company down.

What the Phelps brothers spent billions of dollars to learn will be presented in this chapter. Investment decisions should be based upon careful analysis of all advantages and disadvantages—adjusted for time and risk.

The story of Phelps Products illustrates the investment decision of the firm, and the investment decision represents the single most important method of achieving the firm's objective—maximizing shareholder wealth. In this chapter we discuss how this objective can be achieved, and how the decision to invest can often change the wealth of the firm's shareholders.

CREATING VALUE

Table 6.1 lists twenty firms whose successful investments have resulted in powerful brand recognition in the marketplace. Everyone has heard of these brands; indeed, many of us use these products and services every day. How did these firms judge the potential value of these brands? Why were these products and services brought to the marketplace while competing projects within the firm were never launched? These issues are the focus of Chapter 6.

Should a firm's shareholders approve of an investment opportunity within a corporation that promises to turn $100 today into $110 in one year? While it may be tempting to say yes, shareholders would be wise to first consider this investment against other investment opportunities. For example, shareholders might be able to deposit money in a bank and receive a return greater than the 10 percent offered by this investment. The bottom line is that we can't say if a particular return on investment would (or should) meet with shareholder approval without additional information regarding alternatives.

Let's look at a more detailed example and one with which you are already familiar. Recall Megan Morrison from Chapter 5, the financial analyst for the Gecco Insurance Company, who determined that the bond being considered for purchase by the firm had a price equal to the present value of its future cash flow. In other words, the costs of the bond and the benefits of the bond were equal in present value terms. Most financial assets trade at prices so near the present value of their future cash flows that a corporation's managers have little if any ability to enhance shareholder wealth by trading them. We could say that the investment offers to the shareholders the exact return they would expect to earn on other investments with similar risk— nothing

TABLE 6.1
The Twenty Most Powerful Brands in the U.S.

Rank	Brand	Parent Company
1	Coca-Cola	Coca-Cola
2	Campbell's	Campbell Soup
3	Disney	Walt Disney
4	Pepsi-Cola	PepsiCo
5	Kodak	Eastman Kodak
6	NBC	General Electric
7	Black and Decker	Black and Decker
8	Kellogg	Kellogg
9	McDonald's	McDonald's
10	Hershey's	Hershey
11	Levi's	Levi-Strauss
12	GE	General Electric
13	Sears	Sears
14	Hallmark	Hallmark
15	Johnson & Johnson	Johnson & Johnson
16	Betty Crocker	General Mills
17	Kraft	Philip Morris
18	Kleenex	Kimberly-Clark
19	Jell-O	Philip Morris
20	Tylenol	Johnson & Johnson

Source: From Landor Associates' ImagePower Survey. Copyright © 1990 by Landor Associates. Reprinted by permission.

more and nothing less. Accordingly, the bond investment does not create value or destroy value for the shareholders, but keeps value unchanged.

Gecco's bond is reflective of most financial assets that trade in efficient markets: The price of the asset is equal to its present value. There is nothing special about the Gecco bond. Bonds trading in efficient markets offer returns that investors expect to earn on similar risk investments. This is the reason that modern corporate finance does not view the trading of financial assets to be as important as the management of real assets for the purpose of increasing firm value and therefore shareholder wealth.

⧗ Most financial assets trade at prices so near the present value of their future cash flows that a corporation's managers have little if any ability to enhance shareholder wealth by trading them.

A different type of investment is one in real assets—for example, an investment in plant and equipment. Real asset investments are generally referred to as **projects**, and the analysis of projects is known

projects
Investments in real assets.

capital budgeting analysis
The analysis of projects within the firm, such as the purchase of new plant and equipment.

as **capital budgeting analysis**. An important difference between real asset investment and financial asset investments is the competitive forces of the respective markets where the assets trade. Lack of competition creates the potential for a project to increase shareholder wealth. While millions of individuals and corporations have excellent access to the financial markets where financial assets trade, only a relatively few have access to many of the real goods markets where real assets trade.

⧗ Lack of competition creates the potential for a project to increase shareholder wealth.

Example 6.1 _____ You recognized the Eastman Kodak Company, a maker of cameras and camera equipment, as one of the firms with a powerful brand recognition listed in Table 6.1. Kodak's decision to manufacture and market a camera on a global basis is, realistically speaking, available to only a limited number of firms. Although, of course, there are thousands of firms for which a camera project might be possible, such a project would typically be considered only by a firm with a market reputation or expertise in a related technology. Moreover, when a project is available to only a small number of firms, there is a possibility that a lack of competition will create a superior investment opportunity, thereby increasing shareholder wealth.

To be sure, very few firms have the capital and market position to introduce successfully a new product such as an instant camera with its own film. Since so few firms have this alternative, the lack of competition creates the potential for large benefits—or large losses. ⏎

Patents represent another avenue by which firms establish a competitive advantage in the real goods market. Due to patent protection, there may be some projects that only a single firm can consider. For example, the NutraSweet subsidiary of the Monsanto Company held 75 percent of the artificial sweetener market worldwide in the 1980s, deriving its market power from a patent issued in 1969 on aspartame.[2] This example illustrates how patents can remove competition (in the short run) and create the potential for very large benefits.

Perhaps another source of superior investment opportunity is the ability to compete in a market using superior management. For exam-

---

2. The patent on NutraSweet expired on December 14, 1992. Competing firms then had an opportunity to market their own version of the product.

ple, competitors within a particular industry or geographical region may have inefficient management, such that an efficiently managed firm might be able to increase shareholder wealth by expanding to compete against them.

Thus, opportunities exist to invest in the real asset market and create wealth. But how can financial managers recognize wealth-creating projects? The rest of this chapter is devoted to answering that question.

Keeping Score

This section discusses alternative ways to measure value creation. The models developed assume that all of the costs and benefits of a project can be expressed as dollar values at various points in time. This concept is illustrated in the time line below. The project is represented by costs of $10,000 today and produces numerous future cash inflows:

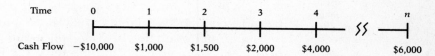

Time	0	1	2	3	4		n
Cash Flow	−$10,000	$1,000	$1,500	$2,000	$4,000		$6,000

Later we'll discuss why it is reasonable to believe that any cost or benefit can be expressed in terms of dollars. The key for now is to understand that this chapter addresses a straightforward question: Given the cash flows of a project (as illustrated above), would acceptance of the project increase, decrease, or leave unchanged shareholder wealth?

The Required Rate of Return in Project Analysis

required rate of return
The minimum rate of return that an investor would accept in order to invest in a project of a particular risk.

Most capital budgeting models require the discount rate to be estimated. The discount rate is the interest rate used to discount future cash flows. Throughout this chapter we will refer to the discount rate as the required rate of return on a project. The **required rate of return** is the minimum rate of return that an investor would accept in order to invest in a project of particular risk. For example, bond investors require a higher rate of return on corporate bonds than on Treasury bonds. The reason for the differential is risk—the risk that a corporation will fail to meet promises is greater than the risk that the government will fail to repay an investor. In general, the higher the risk, the higher would be the required rate of return. Although we defer the full discussion of risk to Module 3, it is important to see that risk enters the capital budgeting analysis through the discount rate and estimations of the cash flows.

A Summary of Value Creation

To summarize, investments in real assets offer the potential for unique advantages and can allow firms to exploit projects whose benefits truly exceed costs. In cases such as these, we say that the project has increased shareholder wealth. On the other hand, firms also wish to avoid projects that decrease shareholder wealth.

We next discuss alternative capital budgeting models. Generally speaking, capital budgeting models are designed to help identify and compare project costs with project benefits. The goal of capital budgeting is to identify those projects whose benefits exceed their costs.

NET PRESENT VALUE

net present value
A capital budgeting model that compares the present value of the project's benefits with the present value of the project's costs. The difference between benefits and costs is the net present value of the project.

The premier capital budgeting model is called the **net present value** (*NPV*) model. One advantage of *NPV* is the way it incorporates the time value of money, measuring benefits and costs in terms of present values. *NPV* transforms all of the project's cash flows through time to the same commodity so that costs can be subtracted from benefits.

Our initial examples of *NPV* will assume that the costs of the investments are paid today at time zero. The initial investment might be the purchase of a machine or of raw materials necessary for production. The project's benefits will be represented by future cash flows received when the product or service is sold and payment is received. The future benefits are pulled back by discounting future cash flows using the required rate of return appropriate for the project. Costs are then compared with benefits:

$$NPV = PV \text{ of Benefits} - PV \text{ of Costs.} \qquad ; \qquad (6.1)$$

A positive *NPV* means that the project's benefits exceed costs, and the decision to undertake the project increases the value of the firm and shareholder wealth. A negative *NPV* means that the project's costs exceed benefits, and the decision to undertake the project would decrease the value of the firm and shareholder wealth. A *NPV* of zero means that the project's benefits are equal to costs, and the decision to undertake a project does not increase or decrease the value of the firm or the wealth of the shareholders. From the perspective of shareholder wealth maximization, positive *NPV* projects should be accepted, negative *NPV* projects should be rejected, and firms should be indifferent toward accepting or rejecting zero *NPV* projects.

The *NPV* rule follows from the third economic principle, the law of conservation of value. If a project whose benefits exceed its costs is added to the existing assets of a firm, the value of the firm's assets with the project must equal the original value of the firm's assets plus the value of the project. In the case of a positive *NPV*, the firm's new asset value will be greater than its original asset value by the amount of the *NPV*.

The *NPV* Rule in Capital Budgeting

It is best to view a project or any other type of financial decision as a set of cash inflows and outflows at various points in time. The cash flows are the incremental cash flows that result from undertaking the project, where **incremental cash flows** are those benefits that would not have been received, or those costs that would not have been incurred, if a project had not been undertaken. Chapter 14 will detail the issues involved in determining the precise cash flows of a project. For now, view the capital budgeting decision as whether or not it is beneficial to accept a given stream of inflows and outflows.

> **incremental cash flows**
> Benefits that would not have been received, or those costs that would not have been incurred, if a project had not been undertaken.

The net present value rule in cash flow form is:

$$NPV = C_0 + \frac{CF_1}{(1+r)^1} + \frac{CF_2}{(1+r)^2} + \frac{CF_3}{(1+r)^3} + \cdots + \frac{CF_n}{(1+r)^n}, \qquad (6.2)$$

where C_0 represents the initial (period zero) cash flow and is usually negative, CF_1 through CF_n represent the incremental future cash flows that result from undertaking the project and are usually positive, and r is the project's required rate of return.

Example 6.2 —————— Consider a new comedy film being considered by Universal Studios. Universal estimates the cost of producing the film to be $25 million, all payable in the current period. Ticket sales are estimated to be $15 million in year one and $10 million in year two, at which point the film will be taken out of circulation and its rights sold to cable companies for $8 million in year three. No other revenues are expected after year three. The project's required rate of return is 12 percent.

The cash flows for the film project and the project's *NPV* are shown in Table 6.2. The movie project's single cash outflow in the current period is $25 million, and the present value of the three future cash inflows, discounted at 12 percent, is $27.059 million. The *NPV* of the movie project is $2.059 million ($27.059 million minus $25 million) and should be accepted as it increases the wealth of Universal Studios' shareholders.

Workshop 6.1 illustrates how *NPV* calculations can be simplified when discounting special cash flow streams such as annuities. The workshop also presents a quick method for discounting an uneven cash flow stream. ↵

TABLE 6.2
The NPV of Universal's New Movie Project

A Time Line View of the Project's Cash Flows

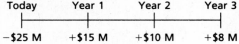

Today	Year 1	Year 2	Year 3
−$25 M	+$15 M	+$10 M	+$8 M

Worksheet for Calculating the *NPV*

Year	Cash Flow	$\frac{1}{(1.12)^n}$	Present Value
0	−$25 M	1.0000	−$25.000 M
1	+$15 M	0.8929	+$13.393 M
2	+$10 M	0.7972	+$ 7.972 M
3	+$ 8 M	0.7118	+$ 5.694 M

Present Value of the Initial Investment	−$25.000 M
Present Value of the Inflows	+$27.059 M
Net Present Value	+$ 2.059 M

COMPETITORS OF *NPV*

NPV is the premier capital budgeting rule because it relates directly to the objective of maximizing shareholder wealth. However, for a variety of reasons, alternative models of capital budgeting are utilized by corporations. Some of these models are preferred because of their simplicity, others because of corporate tradition. This section discusses the competitors of *NPV*.

The Profitability Index

The profitability index (*PI*) is *NPV* in ratio form. Instead of subtracting the present value of costs from the present value of benefits, the present value of the benefits is divided by the present value of the costs (ignoring the negative sign):

$$PI = \frac{\sum_{t=1}^{n} C_t/(1+r)^t}{|C_0|}, \tag{6.3}$$

profitability index
A capital budgeting model constructed by dividing ratio of the present value of the project's benefits by the present value of the project's cost.

where C_t represents cash inflows through time, C_0 represents current cash flows and is usually negative, r is the discount rate, and t represents a period in time. The **profitability index** is a ratio of benefits to costs: a *PI* value greater than one defines a project whose benefits

NPV with Even and Uneven Cash Flow Streams

Chapter 5 discussed and illustrated shortcuts when discounting particular cash flow streams. A good example of such a shortcut was the case of an equal cash flows stream through time—or the case of an annuity—where the entire stream was discounted in one step. If the cash flows in the *NPV* analysis represent an annuity, then shortcut methods can be used.

For example, consider a project whose initial investment is $25 million and which promises three annual cash inflows starting in year one of $12 million each. If the project's required rate of return is 12 percent, the *NPV* can be determined as follows:

$$NPV = -\$25 \text{ M} + \$12 \text{ M} \left[\frac{1}{r} - \frac{1}{r(1+r)^n} \right],$$

where the bracketed expression is the formula for the present value of an annuity. Substituting 12 percent for r and 3 for n provides the *NPV* of the project:

$$NPV = -\$25 \text{ M} + \$12 \text{ M} \left[\frac{1}{.12} - \frac{1}{.12(1.12)^3} \right] = -\$25\text{M} + \$12\text{M} \left[2.4018 \right] = \$3.822 \text{ M}.$$

Thus, given an annuity stream of cash inflows, *NPV* can be calculated in one step.

Although annuities make *NPV* analysis easier, we can't always expect cash flow streams to be equal. In fact, a general rule is that the more complex the *NPV* analysis, the more likely it is for an uneven cash flow stream to result. Uneven streams of cash flows must be discounted one at a time. For those looking for a shortcut, we offer the following process for discounting an uneven stream on an ordinary calculator.

The idea behind the shortcut we are about to present is best seen with an analogy. Suppose a person were asked to take a truck and go pick up a number of packages down a certain road. Suppose that some of the packages were at a location one mile down the road, some were two miles down the same road, and so forth up to perhaps five miles down the road. What would be the most efficient method of hauling the packages (assuming that they could all be fitted on the same truck)?

Rather than make separate trips, it should be obvious that the best method would be to make a single trip for all the packages (unless the person was paid by the hour!). For example, the person could:

(continued on next page)

Workshop 6.1 *(continued)*

1. Drive to the furthest location and load the packages.
2. Drive back to the second furthest location and load the packages.
3. Drive back to the third furthest location, and so forth.

When we discount future cash flows we are in effect moving the cash flows back to the present time. Rather than making a separate trip or present value for each cash flow, it is better to bring back all of the cash flows using a single trip.

Thus, a present value problem for a stream of uneven cash flows can be solved as follows:

1. Enter the final cash flow into the calculator.
2. Move the cash flow "back" one year by dividing it by $1+r$.
3. Add on the second-to-last cash flow to the previous result.
4. Move the new result "back" one year by dividing it by $1+r$.
5. Continue the process until the initial outlay is subtracted out.

For example, consider the following project and cash flows:

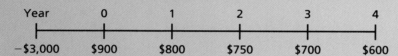

Year	0	1	2	3	4
	$-\$3,000$	$\$900$	$\$800$	$\$750$	$\$700$	$\$600$

Using a discount rate of 12 percent, the keystrokes would be:

$$600 \div 1.12 = + 700 = \div 1.12 = + 750 = \div 1.12 = + 800 = \div 1.12 =$$
$$+ 900 = \div 1.12 = -3000 = \text{(the answer: } -\$239.52\text{).}$$

Quite a savings of time and a definite hit at a good party! In fact, the keystrokes can be further simplified on most calculators by noting that (1) many of the equal signs are unnecessary, and (2) it is easier to place $(1+r)$ into the memory and then simply hit the recall memory key after each "÷". Since calculators vary, this shortcut may need some experimentation.

exceed costs, and a *PI* value less than one defines a project whose costs exceed benefits. A profitability index equal to one implies that costs are equal to benefits.

Example 6.3 —————————— The *PI* for Universal Studios' movie project is:

$$PI = \frac{\$27.059 \text{ million}}{\$25 \text{ million}} = 1.0824.$$

The profitability index for the Universal movie project is greater than one, meaning that benefits exceed costs and the project is acceptable. Given that the profitability index is a ratio, it provides in percentage form the extent to which benefits exceed costs. As shown above, benefits are 8.24 percent greater than costs. ↵

The final decision on the movie project is the same for both *NPV* and the *PI*. This is no coincidence! Any project with a positive *NPV* will also have a *PI* greater than one, and any project with a negative *NPV* will also have a *PI* less than one. Thus, in the analysis of a particular project, both the *NPV* and *PI* rules will lead to the same decision.

However, a potential shortcoming of the *PI* is revealed when, instead of evaluating a single project, the firm evaluates groups of projects and must choose from a subset of the group. As a percentage, the *PI* may overstate the attractiveness of certain projects while understating the attractiveness of others. This shortcoming will be described in detail later in this chapter.

The Internal Rate of Return

internal rate of return
A capital budgeting model represented by the discount rate that equates the present value of the costs with the present value of the benefits from the project.

The most popular competitor to *NPV* is the **internal rate of return** (*IRR*) method. Computing the *IRR* is tantamount to answering the following question: If we viewed the project like a bank account, what interest rate would the bank have to offer in order to produce the same benefits and costs as the project? The *IRR* can also be described as the discount rate that makes *NPV* equal to zero, or alternatively the discount rate that equates the present value of the costs with the present value of the benefits from the project.

There are two steps to evaluating projects based on the *IRR*: (1) calculating the *IRR*, and (2) comparing the *IRR* to the required rate of return. Acceptable projects are those whose *IRR* is greater than the required return. Projects should be rejected if the *IRR* is less than the required rate of return. Shareholders are indifferent when the *IRR* is equal to the required rate of return.

The first step is to determine the *IRR*, which is illustrated in Formula (6.4). Let C_0 be the project's initial investment, and CF_1 through CF_n be the project's future cash inflows. The internal rate of return is the interest rate that equates the right-hand side and left-hand side of the equation:

$$C_0 + \frac{CF_1}{(1 + IRR)^1} + \frac{CF_2}{(1 + IRR)^2} + \frac{CF_3}{(1 + IRR)^3}$$
$$+ \cdots + \frac{CF_n}{(1 + IRR)^n} = 0. \quad (6.4)$$

There are generally two approaches to solving for the *IRR*. The first relies on a trial and error search process similar to that demonstrated for a bond's yield to maturity. The second allows the trial and error process to be performed by an advanced financial calculator programmed to execute the search for you.

Notice the relationship between Formula (6.4) and the *NPV* formula. Solving for the *IRR* may be defined as finding the discount rate that, when plugged into the *NPV* formula, gives an *NPV* of zero. It is important, however, to distinguish between the *IRR* and the discount rate used in the *NPV* method. The *IRR* gets its name because the rate is internal to the project. However, in the *NPV* model, the discount rate is a measure of the project's required rate of return and comes from the market. When using Formula (6.4) to find the *IRR*, the user searches for the unique discount rate that makes costs equal to benefits. Once estimated, the *IRR* is compared to the required rate of return from the market in order to make an accept-reject decision on the project.

Example 6.4 ———— The amount of work required in determining the *IRR* depends on the project's cash flow stream and on the availability of a sophisticated financial calculator. We will assume that a sophisticated financial calculator is not available and demonstrate the *IRR* procedure using the trial and error process.

To determine the *IRR* of the Universal movie project, we insert the cash flows of the project into Formula (6.4):

$$- \$25M + \frac{\$15}{(1 + IRR)^1} + \frac{\$10}{(1 + IRR)^2} + \frac{\$8}{(1 + IRR)^3} = 0.$$

The *IRR* is the precise interest rate that satisfies the above equation. The trial and error process, illustrated in Table 6.3,

TABLE 6.3
Determining the IRR by Trial and Error

Interest Rate	PV of Outflow[a]	PV of Inflows[b]	NPV
10%	$25.000	$27.911	$2.911
11%	$25.000	$27.479	$2.479
12%	$25.000	$27.059	$2.059
13%	$25.000	$26.650	$1.650
14%	$25.000	$26.252	$1.252
15%	$25.000	$25.865	$0.865
16%	$25.000	$25.488	$0.488
17%	$25.000	$25.121	$0.121
18%	$25.000	$24.763	−$0.237

[a] The interest rate does not change the present value of the outflow because the outflow occurs at time zero.

[b] The inflows must be discounted individually. The shortcut method demonstrated in Workshop 6.1 will speed up the process.

selects an initial guess followed by subsequent guesses until the *IRR* is found.

With an initial guess of 10 percent the present value of the inflows of $27.911 million is greater than the $25 million outflow. Remember, our goal is to make the numbers equal. Our next guess for the *IRR* should be higher than 10 percent because we need to lower the present value of the inflows. At 11 percent, the present value of the inflows is $27.479 million, closer to $25 million but still too high. The trial and error process continues until we hit a guess of 18 percent. At 18 percent, the present value of the inflows is $24.763 million, lower than the $25 million present value of the outflow. Thus, the *IRR* is between 17 percent and 18 percent. The exact *IRR* is 17.334 percent.[3]

The *IRR* of 17.334 percent is greater than the 12 percent return investors would require to earn on such a project. Because the *IRR* exceeds the required rate of return, the project will increase the value of the firm and should be accepted.

If an advanced financial calculator is available, the *IRR* can be found by inputting into the calculator the cash outflow and the series of cash inflows. The calculator will then grind through the trial and error process illustrated in Table 6.3 to solve for the *IRR* of 17.334 percent. ↵

---

3. Interpolation can be used to find the precise *IRR*. However, in most cases, investment decisions using *IRR* will not require the exact solution; therefore the *IRR* can be approximated to the closest integer value.

It should be noted that there are two specialized cases where computing the *IRR* does not require a trial and error method. The first is the case of a single cash outflow and a single cash inflow. The second is the case of an annuity of inflows. In both cases, the *IRR* may be found by using the mathematical calculations given in Chapters 4 and 5.

net present value profile
A graph demonstrating the net present value of a project at different discount rates.

The Net Present Value Profile.   The **net present value profile** graphs the trial and error process for finding the *IRR*. The net present value profile for the movie project is presented in Figure 6.1.

The *NPV* profile locates the *IRR* graphically. Because the *IRR* is the discount rate that makes *NPV* zero, the *IRR* is represented by the point where the profile crosses through the horizontal axis measuring the discount rates. This occurs between 17 and 18 percent on the figure, corresponding to our solution of 17.334 percent above. Also note that at zero percent, the *NPV* is equal to the sum of the cash flows.

Payback

The capital budgeting methods discussed thus far are called discounted cash flow (DCF) methods. Net present value, the profitability index, and internal rate of return all discount future cash flows back to the present so that these cash flows can be properly compared. The

FIGURE 6.1
The NPV Profile for the Universal Studios Movie Project

The *NPV* profile shows the relationship between *NPV* and the discount rate. The discount rate that makes *NPV* = $0 is also known as the *IRR*.

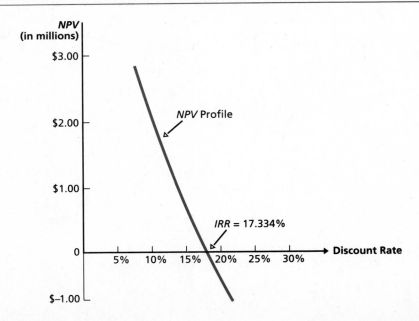

payback model, discussed below, does not discount cash flows and thus fails to treat dollars through time as different commodities. As you might expect, we view this as a serious shortcoming. Nevertheless, surveys have found that corporations use the payback rule, especially in combination with other capital budgeting rules, when making investment decisions.

payback
A capital budgeting model that answers the question: How long will it take to re-coup the initial investment?

Payback answers the question: How long will it take in order to recoup our initial investment? The shorter the period of time needed to get your money back, the shorter the payback. The simplicity of the payback model has a certain appeal. Indeed, it would not be surprising to find even the most ardent critics applying its logic when making certain types of financial decisions.[4] Further, compared with *NPV* and *IRR*, the concept of payback is easier to grasp and is therefore easier to apply. We warn, however, against adopting the payback model because of its simplicity. As we will soon see, simplest is not always best!

Example 6.5 ——————— Recall the cash flows associated with the Universal movie project:

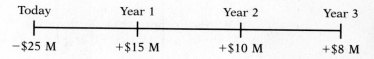

Today	Year 1	Year 2	Year 3
−$25 M	+$15 M	+$10 M	+$8 M

The project recovers the $25 million investment in two years, defining a two-year payback. Universal must now use the information contained in payback to make an accept–reject decision on the movie project. ↵

Is a particular payback, say two years, good or bad? Said differently, would it be wise for Universal to accept projects with a two-year payback, or should it only accept projects with a payback less than two years? If projects with a two-year payback are acceptable, would a three-year payback also be acceptable? What about a ten-year payback?

These questions reveal one of payback's shortcomings. Firms using the payback model to make accept–reject decisions on projects must decide on a payback cutoff criterion. For instance, setting the cutoff criterion at three years would lead Universal to accept the movie project. But this criterion is arbitrary. A payback acceptable to one firm could be unacceptable to others. Further, there is no direct

---

4. For instance, homeowners will often put replacement decisions or energy conservation decisions in the context of payback. In fact, we wonder how many finance professors have justified a major household purchase, say the conversion of oil heat to natural gas, by applying the payback method.

linkage between a project's payback and its value. Projects accepted through the payback model could increase firm value, decrease firm value, or leave the value of the firm unchanged.

A second shortcoming of the payback model is that it ignores all cash flows that occur after the payback period. This shortcoming is illustrated by examining the cash flows of two different projects, A and B:

	Today	Year 1	Year 2	Year 3	Year 4	Payback
Project A:	−$100	+$60	+$40	+$40	+$40	2 Years
Project B:	−$100	+$40	+$40	+$40	+$400	3 Years

Project A's payback is shorter and thus is superior to Project B's payback.[5] In fact, if the firm's payback criterion is to accept any project with a payback of two years or less, Project A would be accepted and Project B would be rejected. But this decision fails to consider Project B's huge cash inflow in year four! Indeed, when considering all the cash flows, Project B is clearly superior to Project A. Unfortunately, as we said, the payback model fails to consider cash flows beyond the payback period.

We can expose this shortcoming of payback by comparing the *NPV* of the two projects. Using a discount rate of 10 percent:

$$NPV\,A = -\$100 + \frac{\$60}{(1.1)^1} + \frac{\$40}{(1.1)^2} + \frac{\$40}{(1.1)^3} + \frac{\$40}{(1.1)^4} = \$44.98.$$

$$NPV\,B = -\$100 + \frac{\$40}{(1.1)^1} + \frac{\$40}{(1.1)^2} + \frac{\$40}{(1.1)^3} + \frac{\$400}{(1.1)^4} = \$272.70.$$

From the standpoint of shareholder wealth maximization, Project B, with the higher *NPV*, is the clear winner.

The third and final shortcoming of payback is that it ignores the time value of money. This shortcoming is illustrated by examining the cash flows of two different projects, C and D:

	Today	Year 1	Year 2	Year 3	Year 4	Payback
Project C:	−$100	+$90	-0-	-0-	+$30	4 Years
Project D:	−$100	+$30	+$30	+$30	+$30	4 Years

---

5. Defining a three-year payback for Project B assumes that all cash flows come at the end of the year. With more detailed information, we might be able to define payback more precisely. For example, if Project B's cash flows arrive continuously over the years, its payback would be 2.5 years.

Both projects offer a payback of four years, so that the firm using the payback method would view them as roughly equivalent. But the payback model adds and subtracts dollars through time as if they were the same commodity, thus violating the principle of the time value of money. From the standpoint of present values, Project C's cash flow stream is preferred because most of its inflows occur in year one.

We can again expose this shortcoming of payback by comparing the *NPV* of the two projects. Using a discount rate of 10 percent:

$$NPV\ C = -\$100 + \frac{\$90}{(1.1)^1} + \text{-0-} + \text{-0-} + \frac{\$30}{(1.1)^4} = \$2.31.$$

$$NPV\ D = -\$100 + \frac{\$30}{(1.1)^1} + \frac{\$30}{(1.1)^2} + \frac{\$30}{(1.1)^3} + \frac{\$30}{(1.1)^4} = -\$4.90.$$

From the standpoint of shareholder wealth maximization, Project C's *NPV* is not only greater than Project D's, but Project D decreases shareholder wealth.

The Accounting Rate of Return

Analysts who tend to focus on accounting numbers often evaluate projects according to the accounting rate of return model. The logic underlying the accounting rate of return is that an objective of the firm is to produce high profits on investments, so it is wise to invest in assets that produce high average profits.

accounting rate of return
A capital budgeting model defined by a ratio of average accounting profits over the project's life divided by some estimate of the average annual investment.

depreciation
The reduction in the value of an asset using accounting rules.

The **accounting** (or average) **rate of return** is a ratio of some measure of average accounting profits over the project's life divided by some estimate of the average annual investment. Accounting profits are defined as revenues less expenses, taxes, and depreciation, where **depreciation** is a reduction in the value of an asset using accounting rules. The average annual investment takes into account the decline in the investment through time due to depreciation. Once computed, the accounting rate of return is compared to some benchmark in order to decide if the project should be accepted or rejected.

Example 6.6 _____ Table 6.4 shows how the accounting rate of return is computed. Methods of computing the accounting rate of return differ. In Table 6.4, depreciation is calculated by the straight line method, whereby the initial investment of $90 million depreciates by $30 million per year. The annual investment starts in year 0 at $90 million and depreciates by $30 million per year to a value of zero at the project's end. Thus the investment lasts for four years. The average annual investment is $45 million. The accounting rate of return is $13.33 million

TABLE 6.4
Computing the Accounting Rate of Return (all values in millions)

Part 1: Determining Average Annual Accounting Profits

	Year 1	Year 2	Year 3
Revenues	$100	$70	$70
Expenses Plus Taxes	$ 50	$30	$30
Cash Flow	$ 50	$40	$40
Less Depreciation	$ 30	$30	$30
Accounting Profit	$ 20	$10	$10

$$\text{Average Accounting Profit} = \frac{\$20 + \$10 + \$10}{3} = \$13.33$$

Part 2: Determining the Average Annual Investment ($90 M outlay)

	Year 0	Year 1	Year 2	Year 3
Investment: Start of Period	$ 90	$90	$60	$30
Depreciation	$ 00	$30	$30	$30
Investment: End of Period	$ 90	$60	$30	$00

$$\text{Average Annual Investment} = \frac{\$90 + \$60 + \$30 + \$00}{4} = \$45.00$$

Part 3: Determining the Average Accounting Rate of Return

$$\text{Average Accounting Rate of Return} = \frac{\$13.33}{\$45.00} = 29.6\%$$

divided by $45 million, which equals 29.6 percent. The firm would then compare the accounting rate of return of 29.6 percent to some benchmark in order to decide if the project is acceptable or not.

The accounting rate of return method suffers from many serious shortcomings. First, like payback, it requires the use of an arbitrary decision rule. In our example, the firm must decide whether 29.6 percent is acceptable or not. There is no decision rule that can be applied equally across all firms, nor is there a way to link the accounting rate of return with firm value.

Second, because accounting rate of return does not discount future cash flows, it violates the time value of money principle. The $20 million of profit in year one is added to the $10 million of profit in years two and three to get the total profit of $40 million. Reversing the timing of the cash flow stream would give us the same total profit, even though the time value is clearly different.

Third, the rate of return measure depends on the accounting rules used to depreciate the investment through time. The project above used the straight line depreciation method. Alternatively, the firm could choose to use some other depreciation method, and that choice would have a significant impact on the measure of return. Modernists strongly believe that cash flows measure value far better than accounting numbers. ◄┘

NPV VERSUS *IRR*—WHICH METHOD IS BEST?

The previous sections highlighted two models of capital budgeting, the *NPV* model and the *IRR* model. While *NPV* is theoretically superior, the *IRR* enjoys widespread use. Both models are designed to determine whether the proposed project adds to or subtracts from the value of the firm. However, unlike the *NPV* model, which measures the change in firm value in dollars, the *IRR* measures the prospective return of the project to the firm.

In many circumstances, the two models lead us to the same conclusion— either to accept or reject the project—so it wouldn't matter which model is used. An argument for using the *IRR* is that most financial managers prefer to speak of projects in terms of rate of return, not in terms of dollar values. A counterargument would recommend *NPV* because it measures the change in wealth as a result of undertaking the project.

The important distinctions between the two models arise when they lead to different decisions. In some circumstances, shortcomings inherent in the *IRR* model will direct the financial manager to accept a project that should be rejected, or to incorrectly rank one project as better than another. Thus, extra care must be taken when using the *IRR* in capital budgeting.

Accept-or-Reject Projects Versus Ranking Projects

accept-or-reject projects (independent projects)
Projects whose accept-or-reject decision can be made without affecting other projects.

ranking projects (mutually exclusive projects)
Projects whose accept-or-reject decision affects other decisions.

In order to clarify the reasons for preferring *NPV*, we begin by drawing a distinction between two types of decisions that might be made. **Accept-or-reject projects** represent decisions that can be made without affecting other projects. These are also known as **independent projects**. **Ranking projects** or **mutually exclusive projects** represent decisions that cannot be made in isolation because they affect other decisions. Projects are mutually exclusive if acceptance of one would preclude acceptance of the other. While both the *NPV* model and the *IRR* model have no problems with accept–reject decisions, only *NPV* ranks mutually exclusive projects correctly.

Example 6.7 ————————— Universal Studios might reason that, for marketing reasons, producing the comedy film under consideration excludes the production of all other comedy projects for at least six months. Or perhaps they only have enough directors, writers, actors, or facilities for one comedy project. Universal therefore cannot simply accept or reject each comedy movie but instead would have to decide on which comedy movie is best to produce. This will necessitate a ranking of movie projects, since their mutually exclusive nature precludes the acceptance of more than one project.

Let's suppose Universal narrows its choice to two comedy movie projects, referred to as Movie Project One and Movie Project Two. Both are three-year projects, and both require a rate of return of 12 percent. However, the two projects have different cash flows streams. Movie Project One has an initial investment of $25 million and cash flows that decrease through time. Movie Project Two has an initial investment of $5 million and level cash flows. The cash flows of the respective projects are given in Table 6.5, along with their *NPV*s, *IRR*s, and *PI*s.

Movie Project One has a higher *NPV* and thus the acceptance of One over Two results in a greater increase in firm value. However, Movie Project Two has a higher *IRR* and thus the acceptance of Two over One results in a greater percentage rate of return on the money invested. Of the two, shareholders should prefer Movie Project One because it results in a higher level of shareholder wealth. Movie Project Two might allow for higher bragging rights ("My rate of return beat yours"), but Project One puts more wealth in the shareholders' pockets.

The conflict results from the fact that *NPV* measures dollar gains while *IRR* measures percentage returns. As a percentage, the *IRR* rule can produce more dramatic numbers for projects of smaller investments ($5 million versus $25 million) and for projects with short time lengths. The *NPV* rule, which is a measure of the change in shareholder wealth as a result of accepting a project, does not suffer from these shortcomings and can thus correctly rank mutually exclusive projects.

The above conflict is known as the *scale problem*. The *IRR* model ignores the scale of the project. In other words, it correctly measures a rate of return, but is biased toward short-term, small-investment projects.

Scale can be exemplified as follows. Which is better, an investment that costs $1.00 today and pays back $1.25 in six months, or an investment that costs $100 today and pays $120 in a year? The *IRR* of the first project is 56.25 percent, while the IRR of the second project is 20 percent. The *IRR* method ranks the first project ahead of the second.

But *IRR* ignores scale differentials. Using a discount rate of 10.25 percent, the *NPV* of the first investment is $0.19 and the *NPV* of the second investment is $8.84. The *NPV* method recognizes that the first project's return is for a shorter time period and is based on such a small investment that there is little net benefit. While these examples give the appearance that scale differences are easy to spot, in practice it can be difficult since scale is determined by both the magnitude and timing of the cash flows. ↩

The profitability index also suffers from scale problems. Table 6.5 computes the profitability index of Movie Projects One and Two. Because the *PI* is also a ratio or percentage, *PI* can rank mutually exclusive projects incorrectly. Under the *PI* rule, Movie Project Two, with a *PI* of 1,201, is preferred over Movie Project One, with a *PI* of 1.082. Project Two has a higher net benefit expressed as a percentage of cost, but a lower *NPV*. The correct decision is to choose Movie Project One, the higher *NPV* project.

Methods exist to help the *IRR* and the *PI* rank mutually exclusive projects correctly. For example, a procedure known as computing the *IRR* of the incremental investment—a method of focusing on the marginal effects between two projects instead of analyzing the projects separately—will correct this shortcoming. The technique of incremental investment will be demonstrated in detail in Chapter 14.

In summary, situations exist when projects, judged individually to be acceptable, must be rank-ordered and must compete against each other. These are called mutually exclusive projects. In these cases, *NPV* will more accurately rank the projects and is preferred to the *IRR* and to the *PI*.

Capital Rationing.   There is another reason that projects might need to be ranked. It is sometimes claimed that a firm cannot or should not accept all projects with positive *NPV*s. The explanation is

TABLE 6.5
Two Mutually Exclusive Movie Projects

	Today	Year 1	Year 2	Year 3
Movie Project One	−$25 M	+$15.0 M	+$10.0 M	+$ 8.0 M
Movie Project Two	−$ 5 M	+$ 2.5 M	+$ 2.5 M	+$ 2.5 M

Capital Budgeting Models

Project	NPV	IRR	PI
One	$2.059 M	17.33%	1.082
Two	$1.005 M	23.33%	1.201

that the firm has a shortage of capital to fund projects, caused either by an unwillingness of investors or lenders to provide additional capital or by an internal decision that the firm must limit growth. This is known as **capital rationing**.

capital rationing
A shortage of investment capital caused either by an unwillingness of external entities to provide additional capital or by an internal decision that the firm must limit growth.

Neither argument is persuasive when one considers the definition of *NPV*. The *NPV* of a decision should include all benefits and costs. If someone attempts to argue that a positive *NPV* project should be rejected, what is really being said is that some costs were not included in the computation of the *NPV*, such as the costs associated with rapid growth. But remember, an *NPV* analysis should include all costs and benefits.

For example, a firm might decide to spend only $25 million on new projects even if it means that positive *NPV* projects will be rejected. Usually what is happening is that management believes that investment beyond $25 million would strain the firm's ability to manage the investments correctly. Thus, there is a hidden cost in too much investment inasmuch as management's time will become stretched out over so many projects that all will not perform as well as planned. When the cost of too rapid growth is included in the analysis, management believes that projects bringing total investments to over $25 million will have greater costs than benefits.

Modernists believe that even these costs should be estimated and inserted into the *NPV* analysis. Only when all benefits and costs are included can management be assured that they are maximizing shareholder wealth.

Nevertheless, practically speaking, projects are sometimes ranked and selected from best to next best, and so forth, until the capital runs out. In this case, ranking becomes especially important. We can expect conflicts in ranks between the *NPV* and the *IRR* rule if the time patterns of cash flows from the projects differ greatly or if the amounts or size of the capital investments are significantly different, or both. Once again, the source of the conflict rests with the *IRR* rule's inability to handle scale differences. Accordingly, *NPV* is the method of choice.

NPV Versus *IRR* for Nonstandard Projects

standard project
A project whose cash flow stream begins with one or more cash outflows and is followed only by cash inflows.

borrowing project
A project whose cash flow stream begins with a cash inflow and is then followed by cash outflows.

A final instance in which *NPV* demonstrates its superiority to *IRR* is the case of nonstandard projects. In this text we define a **standard project** as one that begins with one or more cash outflows and is followed only by cash inflows. For example, many projects involve the immediate purchase of assets followed by years of net benefits. Nonstandard projects are defined as all other projects.

There are two kinds of nonstandard projects: borrowing projects and multiple sign change projects. A **borrowing project** is a nonstandard project because it begins with a cash inflow and is followed

FIGURE 6.2
Standard Versus Nonstandard

The + sign indicates a cash inflow, and the − sign indicates a cash outflow.

		Time Period				
Type of Project	0	1	2	3	4	5
Standard	−	+	+	+	+	+
Nonstandard						
Borrowing	+	−	−	−	−	−
Multiple sign change	−	+	+	−	−	+

multiple sign change project
A project whose cash flow stream switches through time from inflows to outflows or outflows to inflows more than once.

by cash outflows. A **multiple sign change project** is a project that switches through time from inflows to outflows or outflows to inflows more than once. The differences between standard and nonstandard projects are illustrated in Figure 6.2.

Distinguishing between standard and nonstandard projects facilitates a highly simplified comparison of *NPV* and *IRR*. While both methods work fine for standard projects, only NPV gives consistently correct answers for nonstandard projects. In fact, it is in the case of nonstandard projects that *NPV* demonstrates its clearest superiority over *IRR*.

Borrowing Projects. As we said, borrowing projects are represented by a cash inflow followed by cash outflows. We call these projects borrowing projects because they are the opposite of investment. For example, a firm may decide to sell a portion of its manufacturing process and switch to buying the output from external sources. Proceeds of the sale will bring cash into the firm immediately, but the greater cost of purchasing rather than making will result in subsequent cash outflows.

NPV may be used and interpreted as before. However, *IRR* must be interpreted differently. In borrowing projects, a high *IRR* is bad rather than good because the *IRR* is revealing the cost of borrowing rather than the return on investment. In fact, for borrowing projects, the *IRR* decision rule is reversed: Acceptable projects are those whose *IRR* is less than the required rate of return. *IRR* users must search for low *IRRs* when evaluating borrowing projects.

Example 6.8 _____ Consider The Veggie Market Cafe (or VMC for short), whose specialty is carrot cake. VMC has decided to sell its carrot shredder and to purchase its carrots preshredded. Because carrot shredders are in demand, the VMC can sell the machine for $15,000. However, the firm estimates that it must now pay an extra $5,000 per year for preshredded carrots. If the VMC's

TABLE 6.6
NPV and IRR for Borrowing Projects

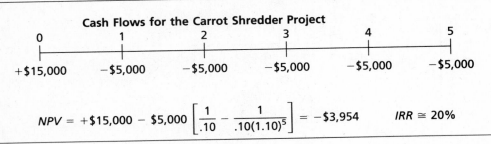

Cash Flows for the Carrot Shredder Project

$$NPV = +\$15{,}000 - \$5{,}000 \left[\frac{1}{.10} - \frac{1}{.10(1.10)^5} \right] = -\$3{,}954 \qquad IRR \cong 20\%$$

carrot shredder was expected to last for five years, should they sell the shredder? Assume that there are no other relevant costs or benefits (the machine has no remaining value if they keep it for five years because it will be worn out), and that the required rate of return for the VMC is 10 percent.

The NPV and IRR of the decision to sell the shredder are provided in Table 6.6. The NPV is negative, directing the VMC to reject the project and to continue to shred its carrots. However, because the IRR is greater than the required rate of return, VMC might be tempted to accept the project. This is the wrong decision! For borrowing projects, the IRR decision rule is the reverse of the normal IRR rule—accept projects whose IRR is less than the required rate of return. Applying the corrected IRR rule for borrowing projects would lead to rejection of the project, the same decision reached by NPV. ↵

Multiple Sign Change Projects.   The second problem—multiple sign changes—is more troublesome. Whenever there is more than one sign change in the cash flow stream, more than one IRR may exist. In other words, there are probably two or more answers that can be found using the IRR formula. In fact, the number of possible IRRs will be equal to the number of sign changes.

There is no problem with using NPV for multiple sign change cash flow streams, but the IRR method becomes difficult to apply. When more than one IRR is calculated, which IRR should be used? There is no way for the IRR model to overcome this particular shortcoming.

Example 6.9 _____ Belchertown Waste Company is developing a temporary site for trash disposal. The landfill, which requires a $5,000 investment to open, is expected to operate for two years and generate cash inflows of $11,500 per year. In the second year the firm must spend $18,050 to cap the landfill. The project's specific cash flows are given below:

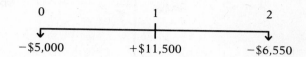

This project changes signs twice, once from negative to positive and another from positive to negative. The two *IRR*s are 3.82 percent and 26.2 percent.

Both 3.82 percent and 26.2 percent satisfy our definition of the *IRR* because they produce an *NPV* of zero. Should Belchertown accept this project on the basis of the high *IRR* or reject it on the basis of the low *IRR*? In this case the *IRR* decision rule would not allow the financial manager to make an accept–reject decision.

The *NPV* profile for the Belchertown Waste Company is provided in Figure 6.3. This *NPV* profile looks very different from the one shown earlier. Note that the line crosses the horizontal axis twice, defining two different *IRR*s. The *NPV* method produces no such dilemma. Using 15 percent as a required rate of return, the *NPV* of the landfill project is +$47.26 and the project is accepted. ↵

In summary, nonstandard projects provide rather strong reasons to prefer *NPV* over *IRR*. Although it is sometimes possible to correct for *IRR*'s shortcomings, the *NPV* method is preferred.

Estimating the Required Rate of Return—
An Advantage to the *IRR*?

Although we have argued for *NPV* over *IRR*, little has been said concerning the difficulty of estimating the required rate of return, a key variable in *NPV* analysis. Because the *IRR* model needs only the cash flows and produces a discount rate, doesn't this give an advantage to the *IRR*?

At first glance the answer appears to be yes. However, in reality, both models have the same demands since a decision for the *IRR* necessitates the required rate of return for comparison. This comparison rate—often referred to as the benchmark or **hurdle rate**—is the same rate used by *NPV* to discount cash flows. Since both methods need the required rate of return, the fact that this variable is difficult to estimate doesn't give one model an advantage over the other, but instead presents a challenge to both models.

hurdle rate
The required rate of return, or the interest rate used in the net present value model to discount future cash flows. It can also be used to determine that good projects are those whose internal rate of return is greater than, or hurdles over, the required rate of return.

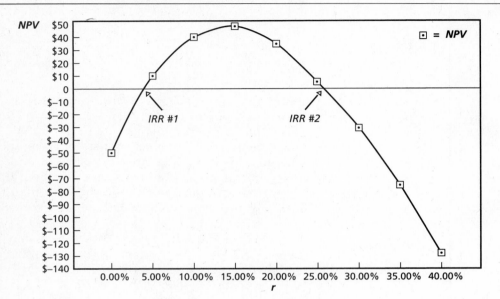

FIGURE 6.3
NPV Profile for Belchertown Waste

With two sign changes in the cash flows, Belchertown Disposal has two *IRR*s.

PROJECT SELECTION AND THE REQUIRED RATE OF RETURN

A true conflict exists within the finance discipline in the debate over how the required rate of return should be measured. The answer of modern finance is that the required rate of return should be derived from the market and should reflect the rate of return investors in the market would require to invest in the project or an asset of equivalent risk.

weighted average cost of capital (WACC)
An attempt to measure the rate of return required by the firm to satisfy its sources of capital.

Traditional finance proposes an alternative: the **weighted average cost of capital** (**WACC**). In a nutshell, the *WACC* is an attempt to measure the rate of return which is required by the firm to satisfy its sources of capital. The *WACC* is discussed in detail and computed in Window 6.1. The logic is that any project that is accepted must be expected to be able to pay for the firm's cost of capital. If a project's *IRR* exceeds the *WACC*, traditionalists reason that it must be good for the firm since it will be more than able to meet the capital expenses the firm now faces.

Although the weighted average cost of capital is intuitively appealing, closer inspection reveals its weakness. The equity and debt costs represent the rates required to be earned by the firm's shareholders

Window 6.1

The Weighted Average Cost of Capital

The purpose of this window is to discuss the issues involved in using the weighted average cost of capital as the required rate of return in capital budgeting analysis. The view of modern finance is that the discount rate should be derived directly from the market. The view of traditional finance is that the cost of capital concept should be used.

The weighted average cost of capital is the cost of the firm's overall financing. In the case of an all-equity firm this would be the return that the firm's shareholders expect to earn on the common stock investment. (Often this number is generated using one of the common stock models of Chapter 5.) If the firm has other securities such as debt, then the cost of capital would be a weighted average of the costs of all the firm's securities. This is known as the weighted average cost of capital.

The weighted average cost of capital is a broad concept that covers a variety of ways to compute the costs of each type of security (their expected return) as well as a variety of ways of computing the weights. For instance, although costs were defined above as market-expected returns, some prefer using accounting numbers that measure the original return the market expected back when the securities were issued. There is also a debate as to the percentages that should be used to weight each security in the weighted average cost of capital. Some people advocate using accounting "book" values, some advocate target values that the firm strives toward, some advocate weights that seem to correspond to the project being analyzed, but most advocate the use of weights based upon current market values. In other words, the weight of each security type is found by dividing the total market value of that security by the total market value of the firm.

Accordingly, the most popular weighted average cost of capital approach taught in traditional corporate finance is the use of market returns on each type of security weighted by market proportions. For example, consider a firm whose assets are financed by both debt and equity in the ratio of 75 percent equity and 25 percent debt. The firm's cost of equity—the rate required to be earned by the firm's shareholders—is 20 percent. The firm's cost of debt—the rate of return required to be earned by the firm's bondholders—is 15 percent. The firm's overall cost of capital, or the *WACC*, would be:

$$WACC = [\% \text{ in Equity} * \text{Cost of Equity}] + [\% \text{ in debt} * \text{Cost of Debt}]$$
$$= [.75 * .20] + [.25 * .15] = .1875, \text{ or } 18.75\%. \tag{6.5}$$

(continued on next page)

Window 6.1 (continued)

Regardless of which costs and weights are used, the objective is the same. The user is attempting to calculate an overall cost of the capital to a firm and then to apply this cost to new projects.

The logic of computing and using the weighted average cost of capital (*WACC*) is that it measures how much the firm is paying for its capital. Accordingly, it would appear that a firm that accepts a project whose return is greater than its *WACC* is making a correct investment decision since the new project is estimated to pay a higher return than is currently being earned by the firm. It would also appear that a firm that rejects a project whose return is smaller than its *WACC* is making a correct investment decision.

However, appearances can be deceiving—especially when risk enters the picture. Differences in risks between projects can make it beneficial for a firm to accept a project whose return is less than its *WACC* and reject a project whose return is greater than its *WACC*. For now, we ask you to think of the required rate of return as a market rate, observed and/or measured in a financial market.

and bondholders—that is, by the firm's capital suppliers—on the firm's currently owned assets. In reality, most firms consist of a large mix of projects (for example, can you think of a one-asset firm?). The *WACC* is therefore appropriate only for firms whose proposed projects are identical in risk to the existing firm's assets such that the required rate of return is the same for each. If the proposed project(s) do(es) not have identical risk with existing assets, then shareholders and bondholders will naturally revise their required rates of return, and the weighted average cost of capital will no longer be appropriate.

The problem of the *WACC* can be better seen in a standard example. It's possible to view a new car as costing, say, $8 per pound. In other words, we can compute an average cost by taking the total cost of a particular car and dividing it by its weight in pounds. Similarly, the *WACC* for a firm measures an average cost of capital for the whole firm.

However, serious mistakes can be made when an average cost is applied to each component. For example, a car's stereo might be worth far more than $8 per pound while the oil and gas in it are worth far less than $8 per pound. In fact, it doesn't make sense to use $8 per pound to measure the value of any component in the car.

Similarly, a firm with a *WACC* of 15 percent should not automatically assume that all of its existing assets or any proposed investments have a required rate of return of 15 percent. It is logical to assume that some of the riskiest assets would have a higher rate of return and some of the safest assets would have a lower rate of return.

SUMMARY

☐ The capital budgeting decision—the decision to invest in real assets or projects—represents the single most important decision in meeting the firm's objective of shareholder wealth maximization.

☐ In highly competitive markets, the price of an asset should equal its present value such that the benefits of investment equal its cost. This is the natural result of competition in which any potential for abnormal profits is competed away.

☐ Some real asset markets are not highly competitive because many projects are available to only a limited number of firms. It is this potential lack of competition for certain projects in terms of real assets that creates the possibility that a project can significantly increase (or decrease) shareholder wealth.

☐ Net present value, or *NPV*, is the present value of future cash benefits minus the initial investment or cost:

$$NPV = PV \text{ of Benefits} - PV \text{ of Costs}.$$

NPV measures the change in the firm's total asset value as a result of undertaking a project. A positive *NPV* adds value to the firm and thus represents an acceptable project. A negative *NPV* subtracts value from the firm and thus represents an unacceptable project. An *NPV* of zero leaves value unchanged and therefore it doesn't matter whether or not it is accepted.

☐ The internal rate of return, or *IRR*, is the discount rate that equates the present value of the costs to the present value of the benefits, in other words the discount rate that sets *NPV* to zero:

$$C_0 + \frac{CF_1}{(1+IRR)^1} + \frac{CF_2}{(1+IRR)^2} + \frac{CF_3}{(1+IRR)^3} + \cdots + \frac{CF_n}{(1+IRR)^n} = 0.$$

Projects with *IRR*s that exceed the required rate of return will add value to the firm and thus are acceptable. Projects with *IRR*s below the required rate of return will subtract value from the firm and thus are unacceptable. If the *IRR* equals the required rate of return, its acceptance or rejection is irrelevant.

☐ Both *NPV* and *IRR* work fine for projects with an immediate cash outflow followed only by cash inflows (standard projects) that are also independent projects whose accept–reject decision will not affect other projects. However, for nonstandard projects or projects requiring ranking, the two methods can produce different decisions. Because the *IRR* method has inherent shortcomings that must be overcome to make correct decisions, it is suggested that the *NPV* method, which has no inherent shortcomings, be used in these cases.

❑ Other capital budgeting models do not apply a discounted cash flow approach. These include payback and the accounting rate of return. These models have serious weaknesses and should be used with extreme care.

❑ The required rate of return must be used either as an input in computing the *NPV* or as a benchmark with which to evaluate the *IRR*. The required rate of return should be estimated or observed in the financial marketplace on securities with risk similar to that of the project under consideration. An alternative to a market-determined required rate of return is the weighted average cost of capital (*WACC*), a measure of the average cost of capital to the firm. However, the *WACC* is inappropriate when the project under consideration has a different level of risk than the average level of risk in the firm's existing assets.

DEMONSTRATION PROBLEMS

Problem 1   Mom and Pop Grocery Stores is considering the purchase of a frozen yogurt machine expected to produce the following cash flows:

C_0	C_1	C_2	C_3	C_4
−$5,000	+2,200	+2,800	+3,400	+1,000

In other words, the machine costs $5,000 today but is projected to produce cash inflows for the next four years as given. Using a required rate of return of 15%, compute the net present value, profitability index, and internal rate of return.

Solution to Problem 1

Net Present Value: The *NPV* is found by substituting into Formula (6.2) with $r = 15\%$. One method of solving the problem is to discount each of the four cash flows using the single cash flow present value techniques of Chapter 4, sum them, and then net out the project cost of $5,000.

Step 1:
Present Value of Year 1 Cash Flow of $2,200 = $1,913.04
Present Value of Year 2 Cash Flow of $2,800 = $2,117.20
Present Value of Year 3 Cash Flow of $3,400 = $2,235.56
Present Value of Year 4 Cash Flow of $1,000 = $ 571.75

Step 2:

Sum the above single cash flow present values: $6,837.55.

Step 3:

Net out the initial cost of $5,000 to compute the *NPV*:

$$NPV = +\$6,837.55 - \$5,000 = \$1,837.55$$

Workshop 6.1 demonstrates a shortcut that significantly speeds up the process into a single step. The keystrokes are:

1000, /, 1.15, =, +, 3400, =, /, 1.15, =, +, 2800, =, /, 1.15, =, +,
2200, =, /, 1.15, =, −, 5000, = ;

which produces the same answer (rounded) of $1,837.55.

Profitability Index: The *PI* is found as the absolute value (i.e., ignoring the negative sign) of the ratio between the answer to Step 2 above and the project's initial cost of $5,000:

Profitability Index = $6,837.55 / $5,000.00 = 1.3675

Internal Rate of Return: The *IRR* is found using trial and error search. The objective is to find the discount rate that produces an *NPV* of $0.

Step 1: Compute the *NPV* of the project at some initial value of the discount rate. Since we have already computed the *NPV* using a discount of 15% as $1,837.55, we will use this as the initial "guess."

Step 2: Use the result of Step 3 from the net present value to formulate an educated guess as to the next value to use in the trial and error process. Since the *NPV* at 15% was positive, we should try a higher discount rate, say 20%. Computing the *NPV* formula as above (except using a discount rate of 20%) produces an *NPV* of $1,227.62. The process is repeated until a discount rate is found that produces an *NPV* of near zero.

For example, since raising the discount rate from 15% to 20% only lowered the *NPV* from $1,837.55 to $1,227.62, our next guess should raise the discount rate about twice more than the initial raise from 15% to 20%. Trying a discount rate of 30% produces an *NPV* of $246.81.

Since the *NPV* is still positive, the next trial should use an even higher discount rate. Since the last trial (using a discount rate 10% higher) lowered the *NPV* by about $1,000, a reasonable estimate would be 33%. A discount rate of 33% produces an *NPV* of only $1.82. Thus the *IRR* is approximately 33%.

Final Solution: All three techniques indicate that the frozen yogurt machine should be purchased. ↵

Problem 2 Compute the weighted average cost of capital of Superstores Inc. The firm is worth $100 million with $60 million of equity and the remainder as debt. The common stock has a dividend yield of 5% (based upon next year's dividend) and a growth rate of 10%. The cost (yield) of the firm's debt is 12%. Find the weighted average cost of capital.

Solution to Problem 2

The weighted average cost of capital, *WACC*, is found using the formula from Window 6.1:

$$WACC = [\% \text{ in Equity} * \text{Cost of Equity}] + [\% \text{ in Debt} * \text{Cost of Debt}]$$

Step 1: The first step is to compute the percentages of equity and debt in the firm, often referred to as the weights. Sometimes these are given directly. In our example, the weights are found by dividing the amount of the equity by the total value of the firm:

$$\% \text{ in Equity} = \text{Equity Value / Total Firm Value}$$

$$\% \text{ in Equity} = \$60 \text{ M} / \$100 \text{ M} = 60\%$$

The percentage in debt forms the remainder of 40% since they must sum to 100%.

Step 2: The second step is to compute the costs of the equity and debt. The equity cost is found in this problem using the tools presented in Chapter 5 and the constant growth perpetuity model. Specifically, the rate of return on common stock formula in Formula (5.10) shows that the required rate of return on (cost of) equity is the sum of the dividend yield (using next year's dividend) and the annual growth rate.

Cost of Equity = Next Year's Dividend Yield + Annual Growth Rate
Cost of Equity = 5% + 10%
Cost of Equity = 15%

Although this problem gave the cost of debt, another problem could ask the student to compute the bond's yield to maturity using the tools presented in Chapter 5.

Step 3: The final step multiplies each weight from Step 1 times each cost from Step 2 and then sums them:

$$WACC = [60\% * 15\%] + [40\% * 12\%]$$

$$WACC = 9.0\% + 4.8\% = 13.8\%$$

Final Solution: The *WACC* is 13.8%. ↵

REVIEW QUESTIONS

1. Why are investments whose potential worth is higher than their cost more likely to be found in the market for real assets than in the market for financial assets?
2. Explain the evaluation of an investment decision using the concepts of costs and benefits.
3. Explain the net present value (NPV) method of evaluating projects. What is its acceptance criterion?
4. Explain the profitability index method of evaluating projects. What is its acceptance criterion?
5. Explain the internal rate of return (IRR) method of evaluating projects. What is its acceptance criterion?
6. What is a net present value profile? What information does it portray?
7. Explain the difference between standard and nonstandard projects. Why is the IRR method troublesome for nonstandard projects?
8. Explain the difference between an accept-or-reject project and a ranking project. What would be the cause of conflicting rankings between the NPV method and the IRR method?
9. What is capital rationing? How does capital rationing affect a firm's choice of acceptable projects?
10. What are the principal disadvantages of the payback method? What (if any) are the principal advantages?
11. What are the principal disadvantages of the accounting rate of return method? What (if any) are the principal advantages?
12. What is the weighted average cost of capital? How does it compare with the project's discount rate?

PROBLEMS

1. Given the following cash flows, determine the net present value (NPV), profitability index (PI), internal rate of return (IRR), and payback for each of the following four projects (assume a discount rate of 10%):

Project	C_0	C_1	C_2	C_3
A	−$100	$ 0	$ 0	$145
B	−$100	$115	$ 0	$ 0
C	−$100	$230	−$120	$ 0
D	−$ 45	$ 20	$ 20	$ 20
E	−$100	$ 30	$ 30	$ 90

2. A ski manufacturer is planning to purchase $500,000 of materials to produce a new line of skis. The skis will be ready for sale in

one year. If the company can sell 10,000 sets for a cash flow of $57.50 a set, should the line be produced? Compute the *NPV* of the project using a required rate of return of 10%, and assume that the skis are produced for one period only.

3. A consultant claims that she can increase employee productivity when automated billing procedures are introduced at law firms. For a $50,000 fee, the consultant states that firm cash flow, now at $1.5 million per year, can be improved by $30,000 each year for five years. Determine the *NPV* of the decision to hire the consultant. Use a required rate of return of 9%.

4. A cookie company wants to expand its retail operations. Based on a preliminary study, ten cookie stores are feasible in various parts of the country. Cash flows at each store are expected to be $150,000 in the first year and grow at 10% per year for the next four years. Each store requires an immediate investment of $500,000 to set up operations. Assuming a required rate of return of 8%, what is the *NPV* of each store?

5. A magazine publisher wants to launch a new magazine geared to college students. The start-up costs are $700,000, and expected cash flows are $200,000 for years 1–4, at which time the magazine project will end. The required rate of return is 7.5%. What is the profitability index for this project?

6. A real estate developer plans to construct and then rent a 15-unit office building. The construction costs are $600,000, and cash flows on all units will be $100,000 annually for five years, at which time the project will end, and the developer will be able to sell the building for $450,000. Calculate the profitability index for the office building using a required rate of return of 12%.

7. The research division of a large consumer electronics company has developed a prototype of a radio that management has decided to produce if the *IRR* exceeds 11%. Production costs in the current period will be $1,399,100. The radios will produce a cash flow of $500,000 a year for four years. Use the *IRR* rule to determine if the project is acceptable.

8. A manufacturer of backpacks plans to introduce a new line. Equipment and production costs total $7,272,727. The company expects a cash flow of $20 per backpack. Sales are estimated at 100,000 in the first year, and are then expected to grow by 10% in each of the following three years. Should the company produce the backpacks if the required rate of return is 12%?

9. An aquarium wants to construct an addition for large tropical fish that will cost $714,568 today and will be completed in three years. Beginning in the fourth year, cash flows will be $400,000 per year for three straight years. What is the internal rate of return on the addition? Should the addition be built if the required rate of return is 11%?

10. A clothing manufacturer anticipates that the market for a certain popular T-shirt will continue to be strong for a few more years. Accordingly, the manufacturer is considering the purchase of equipment that would generate $100,000 in cash flow starting in one year and continuing for three straight years. The machine itself costs $250,000. Initial expenses also include a one-time fee of $710 for a machine maintenance contract and $7,000 for set-up and labor. What is the project's *IRR*? Should the equipment be purchased if the required rate of return is 10%?

11. A real estate developer has just bought an undeveloped parcel of land for $200,000. Although the real estate market is currently slow, he expects that the property will be sold in two years. If improvements costing $15,330 are made now and the land is sold in two years for $275,000, what is its internal rate of return?

12. A small accounting firm is considering the purchase of a computer software package that would reduce the amount of time needed to prepare tax forms. The software costs $1,500. The firm estimates that it will save $750 per year if the software is used.
    a. What is the payback on the computer package?
    b. Instead, the firm may buy a more sophisticated computer package for $3,000. Assuming the same $750 annual savings is relevant, what is the payback on this package?

13. A citrus farmer intends to plant additional lemon or orange trees. The trees would require a $500,000 investment and the farmer can expect to get $250,000 per year in cash flow from the orange trees that would start in year three. Alternatively, the farmer could invest the same amount on lemon trees, which would provide $125,000 per year in cash flow starting in year two. What is the payback for purchase of the lemon trees and the orange trees?

14. An investment at a new trucking firm costs $1,600,000 and is expected to last five years. The investment represents assets that will be depreciated $400,000 per year during years one through four. Revenues are expected to be $600,000 for the first year and $800,000 for each of the next four years. Cash expenses will be $150,000 for the first year and then rise to $300,000 per year for the next four years. What is the accounting rate of return?

15. A snack food manufacturer is planning to introduce three new products simultaneously. Investments and per-year cash flows are given below for each:

	Initial Investment	Cash Flow per Year
A. Potato chips	$ 5 million	$1.60 million
B. Popcorn	$ 2 million	$0.75 million
C. Granola bars	$11 million	$3.25 million

Assuming that the cash flows will be received for five years, compute the *NPV* and the *IRR* (to the nearest integer value) for each project. Use a required rate of return of 10%. Rank-order each project from best to worst.

16. An arts foundation is considering two proposals that have been submitted by its members:

    Proposal 1: Buy a library of animated film classics for $15 million. The collection has to be restored, at no additional cost, which will take three years. In four years, film cash flows are expected to be $6 million a year for five straight years.

    Proposal 2: Buy modern oil paintings for $1 million and then lease them to museums for $100,000 per year starting in year one and continuing for four years. In year five, the paintings would be sold for $2 million.

    Compute the *NPV* and the *IRR* (to the nearest integer value) for each project. Use a required rate of return of 9%. Which proposal is best?

17. A restaurant makes its own pizza crust. However, with the rising cost of labor, the restaurant is investigating the possibility of buying the pizza crust instead of making it internally. The equipment (with a remaining life of five years) and remaining ingredients can be sold immediately for $20,000. The restaurant would spend $5,000 per year for the crusts for five straight years. Assuming that the payment is due at the end of the year and that the required rate of return is 15%, compute the *NPV* for the decision to buy the crust. Now compute the *IRR* for the same decision. What is your recommendation?

18. The manager of a ski resort is planning to open a second site. Demographic and general economic predictions are encouraging for the next three years, but look bleak thereafter. Initial costs are $500,000, and cash flows are expected to be $200,000 per year for the three years. For the fourth year, however, a net loss of $100,000 is projected. What is the *NPV* and *IRR* for the new ski resort? Use a required rate of return of 10%.

19. A computer manufacturer must calculate its cost of capital before deciding on the appropriate method for raising new funds. The company has 58% equity financing at a required rate of return on equity of 13.5%. The remaining 42% is in debt financing at a required rate of return of 8%. What is the firm's weighted average cost of capital?

DISCUSSION QUESTIONS

1. Think of two successful firms, and ask yourself what gives these firms a competitive advantage. Do you think they will continue to be in business in ten years? Why or why not?

2. Respond to the following statement:
   NPV sounds great, but our firm finds it difficult to implement, mostly because we have little idea what required rate of return to apply. For this reason, we prefer to use *IRR*.

3. Respond to the following statement:
   It's clear that modern finance thinks little of the payback method. But I can tell you this. Our firm has done quite well for 50 years relying on that rule, and we intend to continue using it for the next 50 years.

4. The first step in capital budgeting is to convert all advantages and disadvantages into cash flows. Consider the following project where:

   ☐ acceptance of the project will increase the probability of a serious injury or death to an employee,

   ☐ acceptance of the project will increase the probability of a serious injury or death to a customer, and

   ☐ acceptance of the project will cause pollution.

   NPV has been criticized by some as omitting important factors in the analysis. Can *NPV* be used for the foregoing project? Why or why not?

5. Please comment: *NPV* is a terrible and shortsighted financial tool since it ignores the long-term impacts of the decision.

6. How much would you pay for an idea that was guaranteed to pay a risk-free internal rate of return of 100% per year?

Two Great Tastes

As chief financial officer you must approve or reject projects based upon the company's traditional capital budgeting method: the internal rate of return. Recently, your financial analysts calculated the cash flows that would be produced by two projects suggested by the marketing department. Half of the marketing team favored one project and half favored the other project. The cash flow analysis indicated the following cash flows for each project, one called peanut butter and the other chocolate:

	Year 0	Year 1	Year 2	Year 3
		Cash Flows in:		
Peanut butter	−$3,000	$0	$1,000	$0
Chocolate	$0	+$9,053	$0	−$9,053

Both projects look pathetic. The peanut butter project actually has more dollar outflows than inflows. The chocolate project doesn't begin for another year and has future inflows equal to more current outflows.

Nevertheless, in order to evaluate the projects in terms of company policy, you compute the internal rate of return of each project. Sure enough, the internal rate of return of peanut butter is −42.265%. The internal rate of return of chocolate is 0%. Since your company requires a rate of return of 15%, you send out the bad news that both projects are rejected.

Several days later the whole marketing department runs into your office with some startling news. In a seminar on working together, they learned the value of teamwork. They suggest that the two projects be put together to form one great project. None of the revenues or expenses will change, so the combined project looks like this:

	Year 0	Year 1	Year 2	Year 3
		Cash Flows in:		
Combined project	−$3,000	+$9,053	+$1,000	−$9,053

When plugged into the computer, the project produces an internal rate of return of 20%. Since this internal rate of return exceeds the company-required rate of return, it looks like both projects can go ahead.

a. Verify that the internal rates of return have been computed correctly.
b. Find the net present value of each project and the combination using a discount rate of 15%, and
c. Discuss what you would do and why internal rate of return did or didn't work.

MODULE 3

Risk

We begin Module 3 by returning to the corporate objective of shareholder wealth maximization and by noting some of the key results from the first two modules. We learned in Module 1 that financial managers, acting as agents of shareholders, should invest when benefits exceed costs. Module 2 demonstrated the time value of money and introduced net present value (*NPV*) as the premier model for analyzing investment projects. *NPV* measures the change in shareholder wealth as a result of undertaking an investment project by subtracting the present value of the project's costs from the present value of the project's benefits. Positive-*NPV* projects increase shareholder wealth and should be accepted, negative-*NPV* projects decrease shareholder wealth and should be rejected, and zero-*NPV* projects leave shareholder wealth unchanged.

Module 3 now focuses on risk. Risk was introduced in Chapter 2 through the economic principle known as diminishing marginal utility, which implies that investors are risk-averse and establishes a foundation for studying risk-taking behavior. Risk-averse investors bear risk only if rewarded. If investors are risk-averse, the required return on a relatively risky project will be greater than the required return on a relatively safe project.

One of the main objectives of Module 3 is to show how risk can be incorporated into the *NPV* model. Chapters 7 and 8 combine statistical measures of risk with modern portfolio theory. Modern portfolio theory demonstrates that the risk of an asset held alone is different from the risk of an asset held as part of a diversified group of assets. A new model, called the capital asset pricing model, will use modern portfolio theory to estimate an appropriate discount rate for risky cash flows.

Chapter 9 provides an introduction to options. The importance of options comes not only from their widespread trading in the capital markets but also from the fact that options are common components in investment, financing, and working capital management decisions. In fact, the corporate form of organization in itself creates an option: Shareholders have the option of owning the firm or turning it over to the bondholders. Thus, the study of options provides insights into the corporate form of ownership that will be built upon in subsequent chapters, especially in Module 4 on the financing decision.

Chapter 7

Risk and Diversification

T raveler's checks are used as an inexpensive and convenient way of protecting against theft. To the traveler, the time between the purchase of the checks and the use of the money seems short. But for the firms that issue traveler's checks, for example American Express, their revenue comes from the interest income earned between the time they receive payment for the checks and the time the checks are used. This period is called float, and the longer the float, the more interest earned.

In gleaming office towers in major financial centers sit managers whose job is to invest these funds. Their job sounds simple—shopping for the places to store the money at the highest interest rate. But every day these managers must contend with their number-one enemy— risk. High returns must be produced in order to be competitive, but with the promise of high returns comes risk. For example, the money invested may never be returned because the borrower might go bankrupt, or the money received may be less than expected because interest rates have changed. The bottom line is that understanding risk and determining an appropriate rate of return for bearing the risk are central to today's financial decision making.

The definition of finance as the economics of time and risk indicates that risk plays a major role in investment, financing, and working capital management decisions. This chapter will introduce models that allow assets to be classified according to their risk level. Once risk has been identified, other models, such as net present value, can be used to incorporate both time and risk when making corporate financial decisions.

A CONCEPTUAL ANALYSIS OF RISK

When analyzing cash flows, it is best to view dollars to be received at different points of time as different commodities with different values. Comparison of dollars can be made only by transforming future dollars into present dollars. In a similar way, promises of risky dollars are not the same commodity as promises of safe dollars, and a transformation must be made to adjust for risk. Once we learn to transform risky dollars into safe dollars, basic principles can be used to make decisions consistent with the goal of the firm.

Here's a sneak preview of two important results that will be developed over the next two chapters:

portfolio
A combined holding of at least two assets.

1. The risk of an asset held alone is measured differently from the risk of an asset held as part of a group of assets. Groups of assets are known as a **portfolio.** The risk of an asset held as part of a portfolio can be fully measured using a risk measure entitled *beta*, which will be defined in Chapter 8.
2. Risk enters the net present value model through the discount rate or interest rate. The discount rate appropriate for a specific asset depends upon the asset's beta and is found using a model called the capital asset pricing model. The capital asset pricing model will be fully developed in Chapter 8.

Thus, the key to understanding risk is to understand this new risk measure entitled beta and to understand the capital asset pricing model, known by the acronym CAPM (often pronounced: cap em). Although the end result will be straightforward, it is useful for students to understand the reasoning behind the tools used to obtain this end result. We begin with the concept of uncertainty.

What Is Uncertainty?

uncertainty
The inability to forecast which outcomes or states of nature will occur in the future.

Uncertainty is the inability to forecast future outcomes or future states of nature. For example, consider Risk, Inc., a new company whose only project is an attempt to develop a powerful new technology to remove ice cream stains. If the company is successful, we know that the stock will rise to $10 per share—the favorable outcome (or state of nature). If the technology fails, the stock will drop to $0 per share—obviously the unfavorable outcome (or state of nature). Currently, Risk, Inc., is being offered to the public at $5 per share. The uncertainty in this example is that we do not know which of the two outcomes, $10 per share or $0 per share, will occur.

What Is Risk?

risk
The variation in value among uncertain outcomes.

Now let's assume that Mr. Smart has refused to place his money in Risk, Inc.'s stock despite the advice of a stockbroker. We would say that Mr. Smart has decided not to expose his money to this substantial risk. **Risk** is variation in value among uncertain outcomes—in this case the difference between $10 and $0 per share.

Not all securities contain risk. For example, a U.S. Treasury bill promises a guaranteed dollar amount regardless of what happens to Risk Inc.'s new technology or to anything else. We call the Treasury bill investment riskless, as it promises cash flows with certainty.[1] How does Mr. Smart decide in which asset—Risk, Inc., or Treasury bills—to invest? To answer this question, we must consider how investors view risk.

Risk-Averse Behavior

risk-averse
Unwilling to accept risk without the expectation of reward.

Most investors share similar behavior when it comes to risk—they do not enjoy bearing it. This does not mean that people will not take risk, only that they demand extra return for bearing risk. When individuals must be compensated for bearing risk, we say they are **risk-averse.** The vast majority of money in the United States is invested with the attitude that the riskier the investment, the greater must be its expected return or reward.

This is not to say that all risk-averse investors behave in this manner all the time. For instance, we may observe that an investor who is risk-averse by day enjoys taking different types of risk by night, such as buying a lottery ticket or playing casino blackjack. This behavior is due perhaps to the entertainment value that the ticket or game offers. Nevertheless, throughout this text, we will assume that investors behave in a risk-averse manner.

Where Risk Aversion Comes From. For centuries there was no solid explanation for why people are risk-averse. Then in the 1730s, Daniel Bernouilli, a Swiss mathematician, provided an explanation using our second economic principle, diminishing marginal utility. As we have said, diminishing marginal utility means that as people become wealthier and wealthier, a particular amount of money tends to be less and less important to them. For example, to a person who can barely meet the basic economic needs of life, $10 may seem like a great deal of money. However, if that same person were to become wealthy, $10 will be much less important.

---

1. Finance ignores things like thermonuclear war and revolution.

Given diminishing marginal utility, in Bernouilli's explanation, the happiness gained from increases in wealth is less in magnitude than the happiness lost from decreases in wealth. Put simply, people view an unrewarded risk as undesirable because the potential winnings have less value than the potential losses.

Measuring Risk Aversion Using Utility Analysis. Let's return to Mr. Smart. When contemplating the shares of Risk, Inc., Mr. Smart thought about how nice it would be to receive $10 per share and how unpleasant it would be to lose his money. Mr. Smart was applying the economic law of diminishing marginal utility to the investment decision.

Figure 7.1 contains the utility diagram from Chapter 2. It represents the assumed relationship between happiness and money. The two key aspects to utility theory are positive marginal utility —that more money means more happiness—and diminishing marginal utility—that a given amount of money means less and less additional happiness as people become wealthier and wealthier.

Figure 7.1 includes utility values for Mr. Smart. Suppose that Mr. Smart's total wealth is $100,000, without an investment in Risk, Inc. If he purchases 10,000 shares of Risk, Inc., for $5 per share, his wealth would either rise to $150,000 if the stock rose to $10 or fall to $50,000

FIGURE 7.1
Mr. Smart's Utility Curve

Mr. Smart's utility curve illustrates both positive marginal utility and diminishing marginal utility.

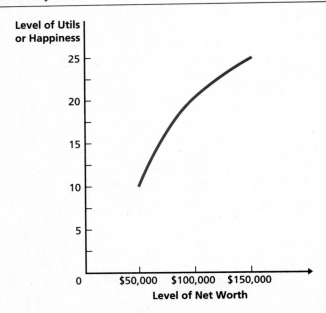

if the stock fell to zero. In terms of dollars, the risk offers equal potential gains and losses of $50,000.

Utility diagrams translate dollar amounts into units (or utils) of happiness. In our example we have attached symbolic levels of happiness to each level of wealth. At $100,000 Mr. Smart enjoys 20 utils of happiness. If Mr. Smart's wealth rises to $150,000, his happiness will rise to 25 utils. If, on the other hand, Mr. Smart's wealth were to fall to $50,000, his happiness would fall to 12 utils.

When viewed in terms of happiness rather than dollars, we see that the potential gain from the investment, measured by five additional utils of happiness, is less than the potential loss from the investment of eight utils of happiness. Even though the dollar gains and dollar losses are equal, Mr. Smart's utility function reveals the problem with risk—that the happiness that could be lost exceeds the happiness that could be gained. Given the characteristic of diminishing marginal utility, Mr. Smart is unwilling to take a risk that in dollar terms appears to offer equal potential for gains and losses.

Why Risk-Averse People Invest in Risky Assets.
Risk is a necessary part of life in general and economic activity in particular. Because most financial decisions involve some degree of risk, we find that risk-averse people will bear risk as long as they are rewarded for doing so.

One way that Mr. Smart could be rewarded for bearing the risk of Risk, Inc., would be if the probability of the stock's rising were greater than the probability of its falling. Another way would be if the stock sold for only $1 per share (instead of $5 per share) such that the potential gain of $9 in the favorable state of nature far exceeded the potential loss of $1 in the unfavorable state. It turns out that Mr. Smart's decision not to invest in Risk, Inc., was based on his assessment that the probability of the stock's price rising to $10 per share was small.

Risky investments will not always produce higher profits when compared with safe investments. If they did, no one would buy the safe investments. Rather, risky investments offer higher expected or average profits than safe investments. These higher expected profits could be a result of high probabilities of moderate success or moderate probabilities of enormously successful outcomes.

Thus, the theory of risk-taking is built upon a tradeoff between risk and expected reward. These tradeoffs between risk and reward are all around us and are made every day. For example, some people accept the risk of driving 80 miles per hour on an interstate highway because the rewards of driving at such a speed are greater than the risks. If the risks increased, say to double the fine for speeding, some people might reassess the risk and reward relationship and decide not to take the risk.

In the 1950s, Harry Markowitz, an economist, demonstrated the insights into the risk and reward tradeoff for financial securities using the tools of math and statistics. In 1990 he earned a Nobel prize for his work. The remainder of this chapter will use these tools.

RETURN AND RISK ON INDIVIDUAL ASSETS

An asset's return is often used as an indication of its performance. Positive returns indicate good performance, and negative returns indicate bad performance. Returns can be thought of as the change in value through time, expressed as a percentage.

> ✗ Asset returns are defined as the change in value through time expressed as a proportion or as a percentage.

For example, consider Woolridge, Inc., a research firm whose stock price is $20 per share today. The annual return on Woolridge Inc., denoted R_W, is expressed as a ratio of the change in price during the year to the old price at the start of the year:

$$R_W = \frac{[\text{End Value} - \text{Start Value}]}{\text{Start Value}}. \tag{7.1}$$

If Woolridge's stock price rises to $22 next year, the return would be:

$$R_W = \frac{[\$22 - \$20]}{\$20} = 0.10 \text{ or } 10\%.$$

To convert a decimal, say 0.10, to a percentage, multiply the decimal amount by 100. For example, if the price of the stock fell from $20 to $19, then the return would be -0.05 or -5 percent.

If the investment includes more than one payment, such as a stock whose end value may include both a price plus a dividend payment, both payments should be added together to get the end-of-period value. These concepts are more thoroughly discussed in Window 7.1.

Distributions of Returns

random variable
In finance, a variable whose value in the future is unknown.

We may now view the risk of an asset as uncertainty regarding the asset's return. Because the return on the asset is unknown, it is referred to as a **random variable.** The relationship between the possible returns of a random variable and the probability of obtaining

FIGURE 7.2
The Normal Distribution of Returns

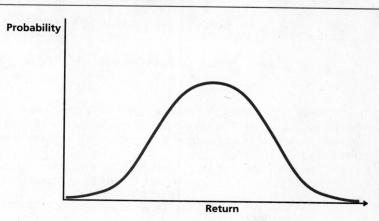

these possible returns is known as a probability distribution. Figure 7.2 illustrates a random variable's return using a special type of distribution called the **normal distribution.**

normal distribution
A probability distribution with a symmetrical or bell-like curve.

The normal distribution illustrated in Figure 7.2 and another similar distribution known as the log-normal distribution are the primary distributions used for return analysis. These distributions are used in developing a framework for describing how an investor would make decisions regarding the tradeoff between risk and the reward for bearing risk.

Statistics contains many useful tools for analyzing the tradeoff between risk and reward. The two primary tools we will use are: (1) the mean or expectation to describe the level of return offered, and (2) the standard deviation or variance to describe the dispersion or degree of uncertainty of the return.

Mean Returns

We are all familiar with the concept of an average such as a grade point average. Mean is another term for average, and expected value is another. The three terms can be used interchangeably.

mean or expected value
The average of all possible values weighted by their probabilities of occurrence.

The **mean** return or **expected value** is the middle of the outcomes on a probability-weighted basis. The formula for the mean return or expected value is the sum of the state-dependent returns multiplied by their associated probabilities:

$$E(R) = \sum_{i=1}^{n} R_i * Prob_i ,$$

(7.2)

Window 7.1

Measuring Security Returns

This window details the calculation of security returns. Many of these calculations were introduced in Chapter 4 as time value of money problems. The returns examined in this window relate directly to financial securities known as common stock and bonds, and will build from Formula (7.1).

Returns from common stock can come from dividend payments and changes in the stock's market value. The common stock return formula can be given as:

$$\text{Common Stock Return} = \frac{[\text{Dividend Received} + \text{Ending Price}] - \text{Starting Price}}{\text{Starting Price}}.$$

For example, suppose you purchase a share of stock for $20 and sell the stock next year for $21. Over the interim, the stock pays a dividend of $2. The percentage return on the stock investment is:

$$\text{Common Stock Return} = \frac{[\$2 + \$21] - \$20}{\$20} = 0.15 \text{ or } 15\%.$$

We could get more precise and break the return into its two components: a dividend return (sometimes referred to as a dividend yield) and a capital gain. In the example above, the dividend return is 10 percent and the capital gain return is 5 percent.

Of course, the selling price could be less than the buying price. In this case, the second component of return would be negative and we would say that the investment produced a capital loss.

Returns from bonds can come from coupon payments and changes in the bond's price when it is sold. The bond return formula can be given as:

$$\text{Bond Return} = \frac{[\text{Coupon Payment} + \text{Ending Price}] - \text{Starting Price}}{\text{Starting Price}}.$$

For example, suppose you purchase a 10-year maturity bond at par for $1,000 that pays a $120 coupon annual payment. Suppose also that at the end of the year the bond's price has fallen to $996 (Quick Quiz: In what direction did market interest rates move?) and you decide to sell the bond at this time. The return on the bond investment is:

(continued on next page)

Window 7.1 *(continued)*

$$\text{Bond Return} = \frac{[\$120 + \$996] - \$1,000}{\$1,000} = 0.116 \text{ or } 11.6\%$$

We could get more precise and break the return into its two components: a coupon return and a capital loss, as we sold the bond for a price less than we paid for it. In the example above, the coupon return is 12 percent and the capital loss is 0.4 percent.

In both examples, the time period of investment was one year, and the rate of return was an annual return. (It is common to quote returns on an annual basis.) However, there is nothing common or conventional about measuring returns over one-year intervals. Some investors buy stock and sell the stock in less than one year; some even buy stock and sell it the next day! The same is true for bonds.

Although the return formulas can be altered to calculate the return over any number of days, it is conventional to report returns as if they were earned over the entire year. For example, an investor who earns a return of 3% over three months might wish to know what the return would have been if the investment were held for the period of one year. Fortunately, returns over any time period can be transformed into annualized returns in one of two ways:

$$\text{Simple Annualized Return} = R_t * 365/t,$$
$$\text{or}$$
$$\text{Compound Annualized Return} = (1 + R_t)^{365/t} - 1,$$

where R_t is the return over the holding period, and t is the number of days in which the investment was held. For example, t is one day in the case where stock is sold the day after it is purchased. The difference between the two annualized return formulas is that the second formula assumes that interest is compounded during the year while the first formula does not.

Returning to the stock example above, suppose you purchase a share of stock for $20 and sell the stock in six months (182 days) for $21. Over the interim, the stock paid a dividend of $2. Although your holding period is six months, what is the annualized return on the stock investment?

It is best to break the problem into two steps. First, apply Formula (7.2) to obtain the holding period return. Next, apply either the simple annualized return or the compound annualized return formula to annualize the holding period return:

$$\text{Step 1: Holding Period Return: } R_t = \frac{(\$2 + \$21) - \$20}{\$20} = 15\%,$$

(continued on next page)

Window 7.1 *(continued)*

Step 2: Simple Annualized Holding Period Return: = 0.15 * 365/182 = 30%,

or

Compounded Annualized Holding Period Return: = $(1.15)^{365/182} - 1 = 32.35\%$.

The effect of compounding interest can be seen from the difference in annualized holding period returns. Under simple interest, the 15 percent return earned over the one-half-year period is doubled to get the annualized holding period return. With compounding, the annualized return is more than double the half-year return because the interest earned over the half-year is assumed to be reinvested along with the original investment over the second half of the year.

This procedure works for any time period, be it one day or 1000 days. However, investors should be aware of the potential for enormous returns when annualizing returns earned over short periods. For example, suppose you buy a share of stock today for $5.00 and sell it next week or in seven days for $5.125 (no dividends are earned). The annualized holding period return would be:

$$\text{Annualized Holding Period Return} = \left[\frac{\$5.125}{\$5.00} \right]^{365/7} - 1 = 2.6239 \text{ or } 262.39\%.$$

This return is realistic only if the investor believes that it is possible on a continuing basis to purchase the stock and sell the stock in one week for a higher price.

where $E(R)$ is the expected or mean return, i stands for a particular state of nature, n is the total number of states of nature, R_i is the asset's return in state i, and $Prob_i$ is the probability that state i will occur.

Example 7.1 ———————— We can calculate the expected or mean return of Risk, Inc., using Formula (7.2). The stock price of Risk, Inc., is currently $5 per share. The uncertainty associated with an investment in Risk, Inc., is captured by the two states of nature. In state success the stock price will rise to $10, and in state failure the stock price will fall to $0, defining the return in each state:

$$\text{Return in State Success: } R_S = \frac{\$10 - \$5}{\$5} = 100\%.$$

$$\text{Return in State Failure: } R_F = \frac{\$0 - \$5}{\$5} = -100\%.$$

In order to compute Risk, Inc.'s mean return it is necessary to know the probability of either state occurring. If the two states are equally likely such that the probability of each state is 0.5, the expected or mean return would be 0%:

$$E(R) = (-100\% * 0.5) + (100\% * 0.5) = 0\%.$$

If the probability of the $10 outcome were 60% and the $0 outcome were 40%, the expected or mean return would be:

$$E(R) = (-100\% * 0.4) + (100\% * 0.6) = 0.20 \text{ or } 20\%.$$

Obviously, in real situations, the number of possible outcomes is far greater than two and the probabilities associated with these possible outcomes are difficult to estimate. However, the concept remains unchanged. ↩

Example 7.2 ——————— Consider Project A and Project B. Project A is an investment in machinery to manufacture a product with a relatively stable market. Project B is an investment in machinery to manufacture a luxury product that is highly sensitive to economic conditions. The returns from each have been estimated for four possible states in the economy: recession, slow growth, moderate growth, and prosperity. The estimates are shown in column 1 of Table 7.1.

Both projects are expected to produce returns of 0 percent in a recession, but in prosperity the return on Project A would

TABLE 7.1

State-Dependent Returns from Projects A and B

	(1)		(2) Probability of State Occurring	(3) Probability-Weighted Return (2) × (3)	
	Annual Return				
State of Nature	Project			Project	
	A	B		A	B
Recession	0.00	0.00	0.20	0.000	0.000
Slow Growth	0.06	0.05	0.30	0.018	0.015
Moderate Growth	0.08	0.10	0.40	0.032	0.040
Prosperity	0.10	0.15	0.10	0.010	0.015
Expected Value				0.060	0.070

be 10 percent while the return on Project B would be 15 percent. These estimates may derive from a sophisticated computer analysis or they may be completely subjective.

The next step is to estimate the probability of each state occurring, which is usually relatively subjective. Once estimated, these probabilities are multiplied by their respective returns to obtain weighted values. As shown in Table 7.1, the sum of these weighted values is the mean or the expected value. The mean of Project A is 6 percent, and the mean of Project B is 7 percent. ◄┘

The Standard Deviation of Returns

The mean is a measure of an average, not a measure of risk. Two investments can have very different risk levels. To measure risk, we need a measure of the amount of dispersion of the returns around the mean return. Such risk measures are known as the **standard deviation** and **variance.**

standard deviation and **variance**
Statistical measures of dispersion and variability.

The variance and standard deviation can be computed using the formula below or using a calculator or computer that has the formula programmed into it:

$$\text{Variance} = \sigma^2 = \sum_{i=1}^{n} [(R_i - E(R))^2 * Prob_i], \qquad (7.3)$$

$$\text{Standard Deviation} = \sigma = \sqrt{\sum_{i=1}^{n} [(R_i - E(R))^2 * Prob_i]}, \qquad (7.4)$$

where the Greek letters σ^2 (sigma squared) and σ (sigma) stand for the variance and standard deviation respectively, R_i is the asset's return in state i, $E(R)$ is the expected or mean return, i stands for a particular state of nature, n is the total number of states, and $Prob_i$ is the probability that state i will occur.

Example 7.3 ——————— Consider Project A and Project B above. Project A has a mean return of six percent while Project B has a mean return of seven percent. Notice that the returns expected in the respective states are different. In the case of Project A, the difference in return between the best and worse states of nature is ten percent, while for Project B the difference is 15 percent. Figure 7.3 illustrates the dispersion of the returns of Projects A and B. The distribution for Project A appears tighter, while the distribution for Project B appears wider.

The calculation of the variance and standard deviation of Project A and Project B is shown in Table 7.2. Columns 1 through 3 of Table 7.2 come directly from Table 7.1. They indi-

FIGURE 7.3
The Distribution of Returns of Projects A and B

Project B has a higher
mean return and higher
dispersion.

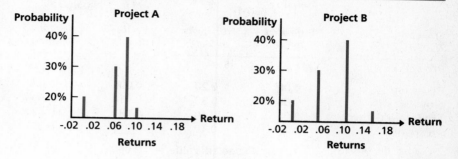

cate, respectively, for each project (1) the estimated return
from the projects under each state (R_i), (2) the probability of
each state occurring ($Prob_i$), and (3) the estimated return
under each state multiplied by the probability of that state
occurring ($R_i * Prob_i$). The sum of these weighted values is the
expected return of Project A and Project B as previously demonstrated in Table 7.1.

Column 4 calculates the return deviation, $R_i - E(R)$, of
each estimated return from its expected return. Column 5
squares each deviation. In column 6, each of the squared deviations is multiplied by the probability of its occurrence ($Prob_i$).
The sum of these weighted squared deviations is the variance
of the distribution. The standard deviation is calculated as the
square root of the variance.

The larger the standard deviation, the wider the probability distribution and the greater the risk. From Table 7.2 we see
that the standard deviation of returns of Project A is 0.03225
and of Project B is 0.04583. ↵

There are two primary methods of computing the variance and
standard deviation. The first is to use a calculator, which will do the
work, and the second is to build a table similar to that shown in Table
7.2. We would encourage you to first learn the concepts by building
tables similar to Table 7.2, and then to seek shortcuts such as those
provided by advanced calculators.

The Normal Distribution. For Project A and Project B there were
only four possible states of nature, whereas in the normal distribution
there are an infinite number of states. The meaning of standard deviation is well known in the case of the normal distribution. For a normally distributed variable, 68 percent of the outcomes fall within one
standard deviation of the mean. For example, if the mean is 12 percent
and the standard deviation is 20 percent, we would say that, although

TABLE 7.2
The Standard Deviation of Returns for Projects A and B

State of Nature	(1) Estimated Return	(2) Probability of State	(3) Weighted Return	(4) Return Deviation	(5) Squared Return Deviation	(6) Weighted Squared Deviation
Project A						
Recession	0.00	0.20	0.000	−0.06	0.0036	0.00072
Slow Growth	0.06	0.30	0.018	0.00	0.0000	0.00000
Moderate Growth	0.08	0.40	0.032	+0.02	0.0004	0.00016
Prosperity	0.10	0.10	0.010	+0.04	0.0016	0.00016
		Expected Value =	0.060		Variance =	0.00104

$$\text{Standard Deviation} = \sqrt{0.00104} = .03225$$

State of Nature	(1) Estimated Return	(2) Probability of State	(3) Weighted Return	(4) Return Deviation	(5) Squared Return Deviation	(6) Weighted Squared Deviation
Project B						
Recession	0.00	0.20	0.000	−0.07	0.0049	0.00098
Slow Growth	0.05	0.30	0.015	−0.02	0.0004	0.00012
Moderate Growth	0.10	0.40	0.040	+0.03	0.0009	0.00036
Prosperity	0.15	0.10	0.015	+0.08	0.0064	0.00064
		Expected Value =	0.070		Variance =	0.00210

$$\text{Standard Deviation} = \sqrt{0.0021} = .04583$$

we expect the return to be 12 percent, an actual return of 12 percent is unlikely. The best we can say is that 68 percent of the time the actual return will be somewhere between −8 percent and +32 percent. Further, for the normal distribution, 95 percent of the actual outcomes will fall within two standard deviations of the mean, and over 99 percent will fall within three standard deviations of the mean. This is illustrated in Figure 7.4.

Risk and Reward

The mean and standard deviation are important in describing the returns offered by a risky asset. The mean appears to be a good measure of the reward that an investor anticipates and, at first glance, it appears as though standard deviation is a good measure of risk.

Recall that the objective of this chapter is to develop a framework for analyzing the way investors make decisions between risk and reward. The concept that investors demand more reward for bearing more risk is illustrated in Figure 7.5. The remainder of this chapter

FIGURE 7.4
Interpreting the Standard Deviation Under the Normal Distribution

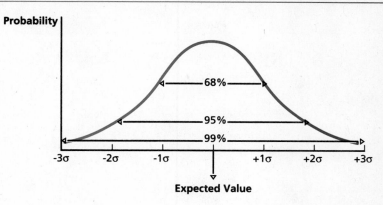

as well as Chapter 8 will determine the proper labels to each axis in Figure 7.5 and what the specific relationship should look like.

Let's return briefly to the discussion of how the investing public views risk. Earlier in this chapter we stated that the vast majority of money in the United States is invested with the attitude that the riskier the investment, the greater is its expected return or reward. Now that we have defined measures of return and risk, we can look to the historical evidence to see if this is true. This is shown in Window 7.2.

The summary provided in Window 7.2 confirms our earlier description of the risk-reward relationship. The higher the risk of the investment as measured by its standard deviation, the higher is its return. Although Window 7.2 does not show year-by-year returns, the

FIGURE 7.5
The Risk-Reward Relationship

With no risk, the expected rate of return is known as the risk-free rate. The expected rate of return is higher as the risk grows higher.

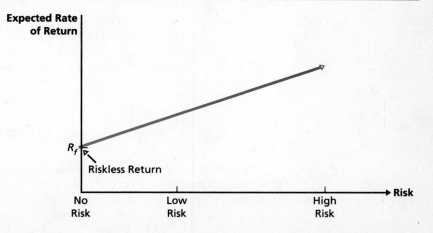

Window 7.2

A Sixty-Year Historical Look at Return and Risk

Security Type	Mean Return	Standard Deviation
1. Common Stocks	12.1%	20.9%
2. Corporate Bonds	5.3%	8.4%
3. U.S. Treasury Bills	3.6%	3.3%

Source: From *Stocks, Bonds, Bills, and Inflation 1989 Yearbook,*™ Ibbotson Associates, Chicago (annually updates work by Roger G. Ibbotson and Rex A. Sinquefield). Used with permission. All rights reserved.

---

greatest dispersion of annual returns is found in common stocks, where returns ranged from +52 percent in 1952 to −43 percent in 1931.

The Problem with Standard Deviation as a Risk Measure

Although the standard deviation at first appears to be a good measure of risk, it has a serious flaw. This flaw, to be demonstrated in the next few subsections, will be revealed when risky assets are combined. When two or more risky assets are combined, the standard deviation of the combination will, in most cases, be less than the average standard deviations of the individual assets. To develop this point further it is necessary to learn some of the results of portfolio theory—an important subset of modern finance.

RETURN AND RISK ON PORTFOLIOS

The previous sections analyzed the calculation of the expected return and the standard deviation of returns for individual assets. It is common, however, for investors to hold groups of assets called portfolios. This section performs similar analysis for portfolios.

Portfolio Returns

The return of a portfolio can be computed by combining the returns of the assets in the portfolio. We refer to the assets in a portfolio as its constituent assets, much as an elected state or national representative refers to the people in his or her district as constituents. If the assets are held in equal proportions, the portfolio return is the simple average of the individual returns. However, if the assets in the portfolio are not held in equal proportions, each asset must be weighted by its percentage representation of the total portfolio value.

Actual Returns.   Consider a portfolio with only two stocks: Disney and MCA. Inasmuch as it is necessary to know the percentages of the portfolio's market value represented by each of the stocks, let's assume that 60 percent of the portfolio's market value is in Disney stock and the remaining 40 percent is in MCA stock.

The return of the portfolio in a given time period can be found by adding 60 percent of Disney's return and 40 percent of MCA's return. For example, if Disney's return is 20 percent and MCA's return is 10 percent, the portfolio's return is 16 percent.

In order to prepare for some more complex concepts to follow, it is useful to introduce some notation. We will denote the percentage of a portfolio's value in a particular asset (such as asset i) as w_i. The letter w stands for weight and the subscript i refers to a particular asset. The formula for w_i is given by:

$$w_i = \frac{\text{Market value of the investment in asset } i}{\text{Market value of the entire portfolio}}. \tag{7.5}$$

Accordingly, the formula for the return of a portfolio (denoted R_p) may be expressed as the weighted average of the returns of the portfolio's constituent assets:

$$R_p = \sum_{i=1}^{n} w_i * R_i , \tag{7.6}$$

where R_P stands for the return of a portfolio, R_i is the return on constituent asset i, and n stands for the number of assets in the portfolio. The summation sign indicates that the weighted returns are summed across the number of constituent assets in the portfolio.

Another way of calculating the return of a portfolio would be to calculate its total market value at the beginning of the period and again at the end of the period, then applying Formula (7.1). However, this method does not illustrate the points of this chapter well and turns out to be slower than the procedures shown in Formula (7.6).

Expected Returns.   As in the case of actual returns, the mean or expected return of a portfolio depends upon the mean or expected returns of the portfolio's constituent assets. In fact, the procedures are identical. The mean or expected return of the portfolio, $E(R_p)$, is a weighted average of the mean returns of the constituent assets as shown below:

$$E(R_P) = \sum_{i=1}^{n} w_i * E(R_i) . \tag{7.7}$$

Expected returns operate just as we would hope. The portfolio's expected return is a blend or weighted average of the expected returns of the constituent assets. Thus, if an asset is added to the portfolio that has a higher expected return than the portfolio's other assets, the portfolio's expected return would rise. Conversely, adding a lower expected return asset would cause the portfolio's expected return to fall.

A First Look at Portfolio Risk

Unfortunately, the simplicity of moving from returns on individual assets to the returns on portfolios does not extend to the portfolio's variance and standard deviation. If it did, this chapter would end at this point and Chapter 8 wouldn't even exist. This subsection is necessary because it explains diversification, a key concept in risk management. **Diversification** is the reduction in a portfolio's risk that occurs when assets are combined into a portfolio and some of the risks of the portfolio's constituent assets cancel each other out.

diversification
The reduction in a portfolio's risk that occurs when assets are combined into a portfolio and portions of the risks of the portfolio's constituent assets cancel each other out.

Diversification.   Consider a sunglasses corporation and an umbrella corporation. Each investment by itself would be risky, since the sunglasses firm's success depends upon sunny days and the umbrella firm's success depends upon rainy days. However, an investor holding both stocks would find little risk since, whether it rains or shines, one of the assets in the portfolio will perform well and will cancel out the bad performance of the other asset. Thus, a portfolio of the two assets would have much less risk than either asset held alone. In contrast, having a sunglasses corporation and a suntan lotion corporation in the same portfolio would provide less diversification, since their risks would not cancel each other out. The amount of diversification in a portfolio will depend upon which assets are in the portfolio and how those assets behave relative to each other.

The Covariance

covariance
A statistical measure of the extent to which two variables move together.

According to the discussion above, portfolio risk must incorporate a statistical measure of diversification known as **covariance.** The formula for covariance is similar to the formula for variance:

$$\sigma_{xy} = \sum_{i=1}^{n} [(R_{xi} - E(R_x))(R_{yi} - E(R_y)) * Prob_i]. \qquad (7.8)$$

The main difference between covariance and variance is that covariance includes two assets, given in the formula by subscripts x and y. Thus, σ_{xy} stands for the covariance between asset x and asset y. The variables R_{xi} and R_{yi} are the returns of assets x and y in state i, $E(R_x)$ and $E(R_y)$ are the expected or mean returns of assets x and y, and $Prob_i$ is the probability that state i will occur.

The covariance of two assets measures the degree or tendency of two variables to move in relationship with each other. If two assets tend to move in the same direction, they are said to be positively correlated and they will have a positive covariance. If the two assets tend to move in opposite directions, they are said to be negatively correlated and they will have a negative covariance. Finally, if they tend to move independently of each other, their covariance will be zero.

Many students find the concept of covariance confusing at first. However, thinking about the importance of diversification in reducing risk makes the concept of covariance clearer. Covariance is a quantitative tool that helps us understand how much diversification will occur.

Example 7.4 _____ The calculation of the covariance of returns for Project A and Project B, introduced in an earlier section of this chapter, is shown in Table 7.3. Columns 1 through 5 of Table 7.3 repeat the analysis shown in a previous table on computing variance. The main difference between the covariance in Table 7.3 and the variance in Table 7.2 is shown in column 6. In Table 7.3, column 6 computes the product of the deviations of each state-dependent return from its respective expected return. In other words, column 6 multiplies Project A's deviation from its expected return by Project B's deviation from its expected return. Each of the products of the deviations is then multi-

TABLE 7.3
The Covariance of Returns Between Projects A and B

	(1)	(2)	(3)	(4)	(5)	(6)	(7)
							Probability-Weighted
		Return	Deviation	Return	Deviation	Product of Deviation	Product
State of Nature	Probability	A	from Mean	B	from Mean	(3) * (5)	(3) * (5) * (1)
Recession	0.20	0.00	−0.06	0.00	−0.07	0.0042	0.00084
Slow Growth	0.30	0.06	0.00	0.05	−0.02	0.0000	0.00000
Moderate Growth	0.40	0.08	+0.02	0.10	+0.03	0.0006	0.00024
Prosperity	0.10	0.10	+0.04	0.15	+0.08	0.0032	0.00032
						Covariance =	0.00140

plied by the probability of each state occurring and is shown in column 7. The sum of the products of the deviations is the covariance between Project A and B.

Covariance measures the degree of the relationship between two variables. Because covariance is based on products of individual deviations and not squared deviations, its value can be positive, negative, or zero. From Table 7.3 we see that the covariance between Projects A and B is 0.0014, indicating that the returns of Project A and Project B tend to move in the same direction. ↵

There are two primary methods of computing covariance. The first is to enter the data into a calculator or computer, which will compute the statistics for you, and the second is to build a table similar to Table 7.3. As with the calculation of variance, we would encourage you to learn how to compute the statistics using the second method. Once you understand how covariance is computed, you will probably want to use the calculator method, as it is much quicker and more reliable.

The Correlation Coefficient

correlation coefficient
A statistical measure of the extent to which two variables move together. The correlation coefficient ranges from positive one, or perfect positive correlation, to negative one, or perfect negative correlation.

A statistic related to the covariance is called the **correlation coefficient.** Like the covariance, the correlation coefficient measures the degree of association between two assets. The sunglasses corporation would be expected to have negative correlation with the umbrella corporation, while the sunglasses corporation would be expected to have high correlation with the suntan lotion corporation.

The correlation coefficient takes the covariance and forces its value to be between negative one and positive one. Negative one is the lowest correlation and indicates that the two assets are exact opposites, while positive one is the highest correlation coefficient and indicates that the assets are clones of each other. Values between these two extremes indicate different degrees of association. The fact that the correlation coefficient is bounded is an advantage because the value of the correlation coefficient itself describes the extent of the relationship or correlation between two variables.

The correlation coefficient is given by:

$$\rho_{xy} = \sigma_{xy} / \sigma_x \sigma_y , \qquad (7.9)$$

where the Greek letter ρ (rho) is the notation for the correlation coefficient between asset x and asset y, σ_{xy} is the covariance between asset x and asset y, and σ_x and σ_y are the standard deviations of assets x and y, respectively.

Example 7.5 _____ The correlation coefficient between Project A and Project B can be determined from the data in Tables 7.2 and 7.3.

$$\rho_{AB} = \frac{\sigma_{AB}}{\sigma_A \sigma_B} = \frac{.0014}{(.03225)(.04583)} = 0.9472.$$

Because the correlation coefficient is close to positive one, its highest possible value, we say that returns expected on Project A and Project B are highly correlated with each other. ◄┘

Calculating Portfolio Variance and Standard Deviation

Knowledge of covariance will come in handy when computing the variance of a portfolio. Although portfolios can be of any size, our examples will illustrate portfolio variance and standard deviation in the case of two assets. The formula for the variance of a two-asset portfolio (using returns and weights as defined in preceding subsections) is:

$$\text{Portfolio Variance} = \sigma_p^2 = w_x^2 \sigma_x^2 + w_y^2 \sigma_y^2 + 2w_x w_y \sigma_{xy}, \quad (7.10)$$

where σ_p^2 is the notation for portfolio variance, σ_x^2 and σ_y^2 are the variances of asset x and y respectively, σ_{xy} is the covariance between asset x and y, and w_x and w_y are the weights of asset x and asset y in the portfolio.

The standard deviation of the portfolio, given by σ_p, may be found by taking the square root of both sides of Formula (7.10). The formula demonstrates that the variance and standard deviation of a portfolio's return depends not only upon the variances of the constituent assets and upon their weights, but also upon their covariance.

Example 7.6 _____ Return to Project A and Project B, whose respective variances and covariances are provided in Tables 7.2 and 7.3. If an investor places an equal amount of money in each of the projects such that the portfolio weights are both 0.5, the portfolio variance from Formula (7.10) would be:

$$\sigma_p^2 = (0.5)^2(0.00104) + (0.5)^2(0.00210)$$
$$+ 2(0.5)(0.5)(0.0014) = 0.001485,$$

and the portfolio standard deviation would be:

$$\sigma_p = \sqrt{.001485} = 0.0385. \quad ◄┘$$

The Relationship Between Covariance and Portfolio Standard Deviation

Of the three terms on the right-hand side of Formula (7.10), the first and second terms represent the effect of the variances of the individual assets on the variance of the portfolio. Notice that all the components of these first two terms are squared so that they must be non-negative. Therefore, portfolios that include stocks with high variances will tend to have high portfolio variances.

It is the third term on the right-hand side of the formula, the part of the formula containing the covariance, that represents the key to how diversification works to reduce risk. As we have said, the covariance term may be positive, negative, or zero depending upon the correlation between the assets. To show the effect of covariance on portfolio risk, it is helpful to analyze three situations: (1) the highest possible covariance, (2) the lowest possible covariance, and (3) any covariance between the highest and lowest.

Figure 7.6 plots the standard deviations and mean returns of two assets given by asset X and asset Y. Asset Y has a higher expected return and higher standard deviation compared with asset X. The lines connecting points X and Y represent possible portfolios that can be formed using assets X and Y in various proportions or weights. For example, points closest to X represent portfolios comprised almost entirely of asset X, while points closest to Y represent portfolios comprised almost entirely of asset Y.

Perfect Positive Correlation. Given the relationship between the covariance and the correlation coefficient, the highest possible covariance occurs when the assets' correlation coefficient rests at the upper limit, that of positive one. This is called perfect positive correlation.

The dotted line between points X and Y on Figure 7.6 plots the possible standard deviations and mean returns achievable by combining asset X and asset Y under perfect positive correlation. Notice that the dotted line is simply a straight line between the two assets. A straight line means that portfolio risk is a weighted average of the individual risks. This illustrates that there are no benefits to diversification when perfectly correlated assets are combined. The intuition is that diversification occurs when the risks of unusual returns of assets tend to cancel each other out. In the case of perfect positive correlation this never happens because the assets always move in the same direction.

Perfect Negative Correlation. Given the relationship between the covariance and the correlation coefficient, the lowest possible covariance occurs when the assets' correlation coefficient rests at the lower limit, that of negative one. This is called perfect negative correlation.

FIGURE 7.6
Diversification Among Two Assets

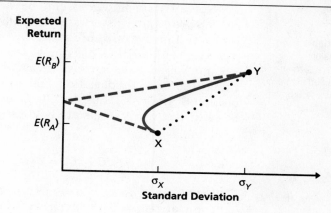

The dashed line connecting points X and Y on Figure 7.6 plot the possible standard deviations and mean returns that would be achieved by combining asset X and asset Y under perfect negative correlation. Notice that the line between X and Y moves directly to the vertical axis, or the point at which the standard deviation is zero. This illustrates "ultimate" diversification—where two assets always move in opposite directions; therefore combining them into a portfolio results in rapid risk reduction, or even total risk reduction![2]

Correlation Between the Extremes.   The final possibility is represented by the solid line in Figure 7.6. This is the more realistic situation in which the assets are neither perfectly positively or perfectly negatively correlated, but instead have some degree of independent movement. The solid line in Figure 7.6 best depicts the situations in this text involving portfolios of stocks or real assets. The solid line is curved in nature, illustrating that combining risky assets into a portfolio produces some degree of diversification as long as these assets are not perfectly positively correlated. However, the line will not touch the vertical axis and therefore will not completely eliminate risk.

Measuring Portfolio Risk with Diversification

The key point to diversification and risk is that when risky assets are combined into a portfolio, a portion of the portfolio's risk is diversified away. The risk that can be removed through diversification is called

---

2. Holding assets in inverse proportions to their standard deviations will result in total risk elimination.

diversifiable risk
The risk that can be removed through diversification.

nondiversifiable risk
The risk remaining even after assets are combined in a well-diversified portfolio. Also known as systematic risk or market risk.

diversifiable risk. Diversifiable risk should be viewed as harmless in the sense that it can be removed by combining assets together.

Not all risk, however, can be diversified away. The risk that remains even after assets are combined in a well-diversified portfolio is called **nondiversifiable risk.** We will see in the next chapter that nondiversifiable risk is also known as systematic risk or market risk.

In Chapter 8, a new risk measure entitled beta is demonstrated. Unlike the standard deviation, beta measures only the nondiversifiable portion of the risk. Thus, beta focuses on only the risk that needs to be rewarded when assets are held as part of a portfolio.

SUMMARY

☐ Risk is variation in value in financial outcomes. People do not want financial risk because their declining marginal utility causes the potential unhappiness from losses to outweigh the potential happiness from gains. Because of this risk aversion, people require higher expected return on assets with greater risk.

☐ Statistics provides several useful tools for analyzing risk, including the mean, standard deviation, variance, and covariance. The expected return of a portfolio is a weighted average of the expected returns of the assets in a portfolio.

☐ The standard deviation of a portfolio is found using the variances, covariances, and weights of the assets in the portfolio. The standard deviation of a portfolio depends upon the covariances between the assets in the portfolio—in other words, the tendency of the assets to move in the same or opposite directions.

☐ When assets that are to some degree uncorrelated are put together in a portfolio, there will be a reduction in the portfolio risk. This reduction is due to diversification. Thus, in situations where different assets are less than perfectly correlated, diversification will reduce some risk and some risk will remain. The risk that is diversified away is entitled diversifiable risk, and the risk remaining is entitled nondiversifiable risk, systematic risk, or market risk.

☐ Beta is a measure of nondiversifiable risk, also known as market risk or systematic risk.

REFERENCES

Bernouilli, D. *Econometrica* 22 (January 1954): 23–36.

Markowitz, H. M. *Portfolio Selection, Efficient Diversification, and Investments.* New York: John Wiley, 1959.

DEMONSTRATION PROBLEMS

Problem 1   The Mom and Pop Grocery Store is incorporated and has shares of stock that are now worth $10 per share. A financial analysis of the store indicates four equally likely states or outcomes:

State	Probability	Share Price	Dividend
Struggling	0.25	$ 5	$0
Status Quo	0.25	$10	$0
Slow Growth	0.25	$12	$0
Good Times	0.25	$14	$1

Compute the mean, standard deviation, and variance of the returns of the common stock of Mom and Pop Grocery Store Corporation.

Solution to Problem 1

The solution is found by first computing the returns for the stock under each outcome or state and then plugging the returns (and their probabilities) into the tables or formulae given in the chapter. We will illustrate the table method since it is clearer.

Step 1: Convert the performance of the stock in each state to a return using the formula for common stock return given in Window 7.1. The four returns are computed as:

Struggling Return	= [$0 + $ 5 − $10] / $10 =	−0.50 or −50%
Status Quo Return	= [$0 + $10 − $10] / $10 =	0.00 or 0%
Slow Growth Return	= [$0 + $12 − $10] / $10 =	0.20 or 20%
Good Times Return	= [$1 + $14 − $10] / $10 =	0.50 or 50%

Step 2: Plug the returns and probabilities into the table given in the chapter as a guide for computing statistics (Table 7.2 will do well):

	(1)	*(2)*	*(3)*	*(4)*	*(5)*	*(6)*
			Weighted	*Return*	*Squared Return*	*Weighted Squared*
State	*Return*	*Probability*	*Return*	*Deviation*	*Deviation*	*Deviation*
Struggling	−0.50	0.25				
Status Quo	0.00	0.25				
Slow Growth	0.20	0.25				
Good Times	0.50	0.25				

Step 3: Compute the mean return, which is found by multiplying each entry in column 1 by the corresponding entry in column 2, and fill in column 3. The mean is entered at the bottom of column 3 as the sum of all the entries in column 3:

State	(1) Return	(2) Probability	(3) Weighted Return	(4) Return Deviation	(5) Squared Return Deviation	(6) Weighted Squared Deviation
Struggling	−0.50	0.25	−0.125			
Status Quo	0.00	0.25	0.000			
Slow Growth	0.20	0.25	0.050			
Good Times	0.50	0.25	0.125			
			Mean = 0.050 or 5%			

Step 4: Fill in the remaining columns of the table. Column 4 is found by subtracting the mean (0.05) from column 1. Column 5 is found by squaring column 4. Column 6 is found by multiplying column 5 by column 2.

State	(1) Return	(2) Probability	(3) Weighted Return	(4) Return Deviation	(5) Squared Return Deviation	(6) Weighted Squared Deviation
Struggling	−0.50	0.25	−0.125	−0.55	.3025	.075625
Status Quo	0.00	0.25	0.000	−0.05	.0025	.000625
Slow Growth	0.20	0.25	0.050	0.15	.0225	.005625
Good Times	0.50	0.25	0.125	0.45	.2025	.005625
			Mean = 0.050 or 5%			

Step 5: Compute the variance by summing all of the numbers in column 6. The sum is 0.1325.

Step 6: Compute the standard deviation by taking the square root of the variance found in step 5, which is 0.364.

Final Solution: The mean is 0.05 or 5%, the variance is 0.1325, and the standard deviation is 0.364. The table method is simply a way of "walking through" the formulas. The answers may also be found using a statistical calculator. ◄┘

Problem 2   SuperStore, Inc., is considering the purchase of two supermarkets at opposite ends of the town of Lehigh, Pennsylvania. The south store has an expected return of 0.12 and a variance of 0.0900, the north store has an expected return of 0.14 and a variance of 0.0625 and together they have a covariance of −0.0500. Compute the expected return (mean) and variance of the portfolio of returns found with $6,000,000 invested in the south store and $4,000,000 invested in the north store.

Solution to Problem 2

The mean or expected return can be found using Formula (7.7), and the variance can be found using Formula (7.10). Both equations require us to begin by computing the portfolio weights.

Step 1: Compute the portfolio weights by finding the percentage of the portfolio invested in each investment. Formula (7.5) provides the method:

Weight in South Store = $6,000,000 / [$6,000,000 + $4,000,000] = 0.60

Weight in North Store = $4,000,000 / [$6,000,000 + $4,000,000] = 0.40

Step 2: Compute the portfolio mean or expected return by plugging the weights and the expected returns into Formula (7.7):

$$E(R_p) = (0.60 * 0.12) + (0.40 * 0.14) = 0.072 + 0.056$$
$$= 0.128 \text{ or } 12.8\%$$

Step 3: Compute the variance by plugging the weights, variances, and covariances into Formula (7.10):

Portfolio Variance = $(0.6^2 * 0.09) + (0.4^2 * 0.0625)$

$$+ (2 * 0.6 * 0.4 * -0.05)$$

Portfolio Variance = $0.0324 + 0.0100 + -0.024$

Portfolio Variance = 0.0184.

Final Solution: The expected return of 12.8% lies in between the expected returns of the individual stores. However, the variance of the combination (0.0184) is much less than the variance of either of the individual stores, because of the very negative covariance between the individual stores and the resulting diversification. ↵

REVIEW QUESTIONS

1. Provide a definition of uncertainty using as an example the investment in a stock.
2. Do all securities contain risk? Provide an example of a security that contains risk as well as one that does not.
3. How do risk-averse investors behave when making investment decisions?
4. Describe declining marginal utility in the context of risk-averse behavior.
5. What does the standard deviation measure?
6. Why might the standard deviation be a flawed measure of risk?
7. The expected return of a portfolio is a weighted average of the portfolio's constituent securities. Is the same true for the standard deviation of the portfolio? Why or why not?

8. Explain why diversification reduces risk in a portfolio. Use as an example a portfolio made up of a sunglasses company and an umbrella company.
9. What does it mean when assets are perfectly positively correlated? How well does diversification work in this case?

PROBLEMS

1. Consider the following alternatives, all of which offer some chance of receiving one dollar at some time in the future:
   A. A safe dollar soon
   B. A risky dollar soon
   C. A safe dollar far into the future
   D. A risky dollar far into the future
   a. Which alternative is generally most valuable?
   b. Which alternative is generally least valuable?
2. Suppose that Olive Oil Corporation offered jobs working on an oil platform out in the ocean for $100,000 per year (with no vacations). The jobs are safe but very boring.
   a. How many years do you think that a typical person would work on the oil platform? Why would they stop?
   b. How many years do you think that a person would work on the oil platform after they won a million-dollar lottery? Why?
3. Melissa has been asked to report the amount of enjoyment that she receives from various levels of wealth. She reports her happiness in utils.

Wealth Level	Happiness in Utils
$100,000	10 utils
$200,000	40 utils
$300,000	50 utils
$400,000	56 utils
$500,000	61 utils

When Melissa's wealth is at risk, her happiness is equal to the expected number of utils. Thus, if she has a 50 percent chance of having $100,000 and a 50 percent chance of $200,000, her happiness is measured by multiplying the corresponding number of utils by each probability and summing them: [(50% × 10) + (50% × 40)] = 25 utils.

Suppose Melissa is offered an investment that has a 60% chance of giving her a profit of $100,000 and a 40% chance of causing a $100,000 loss.
   a. If Melissa currently has $200,000, will she accept the risk? (Hint: Compare her current utils with the expected utils of taking the risk.)
   b. If Melissa currently has $300,000, will she take the risk?

   c. If Melissa currently has $400,000, will she take the risk?

   d. What is the logical reason that Melissa would refuse the risk at some levels of wealth and accept it at others?

4. Abbott Corporation stock sells for $20 per share and Costello Corporation stock sells for $10 per share. Compute the separate returns for the two stocks in each year:

   a. Each stock rises by $4 in year 1.

   b. Each stock falls by $2 in year 2. (Hint: The starting value for year 2 is the ending value from year 1.)

   c. Each stock rises $1 in price and pays a dividend (cash payment) of $1 in year 3.

5. The returns on shares of Lewis Corporation and Martin Corporation are predicted under various economic conditions as follows:

State of Economy	Return on Lewis	Return on Martin
Recession	−10%	−15%
Normal	+5%	+10%
Boom	+35%	+41%

   a. If each economic state has the same probability of occurring, what are the expected returns of each stock?

   b. If the economic outlook improves and the probability of a recession drops to 10%, the probability of normal growth drops to 30%, and the probability of a boom rises to 60%, what are the expected returns of each stock?

6. The returns on shares of Laverne Corporation and Shirley Corporation are predicted under various economic conditions as follows:

State of Economy	Return on Laverne	Return on Shirley
Recession	−20%	−30%
Stagnant	0%	−5%
Moderate Growth	+10%	+10%
Boom	+30%	+65%

Each economic state has a 25% probability of occurring.

   a. What are the expected returns of each stock?

   b. What are the variances of each stock?

   c. What are the standard deviations of each stock?

7. The returns on shares of Ernie Corporation and Bert Corporation are predicted under various economic conditions as follows:

State of Economy	Return on Ernie	Return on Bert
Recession	−5%	−10%
Normal	+0%	+20%
Boom	+25%	+50%

There is a 50% chance of a moderate state and a 25% chance each for a recession and a boom.

a. What are the expected returns of each stock?

b. What are the variances of each stock?

c. What are the standard deviations of each stock?

8. The prices and dividends on shares of Rowan Corporation and Martin Corporation are predicted under various economic conditions as follows:

State of Economy	Probability of State	Rowan Corp. Price	Rowan Corp. Dividend	Martin Corp. Price	Martin Corp. Dividend
Recession	20%	$ 8	$0	$38	$0
Stagnant	30%	$10	$0	$48	$2
Moderate	40%	$12	$0	$63	$2
Boom	10%	$15	$1	$82	$3

The current price of Rowan Corp. is $10.

The current price of Martin Corp. is $50.

a. Compute the returns for each stock in each state.

b. What are the expected returns of each stock?

c. What are the variances of each stock?

d. What are the standard deviations of each stock?

9. The returns on shares of George Corporation and Gracie Corporation are predicted under various economic conditions as follows:

State of Economy	Return on George	Return on Gracie
Recession	-10%	-30%
Moderate Growth	+10%	+10%
Boom	+30%	+65%

Each economic state has an equal probability of occurring.

a. What are the expected returns of each stock?

b. What is the covariance between the stocks?

10. The returns on shares of Jimmy Corporation and Walter Corporation are predicted under various economic conditions as follows:

State of Economy	Return on Jimmy	Return on Walter
Recession	-20%	+40%
Boom	+30%	-20%

There is a 60% chance of a boom and a 40% chance of a recession.

a. What are the expected returns of each stock?

b. What is the covariance between the stocks?

11. Various attributes of three stocks are listed:

	Larry Corp.	*Curley Corp.*	*Moe Corp.*
Price	$20	$20	$40
Expected Return	18%	15%	12%
Variances	.10	.05	.04

The covariance between Larry Corp. and Curley Corp. is 0.03, between Larry Corp. and Moe Corp. is −0.01, and between Curley Corp. and Moe Corp. is −0.01.

a. What would be the weights of a portfolio consisting of 100 shares of each stock?

b. What would be the expected return and variance of a portfolio consisting of 50% Larry Corp. and 50% Curley Corp.?

c. What would be the expected return and variance of a portfolio consisting of 25% Curley Corp. and 75% Moe Corp.?

d. What would be the expected return and variance of a portfolio consisting of 50% Curley Corp. and 50% Moe Corp.?

12. Identify the true statements and the false statements.

a. The popularity of lotteries, casino gambling, and sports betting proves that risky securities are preferred by most investors even when they do not offer a higher return than safe securities.

b. The underlying cause of risk aversion is declining marginal utility.

c. Declining marginal utility proves that money is less important to rich people than to poor people.

d. Risky assets must offer lower expected returns than safe assets in a competitive market.

e. The expected return of a portfolio is the weighted average of the expected returns of the assets in the portfolio.

f. The variance of a portfolio is the weighted average of the variances of the assets in the portfolio.

g. The risk reduction attained through the diversification of a portfolio depends upon the covariances between the assets within the portfolio.

h. If enough securities are added to a portfolio, all risk can be diversified away.

13. Suppose a portfolio has two assets. Asset 1 has a standard deviation of 0.0 and an expected return of 8%. Asset 2 has a standard deviation of 0.22 and an expected return of 18%. The covariance between them is 0.0, since asset 1 has a standard deviation of 0.0. Compute the expected return and standard deviation of a portfolio consisting of:

a. 25% asset 1 and 75% asset 2.

b. 50% asset 1 and 50% asset 2.

c. 75% asset 1 and 25% asset 2.

d. 100% asset 1 and 0% asset 2.

DISCUSSION QUESTIONS

1. Casino games are designed such that the "house" has an advantage over the player. Another way of saying this is that from the player's perspective, the expected return on casino gambling is negative. Casinos are jam-packed every day with willing investors. This is proof that the assumption that individuals are risk-averse is false. Discuss.

2. Since casino gambling can be very risky for gamblers, isn't it also very risky for the casino? Explain.

3. Because diversification works best for assets that are negatively correlated, we should see most investors holding negatively correlated assets in their portfolios. Do you agree?

4. How does the saying "Don't put all your eggs in one basket" relate to this chapter?

5. Consider the St. Petersburg paradox posed by Bernouilli:

   There is a game in which one player flips a fair coin. If the coin reveals heads, the "house" (the person who sets up the gamble) will pay the player $2, and the game is over. If the coin reveals tails, it is tossed again. If the second toss reveals heads, the house pays ($2)^2 to the player and the game is over. If the second toss reveals tails, the coin is flipped again. The game then continues until the first heads appears, and at that time the house pays the player the amount ($2)^n, where n is the number of tosses required to reveal tails.

   a. What is the expected payoff of this game? (Hint: Find the probability of each outcome and multiply this probability by the payoff. The sum of the probabilities times the payoffs is the expected payoff of the game.)

   b. As a player, how much would you pay to play this game?

   c. How can the difference in the answers to (a) and (b) be explained?

Chapter 8

The Capital Asset Pricing Model

The news was quickly spreading around the annual shareholder meeting. It seems that the company's chief financial officer was found to have authorized large investments over the past 15 years that had never paid back a nickel. Further, it was determined that these investments had a 1-in-1000 chance of returning millions of dollars, and a 999-in-1000 chance of returning nothing. One shareholder summed up the mood when he said, "How could this possibly have been a good use of our funds?"

Most concluded that the CFO was speculating with shareholder money. Many likened the characteristics of this investment to that of buying lottery tickets—an investment with an extremely large payoff in one particular state of nature but with a very low probability of receiving such a payoff. However, the conclusion that the CFO was speculating couldn't have been further from the truth. The "investment" turned out to be a fire insurance policy on the firm's headquarters. The insurance offered a large cash payment in the unlikely event of a fire, but because the policy offered a large cash inflow at precisely the time of a large cash outflow to the firm, the fire insurance investment had the effect of decreasing aggregate firm risk.

This example illustrates that the net result of an investment or expenditure on the total risk of the firm cannot be ascertained by looking only at the investment in isolation. The investment in the fire insurance policy seemed to have high risk and yet the investment reduced the total risk of the firm. Proper risk analysis requires a more sophisticated look at risk than simply measuring the variance of the cash flows of an individual investment.

This chapter continues our introduction to risk and builds on the main result of Chapter 7—that total risk can be separated into a diversifiable part and a nondiversifiable part. Diversifiable risk is the portion of risk that disappears as assets are combined in a portfolio.

Nondiversifiable risk is the risk of a portfolio remaining after all possible diversifiable risk is removed.

Chapter 8 will discuss and illustrate a measure of nondiversifiable risk called beta. Finally, beta will be used to accomplish the major objective of risk analysis—to determine how risk can be properly incorporated into investment, financing, and working capital management decisions.

PORTFOLIO MANAGEMENT THEORY

portfolio management theory
A theory describing how and why portfolio managers reduce risk.

Portfolio management theory describes how and why portfolio managers reduce risk. Financial managers use portfolio management theory to make decisions in a risky environment. But to understand how risk enters these decisions we need to know how investors in general—and the stockholders of the firm in particular—view risk.

The Markowitz Model: Risky Assets Only

The pioneering work of Markowitz (1952) determined that investors hold a variety of assets in a portfolio with the objective of diversifying away as much risk as possible. Markowitz extended the statistics of Chapter 7 to develop a portfolio management model, and he demonstrated that investors choose assets in such a way that the risk of those assets matches the investor's level of risk aversion.

In the Markowitz framework, highly risk-averse people, sometimes referred to as widows and orphans, would generally invest all of their money in relatively low-risk, high-quality assets. At the other end of the investment risk spectrum, less risk-averse people would generally accept high levels of risk by investing in lower quality assets.

A Graphical Illustration. The Markowitz model is illustrated in Figure 8.1. The shaded area represents all possible portfolios that investors can form. In other words, all possible or feasible portfolios are shown somewhere within the shaded region. But which portfolio will they hold?

The answer to this question depends, in part, upon the preferences of investors. But there are some portfolios within this shaded region that no rational investor would hold. For example, consider in Figure 8.1 the choice between portfolio A and portfolio Z. Investors will always prefer portfolio A to portfolio Z because portfolio A promises a higher expected return and has the same amount of risk. Now consider the choice between portfolio A and portfolio Y. Investors will always prefer portfolio A to Y because A carries less risk than Y but promises the same amount of expected return.

Extending these examples of choosing between two portfolios based upon return and risk leaves only those portfolios on the dotted

FIGURE 8.1
The Frontier of Risky Portfolios

Asset A dominates assets Y and Z. Assets A and B are on the efficient frontier.

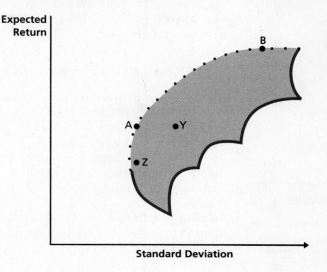

line in Figure 8.1, which represent those diversified portfolios offering the highest return for a given level of risk or the lowest risk for a given level of return. Given the millions of choices represented in Figure 8.1, only those portfolios that lie on the dotted line will be desired by investors. The dotted line is known as the **frontier of risky portfolios.**

frontier of risky portfolios
Portfolios of risky assets offering the highest return for a given level of risk, or the lowest risk for a given level of return.

Risk Preferences. In the Markowitz framework, investors with different levels of risk aversion hold different portfolios along the frontier. For example, in Figure 8.1, highly risk-averse investors might end up holding portfolio A, while investors more tolerant of risk might end up with portfolio B. The risk-versus-return tradeoff is different at each point along the dotted line in Figure 8.1. Therefore, each investor perceives a potentially different expected change in return for a given change in risk since the slope of the dotted line changes.

Corporate Financial Decisions. The main result in the Markowitz framework is that the particular portfolio of risky assets held by the investor depends upon the investor's risk preference. This framework, however, presents a problem for corporate managers who must make decisions for shareholders with differing levels of risk aversion. Whose risk tastes should the manager satisfy when choosing among different investments? Unfortunately, there is no definitive answer to this question in the Markowitz framework.

For example, a particular project might be considered a great opportunity by the firm's high-risk shareholders, but too risky by the firm's low-risk shareholders. And even if shareholders were originally attracted to firms with particular risk strategies, a problem would occur if the firm uncovered a great opportunity that only the particular firm could exploit, but which had the wrong level of risk for most of its shareholders.

An Alternative Framework: Risky and Risk-Free Assets

The solution to the financial manager's dilemma in using the Markowitz model was provided through a slightly different framework introduced by James Tobin (1965). Tobin noted that portfolios could comprise risk-free assets as well as risky assets. We define a risk-free asset as a short-term, fixed income security with little or no risk of default. The ideal example would be a U.S. Treasury bill as detailed in Chapter 4 in Window 4.1.

capital asset pricing model (CAPM)
A model specifying the relationship between risk and expected return. In the *CAPM* model, the only risk that matters is nondiversifiable risk, also known as systematic risk or market risk, which is the variation in the asset's return that is correlated with the market.

Adding the Risk-Free Asset. Combining risk-free and risky investments simplifies the relationship between risk and expected return. This is illustrated in Figure 8.2, where we show the effect of combining a risk-free asset with risky portfolio A. Note that the risk-free asset is on the vertical axis because its risk, measured by its standard deviation, is zero. The line between the risk-free asset and any risky asset is a straight line, since no diversification takes place.

This new relationship between risk and return is known as the **capital asset pricing model (CAPM)**. According to the *CAPM* rela-

FIGURE 8.2
Combining the Risk-Free Asset with Risky Portfolios

Adding the risk-free rate to the frontier of risky assets alters the relationship between expected return and risk.

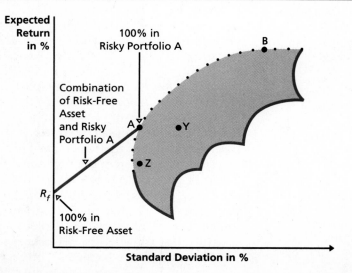

tionship, investors no longer choose only between the risky portfolios along the dotted line, but instead choose how much money to put into risk-free assets and how much to put into risky assets. Points on the solid line near risky portfolio A represent portfolios with most of the money placed in portfolio A. Points in the middle tend to represent a balance between the risk-free asset and the risky portfolio A.

Adjusting for Risk in a CAPM Framework.   How do investors adjust for risk in a *CAPM* framework of risky and risk-free portfolios? The answer is different from that utilizing the Markowitz model, where investors searched for the particular portfolio of risky assets that matched their risk preferences. In the *CAPM* framework, investors adjust the risk in their portfolio by adjusting the percentages of their portfolio held in risky assets versus the risk-free asset.

According to the *CAPM*, the decision of how much money to put in risky assets and how much to put in the risk-free asset is the most important decision investors make regarding risk. This decision is usually called the **asset allocation decision.** For example, low-risk investors typically reduce their risk exposure by placing a limited portion of their money in risky assets and most of their money in the risk-free asset. Although some investors may try to adjust the level of risk by investing primarily in certain types of risky assets, the vast majority of money invested in U.S. capital markets is invested while making use of the risky-versus-riskless-asset decision as the primary risk-management tool.

The Market Portfolio

In the *CAPM* relationship, investors adjust risk by choosing among risky assets and the risk-free asset. But which risky assets? From the millions of risky assets in Figure 8.1, our objective is to see why one portfolio exists that will satisfy the tastes of all investors. This unique portfolio is called the **market portfolio.**

We already know that most of these risky portfolios can be eliminated from contention because they are clearly inferior to other risky portfolios. This led us to consider only those risky portfolios along the frontier represented by the dotted line in Figure 8.1. However, given the availability of the risk-free asset, we know from Figure 8.2 that risk-versus-return opportunities are given by a straight line. Hundreds of straight lines could be drawn, each combining the risk-free asset with one of the risky portfolios along the dotted line. The key is to find which risky portfolio (and therefore which straight line) is best for investors. This is illustrated in Figure 8.3.

Using Figure 8.3, the choice of a particular risky portfolio is a matter of which straight line is best. Said differently, the investor must decide which line offers the best combination of risk and return. We

---

asset allocation decision
The decision as to how much money to put in risky assets and how much to put in risk-free assets. According to the *CAPM* model, the asset allocation decision is the most important decision investors make in terms of risk.

market portfolio
The unique portfolio of risky assets along the efficient frontier that satisfies the tastes of all investors.

Investors must now choose in which portfolio of risky assets to invest.

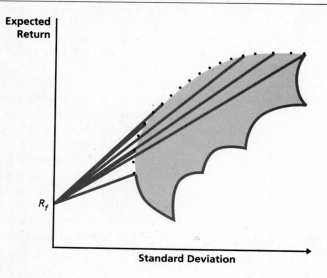

capital market line
The particular combination of the risk-free asset and the diversified portfolio of risky assets offering the highest slope.

see that one line is best in the sense that it offers the highest expected return for a given level of risk. This unique line is known as the **capital market line** and is shown again in Figure 8.4. The particular risky portfolio along the capital market line is given the name portfolio M, which stands for the market portfolio. As we have said, the

FIGURE 8.4
The Market Portfolio

The market portfolio is the portfolio of risky assets that offers the best choice among all risky portfolios.

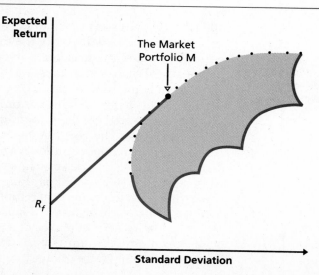

market portfolio is defined as the portfolio that includes all risky assets.

How did we know that this portfolio must be the market portfolio? Since every investor is striving for the same goal—the highest return for bearing risk—and since every investor is competing to purchase the same assets, we can deduce that portfolio M must be comprised of all risky assets, or the market portfolio.

Each asset in the market portfolio is held in proportion of its total value relative to the total of the values of all tradeable risky assets combined. For example, if the stock of General Motors Corporation is one percent of all risky assets, then the market portfolio will be made up of one percent General Motors stock. The market portfolio is therefore made up of all risky assets held by all investors. More on the market portfolio is provided in Window 8.1.

Summary and Illustration of Risk

The key result of the *CAPM* framework is that there are two potential types of risk within the total risk of an asset, (1) diversifiable risk, which is the variation in an asset's return that has no correlation with the overall market, and (2) nondiversifiable risk, also known as systematic risk or market risk, which is the variation in the asset's return that is correlated with the market. We end this section with an illustration of this important concept.

Example 8.1 ——————— Suppose that an investor is considering the purchase of a very small grocery or convenience store. What are the risks this investor faces? What are the most serious risks and the less serious ones? Take a moment before proceeding and try to come up with a brief ranking of these risks.

Of course to some extent these answers are subjective and would depend upon specific circumstances, but here is our list:

1. The risk that another food store will open nearby.
2. The risk of poor management, fire, theft (customer or employee), storm, or other disaster.
3. The risk of a serious loss of traffic due to a new highway, a detour, a bridge in repair, and so forth.
4. The risk that the local neighborhood will decline in population, income, or tendency to use "convenience" stores.
5. The risk that the overall economy will slide into a serious recession.

Perhaps your list contains other risks or has them in different order. However, we hope that you agree with this impor-

Window 8.1

The Market Portfolio

Our development of the market portfolio relied on both theory, or the way in which diversification reduces risk, and reasoning, or the way in which investors will search for the highest return given a level of risk. But does the market portfolio exist in the real world? While we would not expect every investor to hold the market portfolio, there are several reasons to believe that the overall market portfolio is the key portfolio for most investors.

First, it seems reasonable to believe that if all investors are striving to diversify away as much risk as possible, then they will use all available assets. Second, since all investors will be driven by the same instincts, such as their desire for high returns and their aversion to risk, each risky asset must adjust in price through supply and demand forces such that it is included in the portfolio. If a risky asset were priced too high, no one would demand it and its price would fall. Conversely, if it were underpriced the demand would exceed the supply and the price would be driven upward.

Suppose, then, that you wanted to invest in the market portfolio. Can this be done? The answer is that you can get close enough in most circumstances. If you define the market portfolio in its strictest sense to include all tradable assets, such as all stocks, all bonds, all precious metals, all real estate, all art, and all other valued assets, then the answer is probably no. A portfolio that includes everything does not exist.

If, however, you define the market portfolio to include a representative sampling of common stocks, then the answer is yes. Large diversified common stock portfolios do exist. Three popular hypothetical portfolios that attempt to replicate the entire stock market are:

(continued on next page)

tant point: Most of the major risks a convenience store faces are not related to the overall economy of the nation, or the world. In fact, if we were to guess, we would estimate that only a few percentage points of the store's overall risk could be attributed to the systematic movements of national or world economies. This means that most of the major risks are diversifiable.

Now let's consider an investor who is considering purchasing stock in a corporation owning thousands of conve-

Window 8.1 *(continued)*

The S&P 500 Index: An index including 500 widely held common stocks. Stocks held in the S&P 500 are value weighted, such that the larger the firm, the larger its representation in the index.

The Nasdaq Composite Index: An index of stocks that trade over-the-counter (OTC). These stocks tend to be smaller than those included in the S&P 500 index. This index is also value weighted.

The Wilshire 5,000 Index: The broadest of all stock indices, the Wilshire index is made up of 5,000 different securities, including all New York Stock Exchange and American Stock Exchange stocks, and most OTC stocks.

Other popular indices include international stock portfolios. One important fact concerning all of these indices is that they correlate highly with one another, providing some proof that they are all attaining the same goal—a portfolio that behaves as if it contained all assets. Investment companies set up mutual funds that replicate these indices so that even small investors can invest in a representative portion of the market portfolio at low cost.

Finally, you may be surprised that the foregoing discussion did not include the most popular of all indices, the Dow Jones Industrial Average. The reason it was not included is that it is an index of only 30 industrial firms. However, even with its limited sample, studies have shown that the Dow index correlates highly with the larger indices, suggesting that most of the benefits of diversification can be achieved through a small number of holdings.

nience stores throughout the world. What would be the risks that this investor would face?

It seems clear that probably the number-one risk would be the risk of a nationwide recession. Perhaps other risks would include concerns about potentially poor management, or competition from another convenience store chain, or a major change in consumer attitudes regarding convenience stores. But what happened to the risks of lost traffic or disasters? The answer is that they were diversified away. Surely a chain of thousands of convenience stores will have a portion of their stores afflicted by such store-specific risks, but, on the other hand, a portion of their other stores will actually benefit by certain traffic pattern changes or as a result of disasters afflicting their nearest competitor.

A chain of thousands of stores will diversify most of the risks away, leaving primarily systematic risk. This illustrates diversification, or the grouping of assets to reduce risk. In the case of large corporations, not only do the corporations have hundreds or thousands of projects, whose diversifiable risks tend to vanish as the corporation is viewed as a whole, but the shareholders of the corporation can have tens or hundreds of different stocks in their portfolio—creating even more diversification. ◄┘

The vast majority of the shares of common stock in the United States is held in large and highly diversified portfolios such as pension funds, mutual funds, insurance companies, and endowments. Within these funds, the diversifiable risks of the individual stocks are completely removed. The systematic risk remains and is what concerns the investor. The owners of these stocks are most concerned with overall movements in the market. The required return of a common stock should not depend upon diversifiable risks but upon the only type of risk that will ultimately affect the returns of the diversified investor—systematic risk. The consequence of this reasoning is that diversifiable risk can be ignored.

✗ The required return of a common stock or on a project within a large publicly traded corporation should not depend upon diversifiable risks but upon the only type of risk that will ultimately affect the returns of the diversified investor—systematic risk.

The next section details how systematic risk can be measured.

BETA

beta
A measure of systematic risk, or risk that cannot be diversified away by forming portfolios. Specifically, beta is a measure of correlation with the overall market.

We have detailed the importance of systematic risk and the unimportance of diversifiable risk. Fortunately, there exists a rather remarkable measure of systematic risk, a measure called **beta.** A beta of zero means no systematic risk while a beta of one denotes the same level of systematic risk as the overall market. Given the beta of an asset, we may calculate the expected return of the asset by plugging the beta into the *CAPM* model:

$$CAPM: E(R_i) = R_f + \beta_i \, [E(R_m) - R_f], \tag{8.1}$$

where $E(R_i)$ is the expected return of asset i, R_f stands for the risk-free rate of return, β_i is the notation for the beta of asset i, and $E(R_m)$ is the expected return on the market portfolio. The proof of the *CAPM* is provided in the appendix to this chapter.

Scholars may debate whether the nondiversifiable risk can be captured using the single-risk measure of the *CAPM*, but the concept of pricing only nondiversifiable risk is well illustrated using the *CAPM*. More advanced models, such as the **arbitrage pricing theory,** discuss concepts that attempt to provide multiple risk measures for non-diversifiable risk.

Although the theory and development of the *CAPM* are rather complex, Formula (8.1) presents a simple relationship between risk and expected return.

arbitrage pricing theory
A model of risk and expected return that includes multiple measures of systematic risk.

Systematic Risk and Beta

Recall from Chapter 7 the statistical concept known as covariance, which was defined as a measure of correlation between two variables. The beta of a stock or of any other investment is defined by the covariance between the stock's returns and those of the market, divided by the variance of the market's return:

$$\beta_i = Cov\,(R_m, R_i)\,/\,Var\,(R_m), \qquad (8.2)$$

where *Cov* stands for covariance, *Var* stands for variance, i stands for an individual asset, and m stands for the market portfolio of all assets. From our notation used in Chapter 7, we can write the formula for beta as:

$$\beta_i = \sigma_{mi}\,/\,\sigma_m^2 \,.$$

The numerator of Formula (8.2) measures the amount of risk that an individual stock brings into an already diversified portfolio. The denominator represents the total risk of the market portfolio. Beta therefore measures systematic risk relative to the risk of the overall market. (The mathematics of computing both the covariance and variance have been fully covered in Chapter 7.) Window 8.2 provides an example of using these statistical measures to compute the beta for McDonald's Corporation.

There are several important features of beta. First, it can be easily interpreted. The beta of an asset may be viewed as the percentage return response that an asset will have on average to a percentage movement in the overall market. For example, if the market were to rise by one percent in response to certain news, a stock with a beta of 0.95 would be expected on average to rise 0.95 percent, and a stock with a beta of 2.00 would be expected to rise 2.00 percent. The risk-free asset has a beta of zero and therefore its return would not be

Window 8.2

Calculating Beta

This window details the calculation of beta, given in formula form as:

$$\beta_i = Cov(R_i, R_m) / Var(R_m).$$

We know that our calculation will require a covariance and a variance term. The most common procedure in estimating beta is to use what is known as the ex-post method of calculation. In the ex-post method, historical data are used to estimate various statistics. This contrasts with the method discussed in Chapter 7, which used states of nature and their associated probabilities to estimate the statistics. The ex-post method is commonly used when the number of potential states of nature is enormous, and the ability to attach probabilities to those states is difficult.

In our example, we will show how to estimate the beta for the McDonald's Corporation, or Stock MD for short. Our first step is to collect past data for Stock MD and for the market portfolio, or Stock m. We will use the S&P 500 as a proxy for the market portfolio. Our example will use nine years of past data, mostly for illustrative convenience. However, a better approach would be to use more data points measured over shorter intervals of time, say 60 monthly observations instead of nine annual observations.

The following worksheet provides the necessary calculations. These data are in decimal form, such that, for example, 10 percent is stated as 0.10.

(1)	(2) Return on McDonald's	(3) Return on Market	(4) McDonald's Deviation	(5) Market Deviation	(6) Market Deviation Squared	(7) Cross Product
Year	R_{MD}	R_m	$R_{MD} - \bar{R}_{MD}$	$R_m - \bar{R}_m$	$(R_m - \bar{R}_m)^2$	$(R_{MD} - \bar{R}_{MD})(R_m - \bar{R}_m)$
1977	−0.0388	−0.0392	−0.1113	−0.1153	0.0133	0.0128
1978	−0.1019	−0.0204	−0.1744	−0.0965	0.0093	0.0168
1979	−0.0620	0.0729	−0.1345	−0.0032	0.0000	0.0004
1980	0.1238	0.1553	0.0513	0.0792	0.0063	0.0041
1981	0.3411	0.0756	0.2686	−0.0005	0.0000	−0.0001
1982	−0.0765	−0.0625	−0.1490	−0.1386	0.0192	0.0207

(continued on next page)

Window 8.2 (continued)

(1) Year	(2) Return on McDonald's R_{MD}	(3) Return on Market R_m	(4) McDonald's Deviation $R_{MD}-\bar{R}_{MD}$	(5) Market Deviation $R_m-\bar{R}_m$	(6) Market Deviation Squared $(R_m-\bar{R}_m)^2$	(7) Cross Product $(R_{MD}-\bar{R}_{MD})(R_m-\bar{R}_m)$
1983	0.1676	0.3416	0.0951	0.2655	0.0705	0.0252
1984	−0.2677	0.0000	−0.3402	−0.0761	0.0058	0.0259
1985	0.5665	0.1615	0.4940	0.0854	0.0073	0.0422
Total					0.1317	0.1480
Average	0.0725	0.0761				

Columns 2 and 3 provide the annual returns over the nine-year period for McDonald's (stock MD) and for the market (stock M). In columns 4 and 5, each of the average or mean returns is subtracted from annual returns. For example, the value of −0.1113 in column 3 for 1977 is stock MD's return of −0.0388 less stock MD's average return of 0.0725. Column 6 squares each of the annual deviations of the market from its average return. Column 7 multiplies stock MD's annual deviation from its average with the market's annual deviation from its average (column 4 multiplied by column 5).

The covariance between McDonald's and the market is found by averaging column 7:

$$Cov(R_{MD}, R_m) = 0.1480 / 9 = 0.0164.$$

The variance of the market is found by averaging column 6:

$$Var(R_m) = 0.1317 / 9 = 0.0146.$$

The beta of McDonald's, from Formula (8.2), is:

$$Cov(R_{MD}, R_m) / Var(R_m) = 0.0164 / 0.0146 = 1.123$$

Now that we've taken you through this rather lengthy procedure, we should mention that an easier method exists. Students with some background in statistics might recall that the formula for beta is the same as the formula for the slope coefficient of a linear regression of the returns of the asset (as the y or dependent variable) against the returns of the overall market (as the x or independent variable). Programs exist that will easily perform such a regression and produce an estimate of beta.

TABLE 8.1
Estimated Betas of Well-Known Corporations

Corporation	Beta
American Express Corporation	1.35
Digital Equipment Company	1.30
Ford Motor Company	1.26
K mart	1.15
General Electric	1.09
Procter & Gamble	0.80
Anheuser Busch	0.58
Consolidated Edison	0.32

expected to change with movements in the overall market. The return on a portfolio with a beta of one would be expected to change in the same amount as the change in the overall market.[1]

Example 8.2 _____ Table 8.1 lists the estimated betas of some well-known corporations. The highest betas are of the American Express Company, the Ford Motor Company, and Digital Equipment. Companies with high betas have stock returns that are highly sensitive to market-wide factors such as general economic activity and interest rates. The lowest betas are of the Procter & Gamble Company, Anheuser Busch, and Consolidated Edison. Companies with low betas have stock returns that are less sensitive to market-wide factors. ↵

The second feature of beta is that it is the slope coefficient of a linear regression of the returns of the asset as the *y* or dependent variable against the returns of the overall market as the *x* or independent variable. For those familiar with the concept of linear regression, you now have another way to compute beta.

Third, the beta of a portfolio is a weighted average of the betas of the constituent assets. This is true even though the total risk of a portfolio is not the weighted average of the total risk of the constituent assets. Since beta measures only the systematic risk of an asset, and since the systematic risk does not diversify away as assets are combined into a portfolio, we can compute the portfolio beta as a weighted average:

$$\beta_p = \sum_{i=1}^{n} w_i \, \beta_i \,, \tag{8.3}$$

_____

1. Of course, the same concept can be extended for movements in the market of more than or less than one percent. For instance, if the market falls two percent, a stock with a beta of 1.5 would have an expected decline of three percent.

where β_p stands for the beta of the portfolio, w_i is the percentage of the portfolio invested in asset i, β_i is the beta of asset i, and n is the number of constituent assets in the portfolio. We will provide a proof of Formula (8.3) in the chapter appendix.

In summary, beta measures systematic risk. It is used in the *CAPM* to compute an estimate of the expected return for a risky asset. Beta is easy to compute, interpret, and use in portfolio management.

Using Beta to Calculate Expected Rates of Return

The purpose of this section is to demonstrate how the corporate manager can use Formula (8.1), called the *CAPM*, to make financial decisions:

$$E(R_i) = R_f + \beta_i \, [E(R_m) - R_f].$$

The *CAPM* relationship provides an estimate of the return that investors expect to earn on a stock or project with a particular beta.

Previous sections have detailed the importance of systematic risk and how it can be measured using beta. Later in this chapter we will detail how to calculate the beta of a project. For now, let's assume that we know the beta. Once you've measured an investment's beta, how much return should you demand for holding the asset?

The *CAPM* relationship is represented by the straight line in Figure 8.5. The name of this relationship is the security market line *(SML)* or simply the capital asset pricing model itself. Remember, Figure 8.5 is simply a graphical representation of Formula (8.1). From Figure 8.5 we see that R_f, or the risk-free rate, is the line's intercept,

FIGURE 8.5
The Security Market Line

The security market line provides a linear relationship between expected return and risk given by beta.

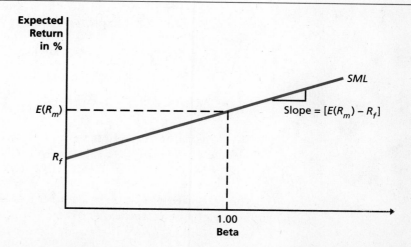

and the bracketed expression $[E(R_m) - R_f]$ is the line's slope. The beta for asset i determines where on the line the asset is placed.

There are three key points to the security market line. First, the expected return of an asset with a beta of zero is equal to the risk-free rate. The reason is that the risk-free asset also has a beta of zero and, from the law of conservation of value, competition will force assets of equal risk to offer the same expected return. Second, the expected return of an asset with a beta of one is equal to the expected return of the market as a whole. The reason is that, by definition, the beta of the market is one, and owing to competition all other assets with a beta of one must offer the same expected return. Third, all other combinations of betas and expected returns lie along a straight line between and beyond these two points. This is proven in the chapter appendix.

Example 8.3 _____ We can estimate the expected return of any risky asset by plugging its beta into Formula (8.1) along with an estimate of the risk-free rate and the expected return of the market. Let's illustrate the mechanics of using the *CAPM*. Consider two assets, A and B. Asset A has a beta of 0.7, and asset B has a beta of 1.0. The risk-free rate is 7 percent, and the return expected to be earned on the market portfolio is 15 percent. The *CAPM* provides an estimate of the expected return of the two assets:

$$E(R_A) = 7\% + 0.7\,[15\% - 7\%] = 12.6\%\,.$$
$$E(R_B) = 7\% + 1.0\,[15\% - 7\%] = 15.0\%\,.$$

It is no coincidence that asset B has a higher beta and a higher expected return. According to the *CAPM*, assets with higher betas offer higher expected returns when compared with assets with lower betas. This must be true because beta is our measure of risk and we know that higher risk must be rewarded with higher expected return in a world of risk-averse investors.

Now let's consider asset C, whose beta is 0.0. From Formula (8.1):

$$E(R_C) = 7\% + 0.0\,[15\% - 7\%] = 7.0\%\,.$$

This illustrates that assets without systematic risk (i.e., assets with betas of zero) have expected returns equal to the risk-free rate. ◄┘

The objective of Chapters 7 and 8 has been met. We now have a way of determining the expected return of any risky asset using its

Window 8.3

Solving for *CAPM* Variables

The *CAPM* presents a simple relationship between risk and return:

$$E(R_i) = R_f + \beta_i \, [E(R_m) - R_f]$$

The text illustrates that the *CAPM* can be used to estimate the return on an asset given three variables: (1) the risk-free rate of interest (R_f), (2) the expected return on the market portfolio $E(R_m)$, and (3) the asset's beta. For example, if the risk-free rate is 7 percent, the return on the market is 15 percent, and the asset's beta is 0.80, then the asset's return according to the *CAPM* is:

$$E(R_i) = 0.07 + 0.8[0.15 - 0.07] = 0.134.$$

This window demonstrates that through algebraic manipulation, the *CAPM* can be used to solve for the risk-free rate, the return on the market, and for beta, given an estimate of the asset's return:

$$R_f = \frac{E(R_i) - \beta_i * E(R_m)}{1 - \beta_i} \quad \text{so that } R_f = \frac{0.134 - (0.8 * 0.15)}{1 - 0.8} = 0.07.$$

$$\beta_i = \frac{E(R_i) - R_f}{E(R_m) - R_f} \quad \text{so that } \beta_i = \frac{0.134 - 0.07}{0.150 - 0.07} = 0.8.$$

$$E(R_m) = \frac{E(R_i) + R_f(\beta_i - 1)}{\beta_i} \quad \text{so that } E(R_m) = \frac{0.134 + 0.07(0.8 - 1)}{0.8} = 0.15.$$

beta, the expected return on the market portfolio, and the risk-free rate. Formula (8.1) is often the foundation for many homework and exam questions. The equation has four variables: (1) the expected return of a risky asset, (2) the risk-free rate, (3) the beta, and (4) the expected return on the market. In most *CAPM* problems, we are given any three of the variables and asked to solve for the fourth. Window 8.3 shows how to use the *CAPM* to solve for the risk-free rate, for the expected return on the market, and for beta. Students whose algebra is a little rusty should practice solving for all four possible missing values.

We have finished detailing the major aspects of the *CAPM*, and will now discuss some of its additional aspects and results. We conclude the chapter by showing specifically how the *CAPM* can be implemented for projects in the firm's capital budgeting decision.

The *CAPM* and Corporate Risk Management

You may recall that, in the Markowitz model, different investors had different risk-return preferences. Whose preferences should a corporate manager utilize when a firm has many heterogeneous shareholders?

According to the *CAPM*, because the security market line is a straight line, all investors will have the same risk-versus-return trade-off. This is true because the slope between risk and expected return is equal regardless of where on the line the investor decides to be. Thus the corporate financial manager now has no problem in understanding the risk aversion of the shareholders—they are all equally risk-averse. This leads us to an important concept called **separation,** meaning that corporate risk decisions can be separated from stock ownership. The following information will explain why the model looks the way it does.

separation
The notion that corporate risk decisions can be separated from the risk preferences of the individual stockholder.

Why All Securities Lie on the Security Market Line.   All securities lie on the security market line for two reasons. First, because of competition, investors are always looking for extra return without bearing added risk. The second reason is that since beta operates in a linear fashion, expected returns must be linear in beta. (We'll defer this proof to the chapter appendix.)

But what about the role of competition? Suppose that you have some cash and are planning to add a stock to your portfolio. You are torn between two stocks, A and B, but have enough money to invest in only one. Suppose, also, that when you compute the beta and expected return on each, and plot them on a risk-return graph, the risk-return tradeoff between the two stocks is as shown in Figure 8.6.

In deciding between stock A and stock B, you have an easy decision to make. Both A and B have the same beta and therefore would have exactly the same effect on the risk of your portfolio. Because stock B offers higher expected return, it is the obvious choice. Adding stock B to the portfolio will result in a higher expected return for the portfolio, as compared with adding stock A. You love a good deal, so you call your broker with an immediate request to purchase stock B.

Unfortunately, such dreams are unlikely to come true in competitive financial markets. The person intending to sell an asset would never sell stock B at a price that would mean giving up a superior return. There would therefore be pressure from buyers trying to buy

FIGURE 8.6
An Example of the Effects of Competition

Competitive forces will drive the expected return of A up to the *SML* as well as drive the expected return of B down to the *SML*.

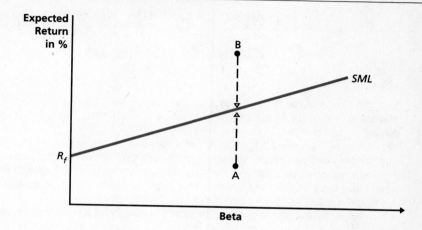

B rather than A, and from sellers refusing to sell B and trying to sell A. These pressures would combine to force the price of B up (and therefore its expected return down) and to force the price of A down (and therefore its expected return up). These pressures would force A and B to offer equal expected returns since they have equal systematic risk.

The lesson to be learned is that U.S. capital markets comprise thousands, even millions, of investors, all operating with similar information and all looking for good deals. In such markets, stocks with identical betas will offer identical expected returns. This will be true for any level of beta, so that the relationship between beta and expected return for all stocks will be a continuous relationship like that given by Figure 8.5. The result that the line is straight is proven in the appendix.

Our analysis, like the *CAPM*, assumes that there is ultimately one type of risk—systematic or market risk. The *CAPM* is also based on the assumption that all investors operate with similar information. We know that this is not true for all stocks in all cases, but we believe it is true for most cases and offer the following evidence: Since we know of no portfolio managers who can endlessly increase their expected returns without bearing additional risks, we conclude that assets with equal risks must offer equal returns.

THE *CAPM* AND CAPITAL BUDGETING

We are now ready to tackle the final objective of the chapter—using the *CAPM* to make optimal capital budgeting decisions. As discussed in Chapter 6, capital budgeting decisions are best made using the net

Window 8.4

Determining Project Betas

In order to estimate the beta of a project when past product prices cannot be observed, it is usually necessary to observe the publicly traded securities of a corporation with assets similar to the project.

Suppose, for example, that we are considering opening a brewery. We first find the market prices of securities of a publicly traded corporation whose primary asset is a brewery. Suppose we observe a brewery whose stock has a beta of 0.8 and debt with a beta of 0.1, where the beta of the debt is estimated in a fashion similar to the beta of a stock, as shown in Window 8.2.

We know that the value of the firm's assets must always equal the value of the firm's liabilities, plus the value of the firm's equity. This is a result of our fourth economic law, the law of conservation of value. The beta of the assets must therefore equal the combination of the betas of the stocks and bonds as shown in Formula (8.3):

$$\text{Beta of Assets} = [(\% \text{ Bonds}) \times \beta_b] + [(\% \text{ Stock}) \times \beta_s].$$

where β_b is the beta of the brewery's bonds, β_s is the beta of the brewery's stock, and % stands for the percentage of the firm's assets financed by bonds or stock. For example, if the brewery has one-third of its assets financed by bonds and two-thirds financed by stock, from the information given above:

$$\text{Beta of Assets} = [(1/3) \times 0.1] + [(2/3) \times 0.8] = 0.567$$

Thus, the beta of the project would be 0.567, estimated by observing the betas of securities of corporations with similar projects already in place.

present value (*NPV*) model, and therefore our discussion focuses on applying the *CAPM* to *NPV* analysis.

The previous sections have established the point that if the beta of a project is known, its expected return can be estimated using the *CAPM*. In this section we concentrate on how to estimate the project's beta. Once the beta of the project is estimated, we can use Formula (8.1), or the *CAPM*, to generate the project's expected rate of return. We can then use the estimate of the project's expected rate of return as the denominator in the *NPV* formula.

At this point, everything should be clear except how to estimate the beta of the project. It was shown in Window 8.2 that the beta of a stock can be calculated using a linear regression of the stock's returns on the market's returns. But for almost any project this would be impossible, since projects are not publicly traded with a track record of historical returns.

The standard method of finding the beta of a project is to find a publicly traded corporation whose overall assets have a level of risk similar to the project under consideration. For example, if the project involved a certain industry, then the objective would be to find a corporation with as much of its assets as possible in the same industry as the project under consideration.

The project's risk will be equal to the risk of the similar firm's assets (the risk of the firm's assets is found by combining the risks of all of its securities). This is detailed in Window 8.4.

Thus, the *CAPM* provides an equation that allows the capital budgeting decision to be made in a way whereby shareholder wealth can be maximized. Let's review the steps in this process. First, estimate the beta of the project using a methodology such as found in Window 8.4. Next, use the estimated beta, estimates of the risk-free rate, the expected return of the market, and the *CAPM* to estimate the required rate of return for the project. Finally, use the required rate of return as the discount rate in the computation of the project's *NPV*. The use of the *CAPM* for capital budgeting is more fully discussed in Chapter 15.

SUMMARY

☐ Risk comes in two varieties: diversifiable risk, which will vanish and therefore can be ignored in terms of required rates of returns, and systematic risk, which does not vanish.

☐ Beta is a measure of an asset's systematic risk and is calculated by:

$$\beta_i = Cov\ (R_m, R_i)\ /\ Var\ (R_m).$$

The numerator of beta's formula measures the amount of risk that an individual stock brings into an already diversified portfolio. The denominator represents the total risk of the market portfolio. Thus, beta measures the systematic risk of an asset in relation to the systematic risk of the market.

☐ Because the beta of the overall market is equal to one, assets with betas greater than one signify a level of systematic risk greater than the overall market, and assets with betas less than one signify a level of systematic risk less than the overall market.

◻ Given an asset's beta, we can use the *CAPM* to determine the asset's required rate of return:

$$E(R_i) = R_f + \beta_i \, [E(R_m) - R_f].$$

The *CAPM* should not be viewed as an extremely accurate and unquestioned method of finding this rate—rather it should be viewed as a good tool for separating risks into those that do and don't require rewards and for estimating the amount of return that the market requires for bearing a particular level of systematic risk.

REFERENCES

Lintner, J. "The Valuation of Risk Assets and the Selection of Risky Investments in Stock Portfolios and Capital Budgets." *Review of Economics and Statistics* 47 (February 1965): 13–37.

Markowitz, H. M. "Portfolio Selection." *Journal of Finance* 7 (March 1952): 77–91.

Sharpe, W. F. "Capital Asset Prices: A Theory of Market Equilibrium Under Conditions of Risk." *Journal of Finance* 19 (September 1964): 425–442.

Tobin, J. "Liquidity Preference as Behavior Toward Risk." *Review of Economic Studies* 25 (February 1965): 65–86.

DEMONSTRATION PROBLEMS

Problem 1   The common stock of SuperStore, Inc., has generated substantially different returns in the last five years. These returns are shown below, along with the corresponding returns for the stock market as a whole.

Year	SuperStore, Inc., Return	Market Return
1	0.12	0.30
2	0.40	0.15
3	−0.10	−0.15
4	−0.20	0.00
5	0.38	0.45

Compute the beta of the common stock of SuperStore, Inc., based upon these five years of returns.

Solution to Problem 1

The beta of an investment is equal to the covariance of the investment with the market divided by the variance of the market. These statistics are now computed using the table method demonstrated in Window 8.2.

Step 1: Form a table similar to that in Window 8.2 and fill in the returns that are given:

(1) Year	(2) Return on SuperStore	(3) Return on Market	(4) SuperStore Deviation	(5) Market Deviation	(6) Squared Market Deviation	(7) Cross Product
1	0.12	0.30				
2	0.40	0.15				
3	−0.10	−0.15				
4	−0.20	0.00				
5	0.38	0.45				

Step 2: Compute the average return for both column 2 and column 3 (separately) by summing the returns in each column and dividing by the number of years (5). Thus, the average return for column 2 (SuperStore) is found by dividing the sum of the returns (0.60) by 5, equaling 0.12. The average return of column 3, the market, is found by dividing the sum of the returns (0.75) by 5, equaling 0.15.

Step 3: Subtract each average return from each column to form columns 4 and 5. If you have done the math correctly (and if the problem doesn't involve unequal probabilities), the sum of the deviation columns should be zero. This is a convenient method for checking your math.

(1) Year	(2) Return on SuperStore	(3) Return on Market	(4) SuperStore Deviation	(5) Market Deviation	(6) Squared Market Deviation	(7) Cross Product
1	0.12	0.30	0.00	0.15		
2	0.40	0.15	0.28	0.00		
3	−0.10	−0.15	−0.22	−0.30		
4	−0.20	0.00	−0.32	−0.15		
5	0.38	0.45	0.26	0.30		
Average	0.12	0.15				

Step 4: Complete the entries for columns 6 and 7. Column 6 is found by squaring each entry in column 5. Column 7 is found by multiplying column 4 by column 5. All of the entries in column 6 must be greater than or equal to zero. However, be careful to make sure that the entries in column 7 have the correct sign. Finally, average columns 6

and 7 separately to form the variance of the market in column 6 and the covariance between the assets in column 7. These columns are averaged by summing them and then dividing by the number of entries (e.g., 0.2250 / 5 = 0.0450 for column 6).

(1)	(2)	(3)	(4)	(5)	(6)	(7)
					Squared	
	Return on	Return on	SuperStore	Market	Market	Cross
Year	SuperStore	Market	Deviation	Deviation	Deviation	Product
1	0.12	0.30	0.00	0.15	0.0225	0.0000
2	0.40	0.15	0.28	0.00	0.0000	0.0000
3	−0.10	−0.15	−0.22	−0.30	0.0900	0.0660
4	−0.20	0.00	−0.32	−0.15	0.0225	0.0480
5	0.38	0.45	0.26	0.30	0.0900	0.0780
Average	0.12	0.15			0.0450	0.0384

Final Solution: The beta is found by dividing the covariance (0.0384) by the variance of the market (0.0450), which equals 0.8533. Notice that the returns of SuperStore tend to move in the same direction as the market (the beta is positive) but not quite as much as the market (the beta is less than one). ↵

Problem 2 SuperStore, Inc., has four divisions based upon geography. Their financial analysts have computed the betas of the divisions as follows:

Region	Beta
Northeast	1.0
Southeast	1.2
Midwest	0.8
West	1.5

The risk-free rate is 5% and the expected return on the market is 14%. Compute the required rates of return for each division.

Solution to Problem 2
When an asset trades in a competitive market, its expected return must equal the required rate of return of the investors. In this question, we are looking for the required rates of return for divisions within a corporation. These required rates of return should be equal to the expected rates of return that an investor would earn in the marketplace on assets with similar betas. Thus, each required rate of return can be found using the *CAPM* as shown in Formula (8.1). The *CAPM* has four variables. This problem, like many others, provides three of the variables and requires that the fourth variable be computed.

Step 1: Copy Formula (8.1) from the text (or, better, from memory):

$$E(R_i) = R_f + \beta_i \, [\, E(R_m) - R_f \,]$$

Step 2: Fill in the two rates of return that are provided, the risk-free interest rate (R_f) and the expected return of the market $[E(R_m)]$.

$$E(R_i) = 0.05 + \beta_i \, (0.14 - 0.05)$$

Step 3: Solve for the required rates of return by inserting the given betas:

Northeast Division: $E(R_i) = 0.05 + (1.0 * 0.09) = 0.14$ or 14%
Southeast Division: $E(R_i) = 0.05 + (1.2 * 0.09) = 0.158$ or 15.8%
Midwest Division: $E(R_i) = 0.05 + (0.8 * 0.09) = 0.122$ or 12.2%
West Division: $E(R_i) = 0.05 + (1.5 * 0.09) = 0.185$ or 18.5%

Final Solution: Each division has a required rate of return that depends entirely upon its beta. An investment with a beta of 1.0 requires 9% more return than a risk-free investment. Therefore, for each 0.1 increase or decrease in beta we should expect a 0.9% increase or decrease in the required rate of return. ↵

REVIEW QUESTIONS

1. Explain the difference between diversifiable and nondiversifiable risk.
2. Why do we say that some risky portfolios will always be preferred to others?
3. In the Markowitz framework, how do investors decide in which risky portfolio of securities to invest?
4. How do people adjust the risk of their total security holdings in the *CAPM* framework?
5. What is the name given to the unique risky portfolio that all investors are drawn to? Why is it given such a name?
6. Provide both a statistical and a nonstatistical definition for beta.
7. If the market were to fall unexpectedly by 1%, a stock with a beta of 0.75 would be expected to fall on average by 1%. True or false? Explain.
8. Draw the relationship given by the security market line. Label both axes.
9. Explain the procedure of using the *CAPM* in capital budgeting.
10. How is a project beta estimated?

PROBLEMS

1. What is the beta of the risk-free asset and what is the beta of the overall market?
2. The covariance between Eb Corporation's common stock returns and the return on the market portfolio is 0.06. The standard deviation of the market is 0.2. What is the beta of Eb Corporation's common stock?
3. Financial analysts have estimated the returns on shares of Drucker Corporation and the overall market portfolio under various economic conditions as follows:

State of Economy	Return on Drucker	Return on Market
Recession	−15%	−10%
Moderate Growth	+10%	+5%
Boom	+35%	+20%

The analysts consider each state to be equally likely.
   a. Compute the expected return for each column.
   b. Compute the variance of the market.
   c. Compute the covariance between Drucker and the market.
   d. Compute the beta of Drucker Corporation's stock.
4. Using Formula (8.1), called the capital asset pricing model or the security market line, if the expected return of the market is 16%, the risk-free rate is 6%, and the beta of an asset is 0.5, what is the expected return of the asset?
5. What would be the beta of the following portfolios?
   a. 100% risk-free asset and 0% market
   b. 75% risk-free asset and 25% market
   c. 50% risk-free asset and 50% market
   d. 25% risk-free asset and 75% market
   e. 0% risk-free asset and 100% market
6. Use Formula (8.1) to supply the missing values:

	$E(R_i)$	R_f	β_i	$E(R_m)$
a.	?	8%	1.0	18%
b.	?	8%	0.5	18%
c.	?	8%	1.5	18%
d.	?	6%	0.8	20%
e.	?	7%	−0.9	15%
f.	14%	9%	?	19%
g.	12%	8%	?	24%
h.	22%	10%	?	18%
i.	−2%	8%	?	18%
j.	15%	5%	1.0	?

	$E(R_i)$	R_f	β_i	$E(R_m)$
k.	10%	5%	0.5	?
l.	18%	9%	0.9	?
m.	22%	7%	1.2	?
n.	−2%	6%	−1.1	?
o.	6%	?	0.0	14%
p.	14%	?	0.5	18%
q.	25%	?	2.0	15%
r.	−5%	?	−1.5	14%

7. Various attributes of three stocks are listed:

	Arnold Corp.	Ziffel Corp.	Douglas Corp.
Price	$25	$40	$35
Expected Return	10%	12%	14%
Covariances with the Market	0.03	0.04	0.05

The variance of the market portfolio is 0.04.

a. What would be the portfolio weights of a portfolio consisting of 100 shares of each stock?

b. What would be the expected return of a portfolio of 100 shares of each stock?

c. What is the beta of each stock?

d. What would the beta of a portfolio of 100 shares of each stock be?

e. What would the beta of a portfolio of these three stocks be if the expected return of the portfolio were 11%?

8. It is possible to compute means, variances, betas, and so forth using historical data as shown in Window 8.3. For our purposes the procedure is identical to the case of various economic states where each economic state is equally likely. Consider the following history of returns:

	Coca-Cola Company	S&P 500
1981	4.13%	−9.73%
1982	49.74%	14.76%
1983	2.88%	17.27%
1984	16.59%	1.40%
1985	35.38%	26.33%
1986	34.09%	14.62%
1987	1.00%	2.03%
1988	17.05%	12.01%
1989	73.15%	27.25%
1990	20.40%	−3.15%

a. Compute the mean of each return series (Hint: Treat each outcome as having the same probability of recurring—in this case 10%).

b. Compute the beta of Coca-Cola Company (Hint: First compute the covariance between them and the variance of the market).

9. What combination of the risk-free asset and the market portfolio would have the same beta as the following stocks?
   a. A stock with a beta of 0.5
   b. A stock with a beta of 0.9

10. If the risk-free asset offers an expected return of 6% and the overall market offers a required return of 18%:
    a. What would be the required returns of the two stocks in problem 9?
    b. What would be the required returns of the two portfolios determined as answers to problem 9?

11. If a stock had an expected return greater than it should according to the *CAPM*, would it be overpriced or underpriced? What should we expect to happen to its price in an efficient market?

12. Both Oliver Corporation and Lisa Corporation have debt with a beta of 0 and equity with a beta of 1.2.
    a. What is the beta of Oliver Corporation's assets if the corporation's debt is 30% of its securities and the equity is 70% of its securities?
    b. What is the beta of Lisa Corporation's assets if the corporation's debt is 50% of its securities and the equity is 50% of its securities?

13. The Haney Corporation is considering a major capital expenditure on a project. The current risk-free interest rate is 8% and the expected return on the overall market is 18%. What required rate of return should the corporation use as a discount to its *NPV* analysis if:
    a. The risk of the project is identical to the risk of the Oliver Corporation in problem 12?
    b. The risk of the project is identical to the risk of the Lisa Corporation in problem 12?

DISCUSSION QUESTIONS

1. When is the expected rate of return equal to the required rate of return? When are they different?

2. *CAPM* theory leads to the conclusion that all investors hold the same portfolio of risky assets—the market portfolio. Today, billions of investment dollars are "indexed" or placed into portfolios that seek to replicate the market as a whole. However, some peo-

ple don't diversify at all. What does this evidence say about *CAPM* theory? Explain.

3. Ricky "All Eggs in One Basket" Jordon has his cash invested in one stock. The beta of his stock is 0.5. Ricky concludes that his investment is half as risky as the market as a whole. Is he correct? Explain.

4. Respond to the following comment:

    Our company's products are unique. Therefore, the *CAPM* is of little use to us in our capital budgeting analysis.

5. Select a product, make an ordered list of the largest risks its producers face, and then estimate the extent to which these risks are diversifiable or systematic.

6. If an asset has a negative beta, will it offer a higher or lower expected return relative to the risk-free rate? Would anyone ever invest in an asset whose expected return is less than the risk-free rate?

7. Respond to the following comment:

    The *CAPM* is ridiculous; actual returns do not lie in a straight line against beta.

APPENDIX

Why Expected Returns Lie in a Straight Line Against Beta

The purpose of this appendix is to derive the *CAPM* with a minimum of math, as some mathematical proofs of the *CAPM* are very difficult to follow. We demonstrate that the linearity of beta and the formulae that use beta are sufficient to derive the *CAPM* under the potentially tricky assumption that assets with identical betas must have identical returns.

We begin by proving that beta operates in a linear fashion—which is to say that the beta of a portfolio is a linear combination of the betas of the constituent assets. Recall Formula (8.2):

$$\beta_i = Cov(R_i, R_m) / Var(R_m).$$

This is the definition of beta and says that the beta of an asset depends upon its covariance with the market divided by the market's variance. Now let's look at the formula for the return of a portfolio of two assets using weights as in Chapter 7:

$$R_p = (w_1 \times R_1) + (w_2 \times R_2). \tag{A8.1}$$

where R_p is the return on a portfolio, w_1 and w_2 are the percentages invested in assets 1 and 2, and R_1 and R_2 are the returns of assets 1 and 2.

The beta of the portfolio in terms of the portfolio's constituent assets can be found by inserting R_p from Formula (A8.1) in place of R_i from Formula (8.2):

$$\beta_p = Cov([w_1 R_1 + w_2 R_2], R_m) / Var(R_m). \tag{A8.2}$$

Formula (A8.2) becomes:

$$\beta_p = w_1[Cov(R_1, R_m)/Var(R_m)] + w_2[Cov(R_2, R_m)/Var(R_m)]. \tag{A8.3}$$

Recognizing the formula for beta, Formula (A8.3) reduces to:

$$\beta_p = (w_1 \beta_1) + (w_2 \beta_2). \tag{A8.4}$$

As promised, we have proved that the beta of a portfolio is equal to the weighted average of the betas of the constituent assets. Note that Formula (A8.4) is simply the two-asset case of Formula (8.3). Obviously, the math could be performed for any size portfolio.

Now let's assume that asset 1 is the risk-free asset with a beta of zero and that asset 2 is the overall market and therefore has a beta of one. The beta of this special portfolio reduces as shown in Formula (A8.5):

$$\beta_p = w_2, \tag{A8.5}$$

where β_p is the beta of a portfolio with w_1 percent in the risk-free asset and w_2 in the overall market.

Thus the beta of the portfolio is equal to the percentage of the portfolio invested in the market. If the portfolio is 0% invested in the market then the beta is 0, if it is 25% invested in the market then the beta is 0.25, and if it is 100% percent invested in the market the beta is 1.00.

The expected return of this portfolio can be found using the formula from Chapter 7 for the expected return on a portfolio:

$$E(R_p) = (w_1 * R_f) + (w_2 * E(R_m)).$$

Inserting $(1-w_2)$ for w_1, B_p for w_2, and rearranging produces the familiar *CAPM*:

$$E(R_p) = R_f + \beta_p \, [E(R_m) - R_f].$$

This equation demonstrates that the expected return of our portfolio, which has w_1 percent in the risk-free asset and w_2 percent in the market, *adheres* to the *CAPM*. The beta of the portfolio is β_p. If we assume that the expected return of all assets with equal betas must be equal, then the expected returns of all assets must lie on the straight line depicted in the *CAPM* equation. For beta values of less than zero or greater than one, some concepts beyond the scope of this text would be required.

The critical assumption was that assets with equal betas must offer equal expected returns. This concept is detailed in the main text of Chapter 8. The implications of this concept are complex and beyond the scope of this text.

However, it is worth noting that there may be systematic types of risk other than market risk. The arbitrage pricing model has been developed to demonstrate the effects of multiple sources of systematic risk. It is a useful concept for advanced courses—but for the purposes of this text one systematic risk factor (the market) is enough!

Chapter 9

Introduction to Options

Thomas Donaldson, a senior finance major, has been managing his family's investment portfolio for three years with good success. His overall philosophy is to take well-calculated risks, and his latest strategy is to invest in stock options. Specifically, he is proposing a position in a combination of options known as a straddle. Here's how the straddle works: The investor purchases two types of stock options—a call option and a put option. The call option becomes profitable if the stock market goes up, while the put option becomes profitable if the stock market goes down. The straddle loses money if the stock market does not change substantially from its current position.

The reaction of the Donaldson family to this new investment strategy was summed up by his mother, who said "Thomas, this sounds crazy. On the one side, we win if the market goes up, but on the other side, we win if the market goes down. It's like placing two wagers on the upcoming football game—one on the home team and one on the away team. How can we possibly come out ahead?"

Thomas explained that the genius of this strategy is timing: "The Presidential elections are coming up, and most everyone expects a close race this year. While I can't predict who will win, I can say that the stock market will react strongly to the election results. The way I see it, the market goes way up if the Republican wins, in which case we make more money on the call option than we lose on the put option. On the other side, the market goes way down if the Democrat wins, making us more money on the put option than we lose on the call option. In other words, I know the market will move, and the straddle allows us to profit no matter what happens."

Understanding the straddle requires option pricing theory—the subject of this chapter. Chapter 9 introduces options on common stock, and links the concept of an option to the value of the equity of a firm. Much of the material in this chapter, from option terminology to the basics of option contracts, is new. While the material may require more than one reading, options are becoming such an important part of the study of finance that the time spent will be well worth the effort.

THE IMPORTANCE OF OPTION THEORY

There are three reasons why the study of options is important. First, options are a common component in many corporate finance decisions. For example, when a corporation purchases land, leases space, or makes major purchases such as airplanes, it is common for the corporation to obtain options for more land, more space, or additional airplanes that allow the corporation to lock in future purchase prices in the event of expansion. Further, corporations often attach options to their securities that enable the holder to buy more securities or to trade their securities for other securities.

Similarly, the corporation may issue securities and require that the purchaser allow the corporation the option to buy them back. Many of the corporation's contracts—including employment contracts, supply contracts, distribution contracts, insurance contracts, and so forth—contain provisions that allow one or more of the parties in the agreement to make a decision about whether or not to terminate, extend, or modify the agreement. These are all options.

Second, the financial markets allow widespread trading of options. Organized option trading, which began in 1973, now consists of hundreds of millions of contracts per year on over a dozen U.S. options exchanges. For example, investors can use options to buy or sell financial securities including common stock, government bonds, and commodities. As mentioned above, the trading of options has exploded in popularity in recent years and is an important building block in the risk management of corporations and investment portfolios.

Third, the corporate form of the business organization itself creates an option. The equity of the corporation is an option in the sense that shareholders can either continue to own a firm or can walk away from the corporation by declaring bankruptcy. Thinking about the equity of a firm as a call option allows for new insights concerning the value of the firm.

Our main objective in this chapter is to provide you with the tools necessary to understand how options are valued. We will begin with a discussion on the mechanics of options. Eventually the Black-Scholes Option Pricing Model—a new and dramatic breakthrough in finance—will be presented. Finally, options will be applied to some of the most common situations in corporate finance.

THE MECHANICS OF OPTIONS

The key to understanding the option contract is that, while many contracts require you to act, an option gives its holder the opportunity to act without an obligation. A financial option is a contract that offers the holder the choice either to accept a transaction or to decline the transaction. The terms of the option usually include a specific transaction price and a time limit or date of expiration.

This chapter emphasizes **call options**. A call option gives its holder the opportunity either to buy something, such as 100 shares of common stock at a certain price, or to do nothing and therefore not transact. The call option will include a time period, at the end of which the option expires or ends. Another common type of option, known as a **put option,** gives its holder the choice of either selling something or not transacting.

> ✕ A financial option is a contract that offers the holder the choice to either accept a transaction or to decline the transaction. The terms of the option usually include a specific transaction price and a time limit or date of expiration.

Options exist in many forms, and many have entered into option contracts without thinking much about them. For example, at one time you may have placed a fee, say $25, with a landlord to guarantee an apartment up to a certain date at a specified monthly rent. The fee (or deposit) essentially holds the apartment until you move into the apartment and pay another sum of money. This deposit is very much like a call option, as it gives you the right to the apartment at a specified price. If you act in time, you pay the next sum of money and the apartment is yours. If you choose not to act, you walk away from the rental deal, losing only the deposit.

There is a new vocabulary to learn when dealing with options for the first time. Window 9.1 explains much of the terminology in detail and highlights the most important terms which you will need to know to understand this chapter. You should review the option terminology in Window 9.1 before proceeding.

A Graphical Look at Options

Chapters 7 and 8 discussed the pioneering work in portfolio theory. The development of the theory assumed that prices of financial assets follow the familiar normal or bell-shaped distribution. The tails of the normal distribution run from negative infinity to positive infinity. In more modern and technical work, stock returns are usually assumed to form a related distribution entitled the **lognormal distribution**.

call option
A security that gives its holder the opportunity either to buy something, such as 100 shares of common stock at a certain price, or to do nothing and therefore not transact. The call option will include a time period at the end of which the option expires or ends.

put option
A security that gives its holder the opportunity either to sell something, such as 100 shares of common stock at a certain price, or to do nothing and therefore not transact. The put option will include a time period at the end of which the option expires or ends.

lognormal distribution
A statistical distribution in which the variables can take on only positive numbers.

Window 9.1

Option Terminology

Call options give the buyer the right to buy an asset at a specific price on or before a certain date. For standard options on common stock, each option permits the holder to purchase 100 shares of stock. The purpose of this window is to review the terminology of options and option trading. Some of these definitions will be illustrated using actual call option prices taken from the *Wall Street Journal* for the IBM Corporation:

IBM Call Option Prices—April 18, 1990

NY Close	Strike Price	April	May
111	100	11⅛	11½
111	105	6¼	6¾
111	115	⅞	1½

1. Strike Price or Exercise Price: The price at which the stock underlying the call option can be purchased. The terms strike price and exercise price can be used interchangeably.

For the IBM option, three different strike or exercise prices are illustrated—$100, $105, and $115. If you purchased the IBM $100 strike option, you could, until expiration, purchase IBM stock for $100 no matter what the current price of IBM. It is typically the case that many different strike prices are available for each tradable option.

2. Option Premium: The amount the buyer of an option has to pay for the right to purchase or sell the stock at the specified price by a specified date. The option premium is also referred to as the option price.

Six different premiums are listed for IBM. For the strike price of $100, the call premiums are $11.125 for April and $11.50 for May. For the strike price of $105, the premiums are $6.25 for April and $6.75 for May. For the strike price of $115, the premiums are $0.875 for April and $1.50 for May. If you wanted to purchase the $100 strike April expiration option, it would cost $11.125.

3. Expiration Date: The last day an option can be exercised. The option becomes worthless after this date is reached. Option exchanges have exact times and dates that define expiration.

For IBM, two different expiration dates, April and May, are listed. IBM options trade on the American Stock Exchange, and these options expire at 4:00 P.M. on the third Friday

(continued on next page)

Window 9.1 (continued)

of the month. The premium for the May option is always higher than the premium of the April option, as the May option has a longer life.

4. In-the-Money Call Options: Options whose underlying stock price is currently above the exercise price.

    For IBM, the current market price is $111. Four of the six options listed are in the money. Both the $100 and $105 exercise price are below the current stock price.

5. Out-of-the-Money Call Options: Options whose underlying stock price is currently below the exercise price. These options will have some value as long as investors believe that there is a chance that, by expiration, the option will be in the money.

    For IBM, the $115 exercise price options are out of the money. The value of IBM would have to rise above the exercise price in order for the option to have value at expiration. These out-of-the-money April and May IBM options have some value because investors believe that, before expiration, IBM's stock price might rise above $115 per share.

6. At-the-Money-Call Options: Options whose underlying stock price is currently equal to the exercise price.

7. Call Option Writer: The individual who created and sold the call option and pays any profits of the call option to the buyer. For this guarantee, the call option writer receives the premium from the option buyer.

8. Covered Call Option: Call option for which the writer owns the underlying stock.

(continued on next page)

The lognormal distribution, illustrated in Figure 9.1, looks similar to the normal distribution but is flattened or skewed to the right. In Figure 9.1, the potential range of stock prices on the horizontal axis runs not from negative to positive infinity but from zero to positive infinity. Given limited liability, stock prices cannot go lower than zero.

Example 9.1 _____ Suppose that a call option on the stock in Figure 9.1 exists such that the option allows the holder to purchase shares of stock for $20. Using option terminology, we say that the

Window 9.1 *(continued)*

9. Naked Call Option: Call options for which the option writer has no holdings of the underlying stock.

10. Option Clearinghouse: The corporation that handles all option transactions on the exchange. The clearinghouse guarantees that all prior commitments, especially those of the option writer, are fulfilled. If the writer fails to deliver the underlying stock to the buyer at the exercise price, the clearinghouse steps in and absorbs the loss. The clearinghouse therefore becomes the seller to every buyer. To safeguard the clearinghouse from losses, option writers are required to keep good-faith deposits, called margin, with the exchange.

11. Index Options: Call options whose underlying security is an index of stocks instead of a single stock. The value of the call option rises and falls with an index of stocks, such as the S&P 500 index, instead of with a single stock like IBM.

12. Option Combinations: One of the interesting features of options is their ability to be combined with stocks or with other options to create portfolios with different payout streams. Popular option combinations include:

> **Straddle:** A call option and a put option on the same stock with the same exercise price and the same expiration date.
> **Strip:** Two put options and a call option, all on the same underlying security, all with the same exercise price and expiration date.
> **Strap:** Two call options and a put option, all on the same underlying security, all with the same exercise price and expiration date.
> **Spread:** The purchase of one option and the simultaneous sale of another option on the same underlying security at a different exercise price or different expiration date.

option's exercise price is $20. Because the call option gives the holder the right to buy stock at $20, the value of the option will depend on the value of the underlying stock. The option is more valuable when the price of the stock is near or above $20 and has little or no value if the stock falls far below $20. For example, if the price of the stock should move to $25, the holder of the call option can exercise the option, purchase stock for $20, and sell the stock in the open market at $25, making $5 in the process. ↵

FIGURE 9.1
The Lognormal Distribution

The lognormal distribu-
tion illustrates the range
of potential stock prices
along with their associ-
ated probabilities.

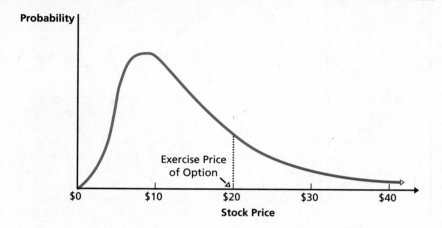

Figure 9.2 illustrates the option payout distribution, or the value
of the call option against the price of the underlying common stock.
Notice that there is a significant chance that the option will be worth
zero because the stock will be worth $20 or less. This is shown in the
unshaded portion of the bottom diagram in Figure 9.2, and illustrates
the concept that at expiration an option whose exercise price is above
the stock price is worthless. The logic is that since the option entitles
its holder to buy the stock at $20, and since the stock can be bought
in the market for $20 or less, there is no value to using or having the
option. After all, would you be willing to leave a deposit with a landlord for the right to rent an apartment for $500 if the apartment can
be rented without such a deposit for $450?

Note, however, that if the final stock price is above $20 the option
has value. In fact, the greater the stock price, the more valuable the
option. This is illustrated in Figure 9.3, where the value of the call
option is shown with the price of the stock. Notice that the value of
the option at expiration is $1 for each $1 by which the stock price
exceeds the $20 exercise price. For example, if at the expiration date
of the option the price of the stock is $8 over the exercise price, the
option will be worth $8.

Figure 9.3 illustrates an important feature about call options. The
worst that can happen when you purchase an option is that it expires
worthless, resulting in a loss equal to the price or premium of the
option. Said another way, the most you can lose when you purchase
the call option is the call premium, the price you paid for the option.
Even if the stock price went to zero, you would lose no more than your
original investment. An option can never have a negative value to its
owner. Owning an option gives you the right to purchase stock at a
specific price and carries no obligation.

FIGURE 9.2
The Option Payout Distribution at Expiration

With an exercise price of $20, the option is valuable at its expiration only if the stock price rises above $20. The option is worthless at its expiration (has a value of $0) at all stock prices below $20 per share.

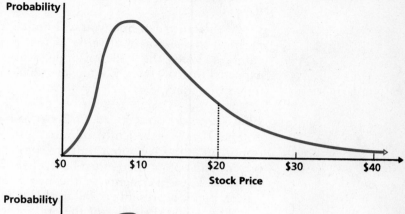

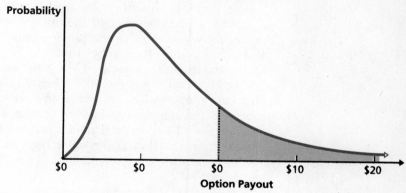

FIGURE 9.3
The Value of a Call Option at Expiration

The option's price at expiration rises by $1 for each $1 that the stock price rises above $20 (the exercise price).

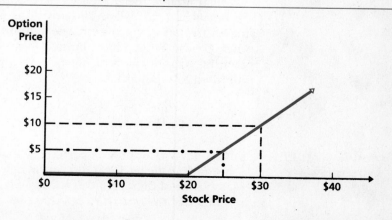

⌛ The worst that can happen when you purchase an option is that it expires worthless, resulting in a loss equal to the price or premium of the option.

At the other extreme, you will notice from Figure 9.3 that there is no limit to the potential value of the option. As the stock climbs in value, so does the call option. Obviously, the stock price is not expected to grow from $20 to, say, $2000, but theoretically there is no upper boundary.

Who Pays the Profits to Call Option Buyers?   The limited loss potential and theoretically unlimited profit potential make owning an option an attractive opportunity to some investors. However, for every buyer of an option there must be a seller of the option who is obligated to make these payments to the buyer. Every dollar of gain to the option buyer represents a dollar of loss to the option seller.

Why would the seller of the option, who has an obligation to the option buyer, ever offer the buyer a security with limited losses and unlimited gains? (Remember that unlimited gains to the buyer means unlimited losses to the seller.) The seller or writer of an option in effect pays all the cash flows the option buyer receives. Thus, the worst thing that can happen when you write an option is that you will be responsible for paying out the buyer's (perhaps considerable) profits. The answer is that the seller is paid a fee, known as the option premium, for taking this risk and the seller hopes that the stock price will not rise beyond the exercise price.

⌛ The seller or writer of an option in effect pays all the cash flows the option buyer receives. Thus, the worst thing that can happen when you write an option is that you will be responsible for paying out the buyer's (perhaps considerable) profits.

In summary, there are two participants in every option contract: the buyer and the seller. The positions of the two parties are mirror images in that any profit on one side must be offset by a loss on the other. Option buyers have limited loss potential and unlimited profit potential. Option writers have limited profit potential and huge or unlimited loss potential.

Call Option Pricing Prior to Expiration

Example 9.2 _____ Consider a coupon or certificate that allows you to purchase an airline ticket for $200 on or before a certain date. In the parlance of finance, this certificate is a call option allowing the holder of the option to purchase an airline ticket for the exercise price of $200. The certificate allows for travel during a certain vacation period, and ticket prices during that vacation period vary from year to year, based upon competition, the economy, and fuel costs. Past prices have varied from $100 to $300 per ticket; future ticket prices are unknown.

How much would such a certificate be worth prior to its expiration? It is clear that the certificate is worth something. In the event that ticket prices at travel time are greater than $200, the certificate will have value. However, there is a limit to the value of the certificate since it is almost impossible for the airline ticket to rise above $300 by the next vacation period.

If you were buying the airline certificate (or call option), how much would you pay? If you owned several of the certificates, what events would cause you to make or lose money? Before introducing a model to help answer these questions, let's apply some common sense. The value of the certificates will rise if airline ticket prices rise or even if ticket prices become much more uncertain because of some international crisis. Conversely, if ticket prices drop significantly, the coupon will also fall in value and may eventually be worthless. Perhaps a "ball park" value to the certificates would be $20 to $30 each. This type of rough analysis would be adequate for occasional transactions. However, many economic exchanges involve options too important to estimate. The next section will introduce a model that provides the sophisticated analysis required by modern corporate financial management. ↵

THE BLACK-SCHOLES OPTION PRICING MODEL

In the early 1970s Fisher Black and Myron Scholes derived an option pricing model, based upon a tremendous insight, that revolutionized not only the study of option pricing but even the option industry itself. Today, with the help of the **Black-Scholes option pricing model,** option trading is a massive and highly sophisticated component of finance.

Black-Scholes option pricing model
A model for valuing options based upon five variables: the value of the underlying asset, the time to expiration of the option, the option's exercise price, the volatility of the underlying asset, and the risk-free rate of interest.

Newer models have attempted to fine-tune pricing in certain specific situations, but the Black-Scholes model remains the industry standard. The next part of this section will explain the underpinnings of the Black-Scholes model.

Systematic Risk and Option Pricing

Like any asset, the value of an option is the present value of the future cash flows adjusted for time and risk. The key is to estimate the future cash flows and to find a proper interest rate for discounting. The Black-Scholes model proved that the price of the option did not depend upon whether the risk is systematic or unsystematic or upon people's attitude toward risk. Black and Scholes proved that options are priced as if no one cared about risk, or in other words as if everyone were risk-neutral rather than risk-averse.

The lack of distinction between systematic and unsystematic risk in the Black-Scholes option pricing model seems very strange given our treatment of risk. At first glance it would seem that the formula for the price of a call option would include beta or some other measure of systematic risk. It doesn't. And it is not that people don't care about risk: There is a good effect and a bad effect of systematic risk within an option, and these two effects cancel each other out.

The price of a call option on common stock may be viewed as the present value of the option's cash payouts at its expiration. These cash payments depend on the price of the common stock, also known as the price of the underlying asset. The good effect of systematic risk in the underlying asset is that high systematic risk, or high beta, translates into a higher expected rate of return for the underlying asset and therefore higher expected future cash flows from the option. The bad effect of systematic risk in the underlying asset is that high systematic risk in the underlying asset means that the future cash flows of the option will also have high systematic risk and therefore must be discounted at a higher rate.

The Black-Scholes magic is that these two systematic risk effects cancel each other out, leaving a model that generates an option price which seems to ignore systematic risk but which actually works whether or not systematic risk exists.

Foundations of the Black-Scholes Option Pricing Model

Because many of the details of the Black-Scholes model are well beyond the scope of this book, we'll summarize what is important. First, the Black-Scholes option pricing model is an accurate way of computing the price of an option that fully accounts for both the time value of money and risk. Second, there are five variables that determine an option price: (1) the price of the underlying asset, (2) the exercise price of the option, (3) the time to expiration, (4) the standard deviation of the returns of the underlying asset, and (5) the risk-free interest rate. Third, given these five variables, the model uses a complicated formula to provide an option price.

Because of its complexity, the model itself has been placed in the appendix to this chapter. However, it can be easily programmed into a computer or even an advanced calculator and therefore can be convenient to use. The user inputs the five variables and asks for the option price to be calculated. (Some readers may wish to study the appendix before continuing.)

The Five Variables in the Black-Scholes Option Pricing Model

This subsection examines in more detail the five variables that determine the value of a call option in the Black-Scholes model.

The Price of the Underlying Asset.   One of the most important relationships in option pricing theory is between a call option price and the price of the underlying asset, in that they tend to move in the same direction. In the Black-Scholes model, the price of a call option rises at an increasing rate as the price of the underlying asset rises. With everything else held constant, a call option premium will, in theory, rise more than 0 cents and less than $1 for each $1 rise in the underlying asset (prior to its expiration).

Figure 9.4 illustrates the relationship between a call option price and the price of the underlying asset, with everything else held constant. The difference between Figure 9.3 and Figure 9.4 is that in Figure 9.4 the value of a call option is shown before expiration, while Figure 9.3 illustrates the value of the call option at its expiration date.

Notice that the slope of the call option is always positive, so that increases in the stock price always lead to increases in the call option price. When the stock price is very low, the slope of the line is nearly flat, illustrating that the price of the call is less responsive to changes in the stock price at this range. In other words, for a near-zero stock price, the exercise price of the option is well above the current stock price, such that the option is way out-of-the-money and will not change much as the underlying stock price changes.

When the stock price is very high, the slope of the line is very steep, illustrating that the call price moves in a nearly one-to-one rela-

FIGURE 9.4

Call Option Sensitivity to the Price of the Underlying Asset

The value of the option prior to its expiration is higher as the price of the underlying asset rises.

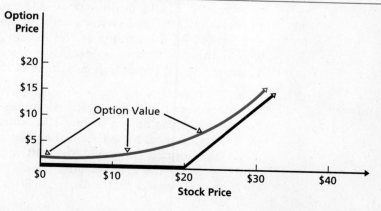

tionship with the stock price at this range. In other words, when the exercise price of the option is well below the current stock price and the option is way in-the-money, owning an option is not very different from owning the underlying security.

The Option's Exercise Price. The exercise price of the option does not change throughout the life of the option. However, it is important to know the effect of alternative exercise prices in comparing different options. In the Black-Scholes model, the price of the call option is inversely related to the option's exercise price, because the call option becomes profitable only when the stock price exceeds the exercise price. When the exercise price is high relative to the stock price, the stock price has to rise more to become valuable. When the exercise price is low relative to the stock price, the stock price has to rise less to become valuable.

The Standard Deviation of the Underlying Asset. The total risk or volatility of the underlying asset can be measured by the standard deviation of the returns of the underlying asset. The Black-Scholes model illustrates that call option prices rise as the standard deviation or total risk of the underlying asset rises. It may seem that this concept runs counter to the concepts of risk aversion detailed in Chapters 7 and 8, since the option price rises in response to increased risk, but in actuality it reflects the real essence of an option.

As we have said, an option is a claim on an asset that permits the holder to have large or unlimited profit potential with limited loss potential. The worst thing that can happen to an option holder is that the option expires without value and the option holder loses the entire investment. However, the profit potential is limitless because the holder benefits from price increases in the underlying asset.

Figure 9.2 illustrated the idea that a call option has the potential for limited loss and virtually unlimited profit. Thus, if the underlying asset becomes much more volatile, the option's upside potential will be increased, but the option's downside potential is limited. Therefore, an increase in the underlying asset's standard deviation, which can be represented by a widening of the distribution in Figure 9.2, acts to benefit the call option holder, who gains higher profit potentials. Again, the worst the option can do remains to expire without value.

Example 9.3 ———— Suppose that for your graduation present your rich uncle has given you the option to buy 100 ounces of gold from him at $400 an ounce. Note that if the price of gold stays at or near $400 an ounce, the graduation gift will have little to no value. However, if the price of gold begins to fluctuate wildly, then the option could become extremely valuable. As the holder of

FIGURE 9.5
Call Option Sensitivity to Underlying Volatility

The value of the option
is higher as the volatility
of the underlying asset
increases.

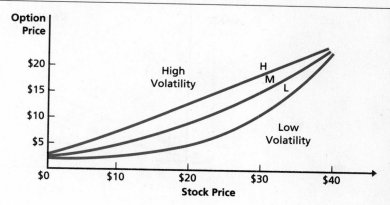

the option, you would rather see the price of gold fluctuate
upward than stay stable since if it remains stable your option
will have little value. If the price of gold rises substantially, you
have the chance at a great graduation gift but not much to lose
if the price goes down. ◄┘

Figure 9.5 illustrates the idea that higher standard deviation in the
underlying asset produces higher call option prices. The curve labeled
"M" is designed to illustrate the relationship between an option price
and its underlying asset price when there is a moderate amount of
volatility in the underlying asset. The curve labeled "L" illustrates the
same relationship in the case of an underlying asset with low volatility,
and the curve labeled "H" illustrates the case of high volatility.
Figure 9.5 illustrates that regardless of the underlying asset's price
relative to the strike price, the higher the volatility of the underlying
asset, the higher is the price of the option, a point that will be utilized
in future chapters.

The Time to Expiration.   The effect of time to expiration on the
value of a call option is straightforward. Since most options allow the
holder to exercise the option at any time during its lifetime, a long-
term option is worth more than a short-term option. The importance
of having more time to expiration is that it provides a longer period
for the underlying asset to achieve substantial price movements.
Remember: The key to an option is that it permits the holder to benefit
virtually limitlessly from price movements in one direction but it limits the losses from price movements in the opposite direction. Thus,
a longer time to expiration gives the option holder a wider opportunity
for the underlying asset to move. The effect of longer time to expira-

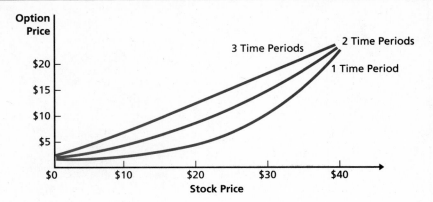

FIGURE 9.6
Call Option Sensitivity to Time to Expiration

The value of the option is higher with increasing time to maturity of the option.

tion is very similar to the effect of more volatility, shown graphically in Figure 9.6.

The Risk-Free Interest Rate. The risk-free interest rate is also a determining factor in the price of options, according to the Black-Scholes model. To understand why the interest rate affects option prices, think again about what call options represent. Suppose that you believe a certain stock will increase in value in the future, and you have decided today to invest money in the stock. Your choice of investment is to buy the stock, or buy a call option on the stock.

If you buy the stock, your investment today for each share of stock will be the current stock price. However, if you buy call options, your investment today is the call premium, and your future investment if you exercise the option is the exercise price of the option. This comparison illustrates that buying options is like buying the stock on borrowed money—you have effectively bought now but do not have to pay the exercise price until later.

The higher the risk-free interest rate, the more advantage there is to owning a call option, because the present value of the exercise price is less if the risk-free interest rate is higher. Thus, call option prices will rise slightly when the risk-free interest rate rises and vice versa.

Summary of the Black-Scholes Option Pricing Model

We discussed each of the five variables that determine option prices. Four of the variables, the price of the underlying asset, the standard deviation of the underlying asset, the time to expiration, and the riskless interest rate, were shown to be positively related to option prices. Only the exercise price is inversely related to the option price. The next section provides a simplified financial example.

OPTION PRICING—A TWO-STATE EXAMPLE

Recall Risk, Inc., from Chapter 7, which had a chance of being worth either $10 per share or $0 per share, depending upon whether or not it was successful in developing a new technology. Let's assume the stock is now selling for $4 per share. The purpose of this section is to discuss how much a call option on the stock would be worth.

Let's consider two call options on Risk, Inc. In one case there is a call option on Risk, Inc., with an exercise price of $10, and in the other there is a call option on Risk, Inc., with an exercise price of $0. How much would these call options be worth?

The call option with a $10 exercise price would be worth $0, as there is no value to an option to buy something for $10 that has no chance of rising above $10 before the option expires. This is true, given that Risk, Inc., will be worth either $10 or $0. The call option with a $0 exercise price is worth the same as the value of the stock, or $4. The reason is that there is no chance that the stock will drop below the exercise price of $0. In this case, the call option is, in effect, identical to owning the stock.

A more interesting case is a call option on Risk, Inc., with a strike price between $0 and $10. For example, a call option with a strike price of $5 will pay either $5 if the stock price goes to $10 or $0 if the stock price falls to $0. In this simplified example the value of the call option on Risk, Inc., can be determined exactly. In this case, the call option pays off exactly half as much as the stock. If the price of Risk, Inc., stock rises to $10, the call option is worth half its value or $5. If the price of the stock falls to $0, the option is worth half its value or $0. Therefore, the call option is worth exactly half as much as the stock, or $2. Two call options with a strike price of $5 would cost a total of $4, and offer the exact payoff as a share of the stock—also $4.

This example from a highly simplified two-state model demonstrates several points regarding option theory.

1. The price of an option does not depend upon whether the risk is systematic or diversifiable, and it doesn't depend upon the degree of risk aversion of market participants.
2. The upper bound to the price of a call option is equal to the price of the underlying asset. This was demonstrated in the case of a $0 exercise price, where the potential payout of the call option was identical to the potential payout of owning the stock. From the law of conservation of value, we know that identical cash flow streams must have identical values. In other words, in this case, the value of the call option must be equal to the value of the underlying asset.
3. The lower bound to the price of a call is zero. This was demonstrated in the case of a $10 exercise price. Because

there was no chance of the option being in-the-money, the option would never have any value. However, the call option can never have a negative value because the option buyer isn't obligated to do anything.

AN APPLICATION OF OPTION THEORY TO THE EQUITY OF A FIRM

We now examine how options can be used to better understand the value of the common stock of a firm. As discussed in Chapter 1, the balance sheet view of a firm using market values is:

$$Equity = Assets - Liabilities.$$

The shareholders are best viewed as owning the firm's assets subject to the claims of debt holders. An alternative and extremely useful view of the position of equity holders is that they have a call option on the assets of the firm. If the firm's assets turn out to be worth more than the value of the debt holder's claim, the equity holders will exercise their option by paying off the debt holders and taking over ownership of the assets. If, on the other hand, the firm's assets turn out to be worth less than the debt holder's claim, the equity holders will walk away from the firm—or declare bankruptcy—allowing their option to the ownership of the firm's assets to expire worthless.

Thus, the ability of a corporation's equity holders to declare bankruptcy is tantamount to owning a call option. Just as in the case of a traditional call option, if the assets do extremely well, the equity holders can benefit greatly. If the assets do extremely poorly, the losses of the equity holders are limited to the dollar amount they invested in the equity. The length of the equity holder's option is the time to maturity of the debt.

Figure 9.7 shows the relationship between equity values and asset values when the debt is maturing. Note the similarity between the payout to equity holders in Figure 9.7 and the payout to traditional call option holders in Figure 9.3.

Example 9.4 ———————— From Figure 9.7, suppose that the face value of the firm's debt is $10 million. If the assets of the firm are worth less than $10 million when the debt matures, the equityholders will declare bankruptcy and the value of the equity will tend toward zero. On the other hand, if the assets are worth more than $10 million, the equityholders will pay to the debtholders their promised payment and the value of the equity will be the excess of the assets' original value over the $10 million. ↵

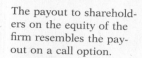

FIGURE 9.7
The Equity of the Firm as a Call Option

The payout to sharehold-
ers on the equity of the
firm resembles the pay-
out on a call option.

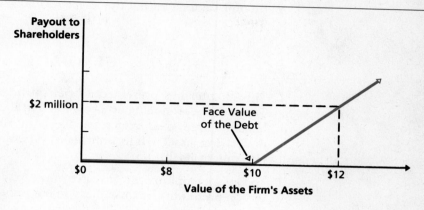

Value of the Firm's Assets

Table 9.1 illustrates the equity of the firm as a call option. The first column lists the five variables that determine an option price according to the Black-Scholes option pricing model. The second column lists the meaning of these five variables in the traditional case of a call option on a share of stock. The third column lists the meaning of the five variables when the equity in a firm is being viewed as a call option.

The idea that the equity of a firm should be viewed as a call option on the firm's assets is most useful when the firm has a substantial amount of debt and therefore a relatively high probability of bankruptcy. The concept is weakened by the tendency of most firms to have a variety of debt issues with different maturities and interest payment dates so that there is no single point in the future at which expiration

TABLE 9.1
Option Variables as Related to the Value of the Firm

Generic	Call Option on Stock	Equity as a Call Option
(1) The option's exercise price	Price at which stock can be purchased	Face value of debt
(2) The price of the underlying asset	Price of stock	Value of firm's assets
(3) The standard deviation of the underlying asset	Volatility of stock	Volatility of firm's assets
(4) The time to expiration	Time to option's expiration	Time to maturity of firm's debt
(5) The risk-free interest rate	Risk-free interest rate	Risk-free interest rate

will occur. Nevertheless, in Chapters 11 and 12, the application of option pricing theory to the equity of a firm will prove to be a useful method of understanding the effects of bankruptcy potential.

SUMMARY

☐ This chapter has presented a brief introduction to option pricing. The essence of owning an option is that it provides the potential to benefit a great deal from a particular movement in the value of an underlying asset while limiting the potential loss to the option investment itself.

☐ To own an option the investor must pay a price, known as the option premium, for this ability to have potentially huge profits and limited losses.

☐ There is a powerful model for pricing options developed by Black and Scholes. The Black-Scholes model estimates an option price using five variables as inputs: (1) the option's exercise price, (2) the price of the underlying asset, (3) the standard deviation of the underlying asset, (4) the time to the option's expiration and (5) the risk-free interest rate.

☐ Call options rise in value between $0.00 and $1.00 for each $1 rise in the value of the underlying asset (everything else held equal) and fall in value between $0.00 and $1.00 for each $1 fall in the value of the underlying asset.

☐ Call options rise in value when the standard deviation of the underlying asset increases and fall in value when the standard deviation of the underlying asset falls.

☐ The equity of a firm can be viewed as a call option on the firm's assets. If the value of the firm's assets is greater than the value of the firm's debt, the equity holders will exercise their option, make promised payments to bond holders, and continue to hold the equity. If the value of the firm's assets is less than the value of the firm's debt, the equity holders will choose not to exercise their option but rather walk away from the firm by declaring bankruptcy.

REFERENCE

Black, F., and M. Scholes. "The Pricing of Options and Corporate Liabilities." *Journal of Political Economy* 81 (May–June 1973), 637–654.

DEMONSTRATION PROBLEMS

Problem 1   a. SuperStore, Inc., common stock is trading for $50 per share. Call options are being traded on the stock with a strike price or exercise price of $50. Find the value (payoff) to the call option at expiration for the following potential prices for SuperStore, Inc., stock: $0, $10, $20, . . . , $100.

    b. Mom and Pop Grocery Store has $50,000 of assets and $50,000 face value of debt. Therefore, including the debt, the value of the store's equity appears to be zero. However, Mom is experimenting with some radically new marketing concepts that will significantly change the value of the store. Find the value to the store's equity (its assets minus its $50,000 debts) for the following potential values to the firm's assets: $0, $10,000, $20,000, . . . , $100,000.

Solution to Problem 1

These questions address the same issues that are addressed in Figure 9.3. In other words, given the value of the underlying asset, find the value of the call option (at expiration).

Step 1: From the text, the value of a call option at expiration is equal to zero if the underlying asset is worth less than the strike price, and it is worth the difference between the price of the underlying asset and the strike price if the underlying asset is worth more than the strike price. Therefore, subtract the strike price from each potential outcome in part (a). The option payout will be the greater of this value and zero as shown below:

Value of Underlying Asset	Strike Price	Underlying Asset Minus Strike Price	Greater of Zero and the Difference
$0	$50	-$50	$0
$10	$50	-$40	$0
$20	$50	-$30	$0
$30	$50	-$20	$0
$40	$50	-$10	$0
$50	$50	$0	$0
$60	$50	$10	$10
$70	$50	$20	$20
$80	$50	$30	$30
$90	$50	$40	$40
$100	$50	$50	$50

Step 2: The value of the equity of Mom and Pop Grocery Store can be similarly determined by subtracting the face value of the debt from the value of the firm's assets. The value of the equity will be the greater

of this value and zero since the lowest value that a corporation's stock can have is zero.

Value of Store's Assets	Face Value of Debt	Asset Value Minus $50,000 Debt	Greater of Zero and the Difference
$0	$50,000	−$50,000	$0
$10,000	$50,000	−$40,000	$0
$20,000	$50,000	−$30,000	$0
$30,000	$50,000	−$20,000	$0
$40,000	$50,000	−$10,000	$0
$50,000	$50,000	$0	$0
$60,000	$50,000	$10,000	$10,000
$70,000	$50,000	$20,000	$20,000
$80,000	$50,000	$30,000	$30,000
$90,000	$50,000	$40,000	$40,000
$100,000	$50,000	$50,000	$50,000

Final Solution: Notice that the payout to a call option holder is extremely similar to the payout to the shareholder of a volatile firm with a great deal of debt. In both cases, the payout is greatest for extremely high outcomes in the value of the underlying assets. Also, in both cases the losses due to declines in the value of the underlying assets are limited. In the case of a traditional call option, the option holder simply allows the option to expire worthless. In the case of a shareholder of a firm whose debt greatly exceeds its assets, the shareholder can declare bankruptcy. ◄┛

Problem 2   A call option is trading which permits the holder to purchase Cantwell Corporation's common stock at $20 per share. The option has 0.5 years to expiration, the risk-free rate is 5%, and the standard deviation of the stock's returns is 0.30. Use the Black-Scholes formula to compute the value of the option if Cantwell Corporation stock is now selling for $25 per share.

Solution to Problem 2
The solution follows the procedure given in the appendix to Chapter 9, which solves the Black-Scholes option pricing model:

$$\text{CALL} = [P \cdot N(d_1)] - [EX \cdot N(d_2) \cdot e^{-rt}]$$

Step 1: Calculate the value of d_1 using the formula for d_1:

$$d_1 = [ln(P/EX) + (r + .5\sigma^2)t] / \sqrt{\sigma^2 t}$$
$$d_1 = [ln(\$25/\$20) + (0.05 + .045)0.5] / \sqrt{0.3^2 0.5}$$
$$d_1 = [.22314 + (0.095)0.5] / 0.2121$$
$$d_1 = 1.276$$

Step 2: Calculate d_2 from d_1:

$$d_2 = d_1 - \sqrt{\sigma^2 t}$$
$$d_2 = 1.276 - \sqrt{.3^2 .5}$$
$$d_2 = 1.276 - 0.2121$$
$$d_2 = 1.064$$

Step 3: Use d_1 and d_2 to look up $N(d_1)$ and $N(d_2)$ in Table 9.2:

$$N(d_1) = N(1.276) = 0.899$$
$$N(d_2) = N(1.064) = 0.8563$$

Step 4: Using $r = 5\%$ and $t = 0.5$, compute e^{-rt}:

$$-rt = -0.05 \cdot 0.5$$
$$-rt = -0.025$$
$$e^{-rt} = e^{-0.025}$$
$$e^{-rt} = 0.9753$$

Step 5: Plug the above results into the Black-Scholes equation:

$$CALL = [P \cdot N(d_1)] - [EX \cdot N(d_2) \cdot e^{-rt}]$$
$$CALL = [\$25 \cdot .899] - [\$20 \cdot .8563 \cdot .9753]$$
$$CALL = \$22.475 - \$16.703$$
$$CALL = \$5.77$$

Final Solution: The value of the call option is approximately $5.77. Notice that if the option expired today it would be worth $5, since the underlying asset price exceeds the strike price by $5. Also, the option is rather far into the money, meaning that its actual price will sell near its price if it were expiring today. Thus, the value of $5.77 seems reasonable. ↵

REVIEW QUESTIONS

1. What is the difference between a call option and a put option?
2. How are call options related to the equity value of the firm?
3. What does a call option give to the option holder?
4. What is an option seller?
5. List the five variables from the Black-Scholes model that determine option values.
6. Describe the relationship between the value of a call option and the exercise price of the option.

TABLE 9.2
Standard Cumulative Normal Probabilities

This table calculates values of $N(d)$ given values for d through a five-step process:

Step 1: If d is negative, remove its negative sign (i.e., use its absolute value).

Step 2: Look at the first column labeled "tenths." Find the row corresponding to the number of tenths in the value d.

Step 3: Find the column with the same number of hundredths at the top.

Step 4: If d was positive, the entry in the appropriate row and column is $N(d)$. If d was negative, subtract the number in the table from 1.

Step 5: For greater accuracy, interpolate using thousandths.

Tenths	0.00	0.01	0.02	0.03	0.04	0.05	0.06	0.07	0.08	0.09
					Hundredths					
0.0	.5000	.5040	.5080	.5120	.5160	.5199	.5239	.5279	.5319	.5359
0.1	.5398	.5438	.5478	.5517	.5557	.5596	.5636	.5675	.5714	.5753
0.2	.5793	.5832	.5871	.5910	.5948	.5987	.6026	.6064	.6103	.6141
0.3	.6179	.6217	.6255	.6293	.6331	.6368	.6406	.6443	.6480	.6517
0.4	.6554	.6591	.6628	.6664	.6700	.6736	.6772	.6808	.6844	.6879
0.5	.6915	.6950	.6985	.7019	.7054	.7088	.7123	.7157	.7190	.7224
0.6	.7257	.7291	.7324	.7357	.7389	.7422	.7454	.7486	.7517	.7549
0.7	.7580	.7611	.7642	.7673	.7704	.7734	.7764	.7794	.7823	.7852
0.8	.7881	.7910	.7939	.7967	.7995	.8023	.8051	.8078	.8106	.8133
0.9	.8159	.8186	.8212	.8238	.8264	.8289	.8315	.8340	.8365	.8389
1.0	.8413	.8438	.8461	.8485	.8508	.8531	.8554	.8577	.8599	.8621
1.1	.8643	.8665	.8686	.8708	.8729	.8749	.8770	.8790	.8810	.8830
1.2	.8849	.8869	.8888	.8907	.8925	.8944	.8962	.8980	.8997	.9015
1.3	.9032	.9049	.9066	.9082	.9099	.9115	.9131	.9147	.9162	.9177
1.4	.9192	.9207	.9222	.9236	.9251	.9265	.9279	.9292	.9306	.9319

	.00	.01	.02	.03	.04	.05	.06	.07	.08	.09
1.5	.9332	.9345	.9357	.9370	.9382	.9394	.9406	.9418	.9429	.9441
1.6	.9452	.9463	.9474	.9484	.9495	.9505	.9515	.9525	.9535	.9545
1.7	.9554	.9564	.9573	.9582	.9591	.9599	.9608	.9616	.9625	.9633
1.8	.9641	.9649	.9656	.9664	.9671	.9678	.9686	.9693	.9699	.9706
1.9	.9713	.9719	.9726	.9732	.9738	.9744	.9750	.9756	.9761	.9767
2.0	.9772	.9778	.9783	.9788	.9793	.9798	.9803	.9808	.9812	.9817
2.1	.9821	.9826	.9830	.9834	.9838	.9842	.9846	.9850	.9854	.9857
2.2	.9861	.9864	.9868	.9871	.9875	.9878	.9881	.9884	.9887	.9890
2.3	.9893	.9896	.9898	.9901	.9904	.9906	.9909	.9911	.9913	.9916
2.4	.9918	.9920	.9922	.9925	.9927	.9929	.9931	.9932	.9934	.9936
2.5	.9938	.9940	.9941	.9943	.9945	.9946	.9948	.9949	.9951	.9952
2.6	.9953	.9955	.9956	.9957	.9959	.9960	.9961	.9962	.9963	.9964
2.7	.9965	.9966	.9967	.9968	.9969	.9970	.9971	.9972	.9973	.9974
2.8	.9974	.9975	.9976	.9977	.9977	.9978	.9979	.9979	.9980	.9981
2.9	.9981	.9982	.9982	.9983	.9984	.9984	.9985	.9985	.9986	.9986
3.0	.9987	.9987	.9987	.9988	.9988	.9989	.9989	.9989	.9990	.9990

Example: If $d = 0.51$, look in the row with tenths = 0.5 and the column with hundredths = 0.01 to find $N(0.51) = 0.6950$. If $d = -0.89$, locate the value corresponding to 0.89 (0.8133) and subtract it from 1 to determine that $N(-0.89) = 0.1867$.

7. Describe the relationship between the value of a call option and the underlying standard deviation of the stock.
8. Describe the relationship between the value of a call option and the option's time to maturity.

PROBLEMS

1. The Last Resort Hotel sells, for $25, a coupon that allows the holder to stay for one week for $350. Currently the regular price of a one-week stay is $450, but the price varies a great deal due to travel conditions. The coupon is good for one year.
   a. What is the call option in the above discussion?
   b. What are the five variables that would determine the value of the above call option?
2. The following option prices were listed for the Jennings Corporation on August 29:

Jennings Corporation — Call Option Prices

NY Close	Strike Price	September	October
$46	$40	7½	6⅞
$46	$45	1½	1⅛
$46	$50	¼	½

   a. From the call options above, identify those that are "in the money" and those that are "out of the money."
   b. Explain why the September option with a strike price of $50 has value.
   c. Explain why the October options have prices or premiums that are higher than those for the September options.
3. A November call option for the Rather Corporation has a price or premium of ¹⁄₁₆. The closing price of Rather's stock is $1.50, and the option's exercise price is $3.00. Is the option "in the money," "out of the money," or "at the money"? Explain.
4. Brokaw, Inc., has a call option that expires in two months. Brokaw's stock is currently trading at $53. The exercise price of the call option is $35. Which of the following call option prices are possible: $2, $12, or $20? Explain.
5. Reno Corp. has common stock trading at $50 per share. Suppose you purchase one share of Reno.
   a. Determine the profit or loss on your stock investment in Reno if when you sell the stock the price per share is: $0; $50; $60; or $100.
   b. Make a graph of the profit or loss from your stock investment at each of the prices listed in part (a). Place the four potential stock prices from problem 2 on the horizontal axis, and the

profit or loss from each of these four potential stock prices on the vertical axis.

6. Reno Corp. (problem 5), whose stock is currently trading at $50 per share, also has a call option with a strike price of $50. The call option premium is $10.
   a. Determine the profit or loss on an investment in one Reno call option if at the option's expiration the stock price is: $0; $50; $60; or $100.
   b. Make a graph of the profit or loss from investing in the Reno call option. Place the four potential stock prices on the horizontal axis, and the option's profit or loss from each of these four stock prices on the vertical axis.
   c. Compare the graph in problem 6(b) to the graph in problem 5(b). Relate these graphs to the risk of a call option vis-à-vis the risk of stock investments.

7. Consider Black Jack Harry, an investor who writes (sells) the call option on Reno that you bought in problem 6.
   a. Determine the profit or loss on Harry's call writing investment if at the option's expiration the stock price is: $0; $50; $60; or $100.
   b. Make a graph of the profit or loss from writing the Reno call option. Place the four potential stock prices on the horizontal axis, and the option writer's profit or loss from these four stock prices on the vertical axis.
   c. Compare the graph in problem 7(b) to the graph in problem 6(b). Relate these graphs to the differences between purchasing and writing call options.

8. Assume that there is a call option on IBM Corp. with a strike price of $100 and an expiration date of June 18. What would the call option be worth on June 18 if the stock is worth:
   a. $112
   b. $102
   c. $92
   d. $100

9. Assume that there is a call option on Eastman Kodak Corporation (EK) with a strike price of $50 and an expiration date of July 20. What would the call option be worth on the following dates and at the following stock prices? (Some of your answers should be in the form "greater than $3.")
   a. On July 20 EK is $52
   b. On July 1 EK is $52
   c. On July 20 EK is $50
   d. On June 1 EK is $50
   e. On July 20 EK is $48
   f. On June 15 EK is worth $48

10. Make a graph of the value of a call option on its expiration date.

Place the underlying stock price on the vertical axis and the call option price on the horizontal axis. Assume that the strike price is $50.

11. What will happen to the value of a call option on a share of stock if everything else stays constant and:
    a. The underlying stock price rises?
    b. The volatility of the underlying stock rises?
    c. The time to expiration of the option is extended?
    d. The risk-free interest rates rise?
    e. The strike price is increased?
    f. The beta of the underlying stock rises but the total variance remains constant?

12. IBM Corp. is selling at $100 per share, and some strange call options begin trading that have widely varying strike prices and expiration dates.
    a. What is the maximum price that any of the call options can sell for?
    b. What is the minimum price that any call option can sell for?

13. Would the owner of a call option hope that the underlying stock price will rise or fall (select one)? What about a person who has written or sold the call option and doesn't own the underlying stock?

14. Fill in the blanks from the following list: strike price, stockholders, time to expiration, variance of the firm's underlying asset, call option price, price of underlying assets, debt, debtholders, call option.

    The common stock of a corporation with debt may be viewed as a _____ on the firm's assets. If the _____ wish to exercise their call option, they simply pay off the firm's _____ by paying them the face value of the firm's _____, which represents the exercise or _____ of the option. The time to maturity of the debt may be viewed as the option's _____. The firm's stock price may therefore be computed as a _____, and it will rise whenever there is a rise in the risk-free interest rate, a rise in the firm's _____, or an increase in risk causes the _____ to increase.

15. Using the Black-Scholes option pricing model, compute the values for call options, given the five variables:

	Strike Price	Underlying Asset	Variance of Underlying Asset	Time to Expiration	Risk-free Interest Rate
a.	$20	$16	0.40	0.25	0.10
b.	$20	$18	0.40	0.25	0.10
c.	$20	$20	0.40	0.25	0.10
d.	$20	$22	0.40	0.25	0.10
e.	$20	$24	0.40	0.25	0.10

16. Using the answers to problem 15, make a graph with option prices on the vertical axis and the price of the underlying asset on the horizontal axis.

17. Assume that you observed that a call option has a price of $2.00 when the underlying asset has a price of $20, the strike price is $20, the time to expiration is 0.25 years, and the risk-free interest rate is 0.10 (i.e., 10%). Using the Black-Scholes option pricing model and trial and error, estimate what the variance of the underlying asset must be. (Hint: Plug in guesses of the variance until the model's answer is near the given option price.)

DISCUSSION QUESTIONS

1. Respond to the following statement:

    Call options sound great! Just think, their gains are unlimited but their losses are limited. I just don't understand why option writers would offer such fantastic opportunities.

2. The chapter explains that the firm's equity holders have a call option on the assets of the firm. The text also teaches us that the value of a call option increases with an increase in risk. Putting these two concepts together seems to suggest that the firm's equity holders are better off when the firm's assets take on additional risk. But isn't risk bad? Explain.

3. Can a call option have a negative value?

4. Is option trading speculation and should it be legal?

5. Respond to the following statement:

    It is said that when options reach their expiration date an investor's position is terminated and often the investor can be forced to accept a loss. In contrast, an investor in stocks can always wait until the stock returns to profitability.

6. Dollar price changes in options are almost always less than dollar price changes in the underlying asset, implying that options are less risky compared to the underlying asset. However, percentage price changes in options are almost always greater than percentage price changes in the underlying asset, implying that options are more risky. Which is correct?

APPENDIX

The Black-Scholes Option Pricing Model

The Black-Scholes option pricing model produces an option price from five variables. The key complexity to the model is the use of the cumulative normal probability function: $N(d)$. The function $N(d)$ is the probability that a standard normally distributed variable will have a value equal to or less than the quantity d. The Black-Scholes formula also shows how d can be calculated.

The value of $N(d)$ is equal to zero when d is equal to negative infinity and is equal to one when d is equal to positive infinity. The value of $N(d)$ can be found from a table of cumulative probabilities of the standard normal distribution function or by using a sophisticated calculator or computer.

The Black-Scholes option pricing model is:

$$\text{CALL} = [P \cdot N(d_1)] - [EX \cdot N(d_2) \cdot e^{-rt}]. \qquad \text{(A9.1)}$$

where:

CALL = price of the call option (the premium)
P = price of the underlying asset,
$N(\cdot)$ = cumulative normal probability function,
EX = exercise price of option,
e = the exponential function,
r = risk-free interest rate (continuously compounded)
t = time to expiration,
$d_1 = [ln(P \div EX) + (r + 0.5\sigma^2)t] \div \sqrt{\sigma^2 t}$
$d_2 = d_1 - \sqrt{\sigma^2 t}$
σ^2 = variance of the price changes of the underlying security.

Looking at the model you may now think that the best way to use it is through a computer program. However, it really isn't as hard as it looks at first. Follow these steps:

1. Calculate the value of d_1 using its formula and write it down,
2. Use d_1 to calculate the value of d_2 and write it down,
3. Convert d_1 and d_2 to $N(d_1)$ and $N(d_2)$, using Table 9.2, and write them down,
4. Calculate e^{-rt} and write it down, and
5. Plug these values into the model.

For example, using the following values:

$$P = \$95.00,$$
$$E_x = \$100.00,$$
$$t = 0.25,$$
$$\sigma = 0.20, \text{ and}$$
$$r = 0.10,$$

the call option value is determined as follows. First, determine the values for d_1 and d_2:

$$d_1 = \frac{ln(\$95 \div \$100) + (0.1 + 0.5\,(0.04))0.25}{\sqrt{0.04(0.25)}} = \frac{-0.0513 + 0.03}{0.1} = -0.213$$

$$d_2 = -0.213 - \sqrt{0.04\,(0.25)} = -0.313.$$

Next, determine the values for $N(d_1)$ and $N(d_2)$. Remember that $N(d_1)$ and $N(d_2)$ represent the probability that a standard normally distributed random variable will have a value less than or equal to d_1 or d_2.

$$N(d_1) = N(-.213) = 0.4157.$$
$$N(d_2) = N(-.313) = 0.3772.$$

The value of the call option therefore is:

$$CALL = \$95\,(0.4157) - \$100\,(0.3772)\,e^{-0.1(0.25)}$$

where $e^{-0.1(0.25)} = 0.9753$.

$$CALL = \$39.49 - \$36.79 = \$2.70.$$

If the current stock price were \$105 instead of \$95, the call price would be determined as follows.

$$d_1 = \frac{ln(\$105 \div \$100) + (0.1 + 0.5\,(0.04))0.25}{\sqrt{0.04(0.25)}} = \frac{0.0448 + 0.03}{0.1} = 0.788$$

$$d_2 = 0.788 - \sqrt{0.04(0.25)} = 0.688.$$
$$N(d_1) = N(0.788) = 0.7846.$$
$$N(d_2) = N(0.688) = 0.7542.$$

The value of the call option therefore is:

$$CALL = \$105\,(0.7846) - \$100(0.7542)\,e^{-0.1(0.25)}$$
$$CALL = \$82.38 - \$73.56 = \$8.82.$$

"And the Winning Envelope Is . . ."

Two envelopes are available to you called Envelope A and Envelope B. There are only two things you know about these envelopes:

1. One of the envelopes contains ten times as much money as the other envelope, and
2. Neither envelope contains more than $10,000.

You do not know which envelope has more money since the placement of the money in each envelope was done with perfect randomness.

You are given two alternatives:

a. You may select Envelope A first and stop the game by keeping the money. You can, however, give up the money and switch to Envelope B, which is unopened. If you switch to Envelope B you must accept whatever is in Envelope B and stop the game.

b. You may select Envelope B, keep the money, and the "game" is over.

Which alternative would you select?

If you selected alternative (a), in what case(s) would you decide to switch to Envelope B and in what case(s) would you keep Envelope A?

For an especially difficult challenge, how would your answer change if there were no limit on the amount of money that could be in either envelope (in other words, delete the second of the two facts that are known).

MODULE 4

The Financing Decision

The first three modules focused almost exclusively on the management of corporate assets. To meet the objective of shareholder wealth maximization, financial managers should invest in projects whose benefits exceed costs, or projects with a positive net present value. Net present value was shown to take into account both the time value of money and risk.

Module 4 shifts the focus from the investment decision to the financing decision. Corporations issue securities to finance their assets. These securities—represented generally by bonds and stocks—come in hundreds of different varieties. Does the choice of a particular set of financing instruments matter? In other words, can firm value be maximized through a particular mix of bonds and stocks? How much time should financial managers spend on the financing decision? How high a dividend should the firm pay to the shareholders? These are all examples of questions that relate to the financing decision.

As in the module on Risk, we offer a preview of the important results that will be developed in the next three chapters:

☐ Financial leverage is created when the firm borrows money in the form of debt. Financial leverage changes the risk of holding the firm's debt and equity securities, but does not change the risk of the firm as a whole (Chapter 10).

☐ Using the restrictive assumptions of a perfect market, the decision of how to finance the firm's assets is irrelevant. The implication of this is that corporate managers should spend little time on how to raise money and most of their time on how to invest the money raised (Chapter 10).

☐ When the restrictive assumptions of a perfect market are relaxed, the conclusion above no longer holds. In such a case, the decision of how the firm finances its assets can change the value of the firm and therefore shareholder wealth (Chapter 11).

☐ The dividend policy of the firm is the decision of which portion of the firm's earnings to pay to shareholders and which portion to retain inside the firm. Under the restrictive assumptions of a perfect market, this decision is irrelevant. However, when the restrictive assumptions of a perfect market are relaxed, the dividend decision can change the value of the firm and shareholder wealth (Chapter 12).

Chapter 10

Financial Leverage

During the late 1980s there was an explosion in the use of a type of bond known as a junk bond, which may be defined as a risky corporate bond. The reason junk bonds are risky is that the corporation usually has issued so much debt that there is a higher than average probability that the corporation will default on some or all of its promised debt payments.

Most junk debt originated from corporate ownership or management battles, especially mergers, in which the corporation's existing assets were purchased from the original owners. Hundreds of billions of dollars changed hands in these mergers and other deals. For example, in one of the largest such corporate ownership changes, the assets of RJR Nabisco, Inc., were purchased with almost $30 billion of new debt such that the assets of the new company were backed by almost 95 percent debt and only 5 percent equity. The investment bankers who acted as intermediaries between the issuing corporation and bond investors earned large and in some cases outrageous transactions fees. A certain percentage of junk bond investors lost money when the issuing corporations experienced financial distress and stopped making promised payments. The media were filled with editorials that decried runaway debt usage by corporations.

The use of junk bonds to finance an acquisition is an example of a corporate financing decision. Other less dramatic examples of corporate financing decisions include the issuing of bonds to finance new projects. Increasingly, financing has become a centerpiece of corporate news stories. Modern finance, however, offers some surprising answers to questions concerning the importance of corporate financing decisions.

AN OVERVIEW OF CORPORATE FINANCING

Chapter 10 follows the balance-sheet view of the firm, emphasizing that a corporation contains assets financed by both debt and equity. As we said early on, the two most important decisions facing financial managers are how to raise the needed money, known as the financing decision, and which assets to acquire with the money raised, known as the investment decision.

Chapter 6 discussed the firm's investment decision through capital budgeting. In a nutshell, the firm compares the costs of investment with the benefits of investment. Good projects are those whose present value of benefits exceeds the present value of costs—in other words, those with a positive net present value (*NPV*).

This module now shifts to the other major decision—where to obtain the money to invest in positive-*NPV* projects. The decision of where to raise money is called the **financing decision**, the capital structure decision, or the debt to equity decision. These three terms are often used interchangeably.

The Walt Disney Company provides a good example of the types of securities a firm typically uses to raise capital. Disney's capital structure, shown in Chapter 1, includes four varieties of debt securities—bank loans, commercial paper, bonds, and accounts payable—and two varieties of equity securities—common stock and preferred stock. Disney is typical of other corporations in the use of many dif-

financing decision
The decision as to which securities the firm will issue in order to raise money to finance the firm's assets. The financing decision is also known as the capital structure decision or the debt-to-equity decision.

TABLE 10.1
1990 Long-Term Debt of Westinghouse Financial Services, Inc.

Type of Security	Dollar Amount (in millions)
Commercial paper supported by variable-rate revolving credit agreements	$1,303
Medium-term notes due through 2000	2,464
Federal Home Loan Bank advances	70
Variable-rate bank loan due 1992	299
Variable-rate bank loan through 1993	79
Variable-rate senior notes due 1995	200
8 7/8% senior notes due 1995	150
6 3/4% yen note due 1996	74
8 3/8% senior notes due 1996	100
8 7/8% senior notes due 2014	150
Other	271
	$5,160

Source: From The Westinghouse Corporation Annual Report, 1990. Reprinted by permission of Westinghouse Electric Corporation.

ferent types of securities in their capital structure. For example, Table 10.1 lists the debt included in the balance sheet category "long-term debt" of Westinghouse Financial Services, Inc., in 1990. These eleven categories do not include short-term debt and other financing commitments of the firm.

Window 10.1 provides some detail on common types of securities used in firm financing.

The fact that firms often choose to finance their assets with many different types of securities appears to indicate that how a firm is financed is very important. In other words, casual observation might suggest that wealth can be created or lost by making good or bad financing decisions. However, these issues need to be examined carefully. By the end of this chapter we hope that you will be convinced that how a firm is financed is not nearly important as how it invests and how it is operated.

To provide an analogy to corporate financing decisions, consider the decision to purchase a car. Most people spend 99 percent of their time deciding on which car manufacturer, which car dealership, which car model, and which car options are most desirable, and one percent of their time deciding which financing option is best. The reason that financing is relatively unimportant is that most car loans offer similar interest rates. One loan choice is about as good as any other loan choice.

In the case of corporate financing, we will discuss whether a firm's particular choice of instruments is as good as any other choice. One key question is whether or not financing can affect firm value. In other words, this module examines whether it matters which types of securities and quantities of securities a corporation uses to raise capital, and the answer to this question involves a complex set of issues. The approach of modern corporate finance is to build logically from a very simple model to more complex models. The simplest model—one in perfect capital markets—provides such a logical starting point.

Financing in Perfect Markets

perfect markets
Markets that operate under highly restrictive assumptions such as zero tax rates, no transactions cost, and full information of all market participants.

The initial model describes behavior in an environment of **perfect markets**. Perfect markets are synonymous with a set of highly restrictive assumptions regarding how securities are traded, how information is received, and how individuals make decisions.[1] Most notable for this discussion is that no corporate or personal income taxes are

---

1. Perfect market assumptions can be summarized as follows: First, markets are frictionless in the sense that there are no costs of transacting, no taxes, and no regulations. Second, information regarding securities and markets is free and understood by all participants.

Window 10.1

The Menu of Financing Securities

This window describes financial securities that make up a firm's capital structure. The securities listed here are the more common types and are not meant as an all-inclusive list.

A. Short-Term Securities

1. Accounts Payable: Credit extended by suppliers for the purchase of raw materials and other goods used for the firm's normal operations. The level of accounts payable will fluctuate with the firm's level of purchases. Terms of credit are usually very short term, with 30 days serving as the standard.

2. Notes Payable: Securities usually issued to banks to cover seasonal expenditures related to the firm's working capital.

3. Commercial Paper: Securities issued by financially secure corporations with maturities that range up to 9 months. Commercial paper is usually backed by the value of the firm's assets.

B. Long-Term Securities—Bonds

1. Debentures: Bonds or debt obligations of the firm whose payment is backed only by the earnings of the firm.

2. Secured Bonds: Bonds whose payment is backed by specific assets. A common type of collateral backing a bond is the issuer's property.

(continued on next page)

paid. Perfect market assumptions, admittedly unrealistic, help to set in place a foundation with which to build more realistic models of capital structure. As part of this foundation, modern finance has proven that, in perfect markets, capital structure does not affect the value of the firm. This is to say that one package of financing securities, such as all equity capital and no debt, is as good as any other package, such as half equity capital and half debt. The form of financing is said to be irrelevant.

Window 10.1 *(continued)*

3. Callable Bonds: Bonds that can be redeemed by the issuer before maturity. Issuers who exercise their option to call usually pay a special fee or a premium to the holder at the time of the call.

4. Convertible Bonds: Bonds that, at the option of the holder, can be converted into another security, usually shares of common stock.

5. Floating-Rate Bonds: Bonds whose coupon interest rate is tied to an interest rate index and thus can change through time. For example, the bond's coupon payment may be set 2 percent higher than the 90-day Treasury bill rate.

6. Income Bonds: Bonds whose coupon payments are not fixed but instead change with the income of the firm. Insufficient income would relieve the firm from making payments to the bondholders, while higher-than-expected income would generate higher payments to the bondholders.

7. Zero Coupon Bonds: Bonds that pay no coupon payment. Zero coupon bonds are sold at a price far below their value at maturity. The difference between the bond's selling price and the bond's purchase price represents the return earned on the bond.

C. Long-Term Securities—Stocks

1. Common Stock: Securities that represent ownership in a corporation. Holders of common stock are given the right to vote for the firm's board of directors, and they are entitled to share in the residual profits of the firm (after all other claims have been paid), and are thus referred to as residual claimants.

2. Preferred Stock: Stock that pays dividends at some specified rate and whose shares must receive dividends before the holders of common stock.

⌧ Modern finance has proven that in perfect markets, capital structure does not affect the value of the firm.

An important implication of this is that managers should spend most of their time on the investment decision, such as which assets to acquire, and very little time on the financing decision, such as how those assets should be financed. The rest of this chapter will detail the analysis that leads to this conclusion.

The Traditionalist Versus the Modernist Positions on Capital Structure

Nowhere in corporate finance is the distinction between traditional finance and modern finance more clear than in the financing decision.

Simply put, traditionalists believe that financing decisions are very important and that the firm should search for the package of securities that minimizes the aggregate cost of obtaining capital for the firm. This package of securities is known as the optimal capital structure. The traditionalist position is not based upon careful model construction, deductive reasoning, and empirical validation. Rather, traditionalists make general observations about the firm's financing alternatives and then draw inferences regarding how a firm arrives at an optimal capital structure.

The traditionalists' position is illustrated in Figure 10.1(a), where it is shown that the firm's cost of capital changes as the use of debt financing inside the firm changes, and in Figure 10.1(b), where it is shown that that firm value is maximized at some optimal level of debt financing.

Modernists take a much different and, at least initially, a much simpler approach. Modernists claim that the decision is irrelevant—that there is no ideal or optimal capital structure. This is illustrated in Figure 10.2, for both the cost of the firm's capital and the value of the firm.

FIGURE 10.1
The Traditionalists' View on Financing and Firm Value

According to the traditionalists' view on financing, firm value is maximized at the point at which the cost of capital is minimized. Managers should search for the optimal debt level of the firm.

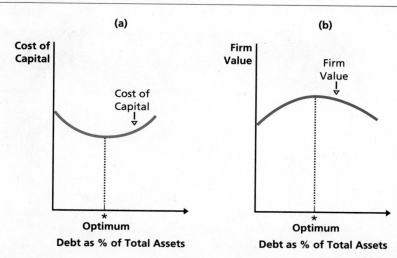

FIGURE 10.2
The Modernists' View on Financing and Firm Value

According to the modernists' view on financing, firm value is not related to the choice of financing. One capital structure is as good as any other capital structure.

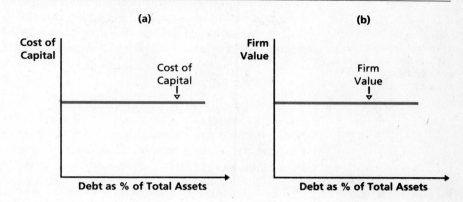

Modernists believe that, in certain conditions, the firm's cost of capital is the same for any financing mix so that it doesn't matter what types of securities the firm issues or when it issues them. At a minimum, modernists believe that corporate financial managers can do far more to maximize shareholder wealth by properly managing the firm's real assets than by transacting in financial markets.

The remainder of this chapter will explore the traditionalist and modernist positions in detail. Because both positions are based on financial leverage, or on the use of debt financing, and the effect of financial leverage on the firm, we must first explore the mechanics of financial leverage. Thus, whether you are a modernist, a traditionalist, or just intend to complete the course successfully, understanding the mechanics of financial leverage is important.

THE MECHANICS OF FINANCIAL LEVERAGE

financial leverage
The use of debt. Financial leverage is created when the firm borrows money in the form of debt.

Everyone should be familiar with the concept of physical leverage, which permits heavy objects to be lifted with relative ease—for example, the use of a car jack to change a tire. The key to leverage is that all of the energy from a large movement, such as the pumping of a jack's handle, is concentrated into a smaller and more powerful movement. The **financial leverage** that results from the use of debt is much like physical leverage.

> ⚡ Financial leverage manipulates risk as physical leverage manipulates energy.

Being Unlevered: The Case of No Debt

To understand the concept of financial leverage, let's begin by considering a firm that uses no debt at all. We can call this firm an all-equity firm, or an **unlevered firm.** Because this firm has no debt, its basic balance sheet relationship is simplified:

unlevered firm
A firm that finances its assets with equity capital only such that there is no debt in its capital structure.

$$\text{The Unlevered Firm: Assets} = \text{Equity}. \qquad (10.1)$$

For unlevered firms, owning a portion of the firm's equity is effectively the same as owning a portion of the firm's assets. In other words, because the equity holders own 100 percent of the assets of the firm, the risk and return characteristics of the firm's equity are essentially equal to the characteristics of the assets.

Example 10.1 _____ Consider an individual who sets up a corporation to own and rent out houses. The individual puts up money or equity capital to start the business in the amount of $100,000 and uses this capital to purchase a $100,000 house. The risk and return of the individual's $100,000 in equity capital is identical to the risk and return of the house. If the house, which is the firm's only asset, rises in value by 20 percent to $120,000, then the individual's equity in the firm also rises by 20 percent to $120,000. If the rental of the house produces an $18,000 per year cash flow, then the equityholder will be entitled to the entire $18,000 cash flow. Because we are in a perfect market, there are no taxes. The return on the house, expressed as a percentage, is:

$$\text{Return to Equityholder} = \frac{\$18,000}{\$100,000} = 0.18 \text{ or } 18\%. \quad \hookleftarrow$$

Being Levered: The Case of Debt

Now let's consider that in addition to raising money by issuing equity, the firm borrows money in the form of debt. In the balance-sheet view of the firm, the firm's assets are now financed by both debt and equity. The effect of this borrowing is termed financial leverage, and a firm that borrows is often called a **levered firm.**

levered firm
A firm that finances its assets with both debt and equity capital such that there is debt in its capital structure.

The best way to understand the use of debt and equity is to view debt as having low risk and to view equity as having high risk. Because debtholders have prior claims to the firm's cash flows, they usually expect to receive their promised payments and thus are in a less risky position vis-à-vis the equityholders. Remember that equityholders are residual claimants and receive cash flows only when all prior claims, including those of bondholders, have been satisfied.

A corporation that has both debt and equity may be viewed as taking the cash flow stream produced by the firm's assets and dividing or partitioning the cash flow into two streams: (1) a low-risk debt stream and (2) a high-risk equity stream:

$$\text{The Levered Firm:} \qquad\qquad\qquad (10.2)$$
$$\text{Assets} = \text{(Low-Risk) Debt} + \text{(High-Risk) Equity.}$$

Example 10.2 ——————— Now let's consider using leverage, or debt, in the previous housing example. Suppose that in addition to equity capital the individual issues a debt security known as a mortgage and uses the proceeds of the debt to purchase assets for the corporation. When money is borrowed, the lender of the money demands a position of priority in receiving the firm's cash flows. The lender, or in this case the mortgage holder or more generally the debtholder, has a fixed claim on the assets of the firm. In contrast, the equityholder has a residual claim.

The equityholder, still with $100,000 to invest, now considers a new set of assets for the corporation. Rather than buying a single $100,000 house with the firm's equity, the corporation might combine the $100,000 in equity with $100,000 in debt and purchase two $100,000 houses. Perhaps each house is financed with $50,000 of debt and $50,000 of equity. The firm's balance sheet looks like this:

$$\text{Assets} \;=\; \text{Debt} \;+\; \text{Equity}$$
$$\$200,000 = \$100,000 + \$100,000.$$

Since the corporation has two houses, the cash flow stream produced by the assets will be twice the cash flow stream of our previous example, in which the corporation purchased one house and didn't use debt. However, now the cash flow stream produced by the firm's assets must be divided or partitioned into debt and equity streams. If the debt were issued at a cost of 10 percent, debtholders would be entitled to interest payments of $10,000 per year (10 percent of $100,000). Equityholders are entitled to whatever cash flow remains after the debtholders' claims have been satisfied.

The $10,000 of promised cash flow to the debtholders changes the financial position of the equityholders. Specifically, we will show that an effect of the financial leverage is to increase the risk of the equityholders' claim.

Let's first examine the good side of financial leverage. If each house produces $18,000 of cash flow, for a total of $36,000 for the two houses, the equityholders will pay $10,000 to the debtholders and be left with $26,000. Expressed as a percentage, the return to the equityholders is:

$$\text{Return to Equityholders} = \frac{(\$36,000 - \$10,000)}{\$100,000}$$
$$= 0.26 \text{ or } 26\%.$$

Notice that this 26 percent return exceeds the 18 percent return earned in the case of the unlevered firm.

Now let's consider the bad side of financial leverage. Suppose the market for rental properties turns bad, and that the rental receipts for the two houses drop from $36,000 to $15,000. Because the debtholders have prior claims, the equityholders must first satisfy the debtholders' claim through a $10,000 interest payment, leaving a residual cash flow of only $5,000. Expressed as a percentage, the return to the equityholders is:

$$\text{Return to Equityholders} = \frac{(\$15,000 - \$10,000)}{\$100,000}$$
$$= 0.05 \text{ or } 5\%.$$

In this case the return of 5 percent falls short of the return earned in the case of the unlevered firm (7.5%). ←

Financial Leverage from the Perspective of Debtholders and Equityholders

We now examine our example of financial leverage from the perspective of both debtholders and equityholders. The debtholders will generally view their claim as virtually assuring a 10 percent return. Their claim is fixed, and although they have no chance of earning a return greater than 10 percent, there is little chance that the real estate market will become so depressed that their promised return is at risk. In fact, the only case in which the debtholders will not receive the 10 percent return is if the corporation defaults on the debt by failing to make the required interest payments. This is a serious consequence and would result in the corporation declaring bankruptcy. Detail on the bankruptcy process is provided in Window 10.2.

In contrast to debtholders, the equityholders view their position as being riskier than just owning a single house, because their position contains leverage. The financial risks of two houses are being borne primarily by the equityholders even though they have only invested an amount of money equal to the value of one house. If things go poorly, the equityholders still owe the debtholders $10,000 per year and thus

Window 10.2

The Bankruptcy Process

We define bankruptcy as a financial situation in which the value of the firm's assets is less than the face value of the firm's debt. However, to be precise, bankruptcy is a complex legal procedure whose details are set forth by the Bankruptcy Act of 1978. In essence, declaring bankruptcy provides temporary protection to the shareholders against legal action taken by the debtholders or creditors.

The bankruptcy process can proceed in one of two ways; liquidation or reorganization. The process of liquidation falls under Chapter 7 of the Federal Bankruptcy Act and is best used when the firm is worth more dead than alive. Under a liquidation, control of the firm's assets is transferred from current management to a court-appointed trustee. The trustee is in charge of selling the assets and distributing its proceeds.

A well defined pecking order exists to determine the position of the creditors in receiving the proceeds of the liquefied assets of a firm. Generally speaking, claims of secured creditors, such as bonds backed by specific assets of the firm, come first. Next in line are employees' claims on wages, claims on the firm's pension plan, and the claims of unsecured or general creditors. Next to last come the claims of preferred stockholders, and, finally, common stockholders.

In contrast to a liquidation, the firm may instead seek to be reorganized, which is governed by Chapter 11 of the Federal Bankruptcy Act. Reorganizations are usually more complicated, as compared to liquidations, and are usually more in the interest of shareholders and creditors low on the pecking order. A reorganization means that the firm is permitted to continue operations while working on a plan for turning the business around.

During reorganization, the firm is operated by either existing management, a group representing the debtors, or a court-appointed trustee. The plan of reorganization must be accepted by the creditors and the court before it can go into effect. The reorganization plan specifies how the creditors' claims will be satisfied through the reorganized firm. In many cases, the creditors exchange their original claims for a new set of claims. For example, bondholders may exchange their $1,000 face-value bond for an amount of, say, $500 and a new bond that promises to start paying interest sometime in the future.

For the sake of keeping the contractual obligations of the firm alive, reorganizations are preferred. Reorganizations make sense if the financial problems of the firm are considered to be temporary—perhaps the result of a local or national economic downturn that is outside the control of the firm's managers. Of course, financial distress that is beyond repair will most likely lead to the liquidation of the firm's assets.

will do much worse than if they had not borrowed the money. If things go well, the equityholders can earn much greater cash flows than if they owned a single house.

The association between the concepts of physical leverage and financial leverage should now be clear. A small amount of physical leverage may allow its users to concentrate two times their normal force into their work. Similarly, in the above example, financial leverage is used and twice as much economic risk, such as two houses rather than one, is borne by the equityholders.

The Link Between Financial Leverage and Risk.   We now need to get more specific about financial leverage and its effect on risk. Suppose, for instance, that in the example above each rental house had one unit of risk. Thus, two rental houses have two units of risk, and so forth. Because a corporation is simply a set of contracts, the risk of a firm's assets flows through to the suppliers of capital. In the case of no debt, the risk of the assets flows through on a dollar-for-dollar basis to the equityholders, as next shown:

Unlevered Firm:

Assets		*Debt*		*Equity*
Risk = 1 unit	=	Risk = 0 units	+	Risk = 1 unit
Amount = $100,000		Amount = $0		Amount = $100,000

However, when the corporation issues debt, the risk of the assets becomes partitioned into a high level of risk represented by equity, and a low level of risk represented by debt. If we assume that the debt was risk-free, such that there is no chance of default, then the risk may be diagramed as follows:

Levered Firm with 50% Debt:

Assets		*Debt*		*Equity*
Risk = 2 units	=	Risk = 0 units	+	Risk = 2 units
Amount = $200,000		Amount = $100,000		Amount = $100,000

Notice that the use of debt has the result of partitioning a moderate level of asset risk into securities with lower risk (debt) and higher risk (equity). In this case, the firm used 50 percent debt and we assumed that this doubled the risk of the equity while permitting the debtholders to bear no risk.

Increasing Financial Leverage—The Case of Using More Debt.
The previous situation can be extended by using more than 50 percent debt. For example, the equityholders may be able to use the corporation to buy four or more houses, utilizing borrowed money to finance the added investment.

TABLE 10.2
Financial Leverage and Risks to Equityholders

	0% Debt	50% Debt	75% Debt	90% Debt
Number of homes purchased	1	2	4	10
Total value of homes	$100,000	$200,000	$400,000	$1,000,000
Amount of equity	$100,000	$100,000	$100,000	$ 100,000
Amount of debt	-0-	$100,000	$300,000	$ 900,000
Leverage factor	1.0	2.0	4.0	10.0
Change in equity for:				
20% rise in home values	+20%	+40%	+80%	+200%
20% decline in home values	−20%	−40%	−80%	−100%

leverage factor

The ratio between the firm's assets and the firm's equity.

The effect of more debt is to produce more leverage, so that a large amount of assets is controlled by a small amount of equity. Let's compare the effects of 50 percent debt with the effects of 75 percent debt and 90 percent debt. As shown in Table 10.2, with 50 percent debt, a 20 percent rise in housing prices will be levered into a 40 percent rise in equity. This is because the risk of $200,000 in houses is being levered into only $100,000 of equity, causing a leverage factor of 2 to 1, or 2.0 for short. We define the **leverage factor** as the ratio between the firm's assets and the firm's equity.

Thus, a firm with no debt has a leverage factor of 1.0 rather than 0.0 since the assets in the numerator are equal to the equity in the denominator. A firm with 90 percent debt would have a leverage factor of 10 since the assets in the numerator represent 100 percent of firm value and the equity in the denominator represents 10 percent of the firm value. Another way to view the leverage factor is as the inverse of the ratio of equity to assets.

The use of 75 percent debt would create a leverage factor of 4 to 1, since $400,000 in houses is purchased with only $100,000 of equity. In this case a rise of 20 percent in housing prices would be levered into an 80 percent increase in equity value. In terms of the risk diagrams used earlier, the case of 75 percent debt looks like this:

Levered Firm with 75% Debt:

Assets		*Debt*		*Equity*
Risk = 4 units	=	Risk = 0 units	+	Risk = 4 units
Amount = $400,000		Amount = $300,000		Amount = $100,000

Notice that the risk of all four houses is being concentrated or squeezed into the $100,000 of equity held by the owner. We are still assuming that the debt is risk-free.

As we said, the use of 90 percent debt would create a leverage factor of 10 to 1. Note that $1,000,000 in houses is purchased with only $100,000 of equity. In this case, a 20 percent rise in housing prices would be levered into a 200 percent rise in equity value.

Our examples have demonstrated financial leverage and rising housing values. Housing values can, however, move down as well as up. In the case of no debt, a 20 percent decline in housing prices will force a 20 percent decline in equity. When debt is used, the decline in housing values causes equity to decline by more than 20 percent. As shown in Table 10.2, the decline in equity values is 40 percent in the case of 50 percent debt, 80 percent in the case of 75 percent debt, and 100 percent in the case of 90 percent debt.

An interesting result can be obtained by comparing, with 90 percent debt, the change in the value of the equity as housing values move up and down. When housing values increase by 20 percent, equity value increases by 200 percent. Yet when housing values decline by 20 percent, equity value decreases by only 100 percent. Why is the change in equity value greater for increases in value than for decreases in value? The reason is that, because of limited liability, the most equity can lose is its full value.

Another result of limited liability is that, with high leverage, some of the risk of the assets is not transferred to the equityholders but instead is transferred to the debtholders. For example, selecting an arbitrary value of 1.25 units of risk to debtholders, our risk diagram looks like this:

Levered Firm with 90% Debt:

Assets		*Debt*		*Equity*
Risk = 10 units	=	Risk = 1.25 units	+	Risk = 8.75 units
Amount = $1,000,000		Amount = $900,000		Amount = $100,000

High Leverage and Debtholder Risk. There are several important changes that occurred when we assumed that the added leverage would cause the debtholders to begin to bear risk. First, the math becomes "muddy" since a high leverage factor, say 10 to 1, no longer causes the risk of the equity to increase by the same factor. In this rough example we cannot be sure of an exact value for the leverage factor. We illustrated using a factor of 8.75 units of risk in the example above, but the same point could have been illustrated using a leverage factor other than 8.75.

Second, the example brings limited liability into focus. By using the corporate form of business organization, equityholders can transfer risk to debtholders, as is shown in the example above. Finally, the example will help us to make clear one of the great puzzles of corporate finance: If the ten-house example had been entirely equity-financed, the risk diagram would be:

Unlevered Firm with 10 Houses:

Assets		Debt		Equity
Risk = 10 units	=	Risk = 0 units	+	Risk = 10 units
Amount = $1,000,000		Amount = $0		Amount = $1,000,000

Notice that when we compare buying ten houses without debt to buying ten houses with 90 percent debt, the use of leverage causes the risk of each dollar of equity to increase. Specifically, without debt, each $100,000 of equity bears one unit of risk. With debt, the $100,000 of equity bears 8.75 units of risk.

We also noticed that when a firm takes on large amounts of debt, the riskiness of the debt increases. Specifically, with low leverage, the debt bears no risk, but with 10 to 1 leverage, the debtholder begins to bear risk.

Here's the puzzle. If leverage causes each $1 of debt and each $1 of equity to bear more risk, doesn't it have to be true that the total amount of risk has increased? The answer is no. Both the debt and equity of a firm can increase in riskiness without total firm risk changing. With 90 percent leverage, both debt and equity become more risky, but the total risk of debt and equity equals that of the risk of assets. Equityholders bear 8.75 units of risk, while debtholders bear 1.25 units of risk. Total units of risk are, however, equal to the total units in the case of no debt. Financial leverage has not caused the risk of the firm to increase; it has only acted to partition total risk between the firm's debtholders and equityholders.

> ⌛ The risk of the firm is determined by the risk of the firm's assets. The only way to change total risk is to change the assets. Financial leverage will not change total risk—it will only partition it.

Figure 10.3 provides another method of illustrating these relationships for the case of 0 percent, 50 percent, and 75 percent debt. The slopes of the lines reflect the level of risk since they reflect the effect on the equity value, measured on the vertical axis, caused by a change in asset value, measured on the horizontal axis.

In Figure 10.3, the zero percent debt line indicates that a given change in asset value corresponds to an identical change in equity value. For example, a 20 percent increase or decrease in assets corresponds to a 20 percent increase or decrease in equity. Thus, in the absence of debt, the risk of the equity is identical to the risk of the assets. Figure 10.3 also indicates that the use of debt causes asset

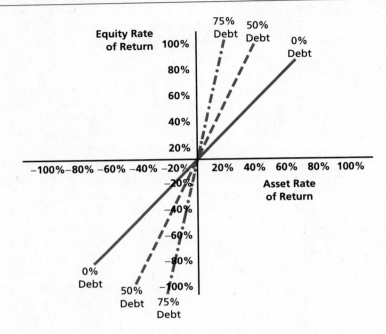

FIGURE 10.3
Financial Leverage and Rates of Return on Equity

The level of debt changes the relationship between the rate of return on equity and the rate of return on assets. The higher the level of debt, the greater the response of the rate of return on equity to a given change in the rate of return on assets.

changes to be magnified or levered into larger equity changes. The steepest line is that of 75 percent debt, illustrating the more dramatic effects of leverage on equity values. For example, a 20 percent increase or decrease in assets corresponds to an 80 percent increase or decrease in equity. For the steep or levered lines, the equity changes are two times greater than the asset changes for the 50 percent line, and four times greater than the asset changes for the 75 percent line.

A Summary of the Mechanics of Leverage

Financial leverage doesn't change the total amount of risk. Rather, it causes the risk of the assets of the firm to be partitioned into risks represented by equity claims and debt claims.

Debt is usually of relatively low risk, while equity is of relatively high risk. A firm with low financial leverage usually has very low-risk debt and only moderately risky equity. A firm with high financial leverage can have both riskier debt and equity. Nevertheless, the firm's total risk depends only on the assets and not on the use of financial leverage.

CAPITAL STRUCTURE AND FIRM VALUE— THE TRADITIONALISTS' VIEW

In our discussion of the mechanics of financial leverage, we concluded that the use of debt partitions the risk of the assets into the firm's debt securities and equity securities. We can now examine the traditionalists' view of the relationship between the use of debt (the capital structure decision) and the expected return on the firm's securities.

In order to isolate the effect of leverage on return, we assume that the risk of the firm's assets stays constant. In other words, the firm has its investment decisions in place, and is now deciding on the particular way to finance those investments.

Figure 10.4 illustrates the traditionalists' view on the effect of leverage on the expected return of both the debtholder and the equityholder. The line r_D represents the cost of debt, the line r_A is the expected rate of return on assets, and the line r_E is the cost of equity.

Traditionalists believe that as a firm moves from a position of zero debt to small amounts of debt, leverage increases the equityholders' risk but does not increase significantly the risk born by debtholders. Because the probability is high that debtholders will receive promised payments, small amounts of debt are considered to be risk-free and debtholders can be persuaded to hold debt at or near the risk-free interest rate (the curve labeled r_D). Traditionalists also believe that the

FIGURE 10.4
A Traditionalist's View on Leverage and Expected Return

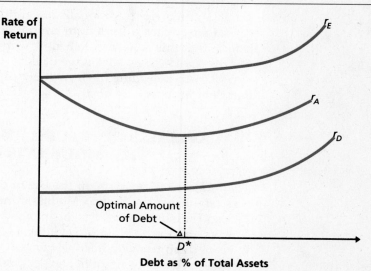

Debt as % of Total Assets

expected return on equity, labeled r_E, will not rise significantly until moderate to large amounts of debt are used.

What about the expected rate of return of the firm as a whole— the curve labeled r_A, which can be viewed as the weighted average of the firm's debt cost, or r_D, and equity cost, or r_E? Traditionalists believe that because debt is cheaper, combining equity with reasonable amounts of debt results in a reduction in the firm's overall cost of capital, or r_A. This would of course be good news because the value of the firm is higher when a lower discount rate is applied to its cash flow stream. Thus, under the traditionalists' argument, the goal of corporate management is to "tinker" with the use of debt in order to find the range of debt that minimizes the firm's cost of capital and maximizes firm value. This amount of debt, sometimes called the firm's **debt capacity**, is given by D^* in Figure 10.4.

Traditionalists believe, however, that too much debt can be a bad thing. Look what happens to the cost of both debt and equity as debt levels go from low to high. First, the cost of debt, which initially did not rise much, now starts to rise substantially as debtholders become highly concerned about the firm's ability to generate enough income to cover promised debt payments. The debtholders' concern is translated into higher required rates of return on debt.

Second, at high debt levels, the cost of equity also rises quickly because equityholders know that high amounts of debt are accompanied by high amounts of fixed interest payments, increasing the chance that they as residual claimants will end up with little or no return on their investment. Thus, following the traditionalists' argument, the overall cost of capital of the firm begins to rise at high levels of debt.

To summarize, traditionalists search for the combination of securities that creates a minimum overall cost of capital. Traditionalists believe that this is accomplished by using an amount of leverage that utilizes the low cost advantage of debt, but which keeps the amount of debt from exceeding the firm's debt capacity and becoming so risky that debt becomes too costly.

debt capacity
The notion that there is some range of debt that maximizes the value of the firm.

CAPITAL STRUCTURE AND FIRM VALUE— THE MODERNISTS' VIEW

The modernists' position on the use of debt and the value of the firm was established by Franco Modigliani and Merton Miller in the late 1950s. Their contributions to finance were so important that their concepts and propositions are known simply by their initials: M&M. Each of them has won a Nobel prize in economics, and the following analyses are highly simplified expositions of the concepts set forth in their work.

In a nutshell, the modernist position states that, under ideal conditions, all capital structures produce the same total cost of capital to the firm and the same total firm value. Said differently, modernists believe that the financing decision is irrelevant.

The modernist position is illustrated in Figure 10.5. In contrast to the traditionalists' position shown in Figure 10.4, there is no dramatic point at which the cost of equity rapidly rises. The required rate of return on equity rises less quickly when greater debt usage begins to transfer some of the firm's risks to the debtholders.

Notice, in Figure 10.5, that the required return on equity (r_E) begins to flatten out or rise less steeply at higher and higher levels of debt. This reflects the fact that as debtholders begin to bear more and more risk, the increased risk borne by equityholders is reduced.

Within the modernist viewpoint there is no optimum capital structure, and firms do not have a debt capacity. It is not necessary to borrow money nor is it unwise to borrow a great deal of money. The key to this viewpoint is that no matter how a firm partitions the risk of its assets among its securities, the market will still charge the same total amount of money for bearing the same total amount of risk. The logic is that since the risk of the firm's assets is not changing, the overall cost of the firm's capital also will not change.

The modernists' position has been carefully and rigorously developed using models and deductive reasoning. As the years have progressed, the modernist position has been demonstrated in different ways and is becoming easier to understand. We will set forth the modernist arguments in three different ways. Each argument, however,

FIGURE 10.5

A Modernist's View on Leverage and Expected Return

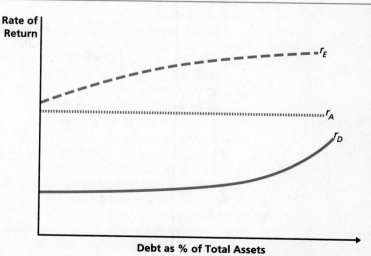

Rate of Return

r_E

r_A

r_D

Debt as % of Total Assets

leads to the same conclusion: The firm's capital structure decision can neither create or destroy wealth—it is irrelevant.

Capital Structure Irrelevancy Using Market Efficiency and Net Present Value

In an efficient capital market, as introduced in Chapter 2, numerous well-informed investors compete to increase their wealth in a marketplace such that financial securities trade at prices that are neither too low nor too high. If a security is trading at a wrong price, then one side of the trade would be making extra money, known as a positive *NPV*, and the other side of the trade would be losing extra money, known as a negative *NPV*. This type of mispricing and the transfer of wealth that would result cannot continue in an efficient market.

The implication of market efficiency is that the *NPV* of a security issued in an efficient market is zero. Investors in an efficient market would never purchase a security with a negative *NPV*, and firms would have no reason to sell a security at a price so low as to create a positive *NPV* for the investor. If, by chance, someone did offer to sell a security at too low a price, buyers would quickly compete to purchase the security, thereby driving the price up until its *NPV* was zero again. The way in which securities are issued is discussed in Window 10.3.

In an efficient market, wealth cannot be increased on a consistent basis by buying and/or selling mispriced securities. Let's examine market efficiency from the standpoint of the shareholders of a corporation that is issuing securities to investors. Because a corporation is simply a set of contracts through which people transact, when we say that a corporation issues a security, we are really saying that shareholders, acting through a particular set of contracts known as a corporation, are selling securities. Can shareholders hope to sell securities at prices generating positive *NPV*s?

The lesson of market efficiency with respect to this question states that the answer is no. No matter what type of security a corporation issues, or when it is issued, if it is auctioned in a competitive market or if it is issued in such a way as to create an equivalent result, the *NPV* to both the buyer (the investor) and the seller (the shareholders) will be forced to zero. Said differently, shareholders will issue securities to investors at a price equal to the present value of the security's promised cash flows.

The opposing view to that of an efficient market is that shareholders sell securities to investors at a price greater than the present value of the security's promised cash flows. However, a positive *NPV* to the shareholder must be a negative *NPV* to the investor. The view that shareholders issue securities with positive *NPV*s is tantamount to claiming that investors desire types of securities that have negative *NPV*s. Can these investors really be so misinformed?

Window 10.3

Issuing Securities—The Investment Banking Process

This window discusses how corporations issue securities. Chapter 1 established that an advantage of the corporate form of business over sole proprietorships and partnerships is its ability to raise additional money for purposes of investment. Of course, sole proprietorships and partnerships can also raise money through banks and through arrangements with private investors, but on a smaller scale and at higher costs. Corporations often issue new shares of stock or bonds. We begin by describing how common stock is issued.

For example, consider Arctic Bay Airlines, the only major air carrier servicing the Baffin Bay area in northern Canada. The company's founders recognized the growing interest in vacationing in the Arctic. Indeed, Arctic Bay's business had grown to the point at which it needed money to purchase a second airplane, so the founders decided to raise the money by issuing shares of stock to outside investors. Because Arctic had no shares trading, the issue would be a primary issue. As you will remember, primary issues of stock contrast with secondary issues, or additional shares of stock for companies whose shares are already trading in the market.

The founders of Arctic Bay, while they are experts in the airline business, know little about issuing securities. The firm, therefore, seeks the advice of experts, known as investment bankers.

Investment bankers serve as a conduit, or intermediary, between the issuer of securities and the investment public. Some well-known investment bankers include Goldman Sachs, Merrill Lynch, and Salomon Brothers. In some cases, the investment banker will purchase the stock from the issuing company at one price and distribute it to the public at a higher price. The difference in price represents the profit to the investment banker. In other cases, the investment banker will enter a best-efforts arrangement, promising to sell as much of the new stock issue as possible without guaranteeing its success. The investment banker's fee is an agreed-upon percentage of the proceeds.

For primary issues of stock, the role of the investment banker begins with preparing the registration statement, the necessary paperwork required by the Securities and Exchange Commission. Next, the investment banker assists the firm in setting the initial price per share for the stock, which is a complex part of primary offerings. Setting the initial offering price too low will underprice the issue, making it easier to sell the stock on the

(continued on next page)

Window 10.3 (continued)

market but depriving the firm of receiving maximum return from the stock issue. On the other hand, setting the initial offering price too high will overprice the issue and jeopardize the success of the sale of stock to investors.

Issuing costs come in two main types: (1) the compensation earned by investment bankers in the form of the spread between the price paid to the issuer and the offering price to the public, and (2) administrative fees. Studies have found that issuing costs as a percent of the gross proceeds average 6.2 percent, but are greater for smaller issues. In other words, the fixed costs of issuing securities tend to be high. The total costs for issues of $1 million are over 15 percent, while the total costs for issues greater than $100 million are 4 percent.

Bond issues share many of the characteristics of stock issues. After a registration statement is filed with the Securities and Exchange Commission, the securities are sold to investors. The registration statement must include an indenture—a written agreement between the corporation and the bondholders—which will usually include: (1) the basic terms of the bond, including the maturity date, the face value, the coupon rate, and how it is to be paid, (2) any collateral that the firm uses to protect the bondholder, (3) any restrictions that the debt issue places on the firm, and (4) any call provisions.

Clear thinking tells us that the answer is no. Institutions such as pension funds, insurance companies, and mutual funds purchase most of the securities issued by major corporations. These institutions are managed by experienced and highly intelligent professionals who cannot be consistently fooled into purchasing securities with negative *NPV*s.

Thus, modernists believe that major U.S. securities markets are reasonably efficient and that money cannot be made on a consistent basis by attempting to buy or sell securities at market prices. Modernists believe, further, that this principle generally holds for the issuance of securities by corporations as well, since a corporation is only a set of contracts. Thus, when shareholders use a corporation to issue a security in a perfect market, there is no wealth created, lost, or transferred.

Capital Structure Irrelevancy Using Arbitrage

Another method of defending the irrelevance of capital structure is to consider what would happen if irrelevancy failed to hold. Modernists believe that investors known as arbitragers would enter the market

arbitragers
Investors who search for extremely quick and low-risk profits.

and force irrelevancy in the capital structure. An **arbitrager** is someone who searches for extremely quick and low-risk profits. The modernist belief is that no matter what combination of securities is issued, the combined value of the securities will be equal to the value of the firm's assets.

The key to the arbitrage argument is that the person who buys up all of the securities of a corporation, both debt and equity, has, in essence, removed the partitioning of the firm's assets into debt and equity and owns all the firm's securities. Thus, competition will force the total value of the securities to equal the value of the firm's assets. If, instead of purchasing all the firm's securities, investors simply purchase a particular percentage of each security, they are in a position equivalent to having direct ownership of that percentage of the firm's assets.

It should be obvious that, if an investor buys up all the securities of the firm, the investor will receive all the cash flows from the firm's assets. Now let's imagine that an investor buys up half of the firm's securities. It is clear that one-half of the securities would entitle the investor to exactly half of the cash flows from the firm's assets. In the same manner, an investor who holds any portion of the firm's securities is in a position equivalent to owning directly the same portion of the firm's assets. This is illustrated in Table 10.3

Table 10.3 demonstrates the partitioning under different economic scenarios such as recession, slow growth, moderate growth, and boom. An investor who owns 10 percent of the firm's equity and 10 percent of the firm's debt would receive exactly 10 percent of the cash flows from the firm's assets, which is equivalent to owning 10 percent of the assets directly.

Example 10.3 —————— Consider Partition, Inc., a fictitious firm with $2,000,000 in assets financed by two different types of securities. Capital structure irrelevance states that the total value of the two types of securities added together must equal $2,000,000, no matter how they are divided. This can be proven through arbitrage.

TABLE 10.3
Partitioning the Firm's Assets into Debt and Equity Claims: Promised Debt Payment = $50

	Recession	Slow Growth	Moderate Growth	Boom
Value of assets	$40	$100	$120	$140
Payoff of debt	$40	$ 50	$ 50	$ 50
Payoff of equity	$ 0	$ 50	$ 70	$ 90
Payoff of both debt and equity	$40	$100	$120	$140
Value of 10% of assets	$ 4	$ 10	$ 12	$ 14
Payoff of 10% of debt and equity	$ 4	$ 10	$ 12	$ 14

If Partition's securities were selling for an amount less than the $2,000,000, arbitragers would purchase all of the securities, take control of the assets, sell the assets for $2,000,000, and make a quick profit. The fact that arbitragers have not done this establishes that the securities are not underpriced.

The argument that the securities of Partition, Inc., cannot be overpriced is not as easy to demonstrate but also can be shown through arbitrage. In this case, arbitragers can take advantage of overpriced securities either by creating new corporations or by short-selling the securities. For example, the arbitragers could use $2,000,000 of assets to start a new corporation and use the optimal capital structure to issue similar securities that would also sell for more than $2,000,000, thus earning their profit. Alternatively, there is a process called short-selling, detailed in Window 10.4, which would permit the arbitragers to profit. Once again, the absence of such activities in a free and well-functioning market establishes that securities are not significantly overpriced.

One rebuttal to this argument is that the purchase or sale of all of the firm's securities must be difficult for practical and legal reasons. However, as shown in Table 10.3, if an investor purchases, for example, one percent of each type of security that a firm issues, then the investor has effectively purchased one percent of the firm's assets even though the investor will not have legal control of the corporation. It may take longer, and be less dramatic, but the arbitrager could still earn profits if capital structure affected firm value.

Perhaps the strongest aspect of this argument is characterized by this question: Would it be possible to intentionally create a capital structure such that the combined securities would sell for less than the firm's assets were worth? Suppose that Masochists, Inc., were run by shareholders who desired to create undesirable securities. Each member of the board constructed the security that in their judgment was worst.

For example, one shareholder from Boston might suggest a bond that would pay interest only if his favorite baseball team won the World Series. Another shareholder might suggest preferred stock that would pay double dividends whenever there was a terrible natural disaster and so forth. Of course, there is one security called common stock that paid whatever was left over.

Would it be possible that Masochists, Inc., could create such a disgusting capital structure that the total value of its securities would be less than the value of the firm's assets? The answer is no!

Remember that it is possible for any investor to purchase a small percentage of each of the firm's securities. No matter how strange each security was, we know that owning and holding together all of the securities is equivalent to owning the firm's assets. In effect, the investors can strip down or remove any partitioning of the firm's cash flows they do not like. In the case of Masochists, Inc., the arbitrager needs to purchase a percentage of each of the securities in order to remove the effects of the partitioning. Thus, capital structure decisions cannot destroy value even if someone tried to.

Capital structure decisions are simply decisions of how to partition or divide the firm's cash flows. If a partitioning is undesirable, then arbitragers can in effect remove it. If a particular partitioning were viewed as so desirable that it increased wealth, then participants would quickly replicate the idea until the added value was removed. The presence of market participants who would engage in such activities and the rarity with which such activities are performed lend support to the belief that little or no shareholder wealth can be created or destroyed by tinkering with capital structure under ideal conditions. ↵

Capital Structure Irrelevance Using Homemade Leverage

The most compelling argument for capital structure irrelevancy is the homemade leverage argument, which states that any leverage decision made by a firm can be dismantled by or replicated by the investor without the corporation's help. There can therefore be little or no economic advantage to having leverage decisions made at the corporate level in a perfect market.

A dairy analogy is useful in understanding the argument of homemade leverage. Back in the days before homogenization, milk separated naturally into cream and skimmed milk. Consumers were able to either use the products separately or mix them for whole milk, low-fat milk, half and half, and so forth. In effect, consumers could very easily create for themselves the variety of milk products we now buy separately. Today, dairies separate the milk products for the consumer, and if they tried to charge a very high price for this service, competition would encourage a return to the days before homogenization, since consumers can do this for themselves.

Just as a dairy now separates milk for us into products with various concentrations of fat, a corporation can partition the cash flows from the firm's assets into securities that contain various concentrations of risk.

The important question is this: If a firm chooses not to partition its cash flows into securities represented by debt and equity, then could investors do it themselves? Alternatively, if a firm chooses to partition its cash flows in a manner considered undesirable by some

Window 10.4

Short-Selling Securities

An accepted viewpoint in financial markets is that the way to make money is to buy low today and sell high in the future. However, it's also possible to make money by first selling high and later buying low. In other words, the markets provide opportunities to sell securities first and buy them back at a later date. This is known as short-selling.

Investors will short-sell if they believe that a security's price is overvalued and will soon fall in price. The short-seller sells a security to another investor at the current price with the hope of buying the security back at a later date at a lower price. The difference between the selling price and the buying price represents the gain or loss to the short seller.

One of the most confusing aspects of short-selling is the notion of selling securities that are not owned. Given that the seller does not have physical possession of the security, isn't selling it impossible? In short-selling, the answer is no. Owners of stocks or other securities often leave the actual stock certificates with their brokerage firms, for safekeeping. The short-seller borrows the securities from the broker and is obligated to return them at a later date. The original owner usually has no knowledge that the securities have been borrowed.

For example, suppose the stock of Neveright is currently selling for $50 per share. Brokerage X has thousands of shares of Neveright in the vault, safekeeping the stock for the investors who expect great things from this company. Suppose that you believe that the share price of Neveright will soon fall to $40 per share and wish to take advantage of this situation. In this case, you borrow 100 shares of Neveright from the broker and sell them in the market for $50. You now have $5,000 from the sale, but also have a liability represented by 100 shares of Neveright that you must return to the vault.

Let's consider the investment aspects of the short-sale. First the good news: If the stock does indeed fall to $40, you go into the market, buy 100 shares of Neveright for $40 a share for a grand total of $4,000, and return the 100 shares to the broker's vault. Compared with the $5,000 you received at the time of the sale, you have just made a $1,000 profit.

Now the bad news. If the stock climbs above its current price of $50, you lose as a short-seller. In fact, you stand to lose $100 for each dollar the stock price rises over its initial value of $50 ($1.00 times 100 shares). If the stock price hits $60, you may decide you've had enough. In this case, you would go into the market, buy 100 shares of Neveright for $60 per share, return the shares to the broker, and suffer a loss of $1,000. Because there is no upper limit to the price of Neveright stock, potential losses to short-selling are unlimited.

investors, can those investors remove the partitions and reconstruct desirable partitions? The answers are yes.

We have already stated in our arbitrage arguments that the investor can completely strip out partitions by purchasing appropriate proportions of each security to replicate the firm's assets. In this section we shall develop the concept more precisely and with greater flexibility by concentrating on one aspect of capital structure, the debt-versus-equity decision.

Example 10.4 ——————— Consider two firms with identical assets. One is an all-equity firm called Boring, Inc. The other firm has significant debt and is called Exciting, Inc. Remember, these firms are considered the same in every way except for the fact that one chooses to include debt in its capital structure and one does not. Is it possible for an investor to use shares of equity in Boring, Inc., to produce the same result as would be obtained by investing directly in Exciting, Inc.? We shall see that the answer is yes, owing to a process called **homemade leverage**.

homemade leverage
The replication of the corporate leverage decision by the investor at little cost.

Similarly, is it possible that an investor could invest in Exciting, Inc., to produce the same investment results as would be obtained from owning shares in Boring, Inc.? We shall again see that the answer is yes, and the process can be called homemade unlevering. Both of these processes demonstrate that since the corporate leverage decision can be replicated or removed by the investor at little cost, there can be no significant advantage for a corporation to levering at the corporate level.

In order to demonstrate these points fully, let's assume that there are three possible states of nature or economic outcomes that investors expect. These states are given by (1) a recession, (2) normal growth, and (3) an economic boom. Since both firms have identical assets, the values of the assets and the cash flows of each firm will be equal to each other regardless of which state occurs. The specific values are shown in Table 10.4.

TABLE 10.4
The Cash Flows and Values of Boring, Inc., and Exciting, Inc.

State	Boring, Inc. Future Cash Flow		Exciting, Inc. Future Cash Flow
Recession	$ 500		$ 500
Normal growth	$ 1,000		$ 1,000
Economic boom	$ 1,500		$ 1,500
Current value of debt	$ -0-	Current value of debt	$ 5,000
Current value of equity	$10,000	Current value of equity	$ 5,000
Current total value	$10,000	Current total value	$10,000

Because Boring, Inc., has no debt, the value of its equity and the cash flow it receives flow directly from the assets. Boring, Inc., has outstanding 1,000 shares of stock such that the equity value per share is equal to the total firm value divided by 1,000.

Exciting, Inc., has $5,000 of debt, which requires an interest payment of $500. Because the debtholders have financed one-half of the assets of the firm, Exciting, Inc., has one-half the number of shares of equity outstanding, or 500 shares. The value of the equity per share is equal to the total equity value divided by 500. The cash flows per share of both Boring and Exciting in each of the three states are given in Table 10.5.

Table 10.5 demonstrates that leverage transfers risk to the equityholders. The greater risk to equityholders is demonstrated by the greater variation in the cash flows per share of Exciting, Inc. In a recession, Exciting's cash flow of $500 is equal to the promised payment to the bondholders, leaving the equityholders with nothing. In a boom, the total cash flow to Exciting, Inc., while equal to that of Boring, Inc., is shared with a fewer number of equityholders so that the cash flow per share is greater. This is illustrated in Figure 10.6.

To illustrate homemade leverage and homemade unlevering, consider that it is possible for an investor to buy shares in either firm and then adjust his or her personal debt usage such that the resulting cash flows will be equal to the cash flows that would be received from owning the other firm's equity. An investor who wants to replicate corporate leverage in a homemade fashion borrows; an investor who wants to unlever or strip away the effects of leverage invests relatively less money in stock and puts the remaining money in bonds—in other words, the investor lends.

Suppose an investor has $500 to invest. One alternative is to purchase ten percent of the equity of Exciting, Inc., for $500—in other words, to purchase 50 shares for $10 per

TABLE 10.5
Financial Leverage and Cash Flows

State	Boring, Inc. (1,000 shares)			Exciting, Inc. (500 shares)		
	Total Cash Flow	Cash Flow to Debt	Cash Flow to Equity per Share	Total Cash Flow	Cash Flow to Debt	Cash Flow to Equity per Share
Recession	$ 500	$ -0-	$0.50	$ 500	$500	$0.00
Normal growth	$1,000	$ -0-	$1.00	$1,000	$500	$1.00
Economic boom	$1,500	$ -0-	$1.50	$1,500	$500	$2.00

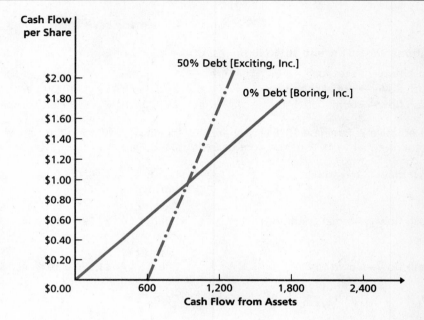

FIGURE 10.6
The Effect of Leverage on Cash Flow to Equity per Share

The cash flow per share to the equityholders of the levered firm changes more for a given change in the cash flow from the assets.

share. However, an equivalent alternative is to purchase ten percent of the equity of Boring, Inc., for $1,000, financing half the purchase by borrowing $500—in other words, to purchase 100 shares at $10 per share. Panel A of Table 10.6 demonstrates that the cash flows from either alternative are identical regardless of which economic outcome occurs. We are temporarily ignoring the effect of risk on the required rate of return and are assuming that the investor can borrow money at the same interest rate as did Exciting, Inc.

In a similar way, Panel B in Table 10.6 illustrates the alternatives available to an investor with $1,000 to invest and who is considering purchasing ten percent of the equity of Boring, Inc., an unlevered firm. However, an equivalent alternative is to purchase, for $500, ten percent of the equity of Exciting, Inc., a firm with debt, and lending $500 by buying bonds— perhaps even bonds of Exciting, Inc. Panel B shows that the cash flows of either alternative are identical regardless of which economic outcome occurs.

The importance of Table 10.6 is that it illustrates that, no matter how a firm partitions the cash flows from its assets into debt and equity streams, the firm is not creating a unique cash

TABLE 10.6
Homemade Leverage

Panel A: Homemade Leverage

Alternative 1: Purchase 10% (50 shares) of the equity of Exciting, Inc., a levered firm.

Cash flow—Recession	$ \quad 0 * 10\% = $ \quad 0 ($0 per share * 50 shares)
Cash flow—Normal conditions	$ \quad 500 * 10\% = $ \quad 50 ($1 per share * 50 shares)
Cash flow—Boom	$1,000 * 10\% = $100 ($2 per share * 50 shares)

Alternative 2: Purchase 10% (100 shares) of the equity of Boring, Inc., an unlevered firm. Borrow an amount equal to 10% of the debt of Exciting, Inc., causing $50 of interest expense.

Cash flow—Recession	Equity:	$ \quad 500 * 10\% =	$ \quad 50 ($0.50 * 100 shares)
	Borrowing:		−$ 50
	Cash flow		$ \quad 0
Cash flow—Normal conditions	Equity:	$1,000 * 10\% =	$100 ($1.00 * 100 shares)
	Borrowing:		−$ 50
	Cash flow		$ 50
Cash flow—Boom	Equity:	$1,500 * 10\% =	$150 ($1.50 * 100 shares)
	Borrowing:		−$ 50
	Cash flow		$100

Panel B: Homemade Unlevering

Alternative 1: Purchase 10% (100 shares) of the equity of Boring, Inc., an unlevered firm.

Cash flow—Recession	$ \quad 500 * 10\% = $ 50 ($0.50 * 100 shares)
Cash flow—Normal conditions	$1,000 * 10\% = $100 ($1.00 * 100 shares)
Cash flow—Boom	$1,500 * 10\% = $150 ($1.50 * 100 shares)

Alternative 2: Purchase 10% (50 shares) of the equity of Exciting, Inc., a levered firm. Lend an amount equal to 10% of the debt of Exciting, Inc., producing $50 of interest income.

Cash flow—Recession	Equity:	$ \quad 0 * 10\% =	$ \quad 0 ($0.00 * 50 shares)
	Lending:		50
			$ 50
Cash flow—Normal conditions	Equity:	$ \quad 500 * 10\% =	$ 50 ($1.00 * 50 shares)
	Lending:		50
			$100
Cash flow—Boom	Equity:	$1,000 * 10\% =	$100 ($2.00 * 50 shares)
	Lending:		50
			$150

Window 10.5

Buying Stock on Margin

Borrowing money through a brokerage firm to buy stock or other securities is known as using margin. Federal regulations (known especially as Regulation T) govern the use of margin.

The key is that the loan is backed by or guaranteed by the securities the investor holds in the brokerage account. The amount of money that can be borrowed is closely governed by the Federal Reserve and individual brokerage firms. Borrowed money can represent up to a particular percentage, say 50 percent, of the total account value.

Regulations also control what securities can be used as collateral, but this generally includes all common stocks of large corporations.

The interest rate charged is set by the individual brokerage firm and is often called the "call rate." The rate may change daily and may depend upon the size of the loan—with large loans being charged a lower rate. Generally, these interest rates are quite competitive and are only slightly higher than money market interest rates.

flow opportunity. Therefore, its securities will not be a set of highly valuable securities that can sell at a premium and therefore provide for a lower cost of capital. We know this because Tables 10.5 and 10.6 illustrate that investors can easily partition the cash flow streams from other firms themselves or can remove any undesirable partitions. ↵

Some people argue that it is somehow easier for a corporation to borrow than it is for an individual to borrow money to purchase stock. This is not true. Window 10.5 details the simple way to borrow to buy stocks, known as using margin.

More sophisticated analyses have been performed that demonstrate capital structure irrelevancy for risky debt as well as risk-free debt. For example, it is clear that an investor who purchases both the debt (even if it is risky) and equity of a firm in the proper proportions can effectively remove the partition and replicate the cash flow stream of the assets. Accordingly, as we have said, all of the firm's securities combined must have the same value as the assets, in a perfect market.

In summary, these three cases have shown that, under certain conditions, the firm's capital structure decision is irrelevant. Firm value is not affected by the choice of financing instruments.

SUMMARY

☐ The study of corporate finance is divided into two primary decisions: the investment decision, or which assets to acquire, and the financing decision, or how those assets are financed. This chapter investigates the effect of the financing decision on the value of the firm.

☐ The financing decision is sometimes called the capital structure decision. Given the objective of maximizing firm value, the question to be explored is whether or not firm value can be affected by the firm's choice of capital structure.

☐ Financial leverage is created when the firm borrows money in the form of debt. A corporation having both debt and equity may be viewed as taking the cash flow stream produced by the firm's assets and partitioning the cash flow into two streams; a low-risk debt stream and a high-risk equity stream.

☐ Under the restrictive assumptions of perfect markets, both modernists and traditionalists agree that leverage affects the risk of equity. Traditionalists conclude that there is an optimal capital structure. Modernists state that capital structure is irrelevant—there is no best mix of securities that a firm issues to finance assets.

REFERENCES

Modigliani, F. and M.H. Miller. "Corporate Income Taxes and the Cost of Capital: A Correction." *American Economic Review* 53 (June 1963), 433–443.

————. "The Cost of Capital, Corporation Finance and the Theory of Investment." *American Economic Review* 48 (June 1958), 261–297.

————. "Some Estimates of the Cost of Capital to the Electric Utility Industry, 1954–1957." *American Economic Review* 56 (June 1966), 333–391.

DEMONSTRATION PROBLEMS

Problem 1   Lindross Salvage Corporation is an all-equity (unlevered) corporation with $10,000,000 in assets and whose performance varies from incurring a loss of $1,000,000 per year to producing a profit of $3,000,000 per year. Please find the range of the rates of return that the shareholders will earn with everything else equal if:

a. Lindross Salvage Corporation remains unlevered, and
b. Lindross Salvage Corporation switches to a capital structure with $3,000,000 of debt and $7,000,000 of equity (assume that the debt has an interest rate of 5%).

Solution to Problem 1
In each case, the problem requires that we determine rates of return for shareholders. In Module 4, we ignore accounting problems and assume that the shareholders' rate of return can be found by dividing the net profit of the firm by the equity of the firm.

Shareholder Rate of Return = Profit or Loss After Interest / Equity.

The profit of the firm is found by subtracting the interest cost of the debt, if any. The equity of the firm is given.

Step 1: For the unlevered firm there is no debt and therefore no interest cost or expense. The range in the unlevered shareholders' rate of return is therefore found simply by dividing the possible profit or loss by the quantity of equity:

Lowest Unlevered Rate of Return = −$1,000,000 / $10,000,000
= −10%.

Highest Unlevered Rate of Return = $3,000,000 / $10,000,000
= +30%.

Step 2: The range of levered rates of return involves the additional step of determining the interest expense and subtracting it from the cash flows produced by the assets. First, the annual interest expense is found by multiplying the interest rate by the amount of debt:

$3,000,000 debt * 5% Interest Rate
= $150,000 annual interest expense

Next, the profit or loss net of interest expense is found by subtracting the annual interest expense from the profit or loss that would have occurred had the firm not used debt:

Low Outcome: Net Loss $= -\$1,000,000 - \$150,000 = -\$1,150,000.$

High Outcome: Net Profit $= +\$3,000,000 - \$150,000 = +\$2,850,000.$

Step 3: Finally, the range of rates of return for the levered firm is determined by dividing the net profit or loss by the value of the levered firm's equity. Note that because the firm has $3,000,000 of debt, only $7,000,000 is needed to fund the firm's $10,000,0000 of assets.

Lowest Levered Rate of Return $= -\$1,150,000 / \$7,000,000$
$$= -16.43\%.$$

Highest Levered Rate of Return $= \$2,850,000 / \$7,000,000$
$$= +40.71\%.$$

Final Solution: The effect of leverage is to widen the range of rates of return from -10% and $+30\%$ to -16.43% and $+40.71\%$. ↵

Problem 2   Using the results of problem 1 above, demonstrate homemade leverage and homemade unleverage for an investor with $1,000,000 by finding:

a. How to use the unlevered equity and homemade leverage to produce the same range of returns as is produced by the levered firm, and
b. How to use the levered firm and homemade unleverage to produce the same range of returns produced by the unlevered firm.

Solution to Problem 2
In the case of homemade leverage, the investor must find how much money to borrow for additional investment (homemade leverage). In the case of homemade unleverage, the investor does not borrow but rather lends or buys bonds. Specifically, the investor must find how much money to invest in equity and how much in bonds (lend).

Step 1: In homemade leverage, the investor must borrow enough to offset the fact that the corporation has not borrowed the "desired" amount. In this case, the unlevered firm has no debt and the levered firm has 30% debt.

The key starting point in this problem is to determine the levered corporation's debt usage as a percentage of its equity. In other words, although the corporation has a debt-to-assets ratio of 30%, we must find the debt as a percentage of equity (the debt-to-equity ratio):

Debt-to-Equity Ratio $= \$3,000,000 / \$7,000,000 = 42.86\%.$

This is the tricky part, because there is a temptation to assume that since the investor has $1,000,000 of his or her own money to invest he or she should simply borrow $300,000 or 30%. However, the borrowed money must be 30% of the total amount invested (including the borrowed money itself!). We find the correct amount to borrow by multiplying the investor's funds times the firm's debt-to-equity ratio:

$$\text{Amount Borrowed} = \text{Amount to Invest} * \text{Debt-to-Equity Ratio}$$
$$\text{Amount Borrowed} = \$1,000,000 * 42.86\% = \$428,571.$$

Thus the total investment by the investor is given as:

$$\text{Original Funds} = \$1,000,000 \quad (70\%)$$
$$\text{Borrowed Funds} = \$428,571 \quad (30\%)$$
$$\text{Total Invested} = \$1,428,571 \,(100\%).$$

Thus, $428,571 in borrowed money leaves the investor with $1,428,571 of total investment and a percentage debt usage of 30%. If the investor had simply borrowed $300,000, the debt usage would have been only 23% ($300,000 / $1,300,000).

Step 2: Now check the result above and prove that homemade leverage works, by showing that the $1,428,571 invested in the unlevered firm produces the same result (after interest expense) as $1,000,000 invested in the levered firm.

First, find the profit or loss for $1,000,000 invested in the levered firm. The range is found by multiplying the returns found in the solution to problem 1 by the $1,000,000 invested. Notice that we use the levered returns since homemade leverage seeks to duplicate levered returns.

$$\text{Lowest Return} = \$1,000,000 * -16.43\% = -\$164,300$$
$$\text{Highest Return} = \$1,000,000 * +40.71\% = \$407,100.$$

Now we check to see if the same results can be found using the performance of the unlevered firm and our homemade leverage. We must find the after-interest expense performance of the borrowed money and investment in the unlevered firm. In order to prove that the results are equal, we must assume that the investor pays the same interest rate as the firm.

	Low Outcome −10%	High Outcome +30%
Total Funds in Unlevered Firm ($1,428,571) Times Outcome	$−142,857	$ 428,571
Interest Expense of Borrowed Funds ($428,571) at 5%	$ −21,428	$−21,428
Total Profit or Loss (rounded)	$−164,300	$ 407,100

Ignoring rounding errors, we have demonstrated that homemade leverage using the unlevered firm produces the same net result as investing directly in the levered firm.

Step 3: Next, we prove that investment in a levered firm using homemade unleverage produces the same result as direct investment in an unlevered firm. In homemade unleverage the investor must limit the amount of money placed in the levered firm's equity and must invest the remaining funds in low-risk debt. The key is to determine how much of the total money (in this problem, $1,000,000) should be placed in the levered firm's equity (the remainder will be invested in bonds earning 5%).

Remember, homemade unleverage attempts to replicate an unlevered firm. If the investor placed $1,000,000 in an unlevered firm, it would be tantamount to directly purchasing $1,000,000 of the firm's assets. However, the levered firm borrows money, so a $1,000,000 investment in the equity of the levered firm would involve greater risk. We will now look for the portion of the $1,000,000 that can be invested in the levered firm's equity so as to produce the same risk exposure as having $1,000,000 in the unlevered firm's equity.

Fortunately, the numbers that we are looking for are directly related to the levered firm's capital structure ratios of 70% equity and 30% debt. Notice that for every $7 of equity that the levered firm has there is a total of $10 of assets. Thus, in order to perform homemade unleverage, the investor simply invests in equity and debt in the same ratio as is found in the firm.

$$\text{Investment in Equity} = 70\% * \$1,000,000 = \$700,000$$

$$\text{Investment in Bonds} = 30\% * \$1,000,000 = \$300,000.$$

Thus, the investor can place $700,000 in the levered corporation's stock knowing that the levered firm will use $300,000 of debt to finance a total of $1,000,000 in assets. This will produce the same result as investing the $1,000,000 directly in the unlevered firm's equity. The investor must place the remaining $300,000 in bonds that pay 5%, to complete the homemade unleverage.

Step 4: Check to see that the homemade unleverage produces the same results as $1,000,000 invested directly in the unlevered firm. First, compute the profit or loss from investing the full $1,000,000 directly in the unlevered firm:

$$\text{Lowest Return} = \$1,000,000 * -10.00\% = -\$100,000$$

$$\text{Highest Return} = \$1,000,000 * +30.00\% = \quad \$300,000.$$

Now we check to see if the same results can be found using the performance of the levered firm and our homemade unleverage. We must combine the performance of the equity investment in the levered firm with the $300,000 invested in bonds.

	Low Outcome −16.43%	High Outcome +40.71%
Total funds in levered firm ($700,000) times outcome	$−1,150,000	$2,850,000
Interest on $300,000 at 5%	$ 150,000	$ 150,000
Total profit or loss (rounded)	$−1,000,000	$3,000,000

Ignoring rounding errors, we have demonstrated that homemade unleverage using the levered firm produces the same net result as investing directly in the unlevered firm.

Final Solution: The homemade leverage solution is to borrow $428,571 in order to invest a total of $1,428,571 in the unlevered firm. This produces the same result as investing $1,000,000 directly in the levered firm. The homemade unleverage solution is to invest $700,000 in the equity of the levered firm and place the remaining $300,000 in bonds (lend). This produces the same result as placing $1,000,000 directly in the unlevered firm. ↵

REVIEW QUESTIONS

1. Describe the "capital structure" decision of the firm.
2. How do traditionalists view the firm's capital structure decision?
3. How do modernists view the firm's capital structure decision?
4. What is financial leverage?
5. Why is the equity of the firm also known as residual claims?
6. Why does the presence of debt change the risk of holding equity in a firm?
7. Explain the term "debt capacity" as it relates to the traditionalists' view of capital structure.
8. What is the modernists'—or the M&M—position on the capital structure decision in perfect markets?
9. What is short selling? What direction of prices (up or down) would benefit the short seller?
10. Explain what homemade leverage is, and how modernists use homemade leverage in their arguments.

PROBLEMS

1. Donny Donruss has set up a corporation to buy and sell baseball cards. Mr. Donruss, the corporation's only shareholder, puts up $50,000 of his savings to begin the business. Calculate the annual return to Mr. Donruss in each of the following two scenarios:

    a. The market for baseball cards goes on a winning streak, and his business produces a cash flow of $15,000 per year.

    b. The market for baseball cards takes a slide, and his business barely squeaks out a cash flow of $2,500 per year.

2. Chris Russo, the arch-rival of Donny Donruss, sets up a competing corporation to buy and sell baseball cards. Chris has only $25,000 to invest in the business, but wants to open a store that is similar to Donny's. In addition to his $25,000, Chris borrows $25,000 from Topps Bank in the form of debt at a cost of 10 percent. Calculate the annual return to Mr. Russo in each of the following two scenarios:

    a. His business hits a home run and produces a cash flow of $15,000 per year.

    b. His business gets "shut out" and squeaks out a cash flow of $2,500 per year.

3. Let's return again to Mr. Donruss and Mr. Russo. Mr. Donruss operates his $50,000 firm using his own equity. Mr. Russo operates his firm with $25,000 of his own money plus $25,000 of debt at a cost of 10 percent interest.

    a. Calculate Mr. Donruss's and Mr. Russo's rate of return if their respective businesses produce a cash flow of $0, $2,500, $5,000, $7,500, or $10,000 (there is a different rate of return for each cash flow for each business).

    b. Plot the relationship between the rate of return on equity (on the "y" or vertical axis) and the four different cash flows in part (a) above (on the "x" or horizontal axis) for each business. Give Donruss a solid line, and give Russo a dashed line. What does your graph tell you about the use of debt and the financial risk of a firm?

4. Bobby Binckman owns and operates Soccer Stores of America. He has $150,000 of his own money in the business as equity capital, but because of the use of debt, the total value of his stores is $750,000. Calculate the percentage of debt in the corporation, and the corporation's leverage factor.

5. Buckley Bookstores, Inc., has $50,000 of equity capital, just enough money to open one store. The firm can, however, open more than one store by taking on debt. Assume that Buckley, Inc., can borrow all the money it needs at a cost of 12 percent. Use this information and the information below to complete the following table.

Number of Bookstores Opened	1	2	3	10
Total Value of the Bookstores	$50,000	$100,000	$150,000	$500,000
Amount of Equity	$50,000	50,000	50,000	50,000
Amount of Debt	-0-	50,000	100,000	450,000
Leverage Factor	?	?	?	?
Percentage of Debt	?	?	?	?

6. Felicia Fish is the sole shareholder in Aquarium City. Her equity in the corporation totals $500,000. However, given her use of leverage, the total value of Aquarium City is $2,000,000. Calculate the change in the value of Ms. Fish's equity in the firm under the following scenarios:
   a. The value of her assets rises by 25 percent.
   b. The value of her assets rises by 100 percent.
   c. The value of her assets falls by 30 percent.

7. Buchanan, Inc., makes "Republican Brand" footwear. The firm is currently unlevered and is valued at $1 million. The business is doing well and a decision has been made to expand. The two key questions are the size of the expansion and how the expansion is financed.
   a. Suppose that the decision is to double the size of the firm, with all expansion funds coming from equity capital. What must the percentage fall in assets be before all of the equity is wiped out?
   b. Suppose that the decision is to double the size of the firm, with all of the expansion funds coming from debt. What must the percentage fall in assets be before all the equity is wiped out?
   c. Suppose the decision is a tenfold increase in the size of the firm with all of the expansion funds coming from debt. What must the percentage fall in assets be before all the equity is wiped out?

8. We can conceptualize the risk of DataTech by assigning 5 units to the risk of the assets—5 units to equity and 0 units to debt. Suppose that the firm expands, using debt such that the firm is five times its original size, and after the expansion we find that the firm's debt can now be assigned 0.5 units of risk. Determine from this information the new amount of risk of the firm's assets as well as the new units of risk assigned to the firm's equity.

9. The table below shows how financial leverage acts to partition risk for these five different firms. Complete the table using the information given.

Assets	=	Debt	+	Equity
Risk = 1 unit	=	Risk = ?	+	Risk = ?
Amount = $1,000		Amount = $0		Amount = $1,000
Risk = 2 units	=	Risk = ?	+	Risk = 2
Amount = $2,000		Amount = $1,000		Amount = ?

Assets	=	Debt	+	Equity
Risk = 5 units	=	Risk = 0	+	Risk = ?
Amount = ?		Amount = $4,000		Amount = $1,000

	Assets	=	Debt	+	Equity
	Risk = 10 units	=	Risk = ?	+	Risk = 8.35
	Amount = $10,000		Amount = ?		Amount = $1,000
	Risk = 5 units	=	Risk = 0.85	+	Risk = ?
	Amount = ?		Amount = $4,000		Amount = $1,000

10. The assets of the Kinsley firm have been partitioned into debt claims and equity claims. The payment on the debt will be $25 unless the firm hits bad times, in which case the debt will pay $20. The payoff to equity will be one of three values: $125 under status quo, $175 in good times, and $0 in bad times. Determine your payoff if you purchase 10 percent of Kinsley's equity and debt under the following three cases: status quo, good times, and bad times.

11. As a keen and insightful investor, you decide to short-sell Atlas Corporation, because you believe that its shares are about to take a dive. Atlas is currently selling for $50 per share. Determine your profit or loss if you sell 500 shares of Atlas short at $50 per share and the price of Atlas:
    a. falls to $40.00.
    b. falls to $ 0.25.
    c. rises to $1,000.00.

12. Tacos Unlimited currently trades at $100 per share. You think the future direction of the share price is south, and decide to sell its shares short.
    a. What is the most you can gain, per share, by selling short?
    b. What is the most you can lose, per share, by selling short?

13. The Thomas Corp. has a total value of $5 million, partitioned between debt valued at $2 million and equity valued at $3 million. There are 1.5 million shares outstanding. Total interest on the debt is $400,000. Calculate the cash flow per share to equity if total firm cash flow is $700,000. Repeat the analysis for a total firm cash flow of $405,000.

14. American Graffiti Corporation has 5 million shares outstanding and debt with interest payments of $1.3 million. How much cash flow would the firm need to earn in order to provide a $3.00 cash flow per share to equity?

15. Two firms, With, Inc., and Without, Inc., have assets valued at $20,000 and are similar in every way except that With, Inc., has $5,000 of debt issued at a cost of 10 percent, and Without, Inc., has no debt. With, Inc., has 750 shares outstanding and Without, Inc., has 1,000 shares outstanding. Total cash flow to each firm will either be $0, $2,000, or $4,000. Calculate the cash flow per share to the equity of each firm under each of the three cash flow scenarios.

16. For firms With, Inc., and Without, Inc., in problem 15 provide a graph of the relationship between cash flow per share to equity (on the "y" or vertical axis) and total cash flow (on the "x" or horizontal axis). Use a solid line for With, Inc., and a dashed line for Without, Inc. What does this graph tell you about leverage and risk to equity holders?

17. Return one last time to firms With, Inc. and Without, Inc. Recall that the firms are identical in every way except that With, Inc., uses debt and Without, Inc., does not. From the information given in problem 15, calculate the level of total cash flow that will give the same level of cash flow per share to equity for each firm. Verify that your answer is the point where the two lines cross on the graph from problem 16.

18. Giants, Inc., is a successful firm that uses leverage and has assets valued at $1 million. Jets, Inc., is another successful firm similar to Giants except that Jets is unlevered. One evening at a party you overhear a shareholder of Giants telling a shareholder of Jets that his firm is better because it uses debt. Use the concept of home-made leverage to convince this rather obnoxious Giants share-holder that because the assets of the two firms are identical, he would be equally as well off by investing in Jets, Inc. and borrowing.

    Set the problem in a way similar to that shown in Table 10.5. That is, assume that Giants, Inc., uses $500,000 of debt at a cost of 10 percent such that interest payments total $50,000. Also assume that three cash flow scenarios exist: bad with $50,000, OK with $100,000, and good with $150,000. The first alternative is to purchase 10 percent of the equity in Giants, and the second alternative is to purchase 10 percent of Jets and borrow an amount equal to 10 percent of the debt of Giants.

19. Although Square and Peg appear to be similar corporations, a look at their respective balance sheets will reveal some differences. Square is unlevered with 500 shares outstanding, while Peg has $2,500 of debt at a cost of 10 percent interest and has 250 shares outstanding. You own 5 percent of the equity of Peg.
    a. Determine the cash flow from your equity investment in Peg assuming that Peg's total cash flow is $500.
    b. Determine the cash flow from equity from the following strategy: Borrow an amount equal to 5 percent of the debt of Peg at 10 percent interest and use the proceeds plus your own money to buy 5 percent of the equity of Square. Assume that Square's total cash flow is $500.

20. Return to the firms Giants, Inc., and Jets, Inc., and that great party you were attending in problem 18. Now suppose that it is a Jets shareholder who tells a Giants shareholder that his firm is better because it is silly to use debt. Use the concept of homemade unlevering to convince this nice but incorrect Jets shareholder

that because the assets of the two firms are identical, he would be equally well off by investing in the equity of Giants and placing the remainder of his or her money in the bank.

Set the problem in a way similar to that shown in Table 10.5. That is, assume that Giants, Inc., uses $500,000 of debt at a cost of 10 percent such that interest payments total $50,000. Also assume that three cash flow scenarios exist: bad with $50,000, OK with $100,000, and good with $150,000. The first alternative is to purchase 10 percent of the equity in Jets, and the second alternative is to purchase 10 percent of the equity of Giants and to lend an amount equal to 10 percent of the bonds of Giants.

DISCUSSION QUESTIONS

1. Respond to the following:

   High debt usage by corporations drives up the riskiness of our country's economic base.

2. Respond to the following:

   Highly levered firms outperformed all equity firms in the mid- to late 1980s and underperformed all equity firms in the early 1990s. How can modernists say that debt is irrelevant?

3. Respond to the following:

   Why are traditionalists incorrect in drawing the required rate of return as bending upward in leverage (a convex shape as shown in Figure 10.4) while modernists are correct in drawing the required rate of return as bending down in leverage (a concave shape as shown in Figure 10.5)?

4. Respond to the following:

   There are some financial managers who pay a great deal of attention to the capital structure decision. Therefore capital structure is relevant.

5. Respond to the following:

   Almost all financial analysts view financial leverage as being an extremely important factor when they analyze a firm. How can it be irrelevant?

The firm's top managers are engaged in a true power meeting. Everyone has assembled to make a final decision on how the firm will raise the $50,000,000 necessary to finance the acquisition of a small public company.

Three investment banking firms from New York City have submitted proposals. One suggests that the firm issue debt to take advantage of current low interest rates. Another suggests an innovative preferred stock issue because they are in heavy demand by institutions. The final investment banking proposal is for the issuance of common stock, because they say this is necessary to prevent the firm's bond rating from deteriorating. But everyone seems to agree that the current market price of the common stock is low.

The chief financial officer presents detailed financial analyses to demonstrate the impact of each idea on the firm's earnings per share and financial ratios. Finally, a consensus emerges—the issue needs further study.

This describes a capital structure decision. Chapter 10 discussed financial leverage and examined the effect of the firm's capital structure on the value of the firm in perfect markets. It was shown that, in the case of perfect markets, the capital structure decision did not affect firm value and was therefore irrelevant. Any mix of financial securities used to finance the firm's assets is as good as any other mix of securities. Securities simply act to divide or partition the cash flows from the assets.

market imperfections
Conditions related to the operations of markets that violate the assumptions of a perfect market. Examples include the payment of taxes and transactions costs.

In this chapter we examine the firm's capital structure decision in imperfect markets. Given certain **market imperfections,** most notably taxes, it will be demonstrated that capital structure can affect firm value, and therefore shareholder wealth. For example, in some cases, levered capital structures, or capital structures that include debt, act to reduce the firm's total tax payment and are preferred to unlevered capital structures.

The first part of the chapter discusses the potential role of taxes on the choice of capital structure, and the second part discusses the potential role of other imperfections on the firm's capital structure choice.

THE RATIONALE FOR CAPITAL STRUCTURE RELEVANCE

Chapter 10 detailed the irrelevancy view of capital structure in perfect markets. It was shown that borrowing money was simply selling debt claims on the firm's assets, just as issuing stock is selling equity claims on the firm's assets. In a well-functioning capital market, competition would force the sales prices of the debt or equity to be equal to their true values, such that securities would be issued with an *NPV* equal to zero. Because managers cannot increase firm value through issuing securities, the capital structure choice is irrelevant.

The irrelevancy conclusion has important implications. Given that corporate managers are faced with two primary decisions—raising money, or the financing decision, and investing money, or the investment decision—capital structure's irrelevancy suggests that managers should spend most of their time deciding which assets to acquire, and little time deciding how to finance those assets. Further, the concept of capital structure irrelevancy vastly simplifies the theory of how to make optimal investment decisions, since capital structure effects can be ignored in the capital budgeting process.

Although the discussion of capital structure in perfect markets was interesting and made things easy, it is now time to bring pertinent market imperfections into our analysis of capital structure. It is important, however, that the effects of these imperfections be developed logically and carefully. The arguments of the investment bankers as to how to raise funds for the hypothetical firm lacked rigor. This chapter helps the reader deduce the differences between valid reasons and dubious reasons for capital structure relevancy.

The No-Free-Lunch Analogy for Capital Structure Relevancy

There is a popular saying in economics—and in everyday life, as well—that there's no such thing as a free lunch. In other words, valuable things always carry a cost. Otherwise they would be free, and people do not regard free things as being valuable, no matter how important they are. This goes for products and services sold in stores, as well as other kinds of commodities such as air, sunlight, and water.

Now let's apply this economic truth to the debate over capital structure. If someone argues that there is an optimal capital structure—one that maximizes the value of the firm—the logical question is where does the value come from? In other words, if shareholders receive added wealth in the form of a higher stock price from a particular mix of financial securities, from whence does this value derive? (Remember, value must come from somewhere, since there are no free lunches.)

This chapter will show that, because of certain imperfections, there are some logical possibilities as to whereof wealth could derive, and that a particular financing decision might make shareholders better off. The best example comes from taxes. It is logical to believe that tax laws might exist that would favor one capital structure over another. In this case, a particular tax-saving financial decision might cause wealth to be transferred from the government, or more accurately from taxpayers through the government, to shareholders. In the case of taxes, the cumbersome nature of government, combined with the difficulty of implementing laws that would tax all capital structures equally, makes it plausible that taxes may affect capital structure.

> ⌛ An acceptable theory of why one capital structure is more valuable than another must include not only an explanation of where the value comes from but also why the other participants allow the wealth to be transferred from them.

Example 11.1 _____ The challenge in the argument of capital structure relevancy is to explain where the value comes from as well as why other participants would allow the wealth to be transferred from them. Let's look at this challenge from the standpoint of the three proposals of the investment bankers presented in the opening of the chapter. Do any of these proposals truly provide value to the firm's shareholders?

The first argument was that debt should be used, since interest rates are low. This rationale implies that interest rates will soon rise and that the same dollar amount of debt issued later will cost the firm more in interest payments. However, the logical question is, why would people willingly purchase the firm's bonds when interest rates are low rather than waiting until interest rates rise? After all, bondholders would surely wish to wait and purchase the bonds after the rates have risen in order to receive the higher interest rate. Would bond investors be so ignorant as to allow the corporation to consistently beat them at an interest rate timing competition? Because we see no logical reason why they would, we dismiss this argument as wishful thinking.

The second argument suggests an innovative preferred stock issue, because such stocks are in heavy demand by investors, or specifically by certain institutions. The argument implies that the demand is so strong that the preferred stock can be issued to investors at a premium. But why would institutions pay a significant amount of extra money for partitioning the cash flows of the corporation? Couldn't the institutions find a less expensive way of obtaining the desired characteristics that the preferred stock offers? Wouldn't competition from other corporations issuing similar preferred stocks have already driven down the reward for issuing them? We suspect that you would be very suspicious of such a claim.

Finally, the third proposal is to use a common stock issue to avoid deterioration in the firm's bond rating, which implies that a good bond rating is valuable. At first this sounds believable, but let's take a closer look. What this argument is really saying is that corporations with good credit ratings can borrow money at positive *NPV*s, while corporations with bad credit ratings are confronted with borrowing at negative *NPV*s. If this is true, then it implies that bond investors—those on the other side of the bond issue—consistently accept negative *NPV*s when investing in high-quality bonds and consistently enjoy positive *NPV*s when investing in low-quality bonds. We have never seen evidence that this is how bondholders behave.

None of these proposals by the investment bankers meet our challenge, so we conclude that none of the proposals would increase shareholder wealth. The remainder of the chapter will present the major arguments regarding the relevance of capital structure that have survived logical analysis and scrutiny. ↵

CAPITAL STRUCTURE WITH CORPORATE TAXES

This section builds a theory of capital structure that includes market imperfections. We begin with taxes. Because the foundation of most of this theory is attributable to the work of Franco Modigliani and Merton Miller (M&M), we will refer to the main analysis of Chapter 10 as M&M without taxes, and will refer to their analysis regarding taxes in this chapter as M&M with taxes.

How Corporate Taxes Are Levied

As discussed in Workshop 3.1, individuals and corporations are taxed on income, and the specific rate of taxation often depends on the income level and residence. The U.S. federal government operates a progressive income tax system, taxing higher income levels at higher marginal tax rates. However, the levels of progressivity are such that corporations with taxable income above $75,000 are taxed at 34 percent. Because most corporations have at least $75,000 of taxable income, throughout most of this chapter we will ignore the lower tax rates and use only 34 percent.

In the discussion in Chapter 3, income refers to taxable income, or revenues less deductible expenses. The firm is permitted to deduct its expenses before it computes its taxes owed, including interest expense, but not including its dividend. It is the ability to deduct interest expense that will drastically alter the results achieved in Chapter 10.

Financial Leverage with Corporate Income Taxes

Let's return to the financial statements of Boring, Inc., and Exciting, Inc., introduced in the previous chapter. Table 11.1 modifies the original analysis to reflect the effect of a 34 percent corporate income tax rate.

The difference between the analysis in Table 11.1 and the corresponding analysis in Chapter 10 is that each corporation must now pay income taxes on profits after interest expense. Since corporations have different amounts of debt, and since interest payments are tax deductible, the otherwise identical corporations pay different amounts of taxes.

Now let's try to replicate the levered firm using homemade leverage as was shown in Chapter 10. Table 11.2 demonstrates the attempt

---

TABLE 11.1
Leverage and Cash Flow per Share

State	Boring, Inc. (1,000 shares)					
	Total Cash Flow Before Interest	*Interest Expense*	*Taxable Income*	*Taxes*	*Net Income*	*After-Tax Equity Cash Flow per Share*
Recession	$ 500	$0	$ 500	$170	$330	$0.33
Normal	$1,000	$0	$1,000	$340	$660	$0.66
Boom	$1,500	$0	$1,500	$510	$990	$0.99
State	Exciting, Inc. (500 shares)					
	Total Cash Flow Before Interest	*Interest Expense*	*Taxable Income*	*Taxes*	*Net Income*	*After-Tax Equity Cash Flow per Share*
Recession	$ 500	$500	$ -0-	$-0-	$-0-	$-0-
Normal	$1,000	$500	$ 500	$170	$330	$0.66
Boom	$1,500	$500	$1,000	$340	$660	$1.32

to replicate the equity cash flows from Exciting, Inc., by buying two times the shares of Boring, Inc., using borrowed money. For simplicity we assume that the equity of each firm still sells for $10 per share. Alternative #1 buys the levered stock directly. As before, alternative #2 attempts to replicate the results of alternative #1 using the other corporation's stock.

Notice that the final results of the two alternatives in Table 11.2 are not equal, and that homemade leverage no longer works. In a recession, alternative #1 breaks even, while alternative #2 loses $17. Similar results occur in normal conditions and a boom. Each outcome in the homemade leverage alternative, alternative #2, is $17 lower than when the corporation does the borrowing. Borrowing through the corporation is therefore preferred to borrowing through homemade leverage. But where, under homemade leverage, does the $17 go?

The answer is that the $17 went to the government. The decision to use homemade leverage rather than corporate leverage means that the tax savings through the deductibility of interest expense in computing the corporation's taxable income is lost. The $50 interest payment multiplied by the 34 percent tax rate equals the $17 of greater taxes paid using homemade leverage.

Modigliani and Miller demonstrated that, when corporate taxes are introduced, there is a tax advantage to using debt, and the optimal capital structure decision is to use as much debt as possible—even up to 100 percent or all debt!

TABLE 11.2
Homemade Leverage with Corporate Income Taxes

Alternative #1: Corporate Leverage

Buy 10% of Exciting, Inc., Equity for $500 (50 shares).

Cash Flow—Recession	50 shares * $0.00 = $ 0.00
Cash Flow—Normal Conditions	50 shares * $0.66 = $33.00
Cash Flow—Boom	50 shares * $1.32 = $66.00

Alternative #2: Homemade Leverage

Buy 10% of Boring, Inc., Equity Using $500 of Borrowed Money *plus* $500 of Original Money (100 shares).

Cash Flow—Recession	Equity	$33.00	($0.33 * 100 shares)
	Borrowing	−$50.00	
	Net Cash Flow	−$17.00	
Cash Flow—Normal	Equity	$66.00	($0.66 * 100 shares)
	Borrowing	−$50.00	
	Net Cash Flow	$16.00	
Cash Flow—Boom	Equity	$99.00	($0.99 * 100 shares)
	Borrowing	−$50.00	
	Net Cash Flow	$49.00	

Example 11.2 —————— Let's imagine a corporation set up by one person who has a great idea about a new way to manufacture a product that cleans props, known as Prop Wash. The paperwork, or articles of incorporation, has been filed but, as of now, the firm does not have any significant assets, liabilities, or equity.

Suppose that the firm wishes to raise $1,000,000 in order to begin the project of demonstrating the new Prop Wash manufacturing process. Since the project will take advantage of a new and valuable technology, it may be reasonable to assume that the value of the firm's assets with the project will rise to $1,500,000. In other words, the project has an *NPV* of $500,000. The $1,500,000 represents the present value of the project's total cash flow stream, ignoring taxes, which are projected to be $150,000 per year forever. (We found this using a discount rate of 10 percent and applying the perpetuity formula.) Because the cash flow is earned year after year forever, its present value is determined by dividing the cash flow by the discount rate.

The individual who set up the corporation has the needed $1,000,000 in his personal bank account and is considering whether the money should be moved inside the firm as equity or debt. Remember, no one else is involved. The investor is simply deciding what paperwork is best for tax purposes. The only difference is that if the money were to be called debt, the firm would be able to pay out cash in the form of interest expense—which for tax purposes would be deductible from income.

Under perfect markets it would make no difference whether the money was contributed as debt or equity. However, with corporate income taxes paid at a rate of 34 percent, the after-tax cash flow stream will depend on whether debt or equity is used. Let's look at the two alternatives: equity and debt.

Calling the Contribution Equity.
If the $1,000,000 is contributed as equity, the corporation's annual cash flow of $150,000 would be fully taxable. The corporation's after-tax income would drop to $99,000, as the tax bill on $150,000 of income is $51,000. The value of the equity would be the present value of $99,000 per year forever, which is $990,000. Thus, the present value of the benefits, $990,000, is less than the present value of the costs, $1,000,000, and the project is unacceptable.

Calling the Contribution Debt.
If, instead, the $1,000,000 is contributed as debt, and if the cost of debt is 10 percent, the

corporation would incur an interest expense of $100,000 per year. The firm would earn a before-tax profit of $50,000, calculated by taking the $150,000 of cash flow and subtracting $100,000 in interest expense. The after-tax profit, after applying a tax rate of 34 percent, would be $33,000 per year. Applying the perpetuity formula, the value of the equity would be $330,000.

Of course, the investor also owns debt securities. The investor's debt holdings would result in $100,000 per year in interest income, and this perpetuity would be worth $1,000,000. The value of both the equity and debt securities is $1,330,000. Thus, the present value of the benefits, $1,330,000, is greater than the present value of the costs, $1,000,000, and the project is acceptable. ⏎

Summary of Financial Leverage and Corporate Taxation

We return to the question being considered in the Prop Wash example—whether funds should be brought into the corporation as equity or debt. If the $1,000,000 investment is contributed as equity, the value of the equity holdings is $990,000. If the $1,000,000 is contributed as debt, the value of the debt claim plus the value of the equity claim is $1,330,000. The difference of $340,000 results from a $34,000 tax reduction, per year forever, as a result of the use of debt.

Illustrating Financial Leverage and Taxes with an M&M Proposition

In the Prop Wash example, the present value of the tax reduction through the use of debt, or $340,000, is equal to the corporate tax rate of 34 percent multiplied by the value of the debt, or $1,000,000. This concept is expressed in the following famous proposition introduced by M&M:

$$V_L = V_U + (T_C * D), \tag{11.1}$$

where:

$$V_L = \text{the value of a levered firm,}$$
$$V_U = \text{the value of an unlevered firm,}$$
$$T_C = \text{the corporate income tax rate, and}$$
$$D = \text{the value of the permanent debt.}$$

This equation shows that the value of a levered firm is equal to the value of an unlevered firm plus the tax shield from debt.

Let's go through the M&M proposition for the Prop Wash example. If the individual uses equity capital by calling the $1,000,000 contribution stock, the value of the firm will be $990,000. This is V_U in Formula (11.1), since the firm would be unlevered. The second part of the formula measures the present value of the tax savings which from Formula (11.1) is given by:

$$\text{Tax Shield from Debt} = (34\% * \$1,000,000) = \$340,000,$$

and the total value of the levered firm is:

$$\$1,330,000 = \$990,000 + \$340,000.$$

Thus, the unlevered firm has a value of only $990,000 and would not be worth the $1,000,000 investment required. However, the $34,000 of annual tax savings produces a present value of $340,000 of perpetual tax savings, which gives the levered firm a value of $1,330,000.

Where Does the Extra Value of Leverage Come From? At first, Formula (11.1) gives the impression that debt adds to the value of the firm by providing a tax shield. While this is in some sense true, it seems to imply that the government subsidizes corporate shareholders who use debt. Perhaps a better way of viewing the tax advantage of leverage is that the use of debt really only reduces the amount of money the government takes from the equityholders. Remember, without taxes, the project had an *NPV* of $500,000. With taxes, the project had an *NPV* of either −$10,000 or +$330,000, depending upon whether the original $1,000,000 is used as debt or equity. Therefore, leverage can reduce taxes.

Regardless of how the story is viewed, the moral is clear. There is a tax penalty to using equity in the M&M corporate income tax model, and there is no tax penalty to using debt. The optimal capital structure is to use as much debt as possible so that the government's claim is minimized, thereby transferring the least amount of wealth from the equityholders to the government.

> ⊠ In the M&M income tax model there is a tax advantage to debt, and the optimal capital structure approaches 100 percent debt.

Are Firms Fully Levered? A funny thing happened in the 25 or so years in which the M&M propositions were being taught and refined: There did not seem to be a wild rush by corporations to take on more and more debt in order to take maximum advantage of the tax shield claimed by M&M. Perhaps some firms fully understood the advantage to debt before the M&M work was published, but, even so, most corporations were far short of 100 percent debt.[1] Thus, it appears that the M&M model with taxes does not explain completely how firms make the capital structure choice.

THE MILLER TAX MODEL

Miller tax model
A theory of capital structure, attributed to Merton Miller, that assumes that the tax advantage to debt at the corporate level is offset by the tax disadvantage to debt at the personal level.

In 1977, Merton Miller proposed an alternative model which, in addition to corporate taxes, included personal taxes—or income taxes on individuals. This model is known as the **Miller tax model.** Within this model, Miller argued that the tax advantage to debt at the corporate level was actually offset by the tax disadvantage to debt at the personal level. The result in the Miller tax model is that capital structure returns to being irrelevant.

> ✗ In the Miller tax model, the tax advantages to debt at the corporate tax level are offset by the tax disadvantages to debt at the individual income tax level, such that capital structure is irrelevant to firm value and shareholder wealth.

The crux of Miller's argument rests on the idea that the income tax laws for individuals tend to place a higher tax on interest income received from debt than on dividend plus capital gain income received from equity. The reason personal income tax laws provide relief to equityholders is the belief that equityholders are taxed twice—once at the corporate level and once at the individual level. This double taxation of dividends led to tax breaks for equityholders to alleviate the burden. In effect, Miller argued that the tax breaks allowed to lessen the burden of double taxation could be used so vigorously that the personal tax on equity was tremendously reduced. This considerable tax advantage to equity at the personal level fully offsets the government's tax penalty on equity at the corporate level.

Miller developed an equation to describe the value of a levered firm that introduced tax rates on individual income from debt and equity:

$$V_L = V_U + \left[1 - \frac{(1 - T_C)(1 - T_E)}{(1 - T_D)} \right] D, \qquad (11.2)$$

where:

V_L = the value of a levered firm,
V_U = the value of an unlevered firm,

---

1. Of course, a firm that is 100 percent debt financed would be "owned" by the debtholders. In this case the IRS would likely treat the capital as equity.

T_C = the corporate income tax rate,
T_E = the individual tax rate on equity income,
T_D = the individual tax rate on debt income, and
D = the value of the permanent debt.

Formula (11.2) expresses the value of the levered firm as the value of the unlevered firm plus the value of the tax shield.

Notice the difference between the Miller tax model and the M&M with taxes model. By introducing personal taxes, given in the model by T_E and T_D, the increase in firm value related to debt financing is not simply $T_C \times D$. Instead, T_C is replaced by the bracketed expression:

$$\left[1 - \frac{(1 - T_C)(1 - T_E)}{(1 - T_D)} \right].$$

The tax advantage to debt is defined by this bracketed expression multiplied by the amount of debt, or D in Formula (11.2). In Miller's model, the tax advantage to debt is reduced as long as T_E is less than T_D.

There are two extreme cases to Miller's model. First, if individual income tax rates, both T_D and T_E, are set equal to zero or are set equal to each other, Formula (11.2) simplifies to being identical to Formula (11.1), the M&M model with taxes. (You may prove this to yourself by substituting and simplifying.) In other words, when personal tax rates are such that there is no personal tax disadvantage to debt, then the effect of debt is the same as in the original M&M model.

Second, when the differences in the tax rates are such that:

$$(1 - T_D) = (1 - T_C) * (1 - T_E),$$

then Formula (11.2) reduces to $V_L = V_U$, which means that capital structure returns to being irrelevant! In other words, this is the Miller tax model discussed above, where there is no net tax advantage to debt. You may check this by inserting the right-hand side of the formula above in place of $(1 - T_D)$ in Formula (11.2) and simplifying.

Prop Wash and the Miller Tax Model

We return to our Prop Wash example to illustrate the conditions given by the Miller model. Suppose that the individual who set up the firm was in the 34 percent tax bracket for interest income, such that T_D = .34, but was able to shelter equity income such that the equity income was tax free at the individual income tax level in a present value sense. With tax-free equity income, the variable T_E in Formula (11.2) is equal to zero. Since the tax rate on corporate income, given by T_C, is 34 percent, the tax advantage to debt vanishes.

You recall from the Prop Wash example that the issue was whether the person should contribute $1,000,000 in the form of equity or debt. We found that when equity financing was used, the value of the firm was $990,000, but when debt financing was used the value was $1,330,000. Now let's introduce personal taxation. We do this by switching to the Miller tax model. The individual's tax bill now must include the $100,000 of interest on the debt. Given the 34 percent personal tax rate on debt interest, new taxes of $34,000 are collected, and the present value of the $34,000 tax perpetuity is $340,000. When this personal tax liability from debt is subtracted from the $1,330,000 firm value, the result is $990,000. This is the same as it was without debt and therefore proves the result of the Miller tax model, which is that debt usage is irrelevant to firm value. The new value of the levered firm can be shown using Miller's equation:

$$\$990,000 = \$990,000 + \left[1 - \frac{(1-.34)(1-.00)}{(1-.34)}\right]\$1,000,000,$$

illustrating that the value of the firm is the same with or without the use of debt, and that the capital structure choice is irrelevant.

We have analyzed the Miller tax model under two extreme cases, one that produces no tax advantage to debt and another that creates a situation in which the firm should be 100 percent debt financed. Of course, the more likely situation is somewhere between these two extreme cases. When the individual tax rate on debt is greater than the individual tax rate on equity such that T_D is greater than T_E, the gain to the firm from using leverage decreases. Thus, the importance of Miller's model depends on the prevailing corporate and personal tax rates. Window 11.1 details the current corporate and personal tax structure as it relates to Miller's model.

Another illustration of the Miller tax model can be found by inserting personal taxes into the example of homemade leverage using Boring, Inc., and Exciting, Inc. Recall that when corporate tax rates were considered, homemade leverage failed to replicate corporate leverage because the corporate tax advantage to debt was lost. Table 11.3 illustrates the combined effects of corporate and personal taxes on homemade leverage assuming that the personal tax rate on debt income is 34 percent, the personal tax rate on equity income is 0 percent, and the corporate tax rate remains at 34 percent.

Table 11.3 shows that the individual receives the same after-tax net cash flow whether corporate or homemade leverage is used. The shareholder's tax advantage of using debt at the corporate level can now be achieved using personal tax savings. This illustrates the Miller tax model result of capital structure irrelevancy, since corporate capital structure decisions are rendered useless by the ability of individuals to repartition the firm.

Window 11.1

Current Income Tax Rates and the Miller Model

The Miller tax model introduces the potential disadvantage to investing in debt when considering personal taxes on debt income. In its purest form, Miller's model shows that the personal tax disadvantage completely offsets the corporate tax advantage of debt such that the capital structure decision is once again irrelevant. This window provides some detail into the U.S. tax code and how it relates to Miller's model.

The Tax Reform Act (TRA) of 1986 had a significant impact on the variables contained in the Miller model, most notably the removal of the distinction between the personal tax rate on ordinary income and the personal tax rate on long-term capital gains. While the reintroduction of this tax break is proposed and debated each year, it is currently not in effect for federal income tax purposes. Some people argue, therefore, that the 1986 changes removed most of the punch of the Miller tax model.

However, there are still personal tax advantages to owning stocks rather than bonds, such that personal taxes act to reduce the total tax advantage to debt. Perhaps the most important advantage is that since the gains from holding stocks are taxed when the stocks are sold, stock investors can set the time when they want to declare profits. Wise investors can carefully time the sale of their stocks to minimize total taxes. Let's take a closer look at how stock investors can minimize or even eliminate personal income taxes on their equity holdings in this way.

Consider an investor who has $100,000 to invest in stocks. Stocks tend to pay a portion of their return in the form of dividends, or distributions of current earnings to shareholders, and perhaps a larger portion in price appreciation as profits are retained and reinvested. Suppose, further, that the investor not only buys $100,000 worth of stock but also borrows money (see the use of margin in Window 10.5) to purchase additional stock. The amount of money borrowed is such that each year the total interest expense on the margin borrowing approximately equals the amount of dividends received on all the stocks.

Each year the investor expects that some stocks will go down and that (ideally) most will go up. Each year the investor sells only those stocks that have gone down—and only enough to be able to declare the maximum allowable $3,000 loss for personal income taxes. If the investor doesn't need cash, the money from the proceeds of the sale of stock is used to buy more stock. And if the investor needs even more cash, the stocks that haven't gone up or down can be sold without incurring any income tax. Notice that the investor isn't really losing on the total portfolio by selling the stocks that fell, but is simply recognizing only the losses for tax reasons. There may be tremendous profits occurring elsewhere in the portfolio.

(continued on next page)

Window 11.1 (continued)

Finally, many years later, the investor will be left with the winners— the stocks that have gone up a great deal. In order to minimize the income tax on selling these winners, the investor may (1) time the sales for those years in which income or tax rates are low, say in retirement, (2) hold the stocks until death and pass the stocks to beneficiaries such that no taxes are ever paid on the gain, or (3) donate the stocks to a charity in lieu of cash (if the investor were going to donate cash anyway). Thus, whether the investor turns out to be rich, poor, or dies early, even the profitable stocks won't cause a big income tax liability.

Notice that the investor enjoys many early years of being able to benefit tremendously from an annual tax loss of $3,000. The tax on dividend income is eliminated by the deductibility of the margin interest expense. Finally, the investor might realize ultimate profits in a way that causes little or no taxes.

In a present value sense, the investor might even be able to have a negative net tax liability. At a minimum, it should be recognized that common stocks offer personal income tax advantages.

Which Model Is Best: M&M or Miller?

As we have stated, the M&M with taxes model argues that there is a large tax advantage to using debt. The Miller argument is that this tax advantage at the corporate level is offset by the tax disadvantage to debt at the personal level.

Numerous studies have failed to establish either model as being correct. Perhaps the view for now should be that the tax advantage to debt at the corporate level is at least partially offset by tax disadvantages to debt at the personal level. Viewed together, perhaps there is a small tax advantage to debt. However, there are other imperfections that will be discussed throughout the remainder of this chapter. Perhaps there are certain other disadvantages to debt that offset any remaining tax advantage.

BANKRUPTCY AND CAPITAL STRUCTURE

One view of bankruptcy, often called the traditionalist view, states that bankruptcy most often occurs when cash flows from the firm's assets are insufficient to cover the cash expenses—including the cash flows

TABLE 11.3
Homemade Leverage with Corporate and Personal Taxes

Alternative #1: Corporate Leverage
Buy 10% of Exciting, Inc., Equity for $500 (50 shares)

	Recession	Normal	Boom
Pretax cash flow	$0.00	$33.00	$66.00
Personal taxes*	-0-	-0-	-0-
After-tax cash flow	$0.00	$33.00	$66.00

Alternative #2: Homemade Leverage
Buy 10% of Boring, Inc., Equity Using $500 of Borrowed Money *plus* $500 of Original Money (100 shares)

	Recession	Normal	Boom
Pretax cash flow	$33.00	$66.00	$99.00
Interest expense	-$50.00	-$50.00	-$50.00
Tax shield on borrowing†	$17.00	$17.00	$17.00
After-tax cash flow	$0.00	$33.00	$66.00

* The personal tax on equity is assumed to be zero.
† Assumes that the individual can deduct $50 interest expense when filing personal tax returns. Tax rate is 34%.

owed to the firm's debtholders. Most people think of bankruptcy as being bad, and since using lots of debt can increase the probability of bankruptcy, it must be that using too much debt is bad.

The modernists' view, on the other hand, recognizes that bankruptcy is a legal event and does not destroy or create value. Therefore, ignoring legal costs and in well-functioning markets, modernists do not perceive increased chances of bankruptcy as a reason to restrain the use of debt.

To provide an analogy, some people hate being in hospitals—perhaps because it brings up memories of their previous pain or that of a loved one. Would it be logical, therefore, for them to move to an extremely remote part of the world where it would be virtually impossible to make use of a hospital? The answer is clearly no. The individuals don't really hate hospitals; they really hate the pain associated with events necessitating hospital visits. Avoiding the hospital will not reduce the amount of pain. The fact is that hospitals actually reduce long-term pain.

Similarly, bankruptcy itself is not value-destroying or painful—it is a legal event. The pain associated with bankruptcy is actually a result of the operational losses that are occurring, and bankruptcy does not cause these losses. Equityholders should view bankruptcy as a tool—not as a disaster—and a useful tool at that. In fact, if the shareholders truly believe that the chance of the firm going bankrupt is zero, then they should consider a different organizational form, such as a partnership, as there may be tax benefits to partnerships not enjoyed by corporations.

The idea that bankruptcy is the friend of an equityholder becomes clearer when one realizes that bankruptcy is what a corporation declares in order to protect its shareholders from being liable for the debts of the corporation. Alternatively, bankruptcy is a legal tool that an equityholder can use when confronted with unpaid creditors, expensive union contracts, massive lawsuits, high property taxes, and so forth. The financial news abounds with examples of major corporations that are using bankruptcy as a tool to benefit shareholders. In fact, when a major firm declares bankruptcy, the value of its equity usually rises.

Example 11.3 _____ Consider two firms: TTMAR, Inc. (Take the Money and Run) and NSS (Not So Swift) Partners. Both firms have identical assets of land, equipment, and cash that will permit the development of a gold mine. TTMAR, Inc., is organized as a corporation—giving its owners limited liability. NSS Partners is a partnership in which all partners bear unlimited liability.

TTMAR, Inc., begins the venture in earnest. Money is borrowed, long-term union contracts are signed, and reasonable amounts of insurance are purchased. The owners feel that if they strike gold, there will be plenty of money to pay the interest expense and labor costs. However, they also know their losses are limited. If they fail to strike gold, they simply declare bankruptcy—or perhaps they can threaten to declare bankruptcy, so that creditors will wait and union officials will renegotiate contracts while further exploration of recovery is under way.

NSS Partners is in a different situation. Although all will be well if they strike gold, they not only fear that they will not strike gold, but also that a serious accident, such as a mine collapse, will wipe out the assets of the company and expose every investor to losing all of his or her personal wealth.

TTMAR, Inc., and NSS PARTNERS illustrate the value and importance of being able to declare corporate bankruptcy. It should, however, be noted that bankruptcy rules do not provide protection in cases of fraud or for corporate officers or shareholders involved in management. ↵

Bankruptcy and Option Theory

Chapter 9, on option theory, discussed the idea that equity can be viewed as a call option on the firm's assets. Option theory can be an important tool in understanding the effects of corporate bankruptcy. If the assets of a corporation have value greater than the face value of the firm's debt, the equityholders will exercise their option, pay off the debtholders, and claim the residual cash flow. If the assets have insufficient value when a debt payment is due, the equityholders can simply let their option expire—in other words, declare bankruptcy.

One of the important points of Chapter 9 was that the value of an option increases as the volatility of the underlying asset increases. In terms of the equity of a corporation, this means that the equity of a firm with substantial debt will increase in value if the firm increases the riskiness of its assets. This is an important point embodying the essence of option theory and bankruptcy.

Let's consider the effects on debtholders and shareholders of a levered firm that substantially increases the riskiness of its assets. The debtholders will receive their promised payments only if the assets don't fall too much in value, so if the assets' value substantially decreases, the debtholders stand to lose. Thus, if the riskiness of the firm's assets is increased, the value of the debt must fall. But the value of the assets is still the same—only their risk has changed. Thus, the loss in value to the bondholders flows as a gain to the stockholders. The stockholders gain because the greater risk has increased their profit potential, while limited liability has protected them from potential losses.

In summary, an increase in the risk of the assets of a firm will cause the value of the equity to rise and the value of the debt to fall. This is a direct wealth transfer from those who don't have the option, the debtholders, to those who own the option, the equityholders. Of course, debtholders are smart enough to understand the potential for this wealth loss and will likely take steps to protect themselves.

For example, would a person with assets currently worth $50,000 take a gamble of flipping a coin to win or lose $50,000? Most of us would agree that the gamble would be foolish, for reasons fully developed in Chapter 7. However, suppose that the person could set up a corporation with $10,000 and take the gamble through the corporation. If the corporation wins the flip, the investor gains $50,000 through his or her ownership of the corporation. But if the corporation loses the flip, bankruptcy can be declared, and the person will lose only $10,000. Most people would agree that this is an excellent risk, since the $50,000 of profit potential remains, but the loss potential has been reduced to $10,000 by the limited liability that corporations have through bankruptcy. Of course, it would be difficult to find somebody foolish enough to offer such a gamble to this corporation.

Risky Projects and the Games Shareholders Can Play

Consider a stockholder of a corporation called Dewey, Cheatum, and Howe, which manufactures fish scalers. The chief economist is predicting that the firm faces extremely volatile times ahead—either sales and profits will skyrocket or they will plummet, based upon a number of economy-wide and industry factors.

The firm has a substantial amount of debt, a very long-term and expensive union contract, high property taxes, and a potentially huge legal liability revolving around a test case now being tried. At this time there are two proposals the firm is considering: (1) a safe proposal and (2) a risky proposal.

Those advocating the safe proposal argue that, with such difficulties and uncertainties ahead, the firm should prepare itself for potential disaster by issuing lots of stock, using half of the money to pay off all of the debtholders and keeping the other half of the money in low-risk, cash-equivalent securities in order to be protected from future disasters. They note that this strategy will best guarantee the survival of the firm.

Those advocating the risky proposal take the opposite position. They suggest that all available cash be sent immediately to the shareholders as a cash distribution or dividend, arguing that in the next few years it will be revealed whether the firm will enjoy massive profits or losses. If there are profits, they can be shared among the equityholders. Since there would be fewer equityholders under this proposal, each will receive a huge wealth increase. (Note that debt expenses and labor costs are already locked in.) On the other hand, if the firm begins to experience massive losses, they can always declare bankruptcy. Therefore, the huge up-side potential profit dwarfs the down-side potential losses. Further, if times get really tough, perhaps the firm can bluff bankruptcy and use the lack of cash as a reason to negotiate cost savings with the union, the people suing them, the local tax authorities, and perhaps even the creditors.

As a shareholder, which proposal would you support? Option theory teaches us that in cases such as these there is tremendous incentive to use bankruptcy potential to transfer wealth from other people to a firm's shareholders.

However, in other cases there may be large costs attached to an increased potential for bankruptcy that would affect the decision. Perhaps if Dewey, Cheatum, and Howe accept the high-risk proposal, the firm would suffer significantly by losing key employees who might seek long-term employment potential with other firms, or would lose large customers who do not want to depend upon a firm that is near bankruptcy. If consumer confidence in a firm's ability to continue its product lines, for example computers or cars, is low, it may be extremely difficult to attract and retain distributors and customers.

Summary of Bankruptcy

The point of this section on bankruptcy is that, although debt may increase the probability of bankruptcy, that, by itself, is not necessarily a bad thing from the shareholder's perspective. In fact, bankruptcy laws protect shareholders and should be used wisely. It is possible that some firms will find that, by using debt and by taking advantage of bankruptcy laws, they can make their shareholders better off. If shareholders are better off, then it must be that some other group is made worse off. What group allow themselves to be taken advantage of by shareholders using bankruptcy laws?

Bondholders are smart people who will likely go to great lengths to protect themselves from being taken advantage of by shareholders. For instance, bondholders place restrictions on the firm when it borrows in the form of actions written into the bond contract, or by demanding a high interest rate up front to offset such risks. Accordingly, equityholders attempting to use bankruptcy and capital structure to maximize shareholder wealth will probably not be successful in transferring wealth from new bondholders.

However, other groups may not be so well protected. Labor unions, for example, tend to allow themselves to be put into positions in which bankruptcy laws can be used against them to void contracts. Local governments and even the federal government may find themselves subsidizing firms that are so large that their failure is deemed to be contrary to the public good. Clearly, legal claimants can be hurt by the use of bankruptcy by corporations.

The total effect on shareholder wealth from high leverage and its resulting bankruptcy potential will depend upon individual circumstances. The bottom line on our bankruptcy discussion is that capital structure may matter in certain extreme cases in which bankruptcy laws can cause wealth transfers to or from shareholders. The key is to look carefully for transfers of wealth that may occur.

TRANSACTIONS COSTS, AGENCY COSTS AND INFORMATION SIGNALING

There are numerous and lengthy issues concerning capital structure that go beyond taxes and bankruptcy costs. In this section we will briefly explore a few of them.

transactions costs
The costs associated with issuing or trading securities such as debt and equity.

Transactions costs, such as the costs of issuing debt and equity or the cost of using homemade leverage, can make capital structure relevant. For small firms, the transactions cost of obtaining capital can be huge. However, for a major firm with access to the U.S. financial markets it seems clear that there is far more money to be made for shareholders by making wise investment decisions than by attempting to minimize aggregate transactions cost by adjusting the firm's capital structure.

agency costs
The costs involved whenever one person hires another person to perform a task.

Agency costs are involved whenever one person hires another person to perform a task. Obviously, individuals attempt to do what they perceive is best for their interests. The person doing the hiring is called the principal, and the person hired is called the agent. In the case of corporate finance, the principal is usually the shareholder and the agent is the firm's management. Agency costs are involved because the manager's objectives differ from the principal's objectives.

In capital structure analysis, debtholders enter as a third party. The debtholders have still another objective—maximizing the probability that they will be paid. As is obvious from the section on bankruptcy, this objective may run counter to the objectives of the shareholders. Some capital structure arguments are based upon the costs involved in these conflicts. This chapter will not explore these issues, but in Chapter 12 there will be a rather substantial discussion of agency costs and dividends.

information signaling
An action taken by the management of a firm that conveys information.

Finally, it is important to realize that the firm's capital structure decisions may involve **information signaling** to the market—causing security prices to change even if the capital structure decision itself does not change true shareholder wealth. For example, if a firm issues debt rather than stock, its stock price might rise. This is because it might signal that the firm's managers believe that the stock is underpriced and therefore do not wish to issue new stock. Or it could signal that the firm is doing very well and needs some tax benefits from debt. The theories and models are numerous and complex.

Some people argue that information signaling is a reason that firms make capital structure decisions. That argument is controversial, but most agree that capital structure decisions do, in fact, signal information whether or not information signaling was the reason for the decisions.

WRAPPING UP

We began with the question: Can the financing decision affect the value of the firm? After two chapters of analysis we are still left without a definitive answer to this question.

Let's summarize what we have learned. First, while financial leverage doesn't change the total amount of risk to the firm, it does cause the risk of the assets to be partitioned into equity risk and debt risk. At low levels of financial leverage, the risk is borne principally by the equityholders. At high levels of financial leverage, the increased risk is shared by both the equityholders and the debtholders. While we cannot determine the point at which the debtholders begin to share (too much) risk, we can point out that debt usage differs significantly across industries. As shown in Table 11.4, financial leverage, measured by the ratio of debt to total assets, is as low as 27 percent for the drug industry, and as high as 92 percent for the banking industry. This evidence suggests that different industries and different groups of assets can support different amounts of debt.

TABLE 11.4
Debt Usage Across Industry—1987

	Drug	Utilities	Retailing	Banks
Debt/Total Assets	27%	48%	51%	92%

The system of taxing business income at the federal level provides an incentive for taking on debt. Because the interest payments from debt are tax deductible, firms with debt in their capital structures pay less tax, leaving more after-tax cash flow compared with identical unlevered firms. But the system for taxing shareholders and bond-holders at the personal level may provide a disincentive for investing in debt. If the personal tax on interest income from debt is high relative to the personal tax on income from stock, the tax advantage to debt at the federal level may be completely eliminated by the tax disadvantage to debt at the personal level.

Last, transactions costs, agency costs, and information signaling may provide situations whereby financial leverage will affect firm value.

While finance does not offer an unambiguous answer to the question of capital structure, it does offer useful insights. The well-trained financial manager should understand the logical method of approaching such issues on behalf of the shareholders rather than expecting to apply a simple universal formula to generate an optimal capital structure. Understanding the discussions in this chapter is a starting point for developing the ability to think clearly through these issues.

SUMMARY

☐ This chapter examines the firm's capital structure decision in imperfect markets. Given certain market imperfections, most notably taxes, it was demonstrated that capital structure can affect firm value and therefore shareholder wealth.

☐ An acceptable theory of why one capital structure is more valuable than another must include an explanation not only of where the value comes from but also of why the other participants allow the wealth to be transferred from them.

☐ Modigliani and Miller, in their M&M with taxes model, demonstrated that when corporate taxes are introduced, there is a tax advantage to using debt.

☐ The Miller tax model adds to corporate taxes the payment of personal taxes, or income taxes on individuals. Within this model,

Miller argued that the tax advantage to debt at the corporate level was actually offset by the tax disadvantage to debt at the personal level. The result, in the Miller tax model, is that capital structure returns to being irrelevant.

☐ Although debt may increase the probability of bankruptcy, that by itself is not necessarily a bad thing from the shareholder's perspective . It is possible that some firms will find that, by using debt and by taking advantage of bankruptcy laws, they can make their shareholders better off.

☐ The total effect on shareholder wealth from high leverage and its resulting bankruptcy potential will depend upon individual circumstances. Although bondholders will likely protect themselves from the use of bankruptcy, other groups may not be so well protected. Labor unions, for example, tend to allow themselves to be put into positions in which bankruptcy laws can be used against them to void contracts. Local governments and even the federal government may find themselves subsidizing firms that are so large that their failure is deemed to be contrary to the public good.

REFERENCE

Miller, M.H. "Debt and Taxes," *Journal of Finance* 32(May 1977), 261– 276.

DEMONSTRATION PROBLEMS

Problem 1   Return to Lindross Salvage Corporation introduced in the Chapter 10 Demonstration Problems. Recall that Lindross Salvage Corporation is an all-equity (unlevered) corporation with $10,000,000 in assets and whose performance varies from producing a loss of $1,000,000 per year to producing a profit of $3,000,000 per year.

In Chapter 10, the use of homemade leverage and homemade unleverage was demonstrated in a perfect market. Using a corporate tax rate of 40% and no personal taxes (an M&M tax world), compare the after-tax returns between a $1,000,000 investment in unlevered Lindross Salvage Corporation using homemade leverage and a $1,000,000 direct investment in Lindross Salvage Corporation in which Lindross Salvage Corporation switches to a capital structure with $3,000,000 of debt and $7,000,000 of equity (assume that all debt has an interest rate of 5%).

Solution to Problem 1
The problem suggests that the homemade leverage computations in Chapter 10 be performed in the presence of corporate taxation of 40%.

We first compute the after-tax performance of a direct investment in a levered firm and then, in Steps 2 and 3, we find the after-tax performance of homemade leverage.

Step 1: First, the after-tax performance of the levered firm is found. The after-tax profit or loss net of interest expense is found by subtracting the corporate taxes from the profit or loss that was shown in Chapter 10 for the case of no taxes.

	Low Outcome	High Outcome
Profit before interest and taxes:	$-1,000,000	$+3,000,000
less interest	$150,000	$150,000
Profit before taxes:	$-1,150,000	$+2,850,000
less taxes	$460,000	$ 1,140,000
Net profit	$ -690,000	$+1,710,000
Return to levered firm shareholders	-9.857%	+24.429%

The third line can be taken directly from the solution in Chapter 10. The fourth line represents taxes at 40%. Federal income tax laws allow certain losses in certain years to offset taxable profits in other years. The final line expresses the profit or loss as a percentage return to the equity investor, assuming that there is $7,000,000 of equity. Notice that income taxes are computed after interest has been deducted.

The percentage returns can be multiplied by $1,000,000 to obtain the range of profits and losses for the investor from directly investing in the levered firm:

	Low Outcome	High Outcome
Profit or loss to $1,000,000 investment	$ -98,570	$ +244,290

Step 2: Compute the after-tax returns to shareholders in the unlevered firm when the firm is taxed at 40%.

	Low Outcome	High Outcome
Profit before interest and taxes:	$-1,000,000	$+3,000,000
less taxes	$400,000	$ 1,200,000
Net profit	$ -600,000	$+1,800,000
Return to levered firm shareholders	-6.000%	+18.000%

Notice that the corporate taxes directly reduce the magnitude of each return by 40% for the unlevered firm.

Step 3: Next, the range of rates of return for homemade leverage is determined. Recall that in the solution to demonstration problem 2 in

Chapter 10, it was established that homemade leverage would require the investor to borrow money and invest in an unlevered firm. Specifically, we found:

$$\text{Amount Borrowed} = \$1,000,000 * 42.86\% = \$428,571.$$

Thus the total investment by the investor is given as:

Original Funds	= $1,000,000	(70%)
Borrowed Funds =	$428,571	(30%)
Total Invested	= $1,428,571	(100%)

The returns to the homemade leverage strategy are found by applying the returns in step 2 to the above investment ($1,428,571) in the unlevered firm and subtracting the interest expense on the borrowed money ($428,571 at 5% per year).

	Low Outcome −6%	High Outcome +18%
Total funds in unlevered firm ($1,428,571) times outcome	$ −85,714	$ 257,143
Interest expense of borrowed funds ($428,571) at 5%	−21,428	−21,428
Total profit or loss	$ −107,142	$ 235,715

Final Solution: Notice that the outcomes from direct investment in a levered firm ($−98,570 and $+244,290) differ from the outcomes using homemade leverage ($−107,142 and $235,715). The difference is that homemade leverage produces approximately $8,572 less cash in each outcome, and this is due to the lost tax deduction, since the interest payment is deductible for the levered firm but not deductible to the individual using homemade leverage. We can verify the lost tax deduction as the amount of interest expense ($21,428) times the tax rate (40%). ↵

Problem 2   Repeat problem 1 using a Miller tax world. Specifically, using a corporate tax rate of 40%, a personal income tax rate of 0% on equity income, and a personal tax rate on interest income of 40%, compare the after-tax returns between a $1,000,000 homemade leverage investment in unlevered Lindross Salvage Corporation and a $1,000,000 direct investment in Lindross Salvage Corporation in which Lindross Salvage Corporation switches to a capital structure with $3,000,000 of debt and $7,000,000 of equity (assume that all debt has an interest rate of 5%).

Solution to Problem 2

We repeat the solution performed in problem 1, except that we incorporate personal income taxes. Any interest paid by the investor can be deducted from his or her personal tax returns. However, equity income to the investor is not taxed. We first compute the after-tax performance of a direct investment in a levered firm and then, in steps 2 and 3, we find the after-tax performance of homemade leverage.

Step 1: First, we note that the after-tax performance to the investor of a direct investment in the levered firm is exactly the same as was found for an M&M tax world. In other words, a $1,000,000 investment in a levered firm will have no effect on personal income taxes since we have assumed that the tax rate in equity income is zero.

	Low Outcome	High Outcome
Profit before interest and taxes:	$-1,000,000	$+3,000,000
less interest	$150,000	$150,000
Profit before taxes:	$-1,150,000	$+2,850,000
less taxes	$460,000	$1,140,000
Net profit	$ -690,000	$+1,710,000
Return to levered firm shareholders	- 9.857%	+24.429%
Profit or loss to 1,000,000 investment	$ -98,570	$ +244,290

Step 2: Next, we note that the introduction of personal taxes does not change the before-tax returns from investing in the unlevered firm. For convenience, the results that were determined in the solution to question #1 above are repeated:

	Low Outcome	High Outcome
Profit before interest and taxes:	$-1,000,000	$+3,000,000
less taxes	$400,000	$ 1,200,000
Net profit	$ -600,000	$+1,800,000
Return to levered firm shareholders	- 6.000%	+18.000%

Step 3: Finally, we see the difference when we find the total after-tax returns to the homemade leverage strategy, since we must alter the analysis to take into account the effects of personal taxation on the use of debt by the investor. Recall that the total investment by the investor is:

$$
\begin{aligned}
\text{Original Funds} &= \$1,000,000 \ \ (70\%) \\
\text{Borrowed Funds} &= \ \$428,571 \ \ \ (30\%) \\
\text{Total Invested} &= \$1,428,571 \ (100\%).
\end{aligned}
$$

The returns after personal (and corporate) taxes to the homemade leverage strategy are found by applying the returns in step 2 to the investment ($1,428,571) in the unlevered firm and subtracting the interest expense on the borrowed money ($428,571 at 5% per year). However, we must now take into account that the investor will be able to reduce his or her personal income taxes using the deduction for interest paid.

	Low Outcome −6%	High Outcome +18%
Total funds in unlevered firm ($1,428,571) times outcome	$ −85,714	$ 257,143
Interest expense of borrowed funds ($428,571) at 5%	$ −21,428	$ −21,428
Tax deduction for interest expense at 40% tax rate	$ 8,571	$ 8,571
Total profit or loss (rounded)	$ −98,571	$ 244,286

Final Solution: Notice that the outcomes from direct investment in a levered firm ($−98,570 and $+244,290) are identical (ignoring rounding errors) to the outcomes from homemade leverage. The reason is that the tax advantage to using debt at the corporate level has been matched by a tax advantage to using debt at the personal level, since both levels have a tax rate of 40%. ↵

REVIEW QUESTIONS

1. Why do we say that the government is a claimant to the firm's assets?
2. Describe how deductions act to reduce the firm's tax burden.
3. Assume an M&M tax model and explain why the optimal capital structure is one with 100 percent debt.
4. Assume a Miller tax model and explain why the capital structure decision can be irrelevant.
5. Why do the traditionalists argue that too much debt is bad?
6. Why do modernists argue that bankruptcy is a good friend to shareholders?
7. Explain how it is possible that the equity value of a firm can increase at the time the firm announces bankruptcy.
8. Use the call option concept to characterize the equity value of a firm close to bankruptcy.
9. What are agency costs?

PROBLEMS

1. Marley, Inc., has total cash flow before tax of $900,000 and no debt. Compute Marley's corporate taxes and cash flow after tax if all corporate income is taxed at 34 percent.

2. Moon Lighting Company is unlevered with 2 million shares outstanding and total cash flow before taxes of $725,000. Compute Moon's taxes owed, net income after tax, and after-tax equity earnings per share if all corporate income is taxed at 34 percent.

3. Suppose that the Moon Lighting Company makes a decision to partition its assets into equity and debt. The firm issues $2 million of debt at a cost of 15 percent. The partitioning does not change the firm's total cash flow before taxes; it remains at $725,000. However, the number of shares outstanding has been reduced from 2 million to 1 million.

   a. Compute Moon's taxes owed using a tax rate of 34 percent. What accounts for the difference between the taxes owed here and those owed in problem 2?

   b. Compute Moon's net income after tax and after-tax equity earnings per share.

4. Magnum Headache, Inc., is unlevered, with equity valued at $7 million and with 3.5 million shares outstanding. The firm's cash flow before tax is $1 million. The corporate tax rate is 34 percent. Magnum is considering an exchange of 1 million of its equity for $2 million in debt with an annual interest expense of 10 percent—in other words an opportunity to become levered. Of course, the change will not affect the firm's cash flow. Calculate the after-tax equity earnings per share for Magnum unlevered and for Magnum levered.

5. Return to Magnum Headache, Inc. It turns out that the firm exchanged equity for debt and became levered, and has decided to make the leverage decision permanent by keeping the debt forever. Using Formula (11.1), calculate the new value of Magnum as a levered firm.

6. Boomer's Boogie Boards is currently unlevered, has equity valued at $5 million, and has total cash flow before tax of $1 million. Boomer's CEO suggests that, in order to save on taxes, the firm should issue debt and use the proceeds to retire shares of stock. The capital structure change results in $2 million of new debt with an annual interest expense of 12 percent.

   a. How much in taxes will Boomer save, per year, as a result of the decision to issue debt? Use a corporate tax rate of 34 percent.

   b. Suppose that the debt is permanent, and determine the new value of the firm.

7. Woody's Fish and Tackle is a firm whose equity is valued at $20 million and is levered with $10 million in permanent 10 percent interest debt. How much of Woody's value is derived from the present value of tax savings if the corporate tax rate is 34 percent?

8. Carla's Traveling Circus, Inc., provides entertainment to small cities and towns. The firm, valued at $1.5 million, is levered with $700,000 of debt. Although the corporate tax rate is currently 34 percent, there is speculation that the rate will be raised to 40 percent. Calculate the change in the value of the tax shield if the tax rate increases.

9. Campbell Nuts, Inc., is unlevered with 10,000 shares outstanding. The firm is facing three cash flow scenarios: (1) recession, (2) normal, and (3) boom. Given a corporate tax rate of 34 percent, complete the following table.

State	Total Cash Flow Before Tax	Taxes	Net Income	After-Tax Equity Ownership per Share
Recession	$4,000	?	?	?
Normal	?	?	$5,280	?
Boom	?	$4,760	?	?

10. Campbell Nuts, Inc., has added a new look to its balance sheet— debt! The firm now has $25,000 of debt, with an annual interest expense of 12 percent. The number of shares outstanding has been reduced to 7,500. The firm continues to face the three cash flow scenarios given in problem 9. Given a corporate tax rate of 34 percent, complete the following table:

State	Total Cash Flow Before Tax	Interest Expense	Taxable Income	Taxes	Net Income	After-Tax Equity Earnings per Share
Recession	$4,000	$3,000	?	?	?	?
Normal	?	?	$5,000	?	?	?
Boom	?	?	?	$3,740	?	?

11. A certain group of shareholders of Campbell Nuts, Inc., are not convinced that financial leverage was a good idea. They make the point that, at a certain level of total cash flow before tax, the shareholders are better off without debt. Help this group of shareholders make their point by computing the level of total cash flow before tax that would make shareholders indifferent between being unlevered and levered. (Hint: Using the formula for EPS and using given values, set unlevered, after-tax equity earnings per

share equal to levered after-tax equity ownership per share, and solve for total cash flow before tax.)

12. Recall the firms Square and Peg from problem 19 in Chapter 10, two firms similar in every way except for their respective capital structures. Square is unlevered with 500 shares outstanding, while Peg has $2,000 of debt with an annual interest expense of 10 percent and has 250 shares outstanding. Suppose that you own 5 percent of the equity of Peg because of its use of leverage. The corporate tax rate is 34 percent.
    a. Determine the cash flow from your equity investment in Peg, assuming that Peg's total cash flow is $500.
    b. Determine the cash flow from equity from the following strategy: Borrow an amount equal to 5 percent of the debt of Peg at 10 percent annual interest expense and use the proceeds plus your own money to buy 5 percent of the equity of Square. Assume that Square's total cash flow is $500.
    c. Compare your answers from (a) and (b) above. Why is it that homemade leverage no longer works?

13. Recall firms Giants and Jets from problem 18 in Chapter 10. Giants, Inc., is a successful firm that uses leverage and has assets valued at $1 million. Jets, Inc., is another successful firm similar to Giants except that Jets is unlevered. Show that homemade leverage no longer works if corporate income is taxed at 34 percent. Explain briefly why this is true.

    Set the problem in a way similar to that shown in Table 11.2. That is, assume that Giants, Inc., uses $500,000 of debt with an annual interest expense of 10 percent such that interest payments total $50,000. Also assume three cash flow scenarios: bad, with cash flows of $50,000; OK, with cash flows of $100,000; and good, with cash flows of $150,000. The first alternative is to purchase 10 percent of the equity in Giants, and the second alternative is to purchase 10 percent of Jets and borrow an amount equal to 10 percent of the debt of Giants.

14. Elizabeth Smith has an investment of one percent of the bonds of CNS, Inc. CNS has debt totaling $1 million, issued at 9 percent interest. Calculate Elizabeth's tax bill on her interest income, assuming that she is in the 34 percent tax bracket.

15. Emerson Electronics, whose value as an unlevered firm would be $10 million, has $1 million of debt outstanding. Use Formula (11.2) to calculate the levered value of Emerson under the following tax scenarios:
    a. The personal tax rate on equity income, T_{PE}, is 34 percent.
       The personal tax rate on debt income, T_D, is 34 percent.
       The corporate tax rate, T_C, is 34 percent.
    b. The personal tax rate on equity income, T_{PE}, is 0 percent.
       The personal tax rate on debt income, T_D, is 34 percent.

The corporate tax rate, T_C, is 34 percent.

c. The personal tax rate on equity income, T_{PE}, is 10 percent.
    The personal tax rate on debt income, T_D, is 34 percent.
    The corporate tax rate, T_C, is 34 percent.

16. In a particular economy, equity income is taxed at 34 percent, debt income is taxed at 34 percent, and corporate taxes are also taxed at 34 percent. How much value per dollar of debt will leverage add to a firm that is currently unlevered? (Hint: Use the bracketed expression of Formula (11.2) and substitute $1 for D.)

17. In a particular economy, equity income is taxed at 0 percent, debt income is taxed at 34 percent, and corporate taxes are also taxed at 34 percent. How much value per dollar of debt will leverage add to a firm that is currently unlevered? (Hint: Use the bracketed expression of Formula (11.2) and substitute $1 for D.)

18. In a particular economy, equity income is taxed at 15 percent, debt income is taxed at 34 percent, and corporate taxes are also taxed at 34 percent. How much value per dollar of debt will leverage add to a firm that is currently unlevered? (Hint: Use the bracketed expression of Formula (11.2) and substitute $1 for D.)

19. Return once more to Giants, Inc., and Jets, Inc., in problem 13. Redo the homemade leverage analysis incorporating personal taxes. Assume that the personal tax on debt income is 34 percent, and the personal tax on equity income is 0 percent. Set the problem up in a way similar to that shown in Table 11.3.

DISCUSSION QUESTIONS

1. A newspaper article quoted a stockholder of a corporation as saying, "The firm is in financial distress—and I view bankruptcy as a friend to the shareholder." It almost sounds as if the stockholder is saying that bankruptcy is a good thing, but we all know that it isn't. Why would bankruptcy be referred to as a friend?

2. A politician was heard arguing that a major reason we see firms "levering" is because of the advantage to debt in the corporate tax code. Describe the advantage the politician is referring to. Do you think the politician has a legitimate point, and if he does, how might the corporate tax code be amended to remove this debt advantage?

3. The chapter argues that when a levered firm increases the riskiness of its assets, the value of the firm's debt decreases such that wealth is transferred from bondholders to stockholders. But levered firms increase their risk all the time. Think of some ways that bondholders can protect themselves from this potential loss in value.

4. The Almost Gone Corporation produces computers and is near bankruptcy. The shareholders argue that it is in their best interest is to "roll the dice" with whatever capital the firm has left and invest in some extremely risky but negative-*NPV* projects.
   a. Use the feature of limited liability to explain why shareholders, in this case, might have the incentive to invest in certain projects even if *NPV* were negative.
   b. Can you think of a positive-*NPV* project that the shareholders would reject?
   c. From the standpoint of operating the business as a "going concern," discuss some costs to the shareholder's strategy.
5. The board of directors of Lucky, Inc., has just decided to issue additional stock to raise capital for an expansion project. At the same time it is revealed to the board that some land owned by the firm, once considered to be worthless, might contain significant amounts of crude oil worth millions, but that this information must remain confidential for several months. Convince the board that given this new information, they should scrap the plan to issue new stock and issue bonds instead.

Chapter 12

The Dividend Decision

U SF&G is a large insurance corporation headquartered in Baltimore, Maryland. The top management of USF&G was very proud of the company's long history of regularly distributing profits to the shareholders. These cash payments, or dividends, had been sent regularly to shareholders since 1939.

In the late 1980s, things were not going well for insurance companies, and USF&G was no exception. Nevertheless, top management held tenaciously to its large and regular dividends. In fact, by 1990, the stock price had fallen by 67 percent compared to its level in 1989, yet the dividend remained at $3.00 per share per year, the same as in 1989.

Debate raged that the top management of USF&G was destroying the company with its refusal to lower the dividend. Finally, top management was replaced and the dividend was lowered. Huge cost savings programs followed and large layoffs were implemented. Some people even began to question if USF&G would survive.

Chapters 10 and 11 analyzed the firm's capital structure decision—what types and amounts of securities the firm may want to issue to finance its assets. This chapter analyzes the firm's dividend decision—what types and amounts of dividends the firm may want to distribute to its shareholders. The firm's dividend policy will, therefore, refer to decisions regarding the general level and timing of distributing cash to the shareholders.

We analyze the dividend decision in a manner extremely similar to that of the capital structure decision. Accordingly, you will want to review Chapters 10 and 11 before reading this chapter.

AN OVERVIEW OF THE FIRM'S DIVIDEND DECISION

dividend
A distribution from the corporation's assets to the shareholders on a pro rata basis.

cash dividend
A distribution of cash from the corporation's assets to the shareholders.

A **dividend** is a distribution from the corporation's assets to the shareholders on a pro rata basis. Thus, if you owned one percent of the firm's stock, you would receive one percent of the amount of the distribution. The most common type of dividend is the **cash dividend,** which is a distribution of cash to shareholders. Most of this chapter will be focused on cash dividends, which, stated differently, are transfers from the firm's cash balance into the personal cash balances of its shareholders. The payment of cash dividends is similar to the action of a store owner who may, on occasion, transfer money from the store's cash drawer to his or her wallet.

In addition to cash dividends, corporations issue other types of dividends, such as extra dividends, special dividends, liquidating dividends, and stock dividends, on an annual or irregular basis. Window 12.1 lists and describes the terminology of dividends.

The firm's dividend payment procedure is spread out over a number of weeks and follows the following sequence. The board of directors meet and declare a dividend of a certain amount to be paid at a certain date in the future. The date when this decision is made public is known as the **announcement date.** The dividend will be sent to all shareholders who own the stock on a particular day—the **record date.** Dividends will be paid to every shareholder listed on the corporate record on the record date.

announcement date
The date when the firm announces the dividend payment.

record date
The date on which shareholders listed on the corporate record will receive the announced dividend.

ex-dividend date
The fourth business day prior to the date of record. The stock trades without the dividend on the ex-dividend date with the result that new purchasers will not receive legal right to the declared dividend if they purchase the stock on or after this date.

Because it normally takes five business days after stock is sold to record the new owner on the corporate record, certain investors who purchase stock near the record date will risk not receiving the dividend. To avoid this potential dividend payment problem, the legal right to dividends remains with the stock until four business days prior to the date of record. The fourth business day prior to the date of record is known as the **ex-dividend date.** On the ex-dividend date, the stock trades "without" dividend, such that new purchasers—on or after this ex-dividend date—will not receive legal right to the declared dividend.

Because investors purchasing stock on or after the ex-dividend date do not receive the dividend, the stock price falls by the amount of the dividend (approximately) on the ex-dividend date. Thus, there is no immediate monetary advantage to purchasing the stock before the ex-dividend date. Dividend checks are mailed to all shareholders about two weeks after the record date. This is known as the **payment date.**

payment date
The date when dividend checks are mailed to all entitled shareholders.

Example 12.1 _____ Suppose that on March 3 the board of directors of the Joepa Corporation announce a quarterly dividend of $0.50 per share ($2.00 annually) to be paid to anyone on the corporate record

Window 12.1

Dividend Terminology

Regular Dividend: Dividends paid on a regular basis, such that shareholders expect the firm to continue such dividend payments in the future.

Extra Dividend: Made in addition to the firm's regular dividend, an extra dividend is paid without an expectation that the firm will continue making the payment in the future.

Special Dividend: Reserved for unique situations, this type of dividend would not be expected to continue in the future.

Liquidating Dividend: A distribution of assets in the form of a dividend, made by companies that expect to terminate operations.

Stock Dividend: A dividend in the form of additional shares of the firm's stock.

Dividend Payout Ratio: The percent of residual cash flow, or earnings, paid to shareholders in the form of dividends. Companies that choose to reinvest all residual cash flow will have zero payout ratios, while companies that choose to distribute all residual cash flow in the form of dividends will have 100 percent dividend payout ratios. Other companies will have dividend payout ratios between zero and 100 percent.

Dividend Yield: A ratio represented by the firm's annual dividend divided by the firm's stock price.

Dividend Reinvestment Plans: The automatic reinvestment of the shareholder's dividends into additional shares of the firm's stock. Dividend reinvestment plans represent an inexpensive way of purchasing additional shares of stock, as most companies absorb the brokerage fees or transactions costs involved in the purchase. Also, some companies offer the stock through these plans at a discount from the current market price.

as of Friday, March 16. Joepa stock trades currently for $25 per share. The announcement date is March 3, and the date of record is March 16.

The ex-dividend date is four business days prior to the record date, or Monday, March 12. Investors who purchase Joepa stock on or after this ex-dividend date will not receive the $0.50 per share dividend. To compensate for this, the share price will fall from $25 to $24.50 per share when the stock begins trading on March 12.

Buy and sell orders that have been placed on an exchange will be marked down by the amount of the dividend. Ignoring taxes, you would be indifferent between paying $25 for a share of Joepa and receiving a $0.50 dividend, or paying $24.50 per share and receiving no dividend. Dividend checks are mailed to the shareholders on March 31, the payment date. ←

Why Are Dividends Special?

How much would you pay for a cow if no one could consume its milk or meat? How much would you pay for a car if no one could drive it? Similarly, how much would you pay for a share of stock that will never pay a dividend?

Recall from Chapter 5 that the value of a share of stock is equal to the present value of the stock's future cash dividends. Ignoring situations such as liquidations and mergers, cash dividends are the only value that stocks provide directly to investors. Although investors often expect to receive capital gains as part of the return on a common stock investment, the ability of your stock to rise in price and be attractive to other investors is based ultimately upon the expected dividends that the stock will offer to future investors.

Another indication of the importance of dividends is the change in the market price of a stock when a corporation unexpectedly changes its dividend policy. Empirical studies examining changes in stock prices in response to dividend announcements have generally found that stock prices rise when firms announce dividends higher than expected and fall upon announcement of dividends lower than expected. The importance of studying dividends is emphasized by the fact that dividends affect both the firm's capital structure and its assets. Because dividends are distributions of cash, they reduce the firm's assets. The dividend also reduces the retained earnings or equity of a firm, thereby increasing the firm's ratio of debt to equity.

The Dividend Payment Flow

The operating profits from the firm's assets minus the cash flows payable to the firm's debtholders and governments form the total return or net income available to the firm's equityholders. The dividend decision divides this cash flow into that portion sent to the shareholders as a dividend and that portion retained inside the firm and used for other purposes, such as to purchase new assets or to pay off some debt. The amount of the net income that stays within the firm is referred to as retained earnings. Figure 12.1 illustrates this concept.

Thus, the firm's dividend policy is the decision as to which portion, if any, of the firm's earnings should be sent to the shareholders as a dividend and which portion should remain inside the firm as retained earnings. Since the money retained inside the firm generally belongs to the shareholders, and since the decision ultimately rests with the firm's owners, the dividend decision can be viewed as the choice of where the shareholders would prefer to have their money— inside or outside the firm. This is the modernists' view. The money used to pay the dividend always belongs to the shareholder; only its location changes.

In contrast, as we learn in the following section, traditionalists view a dividend as a reward or wage to the firm's owners. Traditionalists believe that dividends are important and that an optimal dividend policy for each firm usually exists. As in the capital structure arguments of Chapters 10 and 11, modernists believe that, in perfect markets, the firm's dividend policy is irrelevant. In a world of market imperfections—especially taxes—modernists carefully construct models that demonstrate either relevance or irrelevance to dividends, depending upon the assumed imperfections.

FIGURE 12.1
A Dividend Flow Diagram

Dividends are paid only after all fixed obligations have been met. Any amount not paid as a dividend is funneled back into the firm to finance future investment.

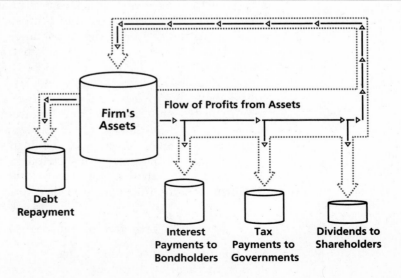

THE TRADITIONALISTS' VIEW
OF CASH DIVIDENDS

The most common traditionalist view is that dividends are good for shareholders, and that the goal of an optimal dividend policy is to pay out as much cash in the form of dividends as possible while still maintaining the optimal growth and capital structure of the firm.

bird in the hand theory
A theory of dividend payments suggesting that a shareholder would prefer to receive a dollar of dividends today over the hope of more than a dollar of dividends in the future. The argument is that most shareholders prefer a sure amount of cash today to an unsure amount of dividends and capital gains in the future.

The traditionalists' idea that dividends are good for shareholders is often referred to as the **bird in the hand theory,** in reference to the popular saying that a bird in the hand is preferred to two birds in the bush. In terms of finance, this suggests that a shareholder would prefer to receive a dollar of dividends today rather than the hope of more than a dollar of dividends in the future. The argument is that most shareholders prefer a sure amount of cash today to an unsure amount of dividends and capital gains in the future. Following the traditionalists' view, the firm's managers should attempt to pay out as much in dividends as they can in order to reward the shareholders without jeopardizing other objectives.

In the traditionalists' model, the shareholders' desire to be rewarded by dividends also forces management to try hard not to cut the dollar amounts of dividends. Managers reason that no one likes a cut in pay, and shareholders certainly don't want a cut in their reward. Managers are also reluctant to raise dividend payouts in response to a rise in the firm's earnings unless or until they are convinced that the new higher earnings level can be preserved, and, therefore, that a new higher dividend payout is likely to be sustained.

The reluctance to both cut and raise dividends motivates firms to create an optimal dividend policy whereby there is a regular dividend with periodic increases but with rare (if ever) decreases. The normal percentage of earnings for a large corporation to distribute in the form of dividends is approximately 50 percent. Thus, a stock whose net income divided by the number of shares of common stock is $4.00 might have an annual dividend of $2.00 per share. This dividend would probably be distributed as $0.50 per share every three months.

dividend payout ratio
The percent of residual cash flow, or earnings, paid to the shareholders in the form of dividends.

Traditionalists have developed numerous models and performed numerous surveys and empirical tests to determine how firms establish their dividend policy and which dividend policy is optimal. The most popular view is that the general level of dividends, called the **dividend payout ratio,** and the speed with which dividends adjust to new earnings levels are determined mostly by the types of assets the firm owns and its plans for the future.

Casual observation does indicate that younger, higher-risk and research-oriented firms tend to pay less of their earnings as dividends. The stocks in these firms are referred to as growth stocks, since their low dividends mean that most or all of their return must come from growth in the share price. In contrast, older, more stable, and low-technology firms tend to pay more of their earnings as current dividends. These stocks are referred to as income stocks, since much of their return comes from immediate dividends or current income.

THE MODERNIST VIEWPOINT— THE M&M MODEL WITHOUT TAXES

At about the same time that Franco Modigliani and Merton Miller were developing their famous propositions regarding the irrelevance of capital structure, they also developed similar propositions for dividends and dividend policy. In perfect markets, M&M demonstrated that dividends and dividend policy are irrelevant. As in Chapter 11, we will refer to this view as the M&M without taxes model.

Understanding dividend irrelevance is much simpler than understanding capital structure irrelevance. A dividend is simply a movement of shareholder wealth from inside the firm to outside the firm. Shareholders have always owned the money and are simply taking it home with them.

homemade dividend
An action by the individual investor that replicates or negates a dividend decision by the firm.

The simplest proof of dividend irrelevancy is the **homemade dividend** argument, which shows that any dividend action by a firm can be replicated or negated by the individual investor.

Homemade Dividends in a Perfect Market

Example 12.2 ——————— Consider an investor with 500 shares of Skyhook, Inc., a stock that trades for $40 per share. The investor has a total equity value of $20,000. Table 12.1 shows the balance sheet of Skyhook, Inc., in terms of market values. Skyhook has no debt, so

TABLE 12.1
Balance Sheet of Skyhook, Inc.

Assets	
Cash and marketable securities	$40,000
Other assets	$360,000
Total assets	$400,000

Liabilities and Owner's Equity	
Debt	$0
Equity (10,000 shares)	$400,000

Value of equity per share = ($400,000/10,000 shares) = $40

in effect the shareholders own all the assets of the firm. Note that the $40 of equity value per share is associated with $4 per share in cash and marketable securities and $36 in other assets.

The purpose of this section is to demonstrate dividend irrelevancy using homemade dividends. We will show that the investor can either negate a dividend that is undesired or can replicate a desired dividend. Thus, if any dividend action of the firm can be easily negated and if investors can create their own dividends, the specific dividend payment policy of the firm must be irrelevant.

First, let's consider the case of an unwanted cash dividend in a perfect market. Suppose that Skyhook pays a cash dividend of $0.50 per share on January 1. What will happen to the firm's balance sheet and share price? Table 12.2 demonstrates that the value of the firm's assets drops by the amount of the cash dividend, or by $5,000 (10,000 shares * $0.50 per share), and the value of its shares will decline to $39.50.

The investor now owns $19,750 worth of stock (500 shares times $39.50 per share) and a $250 dividend check (500 shares times the $0.50 per share dividend) for a total of $20,000. The wealth of every investor in the firm will be unchanged since the new value of the stock ($39.50) plus the cash dividend ($0.50) has the same value as the stock had before the dividend ($40.00).

But what if the investor did not want his or her investment in the firm's stock reduced? The answer is that the investor could negate the dividend by using the dividend check to purchase new shares of stock. For example, the investor could use the $250 check to purchase 6.33 shares of stock (note that in

TABLE 12.2
Balance Sheet of Skyhook After Dividend

Assets	
Cash and marketable securities	$35,000
Other assets	$360,000
Total assets	$395,000

Liabilities and Owner's Equity	
Debt	$0
Equity (10,000 shares)	$395,000

Value of equity per share = ($395,000/10,000 shares) = $39.50

a perfect market there are no brokerage or transaction fees and shares can be divided limitlessly). The investor would now have 506.33 shares of stock worth $39.50 per share for a total of $20,000, and the dividend is negated.[1]

The other type of homemade transaction is the creation of a desired dividend when the firm does not pay a cash dividend. In the previous example, suppose Skyhook decided not to pay a dividend. How could the investor raise the desired $250 in cash? The answer is that the investor could sell 6.25 shares of Skyhook stock and receive a $250 check for the sale. The investor's stock would now be worth $19,750 (493.75 shares times $40.00 per share)—the same amount of cash and stock the investor would have had if Skyhook had paid the $0.50 per share dividend.

Sometimes it is argued that a homemade dividend is not the same as a corporate dividend because in the case of a homemade dividend the investor's stock in the company is declining from 500 shares to 493.75 shares, while if the company pays a dividend the investor retains 500 shares of stock. The fallacy in the argument is that, although the number of shares drops in the case of a homemade dividend, the dollar size of the investment is not affected by whether the dividend is homemade or not. It's the dollar size of the investment, not the number of shares, that matters.

It is also argued that such homemade dividends could eventually cause the investor to have to liquidate all of the stock by selling shares a little at a time. Once again, this argument rests on the number of shares held rather than on the dollar size of the investment. A firm reinvesting its residual cash in non-negative-*NPV* projects will find its share price rising. As the price per share rises, the investor will be liquidating fewer and fewer shares each time to create the desired dividend. The number of shares held will not go to zero and the investor's dollar investment will be growing just as if the company paid a dividend and he or she retained 500 shares of the dividend-paying stock. ↵

---

1. One difference in Skyhook after the dividend payment is that it now has a lower percentage of its assets invested in cash (and therefore has higher risk). It should be noted, however, that Skyhook is expected to produce cash throughout the year from its operations, and its cash balance is expected to return to its level prior to the dividend payment. In other words, the decline in Skyhook's cash account is temporary, and occurs in regular fashion at the time of dividend payments.

In summary, modernists believe that, in a perfect market, dividends do not change shareholder wealth, only its location. Since we are not including transactions costs in this argument, the shareholder can easily adjust the location of wealth with or without the company's help; therefore, dividends and dividend policy are irrelevant.

How Can the Firm's Dividend Policy Be Irrelevant?

You may still find it surprising to read that the firm's dividend policy can be irrelevant. Recall that in Chapter 5 it was argued the value of the firm is the discounted value of its future dividend stream. In fact, using the perpetual growth model, the dividend payment played a major role in determining the value of a share of stock:

$$\text{Price per Share} = \frac{DIV_1}{r_E - g},$$

where DIV_1 is the next year's dividend, r_E is the expected return on the stock, and g represents the constant growth rate in annual dividends.

In the long run, however, dividend policy really answers the question of when dividends are to be paid. If the current dividend is increased, there will be less money to reinvest and the growth rate in dividends will fall. In other words, more dividends today means relatively fewer dividends in the future. In terms of the model above, the rise in dividends will be completely offset by the fall in the growth rate, leaving the share price unchanged. Conversely, a cut in current dividends will generally lead to a rise in the growth rate of future dividends.

Example 12.3 —————— Suppose that the value of Skyhook could be calculated using the perpetual growth model above by inserting the $2 annual dividend, a required return on stock of 10 percent, and a growth rate in annual dividends of 5 percent:

$$\$40 = \frac{\$2}{.10 - .05}.$$

If Skyhook lowered its dividend to $1, the growth rate in annual dividends would be expected to rise to 7.5 percent due to the increase in retained earnings. The lower dividend and the higher growth rate in future dividends produces the same share price of $40:

$$\$40 = \frac{\$1}{.10 - .075}.$$

Conversely, if the dividend were raised to $4, we would expect the growth rate in future dividends to fall to zero. A dividend of $4 and a growth rate of zero percent keeps the stock price at $40 (with the expected return remaining at 10 percent):

$$\$40 = \frac{\$4}{.10 - .00}.$$

For Skyhook, the dividend policy did not change the total present value of the future dividends. Only the timing of these dividends was changed. ↵

What About Superior Investment Opportunities?

Let's take a look at one of the more popular rebuttals to the modernist argument of dividend irrelevancy. Sometimes it is argued that one reason dividend policy matters is that high dividends can create a situation in which the firm is unable to invest in all available positive-*NPV* projects. With high dividend payments, too much of the firm's income is being paid to the shareholders rather than retained and reinvested. In a similar way, it is sometimes argued that the payment of low dividends can cause the firm to invest in negative-*NPV* projects because of a lack of good ways to use the firm's cash.

Dividend policy should, however, be viewed in a perfect market as separate from the optimal investment policy. As detailed in Chapter 6, the optimal investment policy is to invest in all positive-*NPV* projects and turn down all negative-*NPV* projects. This can be accomplished regardless of dividend policy in a perfect market.

For example, if the firm pays too large a dividend such that retained earnings cannot finance all its great projects, then the firm can issue new securities to raise the needed funds. In well-functioning markets, the firm knows that it will raise the funds by issuing securities at a competitive price. The securities of and by themselves will not increase or decrease the value of the firm, because the *NPV* of issuing securities in a perfect market is zero. Since the equityholders are the residual claimants of the firm, all wealth created from the positive *NPV*s of the great projects will flow to the equityholders.

On the other hand, if the firm pays too small a dividend such that there are still retained earnings left after the last positive-*NPV* project has been undertaken, the firm can always invest the remaining cash in competitively priced securities whose *NPV* is zero, leaving shareholder wealth unchanged.

Summary of the Modernist Viewpoint on Dividend Policy

As we have seen, the homemade dividend argument demonstrates that a corporation's dividend policy is irrelevant to an investor in a perfect market. We have also shown that a corporation's dividend policy should have no effect on the firm's investment decision. Regardless of the firm's dividend policy, it should invest in all positive-*NPV* projects, reject all negative-*NPV* projects, and use zero-*NPV* projects such as buying, selling, and issuing financial securities to maintain the desired cash.

You should not be surprised to learn that some of the arguments set forth in a perfect market might not hold in an imperfect market. The purpose of the remaining sections of this chapter is to discuss important imperfections in detail. We begin with taxes, since they are the most important, and then detail other effects such as bankruptcy costs, agency costs, and other imperfections.

MARKET IMPERFECTIONS AND DIVIDEND POLICY

We now consider dividend policy in a more realistic world of market imperfections. This is especially important given that dividend policy, like capital structure policy, is simply paperwork. By paperwork we mean that dividends do not create or destroy wealth—they can, at best, merely transfer wealth since there are "no free lunches." Therefore, any argument claiming that shareholder wealth is enhanced must also show whose wealth is being lost.

The modernists' tax arguments regarding dividends parallel very closely the arguments regarding capital structure. The analysis has the same two models: (1) the M&M with taxes model and (2) the Miller tax model.

The M&M Model with Taxes

We begin with the M&M with taxes model. As in the case of capital structure discussed in Chapter 11, the M&M with taxes model was set forth in the pioneering work of Modigliani and Miller in the late 1950s and early 1960s.

Unlike the M&M with taxes model for capital structure, there are no direct tax implications to dividend policy related to corporate income tax laws. Corporations must pay income taxes on their entire net income regardless of whether the income is paid out to the shareholders as dividends or reinvested in the firm's assets as retained earnings. Therefore, any or all tax implications from the firm's dividend policy derive from the payment of personal income taxes.

The dividend policy decision is viewed as the decision as to which proportion of the shareholder's return in the near future will be in the form of dividend income and which proportion will be in the form of retained earnings leading to capital gains. The standard view used in the M&M with taxes model of taxing equity at the individual or personal income tax level is that investors pay a higher tax on dividend income than they do on capital gains. This view was widely held prior to the income tax revisions of 1986 and is still argued by some as a result of the ability to time capital gains (as detailed in Chapter 11). For instance, although personal tax rates on dividends and capital gains are currently identical, investors can put off realizing a capital gain and therefore delay paying a tax by not selling appreciated stock, but usually they cannot put off the payment of taxes on dividends received in the current year.

At first glance, the ability to delay and time the realization of capital gains may appear to be trivial. However, wealthy investors in high tax brackets can utilize this feature to create important tax advantages. Thus, the M&M with taxes model for dividends stresses the concept that dividends are taxed at a higher rate in terms of present values than are capital gains and, therefore, investors will prefer to receive no dividends.

⚡ In an M&M with taxes model, a zero percent dividend payout policy will maximize shareholder wealth.

Example 12.4 ——————— Recall the Skyhook, Inc., example in which the investor was indifferent between a $250 corporate cash dividend and a homemade dividend created by selling off $250 worth of stock. In the M&M with taxes model, the homemade dividend offers a higher after-tax cash flow to the investor, which is illustrated in Table 12.3.

In present value terms, and realizing that taxes on capital gains in the future could be avoided through the techniques of Chapter 11, the tax liability of the investor is minimized by a zero percent dividend payout. Therefore, this represents the firm's optimal dividend policy.

Thus, our first market imperfection—that of personal income taxes that favor capital gains—forces shareholder wealth to be maximized by a dividend policy of zero dividends. Because the individual's tax bill is smallest when the firm pays no dividends, the increased wealth of the shareholders comes from a wealth transfer from the government to the individual. ↵

TABLE 12.3
The Payment of Personal Taxes on Dividends

Situation 1: Investor receives a $250 cash dividend from Skyhook, Inc.
Investor's tax bracket = 30 percent.

Dividend payment	$250.00
Tax on dividend	75.00
After-tax cash flow	$175.00

Situation 2: Investor creates a "Homemade Dividend" of $250 by selling stock.
Stock's original purchase price = $24 per share.
Investor's tax bracket = 30 percent.

Proceeds from the sale of stock	$250.00
Original purchase price of stock	$150.00
Capital gain	$100.00
Tax on capital gain (30 percent)	30.00
Proceeds from sale minus tax	$220.00

Result: Homemade dividend pays $45 less in tax and is the preferred choice.

THE MILLER TAX MODEL

Despite the widespread teachings of the M&M propositions, firms continue to pay dividends. Part of the explanation is that the United States Internal Revenue Service (IRS) exerts pressure on firms not to avoid dividend payouts for tax-avoidance purposes. But clearly funds distributed as a result of the tendency of corporations to pay dividends vastly exceed the amounts that would be explained by pressure from the IRS.

When Merton Miller established what is known as the Miller tax model in 1977, he created a model that has important implications for dividends as well. These implications were then fully developed by Miller and Scholes in 1978.

In the Miller tax model, it is argued that the tax advantages of capital gains—the investor's ability to best time these gains or to pass the capital gains on through an estate—can be used by investors to create such a powerful tax savings that, for all practical purposes, the personal income tax on capital gains is zero. Miller argues that there were so many tax breaks available to taxpayers that even the tax on dividends can be sheltered easily by the investor. In other words, the taxes on dividends can be avoided using the extraordinary tax breaks from capital gains and other tax-advantaged investments. In this model, the dividend payout decision is irrelevant since investors can avoid any income taxes on their equity returns.

> ⏳ In the Miller tax model, the dividend payout decision is irrelevant since investors can avoid any income taxes on their equity returns.

Example 12.5 ———— Returning to Skyhook and under the Miller tax model, the investor could make portfolio adjustments and ultimately pay no additional income taxes, even if the firm paid a dividend of $250. In Chapter 11, Window 11.1 discussed in detail a portfolio strategy that could accomplish the elimination of taxes on all forms of equity income. Since the investor can avoid any and all taxes on the equity portfolio, it will make no difference to the investor whether or not the firm pays a dividend. Again, dividend policy is irrelevant. ↩

A Summary of the Two Tax Models for Dividends

Are the tax advantages to capital gains under current tax laws such that investors would prefer low-dividend-payout stocks? In other words, does the M&M with taxes model hold? Or are the tax loopholes so great as to make taxes irrelevant at the personal level? Modernists are not sure of the answers to these questions, but they are sure that these logical arguments are the best way of analyzing the problem.

It is obvious that, under current tax laws, there are not millions of investors in high tax brackets frantically fighting with the managers of corporations to stop paying dividends. Rather we find that investors who are in search of tax breaks can find them without having to search out firms with extraordinarily low dividend payout policies. Thus, there doesn't appear to be a large tax penalty to dividends.

Remember, a firm's dividend policy is paperwork rather the creation or destruction of real assets. Therefore, dividend policy can only transfer wealth, not create it. In this section we have discussed whether tax laws allow shareholders to use dividend policy to transfer wealth from the government. Since there is no strong evidence to the contrary, it is safe to conclude that, under current tax laws, whether or not a particular firm pays high or low dividends is not an extremely important issue.

DIVIDENDS AND BANKRUPTCY

All of the discussions in this chapter so far have ignored bankruptcy. In other words, the debt of the corporation has been assumed to be risk-free. This section will examine the effects of bankruptcy and financial distress on dividend policy.

Issues of dividends and bankruptcy are virtually identical to the issues regarding debt and bankruptcy. The payment of dividends reduces equity in the firm as well as the cash balance of the firm. Thus, when a firm pays a dividend, it loses cash, one of its safest assets, and increases its financial leverage. Both of these effects would tend to increase the probability of bankruptcy. Since traditionalists view bankruptcy as bad, their position is that a firm should avoid dividend payments that would significantly increase that probability.

Modernists believe that dividends do not create or destroy wealth—they can only transfer it. If some large dividends increase the probability of bankruptcy substantially, it would be worthwhile to examine whether this could benefit shareholders by transferring wealth from other people such as creditors or unions. Whether a dividend can increase shareholder wealth depends upon the specifics of the situation, as was found in the discussion in Chapter 11 regarding debt.

Bankruptcy and Option Theory

In the absence of other effects, option theory provides a tremendous insight into the dividend controversy. You will recall that one of the major points of Chapter 9 was that a call option fell by more than $0.00 but by less than $1.00 when the underlying asset dropped in value by $1.00. In terms of corporate finance, the firm's equity is the call option and the firm's assets are the underlying asset. This means that the equity of a levered firm, which is a call option on the firm's assets, will drop by less than $1 when the firm's assets are reduced by $1—which is exactly what a dividend does. Thus, a shareholder of a levered firm can receive a $1 dividend and expect that the market value of the equity will drop by less than $1—making the shareholder wealthier!

Where does the shareholder's wealth increase come from? The answer is that it comes from the people who don't hold the option— the debtholders.

Example 12.6 _____ Let's examine in detail how this can happen. Suppose that Skyhook, Inc., has a very similar competitor named Cloudhook, Inc. The only difference between the two firms is that while Skyhook has no debt, Cloudhook is loaded with debt, as shown in Table 12.4.

Now let's suppose both firms experience financial distress, causing them to liquidate most of their assets by selling their buildings, land, and so forth and to move to a rented facility. As part of the liquidation, both firms send $300,000 to their shareholders in the form of a cash dividend. Table 12.5 shows the new balance sheets that would result after the dividend.

TABLE 12.4
Balance Sheets of Skyhook and Cloudhook

Assets	Skyhook, Inc.	Cloudhook, Inc.
Cash and marketable securities	$40,000	$40,000
Other assets	$360,000	$360,000
Total assets	$400,000	$400,000
Liabilities and Owners' Equity		
Debt	$-0-	$300,000
Equity	$400,000	$100,000

The value of the equity of Skyhook dropped by the full $300,000. In other words, the dividend caused no wealth transfer between people—it simply moved the shareholders' money from inside the firm to outside the firm, in the shareholders' personal accounts.

However, notice that the equity of Cloudhook dropped by only $99,000 (from $100,000 to $1,000). Cloudhook's shareholders are far better off, since they received a $300,000 dividend that was only partially offset by a $99,000 drop in equity. How did the stockholders become better off? As explained above, the stockholder's $201,000 wealth increase came from the debtholders, who saw the value of their bonds drop by $201,000. ↵

This example demonstrates that, in theory, stockholders of a levered firm can use dividends to transfer wealth from bondholders to themselves. The driving force is bankruptcy. The removal of so much cash from the firm hurts the value of the bonds tremendously, since it is virtually certain that the firm will declare bankruptcy and the

TABLE 12.5
Balance Sheets of Skyhook and Cloudhook After Dividend

Assets	Skyhook, Inc.	Cloudhook, Inc.
Total assets	$100,000	$100,000
Liabilities and Owners' Equity		
Debt	$-0-	$ 99,000
Equity	$100,000	$ 1,000

bondholders will receive less than they are owed. But, again, wealth hasn't been destroyed; it was simply transferred—in this case from the bondholders to the stockholders.

In the real world, few such startling opportunities exist, since bondholders are careful to protect themselves before they lend money and governments usually impose laws to protect bondholders from such outrageous cases.

However, other less obvious cases exist, allowing shareholders to benefit from profits by using dividends to distribute them outside the levered firm while keeping the corporation lean on cash. For example, in the case of a potential lawsuit against the firm, legal claimants may settle quickly or not even file a lawsuit if they know that the corporation couldn't pay a large cash award. Also, labor unions may negotiate more easily due to the fact that a tough stance could force the firm into bankruptcy. And governments are known for using taxpayers' money to assist a struggling firm. Of course, cases such as these raise ethical issues that shareholders need to explore.

As in the case of the capital structure decision, the ultimate question of whether bankruptcy and dividends can be used to maximize shareholder wealth must be decided on a case-by-case basis. Most creditors are not fools and therefore are not easily separated from their money. However, the idea of distributing equity by way of dividends outside the firm in the face of huge debt, large lawsuits, unfavorable union contracts, and so forth seems to be plausible.

DIVIDENDS AND AGENCY COSTS

As discussed in Chapter 11, an agency relationship and agency costs arise when a principal, or shareholder, hires an agent, or manager, to perform a service such as run the firm. Such arrangements may create conflicts in objectives and therefore result in costs. Agency costs are related to both the cost of trying to align objectives and the costs associated with unaligned objectives.

Previously it was stated that a dividend represents the decision that the shareholder's wealth is to be held outside rather than inside the firm. In terms of agency theory this decision takes on more importance. The big difference is that, if the earnings are retained inside the firm, an agent has direct and immediate control over these earnings. If the earnings are paid as dividends, the control of these earnings is in the hands of the principals.

Agency models explain whether agents will correctly invest retained earnings, from a shareholder perspective, by accepting only positive *NPV* projects or will squander some of the money on negative *NPV* projects. Managers might be tempted to squander money on negative *NPV* projects in order to derive personal benefit from them.

Examples that come to mind would be lavish executive dining rooms, projects to employ friends and relatives, and pet projects such as wineries, branch offices in Hawaii, and so forth.

Models that attempt to explain the effects of these agency costs differ from finding that retained earnings are squandered to finding that the same amount of money will be squandered whether the firm retains its earnings or has to raise the money by issuing securities. In other words, it isn't clear that agency costs can directly explain firm dividend policy. However, the importance of understanding and effectively setting up agency relationships in modern business is clear. It is possible that agency relationships and the compensation schemes that are set up are the single most important issue in corporate finance.

DIVIDENDS AND INFORMATION SIGNALING

As we have previously stated, many scholars believe that dividend payments contain a signal about the financial strength of the firm. Information-signaling models and concepts begin with the idea that managers have inside and valuable information regarding the firm that the public does not know. Such information would include unpublished sales and costs figures, knowledge regarding how projects are proceeding, and what types of new projects are being considered.

Managers may be reluctant to announce such news explicitly for fear of disgruntled investors or even lawsuits if things don't turn out well—or perhaps (more likely) they wish to keep the specifics of the information from their competitors. Accordingly, the public's awareness of such information must be achieved by observing the actions of the managers.

Earlier in the chapter it was argued that, because managers dislike lowering dividends, they are very reluctant to raise dividends until they are rather sure that new dividend and earnings levels can be sustained. Accordingly, dividends are an important signal regarding management's view of the prospects for the firm.

Dividend increases generally signal good news, and dividend cuts or even failure to raise dividends at times may be viewed as bad news. The firm's stock price generally responds by rising on announcements of dividend increases and falling on announcements of dividend cuts. This doesn't mean that the dividend itself creates shareholder wealth, but rather that the dividend signals to the shareholders that the managers believe the firm is worth more than the market perceives.

On the other hand, dividend increases can signal bad news. For instance, a dividend increase could signal that the firm doesn't have good projects in the works and therefore is paying out cash in the form of a dividend. Similarly, dividend cuts can signal the good news that the firm has great projects and needs cash to finance them. When a signal can be interpreted in more than one way it is called an ambiguous signal. Moreover, most signals are ambiguous and need to be examined empirically.

The bottom line on information signaling is that a dividend decision can affect the firm's stock price even though the dividend itself doesn't create, destroy, or transfer wealth. For example, when a firm announces that it has discovered oil, we would expect its stock price to rise. However, the announcement itself did not create value; the value was always there in the form of undiscovered oil. The announcement simply revealed the information.

Information signaling certainly explains why security prices often move substantially in response to actions that modernists believe are irrelevant. Some even argue that the reason managers make certain dividend decisions is in order to signal certain information to the market. However, most people believe that information signaling does not provide a powerful reason to prefer one particular dividend policy over any other.

STOCK DIVIDENDS AND STOCK SPLITS

In a stock dividend—as opposed to a cash dividend—the firm issues additional shares to each shareholder based upon the number of shares currently held. For example, in a 10 percent stock dividend, each investor would receive additional shares to increase share holdings by 10 percent: An investor with 500 shares would receive 50 new shares. Note, however, that no cash has moved outside the firm, and since all shareholders own now 10 percent more total shares, each investor still holds the same percentage of the firm's equity. Accordingly, we would expect the share price to fall in response to the stock dividend—in this case by approximately 10 percent.

Stock dividends do not change anyone's wealth—in the same way that cutting a pie into twice as many pieces does not create more pie. Regardless of how many times the pie is sliced, the total size remains constant. This can also be shown through the balance-sheet relationship:

$$Assets = Debt + Equity.$$

Because the stock dividend has no effect on either assets or debt, there can be no effect on equity. In the case of a stock dividend, the value of each share drops, while the number of shares rises, leaving total value unchanged. Thus, stock dividends are clearly irrelevant in a perfect market.

Window 12.2

The Mechanics of Stock Dividends and Stock Splits

Stock Dividend: Consider the Malta Corporation, currently with 1,000 shares of stock outstanding, each trading at a market price of $10. To simplify matters, Malta is unlevered, such that the total value of the firm is $10,000. Malta announces that each shareholder will receive a 10 percent stock dividend. You currently own 10 shares of Malta, and the market value of your holdings is $100.

Stock Split: Consider the Yalta Corporation, currently with 1,000 shares of stock outstanding, each trading at a market price of $10. To simplify matters, Yalta is unlevered, such that the total value of the firm is $10,000. Yalta announces a 2-for-1 stock split, such that for each share originally owned, Yalta will issue one additional share. You currently own 10 shares of Yalta, and the market value of your holdings is $100.

Reverse Stock Split: Consider the Falta Corporation, currently with 1,000 shares of stock outstanding, each trading at a market price of $10. To simplify matters, Falta is unlevered, such that the total value of the firm is $10,000. Falta announces a 1-for-2 reverse stock split, such that for each two shares originally owned, Falta will take one share away. You currently own 10 shares of Falta, and the market value of your holdings is $100.

The key in each of these situations is that total market value does not change, just the ratio of shares. The stock price after the stock dividend, stock split, and reverse stock split can be found as the product of the old price and the ratio of the number of shares:

(continued on next page)

stock split
A large stock dividend. For example, in a 2-for-1 stock split, the number of each shareholder's shares is doubled, and the price per share falls to half its original level. No money changes hands nor does the percentage ownership of each shareholder change.

A **stock split** is a large stock dividend. For example, in a 2-for-1 stock split, the number of each shareholder's shares is doubled, and the price per share falls to half its original level. There is also such a thing as a *reverse stock split*, in which the number of each shareholder's shares is reduced, and the price per share rises from its previous level. Once again, no money changes hands nor does the percentage ownership of each shareholder change. Window 12.2 details the mathematics of stock dividends, stock splits, and reverse stock splits.

Window 12.2 *(continued)*

$$\text{New Stock Price} = \text{Old Stock Price} * \frac{\text{Old Number of Shares}}{\text{New Number of Shares}}.$$

For Malta (stock dividend), the new stock price is

$$\$10 * \frac{1}{1.1} = \$9.09,$$

and the total market value of your investment is 11 shares * $9.09 = $100, the same as before.

For Yalta (stock split), the new stock price is:

$$\$10 * \frac{1}{2} = \$5.00,$$

and the total market value of your investment is 20 shares * $5 = $100, the same as before.

For Falta (reverse stock split), the new stock price is:

$$\$10 * \frac{2}{1} = \$20.00,$$

and the total market value of your investment is 5 shares * $20 = $100, the same as before.

Traditionalists usually view stock dividends as means by which managers of firms with limited cash reward their shareholders without having to pay large cash dividends. Additionally, stock splits and stock dividends may be viewed as an attempt by managers to lower the market price of the stock toward a preferred dollar and cent level—perhaps because it requires lower brokerage fees to trade. Another aspect of stock dividends is that if the cash dividend is kept constant on a per share basis, a stock dividend is tantamount to a cash dividend increase, since each investor will receive the cash dividend on more shares.

To repeat, stock dividends and stock splits do not significantly create, destroy, or transfer wealth. They are simply types of paperwork that can be used to move prices per share into more desirable levels in order to provide convenience or reduced transactions costs. Important creation of wealth comes from intelligent acquisition and management of real assets.

A FINAL WRAP-UP

Can the firm's dividend policy affect the value of the firm? The traditional view is yes, that dividends are good for shareholders and that the goal of an optimal dividend policy is to pay out as much cash in the form of dividends as possible, while still maintaining the optimal growth and capital structure of the firm.

But the modernist view is that the firm's dividend policy is paperwork, rather than the creation or destruction of real assets. Therefore, dividend policy cannot create wealth. But questions still remain. Do the tax laws allow shareholders to use dividend policy to transfer wealth from the government? Can dividends be a vehicle through which bankruptcy can be used to maximize shareholder wealth? Can dividends be a vehicle through which agency costs can be minimized, or through which information can be signaled?

As in the case of capital structure in Chapter 11, there are no clear answers to these questions. Rather, this chapter has offered a structured framework within which logical analysis can take place. Equipped with this method of thinking and analyzing, the financial manager will be prepared to make decisions for specific cases.

SUMMARY

- Dividend policy is the decision as to which portion of earnings to pay outside the firm to stockholders and which portion to retain inside the firm. Either way, the shareholder is entitled to the wealth—as a current dividend or as a higher future dividend.

- In the absence of market imperfections, the dividend decision is irrelevant. This is best shown through the argument of homemade dividends. There are, however, several market imperfections, such as taxes, bankruptcy, and agency costs, that seem to play an important role in understanding dividends.

- In the M&M with taxes model, the tax disadvantages of dividends in terms of personal income tax drive the optimal dividend policy to a zero percent payout. In the Miller tax model, the tax advantages of capital gains and other breaks are so powerful that personal-equity income taxes are driven to zero and it becomes irrelevant as to whether or not the firm pays dividends.

❑ Dividends remove equity and cash from the firm and therefore may increase the probability of bankruptcy. Although this can have both advantages and costs to shareholders, it would generally appear to be beneficial in cases of huge debt burdens, large lawsuits, and impending business collapse.

❑ Dividends appear to signal information to the market. This is a critical explanation of why security prices tend to change dramatically when a major dividend announcement is made, but does not necessarily say anything about how dividend payments affect firm value.

REFERENCES

Miller, M. H., and F. Modigliani. "Dividend Policy, Growth, and the Valuation of Shares." *Journal of Business* 34 (October 1961), 1–40.

Miller, M. H. "Debt and Taxes." *Journal of Finance* 32 (May 1977), 261–276.

Miller, M. H., and M. S. Scholes. "Dividends and Taxes." *Journal of Financial Economics* 6 (December 1978), 333–364.

DEMONSTRATION PROBLEMS

Problem 1 Miles Corporation has the following balance sheet, expressed in market values:

Assets		Liabilities and Owners' Equity	
Cash	$500,000	Debt	$1,000,000
Fixed assets	$2,500,000	Common stock	$2,000,000
Total assets	$3,000,000	Total debt and stock	$3,000,000

Assuming that there are currently 100,000 shares of common stock, find the current stock price as well as the stock prices that would immediately result from: (a) a $1 cash dividend, (b) a 10% stock dividend, (c) a 2-for-1 stock split, and (d) a 1-for-4 reverse stock split. (Solve each occurrence separately rather than assuming that all four events happened.)

Solution to Problem 1

Step 1: Find the current stock price. The current common stock price may be found by dividing the total value of the shareholders' equity by the number of shares:

Price per Share = Total Equity Value / Number of Shares
Price per Share = $2,000,000 / 100,000
Price per Share = $20.

Step 2: Find the stock price after a $1 cash dividend. The price per share of a common stock drops (approximately) by the amount of a cash dividend on the ex-dividend date as discussed in the text.

New Share Price = Old Share Price − Cash Dividend
New Share Price = $20 − $1
New Share Price = $19.

This can be verified by putting together a new balance sheet:

Assets		Liabilities and Owners' Equity	
Cash	$400,000	Debt	$1,000,000
Fixed assets	$2,500,000	Common stock	$1,900,000
Total assets	$2,900,000	Total debt and stock	$2,900,000

The cash balance has declined by $100,000 to reflect the payment by the corporation of a $1 per share cash dividend on 100,000 shares. The value of the common stock drops by the same amount to keep the balance sheet balanced. The result is that the new total equity value ($1,900,000) divided by the same number of shares (100,000) is $19.

Step 3: The new price of the stock after each of the actions can be found using the procedures and formula shown in Window 12.2:

New Stock Price = Old Stock Price ∗ (Old # of Shares / New # of Shares).

Step 4: For the 10% stock dividend, there will now be 110,000 shares since the number of shares has increased by 10%. Plugging into the equation:

New Stock Price = $20 ∗ (100,000 / 110,000) = $18.18.

Step 5: For the 2-for-1 stock split, there will now be 200,000 shares since the number of shares has doubled. Plugging into the equation:

New Stock Price = $20 ∗ (100,000 / 200,000) = $10.00.

Step 6: For the 1-for-4 reverse stock split, there will now be 25,000 shares since the number of shares has been quartered. Plugging into the equation:

New Stock Price = $20 ∗ (100,000 / 25,000) = $80.00.

Final Solution

Current Stock Price	$20.00
(a) After cash dividend	$19.00
(b) After stock dividend	$18.18
(c) After stock split	$10.00
(d) After reverse stock split	$80.00 ↵

Problem 2 Return to Miles Corporation, which has the following balance sheet expressed in market values:

Assets		Liabilities and Owners' Equity	
Cash	$500,000	Debt	$1,000,000
Fixed assets	$2,500,000	Common stock	$2,000,000
Total assets	$3,000,000	Total debt and stock	$3,000,000

Continue to assume that there are currently 100,000 shares of common stock. However, let's assume that Miles Corporation has decided not to pay any cash dividends to their shareholders—as a method of demonstrating the firm's financial troubles to their labor union as negotiations draw near. Joan owns 1,000 shares of Miles Corporation stock and counts on the $1 per share dividend to meet ordinary living expenses. Joan paid $20 per share for the stock and is in a 30% income tax bracket. Given this information:

a. Demonstrate homemade dividends with no taxes,
b. Compare (1) the after-tax value of Joan's investment using homemade dividends with (2) the after-tax value assuming that a dividend is paid in an M&M tax world (with no taxes on capital gains), and
c. Compare (1) the after-tax value of Joan's investment using homemade dividends with (2) the after-tax value assuming that a dividend is paid in a Miller tax world (with no tax on any equity income).

Solution to Problem 2

Step 1: First, demonstrate homemade dividends with no taxes. Joan now owns 1,000 shares at $20 per share for a total value of $20,000, and she wants a $1 per share dividend so she can have $1,000 cash even though she knows that the share price will drop by the $1 if the firm pays a $1 dividend. Thus, Joan wants to move from the left side to the right side of the following illustration:

Where Joan is:		Where Joan wants to be:	
Cash	$0	Cash	$1,000
Stock	$20,000	Stock	$19,000

Examining the above illustration, it is clear that Joan can obtain the $1,000 cash that she desires by selling 50 shares of stock at $20 each:

Proceeds from sale of 50 shares at $20 each $1,000
Remaining value of 950 shares at $20 each $19,000

This is the same result as would be obtained if the firm has issued a $1 dividend:

Cash from $1 per share dividend on 1,000 shares $1,000
Remaining value of 1,000 shares at $19 each $19,000

Step 2: Next, we compare the homemade dividend strategy on an after-tax basis with an actual corporate cash dividend. Assuming an M&M tax world, investors are fully taxed on dividend income but income from capital gains is untaxed.

First, find the after-tax proceeds from selling 50 shares:

Proceeds from sale of 50 shares at $20 each $1,000
Remaining value of 950 shares at $20 each $19,000
Total after-tax value $20,000

Now, find the after-tax value of receiving a cash dividend from the corporation:

Cash from $1 per share dividend on 1,000 shares $1,000
Tax liability on $1,000 dividend at 30% .... $−300
Remaining value of 1,000 shares at $19 each $19,000
Total after-tax value $19,700

Thus, in an M&M tax world, the investor is better off not receiving a cash dividend so that the $300 tax liability can be avoided.

Step 3: Finally, we compare the homemade dividend strategy on an after-tax basis with an actual corporate cash dividend in a Miller tax world with no tax on equity income. First, find the after-tax proceeds from selling 50 shares:

Proceeds from sale of 50 shares at $20 each $1,000
Remaining value of 950 shares at $20 each $19,000
Total after-tax value $20,000

Now, find the after-tax value of receiving a cash dividend from the corporation:

Cash from $1 per share dividend on 1,000 shares $1,000
Tax liability on $1,000 dividend .... $ 0
Remaining value of 1,000 shares at $19 each $19,000
Total after-tax value $20,000

Thus, in a Miller tax world, the investor is equally well off receiving a cash dividend as liquidating shares since there are no personal taxes on either dividends or capital gains.

Final Solution: Homemade dividends are equally attractive as corporate cash dividends without taxes or in a Miller tax world. Only in an M&M tax world, where it is assumed that capital gains offer a tax advantage and that dividends are taxed, is there a disadvantage to cash dividends and therefore an incentive to use homemade dividends. ↵

REVIEW QUESTIONS

1. Describe the dividend decision as a transfer of cash from inside to outside the firm.
2. Contrast the following terms: (a) regular cash dividend, (b) extra dividend, (c) special dividend, (d) stock dividend.
3. What is the ex-dividend date, and what will happen to the market price of the stock on the ex-dividend date? Why?
4. What are retained earnings, and how do they relate to the firm's dividend policy? (Hint: Think of shareholders as residual claimants.)
5. Describe how homemade dividends can undo the firm's dividend policy.
6. Why do M&M maintain that, in the presence of taxes, the dividend payout ratio should be zero percent?
7. Why in the Miller model is it stated that, in the presence of taxes, the dividend payout ratio is irrelevant?
8. How are agency costs related to the payment of dividends?
9. Relate signaling theory and manager's information to dividend policy.
10. Do stock dividends or stock splits, in and of themselves, make shareholders better off? Worse off? Explain.

PROBLEMS

1. Fill in each blank space with a type of dividend payment. Choose from the following: stock, extra, regular, liquidating, special.

   Dividends that shareholders expect to receive on a periodic basis are called _____ dividends. However, other types of dividends exist. For example _____ dividends are paid in addition to regular dividends, and _____ dividends are reserved for special situations. Further, dividends in the form of shares of stock instead of cash are called _____ dividends. Finally, companies that expect to terminate operations may pay a _____ dividend.

2. Fill in each blank with a dividend payment date. Choose from the following: announcement, record, ex-dividend, payment.

   The dividend payment procedure is often spread out over a number of weeks and follows a certain sequence. The date the board of directors meet and make public the firm's intent to pay a dividend is the _____ date. The dividend will be sent to all shareholders who own stock on the _____ date. Because it normally takes five business days after stock is sold to record the name and address of the new owner on the company official list, the fourth business day prior to the _____ date is known as the _____ date. Dividend payments are mailed to the shareholders about two weeks after the _____ date, known as the _____ date.

3. The dividend payout ratio is the percent of the firm's residual cash flow paid to the shareholders in the form of a dividend. The annual dividend is usually divided into quarterly chunks. Simon's Suitcases, Inc. has a payout ratio of 60 percent. Calculate Simon's annual and quarterly dividend if its residual cash flow is $4.00 per share.

4. Alfred is a wise investor who picks stocks on the basis of the firm's dividend payout ratio. He invests in a stock only if the dividend payout ratio is at least 40 percent. Help Alfred determine if he should consider the following four stocks for his portfolio:

   1: Quarterly dividend= $0.30 per share, annual residual cash flow = $ 2.00 share.
   2: Quarterly dividend= $2.50 per share, annual residual cash flow = $22.50 share.
   3: Quarterly dividend= $0.75 per share, annual residual cash flow = $ 4.00 share.
   4: Quarterly dividend= $1.25 per share, annual residual cash flow = $12.50 share.

5. Jim Simpson, the founder of Simpson's Saxophones, knows much about saxophones but little about finance. The other day he was alarmed when his company's stock price, which had been $50 per share, fell to $48.50 per share. The reason he was alarmed was because he knew things were going well for the firm, and that no bad news had been released. Explain to Jim how dividends might explain the movement in share price.

6. McMann's Marble Shoppes has stock currently trading at $8.00 per share. The firm has announced a $0.50 quarterly dividend.
   a. What is McMann's expected price per share on the ex-dividend date?
   b. Ruth purchases 500 shares of McMann stock on the day prior to the ex-dividend date. Jerry purchases 500 shares of McMann stock on the ex-dividend date. Given your answer in part (a), show how these investments are equivalent.

7. Below is the abbreviated balance sheet for DiConcini Boats and Yachts.

Cash	$500,000	Debt	$0
Other Assets	$9,500,000	Equity	$10,000,000

   Shares outstanding = 100,000

   DiConcini has just paid a cash dividend of $1.00 per share. Show what will likely happen to the firm's balance sheet and share price after the dividend payment.

Cash		Debt	
Other Assets		Equity	

8. Recall DiConcini Boats and Yachts. Hatch is an unhappy DiConcini shareholder, as he has no use for the $1 dividend. Hatch owns 1,000 shares. Show how Hatch can (approximately) negate the dividend.

9. Mary-Ellen Kennedy is also a DiConcini shareholder who owns 1,000 shares. Unlike Mr. Hatch, Ms. Kennedy loves dividends. In fact, Mary-Ellen would prefer that the firm double its dividend to $2 per share. Show how she can use homemade dividends to (approximately) achieve her desired dividend.

10. Below is the abbreviated balance sheet for Bryant Mining.

Cash	$ 6,000	Debt	$0
Other assets	$14,000	Equity	$20,000

   Shares outstanding = 2,000

   Bryant has just paid a cash dividend of $1.00 per share. Show what will likely happen to the firm's balance sheet and share price after the dividend payment.

Cash		Debt	
Other assets		Equity	

11. Refer to Bryant Mining in problem 10. Becker Shembo owns 100 shares of Bryant, but he decides that he does not want his invest-

ment in the firm reduced. Show how Becker Shembo can negate the dividend. Repeat the analysis for a $2 dividend payment.

12. The Duke Football Company has equity valued at $60,000, 10,000 shares outstanding, and a current price per share of $6.00. Duke just paid a $1.00 dividend per share. You own 500 shares of Duke. Show how you can negate the dividend.

13. Sacco Genetech has a policy of retaining after-tax income for future growth opportunities. Sacco has equity valued at $500,000 and has 5,000 shares of stock outstanding. As a shareholder with 100 shares, you desire a dividend to meet cash needs. If your cash needs are $500, show how you can use a homemade dividend to realize the $500.

14. Duffie Dog Collars has 600,000 shares outstanding and a market equity value of $2,400,000. The firm has just paid a dividend of $1.00 per share. However, as a shareholder with 1,000 shares, you desire a $3.00 dividend. Use homemade dividends to (approximately) create the desired dividend.

15. Sandusky Real Estate estimates dividends next year at $1.50. The firm's required rate of return on equity is 12 percent. If the firm's rate of growth in annual dividends is 6 percent, calculate the price per share of Sandusky using the perpetual growth model.

16. The Board of Directors of Sandusky Real Estate (see problem 15) announces that next year's dividend, expected to be $1.50, will be lowered to $1.00 in order to retain additional funds for investment purposes. Given a required rate of return on equity at 12 percent, calculate the new growth rate in dividends that would produce the share price of $25.

17. J and J Cowboy Paraphernalia, Inc., pays a dividend of $2.00 per share. All of J and J's shareholders are taxed at the rate of 31 percent. Calculate the after-tax proceeds per share of the shareholder's dividend payment.

18. Elvis Humperdinck is a retired tightrope walker. Mr. Humperdinck relies mostly on his dividend check from RRR Corp. to meet living expenses. He owns 10,000 shares of RRR, which pays a dividend of $1 per share, and he is in the 15 percent tax bracket.
    a. Calculate Mr. Humperdinck's after-tax dividend proceeds.
    b. Suppose that the taxing authorities raise Mr. Humperdinck's tax rate to 25 percent. How much higher would the dividend of RRR need to be in order to keep Elvis's after-tax dividend income the same as it was under the old tax rates?

19. Recall Mary-Ellen Kennedy (problem 9), who owns 1,000 shares of DiConcini, Inc. Ms. Kennedy is in the 31 percent tax bracket.
    a. Compute Ms. Kennedy's after-tax dividend payment per share, assuming that she pays her taxes on time.
    b. Problem 9 illustrated how Ms. Kennedy used homemade dividends to create her desired dividend payment. Show that, con-

sidering personal taxes, Ms. Kennedy would be better off creating the homemade dividend than she would be if the firm increased the dividend. Assume her original purchase price for DiConcini was $70.00 per share.

20. Washington Turf is a large corporation with equity valued at $5 million but no debt. Rust Roofing is also a large corporation with $3 million in debt and $2 million in equity. Both companies are close to bankruptcy. Calculate the maximum amount of a liquidating dividend that each firm can make. In which firm would you rather have a $1,000 investment? Explain.

21. Parcells Pools has 5,000 shares of stock outstanding and a current stock price of $5.00 per share. Parcells has no debt. The company is short on cash and announces that, instead of a cash dividend, the firm will pay a stock dividend—one new share of stock for each 10 held.
   a. Calculate the new share price after the stock dividend goes into effect.
   b. L.T., a Parcells shareholder with 100 shares, wonders what the stock dividend means to him. Show L.T. that the stock dividend does not increase his wealth.

22. Madden Airlines is so strapped for cash that it has decided to scrap any plans for a cash dividend and to "reward" its shareholders with a stock dividend. Madden's share price is currently at $10 per share. There are 10,000 shares outstanding and its equity value is $100,000. Madden decides to keep its shareholders happy by providing 10 new shares for each one share held. Patrick Summerhill, a loyal Madden shareholder, has 10 shares before the stock dividend. Explain to Summerhill both the good news and the bad news of the stock dividend.

23. Ryan's Buddy System, a company specializing in social skills training, makes the big announcement: The firm will split its stock 2-for-1. Ryan's stock is currently at $150 per share, and there are 1,000 shares outstanding.
   a. What will happen to the price of each share upon the announcement?
   b. Demonstrate that a shareholder with 50 shares does not gain by the split.

24. There are some who believe that firms split their stock in order to bring the per share price down to a trading range affordable to most investors. Darlene's Dance Company is currently trading at $180 per share, but would like to see its shares trade at $45. Design a stock split strategy for Darlene to accomplish its trading range objective.

25. Shula Air Attach, a manufacturer of navigational systems, is near bankruptcy with shares trading at $0.25 each. Shula has 100,000 shares outstanding. The firm's founder, sensing that the end is

near, has given up all hope of his goal—to head a firm whose share price is over $100 per share. Show how the founder can obtain his goal through the reverse stock split.

DISCUSSION QUESTIONS

1. Why would the U.S. Internal Revenue Service try to force firms to pay dividends?
2. Which of the following groups of people can be hurt when a firm switches to a high dividend payout strategy in an imperfect market—managers, laborers, creditors, suppliers, pension recipients?
3. How could a stock split signal good news and how could a reverse stock split signal bad news?
4. Stock prices fall by only 20 percent when a firm pays a 25 percent stock dividend. Is this an arbitrage opportunity?
5. Respond to the following:

   Modern corporate finance theory does not apply to firms that currently pay no dividends since obviously the market is pricing their stock based on something other than dividends.
6. Why do the stock prices of large firms that declare bankruptcy usually rise when the announcement is made?

Should Chance Seek Security?

Chance and Security are identical twin sisters (with strange names) who live in the city of Ceteris Paribus, Pennsylvania. It is important, for this problem, to note that it is assumed that these sisters live in a country with well-functioning capital markets. (For the purposes of this problem, assume that they are perfect capital markets.) Further, legal services and other "frictions" involved with bankruptcy do not exist.

Chance and Security have identical high-level management jobs in identical (but separate) small corporations. Both corporations have a single identical building, identical equipment, identical products, identical financial statements, and so forth.

There is one difference between Chance and Security. The corporation that employs Chance has absolutely no fire insurance. The corporation that employs Security is well insured against losses due to fire. The fire insurance policy for Security's firm states that, in the event of a serious fire, the insurance company will pay Security's firm an amount of money equal to the value of the fire damage to the building.

Chance worries that someday there might be a fire that will destroy the building. In particular, she is rather worried that a large, uninsured loss would drive her firm into bankruptcy, and she worries that she would, therefore, lose her job. Jobs like Chance's and Security's are very difficult and costly to find. On the other hand, Security knows that a serious fire would not drive her firm into bankruptcy, since the insurance company can be trusted to provide a prompt and fair settlement.

Chance has sought your advice. Which of the following do you most agree with:

a. Chance should try to talk with other managers of her corporation in order to encourage them to obtain the same type of insurance that Security's firm has,

b. Chance should purchase her own insurance against this loss (assume that this is legal) even though her sister shouldn't purchase such insurance,

c. Chance is in the same position as her sister.

Module 4

Integrative Problem

Therefore, she should do the same thing that her sister does (which may or may not include the purchase of "private" insurance),

d. Chance should incur the expense of switching jobs before it's too late,

e. Chance should seek advice from someone else, or

f. None of the above.

Defend your answer and then attempt to extend the results of this exercise into addressing the following question. In perfect capital markets, who benefits from insurance?

Chapter 13

Corporate Ethics and Shareholder Wealth Maximization

Prerequisites: Chapters 1 and 2

It seemed like a dream come true. Craig had just graduated from college and was offered a job as a stockbroker at a small but rapidly growing East Coast brokerage firm. He knew it was going to be hard work. The firm offered no guaranteed salary—only commissions on sales. At age 22, Craig had no actual investment experience. He did pass the exam required for a license as a stockbroker, paying $500 for the study materials for the training class which the brokerage firm required. He borrowed the money from his parents—confident that his commissions would enable him to pay it back.

The first few days on the job were far different than Craig had imagined. The brokerage firm specialized in newly issued shares of stock in high-technology ventures. Craig's job consisted of "cold-calling" prospective investors and attempting to get them to invest.

The hours were strange. Work began at 5 P.M. Craig's office was one of about 30 desks in a large room filled with computers and telephones. A computer would dial numbers for Craig until someone answered the phone. Craig would then read word-for-word from a script, as he had been trained:

Hi, Mr. _____ : My name is Craig, with America, Motherhood, and Apple Pie Investment Corporation. How are you today? Fine. Listen, Mr. _____ , the reason I am calling is to let you know about our firm. We specialize in the common stock of small and extremely promising high-technology firms. In the past, our recommendations have produced profits for our clients of up to 200 percent per year. Is 200 percent a return which you would be interested in earning? Great, Mr. _____ , we do not have any such opportunities right now, but when the next great opportunity arises, I'll give you another call.

As the evenings wore on, the computer would dial phone numbers in western time zones so that Craig could continue calling prospective clients until 11 P.M. eastern time.

In the first few weeks, success was rare. While Craig did manage to sell about $2,000 of stock, his sales were to his closest relatives and friends. However, by watching the techniques of the superstars in the office, Craig began to learn the proper technique of cold-calling. Any investor who responded favorably to the first phone call would receive a second phone call urgently pressing the customer to invest quickly in a new venture. The key was to make it seem as if it was now or never, that this opportunity might never be presented again.

Craig found that the rewards for success were phenomenal. In addition to commissions, there were monthly sales contests in which one could win trips to the Bahamas. As commissions came in, Craig was able to pay back the $500 loan to his parents and to enjoy a new type of life-style. He took on a large car payment and larger and larger credit card bills. Craig found that even though he was beginning to make good commissions, his rising debt forced him to push potential clients especially hard.

After several months, some problems began to develop. Many of the stocks he had recommended shot upward in price initially, but collapsed soon afterward and became worthless. He was instructed to push clients who did make money into reinvesting profits in new companies instead of cashing in. But he also noticed that often the stocks he was recommending to buy were the same stocks that other brokers in the office were recommending to sell.

A nagging fear in the back of Craig's mind told him that the America, Motherhood, and Apple Pie Corporation was not like the typical brokerage firm and was stretching the rules of investing to the point of being illegal. But what could he do? If he quit, he would lose everything he'd worked hard for over the last six months, and he'd never be able to help his friends and relatives earn back the money that they had lost on his first few recommendations. And how could he ever expect to get a better job if he blew his first one?

Craig knew better than to discuss his concerns at work, as there seemed to be an unwritten office rule against negative or discouraging comments. Further, the other brokers joked about the ignorance and hard luck of their clients. They seemed to feel that the best way to do business was to worry only about themselves.

Craig's dilemma raises the issue of ethical business behavior. Recall our conclusion in Chapter 1—that the purpose of the corporation is to maximize shareholder wealth. Is wealth maximization still an appropriate objective when ethics are considered? Said differently, was it right for the America, Motherhood, and Apple Pie Investment Corporation to sell stock this way? To help answer this question, this chapter discusses ethics and ethical decision making as it relates to corporate finance and the firm's objective.

CORPORATE ETHICS INTRODUCED

Corporate ethics has been and continues to be a topic of prime importance in business. Unfortunately, business ethics is traditionally discussed in the context of proper conduct in specific situations, perhaps through case analyses or through surveying business leaders. Although we can draw interesting inferences from cases and surveys, they fail to provide a proper foundation by which to analyze corporate ethics.

In providing such a foundation, we begin by defining ethics. According to *Webster's New Collegiate Dictionary*, ethics is "the discipline dealing with what is good and bad and with moral duty and obligation." Thus, discussing ethics is by definition exploring right and wrong. **Corporate** (or business) **ethics** explores establishing right and wrong conduct for situations within a corporate or business environment. Examples of business ethics include (1) with what wages and benefits should firms compensate their employees? (2) to what hiring, promotion, and severance practices should a firm adhere? and (3) what role should a corporation play within its community?

corporate ethics
Ethics is by definition exploring right and wrong behavior. Corporate or business ethics explores establishing right and wrong conduct for situations within a corporate or business environment.

This text does not discuss ethics per se. In other words, we are not trying to teach what is right or wrong. Rather, we are attempting to provide students with a framework with which they can use their understanding of ethics to analyze a situation that occurs in business.

For example, Chapter 2 discussed the importance of basing decisions on market prices, and stated that market prices are the product of basic economic principles. Do questions of ethics move us away from using market prices and economic principles? We believe the answer is no, that market values can price ethics just as they can price anything else. Thus, a corporation that maximizes shareholder wealth by maximizing the firm's stock price is making the stock as desirable as possible to investors. We return to this point later in the chapter.

Can Corporations Act Ethically?

We often hear news or commentary suggesting that a certain corporation is practicing unethical behavior. Is this possible? The answer is no! Ethical decisions can be rationally viewed only as being between the people who contract through the corporation—including managers, employees, shareholders, bondholders, customers, suppliers, and so forth.

As discussed in Chapter 1, a corporation is a set of contracts linking people together. Corporations, like all forms of business organizations, are legal abstractions that do not have the ability to hurt or to be hurt. Pieces of paper and documents do not have feelings, emotions, or nervous breakdowns—they can only serve as conduits from one person to another. It is not possible for a legal abstraction to do something right or wrong.

Questions of corporate ethical behavior are therefore questions of actions by one person or group of persons within the corporation with respect to their effect on another person or group of persons. We may, for example, ask if it is ethical of shareholders (people) to seek wealth maximization. In a similar way, we can ask if bondholders (people) are acting ethically by taking control of the firm when it is in financial trouble. But discussing whether a specific company, say Exxon, is unethical must be viewed as imprecise and requires further specification in order to identify clearly the people involved.

TWO APPROACHES TO CORPORATE ETHICS

contractual-rights approach

An approach to the study of ethics in which ethical decisions are applied based upon rights and how those rights should be preserved.

societal-good approach

An approach to the study of ethics whereby ethical decisions are applied based upon whether or not something is viewed as being good for society.

There are two general approaches to applying ethics. The first is the **contractual-rights approach,** in which ethical decisions are applied based upon rights and how those rights should be preserved. The second approach is the **societal-good approach,** wherein ethical decisions are applied based not upon rights but, instead, upon whether or not something is viewed as being good for society.

For example, let's consider the topic of drug testing in the work place, for which the typical question is should employers be allowed to administer drug testing on current or prospective employees? Advocates of the contractual-rights approach would explore this issue by questioning whether employees have a right not to be drug tested and whether employers have a right to hire and retain anyone they want. Advocates of the societal-good approach would explore this issue from the perspective of when and if drug testing leads to a better or worse society.

Other examples of topics involving ethical decisions include universal health care, family leave in the work place, and minimum wage laws, and can be analyzed from the perspective of these two approaches. As authors, we admit that we favor the contractual-rights approach. We will present both approaches, but we must point out that only the contractual-rights approach stands up against the standards of proper analysis discussed in Chapter 1.

The Contractual-Rights Approach to Corporate Ethics

The contractual-rights approach to corporate ethics analyzes behavior on the basis of individual rights, contractually retained. For instance, is it a person's right to drug-test an employee or does it violate the employee's rights? Is health care a right of each employee? Within the contractual-rights approach there is little or no emphasis on whether or not the behavior is good for society.

In discussions of contractual rights, it becomes clear that people differ on what they feel is a true right. For example, from the two lists below, ask yourself which group, List 1 or List 2, represents true rights of individuals.

<table>
<tr><td>List 1</td><td>List 2</td></tr>
</table>

List 1	List 2
1. The right to a decent job.	1. The right to unionize.
2. The right to basic health care.	2. The right to own property.
3. The right to quality child care.	3. The right to pay an agreed-upon wage.

Within the contractual-rights view of business ethics, there is general agreement that List 2 represents true rights and List 1 does not. In the United States, for example, the discussion of contractual rights is greatly simplified because many of the rights of people are clearly understood. Individual rights in the United States are set forth in the U.S. Constitution and the constitutions of the states. The Constitution declares that people have a right to own, keep, and control the property they have earned in exchange for their labor or which they have been lawfully given by others (e.g., parents).

In contrast, the "rights" in List 1 have not been contracted. Further, List 1 forces people to supply resources against their will to other people. For example, the right to health care or child care is tantamount to forcing other people to provide it or to pay for it. Thus, the rights in List 1 are examples of attempts to violate the rights of other persons. The rights in List 2 are contractual, as they represent the rights of people to control their own bodies and property, when rights are defined in their traditional and constitutional sense.

The Societal-Good Approach to Corporate Ethics

The second approach to corporate ethics is the societal-good approach, in which ethically correct decisions are defined as those that produce the greatest overall benefit to society.

Politicians often use this approach when debating or determining matters of public policy. For example, most people support the idea that corporations should be required to pay at least some minimum wage, based on the idea that it is only fair that a corporation provide this minimum pay to its employees. Notice that this argument focuses on what seems fair rather than on whether society has a right to interfere with the wage rate that the corporation's shareholders pay.

Returning to the drug-testing example, advocates of the societal-good approach would debate whether the responsibilities of certain jobs, such as those of airline pilots or other jobs that put people at risk of injury, are important enough to society that testing should be required. If so, testing would become a requirement for these jobs but not for others.

Debating the Two Approaches to Corporate Ethics

Despite the widespread usage and appeal of the societal-good approach, the debate must be analyzed carefully. Consider the fact that the U.S. was founded by applying the contractual-rights approach.

The rich and the poor provide a fertile ground for debating the two approaches to business ethics. Compassionate people hate to see groups suffer in poverty while others live in opulence. In fact, it is the desire to force a fairer distribution of wealth that lies at the heart of most societal-good arguments. However, what many people fail to see is that actions designed to alleviate the economic conditions of the poor can violate individual rights.

Contractual rights belong to everyone—from the poorest to the wealthiest individuals in society. The view that "I" have a right to "my property" but "shareholders" of a corporation do not have the same right to "their property" is implicit in many widely held viewpoints. It is essential that, as we explore business ethics, we keep reminding ourselves that according to the U.S. Constitution, individual rights belong to everyone—even shareholders! To illustrate this important point, we offer the story of Robin Hood in Window 13.1.

Does this mean that in order to adhere to contractual rights a person must stop caring about the poor and doing things for them? The answer is no! The contractual-rights approach does not stand in the way of helping the poor, but rather it says that it is wrong to pass laws that force people to help the poor. Indeed, the U.S., under a system of contractual rights, has one of the highest levels of philanthropic giving in the world.

UNREQUIRED BEHAVIOR (OUGHTTAS) VERSUS REQUIRED BEHAVIOR (GOTTAS)

Before addressing questions of corporate ethics directly, it is useful to draw a distinction between the concepts oughttas and gottas. We seek to differentiate ethical conduct we require from other people (the "got to's" or gottas) from the ethical conduct we do not require from others (the "ought to's" or oughttas). Helping an elderly person cross a street is an oughtta. Not running an elderly person over in a crosswalk with your car is a gotta.

We must keep these two concepts separate in our minds in order to develop a reasoned approach to corporate ethics. We need to separate behavior that we pursue ourselves and wish others would pursue from behavior that we require of other people. Thus, we categorize a particular ethical dilemma as an oughtta or a gotta. Readers will find that this insight changes their view of ethics.

Window 13.1

The Corruption of Robin Hood

Most people are familiar with the story of Robin Hood—or so they think. Many people will describe Robin Hood as the legendary Englishman who stole from the rich and gave to the poor, but it may surprise most readers to know that this is not the original story. Some may recall that the story was a little more complicated than simply stealing from the rich and giving to the poor. In fact, most authorities agree that, in the original stories, Robin Hood was taking money from tax collectors and unscrupulous landowners and returning it to the people from whom it had been stolen. Many readers will never have heard of the original version.

There is a very big difference between these versions. In the "stealing from the rich and giving to the poor" version, Robin Hood is admired based upon the idea that poor people are entitled to money held by rich people—therefore this is not "stealing" but rather is "justice." In the historic version, Robin Hood is admired for risking his life to return stolen money.

What do you believe stealing is? Is it stealing to shoplift from a small store owned by a family but acceptable to shoplift from big corporations such as Sears? Is it stealing to inflate a claim made to a large insurance company? Would it be stealing if someone stole this book from you right now, sold it, and used the money on the premise that he or she needs the money more than you? As you evaluate these questions, we hope you agree that individual rights belong to everyone according to the U.S. Constitution—even the rich.

Oughttas

We start with oughttas, or conduct a person believes is morally correct but which is not legally required. Virtually everyone would agree that, in business, there are many oughttas. For example, people operating within the firm should be courteous to customers and co-workers— saying please and thank you. Also, people operating within the firm should not knowingly sell a product or service that entails certain dangers without providing an appropriate warning. We could cite many more examples of what most people would agree the corporation ought to do.

Example 13.1 _____ Should Sarah, a trusted employee in a small computer firm, give two weeks' notice before leaving the firm for a new job?

Sarah's dilemma is a good example of an oughtta. The key to this oughtta is that no matter how much we agree that providing notice to the firm is proper, and no matter how serious are the consequences to other people of not providing notice, forcing an employee to work for two weeks after announcing that she is leaving (assuming that the employee did not agree to this condition when accepting the job) would be tantamount to forced work, a clear violation of the Constitution's antislavery amendment. Thus, in the theory of contractual rights, an employee cannot be forced to work against his or her will even if a job is crucial within a small and vital business. ↵

Gottas

Gottas represent required behavior. For example, we require people not to murder or steal. While a discussion of oughttas is fun because no one is being forced to do or not do anything, a discussion of gottas is less fun, because it often poses the risk of the denial of one or more persons' rights.

Example 13.2 _____ Can corporations be required to pay income taxes? According to the Sixteenth Amendment to the U.S. Constitution, the answer is yes. The Constitution gives the federal government the right to collect income taxes from people who transact, using the corporate form of business organization. Thus, this is a contractual gotta. Of course, people can debate this question in the context of whether or not this gotta is appropriate, but a firm that organizes as a corporation does not have a choice in the matter; it must pay taxes. ↵

This discussion of oughttas and gottas may seem a little unnecessary for understanding business ethics, but it is essential in drawing a clear line between what a person should do and what a person can be forced by society to do. As we will see in the following section, this helps divide the discussion of ethics into two types of decisions: personal ethical decisions and public-policy decisions.

PERSONAL VERSUS PUBLIC-POLICY DEBATES

We now use the concepts of oughttas and gottas to clarify the issues of corporate ethics. As Craig from the America, Motherhood, and Apple Pie Investment Corporation found out in the opening to the chapter, ethical dilemmas are faced almost daily by individuals and groups of individuals within the corporation. For instance, shareholders face ethical decisions regarding pollution, the fair treatment of customers, the fair treatment of employees, and so forth.

Personal Ethical Decisions

Like Sarah's decision to give notice, many ethical decisions do not involve illegal behavior but instead are personal decisions such as those found in office politics. Most of these issues come down to a conflict between helping yourself and doing what is right for others.[1] How individuals reach a particular decision involves their own ethical belief system, that is, their own beliefs regarding right or wrong conduct.

Sarah's decision whether or not to provide two weeks' notice falls in the category of a personal ethical decision. Because she would not be violating the law or others' rights by leaving the firm without providing two weeks' notice, the decision comes down to her own belief system regarding right or wrong conduct.[2]

Public-Policy Ethical Decisions

A different type of ethical decision is a public-policy ethical decision. Public-policy decisions use the government to turn an oughtta into a gotta. As citizens, we participate in making laws subject to the limits placed by the Constitution, and we can even change the Constitution itself by amending it (with the approval of 75 percent of the states).

In terms of public-policy decisions, think of the government as a set of contracts through which people formulate gottas—requiring certain types of behavior. Many of the current public-policy debates regarding corporations involve the passage of laws to force some type of behavior (e.g., the Americans with Disabilities Act, the Civil Rights Act, and the Clean Air Act). As long as the piece of legislation is constitutional, discussing ethical conduct through these laws is a debate of what is good or bad for society, both within and outside the corporation.

We examined a public-policy ethical decision earlier when we asked whether corporations can be required to pay income tax. People, acting through government, have passed laws that force those

---

1. There is an old joke about someone who was asked to perform unethical behavior for $1,000,000. After a little thought, the person agreed. The person was then asked to perform the same behavior for $20. The person responded: "No, what type of person do you think I am?" The reply was: "We have already determined what type of person you are; now we are simply negotiating the price."
2. Sarah's decision did not involve violating the law. However, sometimes personal ethical decisions can involve breaking the law—such as the decision to speed to avoid being late for an important appointment.

who contract through the corporation to pay taxes. If society believes that this law is bad, then society can change the law and undo this gotta. A more detailed discussion of personal and public-policy ethical decisions is provided in the appendix to this chapter.

CORPORATE ETHICS AND SHAREHOLDER WEALTH MAXIMIZATION

A popular debate in corporate ethics concerns the purpose or goal of a corporation. As detailed in Chapter 1, debating the purpose of the corporation, when this is interpreted literally, doesn't make a great deal of sense, because a corporation is simply a nexus or set of contracts, not a set of people. Although we could detail the goals of all people who contract through corporations, including employees, customers, suppliers, and creditors, we are concerned primarily with discussing the shareholders, because they own the corporation. The key question involves the goal of the shareholders with respect to their decision to contract through a particular corporation.

The goal of any person is to make decisions that produce what they perceive to be the most desirable results. Thus, the goal of a corporation is to achieve the most desirable possible results for its shareholders—which may or may not include concern for other people—depending upon the shareholders' ethical beliefs. As is fully developed in Chapter 2, we would generally expect shareholders to desire the greatest possible market value to their stock and therefore their wealth.

Do shareholders have the right to seek maximization of their wealth? The answer based on contractual rights is clearly yes! Shareholders can do whatever they want with their wealth as long as that doesn't include a violation of society's gottas. The concept of individual private property rights makes the goal of assets or contracts clear—the goal is set by the owner subject to the required behavior or gottas of the society. Shareholders will determine the goal of a corporation, since they own the corporation.

The societal-good approach to corporate ethics, which is often referred to as **the stakeholder view of the corporation,** attempts to force the shareholders to do the good deeds that other people would like to see done. The word stakeholder originates from the concept that anybody affected by a corporation has a stake in the corporation and should therefore be given the right to influence the corporation. While stakeholders have contracts, they are not owners. Arguing against shareholder control is implicitly arguing that society itself owns the property and therefore has the right to determine or influence the corporation's goal. This argument can be presented with

the stakeholder view of the corporation
A view of the corporation originating from the concept that anyone affected by a corporation has a stake in the corporation and should therefore be given the right to influence the corporation.

great intentions, but as the contractual-rights view points out, the stakeholder view violates the rights of the shareholders.

Example 13.3 _____ Given the background of oughttas and gottas, and of personal and public-policy decisions, let's now work through some actual ethical situations facing shareholders within corporations. For example, let's consider the following five corporate ethical questions:

1. Offering leave of absence (paid or unpaid) with job guarantees upon return.
2. Smoking in the work place.
3. Issuing high-risk bonds, sometimes referred to as "junk" bonds.
4. Equal opportunity in hiring practices, especially company policy regarding minority applicants.
5. The disposal of hazardous waste products.

How would these two approaches—societal good and contractual rights—attempt to resolve these ethical issues? The societal-good approach would examine whether laws should be passed to control these behaviors based upon what is best for society. For example, it might be argued that (1) granting a leave of absence is the least a corporation can do to assist its employees through various periods of transition in their lives, (2) secondhand smoke adversely affects the health of all employees, (3) junk bonds have a destabilizing effect on the economy, (4) employment practices need to be fair and equitable, and (5) the local environment must be protected. If widespread agreement exists on these points of view, people might be tempted to work through government and pass laws that guarantee leaves of absence, that ban all smoking in the work place, that restrict the issuance of certain types of bonds, that require that certain hiring standards be maintained, and that restrict haphazard disposal of waste.

In contrast, the contractual-rights approach first asks whether or not these issues restrict individual rights protected by the Constitution. In other words, does the U.S. Constitution allow governments to interfere with these rights? If the answer is no, then from the point of view of contractual rights, people cannot force other people to do these good deeds. If the answer is yes, then from the point of view of contractual rights, people can come together to work through government to regulate certain corporate behavior.

In the U.S., the Constitution protects the right to owner-ship of private property. Shareholders are no exception. Thus, shareholders can't be forced to hire or retain people who need paternity leave or who smoke cigarettes. Further, shareholders have the right to issue debt—including "junk" debt. Because no such contracts exist involving paternity leave, smoking, and junk bonds, these situations fall in the category of personal ethical decisions that the corporation's shareholders must make. Shareholders within one corporation could decide to grant leaves of absence; shareholders within another corpo-ration could decide not to grant such leaves. The same is true for cigarette smoking in the work place or issuing junk bonds.

However, in the areas of hiring practices and hazardous waste disposal, laws have been passed specifying gottas. Soci-ety has acted through government to legislate certain corpo-rate conduct, perhaps because of infringements on the right of people to life and property. These examples illustrate the application of this chapter's principles to contemporary busi-ness ethics debates. In the cases of hiring practices and haz-ardous waste disposal, the corporation faces penalties if spe-cific guidelines are not followed. ↵

CORPORATE ETHICS AND MARKET VALUES

Previously we discussed whether shareholders have the right to seek maximization of their wealth. Now we discuss whether shareholder wealth maximization is an ethical goal. Some would argue that this goal drives corporations toward highly unethical, and perhaps even illegal, activity.

However, an essential point is that market values can price ethics just as they can price all other expected cash flows to the firm. Thus, a corporation that maximizes shareholder wealth by maximizing the firm's stock price is making the stock as desirable as possible to inves-tors. If investors care about ethical issues, they will find the stock of an unethical firm to be less desirable and its stock price will be lower than if it were an ethical firm.

In recent years, it is becoming increasingly clear that many inves-tors do care about ethics. With divestiture from certain countries lead-ing the way, ethical concerns have entered corporate boardrooms throughout the world. Window 13.2 discusses socially responsible investing.

Throughout our society we find that ethics are priced. For exam-ple, hiring someone to perform an unethical task generally costs more than hiring someone to do honorable work. Are shareholders any dif-ferent? If not, then the goal of shareholder wealth maximization

Window 13.2

Pricing Business Ethics

The decade of the 1980s witnessed the introduction of investment funds organized around ethical concerns. For example, mutual funds were created to invest only in corporations meeting certain predetermined guidelines such as the corporation's involvement in military weapons systems, in environmental protection, in doing business in certain countries (e.g., South Africa), and in philanthropic activities. These ethical funds were formed under the premise that ethics are valuable, or that all else being equal, the market places a higher value on ethical concerns.

In terms of investment performance, the evidence on ethics funds is far from clear. There is, however, no evidence to support the argument that ethics funds have outperformed the market, where outperforming would be defined as offering a higher return for the same amount of risk. Indeed, if anything, evidence reports that ethics funds have underperformed the market. And although no conclusive evidence exists on the performance of ethics funds, the demand for them is expected to continue for some time.

forces corporate decisions to be made in a way that most satisfies these investors—including their ethical concerns.

In order to maximize shareholder wealth, corporate decisions must be made using the same ethical beliefs that investors have and use in making everyday investment decisions. In other words, market prices are mirrors of or gauges of the values of the free society that produces them. To claim that maximization of shareholder wealth results in unethical behavior is really to claim that the society trading the stock is unethical. In such cases, the real criticism is against the views of society and is unrelated to corporate finance.

Regardless of whether or not shareholders have standards that encourage managers to act ethically, there are other market pressures exerted on a corporation's ethical conduct. For instance, a corporation labeled with "bad" ethical conduct can be hurt by boycotts or other activist activities. There is also some anecdotal evidence that firms can use stated ethical objectives to achieve success in the marketplace. Ben and Jerry's Homemade, the Vermont ice cream producer introduced in Chapter 1, has achieved phenomenal growth due in part to their business philosophy known as caring capitalism. However, for Ben and Jerry's, as well as for any other corporation, this does not mean that the objective of the firm has changed.

SUMMARY

☐ This chapter discusses corporate ethics and provides a framework for analyzing business decisions involving questions of ethical behavior. While a discussion of the underpinnings of ethics is beyond the scope of this chapter, the purpose here is to provide a way to think clearly through questions of corporate ethics.

☐ Two foundations exist from which to study corporate ethics. The contractual-rights approach analyzes behavior on the basis of contracts. In contrast, the societal-good approach analyzes behavior on the basis of its overall benefit to society, and ethical decisions are those viewed as being good for society.

☐ Under the contractual-rights approach, shareholder wealth maximization remains the appropriate goal of the firm as long as the shareholders, who have the rights of ownership, desire their wealth to be maximized.

☐ Under the societal-good approach, shareholder wealth maximization may or may not be the appropriate goal, depending on whether the objective most benefits society. This viewpoint often advocates stakeholder objectives.

☐ Shareholder wealth maximization does not necessarily force unethical behavior but rather mirrors the ethical standards of the society within which the firm operates.

DEMONSTRATION PROBLEMS

Problem 1   It is often argued that at least some corporations should be required to offer alcohol and drug abuse treatment programs to those employees who voluntarily come forward to request help. Defend this position concisely based upon the societal-good approach.

Solution to Problem 1
The preamble to the U. S. Constitution (see Window 13.4) establishes the broad mission for people to come together through government to promote the general welfare and to insure domestic tranquillity. When an employee operates a train, or a ship weighing hundreds of tons, or a truck, or an airplane, the general public is placed in extreme

danger if that person is impaired by drug abuse. Certainly, within these industries, and perhaps in many others, everyone can be made better off by requiring that the employer treat fairly any employees who voluntarily come forward seeking help.

Treatment programs for those persons voluntarily coming forward is the most cost-effective and successful method for alleviating the problem of substance abuse. Even the corporations will be better off, inasmuch as these programs have been proven to be an effective means of reducing the financial consequences of the abuse of drugs and alcohol.

Final Solution: The federal government must set up clear guidelines through which employees in vital industries will be granted access to programs required for their safety as well as for the safety of the general public, which has a stake in the drug-free performance of their duties. ↵

Problem 2 Discuss the same issue as discussed above in question #1, except this time utilize the contractual-rights approach.

Solution to Problem 2

To claim that an employer must provide drug treatment programs to employees is to claim that an employer must spend shareholder money, unwillingly, to provide for services to employees that the employees did not require when agreeing to employment terms.

The U.S. Constitution clearly sets forth that government shall not violate the rights of its citizens, including the right to own private property. The Declaration of Independence holds that the liberties we cherish are self-evident and unalienable.

When a person acting either alone or as a shareholder of a corporation (the employer) hires another person (the employee), this does not abolish the rights of the employer. The employer still has the same rights and protections under the law (ignoring those rights that the employer may have explicitly waived in the employment contract). In other words, just because a person becomes an employer does not mean that the person gives up the right to free speech, a speedy trial, or anything else. An employer has the right to own private property just as an employee does.

How would parents feel if they were suddenly "socked" with a $50,000 drug treatment bill for a baby-sitter whom they had hired to watch their children? Isn't child care a vital job with a direct effect on the health and well-being of our children?

Final Solution: Laws that require an employer to provide services to employees in excess of those agreed upon in the employment contracts violate the rights of the employers. If drug treatment programs are a cost-effective method of alleviating the problems of employees in vital industries, then competition and litigation will "force" employers to provide those programs whose benefits exceed their costs. ↵

REVIEW QUESTIONS

1. Can a corporation be ethical or unethical? Explain.
2. Explain the difference between an "oughtta" and a "gotta."
3. Explain briefly the role of the Declaration of Independence and the Constitution as they relate to the contractual-rights approach.
4. Explain the property-rights view of business ethics.
5. Distinguish between personal ethical decisions and public-policy ethical decisions.
6. Can the market price ethics? Explain.
7. If a firm has a goal of shareholder wealth maximization, does this mean that only cash flows should be considered in decision making and that ethical considerations should be ignored?

PROBLEMS

1. Based upon your understanding of typical laws, place an "O" in front of those actions better described as "oughttas" (unrequired) and a "G" in front of those actions better described as "gottas" (legal requirements).

    _____ a. Making donations to orphans.
    _____ b. Paying income taxes.
    _____ c. Selling safe and reliable products.
    _____ d. Paying employees wages for work performed.
    _____ e. Producing products that perform as advertised.
    _____ f. Paying wages that permit dignity.

2. Based upon your interpretation of the U.S. Constitution in Window 13.4 on page 429, which of the following are guaranteed rights and which are not rights at all? Use the label "Y" for constitutionally protected rights and "N" for all others.

    _____ a. A job.
    _____ b. Wasting your food or other assets.
    _____ c. Not being fired for voicing one's religious beliefs.
    _____ d. Publicly denouncing the actions of a corporation.
    _____ e. Adequate health care.
    _____ f. Buying, using, and selling property.
    _____ g. Firing workers who join a union.

3. For each issue listed below, indicate whose rights might be violated (e.g., workers, shareholders), and which rights are violated (e.g., property, speech).

   a. Laws that make it illegal for a corporation to pay a worker less than a certain wage (minimum wage legislation).
   b. Laws that limit the ability of shareholders of an existing corporation to sell their firm.
   c. Laws that allow corporations to break their contracts with a labor union when the contract is not in the society's interest.
   d. Laws that prevent discrimination in hiring people.
   e. Laws that prevent employees from being purchased by corporations and forced to work.
   f. Laws that limit corporations from polluting the resources of other people.
   g. Laws that require a corporation to negotiate in good faith with a union that has been properly selected by a majority of employees.
   h. Laws that force corporations not to pollute or deface their land.
   i. Corporate income taxes
   j. Individual income taxes
   k. Social security taxes.
   l. A law that requires only "large" firms to provide reasonable child care and health care to their full-time employees.
   m. A law that requires corporations to sell only the safest possible cars and other products regardless of cost.

4. In which of the following situations do you believe that society generally prices ethics (i.e., requires more money to perform unethical tasks). Answer with a T for true or F for false.

   _____ a. Actors or actresses in sexually explicit shows requiring greater pay than those in documentaries for public TV.
   _____ b. Owners of pawnshops requiring greater returns than owners of soup kitchens.
   _____ c. Slumlords requiring higher returns than luxury apartment owners.

5. Can you think of an ethically wrong thing a corporation (i.e., its shareholders or managers) could do that would lower its stock value even though it caused it to make more money?
6. Make a list of things you do or have done that save money but which put yourself and others in danger. Are you acting ethically?
7. The Keystone Pharmaceutical Company received permission from the FDA to sell Cardizone, a drug that reduces the discomforts of heartache. However, research indicates that the drug can cause serious side effects in a small percentage of potential users.

The company's president calls the board together to discuss Cardizone. Three options are proposed:

a. Drop all plans of selling Cardizone. The risk of serious illness or death, although remote, is a risk that the firm will not be a party to.
b. Place a large warning of the potential side effects on the package. It is expected that such a warning will significantly lower usage but will also greatly reduce liability.
c. Put a rather limited warning on the package. Analysis indicates that such a warning would permit higher sales but would provide less protection from lawsuits.

What would you recommend?

APPENDIX

The Origin of Individual Rights

In Chapter 13, a "gotta" was defined as required behavior. Because gottas often result in the denial of certain rights, it is appropriate to ask where required behavior (gottas) originates. History provides a guide, in that when people have gathered together to form a society, they have contracted with, or required, other people to behave in certain ways. People agree that a certain type of ethical behavior (an oughtta) is so nice that it should be required of everybody—turning it into a contractual gotta.

People may agree to be subjected to these behavior requirements (gottas) in a voluntary manner, such as when a person immigrates into a country or when shareholders decide to organize as a corporation, or in an involuntary manner, such as when one country conquers and annexes another. An ethical question that merits debate is whether people should ever force others to be subjected to certain required behavior against their will. For example, is taxation without representation moral? Unfortunately, such a debate is beyond the scope of this chapter. Accordingly, we will concentrate on the behavior requirements (gottas) as if they have been voluntarily entered. Thus, a gotta is a rule of a particular society which all of the society's people have (perhaps implicitly) voluntarily agreed to abide by or face the consequences.

In the United States, as well as in other countries, there are agreed-upon limits to the behavior people can require of others (which oughttas can be turned into gottas). The founders of the United States defined these limits through the Declaration of Independence and through the Constitution. (Key portions of the Declaration of Independence and the Constitution are listed in Windows 13.3 and 13.4.) The purpose of these limits is to draw a clear line of distinction between what a person should do and what a person can be forced by society to do.

The United States and some other countries emphasize the role of contractual rights in business ethics. However, not all societies base government on individual rights. When government contracts are formed (e.g., the U.S. Constitution) there are two primary foundations or perspectives that people can use in attempting to turn an oughtta into a gotta. The first is a "contractual-rights" perspective and the second is from a "societal-good" perspective. Free-market economics

Window 13.3

Key Portions from the Declaration of Independence

We hold these truths to be self-evident, that all men are created equal, that they are endowed by their creator with certain unalienable **Rights, that among these are Life, Liberty, and the pursuit of Happiness.**—*That to secure these rights, Governments are instituted among Men, deriving their just powers from the Consent of the Governed—that* **whenever any Form of Government becomes destructive of these ends, it is the Right of the People to alter or to abolish it, . . .**

We, therefore, the Representatives of the United States of America, in General Congress, Assembled, appealing to the Supreme Judge of the world for the rectitude of our intentions, do, in the Name, and by Authority of the good of the People of these Colonies, solemnly publish and declare, That these United Colonies are, and of Right ought to be Free and Independent States; that they are absolved from all Allegiance to the British Crown, . . .

(and modern finance) is built primarily upon a foundation of individual rights. Socialism, communism, and countries using these systems are built primarily upon a foundation of management for the "good" of the society. In other words, in deciding whether a person should be allowed to do something, a free society asks whether it is the person's right, while a controlled society, in theory, asks whether or not it is in the best interests of the society.

For example, many people might think it is morally wrong for a newspaper to try to increase its circulation and profits by writing numerous extremely negative (but true) articles and opinions about the personal lives of famous people and their families. But most free societies agree that this is a freedom of the press. In a controlled society, the press might be allowed to write only what the ruling class desires.

The alternative viewpoint to the concept of individual rights is often held outside the free world and is enforced by ruling groups in countries known for communism, socialism, fascism and so forth.

Window 13.4

Key Portions from the Constitution of the United States of America

We the People of the United States, in order to form a more perfect Union, establish justice, insure domestic tranquility, provide for the common defence, promote the general welfare, and secure the blessings of liberty to ourselves and our posterity, do ordain and establish this Constitution for the United States of America.

Amendments

Article I (1791): Congress shall make no law respecting an establishment of religion, or prohibiting the free exercise thereof; or abridging the freedom of speech, or of the press, or the right of the people peaceably to assemble, and to petition the Government for a redress of grievances.

Article IV (1791): **The right of the people to be secure in their persons, houses, papers, and effects, against unreasonable searches and seizures shall not be violated, . . .**

Article V (1791): . . . (no person shall) be deprived of life, liberty, or property, without due process of law; **nor shall private property be taken for public use without just compensation.**

Article IX (1791): **The enumeration in the Constitution, of certain rights, shall not be construed to deny or disparage others retained by the people.**

Article XIII (1865): Section 1. Neither slavery nor involuntary servitude, except as a punishment for crime whereof the party shall have been duly convicted, shall exist within the United States, or any place subject to their jurisdiction.

Article XIV (1868): . . . No State shall make or enforce any law which shall abridge the privileges or immunities of citizens of the United States; **nor shall any State deprive any person of life, liberty, or property, without due process of law;** *nor deny to any person within its jurisdiction the equal protection of the laws.*

Article XVI (1913): The Congress shall have the power to lay and collect taxes on incomes, from whatever source derived, without apportionment among the several States, and without regard to any census or enumeration.

Within this alternative, the permitted uses of property and the permitted behavior of people are based upon whether the results of the permission appear to produce a generally improved or worsened society. Thus, a person is allowed to speak, write, pay wages, receive wages, buy goods, sell goods, and so forth only if the action is viewed as benefiting or at least not hurting the society's overall good.

Of course, the decision as to whether something is good or bad for society, and therefore whether it is legal or illegal, is made usually by the ruling class and the permitted behavior usually changes as the composition of the ruling class changes.

Now we can link the concepts of oughttas versus gottas with the types of governmental foundations: individual rights versus societal good. In a controlled society the gottas will be whatever oughttas the ruling class desires and can impose on the society. In theory, the government can and will impose on society whatever ethical standards it deems are for the good of the society. In contrast, in an individual-rights or free society, the government is limited to imposing on society only those ethical standards that do not interfere with the guaranteed rights of the individuals.

Chapter 14

Estimating Project Cash Flows

Prerequisites: Chapters 1 through 6

Rush Ryan, a senior vice-president of the Orange Electronic Company, was about to make the biggest decision of his career. Rush has the authority to move ahead with a project that could literally change the videocassette recorder (VCR) industry. Orange's project, called "Project Prose," is a VCR that understands spoken commands.

Project Prose is similar in design to other VCRs, with one exception—a voicebox. Users speak into the voicebox and the VCR responds. For instance, once the voice mechanism is activated, the VCR would ask specific questions about taping an upcoming program such as the time to start recording, the time to end recording, and the channel to record. Users could verbally tell the VCR to tape multiple programs over multiple days, and the VCR would play back those instructions for verification.

Marketing research performed by Rush Ryan and his staff found that a surprisingly high percentage of VCR owners do not prerecord programs, due mostly to an inability to follow the taping directions. It was thought that Project Prose's main appeal would be its simplified programming procedures.

The idea of developing a talking VCR originated at the Orange Electronic Company five years ago. The firm has been secretly exploring the technology and has put $7 million into research and development. If Rush decides to attempt to develop Project Prose, an additional investment of approximately $53 million will be required. This would represent the largest single investment project in Orange Electronics' 20-year history. The firm estimates that once development is complete, even if successful, the first generation of Project Prose VCRs won't be ready for 12 to 18 months.

The question before the new-product division is whether or not to accept the project. Given its significance, each of the managers in Rush Ryan's division wants to be sure that the capital budgeting analysis is done carefully and correctly. The firm will base its decision on the project's estimated net present value *(NPV)*. *NPV* is a capital budgeting model that compares the present value of the project's benefits to the present value of the project's costs:

$$NPV = C_0 + \frac{CF_1}{(1+r)^1} + \frac{CF_2}{(1+r)^2} + \frac{CF_3}{(1+r)^3} + \ldots + \frac{CF_n}{(1+r)^n},$$

where C_0 is the cash flow in the current time period and usually represents the initial investment, CF_1 through CF_n are the cash flows from periods one through n, and r is the shareholder's required rate of return on projects of similar risk. Positive-*NPV* projects increase shareholder wealth and should be accepted. Negative-*NPV* projects decrease shareholder wealth and should be rejected. Zero-*NPV* projects neither increase nor decrease shareholder wealth.

As Rush and his staff work through the final analysis for Project Prose, they know that the decision to be made shortly will determine the future of the Orange Electronic Company.

This chapter discusses the process of estimating project cash flows. Recall from Chapter 6 the simplicity of using the *NPV* model in capital budgeting. The initial investment was given by a single cash outflow (C_0), and all subsequent cash flows were labeled project inflows (CF_1 through CF_n). Applying *NPV* was reduced to simple arithmetic.

What Chapter 6 did not discuss was the process of estimating the cash flows that serve as the inputs to the *NPV* model. For instance, think for a moment about the VCR project called Project Prose. Estimating its *NPV* will require the firm to: (1) estimate the probability that the technology can be successfully developed, (2) approximate the demand for this new and unique product over its life, (3) turn all relevant costs and benefits into cash flow estimates, (4) determine when the project should be terminated, and (5) estimate the project's terminal cash flow. Of course we could continue to enumerate complicating factors, but this short list serves to illustrate the complexity of cash flow estimation.

This chapter illustrates the estimation of cash flows and is organized into five sections. Section One discusses what constitutes cash flow and presents a model and an example of cash flow estimation. Section Two estimates cash flow and *NPV* analysis for Project Prose. Section Three discusses the effect of errors in cash flow estimation. Section Four presents "what-if" or sensitivity analysis as a way of dealing with cash flow uncertainty. Section Five summarizes the chapter.

ESTIMATING PROJECT CASH FLOWS

Project cash flow lies at the heart of sound *NPV* analysis. Whether *NPV* is positive, negative, or zero matters little if the model's inputs are not reliable estimates of costs and benefits. The old cliché "garbage in—garbage out" has direct application here.

The first task in estimating cash flow is to identify those costs and benefits that are relevant to the particular project. As a rule, only incremental cash flows should be counted.

> ✗ Only incremental cash flows should be counted (i.e., those that will occur only if the project is accepted).

The rule of counting only incremental cash flows seems trivial. But even seasoned project managers include costs and benefits that are not relevant and/or omit costs and benefits that are relevant. The highlighted rule will force managers to make a judgment on each potential cost and benefit. The rest of this section will discuss how those judgments should be made.

Incremental Cash Flow Versus Accounting Profit

incremental cash flows
Dollar expenditures or dollar receipts that are the direct result of a particular decision.

Incremental cash flows are dollar expenditures or dollar receipts that are the direct result of a particular decision. When determining whether or not an expenditure or receipt is incremental, ask the question: Would the expenditure have been made or the receipt have been realized if the project had not been undertaken? If the answer is no, then the expenditure or receipt is incremental and relevant and should be included as part of the analysis. We can also define incremental cash flow for multiple project firms as cash flow to the firm with the project minus cash flow to the firm without the project.

Cash flow is sometimes confused with accounting profit, even though they can be very different. In fact, it is possible for a project to offer accounting profits while at the same time decreasing shareholder wealth (i.e., having a negative *NPV*). Conversely, projects can have low accounting profits while increasing shareholder wealth (i.e., having a positive *NPV*). The reason for these apparent inconsistencies is that **accounting profit** is a measure of performance based upon accounting rules, while shareholder wealth and *NPV* are measures of performance that are based upon cash flow.

accounting profit
Financial performance based upon accounting rules.

Project cash flows in a particular year are easy to measure. You just add up the dollars brought into the firm as a result of the project, and subtract out the dollars that leave the firm as a result of the project:

$$CF_t = (PI_t - PO_t), \tag{14.1}$$

where CF_t is the cash flow in time period t, PI_t is the sum of the project inflows in time period t, and PO_t is the sum of the project outflows in time period t.

Example 14.1 ——————— Superstores, Inc., is considering adding video rental departments in their stores. Video rentals have been introduced successfully by other supermarket chains, and the management at Superstores believes videos would complement their product line. The cost of adding a video department, mostly in equipment and video purchases, is estimated at $250,000 per store, which will be incurred immediately. Because of required renovations in the stores, rentals are not expected to begin until a year later. The rental facilities are expected to become obsolete in five years and to have no market value at that time. Based on market research, per-store revenues are expected to be $146,000 a year, and per-store expenses are expected to be $46,000 a year. Applying Formula (14.1), project cash flow per store is represented as:

$$\text{Annual Project Cash Flow} = (\$146,000 - \$46,000)$$
$$= \$100,000$$

and the stream of cash flows for the video rental project is:

Superstores' Video Rental Project: Projected Annual Cash

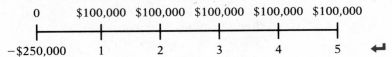

Cash Flow and Taxes

Formula (14.1) does not yet explicitly consider taxes. As discussed in Workshop 3.1, most major corporations, as legal entities, are subject to federal income taxes. Because most profitable corporations have taxable income over $348,850, we assume that the tax rate of 34 percent can be applied for all firms.[1]

———————————

1. The corporate income tax is progressive in that the tax rate increases as taxable income increases. Corporate tax brackets begin at 15 percent for income up to $52,050 and then quickly rise to 34 percent for income over $348,850. A marginal tax rate of 39 percent is phased in for corporate taxable income over $104,100 and then phased out again for corporate taxable income over $348,850. This tax bracket "bubble" has the effect of equating the corporation's average tax rate to its marginal tax rate. See Workshop 3.1 for a worked-out example.

Let's begin by incorporating taxes into cash flow but by ignoring depreciation. The formula for cash flow after tax is:

$$CF_t = (PI_t - PO_t) - T_c(PI_t - PO_t),$$

where T_c stands for the corporate tax rate. Note that the amount of taxes paid (the second part of the formula) depends on the difference between project inflows and project outflows.[2] After-tax cash flow can be written more compactly by factoring out the common term $(PI_t - PO_t)$:

$$CF_t = (PI_t - PO_t)(1 - T_c). \tag{14.2}$$

Formula (14.2) shows that only a portion of project cash flow stays with the firm since the portion T leaves the firm in the form of taxes. The closer the tax rate, T, gets to 1.0 (100 percent), the smaller is the amount of project cash flow that stays with the firm.

Example 14.2 _____ Return to Superstores' video rental project. The cash flows provided earlier were before tax. Given a tax rate of 34 percent, the annual after-tax cash flows from Formula (14.2) are:

$$CF_t = (\$146,000 - \$46,000)(1 - .34) = \$66,000,$$

and the stream of cash flows is given on the time line below:

Superstores' Video Rental Project:
Projected Cash Flows After Tax

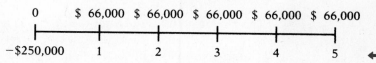

Depreciation (and Other Noncash Expenses) and Cash Flow

Earlier in the chapter we discussed the difference between accounting profit and cash flow. Accounting profits are sometimes difficult to measure and, compared with cash flow, appear to be more compli-

2. Formula (14.2) allows taxes to be positive or negative, depending on the difference between project inflows and project outflows. In our examples we will assume inflows greater than outflows such that taxes are always greater than zero. The U.S. corporate tax system has a negative tax feature, called tax loss carryforwards, that allows corporations to deduct from current year those income losses sustained in previous years.

cated. First, accountants usually treat sales as inflows whether or not the firm has received payment (i.e., whether or not the dollars have arrived at the firm), and they count certain expenses as outflows even if the firm has not yet paid for the expenditure (i.e., whether or not the dollars have left the firm). Second, accountants separate expenditures into two categories—expenses that can be expensed or deducted from revenues immediately, versus those that can be capitalized or deducted from revenues in increments through time. The term used to describe the accounting treatment of capital expenditures is **depreciation**, and different rules exist to determine how capital expenditures are to be depreciated.

depreciation
Reduction in the value of an asset.

Depreciation is an accounting number—the accountant's method of deducting an asset's value through time. For example, Superstores, Inc., may determine that the $250,000 investment in the video rental project will be used up over five years, so we can generally think of the investment losing one-fifth of its value each year. A simple technique for depreciating the machine would be to subtract as depreciation one-fifth of its original value of $250,000, or $50,000, per year. According to this simple technique, the accounting value of the machine would be $200,000 after one year, $150,000 after two years, and so on until the machine's value after five years would be zero. Other depreciation techniques will be considered later in the chapter.

Depreciation introduces a key difference between accounting profits and cash flow. In defining accounting profits, depreciation is treated as an expense throughout the life of the project. Using the simple depreciation method, annual revenues are reduced by the depreciation expense, $50,000, and per-year after-tax, profits are:

$$\text{Profit}_t = (\$146,000 - \$46,000 - \$50,000)(1 - .34) = \$33,000.$$

The five-year stream of after-tax profits is given on the time line below:

Superstores' Video Rental Project: Projected Accounting Profits After Tax

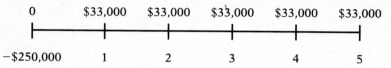

There are two differences between this time line of accounting profits and the previous time line of projected after-tax cash flows. First, the cost of the machinery is expensed over time, not deducted as an immediate lump sum outflow of $250,000 in the present time (time 0). Second, depreciation expense is subtracted from profits each year.

In contrast, cash flow analysis recognizes that depreciation is not an annual out-of-pocket expense because no money leaves the firm. Treating depreciation as a true expense would neglect the timing of the investment represented by the outflow in time zero. The issue is therefore one of timing and not of magnitude; cash flow recognizes the outflow when it occurs, while depreciation recognizes the outflow in increments through time.

There is one hitch. While not a true expense, depreciation is a determinant of cash flow. As an allowable business expense, depreciation reduces the firm's taxable income, and lower taxable income results in lower taxes paid. Accordingly, depreciation works to reduce taxes, a relevant cash outflow. The cash flow formula must be altered by incorporating depreciation's role in reducing taxes:

$$CF_t = (PI_t - PO_t) - T_c(PI_t - PO_t - D_t).$$

In the above formula, D_t is the amount of incremental depreciation expense caused by the project under consideration in period t. The formula demonstrates that depreciation reduces taxes and increases cash flow. We can also write this formula another way by factoring out common terms:

$$CF_t = (PI_t - PO_t - D_t)(1 - T_c) + D_t. \tag{14.3}$$

Formula (14.3) can be factored to illustrate that depreciation is important only in that it reduces taxes.[3] Depreciation expense is removed from cash flow in order to determine taxes owed, and is then added back to avoid double-counting the expenditure.

Example 14.3 _____ For Superstores' video rental project, per-year after-tax cash flow including the depreciation tax shield is:

$$CF_t = (\$146{,}000 - \$46{,}000 - \$50{,}000)(1 - .34) + \$50{,}000$$
$$= \$83{,}000,$$

and the stream of cash flows are given on the time line below:

Superstores' Video Rental Project:
Projected Cash Flows After Tax and the Depreciation Tax Shield

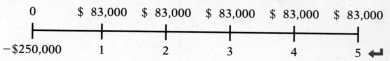

---

3. Another way to write the after-tax cash flow formula with depreciation is:

$$CF_t = (PI_t - PO_t)(1 - T_c) + T_c * D_t. \tag{14.3'}$$

This is sometimes called the "depreciation tax-shield" version of the cash flow formula because it treats depreciation solely as a shield against taxes. The depreciation tax shield is higher the higher the depreciation expense and the higher the tax rate. Formula (14.3′) is algebraically equivalent to Formula (14.3).

Depreciation is not the only type of noncash expense. Other types include the **amortization** of the value of certain intangible assets (e.g., patents and licenses) over time, and the **depletion** of certain assets such as natural resources as they are used. Both amortization and depletion are similar determinants of cash flow because they act to reduce taxable income and subsequently increase cash flow. Accounting rules also provide for the advance recognition of certain revenues and expenses that have been agreed to but have not been completed. These accrued figures represent another difference between accounting numbers and cash flow. Fortunately, these issues can be addressed in a way similar to depreciation, but are beyond the scope of this chapter.

Sunk Costs and Cash Flow

Did you ever hear the story of the gambler who spent his entire life trying to recover the $10 he lost on his first bet? The gambler was applying the empty logic that somehow the lost $10 should matter, whereas the correct way to view the lost $10 is as a sunk cost. **Sunk costs** are costs that have already been incurred and shouldn't influence future behavior. Accordingly, they should not be included as incremental cash flow.

For example, Superstores, Inc., may have spent $50,000 on market research to determine the feasibility of video rental facilities in their stores. Once those research and development costs have been incurred, they are irrelevant to future decisions and become sunk costs. Treating the $50,000 in research and development as relevant to the decision on whether to accept or reject the new project would be analogous to the gambler treating the $10 he lost in his first bet as relevant to subsequent bets.[4]

Project Side Effects and Cash Flow

Project side effects are hidden but relevant costs or benefits that should be factored into cash flow. Project side effects can be easily overlooked. An example of a relevant side effect was introduced in Chapter 6 under the heading capital rationing, where we discussed an often overlooked cost related to excessive growth and the costs related to spreading management too thin. Firms that reject positive-*NPV* projects on the premise that capital needs to be rationed are implicitly incorporating these costs into the analysis.

Overlapping revenues are another example of a project side effect. This is especially important for firms with homogeneous product

---

4. For simplicity we are ignoring the tax consequences of decisions that expense previously capitalized sunk costs.

lines. For example, when introducing Lite Beer, the Miller Brewing Company reasoned that a portion of the revenue stream from the new "lite" product would come at the expense of the revenues from its other beers. The amount of shared revenue should be identified and removed from the revenues of Lite Beer to determine incremental cash flow.

net working capital
The difference between current assets and current liabilities.

Another relevant side effect is the additional investment in **net working capital**, or the difference between current assets and current liabilities. Examples of side effects related to working capital include additional investments in inventory, accounts receivable, and cash needed to support the project. These costs are typically incurred early in the project's life, with the full investment or some portion of this additional investment recovered when the project is terminated.

Summary of Cash Flow Estimation

Incremental cash flows are those costs that wouldn't have been incurred, or those receipts that wouldn't have been received, if the project had not been undertaken. Only incremental cash flows should be included in *NPV*. Applying this rule of thumb when estimating project cash flow will assure not only that all relevant costs and benefits are included, but also that costs and benefits not relevant to the project will be omitted. Once incremental costs and benefits have been identified, Formula (14.3) can be used to determine after-tax cash flow.

ESTIMATING CASH FLOW AND *NPV* FOR PROJECT PROSE

initial investment phase
The first phase of a capital budgeting analysis, which details the project's capital investment.

long-term cash flow phase
The second phase of a capital budgeting analysis, which details the project's inflows and outflows throughout its life.

termination phase
The third phase of a capital budgeting analysis, which details the cash flows associated with the project's end.

The chapter's opening section described the current situation at Orange Electronics: The firm is faced with an accept-or-reject decision on Project Prose, a VCR that understands spoken commands. Rush Ryan, a senior vice-president at Orange—along with his staff in the new project division—is now evaluating the project based on estimated cash flow and its projected *NPV*.

The analysis will be separated into three phases. The first phase, entitled the **initial investment phase**, takes into account the project's capital investment. An example of the format for cash flows that comprise the initial investment phase is shown in Panel A in Table 14.1. The second phase, called the **long-term cash flow phase**, considers the project's inflows and outflows throughout its life. An example of the format for cash flows that comprise the long-term cash flow stage is shown in Panel B in Table 14.1. Finally, the third phase, called the **termination phase**, takes into account cash flows associated with the project's end. One common type of terminal cash flow is the value of the capital investment when the project is terminated, known

TABLE 14.1
The Format for Cash Flow Analysis

Panel A: The Initial Investment Stage

	Year 0
1. Building renovations	————
2. Production equipment	════
3. Total plant costs (1 + 2)	————
4. Start-up costs	————
5. Working capital investment	════
6. Total initial investment (3+4+5)	————

Panel B: The Long-Term Cash Flow Stage

	Year 1	Year 2	. . . . .	Year N
7. Units sold	————	————		————
8. Price per unit	════	════		════
9. Project inflow (7∗8)	————	————		————
10. Project outflow	————	————		————
11. Depreciation	════	════		════
12. Income before tax (9−10−11)	————	————		————
13. Taxes	════	════		════
14. Income after tax (12−13)	————	————		————
15. Depreciation	════	════		════
16. Net cash flow (14+15)	————	————		————

Panel C: The Terminal Cash Flow Stage

	Year N
17. Salvage value	————
18. Tax on sale	════
19. Net salvage value (17−18)	————
20. Recovery of working capital	————
21. Depreciation tax shield	════
22. Net terminal cash (19+20+21)	————

salvage value
The value of a capital investment when the project is terminated.

as **salvage value**. A format showing the types of cash flows that comprise the termination phase is shown in Panel C in Table 14.1.

The Initial Investment Phase

The decision to move forward with Project Prose will necessitate a significant investment over the next 12 months. These investments are listed in Table 14.2. It is anticipated that Project Prose will be housed in an idle building owned by Orange Electronics. Required renovations to the building include the installation of a new climate-control system and a newly designed layout of the production floor. It is esti-

TABLE 14.2
The Initial Investment for Project Prose

	Year 0
1. Building renovations	2,000,000
2. Product equipment	50,000,000
3. Total plant costs (1 + 2)	52,000,000
4. Start-up costs	1,130,000
5. Working capital investment	7,500,000
6. Total initial investment (4 + 5)	60,630,000

mated that these renovations will cost $2 million and will take approximately six months to one year to complete.

Once renovated, the building will be ready for production. The required investment will consist mostly of high-technology machinery, which is estimated to cost $50 million and will represent a significant portion of the project's required initial investment. Orange estimates that the first generation of Project Prose VCRs will be on store shelves within twelve months of the start of the project.

Finally, the initial investment includes *start-up costs*, defined as all other costs related to the project, and an investment in working capital. Start-up costs for Project Prose include employee training, sales force training, and the kick-off of the advertising campaign. The total of training and advertising is estimated at $1.13 million.

The total initial investment for Project Prose, including building renovations, production equipment, training, advertising, and increases in working capital, totals $60.63 million.

The Long-Term Cash Flow Phase

The long-term cash flow phase illustrated in Table 14.1 is an expansion of Formula (14.3). The first generation of Project Prose VCRs is expected to be ready for sale within 12 months of the start of the project. It is expected that Project Prose will last five years, at which time the project will be terminated. These cash flows require substantial analysis. We start with depreciation.

Depreciating the Production Equipment. The $50-million investment in equipment will be depreciated through time. As discussed earlier in the chapter, depreciation is a relevant noncash expense in that it provides a valuable tax shield to the firm.

In calculating depreciation, three decisions must be made. First, the firm must determine the investment's depreciable base. The **depreciable base** is the dollar amount of production equipment that

depreciable base
The dollar amount of an asset that is depreciated through time.

is depreciated through time, and is usually the cost of the capital expenditure.[5] If the full amount of equipment is depreciated, the firm is estimating that the value of the equipment at the end of the project is zero. In other words, the depreciable base is the cost of the asset less its estimated salvage value. Second, the firm must determine the number of years it will take to depreciate the capital expenditure. This decision has been greatly simplified by a system known as the modified accelerated cost recovery system (MACRS). Detail on the MACRS will be given below. Third and finally, the firm must determine the timing of the depreciation. For instance, the firm can depreciate an equal amount each year, or an unequal amount, such that more depreciation is taken in the early years, and less depreciation is taken in the later years.

With these three decisions in mind, Orange Electronics has a number of alternatives in depreciating the VCR equipment. Given a depreciable base of $50 million, the firm can depreciate according to a *straight line depreciation schedule*, which depreciates in equal dollar amounts per year, or according to an *accelerated depreciation schedule*, which depreciates more of the investment in the early years and less of the investment in the later years.

The straight line method is the easiest to calculate:

$$\text{Straight Line Depreciation: } D_t = \frac{1}{n} * \text{Depreciable Base,} \quad (14.4)$$

where D_t is the depreciation in year t, and n is the life of the investment. Assuming an estimated useful life of five years for the video project, and a value of the investment in five years of zero, the straight line method produces depreciation per year of:

$$\text{Straight Line Depreciation: } D_t = \frac{1}{5} * \$50 \text{ million} = \$10 \text{ million.}$$

modified accelerated cost recovery system (MACRS)
Accounting rules developed to simplify the depreciation process for tax purposes. MACRS is adapted from the double-declining balance method of depreciation, which allows more rapid depreciation in the early years and less rapid depreciation in later years.

Depreciating the equipment by $10 million per year for five years depreciates to a value of zero. Said differently, the equipment is assumed to have no value at the end of the project.

A more attractive alternative to the firm would be to depreciate according to the **modified accelerated cost recovery system (MACRS)**, developed to simplify the depreciation process for tax purposes. MACRS is adapted from the double-declining balance method of depreciation, which allows more rapid depreciation in the early

---

5. The depreciable base includes only the cost of equipment, and should not include expenses such as delivery and installation expenses. Nor should the depreciable base include any tax credits such as the investment tax credit.

TABLE 14.3
Depreciating the $50-Million Investment in Project Prose

Year	MACRS Factor	Depreciation (in millions)
1	.2000	$50 * .2000 = $10.00
2	.3200	$50 * .3200 = $16.00
3	.1920	$50 * .1920 = $ 9.60
4	.1152	$50 * .1152 = $ 5.76
5	.1152	$50 * .1152 = $ 5.76
6	.0576	$50 * .0576 = $ 2.88

years and less rapid depreciation in the later years. Because depreciation shields the firm's income from taxes, and because the shield is more valuable in early years due to the time value of money, MACRS provides a more favorable method of depreciation. Window 14.1 provides additional details on the MACRS. Project Prose, with an estimated life of five years, falls into the five-year recovery period class. Table 14.3 shows the depreciation schedule that will be used for Project Prose.

Annual Cash Flow Estimates. Table 14.4 derives cash flow estimates for Project Prose over its five-year life. The numbers in the left margin pick up where Table 4.2 ends and follow the outline in Table 4.1. Net cash flow is computed using Formula (14.3):

$$CF_t = (PI_t - PO_t - D_t)(1 - T_c) + D_t .$$

Project inflows are estimated by multiplying the number of units sold by the price per unit. For instance, it is estimated that Orange will sell 10,000 units in year one at a price of $5,000 per unit, defining cash

TABLE 14.4
Long-Term Cash Flows for Project Prose

	Year 1	Year 2	Year 3	Year 4	Year 5
7. Units sold	10,000	12,000	12,000	9,000	6,000
8. Price per unit	$5,000	$5,250	$5,250	$4,725	$4,725
9. Project inflow (7*8)	50,000,000	63,000,000	63,000,000	42,525,000	28,351,418
10. Project outflow	30,000,000	35,200,000	35,200,000	27,010,000	21,340,567
11. Depreciation	10,000,000	16,000,000	9,600,000	5,760,000	5,760,000
12. Cash flow before tax (9−10−11)	10,000,000	11,800,000	18,200,000	9,755,000	1,250,850
13. Taxes (34%)	3,400,000	4,012,000	6,188,000	3,316,700	425,289
14. Cash flow after tax (12−13)	6,600,000	7,788,000	12,012,000	6,438,300	825,561
15. Depreciation	10,000,000	16,000,000	9,600,000	5,760,000	5,760,000
16. Net cash flow (14+15)	16,600,000	23,788,000	21,612,000	12,198,300	6,585,561

Window 14.1

The MACRS Depreciation Method

The Economic Recovery Act of 1981 defined methods of depreciation for federal income tax purposes. Because the system uses an accelerated method of depreciation, it was referred to as the accelerated cost recovery system (ACRS). The Tax Reform Act of 1986 modified the ACRS and designed a new system called the modified accelerated cost recovery system (MACRS).

Two objectives were accomplished by the depreciation methods given by ACRS and MACRS. First, they provided a standard by defining certain cost recovery periods rather than basing the depreciation schedule strictly on the asset's useful life. Second, the system allowed for more depreciation in the early years and less in the later years (i.e., allows for more rapid depreciation), a more valuable schedule given the time value of money. This was accomplished by allowing most machinery to be depreciated over three to five years. Five of the six recovery periods under MACRS are given below:

| | | | Recovery Period | | |
Year	3-Year	5-Year	7-Year	10-Year	15-Year
1	33.33%	20.00%	14.29%	10.00%	5.00%
2	44.45%	32.00%	24.49%	18.00%	9.50%
3	14.81%	19.20%	17.49%	14.40%	8.55%
4	7.41%	11.52%	12.49%	11.52%	7.70%
5		11.52%	8.93%	9.22%	6.93%
6		5.76%	8.93%	7.37%	6.23%
7			8.93%	6.55%	5.90%

(continued on next page)

inflows in year one of $50 million. Units sold are expected to change year to year, because of market conditions. Orange estimates that sales will increase 20 percent in year two to 12,000 units, but due to competition (competitors are expected to respond with similar products in two years) will never go higher. Sales in year three are expected to remain at 12,000, but are then forecast to fall by 25 percent in year four, and by an additional 33 percent in year five.

It is expected that the price per unit will rise by five percent in year two, but must then hold at that level in year three. As demand

Window 14.1 (continued)

Recovery Period

Year	3-Year	5-Year	7-Year	10-Year	15-Year
8			4.45%	6.55%	5.90%
9				6.55%	5.90%
10				6.55%	5.90%
11				3.29%	5.90%
12					5.90%
13					5.90%
14					5.90%
15					5.90%
16					2.99%

The particular recovery period is determined through the asset's useful life:

Useful Life of	MACRS Recovery Period
Less than 4 years	3 years
Between 4 and 10 years	5 years
Between 10 and 15 years	7 years
Between 16 and 20 years	10 years
Between 20 and 25 years	15 years
Greater than 25 years	20 years

Note that, for example, the five-year recovery period class gets depreciated over six years. This is due to the fact that one-half year's depreciation is recognized on all assets purchased during the year. Thus, for tax purposes, it is assumed that the asset is purchased halfway through the first year, such that a five-year recovery system begins halfway into year one and lasts into year six.

weakens, Orange will have to cut the price per unit by ten percent in year four. Price per unit in year five is forecast to remain at its previous year's level.

Project outflows include both fixed costs, estimated at $10 million per year, and variable costs, estimated to be 40 percent of total cash inflows. For example, estimated project outflows in year one are:

$$PO_1 = \$10,000,000 + .4(\$50,000,000) = \$30,000,000.$$

Project outflows in years two through five are calculated in a similar way. Outflows fall as sales drop off, reflecting the variable costs of production. Taxes are levied at the rate of 34 percent.

The Terminal Cash Flow Phase

The final phase in estimating cash flow for Project Prose occurs in years five and six. The terminal cash flows for Project Prose are given in Table 14.5. The numbers in the left margin pick up where Table 14.4 ends and follow the outline in Table 14.1.

Orange estimates that the machinery used for production can be sold on the market for 11 percent of its original value, or for $5.5 million in year six. The firm depreciated the equipment to a zero value. Thus, the book value of the machine at the end of year five is zero, while the market value of the machine is $5.5 million. In cases such as these, the amount by which the selling price exceeds the terminal book value ($0) represents a taxable gain to the firm. The $5.5-million salvage value will net the firm $3.63 million after tax.

The firm expects to recover a portion of its investment in working capital. It is estimated that the last of its inventory units can be sold to mail-order firms at a discount of 50 percent, or for $3.75 million.

Finally, Orange will depreciate the remaining 5.76 percent (see Table 14.3) of its equipment investment in year six. Depreciation in year six will be used to offset a portion of the firm's income in that year.[6] Given a tax rate of 34 percent, the tax shield from depreciation in year six is:

Depreciation Tax Shield in Year Six = $2,880,000 * .34 = $979,200.

The terminal cash flows in years five and six are represented by the after-tax salvage value, the recovery of working capital, and the year-six depreciation tax shield.

Total Project Cash Flows and *NPV*

Figure 14.1 summarizes the three cash flow phases by placing the project's net cash flows beneath a time line. These net cash flows will be used to estimate project *NPV*. Recall from Chapter 4, The Time Value of Money, that cash flows that occur through time cannot be added to or subtracted from each other. Our analysis of Project Prose has provided a cash outflow followed by six cash inflows. Because the

---

6. We are assuming that the equipment was depreciated during the first half of the year, and sold during the second half of the year.

TABLE 14.5
Termination Cash Flows for Project Prose

	Year 5	Year 6
17. Salvage value	5,500,000	
18. Tax on sale (34%)	1,870,000	
19. Net salvage value (17−18)	3,630,000	
20. Recovery of working capital	3,750,000	
21. Depreciation tax shield*		979,200
22. Net terminal cash flow (19+20+21)	3,750,000	4,609,200

*Depreciation tax shield = $ Depreciation * Tax Rate

$$= \$2,880,000 \quad * \ 0.34$$

$$= \$ \ 979,200$$

cash flows occur in different time periods, they are different commodities that cannot be directly compared. To provide a meaningful comparison, the cash flows must be converted to some common time period, so we use the convention of transforming all cash flows to the present time. The initial investment will occur in year zero, and each of the six cash inflows must be pulled back or discounted to year zero.

Orange will use 10 percent as the project's discount rate or required rate of return. Table 14.6 computes the *NPV* for Project Prose.

The project's investment at time zero is $60,630,000, and the present value of the future cash flows, spanning years one through six, is $68,337,000. Subtracting the present value of the estimated outflows from the present value of the estimated inflows defines *NPV*:

Project Prose *NPV* = −$60,630,000 + $68,337,000 = +$7,707,000.

Because the present value of benefits exceeds the present value of costs, the project has a positive *NPV* and is acceptable.

FIGURE 14.1
A Cash Flow Time Line for Project Prose (cash flows in millions of dollars)

The projected cash flows for Project Prose must be discounted to the present in order to determine the investment's *NPV*.

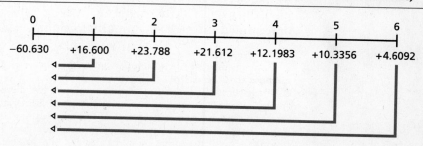

TABLE 14.6
NPV *for Project Prose (r = 10%; cash flows in millions)*

$$NPV = -\$60.630 + \frac{\$16.600}{(1.1)^1} + \frac{\$23.788}{(1.1)^2} + \frac{\$21.612}{(1.1)^3} + \frac{\$12.1983}{(1.1)^4} + \frac{\$10.3356}{(1.1)^5} + \frac{\$4.6092}{(1.1)^6}$$

$$NPV = -\$60.630 + \$15.091 + \$19.660 + \$16.234 + \$8.332 + \$6.4176 + \$2.6018$$

$$NPV = -\$60.630 + \$68.337$$

$$NPV = +\$7.707 \text{ million.}$$

Has Everything Been Included?

Let's take a quick check of the cash flow analysis to make sure everything relevant has been included. We defined an incremental cash flow as any revenue source that would not have been received, or any cost that would not have been incurred, if the project were not undertaken. Our analysis was careful to include the obvious (investment in plant and equipment, fixed and variable expenses tied directly to the project, the revenue stream from sales, and salvage value) as well as the less obvious (start-up costs, tax benefits from depreciation, and additional investment in net working capital).

Rush Ryan calls his staff together to announce the good news of the positive *NPV*. However, at that time, a number of questions surface, the first concerning the facility to be used to house the production process. While it is true that the building is owned by Orange and is currently vacant, someone recalls an offer made by the company across the street to rent out the space for storage. In fact, the company was to pay Orange $250,000 per year in rent for the use of the space. Wouldn't the lost rent relate directly to the decision to accept Project Prose, and, if so, shouldn't the lost rent be included as part of the cash flows of the project?

After some discussion, the consensus is that the foregone rent should be included into *NPV* as an opportunity cost. Because the rent payments are taxable to the firm, taxes at the rate of 34 percent must be subtracted. The after-tax amount of the lost rent payments is $165,000 ($250,000(1−.34)). The present value of the five after-tax rent payments of $165,000 with an interest rate of ten percent[7] can be determined through the annuity formula:

---

7. Using an interest rate of ten percent to present-value the foregone rental payments assumes that the risk of renting out the space to another firm is the same as the risk of Project Prose. It is not a requirement that the two discount rates be the same. If the "rental" project is considered to be less risky than Project Prose, then a discount rate less than ten percent is appropriate. If the rental project is considered more risky then a discount rate higher than ten percent is appropriate. Remember, the discount rate reflects the return required on investments of similar risk.

$$PVA = \$165,000 \left[\frac{1}{.10} - \frac{1}{.10(1.1)^5}\right] = \$165,000 \left[3.7908\right] = \$625,482.$$

The value today of the opportunity cost of lost rent payments is $625,482. This amount can be easily incorporated into project *NPV* because the annuity stream is in the form of a present value. The *NPV* adjusted for the inclusion of the opportunity cost of foregone rent is:

$$\text{Adjusted } NPV = \$7,707,000 - \$625,482 = \$7,081,518.$$

Including this hidden cost does not change the decision, as *NPV* is still positive.

The second question raised by the staff concerns the customers of Project Prose. Will most customers be first-time VCR users who were waiting for the advent of a talking VCR, or will they be VCR users who would have purchased a new VCR even in the absence of Project Prose? If the former case is true, then the analysis does not change. If the latter case is true, then a relevant side effect has been introduced in the form of overlapping revenues, which will occur across the company's product line of VCRs.

A persuasive argument is made that Project Prose is so different from other VCRs on the market that most customers will purchase the product because of its uniqueness. This line of reasoning suggests that this potential side effect can be dismissed. However, the managers in the new-product division understand that this issue is likely to become relevant in the future should Project Prose spawn new generations of talking VCRs.

Finally, someone on the staff mentions that the analysis has failed to consider the cost of researching and developing Project Prose. In fact, given that R & D expenditures totaled $7 million, the inclusion of these costs would reverse the accept-or-reject decision:

$$NPV \text{ Including R \& D Expenditures:}$$
$$\$6,682,518 - \$7,000,000 = -\$317,482.$$

The $7 million in research and development is quickly dismissed as a sunk cost that should not be included in *NPV*. The R & D expenditures, which would have already been incurred regardless of the accept-reject decision of Project Prose, is not an incremental cost and therefore should not be part of cash flow.

At this point, Rush Ryan and his staff at Orange Electronics are satisfied that their cash flow analysis includes all relevant costs and benefits. It is the unanimous decision of the staff to recommend acceptance of the project to the board of directors at the next meeting. Rush is confident that the board will provide the final stamp of approval and that Project Prose will shortly become a reality.

ERRORS IN PROJECT CASH FLOW ESTIMATION

The first part of the chapter discussed what constitutes cash flow and presented a model of cash flow estimation. In this section, we focus attention on the accuracy of cash flow estimates. Estimating incremental cash flows with values that are too high or too low will result in an inaccurate *NPV*.

The second part of the chapter provided estimates of project cash flows and *NPV* for Project Prose. As you recall, *NPV* is the change in shareholder wealth from undertaking a project. But how confident can the shareholders in the Orange Electronic Company be that the decision to produce a talking VCR will increase the value of their shares by $7,081,518?

The cash flows are estimates and are subject to error of a certain degree. Further, because Project Prose is a new product in the industry, the potential for error is greater.

When discussing the potential for errors in cash flow estimation, it is useful to differentiate between errors of two types: (1) managerial bias, and (2) misestimation, both of which will be discussed below.

Managerial Bias

managerial bias
The potential for managers to base their analysis on rosy or optimistic forecasts. Examples of managerial bias include high sales projections and/or low cost projections.

Managerial bias occurs when managers base their analysis on rosy or optimistic forecasts. Examples of managerial bias include high sales projections and/or low cost projections. Managerial bias will result in an *NPV* that is higher than would be expected under more realistic or unbiased cash flow estimates.

It is easy to see how managerial bias can come about. The time and effort spent by managers in developing a new project can create a situation in which managers wish to see their projects accepted. For instance, Rush Ryan of Orange Electronics has a personal stake in Project Prose. Because this project was developed by his staff, the project's success will in some part be his success as well. As this example illustrates, most projects suffer from some degree of managerial bias, the extent depending on the firm and the project being evaluated.

One way of eliminating or reducing managerial bias is to set up a system of checks and balances. For example, each new project may be subjected to questioning from outside or impartial managers. This would be similar to the questions concerning side effects raised by the staff in the new project division. One drawback with this approach is that impartial managers may lack the knowledge to ask the right questions.

Another way to remove or lessen managerial bias is to make arbitrary adjustments in order to project cash flows. For example, the firm may require that cash inflows be adjusted downward and cash outflows be adjusted upward. Acceptable projects would be those whose adjusted *NPV* is still greater than zero after the adjustments.

To incorporate managerial bias, Orange Electronics Company might arbitrarily adjust the initial cash outflow upward by five percent and adjust the present value of the cash inflows downward by five percent. Using the estimates from Table 14.6, the *NPV* adjusted for managerial bias becomes:

NPV Adjusted for Managerial Bias:[8] = −$63,661,500 + $64,325,942
= $664,442.

The adjustment has lowered significantly the *NPV* for Project Prose. However, including this adjustment does not change the decision to accept.

Misestimation

Misestimation is fundamentally different from managerial bias. In managerial bias, revenues are consistently biased upward and costs consistently biased downward. In misestimation, errors in the projection of revenues and costs can be in either direction.

Misestimation reflects the fact that future events are uncertain and that actual outcomes may differ from expected outcomes. For example, Figure 14.2 provides sales estimates of Project Prose against the probability of obtaining a certain sales level. This graph is of a particular type of probability distribution known as a normal distribution. In the center of the distribution is the expected outcome. The distribution is symmetrical so that the probability of obtaining an estimate of a certain magnitude above the expected outcome is equal to the probability of obtaining an estimate of a certain value below the expected outcome.

The expected sales level is 12,000 units. As the distribution moves away from the expected outcome, the probability of obtaining sales at these levels diminishes. In fact, the probability of sales being greater than 20,000 or less than 4,000 in year two is almost zero. However, the probability that sales will fall within 1,000 units of the expected level of 12,000 is high.

Statistical techniques—such as confidence interval estimation—can be used to incorporate misestimation into *NPV*. For instance, managers can determine that they are 90 percent confident that *NPV* will be within a certain range. However, the statistical techniques that allow for such analysis are beyond the scope of this text.

misestimation
Errors in revenues and costs, either too high or too low. Misestimation reflects the fact that future events are uncertain and that actual outcomes may differ from expected outcomes.

---

8. Included in net revenues is the opportunity cost of lost rent payments.

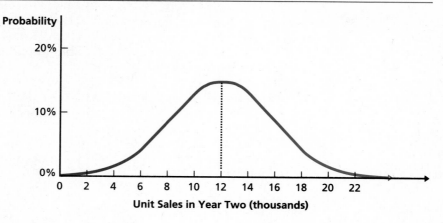

FIGURE 14.2
A Normal Probability Distribution for Project Prose

Although the expected level of sales in year two is 12 thousand units, there is a distribution around this expected level with associated probabilities.

SENSITIVITY ANALYSIS

Cash flow estimation is not an exact science, especially for estimates projecting a number of years in the future. In some cases management would like to know which variables merit a more detailed analysis. For example, if net present value is extremely sensitive to a particular factor, management should study this factor in more detail to develop a more precise estimate.

sensitivity analysis
A technique of isolating factors to which *NPV* is most sensitive.

"What-if" or **sensitivity analysis** is a way of isolating such factors. Sensitivity analysis asks how sensitive is *NPV* to a change in a particular variable holding all other variables constant.

For example, suppose that of all the cash flow estimates of Project Prose, the one that concerns Rush Ryan the most is the projected rate of growth in sales in year two. Year two is a key year as it will gauge the market's response to a talking VCR and will determine the likely sales path through year five. Rush Ryan wonders what the project's *NPV* would be if sales fell short of projection.

This question can be answered by performing a sensitivity analysis on year-two sales growth. Figure 14.3 shows the sensitivity of *NPV* to changes in the growth in sales over year two. Shown in the graph are sales growth rates between −30 percent (a decline in sales of 30 percent from the previous year given by 0.70) and +30 (a rise in sales of 30 percent from the previous year given by 1.30). The 13 points plotted on the graph are 13 *NPV*s, one for each growth rate in five percent increments in year-two sales.

From this sensitivity analysis, we learn that *NPV* will reach as high as $7.7 million if sales growth is 30 percent, but it will reach a low of −$17.5 million if sales growth is −30 percent. Also of interest is the

FIGURE 14.3
Sensitivity Analysis

NPV is sensitive to variables given by sales growth, price growth, production costs, and the discount rate. Sensitivity analysis provides answers to "what-if" questions, such as: "What if price per unit must be set at a level X% below that forecast?"

Sales Growth
0.70
0.75
0.80
0.85
0.90
0.95
1.00
1.05
1.10
1.15
1.20
1.25

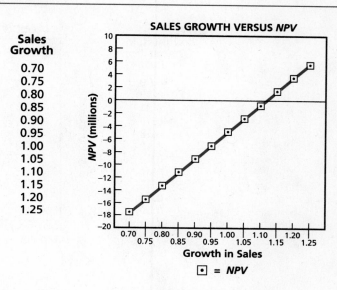

Price Growth
0.90
0.92
0.94
0.96
0.98
1.00
1.02
1.04
1.06
1.08
1.10

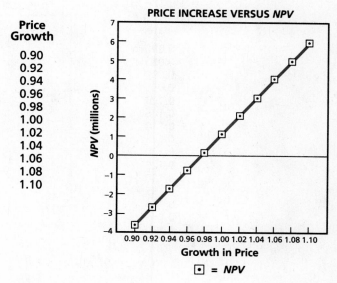

continued

FIGURE 14.3 (continued)

Growth in Production Cost
0.30
0.32
0.34
0.36
0.38
0.40
0.42
0.44
0.46
0.48
0.50

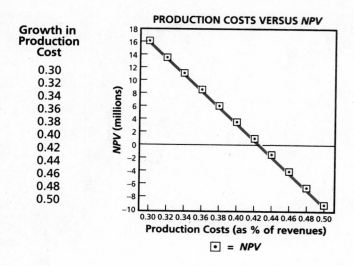

Discount Rate
0.080
0.085
0.090
0.095
0.100
0.105
0.110
0.115
0.120
0.125
0.130
0.135
0.140
0.145
0.150

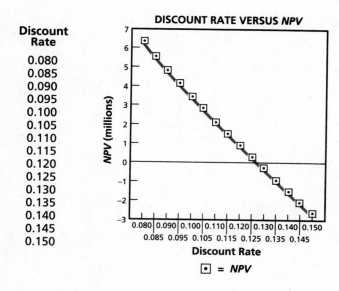

NPV "crossover" point, or the point at which NPV turns from positive to negative. This occurs at a growth rate in sales of approximately 12 percent.

Sensitivity analysis can be performed isolating any one input variable. Figure 14.3 also shows the sensitivity of NPV to projected price increases, to production costs, and to the discount rate.[9] Each of these graphs demonstrates NPV sensitivity to a change in a key input variable, holding all other input variables constant.

To summarize, sensitivity analysis allows managers to isolate NPV sensitivity to a change in a certain variable. A strength of sensitivity analysis is that it addresses, albeit in a crude way, uncertainty. A weakness is that it assumes that all other variables are held constant—it is static as opposed to dynamic. In a real-world scenario, we should expect many variables to change simultaneously. Finally, it should be noted that sensitivity analysis is tedious work, and, because of this, is usually performed using a computer and an electronic spreadsheet. Window 14.2 discusses how the computer spreadsheet is used in performing sensitivity analysis.

SUMMARY

- ☐ Incremental cash flows are dollar receipts or dollar expenditures that relate directly to a particular project.

- ☐ Much of the complexity in project analysis derives from determining which cash flows belong and which do not belong. This is especially true given the fact that certain cash flows, such as additional investment in working capital, managerial time, and overlapping revenues, are less obvious but relevant to the decision.

- ☐ Depreciation and other noncash expenses are important only to the extent that they reduce taxable income and therefore reduce the firm's tax liability.

- ☐ The formula for after-tax cash flow is given by:

$$CF_t = (PI_t - PO_t - D_t)(1 - T_c) + D_t,$$

where PI_t and PO_t are the project inflows and outflows in time t, T_c is the tax rate, and D_t is the amount of depreciation expense taken

---

9. Readers will recognize the similarity between the sensitivity analysis on the discount rate and the NPV profile from Chapter 6. Another way to think of the NPV profile is that it measures the sensitivity of NPV to changes in the discount rate. The point at which NPV moves from positive to negative defines the project's IRR, or the discount rate that makes NPV zero.

Window 14.2

Performing Sensitivity Analysis on a Computer Spreadsheet

Sensitivity analysis is tedious work. Each change in an input variable changes the cash flow stream and *NPV*. For instance, the sensitivity of *NPV* to sales growth in Figure 14.3 was examined against 13 different sales growth assumptions, leading to 13 different cash flow streams and 13 different *NPV*s.

Fortunately, financial tools—called computerized spreadsheets—can perform sensitivity analysis with little input effort. Spreadsheet programs such as Lotus 1-2-3 are designed to perform repetitive tasks quickly and without mathematical error. Properly set up, a spreadsheet program can perform each of the sensitivity analyses illustrated in Figure 14.3 in minutes.

Constructing a computerized spreadsheet to perform sensitivity analysis is similar to constructing a large display of dominoes to be knocked down one by one. Each domino is connected to the next, so that knocking over the first domino starts a chain reaction that doesn't end until the last domino has fallen. The computer spreadsheet connects each cash flow value to the next such that changing one variable starts a chain reaction that doesn't end until every *NPV* has been recalculated.

The chain reaction in the spreadsheet requires each cash flow to be connected. Cash flows are connected from top to bottom (from cash inflows to net cash flow) through the after-tax cash flow Formula (14.3), and are connected from left to right (from year to year) through growth rate assumptions. For example, in the sensitivity analysis for sales growth, second-year sales are estimated as first-year sales augmented by some growth rate, third-year sales are estimated as second-year sales augmented by a new growth rate, and so on for each year of the project's life. In this way, changing the growth in sales over year two will change the sales estimates through year five. With each new sales estimate comes a new set of cash flows and a new *NPV*. Recalculating *NPV* becomes as simple as pushing a key on the computer keyboard.

---

in time t. Depreciation is first subtracted out for tax purposes, but is then added back in to produce after-tax cash flow.

☐ Errors in cash flow estimates can be traced to overly optimistic estimates on the part of managers (managerial bias) or to the fact that actual outcomes differ from estimated outcomes. Overoptimism on the part of managers will bias *NPV* upward and can be corrected by installing a system of proper checks and balances, or, arbitrarily, by adjusting *NPV* downward. Misestimation can be measured through a probability distribution that allows for statistical techniques, such as confidence interval estimation, to be defined.

☐ Sensitivity analysis allows managers to see the sensitivity of *NPV* to a change in one of the key input variables. It is useful in illustrating best- and worst-case scenarios, and also for identifying the *NPV* crossover point, the point at which *NPV* shifts from positive to negative. The shortcoming of sensitivity analysis is that it is static, changing one variable and assuming that all other variables stay constant.

DEMONSTRATION PROBLEMS

Problem 1   A new automotive tuning machine would cost a repair shop $21,000 and would be expected to produce higher revenues of $11,000 per year and higher expenses of $4,000, based upon the additional work brought in. The machine is expected to last for four years, at which time it would be sold as scrap for $1,000. Compute the annual after-tax cash flows and the net present value by assuming a discount rate of 10%, a tax rate of 40%, and that the machine can be depreciated at $7,000 per year for each of the first three years.

Solution to Problem 1
After-tax net cash flows must be determined for the inital investment stage (Step 1), the long-term cash flow stage (Step 2), and the terminal cash flow stage (Step 3). Then they are combined in the final solution. The solution to this problem may be approached by plugging the missing values into Table 14.1, and readers may find Table 14.1 helpful. However, for this simple example, we will demonstrate the solution directly with the equations.

Step 1: The initial investment stage computes the after-tax net value of all immediate cash inflows and cash outflows. In this simplified example, the only immediate cash flow is the $21,000 outflow to cover the cost of the machine. Notice that this outflow is not tax deductible, since it is a capital expenditure. The expensing of this outflow for tax purposes must take place each year using depreciation.

Step 2: The cash flows from the long-term cash flow stage are usually the most difficult and may be found using Formula (14.3) directly or one of its equivalent forms:

$$CF_t = (PI_t - PO_t - D_t)(1 - T_c) + D_t \qquad (14.3)$$

PI_t for each year is the increased cash inflow of $11,000 per year. PO_t is the increased cash expense of $4,000 per year. D_t is the increased depreciation. For years one through three, $D_t = \$7,000$. For year four D_t is $0 since we have assumed that the machine can be fully depreciated in the first three years. Let's start with years one through three by inserting the known values into Formula (14.3):

$$CF_1 = CF_2 = CF_3 = (11,000 - 4,000 - 7,000)(1 - 0.40) + 7,000$$
$$CF_1 = CF_2 = CF_3 = \$7,000$$

Finally, let's solve for year four (CF_4) by again inserting the known values into Formula (14.3) and remembering that $D_4 = \$0$:

$$CF_4 = (11,000 - 4,000)(1 - 0.40) + 0 = 4,200$$

Thus, the after-tax cash flow in years one through three is $7,000, while the depreciation is eliminating taxes, but falls to $4,200 in year four as the machine has been fully depreciated.

Step 3: Compute the cash flow for the terminal cash flow stage. This cash flow is the net after cash flows from ending the project. In this simple example, the only cash flows are the $1,000 that the machine can be scrapped for and the taxes due on this sale. Since the machine has been fully depreciated to a book value of zero (three years of depreciation at $7,000 per year equals the total purchase price), the entire $1,000 of proceeds is taxable. At a tax rate of 40% the tax expense is $400 and the after-tax net cash flow is $600.

Final Solution: Insert the cash flows from each stage into the net present value formula using a discount rate of 10%:

$$NPV = -\$21,000 + \$7,000/1.10^1 + \$7,000/1.10^2 + \$7,000/1.10^3$$
$$+ \$4,800/1.10^4$$
$$NPV = -\$21,000 + \$6,363.64 + \$5,785.12 + \$5,259.20 + \$3,278.46$$
$$NPV = -313.57$$

Notice that the CF_4 of $4,200 was added to the terminal stage cash flow of $600 to produce a single cash flow in year four of $4,800. ◄┘

Problem 2   Repeat the previous problem assuming, however, that the machine can be depreciated in two years at $10,500 per year. Assume that the firm can take advantage of any tax losses on this project in a particular year by offsetting the tax losses against taxable profits on other operations.

Solution

The important difference is that the timing of the depreciation will change from Problem 1, so the present value will change. We will repeat the entire problem with less detail and with the new depreciation numbers.

Step 1: The initial investment stage computes the after-tax net value of all immediate cash inflows and cash outflows. The new depreciation schedule has no effect on this stage, so the only immediate cash flow is still the $21,000 outflow to cover the cost of the machine.

Step 2: The cash flows from the long-term cash flow stage are found by substituting the new depreciation numbers. Recall that D_t is the depreciation. For years one through two, $D_t = \$10,500$. For years three and four D_t is $0. Let's start with years one through two by inserting the known values into Formula 14.3:

$$CF_1 = CF_2 = (11,000 - 4,000 - 10,500)(1 - 0.40) + 10,500$$
$$CF_1 = CF_2 = \$8,400$$

Finally, let's solve for years three and four (CF_3 and CF_4) by again inserting the known values into Formula (14.3) and remembering that $D_3 = D_4 = \$0$:

$$CF_3 = CF_4 = (11,000 - 4,000)(1 - 0.40) + 0 = 4,200$$

Thus, the after-tax cash flow in years one and two is $8,400, but falls to $4,200 in years three and four as the machine has been fully depreciated.

Note that we are assuming that the firm is able to benefit in a tax sense from the full $10,500 of depreciation in each of the first two years even though the machine only produces a gross profit of $7,000 per year. This is because we are assuming that the "additional" $3,500 of depreciation can be used to reduce the overall taxes of the firm.

Step 3: Compute the cash flow for the terminal cash flow stage. This cash flow is the same as above, $600.

Final Solution: Insert the cash flows from each stage into the net present value formula using a discount rate of 10%:

$$NPV = -\$21,000 + \$8,400/1.10^1 + \$8,400/1.10^2 + \$4,200/1.10^3$$
$$+ \$4,800/1.10^4$$
$$NPV = -\$21,000 + \$7,636.36 + \$6,942.15 + \$3,155.52 + \$3,278.46$$
$$NPV = +12.49$$

Notice that the *NPV* is now positive. This reflects the tax advantage of being able to depreciate more quickly and therefore to benefit from the time value of money. ↵

REVIEW QUESTIONS

1. Provide a definition of cash flow. Name two reasons that cash flow can differ from accounting profit.
2. Why is depreciation, defined as a noncash expense, included in the formula for estimating cash flow?
3. Describe briefly how a progressive tax system works.
4. What are sunk costs, and why are they not relevant in cash flow estimation?
5. List three common side effects when estimating cash flow.
6. What are the three phases of cash flow estimation? At which phase(s) would the depreciation tax shield enter in?
7. Why would a firm, for tax purposes, choose an accelerated depreciation method over a straight line depreciation method?
8. List the two types of errors in cash flow estimation and discuss briefly how they are different.
9. What is sensitivity analysis, and how is it useful in making accept-or-reject decisions on projects?

PROBLEMS

1. A marketing research firm with current sales of $400,000 does not expect any growth in sales for the next two years. However, the company anticipates that expenses, currently at $200,000, will increase to $210,000 next year and to $220,500 the year after. Assuming a tax rate of 34%, determine the firm's current after-tax cash flow as well as projected after-tax cash flow over the next two years. Assume there is no depreciation.
2. A distributor of computer software instruction manuals plans to expand distribution. Annual sales are currently $2 million and are expected to be $2.1 million next year and $3.08 million the year after. Assuming that expenses are 80% of sales each year, what are the distributor's current after-tax cash flows and projected after-tax cash flows next year and the year after if the tax rate is 34%? Assume there is no depreciation.
3. MBI Corp. is considering purchasing one of two types of machinery. The first type, costing $800,000, is expected to last for 10 years. The second type, costing $1.2 million, is expected to last for

15 years. Assuming that straight line depreciation is used, what is the annual depreciation schedule for each type of machinery?

4. For the MBI Corp. in problem 3, recalculate the annual depreciation schedule for each type of machinery using the MACRS schedules in Window 14.1 assuming the recovery period = useful life.

5. A travel agent intends to update its computerized reservation system. State-of-the-art computer equipment costs $200,000 and is expected to be used for four years. There is no salvage value. What is the equipment's depreciation schedule for each of the four years, assuming that the MACRS is used and a three-year recovery period?

6. The owner of two pizza restaurants needs to buy a new pizza oven for each restaurant. Each oven costs $300,000 and is expected to last 15 years.
   a. Using the MACRS schedules in Window 14.1, determine the annual depreciation schedule for each oven over the first five years assuming a 15-year recovery period.
   b. Determine the annual after-tax cash flow for the pizza restaurants over the first five years, assuming total cash inflows are a constant $1 million, total cash outflows are a constant $500,000, and the tax rate is 34%.

7. A manufacturer of recyclable paper and paper board is considering the replacement and upgrading of machinery that would improve efficiency. The new machinery costs $2.5 million and is expected to last for five years. Straight line depreciation will be used. Cash inflows, currently at $5 million per year, are expected to increase to $5,750,000 annually if the machinery is purchased. Assuming that the machinery can begin to increase cash inflows in one year, and company expenses are consistently 60% of cash inflows, what is the after-tax cash flow in each of the next five years? The tax rate is 34%.

8. A poster manufacturer wants to introduce a small-size line of movie, concert, and theater posters. To do so, however, requires new equipment, additional personnel, and increased advertising expenses. The equipment costs $2 million and will be depreciated on a straight line basis for four years. Annual cash inflows are expected to increase by $5 million in year 1, by $5.5 million in year 2, and rise 15% per year over each of the next two years. Costs for manufacturing, sales personnel, and advertising will increase by $3,800,000 in year 1, increasing by 5% annually in each of the next three years. What are the after-tax cash flows for the project? The tax rate is 34%.

9. A bus tour company wants to provide excursions to several national and international sports events that will be taking place

throughout the country during the next few years. To make the buses more comfortable and the trips more popular, each of eight new buses will be equipped with a kitchen and a large video screen for movies and sports telecasts.

Each bus costs $200,000 and requires customized equipment that costs an additional $100,000 per bus. All the buses and the equipment have a recovery period of five years. An advertising campaign, which will start immediately, costs $750,000 and will be paid for immediately. Other start-up costs total $30,000.

The sports trips are scheduled for three to ten days and will generate revenues of $100 per day per seat. For the eight video buses, total revenues are expected to be $3,168,000 for the first year and $3,484,800 for the second year (a 10% increase). Operating costs are 30% of total revenues. Personnel expenses, including driver salaries, are $650,000 in year 1 and will increase by 5% in year 2.

The company expects to discontinue operation of its video bus tours after the second year. Each bus will be sold to a university for $35,000 — $30,000 for the bus itself and $5,000 for the equipment.

a. What are the cash flows for the initial investment period?
b. What is the MACRS depreciation schedule for the first two years for all of the buses and the equipment? Depreciate both down to zero, using the five-year recovery period.
c. What are the after-tax cash flows for the two years that the bus tours will be in operation? The tax rate is 34%.
d. What are the termination cash flows in year 2?
e. If *NPV* analysis is used, should the buses be purchased? The required rate of return is 12%.

10. A car manufacturer is considering production of a convertible version of the former Volkswagen "beetle." The marketing VP, an enthusiastic former owner of a "beetle" himself, has been conducting market research on the project. Once the car is available, the marketing VP expects that 50,000 cars at $18,000 per car will be sold in the first year. Sales would then be anticipated to increase 8% per year over the previous year's level.

The cars will be produced and warehoused at only one of the company's several locations. Machinery will cost $100 million, has a useful life of 10 years, and will be depreciated on a straight line basis. Start-up costs, including mechanic's training, are another $13 million. Advertising expenses will amount to $5 million initially and remain at this level annually for the first two years. Manufacturing and employee costs will be 60% of revenues.

a. What is the after-tax cash flow in year 1 if 50,000 cars are sold? The tax rate is 34%.

...he after-tax cash flow in year 2 if 50,000 cars are sold
 The tax rate is 34%.
 year 1 turn out to be 50% lower than expected, what
...er-tax cash flow for the first year?
...keting VP wishes to project sales and expenses in a
...conomic scenario in which both unemployment and
...are high. Consequently, sales would be lower and
...uld be higher. What is the net after-tax cash flow for
...year if sales are 50% lower and manufacturing costs
...instead of 60%, of sales?

11. ...onal airline is performing sensitivity analysis to deter-
...rfect of changes in the price of oil on its cash flow.
...competitive market conditions, the airline cannot raise
...athe price of oil increases but could lower fares if oil
...d consequently, an increase in the per-barrel price of oil
...worbed by the firm, but a sizable decrease in the price
...of cipated to increase revenues. On particular routes, the
...firtes that five million passenger miles are recorded for
...on each passenger mile generates $0.50 in revenue and
...$0er-tax cash flow, assuming that oil costs $19.00 per bar-
...rel h $1.00 increase in the per-barrel price of oil, after-tax
...cas rops by $0.02. For each $1.00 decrease in the per-bar-
...rel oil, one million passenger miles will be added.
 a. ...00 per barrel, what is the total revenue and after-tax
 ...w?
 b. ...A0 per barrel, what is the after-tax cash flow?
 c. ...A0 per barrel, what is the after-tax cash flow?

DISCUSSION QUESTIONS

1. The ...treet Journal makes two announcements on the Walker
 Corp...on. First, Walker reported record-high profits for the last
 fiscal Second, Walker arranged a $50 million credit line over
 the sa fiscal year from Citibank to get the firm through cash
 flow pems. How is it possible that these two events can occur
 simult ously?
2. The E am Company uses straight line depreciation. The firm
 reason at it doesn't matter which depreciation method is used
 because total amount of depreciation is the same under each
 method o you agree or disagree with Eastham?
3. Scnibbl nd Fizz, a firm with an entire line of dishwashing deter-
 gents, is dvertising its newest dishwashing detergent project as
 new and nproved. When analyzing project cash flows, you notice
 that the stimates on the new project make no adjustments for

"side effects." Fro information provided, what mistakes do you think e in its analysis?

4. It was argued that ve an incentive to see their own projects get funde gerial bias). Design an incentive scheme for project at will have the effect of reducing or even eliminating bias.

5. The UpSmith Phar Corporation announced the successful developmen e that can prevent certain forms of cancer. The cost e of the vaccine is inexpensive— as low as $1 by son s. However, the retail price of the vaccine per dose is mith defends this high price as a way to recover resea velopment efforts connected with the cancer vaccine th l over 20 years. Is the firm correct in incorporating thes penditures into the vaccine's sales price?

Chapter 15

Advanced Topics in Capital Budgeting

Prerequisites: Chapters 1 through 6

Emily, the president of Visualized Construction, Inc., was responsible for analyzing the firm's new construction projects. In fact, Emily made all of the the firm's business decisions, while her partner was in charge of on-site project management. Emily enjoyed her job and took pride in the fact that the firm was growing and successful.

Emily studied corporate finance while at college. The most important thing she learned was the net present value (*NPV*) rule—the premier method by which to make new project decisions. However, Emily had recently encountered a situation in which her instincts led her to believe that *NPV* was providing the wrong answer.

The situation was this: Emily had been asked to consider the possible construction of two types of building projects. The first, Project Big, involved a very large building. Project Big appeared extremely lucrative and would be finished in about two years. The second, Project Small, involved twelve small office buildings. The second project would be finished in about six years.

Emily decided to base the decision on *NPV*. Project Big offered an *NPV* of $1,000,000, and Project Small offered an *NPV* of $1,500,000. Because her firm had only one qualified construction manager (her partner), she realized that these were mutually exclusive projects and that she had to decide which of the two (if either) to accept. Emily remembered that *NPV* was supposed to solve all ranking problems caused by scale differentials such as size and length of time. Nevertheless, her instincts told her that the two-year project was better even though it had a smaller *NPV*.

Perhaps Emily's instincts had more to do with her ambition to build a grandiose building than with corporate finance. Or perhaps her instincts were wrong. Or worse yet, perhaps the unthinkable was true—that the *NPV* rule as applied was not correct in its choice of projects!

CHAPTER OVERVIEW—COMPLEXITIES IN CAPITAL BUDGETING ANALYSIS

The opening six chapters of the text presented a highly simplified decision rule for financial managers: Accept all projects with positive *NPV*s and reject all projects with negative *NPV*s. In theory, *NPV* can be used to make all optimal investment decisions since the *NPV* rule measures the change in the wealth of the firm's shareholders by subtracting costs from benefits.

However, in practice, there are complexities that make it virtually impossible to reduce all decisions to a simple *NPV* analysis. (One such complexity, project risk, will not be considered explicitly here but is discussed at length in Module 3.) This chapter will detail some common complexities that arise when making investment decisions using *NPV*. We first consider the problem of using *NPV* to select between projects with unequal lives, such as the Visualized Construction example of deciding between a six-year project and a two-year project; this situation was not discussed in Chapter 6. Users should be aware that *NPV* must be calculated with care when deciding between unequally lived projects.

This chapter will also detail three other special situations that occur within capital budgeting analysis. They are least-cost decisions, inflation, and capital rationing. Of course, there are an unlimited number of complexities that can arise in investment decisions, and no textbook can fully prepare a student for all of them. Nevertheless, this chapter provides a good starting point for tackling some of the more common issues.

PROJECTS WITH UNEQUAL LIVES

For the construction company forced to decide between a six-year project and a two-year project, the projects were mutually exclusive such that the firm could choose one but not both. Mutually exclusive projects were introduced in Chapter 6 as a ranking problem, and a problem that could be solved by selecting the project with the higher *NPV*. In fact, you will remember that Chapter 6 indicated that when ranking projects, *NPV* was clearly superior to other criteria—especially the internal rate of return rule.

However, these results apply only to a special situation in which a certain advantage to short-lived projects was assumed not to exist. In particular, the analysis in Chapter 6 ignored the fact that a short-lived project might offer a firm the advantage of being able to begin a new project sooner than if a longer-term project were accepted. This section will attempt to incorporate this aspect into the analysis.

NPV Versus *IRR:* The Controversy Revisited

Chapter 6 discussed the problem of choosing between two mutually exclusive projects, necessitated perhaps because of the firm's limited space, limited management, or the fact that the projects fill the same market niche. It was demonstrated that the *IRR* can rank projects incorrectly if the projects have unequal scales, which were defined as having either unequal sizes in terms of dollar magnitudes or unequal lives in terms of length of time the projects will run.

Chapter 6 correctly demonstrated that earning, say, 26 percent on a large, long-term project might be preferred to earning 30 percent on a small, short-lived project. After all, would you rather have a summer job that lasted eight weeks and paid $26 per hour or a summer job that lasted only one week and paid $30 per hour? We are sure you agree that the eight-week job is the one to choose. Chapter 6 showed that *NPV* would incorporate the scale differentials and would generate the correct ranking.

The Hidden Reinvestment or Replication Assumption

What our analysis has yet to consider is the possibility that projects can be repeated. Returning to the summer job analogy, is there any situation in which you would prefer a one-week summer job that offers $30 per hour to an eight-week summer job that offers $26 per hour? The answer is yes! Suppose you know that, at the end of the first week, you can get another job paying $26 per hour for the remaining seven weeks. Wouldn't it be better to work one week for $30 per hour and then switch to another job for $26 per hour for the remaining seven weeks?

Using this same line of reasoning, consider Emily and the choice she faces as president of Visualized Construction. What if Visualized Construction, at the end of Project Big, could begin a new project with a potentially positive *NPV*? In this case, the firm might be better off with Project Big in combination with this new project.

In capital budgeting, a simple *NPV* analysis can incorrectly rank unequally lived projects. This can occur if the firm ignores the fact that at the end of the shorter-term project the firm might be able to find new positive *NPV* projects. In finance, this is often called project reinvestment, although it might be better referred to as **project replication.**

project replication
An assumption that projects, at completion, can begin again offering the same *NPV*.

NPV *and Replication.*   In a nutshell, simple *NPV* analysis assumes that investing in the short-term project will not allow the firm to be able to reinvest or get started on any other project with a positive *NPV*. Simple *NPV* analysis implicitly assumes that the selection of the short-term or long-term project will not change the firm's future investment opportunities. This seems rather unrealistic in the case of Visualized Construction during strong economic times, since presumably the two-year project would allow the firm to begin another profitable construction project sooner than if management selected the six-year project.

IRR *and Replication.* Conversely, simple *IRR* analysis implicitly assumes that the firm will be able to reinvest all cash flows at the project's *IRR*. This is also unrealistic, since it would be unusual for a firm always to have sufficient new projects into which it could reinvest each cash flow and which will earn the *IRR* of today's best project. For example, if Project Short is earning a high *IRR*, such as 30 percent, a simple *IRR* analysis implicitly assumes that all cash flows from future projects can be continually reinvested at the rate of 30 percent.

This chapter will discuss a more complex *NPV* analysis that permits the financial manager to utilize a replication assumption between the two extremes mentioned above and, therefore, is more realistic. This more complex *NPV* analysis is to be used in cases in which a financial manager believes that once the shorter-term project is finished, the firm will be able to begin a new project offering a similar *NPV*. Simply put, we will assume that the short-lived project can be replicated as soon as it is finished.

Solving the Problem of Unequal Lives

equivalent annuity approach
A method of comparing unequally lived projects by converting project *NPV* into an annuity stream. Under this approach, a particular level of wealth today (an *NPV*) is shown to be equivalent to receiving some constant level of wealth each year in the future. The preferred project is the one with the highest present value of the annuity string.

The purpose of this section is to detail an advanced capital budgeting approach called the **equivalent annuity approach,** which converts an *NPV* into an annuity stream. In other words, a particular level of wealth today (an *NPV*) can be shown to be equivalent to receiving some constant level of wealth each year in the future. This equivalent annuity allows projects with unequal lives to be directly compared with each other under the assumption that the projects can be replicated when they are completed.

To illustrate, Skyhigh Airlines is considering one of two projects, both with an initial investment of $500,000. Project Short will last three years and has expected cash flows represented by a three-year $258,136 annuity. Project Long will last seven years and has expected cash flows represented by a seven-year $153,382 annuity. Cash flow streams and project *NPV*s using a 12 percent required rate of return are given below:

Skyhigh Airline's Project Short

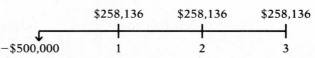

$$\text{Project Short's } NPV = -\$500,000 + \$258,136 \left[\frac{1}{.12} - \frac{1}{.12(1.12)^3} \right]$$

$$= \$120,000.$$

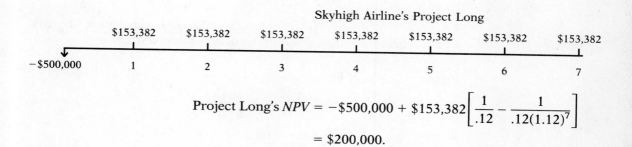

Skyhigh Airline's Project Long

$$\text{Project Long's } NPV = -\$500,000 + \$153,382 \left[\frac{1}{.12} - \frac{1}{.12(1.12)^7} \right]$$

$$= \$200,000.$$

Since these projects use the same facilities, the same personnel, and produce products that fill the same niche in the firm's product mix, only one project can be accepted. However, the financial managers at Skyhigh believe that if the firm selects Project Short, it can either repeat that project in three years or begin a new project in three years that would add similar value to the firm.

Remember that accepting a project with an *NPV* of $120,000 has the same effect on the value of the firm's assets as if the firm received an immediate gift of $120,000. Therefore, accepting Project Short is just like receiving $120,000 in immediate cash while accepting Project Long is just like receiving $200,000 in immediate cash. If the unequal lives of the projects didn't matter, the simple *NPV* rule would show that it is better to take the $200,000 project. But what if projects can be repeated? Should the Skyhigh managers accept a project that produces an *NPV* of $120,000 every three years or should they, instead, accept a project that produces an *NPV* of $200,000 every seven years?

One Approach: The Common Ending Point.   One way to factor replication into the analysis is to repeat each project over and over again—stringing out each project on a time line. In this case, Project Short will repeat every three years, and Project Long will repeat every seven years. The projects should repeat on the time line until they have a common ending point. The common ending point occurs in 21 years such that Project Short is repeated for a total of seven times and Project Long three times.

The next step is to discount the string of *NPV*s to the year the project starts. For example, Project Long is repeated for a total of three times over the span of 21 years, earning an *NPV* of $200,000 in year zero (today) along with two additional *NPV*s of $200,000 in year seven and $200,000 in year 14. The present value of the string of *NPV*s for Project Long is given by:

$$\text{Project Long's } NPV \text{ String} = 200{,}000 + \frac{200{,}000}{(1+r)^7} + \frac{200{,}000}{(1+r)^{14}}.$$

Project Short can be replicated for a total of seven times over 21 years, and the present value of the string of *NPV*s is given by:

$$
\begin{aligned}
\text{Project Short's } NPV \text{ String} \\
= 120{,}000 + \frac{120{,}000}{(1+r)^3} + \frac{120{,}000}{(1+r)^6} + \frac{120{,}000}{(1+r)^9} \\
+ \frac{120{,}000}{(1+r)^{12}} + \frac{120{,}000}{(1+r)^{15}} + \frac{120{,}000}{(1+r)^{18}}.
\end{aligned}
$$

Comparing Project Long's *NPV* string against Project Short's *NPV* string will allow for *NPV* to incorporate correctly the replication assumption.[1] This **common ending point approach** is shown in Figure 15.1.

Given a required rate of return of 12 percent, the present value of the string of *NPV*s for Project Short is greater than the present value of the string of *NPV*s for Project Long. Thus, incorporating replication leads to a decision to select Project Short over Project Long.

common ending point approach
A method of comparing unequally lived projects by replicating the projects until they have a common ending point. The preferred project is the one with the highest *NPV* string.

A Better Approach: The Equivalent Annual Annuity. Although it produces correct results, the common ending point approach can be quite tedious.[2] An easier way to compare these repetitive projects is to convert the *NPV*s of each project into equivalent annuities, then to compare these annuities. For example, with an interest rate of 12 percent, we may use the annuity concept to convert Project Short's *NPV* of $120,000 today into a three-year annuity of $49,961.88. This is shown in the form of a time line in Figure 15.2.

Receiving $120,000 today is equivalent to receiving $49,961.88 each year for three years. If we imagine Project Short being repeated

---

1. Stopping at year 21 is sufficient even though these projects are assumed to continue indefinitely. Extending the analysis beyond year 21, say to year 42 or beyond, will change the magnitude of the respective *NPV*s but not the ranking.
2. For example, if one project ends in seven years, while the other ends in 13 years, the time line will be extended to 91 years, the year of the first common ending point.

FIGURE 15.1
NPV *Using the Common Ending Point Approach (numbers in thousands)*

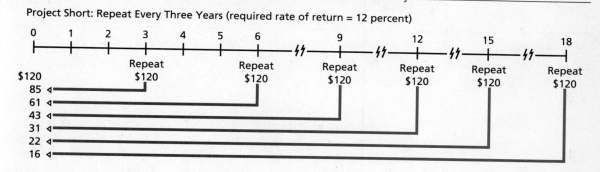

Project Short: Repeat Every Three Years (required rate of return = 12 percent)

$378 = Present value of the string of NPVs

Project Long: Repeat Every Seven Years (required rate of return = 12 percent)

$331 = Present value of the string of NPVs

every three years forever, we can extend the time line out six years and beyond. This is illustrated in Figure 15.3.

Project Long can also be converted into an annuity of approximately $43,823.55. Note that in computing Project Long's equivalent annuity we used its seven-year life. Project Long's equivalent annuity and equivalent perpetuity are illustrated in Figure 15.4.

FIGURE 15.2
Project Short's Equivalent Annuity

The present value of $120,000 is equivalent to a three-year $49,961.88 annuity.

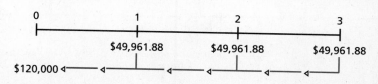

FIGURE 15.3
Project Short's Equivalent Perpetuity

The present value of a repetitive "string" of Project Shorts is equivalent to a $49,961.88 perpetuity.

The usefulness of converting each *NPV* into an annuity of equivalent value is that it permits us to compare the projects directly. Accepting Project Short and repeating it every three years is equivalent to receiving $49,961.88 every year. Accepting Project Long and repeating it every seven years is equivalent to receiving $43,823.55 every year. Now the comparison is easy. We accept Project Short, since this is tantamount to receiving a higher cash flow in every year.

In summary, when a firm must decide between projects having unequal lives, it is often appropriate to assume that the projects can be replicated once finished and to use the equivalent annuity method, which converts each *NPV* into an annuity whose length is equal to the length of the project. The annuities are then compared and the project with the higher annuity is accepted. This method should be used whenever the firm believes that the shorter project's quicker termination will permit the firm to commence projects of similar added value.

FIGURE 15.4
Project Long's Equivalent Annuity and Perpetuity

Equivalent Annuity

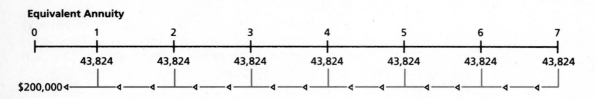

Equivalent Perpetuity

The present value of a repetitive "string" of Project Longs is equivalent to a $43,825.55 annuity.

LEAST-COST DECISIONS

least-cost decision
A capital budgeting decision in which the best process is the one that offers the lowest total cost when time value is included.

Another common investment decision involves the comparison of projects producing the same cash inflows but at different costs. For example, a firm may be deciding between two production processes performing the same job and therefore producing the same benefits. The firm has already decided that it needs a production process; all that is being decided is which production process is best for the firm. In this case, the best process would be defined as the one that offers the lowest total cost when time value is included.

The problem is solved utilizing a **least-cost decision.** Rather than computing the *NPV* of the alternative production processes, the firm computes the total present value of the costs and compares them.

Example 15.1 —————— Vertigo Cabs, Inc., of New York City, is debating whether to buy high-quality cars that will need fewer repairs or low-quality cars that will cost less. High-quality cars cost $15,000 to buy and $2,000 per year to maintain. Low-quality cars cost $10,000 to buy and $5,000 per year to maintain. The life expectancy of both types of cars is three years, after which they are worthless. Which type of car should they buy?

The answer is found by computing the present value of all of the costs for each alternative. Assuming an interest rate of 11 percent, the present value of the costs of the high-quality cars is found by adding the $15,000 cost of the car today with the present value of three $2,000 payments. The annuity formula can be used to determine these present values. The present value of the cost of high-quality and low-quality cars is:

PV Costs for High-Quality Cars

$$= \$15,000 + \$2,000 \left[\frac{1}{.11} - \frac{1}{.11(1.11)^3} \right]$$

$$= \$15,000 + \$2,000 \left[2.444 \right]$$

$$= \$19,888.$$

PV Costs for Low-Quality Cars

$$= \$10,000 + \$5,000 \left[\frac{1}{.11} - \frac{1}{.11(1.11)^3} \right]$$

$$= \$10,000 + \$5,000 \left[2.444 \right]$$

$$= \$22,220.$$

The least-cost alternative is the high-quality cars, whose higher purchase price is more than offset by their lower annual maintenance costs.

Technically, the values in the above example should be listed as negative numbers since they are costs. However, by convention, they are listed as positive numbers and the decision is to choose the project with the smallest present value.

Least Cost and Unequal Lives

It is also common for least-cost comparisons to involve different lives. Usually, one alternative is more expensive but lasts longer than its cheaper and shorter-lived counterpart. Thus, the problem involves both the concepts of a least-cost analysis and an unequal-lives analysis.

Example 15.2 _____ Consider Nittany Manufacturing Inc., which is deciding between two alternative manufacturing processes. Alternative A uses high-quality, all stainless steel equipment that costs $1,350,000, and has an expected life of 10 years and an annual operating expense of $250,000. Alternative B is a cheaper set of equipment that uses a variety of materials, costs only $750,000, and has a useful life of 5 years and annual operating expenses of $350,000. Which alternative is cheaper given that both alternatives produce equal-quality output?

The answer is found by combining the approaches of unequally lived project selection and least-cost decision making. The user computes the total present value of the costs and converts the costs into equivalent annuities. Using an interest rate of 8 percent, the answer is found by selecting the alternative with the lower annuity cost.

Let's apply this solution to Nittany Manufacturing's problem. First, the present values of the costs are:

Alternative A
$$= \$1,350,000 + \$250,000 \left[\frac{1}{.08} - \frac{1}{.08(1.08)^{10}} \right]$$
$$= \$1,350,000 + \$1,677,520 \longrightarrow \$3,027,520.$$

Alternative B
$$= \$750,000 + \$350,000 \left[\frac{1}{.08} - \frac{1}{.08(1.08)^{5}} \right]$$
$$= \$750,000 + \$1,397,449 \longrightarrow \$2,147,449.$$

Alternative A has higher total costs, but we must now adjust these costs for the fact that they cover ten years of production rather than five years. We adjust for the unequal lives by converting each total cost into an equivalent annuity. Following the equivalent annual annuity approach outlined earlier in the chapter, the *PV* of the costs of Alternative A can be converted into a $451,190 annuity:

$$\$3,027,520 = \text{Annuity} \left[\frac{1}{.08} - \frac{1}{.08(1.08)^{10}} \right] \longrightarrow$$

$$\text{Annuity} = \$451,190,$$

while the *PV* of the costs of Alternative B can be converted into a $537,842 annuity:

$$\$2,147,449 = \text{Annuity} \left[\frac{1}{.08} - \frac{1}{.08(1.08)^{5}} \right] \longrightarrow$$

$$\text{Annuity} = \$537,842.$$

If these manufacturing processes can be repeated after completion, we can think of these annuities as representing a perpetual string of costs. Alternative A is the best alternative in that it produces smaller annual costs. This example illustrates a common problem in corporate finance since the more expensive alternative often lasts longer. If this weren't true, the choice of technologies would be easy—always take the less expensive, longer-lasting technology. ↵

INFLATION AND INVESTMENT DECISIONS

A topic of prime importance is the treatment of inflation in investment decisions. As Chapter 3 detailed, inflation occurs when the value of money falls, causing the prices of everything else to rise. In terms of project cash flows, inflation will affect estimated revenues as well as estimated costs throughout the project's life. While Chapter 14 discussed the difficulty of estimating cash flows, inflation can make the task seem especially difficult.

Example 15.3 ————— Let's first consider inflation in the context of personal finance—the retirement decision faced by independent business owners Matthew and Jennifer Fairmont. The Fairmonts have worked all their adult lives owning and operating a clothing store and building its reputation and clientele. The couple's only other asset is their house. Everything that they have earned they have reinvested in the store or have spent raising their children. As they both approach age 62, they begin to question whether they can sell the business and retire.

The Fairmonts are sure of two things. First, they know they can sell the store for $650,000. Second, as they think about their retirement life-style, they know that they must supplement their social security benefits by about $30,000 per year, or $2,500 per month, based upon today's prices.

The Fairmonts have learned that they can use the $650,000 proceeds from the sale of the business to purchase a retirement annuity that will pay them $66,092 per year as long as either of them lives. The annuity is based upon a life expectancy of 30 years and an interest rate of 9.5 percent. The calculations of the annuity are shown in Table 15.1.

As shown, the retirement question can be solved by applying the present value of the annuity formula first presented in Chapter 5. The couple knows the present value of their funds ($650,000), has estimated the amount of time they wish to draw on these funds (30 years), and the rate of interest these funds can earn in the bank throughout their retirement (9.5%). The annuity formula is used to solve for the annuity amount, or $66,092.

The Fairmonts' financial problem appears to have been solved, since the annuity amount of $66,092 per year greatly exceeds their annual cash needs of $30,000. But the analysis has yet to consider inflation. What if high inflation occurs such that the fixed annuity of $66,092 per year purchases less and less each year? Could inflation make $66,092 a poverty level of income? ↵

The Mathematics of Inflation

The tools of Chapter 4 allow for an analysis of the effects of inflation. As discussed in Chapter 3, price indexes are regularly computed using current prices to reflect the changing costs of overall purchases. Inflation is expressed using rates of growth. Mathematically speaking, the growth rate of inflation acts like the interest rate in present and future value analysis. For example, if on January 1 the price index stood at 100.0 and on December 31 the price index stood at 106.2, inflation, expressed as π, is 6.2 percent:

$$106.2 = 100(1 + \pi) \longrightarrow (1 + \pi) = 106.2/100 \longrightarrow \pi = .062.$$

We can calculate the rate of inflation over various intervals by inserting the starting value price index as PV, the ending value price index as FV, the number of years as N, and solving for the interest rate. For example, returning to the Fairmonts, we can readdress their

TABLE 15.1
The Fairmonts' Retirement Annuity

The Facts

Retirement nest egg = $650,000
Length of time of the investment = 30 years
Interest rate to be earned = 9.5%

The Problem

How much can they spend, per year, from their retirement nest egg?

The Procedure

Apply the present value of the annuity formula:

$$PVA = \text{Annuity} \left[\frac{1}{r} - \frac{1}{r(1 + r)^n} \right]$$

$$\$650,000 = \text{Annuity} \left[\frac{1}{.095} - \frac{1}{.095(1.095)^{30}} \right]$$

$$\$650,000 = \text{Annuity} \left[9.8347 \right]$$

$$\text{Annuity} = \$650,000 / 9.8347$$

$$\text{Annuity} = \$66,092$$

retirement income in the context of inflation. What rate of inflation, say over ten years, would turn their $66,092 annuity into the same purchasing power as the $30,000 of income they desire in today's dollars? This can be found by solving the present value formula for the rate of return:

$$\$66,092 = \$30,000(1 + \pi)^{10}$$

$$(1 + \pi)^{10} = \$66,092/\$30,000$$

$$\pi = 2.2031^{1/10} - 1 = 0.0082.$$

This means that if 8.22 percent inflation occurred each year for ten years,[3] the purchasing power of the Fairmonts' income would decline to the same level of purchasing power as $30,000 today. In other words, $66,092 of income ten years from now would be approximately

---

3. We can analyze inflation's effect on purchasing power over periods other than ten years. For instance, for time periods of 20 years and 25 years, the inflation rate that would reduce the purchasing power of $66,092 to $30,000 would have to be 4.03 percent and 3.21 percent respectively.

equiva'ent to $30,000 of income today if inflation were 8.22 percent per year. A higher rate of inflation would push the purchasing power of the Fairmonts' income below $30,000, so that their retirement goal would not be achieved.

Do the Fairmonts need to be concerned with the level of inflation that will occur over their retirement? As we will see, they can protect their retirement income from inflation rather well if they rely on the tendency of interest rates to adjust to the level of inflation.

Interest Rates and the Fisher Effect

In the late 1970s, inflation was causing prices to rise at over 10 percent per year. The dollar you held in your hand on January 1 would buy 10 percent less of most goods and services by December 31 of the same year. Lenders who had lent money to borrowers at interest rates of less than 10 percent found that their money wasn't growing fast enough to keep up with inflation; it was actually declining in value.

Fisher effect
A theory of interest rates stating that the nominal interest rate is composed of the real interest rate plus the expected inflation rate.

A property of interest rates called the Fisher effect became abundantly clear as people adjusted to the unprecedented levels of inflation in the United States. The **Fisher effect** states that the market interest rate can be separated into a real rate of interest and an expected inflation rate. Fisher called the market interest rate the nominal interest rate. It is the nominal rate that we usually use for computing present values.

real rate of interest
The interest rate earned after removing the effects of inflation.

The **real rate of interest** is the rate earned after the effects of inflation, and it reflects purchasing power rather than dollars. When economists use the term "real" they are referring to true purchasing power rather than numbers influenced by inflation. Given the concept of the real rate of interest, the Fisher effect is expressed as:[4]

$$\text{Nominal Rate} = \text{Real Rate} + \text{Expected Inflation Rate}. \quad (15.1)$$

Although it may take a little time for interest rates to adjust, generally speaking, the nominal interest rate adjusts to reflect inflationary expectations.

----

4. Formula (15.1) is really just an approximation and comes from the more precise formula:

$$(1 + \text{Nominal Rate}) = (1 + \text{Real Rate}) * (1 + \text{Expected Inflation Rate}).$$

This formula differs from Formula (15.1) by including a cross-product term between the real rate and inflation rate. The cross product term is usually ignored, which makes the simple addition of the "real" rate with the expected inflation rate to get the nominal rate an approximation.

Estimating the Real Rate of Interest

From the Fisher effect, the real rate of interest is the nominal rate minus the expected rate of inflation. The real rate of interest is the price of borrowing and lending (with inflation removed). Although prices change in response to supply and demand, some argue that the real rate of interest is relatively stable and that it tends to range around two to three percent.

In other words, when there is a very low rate of inflation, such as one or two percent per year, we would expect nominal interest rates to be four or five percent. This is confirmed by applying the Fisher effect shown in Formula (15.1)—adding together the real interest rate and the expected inflation rate. During periods of high inflation, such as ten percent, we would expect that interest rates would rise to twelve or thirteen percent.

Using the Fisher Effect in Investment Decisions

Remember that the typical investment decision is made by discounting estimated future cash flows by market interest rates:

$$NPV = C_0 + \frac{CF_1}{(1 + r)^1} + \frac{CF_2}{(1 + r)^2} + \cdots + \frac{CF_n}{(1 + r)^n}.$$

Inflation can be viewed as having two effects on the above equation. First, inflation will cause the estimated cash flows to increase through time as the prices underlying the cash flows rise. Second, inflation is viewed as being a component of the interest rate, or r in the NPV formula.

For simplicity, let's look at cash flows of an investment that are expected to rise only by the inflation rate. We express this by inserting the inflation rate, given by π, into the numerator of the NPV formula above. Second, we replace the nominal interest rate in the NPV formula with its components, according to the precise form of the Fisher effect:

$$NPV = C_0 + \frac{CF(1 + \pi)}{(1 + \text{real})(1 + \pi)} + \frac{CF(1 + \pi)^2}{(1 + \text{real})^2(1 + \pi)^2}$$

$$+ \cdots + \frac{CF(1 + \pi)^n}{(1 + \text{real})^n(1 + \pi)^n}, \tag{15.2}$$

where CF stands for real cash flows, and real is the real rate of interest.

Notice that the expected inflation rate appears in both the numerator and the denominator of Formula (15.2). Thus, the terms containing the expected inflation rate cancel out and the formula can be rewritten as:

$$NPV = C_0 + \frac{CF}{(1 + \text{real})^1} + \frac{CF}{(1 + \text{real})^2} + \cdots + \frac{CF}{(1 + \text{real})^n}.$$

Rather than performing the analysis in actual or nominal dollars and with nominal interest rates, the analysis can be performed as if inflation did not exist. This is accomplished by using real dollars in the numerator, which is equivalent to estimating future cash flows as if inflation did not exist. The second step is to use the real rate of interest in the denominator—around two percent or three percent.

Example 15.4 _____ Let's return to the Fairmonts' retirement decision and attempt to simplify the analysis, using real numbers. As discussed above, the Fairmonts, like everyone else, are very uncertain as to what the inflation rate will be over the next 30 years. However, they do expect that they will need $30,000 per year measured in today's dollars (i.e., in terms of today's prices). The Fairmonts can obtain an estimate of the dollar amount needed today to meet their retirement needs by working with "real" cash flows and a "real" interest rate of, say, 2.5 percent. The amount needed to be invested today in order to be able to spend $30,000 in today's purchasing power for 30 years can be determined, through the annuity formula, by supplying the annuity amount ($30,000), the interest rate (2.5%), and the time period (30 years) and solving for the present value of the annuity:

$$\text{Fairmonts' Need in } PV = \$30,000 * \left[\frac{1}{.025} - \frac{1}{.025(1.025)^{30}} \right]$$

$$= \$627,909.$$

Since the Fairmonts anticipate having $650,000 of cash when they sell their business, it looks as if they'll be able to fund their retirement needs regardless of the actual subsequent inflation rate. They simply need to keep their money in short-term, very low-risk investments that will offer a return of around two to three percent above the current inflation rate. If the inflation rate rises dramatically, the cash needs of the Fairmonts will also rise. However, by investing their money short term, the Fairmonts will be able to reinvest at the new, higher interest rates caused by inflation and will, therefore, be able to meet both the expenses caused by higher prices and the need to reinvest money to keep up with inflation. ↵

Adjusting for Inflation in a Corporate Context

Corporate investment decisions need to incorporate inflation appropriately. As demonstrated in the retirement example, there are two ways to treat inflation: (1) use nominal dollar values along with nominal interest rates, or (2) use real dollars along with real interest rates.

Nominal decisions, the more common approach, use estimates of cash flows and interest rates that have the effects of inflation added into them. The key to implementing this approach is to make sure that the cash flows are estimated using the same inflation rate that is implied by the discount rate.

Real decisions estimate cash flows using today's dollars and apply a much lower interest rate, the real interest rate, as the discount rate. Economists estimate the real interest rate to be approximately two to three percent before risk adjustment. Thus, the effects of inflation are subtracted out of both the numerator and the denominator. Long-term decisions such as those concerning retirement can sometimes be more accurately estimated using the latter technique.

CAPITAL RATIONING

Our final advanced topic in capital budgeting is capital rationing. As discussed in Chapter 6, capital rationing is the concept that a firm limits the amount of money it will invest in new projects. Modernists look skeptically at capital rationing, believing that firms reject positive-*NPV* projects not because of a lack of funding, but because of hidden costs such as the inability of management to oversee excessive growth efficiently. Therefore, what appears to be a worthwhile project would in actuality put a strain on the firm's resources such that firm value would decline. Nevertheless, capital rationing is often argued to limit investment, and it is discussed in detail in this section.

Capital Rationing and the Profitability Index

One approach to solving this problem is to rely on the profitability index. As discussed in Chapter 6, the profitability index expresses the *NPV* of the project as a proportion by dividing the *PV* of the cash inflows by the immediate cash outflows. Because *NPV* is measured as a proportion of its cost, the profitability index is reasoned to be the ideal way to rank projects when there is a need to ration capital.

Example 15.5 ——————— Consider United Piano, a firm built on a successful history in the musical instrument industry but which in later years expanded into other fields such as financial services. The firm has $100 million of investment capital available for projects

TABLE 15.2
A List of Prospective Projects for United Piano

Project	Investment (in millions)	NPV (in millions)
A	$ 50	$20
B	$ 20	$ 5
C	$ 20	$ 4
D	$ 50	$12
E	$ 70	$ 6
F	$ 10	$ 2
G	$ 25	$ 1
Total	$245	$50

that it considers worthwhile. The financial managers of the firm's various divisions have compiled the list of prospective projects shown in Table 15.2.

If each project were funded, the cost of investment would be $245 million. However, the firm will invest only up to $100 million. How does the firm decide which projects to accept?

Using the profitability index, United Piano's projects would be ranked as shown in Table 15.3. According to the profitability index, the financial manager should begin with the highest ranked project and accept lower and lower ranked projects until the capital has been fully allocated. In the example above, the firm would accept Projects A and B (because

TABLE 15.3
A Ranking of United Piano's Projects Using the Profitability Index

Project	Profitability Index	Rank	Cost (in millions)	NPV (in millions)
A	1.40	1	$50	$20
B	1.25	2	$20	$ 5
C	1.20	4–5	$20	$ 4
D	1.24	3	$50	$12
E	1.09	6	$70	$ 6
F	1.20	4–5	$10	$ 2
G	1.04	7	$25	$ 1

Amount of capital to invest = $100 million
Decision: Invest in project A ($50 million invested, $50 million left)
         Invest in project B ($20 million invested, $30 million left)
         Bypass project D as not enough capital is available
         Invest in project C ($20 million invested, $10 million left)
         Invest in project F ($10 million invested, $0 million left)

they are ranked first and second) but would then find that there would be insufficient funds to accept Project D (which is ranked third). The firm might add Projects C and F so that all $100 million is used.

Unfortunately, this list of acceptable projects would not maximize *NPV*. In this case, the total of the *NPV*s of Projects A, B, C, and F is $31 million. The firm would be better off skipping Project B and investing in only Projects A and D for a total *NPV* of $32 million. ↵

In summary, the profitability index is a simple but imperfect attempt to solve the capital rationing problem. The problem is that projects typically must be either fully accepted or fully rejected—they cannot be partially accepted. A better approach is a procedure known as integer linear programming. The integer linear programming model as it applies to United Piano is presented in the chapter appendix. Integer linear programming is a rather sophisticated solution to the problem of capital rationing. However, as with all the techniques discussed in Chapter 15, there are times when simple *NPV* analysis is insufficient.

SUMMARY

☐ In the simplest model of the firm, the financial manager makes investment decisions by selecting those projects with a positive *NPV*. In theory, *NPV* can be used to solve any problem because it includes all costs and benefits.

☐ In practice, several more advanced tools of *NPV* analysis have been developed to solve common complexities. The problem of unequal lives for projects that can be replicated or projects whose completion would enable acceptance of other equally attractive alternatives can be solved using the equivalent annuity method. The financial manager simply converts the *NPV* of each alternative into an annuity based upon each project's life span. The annuities are then compared directly.

☐ Some problems that produce highly similar benefits can be compared on a least-cost basis. The alternative with the lower total present value of costs is usually the best. In cases of unequal lives, it is usually necessary to convert the costs into equivalent annuities.

☐ Inflation affects the future cash flows of a project and is difficult to estimate. If nominal values are used, the financial manager should be careful that both the cash flows and discount rates reflect a similar inflation expectation. In some long-term decisions it may be useful to estimate cash flows and discount rates as real numbers. Real numbers subtract out the effects of inflation as if the inflation rate were zero.

☐ Capital rationing can be nicely solved using a technique known as integer linear programming. Through this technique, illustrated in the chapter appendix, virtually all common aspects of capital rationing problems can be easily modeled and solved.

DEMONSTRATION PROBLEMS

Problem 1 Lafayette Corporation is considering two mutually exclusive projects with unequal lives. Lafayette anticipates being able to repeat each project each time it is completed. The cash flows are given as:

Cash Inflows for Each Year

Name	Cost	Year 1	Year 2	Year 3	Year 4	Year 5
Danny	−$10,000	+$9,000	+$7,000	+$0	+$0	+$0
Arnold	−$8,000	+$8,000	+$2,000	+$2,000	+$2,000	+$2,000

First, compute the simple net present values and the internal rates of return. Then use the equivalent annuity approach in order to select the best project. Assume that the required rate of return for each project is 12%.

Solution to Problem 1

There are three separate analyses to be performed: simple *NPV*, *IRR*, and the equivalent annuity approach. These will be demonstrated in steps 1 through 3, respectively.

Step 1: Compute the simple *NPV*s by discounting all the cash flows at 12% and summing them. Project Danny has *NPV* = $3,616.07 and Project Arnold has *NPV* = $4,566.70. These answers were found using the simple time value of money techniques of Chapter 6. Note that, according to simple *NPV* analysis, Project Arnold seems better since it has a higher *NPV*.

Step 2: Compute the internal rates of return using the techniques of Chapter 6. In other words, use a trial and error search for each project to find the discount rate that sets *NPV* = $0. Project Danny has *IRR* = 40% and Project Arnold has *IRR* = 43.76%. According to simple *IRR* analysis, Project Arnold appears better.

Step 3: Now compute the equivalent annuities taking into account that Project Danny is a two-year project while Project Arnold is a five-year project. Equivalent annuities are formed by transforming the given *NPV*s into annuity streams that have the same present value.

This is especially easy using financial calculators. For each project, we input the length in years, the interest rate of 12%, the *NPV* as the present value, and compute the annuity amount:

Project Danny: = $3,616.07, N = 2, %I = 12, *CPT PMT*.

The answer is $2,139.62.

Project Arnold: = $4,566.70, N = 5, %I = 12, *CPT PMT*.

The answer is $1,266.85.

Final Solution: The equivalent annuity method demonstrates that Project Danny is superior since its annuity amount is $2,139.62 per year while Project Arnold's is only $1,266.85 per year. ⏎

Problem 2   Lafayette Corporation also struggles with a question of whether to use high-quality vehicles for their fleet that cost more to purchase but less to operate. The cash costs of each type of vehicle are given as follows:

Name	Initial Cost	Year 1	Cash Outflows for Each Year Year 2	Year 3	Year 4
High quality	-$16,000	-$1,000	-$2,000	-$3,000	-$4,000
Low quality	-$12,000	-$2,000	-$3,000	-$4,000	-$6,000

Compute the least-cost vehicle using a discount rate of 15%.

Solution to Problem 2

Step 1: Since both projects involve equal-length lives, this is a simple analysis of which of the two projects has the lower total present value of costs. Notice that all of the cash flows are costs. Thus they should all be added together rather than netted from each other.

Step 2: Present-value all the costs from the high-quality alternative and sum them:

$$PV = -\$16,000 - \$1,000/1.15^1 - \$2,000/1.15^2$$
$$-\$3,000/1.15^3 - \$4,000/1.15^4$$
$$PV = -\$22,641.41$$

Step 3: Present-value all the costs from the low-quality alternative and sum them:

$$PV = -\$12,000 - \$2,000/1.15^1 - \$3,000/1.15^2$$
$$-\$4,000/1.15^3 - \$6,000/1.15^4$$
$$PV = -\$22,068.15$$

Step 4: Since our objective is to minimize costs, the project with the smallest present value should be selected.

Final Solution: Select the low-quality alternative with the smallest total present value of costs: $22,068.15. ↵

REVIEW QUESTIONS

1. Why are some sets of projects mutually exclusive while others are not?
2. How does the *NPV* rule dictate a choice among mutually exclusive projects when projects cannot be repeated?
3. Why might it be true that a project with a lower *NPV* is preferred to a project with a higher *NPV*?
4. How does the equivalent annual annuity approach help solve the unequal lives problem?
5. True or false: Accepting a project with an *NPV* of $1 million has the same effect as the firm receiving a $1 million gift today.
6. How does the equivalent annuity approach differ from the common ending period approach?
7. What is the Fisher effect?
8. Distinguish between the real rate of interest and the nominal rate of interest.
9. Provide an estimate of the real rate of interest.
10. Should firms use nominal or real dollars in capital budgeting?
11. What is capital rationing?
12. Explain how the profitability index is used to solve the ranking problem.
13. [Based on Chapter Appendix] What is integer linear programming?
14. [Based on Chapter Appendix] What is the purpose of the objective function and the constraints in the integer linear programming model?

PROBLEMS

1. Project Jethro has an *NPV* of $100,000 and is expected to last four years. Using a discount rate of 10%, convert this *NPV* into an equivalent annuity.
2. Using a discount rate of 12%, convert the following *NPV*s to equivalent annuities based upon the project lives.
   a. Project Carter with an *NPV* of $10,000 lasting one year.
   b. Project Reagan with an *NPV* of $25,000 lasting two years.
   c. Project Roosevelt with an *NPV* of $30,000 lasting four years.

d. If the White House Corporation can select only one of the projects and if the corporation believes that there will be opportunities to begin new projects with similar *NPV*s once a project terminates, which of the projects should be accepted? Why?

3. Project Enquirer has an *NPV* of $875,000 and is expected to last five years. Project Star has an *NPV* of $1,225,000 and is expected to last seven years. Both projects have a discount rate of 15%. Use the equivalent annuity approach to determine which project should be accepted.

4. Bundy Corporation has two projects under consideration which would use the same facilities and management team: Project Al and Project Peg. The cash flows of the projects are given as follows:

Project Name	Initial Cost	Cash Inflows			
		Year 1	Year 2	Year 3	Year 4
Al	10,000	7,000	6,000		
Peg	20,000	8,000	9,000	10,000	12,000

Bundy Corporation realizes that the shorter life of Project Al would be an advantage because it would enable the firm to begin another profitable project quicker than if Project Peg were accepted, since Project Peg takes longer to finish. Both projects have a discount rate of 10%. Use the equivalent annuity approach to determine which project should be accepted.

5. Island Corporation has two projects under consideration, both of which fill the same niche in its product line: Project Thomas and Project Croix. The cash flows of the projects are given as follows:

Project Name	Initial Cost	Cash Inflows		
		Year 1	Year 2	Year 3
Thomas	200,000	90,000	160,000	
Croix	200,000	80,000	90,000	190,000

Island Corporation asks you to select the better project using the equivalent annuity approach. Both projects have a discount rate of 8%. Determine which project should be accepted.

6. Paterno Corporation specializes in building production facilities in cold and remote locations. The production facilities manufacture equipment used to reel in fishing lines and nets (known as linebackers in the industry). The firm is considering two projects for which it has been asked to work. The first project, labeled "Ground," would involve shipping materials by ground and would take four years to complete. The other project, labeled "Air," would be much quicker but more expensive. The cash flows are given as:

Project Name	Initial Cost	Year 1	Cash Inflows Year 2	Year 3	Year 4
Ground	800,000	300,000	300,000	400,000	500,000
Air	2,000,000	2,000,000	900,000		

Select the better project using the equivalent annuity approach. Both projects have a discount rate of 12%.

7. Three alternatives produce identical benefits to the firm but have the following costs:

Project Name	Initial Cost	Year 1 Cost	Year 2 Cost	Year 3 Cost	Year 4 Cost
A	100,000	10,000	10,000	10,000	10,000
B	120,000	8,000	6,000	4,000	2,000
C	40,000	40,000	40,000	40,000	40,000

Using a discount rate of 14%, compute the total present value of each alternative. Which is cheapest?

8. Jordan Airlines is considering two alternatives for maintaining its fleet of small private jets. The first alternative is to contract with a major airline to perform the necessary maintenance for an annual cost of $1,200,000. The second alternative is for Jordan to construct its own facilities and establish its own maintenance program. The second, "do-it-yourself" alternative will cost less each year (only $500,000) but has large costs to get started—management estimates that it will involve an initial investment of $9,000,000. The time horizon of the problem is 20 years, because by that time a new fleet of jets will be purchased and the facilities and program will have to be completely revised. Which alternative has the lowest present value of costs, given a 13% discount rate?

9. Rose Resorts is debating which type of slot machine to buy for its new casino in Atlantic City. There are two types, a high-quality model that costs $12,000 and is expected to require $1,500 per year of maintenance and a low-quality model that costs $8,000 and is expected to require $2,000 per year in maintenance. Both machines are expected to last ten years. Using a discount rate of 15%, compute the total present value of the costs of the two alternatives.

10. Three alternatives produce identical benefits to the firm but have unequal lives and different costs:

Project Name	Initial Cost	Year 1 Cost	Year 2 Cost	Year 3 Cost	Year 4 Cost
Short	100,000	10,000	10,000		
Medium	160,000	10,000	8,000	6,000	
Long	200,000	40,000	40,000	40,000	40,000

Using a discount rate of 10%, compute the total present value of each alternative and then convert them into equivalent annuity costs. Which is cheapest?

11. Returning to problem 9, if Rose Resorts determines that the high-quality machine would last 15 years and that the low-quality machine would last only 10 years (with initial costs and annual maintenance costs unchanged), which machine would have the lower equivalent annuity cost?

12. Shark Entertainment Corporation has two alternatives under consideration that would provide major entertainment and considerable benefit to the firm. The benefits of the alternatives are equal, but their lives and costs are different. One alternative, code-named "Transfer," will last two years. The second alternative, code-named "Senior," will last four years. The costs of each of the projects are given as follows:

Project Name	Initial Cost	Costs			
		Year 1	Year 2	Year 3	Year 4
Transfer	100,000	90,000	160,000		
Senior	50,000	80,000	120,000	180,000	240,000

Shark Entertainment Corporation asks you to select the better project using the equivalent annuity approach. Both projects have a discount rate of 15%. Determine which should be accepted.

13. Inflation rates can be computed for overall indexes or for individual items. Compute the inflation rate implied by each of the following pairs of prices:

Item	Year	Price	Year	Price
Consumer price index	1940	42.0	1950	72.1
Consumer price index	1950	72.1	1960	88.7
Consumer price index	1960	88.7	1970	116.3
Consumer price index	1970	116.3	1980	246.8
Consumer price index	1980	246.8	1990	385.0
Milk	1965	$1.00	1990	$2.25
Gasoline	1965	$0.35	1990	$1.25
Beer	1975	$1.25	1990	$3.00
House	1950	$5,000	1990	$125,000
Computer	1985	$5,000	1990	$2,000
Tuition (public)	1975	$2,000	1990	$4,000

14. Use the approximate formula for the Fisher effect given in Formula (15.1) to determine the missing values:

	Nominal Rate	Real Rate	Expected Inflation Rate
a.	_____	3%	5%
b.	_____	2%	15%
c.	10%	4%	_____
d.	8%	_____	6%

15. Use the precise formula for the Fisher effect given below in order to revise your answers:

$$(1 + \text{Nominal}) = (1 + \text{Real}) \times (1 + \text{Expected Inflation})$$

	Nominal Rate	Real Rate	Expected Inflation Rate
a.	_____	3%	5%
b.	_____	2%	15%
c.	10%	4%	_____
d.	8%	_____	6%

16. Keuka Corporation is considering a project that costs $1,000,000 and will produce benefits for five years. The first year cash inflow can be rather accurately estimated at $240,000, measured in today's dollars. If the actual first- through fifth-year cash flows are assumed to be the same size ($240,000), what would the *NPV* of the investment be if the appropriate discount rate is 15%?

17. Return to Keuka Corporation in problem 16. Now assume that the cash inflow will rise each year with inflation. Assume that the inflation rate is 10%. Thus the first-year cash inflow will be found by multiplying the $240,000 by (1 + 10%) to obtain $264,000. After the first-year cash inflow of $264,000, each cash inflow is expected to rise by another 10%. Compute:
   a. The second-year cash inflow = _____
   b. The third-year cash inflow = _____
   c. The fourth-year cash inflow = _____
   d. The fifth-year cash inflow   = _____
   (Hint: Each cash inflow must be determined by applying the inflation rate to the previous year's cash inflow.)
   e. Now compute the *NPV* using the cash inflows above, the original project cost of $1,000,000, and the discount rate of 15%.
   f. Why did the *NPV* change relative to problem 16?
   g. Which computation of *NPV* is more reliable?

18. Returning once again to Keuka Corporation (problem 16), let's compute the *NPV* using real cash flows and real interest rates. Thus we use the original cash flow estimate of $240,000 for each of the five years. To start, we approximate the real rate of interest by subtracting the inflation rate (10%) from the nominal interest rate (15%) and obtaining 5%.
   a. Compute the *NPV* using these real cash flows and the real discount rate (5%).
   b. Compute the *NPV* using the real cash flows and a discount rate of 4.55%.
   c. Can you verify that the discount rate used in 18(b) is found by computing the real rate of interest using the precise form of the Fisher effect?

    d. Ignoring rounding errors, compare your answers to 16, 17(e), 18(a), and 18(b). Which is (are) correct?

19. Brooksmel Corporation is considering offering a pension alternative to its employees that is indexed to inflation. In other words, each employee would receive a pension that is increased each year in order to keep up with the inflation rate as measured by the consumer price index. Of course, employees who opt for this plan would have to be willing to accept a lower starting pension. Brooksmel's CFO is attempting to compute the cost of this pension to the firm. Consider Gene, who has worked for Brooksmel for years and is considering retirement soon. For math simplification, consider that Gene's life expectancy is only 8 years.

    a. Compute the present value of Gene's pension if he opts for a fixed pension of $8,000 per year and the interest rate is 10%.

    b. If Gene opts for a pension indexed to inflation, his "base pension" would be $5,000. All of his actual receipts would be higher than this figure and would depend upon the inflation rate. For example, if the inflation rate is 5%, his first-year pension would be $5,250, which is found by multiplying $5,000 by (1 + 5%). If the inflation rate continues at 5%, his second-year pension would be $5,512.50, and so forth. Project his eight annual pension receipts, assuming that the inflation rate starts and stays at 6%.

    c. Now let's solve the problem in real terms. Compute the present value of Gene's pension using a fixed annual cash flow of $5,000 and a discount rate of 4%. This approximate real rate of interest was found by subtracting the 6% inflation rate from the nominal interest rate of 10%.

    d. In order to obtain an exact solution, find the real rate of interest using the precise form of the Fisher effect and solve 19(c) again with the new rate.

20. Plastex Corporation is considering expanding but wishes to control growth by imposing a limit on capital expenditures of $500,000. The capital investment opportunities are given as follows:

Investment Opportunities of Plastex Corporation
(all dollar values are in thousands)

Project	Cost	NPV	Profitability Index	PI Rank	First-Year Cash Flow
1	$200	$50	1.25	1	$ 0
2	$200	$40	1.20	5	$ 5
3	$400	$99	1.2475	2	$10
4	$100	$17	1.17	7	$ 2
5	$100	$19	1.19	6	$ 3
6	$ 50	$12	1.24	3	$20
7	$ 50	$11	1.22	4	$15

a. Use the profitability index to select projects subject to the constraint that the firm can only invest $500,000. In other words, use the *PI* ranking to accept the best project, the next-best project, and so forth until the money is completely used. If a project's cost brings the total cost over the $500,000 limit while money remains, then skip the project and attempt to add a cheaper one.

b. Compute the total of the *NPV*s of the projects selected above.

c. Use your common sense to figure out a better solution—one that produces a higher total *NPV* but still uses only $500,000. Compute the sum of the *NPV*s of this better solution.

d. Why do the answers to (a) and (c) differ and why is the profitability index method flawed?

21. [Based on Chapter Appendix] Using the following notation:

NPV_i = the net present value of Project i,

X_i = the decision variable produced by the software, which has a value of 1 if the project should be accepted and 0 if it should be rejected,

C_{0i} = initial cost of Project i, and

C_{ti} = cash inflow (+) or outflow (−) in period T for Project i.

a. Express the objective function of problem 20.

b. Express the constraint that all the initial costs of the accepted projects must be less than or equal to $500,000.

c. Express the constraint that all the first-year cash flows of the accepted projects must add together to be at least $25,000.

d. Express the constraint that Projects 3 and 4 use the same facilities, so only one of them can be accepted.

e. Express the constraint that the company is required by previous contracts to produce a certain good, which means that the company must accept either Project 4 or 5 (or both).

f. Express the constraint that no more than three projects can be accepted from the group of projects which require supervisors (Projects 3 through 7).

22. [Based on Chapter Appendix] Use integer linear programming software to solve for the optimal solution to problem 20 without incorporating any of the additional constraints in problem 21.

DISCUSSION QUESTIONS

1. If *NPV* has as many difficulties as discussed in this chapter, why shouldn't we learn a different capital budgeting method?

2. Why is it said that using the equivalent annuity method implicitly assumes project replication?
3. In least-cost problems, the present values are always negative. Why would any firm accept a decision when the cash flows are all negative?
4. [Based on Chapter Appendix] When would normal linear programming be a better solution than integer linear programming for the capital rationing problem?
5. What is the exact formula for the error introduced by using the approximation for the real interest rate in the Fisher effect equation?
6. It is said that, when using continuously compounded interest rates, the Fisher effect is given exactly by the equation:

   Nominal Interest Rate = Inflation Rate + Real Interest Rate

   Why would this be true?

APPENDIX

Integer Linear Programming

A mathematical technique known as *integer linear programming* is ideally suited for solving the capital rationing problem. Once the problem is set up, the power of a computer can be used to search for those projects that should be accepted or rejected. Projects that are acceptable are assigned a value of one, while projects that are rejected are assigned a value of zero. The word "integer" refers to the technique's ability to accept a project in total or reject the project. In other words, the technique will not allow some fraction of the project to be accepted while some fraction is rejected. This is ideal for our problem.

We illustrate the technique of integer linear programming using the variables X_1 through X_n, where X_1 signals whether Project One should be accepted, X_2 signals whether Project Two should be accepted, and so forth. When X_1 is assigned the value of one, Project One is accepted. When X_1 is assigned the value of zero, Project One is rejected, and so forth.

THE MODEL'S OBJECTIVE FUNCTION

We first state the objective of the problem. For United Piano (Example 15.5), the objective is to select the combination of projects that produces the highest total *NPV*. The total of the *NPV*s is determined by multiplying each project's *NPV* by its decision variable ($X_i = 1$ to accept, $X_i = 0$ to reject) and summing them:

$$\text{Maximize} \sum_i NPV_i * X_i .$$

The purpose of the technique is to compute which projects should be accepted and which projects should be rejected by setting their decision variable, X_i, to either one or zero. Notice that the equation above adds together the *NPV*s of all the accepted projects, since acceptable projects have a value of X_i equal to one, while unacceptable projects have a value of X_i equal to zero.

The equation above is known as an objective function, since it expresses what the user of the model wants to optimize—in this case the sum of the *NPV*s of the accepted projects.

THE MODEL'S CONSTRAINTS

The integer linear programming model also needs constraints to be placed on the decision variables. Constraints are equations that place limits on the values of the decision variables. Without constraints, the model would accept all projects with positive *NPV*s.

First, linear programming automatically restricts each decision variable to be greater than or equal to zero:

Constraint One: $X_i \geq 0$, for all projects.

Next, we would usually restrict each of the *X*s to be less than or equal to one, since it would be rare that we would have a project that we would be able to accept more than one time.

Constraint Two: $X_i \leq 1$, for all projects.

Since integer linear programming restricts the *X* variables to integer values, the two sets of constraints listed above force the *X*s to have a value of either one (acceptance) or zero (rejection).

We now can address the issue of capital rationing directly. United Piano's problem is that they have only $100 million to invest. We can express this constraint by requiring that the solution have initial cash flows that spend no more than the budgeted amount:

$$\text{Constraint Three: } \sum_i X_i * C_{0i} \geq -\$100{,}000{,}000,$$

where C_{0i} is the initial cash flow (C_0) of Project i. Thus the total initial costs of all accepted projects, given by summing $\{X_i * C_{0i}\}$, must not exceed in absolute value the amount specified by the user. Since the cash flows are negative, we constrain the sum to be greater than a negative number. In other words, the sum must be less negative than the budgeted number.

The objective functions and constraints mentioned above would guide the computer program into providing the optimal solution to the simplified typical capital rationing problem.

OTHER CONSTRAINTS

One important advantage of using integer linear programming to solve capital rationing problems is that many other potential restrictions can be easily incorporated.

For large projects it would be common for cash flows to be negative for several years. Thus the financial manager might want to restrict the sum of the cash flows across projects to be no less than a certain amount in each of the first few years. For example, to constrain the projects to cost no more than $10 million in the first year, to break even by the second year, and to produce a cash inflow of $20 million by the third year, the financial manager would include the following constraints:

$$\text{Constraint Four: } \sum_i X_i * C_{1i} \geq -\$10,000,000,$$

$$\text{Constraint Five: } \sum_i X_i * C_{2i} \geq \$0,$$

$$\text{Constraint Six : } \sum_i X_i * C_{3i} \geq \$20,000,000.$$

Other potential constraints could be that certain combinations of projects could not be accepted together. Projects sharing the same building, personnel, or product niche might have to be limited so that only one of them would be accepted. For example, if Projects A and B were mutually exclusive because they required the same building, we would impose the following constraint:

$$\text{Constraint Seven: } X_A + X_B \leq 1.$$

If only two of the projects C, D, and E could be accepted because they used the same personnel, we would impose the following constraint:

$$\text{Constraint Eight: } X_C + X_D + X_E \leq 2.$$

Finally, perhaps market research or agreements with customers would require that the firm continue to supply at least one of the products produced by certain projects such that at least one of projects B and C has to be accepted:

$$\text{Constraint Nine: } X_B + X_C \geq 1.$$

Other constraints could be included to consider project interaction.

A SUMMARY OF INTEGER LINEAR PROGRAMMING

Integer linear programming is a powerful answer to the problems of capital rationing and project interactions. With the widespread availability of personal computers and the increasing ability and willingness of financial managers to use them, it is clear that integer linear programming is destined to become the standard technique.

TABLE 15.4
The Integer Linear Programming Model

The Problem

United Piano must decide which of the seven projects in Table 15.2 (page 482) to invest in.
United Piano cannot invest more than $100 million.

The Basic Model

Objective function: Maximize $\sum_i NPV_i * X_i$, subject to the following constraints:

$X_i \geq 0$, for all projects.
$X_i \leq 1$, for all projects.
$\sum_i X_i * C_{0i} \geq -\$100,000,000$.

The More Advanced Model

Objective function: Maximize $\sum_i NPV_i * X_i$, subject to the following contraints:

$X_i \geq 0$, for all projects.
$X_i \leq 1$, for all projects.
$\sum_i X_i * C_{0i} \geq -\$100,000,000,$

$\sum_i X_i * C_{1i} \geq -\$10,000,000,$

$\sum_i X_i * C_{2i} \geq 0,$

$\sum_i X_i * C_{3i} \geq \$20,000,000,$

$X_A + X_B \leq 1,$
$X_C + X_D + X_E \leq 2,$
$X_B + X_C \geq 1.$

This appendix demonstrates how the integer linear programming model can be used in a business situation. The complete integer linear programming model is shown in Table 15.4. Given the model's objective function and its series of constraints, the computer will find the ideal set of projects that maximizes *NPV*.

Chapter 16

Financial Analysis and Planning

Prerequisites: Chapters 1 through 6

It has been a busy day at Points of Light, Inc. (POL, Inc.), the nation's only manufacturer of points of light. As part of the firm's ambitious growth program, top management has placed a large order for raw materials, applied for a bank loan, decided to whom to offer a job as an assistant treasurer, and met with a potential new investor. Tomorrow will be a new day during which top management can tackle another set of decisions and responsibilities.

However, each of today's actions has set a number of people in motion to perform the challenging task of financial analysis. The firm that received the order for materials from POL, Inc., the bank that received their loan application, the woman who was offered the job, and the potential new investor all must make important decisions regarding how to contract with POL, Inc.

The consequences of poor financial analysis could be disastrous. To the raw materials supplier it might mean delivery of materials for which the supplier would never receive payment. For the bank it might mean making a loan that will never be repaid. For the prospective assistant treasurer it might mean leaving her current job and moving to a new location for a firm with an uncertain future. Finally, for the prospective investor, it might mean sinking hundreds of thousands of dollars into the equity of a firm that ends up bankrupt.

How do these firms and people make the difficult decision of whether or not to do business with POL, Inc.? In the case of dealing with small firms and in certain other circumstances, the answer is financial analysis.

The purpose of this chapter is to provide an overview of financial analysis and financial planning. The first half of this chapter deals with financial analysis that seeks to extract decision-making information from available knowledge. The second half of the chapter surveys a corporation's financial planning process, in which the corporation develops plans, and forecasts and analyzes the future in search of the optimal financial plan.

Text Modules 1 and 2 serve as prerequisite background material for this chapter. The material in Module 4 (The Financing Decision) is also helpful. For those students who have not yet covered Module 4, or for those students who would like a refresher on the material, Window 16.1, on Debt and Dividends, provides sufficient background.

FINANCIAL ANALYSIS

financial analysis
The process of extracting decision-making information from existing knowledge such as financial statements.

Financial analysis is the process of extracting decision-making information from existing knowledge such as financial statements. Thus, the purpose of performing financial analysis is to facilitate decision making by transforming raw facts into more useful information. For example, it may be possible to use the raw information in financial statements to predict bankruptcy, or some other potential event.

Who performs financial analysis? First, firms perform such analysis on themselves in order to better understand their current performance and to plan for the future. Second, financial analysis is performed by external entities dealing with the firm, in such circumstances as deciding whether to extend credit, accept a job offer, or invest in a firm. Finally, firms such as rating agencies and investment houses may perform financial analysis on other firms as a service to their clients. In many cases, it is more cost effective to have a third party perform a single analysis for all of its clients rather than have each client perform the analysis for itself. This is especially true given the fact that many firms lack the expertise to perform such analysis. Window 16.2 details the most popular sources of financial analysis on firms.

Modernists' View of Financial Analysis

In many cases, the essential information being sought in financial analysis is the probability that the firm will declare bankruptcy or have other serious problems meeting its obligations. Modern corporate finance theory offers some powerful tools—such as option theory—to measure the probability of bankruptcy. (Option theory is briefly introduced in Chapter 9.) Although using option theory to predict bankruptcy is beyond the scope of this text, it is certainly within the scope of most advanced finance courses.

Whatever tools are used in the analysis, modernists believe that it is almost always better to perform financial analysis using market prices rather than accounting numbers, such as those provided by

Window 16.1

Review of Debt and Dividends

A. Debt

The two primary securities used by corporations to raise capital are debt securities and equity securities. Debt and equity are financial securities that differ in risk such that the proportions of debt and equity used by the firm determine who bears the firm's risk.

Debt securities are fixed promises of future cash flows and generally have a lower level of risk. Equity securities—more specifically common stock—are claims to whatever cash flows are left over, if any, after all prior claims have been satisfied. Accordingly, equity securities generally have a higher level of risk.

A firm with a high proportion of debt is said to have high financial leverage. Ignoring the detailed theoretical arguments discussed in Chapters 10 and 11, the use of debt has certain generally accepted results. A firm that uses a high proportion of debt has: (1) a higher probability of going bankrupt, because of being unable to meet its obligations, due to the relatively high interest payments it must make to its debtholders, (2) a higher probability of defaulting on (i.e., being unable to pay) its debt payments such that the debt itself becomes more risky, and (3) more volatile residual cash flows such that the equity claims become more risky.

Alternatively, a firm with a low proportion of debt is said to have low leverage. Low leverage indicates that the firm, under normal operating conditions, will be able to meet its obligations and thus has a lower probability of bankruptcy. This acts to reduce the risk borne by the firm's debt and equity securities.

Thus, analysts view debt usage as an indicator of whether the firm will be able to meet

(continued on next page)

financial statements.[1] For example, the best way to determine a firm's credit worthiness is to analyze the pricing of its existing debt that trades in the marketplace. Whether a financial analyst prefers to use market prices, assuming that the firm's securities are traded in an

---

1. It is generally only in cases where the firm's securities are not actively and competitively traded that market prices should not be given primary consideration. Examples of firms that would not have reliable market prices would be very small firms or "privately held" firms whose securities are not traded by numerous investors at publicly known prices.

Window 16.1 *(continued)*

its obligations. This is not to say that debt usage is bad, rather that it can affect who bears risk. Therefore, a financial analyst needs to take debt usage into account.

B. Dividends

A dividend is a distribution—usually of cash—from the firm to its stockholders. Generally, the dividend is viewed as derived from the firm's profits. Accordingly, the amount of dividends that a firm pays out determines the percentage of profits that will leave the firm and the percentage which will be retained within the firm. The profits retained within the firm are called retained earnings.

The financial planning material of this chapter will utilize the accounting mechanics of dividends discussed above. With reference to the value of the firm, some argue that cash dividends usually do not matter, since the firm's profits belong to the stockholders whether they are paid out as dividends or retained inside the firm. As part of this argument, dividends are simply the transfer of the stockholders' wealth from the firm's cash balances to their private cash balances.

However, the payment of dividends can affect the ability of the firm to meet its obligations. In simple terms and ignoring the theoretical arguments of Chapter 12, it can be argued that high dividends damage the ability of a firm to meet its obligations. The reason for this is twofold. First, dividends cause a reduction in the firm's cash balance, which is viewed as the firm's safest asset. Second, dividends reduce the equity owner's investment in the firm and therefore act to decrease the percentage of equity and increase the percentage of debt in the firm.

How much debt to use and the amounts to pay in dividends are the two most important financing issues to be made by financial management. The ultimate effect of debt and dividends on financial analysis is complex. This window has attempted to touch on enough of the major concepts so that the reader who has not read Chapters 10 to 12 will have a basic understanding of how debt and dividends relate to basic financial-analysis concepts.

active and competitive market, or accounting information found on financial statements are important distinctions.

The argument for using market prices is that self-interest will drive the most talented analysts in the world, equipped with the best information available in the world, to trade any mispriced securities until the mispricing vanishes. Thus the market prices themselves become conduits of the finest information available.

Some analysts tend to distrust accounting numbers since they can be manipulated by management in an effort to conceal troubles.

Window 16.2

Sources of Financial Analysis

Credit-Rating Agencies

1. *Standard and Poor's:* A subsidiary of McGraw-Hill, Inc., Standard and Poor's (S&P) provides a range of financial services, most notably ratings on corporate and municipal bonds and common stocks. S&P ratings classify bonds according to risk classes—triple A (AAA), or most financially secure, to single D (D), or in default. In addition, Standard and Poor's uses the modifiers plus (+) and minus (−) to classify debt securities further. Thus, bond ratings signal the probability of default. Ratings on common stocks range from A+ (most financially secure) to D (in reorganization) and signal the potential for future growth and stability of dividend payments. Other financial information provided by Standard and Poor's includes the compilation of common stock indices (for example, the S&P 500), *The Bond Guide, Earnings Forecaster, New Issue Investor, The Stock Guide*, and *Corporation Records*.

2. *Moody's:* A subsidiary of Dun & Bradstreet, Moody's provides information similar to that provided by Standard and Poor's. Moody's is best known for its corporate and municipal bond ratings, which signal the financial strength of the issuer and the probability of default. Moody's also rates common stocks, providing information on each company's background, its current operations, and the outlook for the future.

(continued on next page)

Instead, these analysts place their greatest trust in market prices, which are determined by people investing real money. For example, if the debt of a firm is regularly being bought and sold at a high price, a modernist would conclude that the firm must have a small chance of going bankrupt—regardless of other indicators. It is argued that indicators other than market prices, such as talk and accounting numbers, are unreliable.

Traditionalists' View of Financial Analysis

Traditionalists tend to distrust market prices from a belief that they are subject to emotions and fads. According to this argument, market prices may be either too high or too low, depending upon the errors

Window 16.2 *(continued)*

Information on Commercial Firms

3. *Dun & Bradstreet:* Dun & Bradstreet is a supplier of credit information on commercial firms, including previous credit history and current credit listings. It also provides financial analysis and other financial information, including *Industry Norms and Key Business Ratios*, which provides basic balance sheet and income statement information as well as ratios for industries.

4. *Value Line Investment Survey:* The Value Line Investment Survey is an advisory service best known for its system of ranking thousands of stocks from One (recommend to buy) to Five (recommend to sell). The Value Line ranking system is updated weekly and is based on relative strength in market price movement, earnings momentum, and unexpected changes in earnings. Value Line also provides other types of firm analysis, including history, current developments, and measures of risk such as firm betas. The beta of the firm is a measure of its systematic risk, as detailed in Module 3.

Information on Individuals

5. *TRW, Inc.:* TRW, Inc., is a major corporate conglomerate producing automobile products, space and defense products, and consumer credit reporting services. Consumer credit reporting provides a credit history for millions of individuals, reporting on amounts of credit outstanding as well as any defaults on past credit.

being made by investors; therefore, information found on financial statements provides better information.

The debate over whether market prices provide better answers to the questions asked by financial analysts or whether accounting numbers are better has gone on for years and will continue. Nevertheless, even modernists agree that, when reliable market prices are not available, the information found on financial statements must be used.

FINANCIAL STATEMENTS

There are two primary types of financial statements that accountants produce to convey financial information regarding a firm: (1) the balance sheet and (2) the income statement. Ordinarily, both statements are reported using accounting numbers or book values. These accounting numbers are generally derived from the cost of each item using the complex rules of accounting.

For example, the accounting or book value of land is usually listed as the cost of the land when purchased rather than its value today. In the case of buildings and equipment, the book values are lowered or depreciated each year according to complicated depreciation rules—even if the true values are rising.

The good news about accounting numbers is that to some extent the practices of how to report values are standardized so that different corporations use generally similar methods. The bad news is that the values can bear little resemblance to the true values being measured. This is especially true when the corporation being analyzed has assets that are very difficult to value, such as patents, trademarks, a good reputation, and so forth.

As discussed briefly in Chapter 1, it is also possible to envision financial statements based upon the market values of each item. If correctly implemented, market-value financial statements would be extremely useful. Unfortunately, the enormous difficulty of reporting accurate market prices of untraded items on a consistent basis and the tremendous potential for misuse virtually eliminate their practical usefulness. Thus, for the remainder of this chapter, "values" will refer to accounting or book values rather than market values. Now let's take a closer look at the two primary financial statements.

The Balance Sheet

balance sheet
A listing of all of the assets of a firm and all of the claims to those assets at a particular point in time.

Many people refer to a balance sheet as a snapshot of the firm, since it attempts to express all items of value at a particular point in time. The **balance sheet** or balance statement is simply a listing of all of the assets of a firm and all of the claims to those assets at a particular point in time. Assets are anything that can produce future cash inflows to the firm and are generally listed first, or on the left-hand side of the statement.

The claims to the firm include all fixed debts or liabilities as well as residual ownerships, known as preferred and common stocks. These claims are listed last, or on the right-hand side, usually under the title "Liabilities and Owners' Equity." The total value of the assets must equal the total value of the liabilities and owners' equity, since all the assets are owned by or claimed by someone. An example of a real-world balance sheet is provided in Chapter 1, Figure 1.2, for the Walt Disney Company.

Difference in Balance Sheet Detail.   The distinguishing aspect of balance sheets is their level of detail. Sometimes students are confused by balance sheets because they expect them to look somewhat similar to each other. However, balance sheets can differ markedly in appearance depending on whether various categories are lumped together or separated out. For example, in its briefest form, the balance sheet for Points of Light, Inc., after their first year in business would look as follows:

Assets	*Liabilities and Owners' Equity*
Total Assets $1,000,000	Common Stock $1,000,000

Alternatively, this balance sheet could be expanded to cover several pages by listing the different types of assets in extreme detail. Thus, the primary difference between various balance sheet formats is their level of detail.

> ✗ The primary difference between various balance sheet formats is their level of detail.

Common Balance Sheet Practices. A convention of balance sheets is that they list assets and liabilities starting with the shortest maturities and ending with the longest maturities. The reason for this is the importance that financial analysts place on the liquidity of the items, which was more fully discussed in Chapter 2.

Another convention is that certain figures are added together or subtracted out to form various subtotals. For example, loosely speaking, assets and liabilities with lifetimes of less than one year are often subtotaled under the headings current assets and current liabilities. Other assets are called fixed assets, while other liabilities are entitled long-term liabilities.

Also, assets that have been depreciated or lowered through time are often listed first at their original purchase prices and then lowered to their depreciated or net values. Finally, two or more balance sheets are often overlaid onto a single statement by including a column of figures for each quarter or year. An example of the detail found in a typical balance sheet is provided in Table 16.1. Remember that a balance sheet is simply a listing of the firm's assets, liabilities, and residual value. The general concept of a balance sheet is easy to understand even though, as we have said, these statements can differ tremendously owing to differences in the level of detail shown.

Complex Aspects of Balance Sheets. Detailed balance sheets usually contain a few tricky aspects, which are summarized below.

1. Assets that can be liquidated within one year and liabilities that may come due within one year are often expanded into numerous entries. This is done to provide detail for analysts studying liquidity.

2. Asset categories such as equipment and buildings, which are depreciated through time, are often listed using three lines. The first

TABLE 16.1
A Detailed Balance Sheet for Points of Light, Inc.

Assets	
Cash and marketable securities	$ 852,000
Accounts receivable	2,324,000
Inventory	9,496,000
Total Current Assets	$ 12,672,000
Equipment	$ 42,939,000
Less accumulated depreciation	17,389,000
Net equipment	$ 25,550,000
Buildings	$ 95,921,000
Less accumulated depreciation	65,838,000
Net buildings	$ 30,083,000
Land	$ 73,012,000
Fixed Assets	$128,645,000
Total Assets	$141,317,000
Liabilities and Owners' Equity	
Accounts payable	$ 1,465,000
Bank loans	3,960,000
Debt due within one year	2,580,000
Total Current Liabilities	$ 8,005,000
Total Long-Term Debt	$ 27,812,000
Common stock (par value $0.10)	$ 1,000,000
Paid-in-surplus of par	99,000,000
Retained earnings	5,500,000
Total Equity	$105,500,000
Total Liabilities and Owners' Equity	$141,317,000

line lists the sum of the original purchase prices of all of the assets in the category. The second line lists the accumulated depreciation, which represents the sum of all of the years of depreciation on all of the assets in the category. Depreciation is an accounting estimate of the decline in an asset's value due to aging and wear. The third and final line lists the net (or subtracted) value. This last line is the true book value of the assets and is the only value that is summed into the total fixed assets and total assets lines.[2]

---

2. When a depreciable asset is sold, its cost is removed from the first line and its accumulated depreciation is removed from the second line. Simpler balance sheets in effect report only the third line. Accounts receivable can also be listed in three lines in order to reflect the fact that some of the money might not be collected.

par value
An arbitrary listing of the value of stock per share on the firm's books. Par value has little economic significance.

3. Common stock is often broken into two or three lines based upon a concept known as **par value.** All three lines added together form the book value of the firm's common equity. Generally speaking, there are two important reasons to separate common equity into three lines. First, with a line listed as common stock (par value $0.10), the user is able to compute the number of shares of common stock in the corporation. The user simply divides the value for the item by the par value per share. From Table 16.1, there are 10,000,000 shares, found by dividing $1,000,000 by $0.10 par value per share. Second, the user can differentiate between common equity that was contributed to the firm by the sale of shares to investors and common equity that was generated by profits through the years. The sum of the common stock and paid-in-surplus of par is the amount of money raised from selling newly issued shares. The third line is the residual ownership, or retained earnings, generated by the firm's profits and cumulated through the years. It represents the sum of all previous profits less all previous dividends.

4. Balance sheets can be condensed by deducting current liabilities from current assets and reporting only net current assets or net working capital. The net working capital is entered as an asset. Thus, the balance sheet is shorter (current liabilities and current assets don't even appear) and the total figures will not really represent all assets or liabilities.

Summary of Balance Sheets

A balance sheet is a listing of the firm's assets, liabilities, and residual value. However, tremendous variations in their format as well as such alternatives as those previously listed may tend to be intimidating. However, with a little practice and by keeping "the big picture" clear in your mind, most balance sheets can be understood.

The Income Statement

income statement
A summary of the firm's profit or loss over a certain time period.

An **income statement** is a summary of the transactions that have added accounting value to the firm, known as profits, or lost accounting value from the firm, known as losses. While a balance sheet tries to express a firm's value at a particular point in time, an income statement attempts to summarize the firm's profit or loss over a certain time period. Thus, an income statement summarizes all of the transactions that affect the accounting value of equity.

Income statements are typically compiled for three-month, six-month, or one-year intervals. Two or more income statements can be listed together using different columns for the financial figures corresponding to different time intervals. A real-world income statement was provided in Figure 1.4 for the Walt Disney Company.

Difference in Income Statement Detail.   As in the case of balance sheets, income statements differ tremendously in format due primarily to the amount of detail they express, such as whether various categories are lumped together or separated out. For example, in its briefest form, an income statement would look as follows:

Total Revenues	$110,600,000
Total Expenditures	$102,788,000
Net Income	$ 7,812,000

Only those types of transactions that earn or lose money are listed. There are many transactions in which a firm may engage that do not make or lose money immediately, and therefore are not listed on the income statement. Examples include borrowing money, issuing stock, repaying debt, or purchasing assets.

There are two primary types of transactions that can earn or lose money. The first is an ordinary operation, which represents the enterprise of the firm in making and selling its products. The second is an extraordinary event, which represents unusual and major transactions producing a profit or loss—such as the sale or loss of a major asset. Most income statements differentiate between these two types of transactions.

Ordinary transactions represented by the production and selling of the firm's products are usually provided in somewhat standard fashion across firms. The firm's revenues are often broken into three lines in order to reflect the expectation that some of the money from the sales will never be collected because some customers will never pay. The first line usually lists the total possible revenues from sales, followed by a second line reflecting an allowance for the money that is typically uncollected. The third line is the difference and is entitled the net sales. For condensed income statements, only the third line might be listed.

Often the firm's ordinary expenses are detailed in the following way:

Cost of Goods Sold
Selling and General Administrative Expenses
Depreciation

The first category represents the variable costs of production, while the second category represents fixed costs of production. Depreciation is often separated out because it is simply an accounting concept and not a cash expense. Of course, there is no limit to the level of detail that could be used to expand this list by breaking out expenses into more specific categories, such as labor versus materials, or into different divisions, product types, and so forth.

Another common practice is to subtotal the revenues and expenses before subtracting interest expense and taxes. The purpose of this is to illustrate how the cash flows being produced from the assets are being divided among the claimants of the firm's cash flows. In this classification, interest goes to bondholders, taxes to the government, and net income to the shareholders.

Earnings Before Interest and Taxes (Operating Income)
−Interest Expense

Profit Before Taxes
−Income Taxes

Net Income

The last figure or line on the income statement is usually viewed as the most important, since it is the accounting measure of the change in the value of the shareholder's wealth, hence the expression "the bottom line." Combining the previous characteristics produces the income statement shown in Table 16.2, which illustrates a moderate level of detail.

Complex Aspects of Income Statements. As with balance sheets, it is important to remember that most income statements are based upon accounting numbers and accounting rules rather than market values and economic principles. For example, a firm may have a tremendous economic gain because the buildings, land, patents, and trademarks it purchased and developed years ago are now worth a great deal of money. However, these gains will not be recognized and reported by accountants until the assets have been sold.

Accountants are quicker to report losses even if the assets haven't been sold. For example, a bank with huge potential losses on its investments must "write off" or declare the losses even though it might not be allowed to report potential profits on other assets that have risen in value but have not been sold.

Worse yet, some major decisions of when to recognize and report transactions can be left to the discretion of management. In effect, this

TABLE 16.2
A Moderately Detailed Income Statement

Sales	$110,600,000
Cost of goods sold	45,427,000
Selling and administrative expenses	39,650,000
Depreciation	10,350,000
Earnings before interest and taxes (EBIT)	$ 15,173,000
Interest on debt	3,337,000
Earnings before taxes (EBT)	$ 11,836,000
Taxes	4,024,000
Net income	$ 7,812,000

allows management, in some cases, to exert an enormous amount of control over the reporting of the firm's performance. The net result is that in certain circumstances the net income of a firm bears little or no resemblance to its true economic performance for the time period.

Another complexity of the income statement is the distinction between completed transactions, represented by revenues or expenses that have been received or paid, and those that have only been *accrued*, represented by revenues or expenses that have not been collected as of the date of the income statement. However, the more serious problem is that many major potential profits and some major potential losses are not reported until and unless a transaction has occurred or been agreed to.

Finally, income statements often express figures such as net income on a per share basis by dividing the total net income by the number of shares of common stock. The statement may also detail payments to preferred stockholders and the amount of the net income paid to the common stockholders as a dividend rather than retained inside the firm.

Summary of Income Statements

In summary, the formats of income statements vary so tremendously that it is easy to become confused. However, all income statements are attempts to measure the profit or loss of a firm over a specified time interval. As with any accounting numbers, they are to be viewed realistically and with recognition of their limitations.

RATIO ANALYSIS

A ratio is one number divided by another number or, in other words, one number expressed as a proportion of another. For example, we might divide the total amount of a firm's debt by the amount of its total assets in order to compute the proportion of the firm's total value which is represented by the debt.

Total debt, say an amount of $853,000, may convey very little information regarding the level of a firm's debt usage or health. For example, $853,000 might be a large amount of debt for a small retail firm but a small amount of debt for a large manufacturer. The number must be adjusted or scaled in order to be transformed into a meaningful measure. Ratios provide the solution.

ratio analysis
The use of values taken from financial statements such as the balance sheet and income statements in order to measure certain aspects of a firm's financial condition.

Ratio analysis refers to the use of simple ratios between numbers, such as those in the balance sheets and income statements, in order to measure certain aspects of a firm's financial condition. The four primary aspects that financial analysts study are: (1) the debt usage of the firm, (2) the liquidity of the firm, (3) the profitability of the firm, and (4) the efficiency of the firm.

Standards for Comparison of Financial Ratios

Before detailing each of the four types of ratios, we first examine the usefulness of the ratio. One of the most troubling aspects of ratio analysis is the difficulty of determining good or bad values. Is there such a thing as a correct value, an optimal value, or even a reasonable range of values?

The answers to these and other related questions depend on how the ratios are used. For instance, after a ratio has been computed for a particular firm, it needs to be compared or judged against some type of target or benchmark ratio. But should these target ratios be taken from theory, from the firm's previous years, or from other firms in the same industry? Do other firms use the same accounting methods? Why should we believe that the other firms in the industry have the correct ratios?

Practices vary and must be tailored to circumstances. Generally, however, a firm's financial ratios are analyzed through time in order to ascertain trends, and then compared with industry averages in order to provide indications as to whether the firm is above or below the levels found in the industry. Thus, a performance ratio that is below that of the year before may not be a danger signal if the industry's ratio has fallen by an even larger extent.

Sources for industry ratios include Dun & Bradstreet, Robert Morris Associates, and the U.S. Commerce Department's *Quarterly Financial Report for Manufacturers*. Many of these industry averages are reported for specific industries grouped by four-digit standard industrialized company (SIC) codes. It is important that the industry used as the benchmark match the industry of the firm. In some cases, this is a straightforward comparison inasmuch as the company being analyzed has one major line of business. In other cases, the benchmark is not easily identified because the company being analyzed has a number of business lines. In cases such as these, analysts usually use as an industry benchmark the firm's major line of business.

Ratios will be illustrated by separating the analysis into four major areas: debt usage, liquidity, profitability, and efficiency. Next to each type of ratio will be the corresponding value for the Walt Disney Company and Walt Disney's industry average.

Financial Ratio Example: The Walt Disney Company

Table 16.3 reports financial ratios for the Walt Disney Company in 1992. Also reported are industry averages as reported in Dun & Bradstreet's *Industry Norms and Key Business Ratios*. Because Disney's

TABLE 16.3
Common Financial Ratios (1992)

	Walt Disney	Industry Average*
Panel A: Debt Ratios		
1. The Debt Ratio $= \dfrac{\text{Total Debt}}{\text{Total Assets}}$	0.57	0.30
2. The Debt-to-Equity Ratio $= \dfrac{\text{Total Debt}}{\text{Total Equity}}$	1.31	0.55
3. The Equity Multiplier $= \dfrac{\text{Total Assets}}{\text{Total Equity}}$	2.3 times	1.8 times
4. Times Interest Earned Ratio $= \dfrac{\text{EBIT}^\dagger}{\$\,\text{Interest}}$	9.3 times	6.5 times
Panel B: Liquidity Ratios		
1. The Cash Ratio $= \dfrac{\text{Cash}}{\text{Current Liabilities}}$	0.43	0.72
2. The Quick Ratio $= \dfrac{\text{Cash} + \text{Accounts Receivable}}{\text{Current Liabilities}}$	1.15	1.00
3. The Current Ratio $= \dfrac{\text{Current Assets}}{\text{Current Liabilities}}$	2.20	1.72
Panel C: Profitability Ratios		
1. Net Return on Sales $= \dfrac{\text{Net Income}}{\text{Total Sales}}$	0.11	0.06
2. Net Return on Assets $= \dfrac{\text{Net Income}}{\text{Total Assets}}$	0.08	0.12
3. Net Return on Equity $= \dfrac{\text{Net Income}}{\text{Total Equity}}$	0.17	0.21
4. Net Profit Margin $= \dfrac{\text{Net Income}}{\text{EBIT}}$	0.70	0.60
Panel D: Efficiency Ratios		
1. Inventory Turnover $= \dfrac{\text{Costs of Goods Sold}}{\text{Inventory}}$	13.4	6.85
2. Days Sales Outstanding $= \dfrac{\text{Receivables}}{\text{Annual Sales}/360}$	62.3 days	14.38 days

*Source: Dun & Bradstreet Information Services, *Industry Norms and Key Business Ratios,* **Desk** Top Edition 1991–92.
†EBIT = Earnings before interest and taxes.

main products include theme parks, full-length films, and consumer products and no one industry benchmark provides a perfect match, for this analysis the main line of business is theme parks and the benchmark industry is amusements and recreation.

Debt Usage Ratios.   As is fully discussed in Module 4 and briefly discussed in Window 16.1, it may be important to study the amount of debt owed by the firm. The most common reason for analyzing debt usage would be to determine the probability that the firm will be able to pay its current and future debts. This information would be useful to current and prospective owners of the firm's debt—including the people who are considering selling their products to the firm on credit.

There are two types of ratios that measure the amount of debt a firm uses. The most common type of debt ratio expresses some measure of the firm's debt as a proportion of some other value in the firm. These ratios, known as the debt ratio and the debt-to-equity ratio, are summarized in Panel A of Table 16.3. Analysts concerned about the firm's debt capacity will focus on debt as a percent of assets. Ratios appropriate for analyzing a particular situation vary and depend upon the purpose of the analysis. For example, the analyst concerned about the ability of the firm to generate cash flow sufficient to make debt payments will focus on ratios that measure interest as a percent of profitability or cash flow. This is known as a coverage ratio, or a ratio measuring the firm's ability to cover fixed interest expense.

Comparisons indicate that Disney has a higher debt usage than the industry average. For example, total debt in relation to total equity is over twice as high for Disney compared with the industry. However, the coverage ratio indicates Disney's superior ability to meet fixed interest expense. Thus, Disney is either generating significantly more income than its peer group, or has locked in debt at relatively low interest rates.

Liquidity Ratios.   As discussed in Chapter 2, the liquidity of a firm refers to its ability to have sufficient cash to meet current and future needs. Thus, liquidity depends upon the amount of the firm's cash, the amount of other assets that can be quickly converted to cash, whether the firm is making or losing money, the amount of obligations that will require repayment in the near future, and the ability of the firm to raise more cash by issuing securities or borrowing money.

The primary purpose for analyzing the liquidity of a firm is to determine whether it has sufficient liquidity to meet its needs and, therefore, whether it would be a wise decision to extend credit to the firm such as by allowing it to purchase products on credit.

Panel B in Table 16.3 lists the most common measures of liquidity. Notice that the three liquidity ratios differ only by their numerator.

Each ratio divides certain liquid assets of the firm by the firm's total current debt. The first ratio includes only the firm's cash, the second ratio adds accounts receivable to cash, and the third ratio includes all of the firm's current assets including inventories. Which ratio or set of ratios a financial analyst will focus on depends upon the purpose of the analysis. The cash ratio might better indicate the firm's ability to meet immediate payments, while the current ratio might be a better indicator of credit worthiness over the next year.

Disney's ratios are similar to industry averages. While the cash ratio is below the industry, the other two liquidity ratios are above the industry. The current ratio indicates that Disney's current assets are over twice that of current liabilities, considered to be in the "safe" range of liquidity.

Profitability Ratios. The most common profitability ratios are shown in Panel C of Table 16.3, measuring net income as a proportion of (1) the firm's sales, (2) total assets, (3) total equity, and (4) earnings before interest and tax (EBIT) respectively. The first two ratios can provide useful insights into the amount of sales or assets that a particular corporation has used to produce a particular income and perhaps whether these sales and assets are being used efficiently.

The third and fourth ratios, the return on equity and the profit margin, are perhaps the most common accounting measures of profitability. The return on equity is the accounting measure of the return to the firm's stockholders, and the profit margin is the accounting measure of the firm's profit as a percent of EBIT.

Disney's profitability ratios are, once again, similar to industry averages. While net income to sales is twice that of the industry, net income to assets is just below the industry average. Return on equity, considered by some to be the most common measure of profitability, shows Disney to be slightly below the average. Overall, these ratios provide a healthy picture of profitability.

Efficiency Ratios. The ratios in Panel D in Table 16.3 measure the efficiency of the firm. For example, the inventory turnover ratio measures the number of times the inventory is turned over or sold. Sometimes the ratio has sales in the numerator, but costs of goods sold is the generally preferred numerator. A high turnover ratio indicates the advantage of not tying up a lot of its capital in inventory. On the other hand, a low inventory can produce a high turnover ratio but may cause problems to the firm such as lost sales and production inefficiencies.

A similar ratio is the days sales outstanding, which measures the amount of the firm's revenues tied up in accounts receivable as well as indicates how many days the firm takes on average to collect its accounts receivable. Disney's high ratio indicates either that the firm's customers are not prompt payers or that the firm does not collect its accounts receivable aggressively.

Disney's inventory turnover is almost three times as high as the industry average. This could indicate that inventory levels are at alarmingly low levels, or it could point to a faulty industry comparison due to the uniqueness of Disney's business.

Problems with Ratio Analysis

In addition to problems relating to inaccuracies of accounting numbers, there is a particular problem with ratios that depend on balance sheet values at a single point in time. Some balance sheet values, such as cash, can change substantially through time and can even be manipulated by management to be at certain levels at the end of an accounting period. Thus, a ratio indicating a low level of cash may be the result of a seasonal variation in sales and not a liquidity problem.

Also, profitability and efficiency ratios should be used with special caution. It should be remembered that there are no absolute standards for efficiency ratios. For example, a high inventory turnover rate and a low average collection period would appear to indicate efficient management. However, the opposite may be true. What appears as high efficiency may actually be a practice that hurts shareholder wealth. A high inventory turnover rate might indicate that the firm has too little inventory and is experiencing lost sales and production delays when inventories run out. A low average collection period might indicate that a firm has a credit policy that is too restrictive. A restrictive credit policy could cause the firm to lose profitable sales because of its reluctance to extend credit to customers.

Systems of Ratio Analysis

Rather than computing a few ratios and comparing them to some standards, some analysts have developed systems for analyzing ratios in an organized fashion. The objective of these systems is to identify strengths and weaknesses of the firm.

⚖ Systems for analyzing ratios, such as the Du Pont system, attempt to identify the firm's strengths and weaknesses.

Du Pont system
A system for analyzing ratios in an organized fashion. The objective of the system is to identify strengths and weaknesses of the firm.

For example, the **Du Pont system** was devised by financial managers of the Du Pont Corporation as a tool for systematic ratio analysis. It breaks down the return on equity into two components:

$$\text{Return on Equity} = \frac{\text{Net Income}}{\text{Equity}} = \frac{\text{Net Income}}{\text{Assets}} * \frac{\text{Assets}}{\text{Equity}}.$$

This simple mathematical identity is intended to assist the financial analyst in separating the equity performance into a measure of the profitability of the assets as represented by the return on assets and a leverage factor.

The Du Pont system then breaks return on assets into further components of profit margin, turnover, and so forth. This systematic method of pulling apart the return on equity is designed to lead the analysts to pinpointing the potential problem areas.

A detailed explanation of the Du Pont system and other systems is beyond the scope of this text. However, students should be aware that such systems exist and may be useful in providing a thorough analysis.

Financial Ratios as a Predictor of Performance

Some analysts use ratios as a method of predicting firm performance. For example, models have been developed using ratios and accounting entries to predict default. These models base their predictions on past history, investigating whether firms that declare bankruptcy share common characteristics. To the extent that these characteristics can be captured in financial ratios, trends in these ratios can be used to predict which firms will or will not default.

Research investigating the ability of financial ratios to predict default has been inconclusive. Perhaps the best that can be said is that ratios can provide insights into predicting which firms will run into financial distress.

SOURCES AND USES STATEMENTS

sources and uses statement
A financial statement that attempts to organize and convey information regarding all of the changes in the components of the firm's balance sheet.

A lesser-known financial statement known as the **sources and uses statement** is extremely important for financial planning. The sources and uses statement attempts to organize and convey information regarding all of the changes in the components of the firm's balance sheet. You may recall that the income statement reflects only those transactions that affect the firm's profit and therefore the value of the firm's equity. The sources and uses statement also includes the transactions that do not immediately affect profits but which can have longer-term implications, such as purchases of assets and raising of capital.

The Sources and Uses Statement as a Summary of Changes in Balance Sheets

The sources and uses statement may be viewed as a summary of the changes between two balance sheets of a firm at different points in time. For example, Table 16.4 lists the balance sheet of Points of Light,

TABLE 16.4
The Balance Sheet for Points of Light over Two Years (in thousands of dollars)

	1993	1992	Change
Assets			
Cash and securities	$ 852	$ 953	− 101
Accounts receivable	2,324	2,200	+ 124
Inventory	9,496	8,386	+ 1,110
Total Current Assets	$ 12,672	$ 11,539	+ 1,133
Equipment	$ 42,939	$ 31,929	+11,010
Less accumulated depreciation	17,389	15,027	+ 2,362
Net equipment	$ 25,550	$ 16,902	+ 8,648
Buildings	$ 95,921	$ 95,921	0
Less accumulated depreciation	65,838	61,687	+ 4,151
Net buildings	$ 30,083	$ 34,234	− 4,151
Land	$ 73,012	$ 73,012	0
Fixed Assets	$128,645	$124,148	+ 4,497
Total Assets	$141,317	$135,687	+ 5,630
Liabilities and Equity			
Accounts payable	$ 1,465	$ 1,166	+ 299
Bank loans	3,960	4,040	− 80
Debt due within year	2,580	2,580	0
Total Current Liabilities	$ 8,005	$ 7,786	+ 219
Total Long-Term Debt	$ 27,812	$ 25,392	+ 2,420
Common stock	$ 1,000	$ 1,000	0
Paid-in-surplus	99,000	99,000	0
Retained earnings	5,500	2,509	+ 2,991
Total Equity	$105,500	$102,509	+ 2,991
Total Liabilities and Equity	$141,317	$135,687	+ 5,630

Inc., for two years. The final column in Table 16.4 shows the changes in each value. The changes are formed by subtracting the earlier balance sheet values from the later balance sheet values.

A sources and uses statement can be formed by transposing the changes illustrated in Table 16.4 into the format of Table 16.5 (along with a few adjustments to be discussed later). All values are transposed as positive numbers. The sign of each value determines its location. All decreases in asset values and increases in liabilities (or equity) are placed under the heading "Sources." All increases in asset values and decreases in liabilities (or equity) are placed under the heading "Uses." The placements are logical, since buying assets and

TABLE 16.5
A Sources and Uses Statement for Points of Light, Inc.
(in thousands of dollars)

Sources		Uses	
Depreciation	$ 6,513	Dividends	$ 3,000
Net income	5,991	Inventory	1,110
Cash	101	Accounts receivable	124
Accounts payable	299	Equipment	11,010
Long-term debt	2,420	Bank loans	80
Total Sources	$15,324	Total Uses	$15,324

paying off debts are uses of money, whereas selling assets and borrowing are sources of money.

Complex Aspects of the Sources and Uses Statement

There are two rather tough "tricks" in creating a sources and uses
statement like the one shown in Table 16.5. First, rather than placing
the change in the retained earnings value in the statement, the user
includes the firm's net income as a source and its dividends as a use.
Note that the change in retained earnings is equal to the net income
minus the dividends.

Second, depreciable assets complicate the sources and uses statement. You may recall from the discussion of the balance sheet that
depreciable assets, such as equipment, are often listed in three lines
such as:

> Equipment
> − Accumulated Depreciation
> Net Equipment

Rather than transposing the third line from above to the sources and
uses statement (the net value of the depreciated asset), the sources and
uses statement usually contains both of the first two lines. As
expected, the first line is listed as a use if it is an increase and a source
if it is a decrease. The change in accumulated depreciation is listed as
a source if it is an increase (which it usually is) or a use if it is a
decrease.

Depreciation is one of the most difficult aspects of a sources and
uses statement. It is important to recognize depreciation as an
unusual item, inasmuch as no money leaves the firm in the form of
depreciation expense. In the sources and uses statement, depreciation
is entered twice with opposite results—which cancel each other out.
Depreciation needs to be negated because it is an accounting number
rather than an actual cash flow.

Depreciation "washes out" of a sources and uses statement because it is subtracted from net income, which reduces a source, and then is added back in as a source. In fact, the only importance of depreciation from the perspective of cash flows is that it is tax deductible and therefore reduces the cash spent on income taxes. The concept that the only real consequence of depreciation is its effect on income taxes is an important insight.

The Starting Format for a Sources and Uses Statement

In order to minimize confusion due to the "tricks" discussed above, students may find it helpful to begin construction of a sources and uses statement by using the format shown in Table 16.6. This format helps guide the student past some of the adjustments necessitated by equity changes and depreciation. The user then transposes the changes in the balance sheet items into their appropriate locations. Remember to transpose all values as positive numbers, using the sign only to determine whether it is a source or a use. The numbers should be transposed according to the following location guideline:

Sources:	Decreased Assets and Increased Liabilities
Uses:	Increased Assets and Decreased Liabilities

The level of detail in the balance sheets determines the level of detail in the sources and uses statement. The primary reason that sources and uses statements look so different results from whether the balance sheets are expanded or condensed.

Formatting Differences in Sources and Uses Statements

There are two major formatting differences in sources and uses statements. First, whether or not short-term assets and liabilities are detailed determines whether the statement is called a sources and uses of cash statement or a sources and uses of funds statement.

If the cash and other current assets and current liabilities are detailed, it is called a sources and uses of cash statement. Table 16.5

TABLE 16.6
A Format for Starting a Sources and Uses Statement

Sources	Uses
Depreciation	Dividends
Net income	. . . . .
. . . . .	. . . . .
. . . . .	. . . . .
. . . . .	. . . . .
Total Sources	Total Uses

was an example of a sources and uses of cash statement, since it explicitly listed the changes in cash and other components of working capital.

If the cash and other current assets and current liabilities are not detailed, it is called a sources and uses of funds statement. Sources and uses of funds statements are constructed from condensed balance sheets that subtract current liabilities from current assets to form a single value entitled net working capital. This statement is simpler and allows the user to focus on the more permanent types of changes that have taken place. Table 16.7 condenses Table 16.5 into a sources and uses of funds statement.

The second major formatting issue is whether all sources and uses are inserted into two lists or whether the "key" value is extracted from the lists and inserted at the bottom of the statement as the difference between the sources and uses. The only difference is in exposition.

For example, in a sources and uses of cash statement, the user can place the cash change at the bottom as illustrated in Table 16.8. In a sources and uses of funds statement, the change in net working capital can be placed at the bottom of the statement as shown in Table 16.9.

Summary of Sources and Uses Statements

As with other financial statements, the variety of formats and detail tends to make the topic appear complex and incomprehensible. Underneath these vastly different appearances, however, each sources and uses statement is essentially the same. Regardless of format, the purpose of a sources and uses statement is clear: It conveys the changes in the balance sheet values in a manner that encourages the user to view the firm as having used cash or funds from various sources.

In order to explain sources and uses statements it is useful to think about a sources and uses statement as resulting from the subtraction of balance sheets at two points in time:

New Balance Sheet − Old Balance Sheet = Sources and Uses

TABLE 16.7
A Sources and Uses of Funds Statement for Points of Light, Inc. (in thousands of dollars)

Sources		Uses	
Depreciation	$ 6,513	Dividends	$ 3,000
Net income	5,991	Net working capital	914
Long-term debt	2,420	Equipment	11,010
Total Sources	$14,924	Total Uses	$14,924

TABLE 16.8
A Sources and Uses Statement with Cash at the Bottom (in thousands of dollars)

Sources		Uses	
Depreciation	$ 6,513	Dividends	$ 3,000
Net income	5,991	Inventory	1,110
Accounts payable	299	Accounts receivable	124
Long-term debt	2,420	Equipment	11,010
		Bank loans	80
Total Sources	$15,223	Total Uses	$15,324
		Change in Cash	−$ 101

However, in order to understand the purpose of a sources and uses statement, it is better to view it as a link through time between balance sheets:

$$\begin{array}{ccc} \text{Current} \\ \text{Balance Sheet} \end{array} + \begin{array}{c} \text{Sources and Uses} \\ \text{Statement} \end{array} = \begin{array}{c} \text{Forecasted} \\ \text{Balance Sheet} \end{array}$$

In the financial planning process of an existing corporation, the sources and uses statement is the focal point of the model because it forces forecasted balance sheets to be balanced.

In the business plan of a new venture, the sources and uses statement is especially useful since it is the tool for estimating future funding needs. Many new business plans incorrectly forecast funding needs as a list of investments and projected initial losses. Without a sources and uses statement, such financial plans are both incorrect and unimpressive to sophisticated venture capitalists considering investing in a new business.

TABLE 16.9
A Sources and Uses of Funds Statement with Net Working Capital at the Bottom (in thousands of dollars)

Sources		Uses	
Depreciation	$ 6,513	Dividends	$ 3,000
Net income	5,991	Equipment	11,010
Long-term debt	2,420		
Total Sources	$14,924	Total Uses	$14,010
		Change in Net Working Capital	$ 914

FINANCIAL PLANNING

financial planning
The process of planning the major financial aspects of a corporation over long periods of time, such as three to five years.

Corporate **financial planning** is the process of planning the major financial aspects of a corporation over long periods of time, such as three to five years. The major financial aspects that financial planning addresses are how much money will need to be raised, how it will be raised, how much money will be invested in fixed assets, how much will be invested in working capital, and how much profit the firm can expect to make.

Corporations have rather precise and detailed short-term plans regarding the sources and use of cash. These shorter-term plans involve a few months to two years and are discussed in Chapter 17 on working capital management.

An Overview of the Planning Process

The concept of corporate financial planning is really quite simple. Most large corporations use an iterative technique in which projections are tested and adjusted in search of the best plan. Let's look at an overview of the process.

First, the user inputs into a particular model a number of assumptions or parameters about how various items such as revenues, expenses, and investments will change through time. Second, these assumptions are used to forecast future balance sheets. Third, a financial analysis technique such as ratio analysis is applied to determine the desirability of the results of the forecast.

The process is then repeated by modifying the assumptions and repeating the forecast and analysis stages until the users are confident that they have found the best available plan. This whole process is computerized so that numerous new forecasts can be generated with just a few changes to the parameters of a computer program.

The computer model used specifies certain relationships between variables and how the variables change through time. For example, one model might assume that revenues will grow at a constant percentage growth rate through time, while a more complex model will allow the user to input two or more stages of growth with different growth rates in each stage.

The Accounting Mechanics of a Financial Planning Model

It is possible to use corporate financial planning models with little or no knowledge of their underlying mechanics just as it is possible to drive a car without knowing how the engine works. However, the best financial managers, like the best race car drivers, understand both how their tools work as well as how to operate them.

TABLE 16.10
Current and Forecasted Financial Statements, Simplified Tools, Inc.
(in thousands of dollars)

Panel A: Condensed Balance Sheet—12/31/94	
Net working capital	$ 80
Fixed assets	830
Total Assets	$ 910
Long-term debt	$ 400
Equity	510
Total Debt and Equity	$ 910
Panel B: 1995 Forecasted Income Statement	
Revenues	$ 187
Expenses	132
Net income	$ 55
Panel C: 1995 Forecasted Sources and Uses of Funds Statement	
Sources	
Net income	$ 55
Depreciation	20
Debt	20
Total Sources	$ 95
Uses	
Dividends	$ 4
Net working capital	8
Fixed assets	83
Total Uses	$ 95

Table 16.10 illustrates highly condensed versions of a firm's current balance sheet as well as the forecasts of the next period's income statement and sources and uses statement, which were produced by a computer model. Notice that the working capital and fixed assets are assumed to increase by 10 percent. In most models, the user would simply input these growth rates and the computer would convert them to dollar values. The user can then alter the figures by inputting alternative growth rates.

Most computerized corporate financial planning models may be viewed as following this process:

1. The inputted forecasts of revenue and expense growth rates (along with tax rates, depreciation, and so forth) are used to forecast the "next" income statement.
2. The income statement is combined with other growth-rate forecasts of assets and liabilities to generate a balanced sources and uses statement.

3. The sources and uses statement is "overlaid" onto the previous balance sheet in order to produce the next balance sheet. This new forecasted balance sheet then becomes the basis upon which to forecast another time period into the future.
4. The computer then returns to step #1 and repeats the process by forecasting another time period into the future until the financial statements have been forecasted for the desired number of periods.

The foregoing discussion emphasized a single forecast in order to simplify the concepts. In actual usage, most financial plans would produce a spectrum of forecasts based upon various scenarios such as high, moderate, and low growth. The spectrum of scenarios is usually input by the user as a range of values for certain parameters such as growth rates.

An Example of Compiling a Forecast

For example, let's look at a highly simplified financial planning model that produces the forecast for only one scenario at a time. The income statement and sources and uses statement from Table 16.10 are produced by the model using the inputted parameters and can be used to construct the next balance sheet as illustrated in Table 16.11.

The computer model would then use the inputted growth rates to forecast the next income statement and sources and uses statement, and the process would repeat itself.

The key financial statement is the sources and uses statement. The model requires that the sources and uses be balanced so that forecasted balance sheets are balanced. We will next show that all of the items in the sources and uses statement except one are explicitly forecasted by the model. The remaining variable is known as the "slack" variable, and it takes on whatever value is necessary to balance the sources and uses statement.

TABLE 16.11
Forecasting the Balance Sheet, Simplified Tools, Inc.
(in thousands of dollars)

Net working capital	$ 88
Fixed assets	893
Total Assets	$ 981
Long-term debt	$ 420
Equity	561
Total Debt and Equity	$ 981

The Slack Variable. All but one of the values in the forecasted balance sheet were explicitly forced into their values by assumptions in the model. It was noted above that the working capital and fixed assets grew at the user-supplied growth rate of 10 percent. It's a little more difficult to realize that the change in the value of the equity was also forced, since it was assumed to be equal to the net income of the firm minus its dividend. (This is the definition of retained earnings and we are assuming that the firm does not wish to issue new stock.)

Thus, all of the items in the sources and uses statement were automatically and directly determined by the parameters inputted by the user, except the change in the debt. In the above model, debt is the **slack variable,** since its value is implicitly determined by the requirement that the sources and uses statement be balanced. In other words, debt took the value necessary to keep the statements balanced.

slack variable
A variable whose value is implicitly determined by the requirement that the sources and uses statement be balanced.

The slack variable is usually the focus of the financial planning process. Different models have different slack variables, but the most common are the amount of debt, the amount of dividends, and the amount of equity.

When debt serves as the slack variable, the model will show the user the amount of debt that will cumulate throughout the years given all of the other decisions such as growth rates, dividend policy, and so forth. Obviously, the user will then analyze the debt usage to determine whether the debt usage would be reasonable.

When the dividend amount serves as the slack variable the model will show the user how much the firm can pay out in dividends given all of the other decisions regarding growth rates, debt usage, and so forth.

Finally, when the equity amount serves as the slack variable, the model will show the user how much equity the firm will have to issue throughout the years or can repurchase, given the other decisions.

Using a Financial Planning Model

Although most financial planning models may be viewed as having a key slack variable whose future values are determined based upon all of the other inputs, the real process of meeting future financial needs of a firm is not as simple as allowing the slack variable to be whatever it needs to be. In the real world, corporations are usually interested in planning all of the variables including the slack variable—whether it is debt usage, dividend payout, or equity usage.

This is where the iterative process becomes so important. After the computer model has generated a financial plan or a range of financial plans, the user then performs a financial analysis to determine if the plan offers an optimal level of profitability and the desired capital structure (debt versus equity financing).

If a variable other than the slack variable appears to be unreasonable, the user can alter this variable by changing the parameters that determine it or its components. Of course, when one variable is changed other variables will be affected, especially the slack variable.

If the forecasted values of the slack variable appear unreasonable, the user can modify the parameters that explicitly determine other variables, which will cause the slack variable to change. For example, if debt usage is the slack variable and the forecasts indicate debt usage that is "too high," the user may alter other parameters—such as lowering the dividend payout rate, lowering the growth rate, and so forth.

This iterative process allows the user to experiment. The goal is to produce a financial plan that is viable for a range of scenarios—which reflects the potential outcomes of variables that are outside the control of the financial manager such as interest rates, general economic performance, and the like.

Summary of the Planning Process

Financial plans differ tremendously with regard to the level of detail, the parameters assumed to affect the firm, and the relationship between the parameters and the firm's performance. Nevertheless, the general concepts remain unchanged.

Some readers may have been surprised to learn that a plan of three to five years is considered to be a long-term plan. But practically speaking, for most corporations it is very difficult to develop realistic projections of significant results much more than five years into the future.

Corporate financial planning is designed to bring together and modify the investment, financing, and operational plans of the firm and to ensure that, under reasonable scenarios, plans can operate together in a sensible fashion.

SUMMARY

- ☐ Financial analysis is the process of using financial information for decision-making purposes. Most of the information used in financial planning comes from financial statements known as the balance sheet, the income statement, and the sources and uses statement.

- ☐ Ratios constructed from financial statements can be used to analyze the debt usage, liquidity, profitability, and efficiency of the firm.

- ☐ Financial analysis is sometimes criticized because it relies on accounting numbers that can be manipulated in many different ways. For example, accounting numbers can be used to show that the firm is profitable when it is not. However, in the absence of reliable market information, there may be no other alternative to accounting statements.

☐ The material in this chapter may at times appear to be reduced to a number of rules that need to be followed. This contrasts to the "way of thinking" approach of other chapters in this text.

DEMONSTRATION PROBLEMS

Problem 1   Harlow Corporation has an especially simple balance sheet since it has no debt:

Harlow Corporation 12/31/94

Assets	*Equity*
$1,000,000	$1,000,000

Harlow Corporation has developed the following projections of net income for the next three years:

1995	*1996*	*1997*
$75,000	$100,000	$125,000

Finally, Harlow Corporation projects that in order to meet future demands it will need to expand its total assets by $50,000 per year.

Use this information to compute sources and uses statements and balance sheets for next year. Assume that Harlow Corporation wishes to avoid debt. Management hopes that its plans for expansion can be met by retaining earnings and then paying out any further income in the form of dividends. For simplicity, ignore taxes and depreciation.

Solution to Problem 1

This is a classic and extremely simplified financial projection. The key to completing the exercise is to begin by forming the sources and uses statement and recognizing that dividends are the "slack" variable in this problem. In other words, we use the sources and uses statement for the purpose of computing the dividend that can be paid. This comprises steps 1 and 2. Then in step 3 we use the sources and uses statement to forecast the next future balance sheet.

Step 1: The sources and uses statement is best begun using a format such as Table 16.6:

Harlow Corporation 1995 Sources and Uses Statement

Sources	Uses
Depreciation	Dividends
Net income	
Total Sources	Total Uses

Step 2: Fill in the information that is known from the problem:

Harlow Corporation 1995 Sources and Uses Statement

Sources		Uses	
Depreciation	$0	Dividends	?
Net income	$75,000	New assets	$50,000
Total Sources	$75,000	Total Uses	?

Notice that net income, depreciation, and changes in assets are already given. In this simplified example, it is relatively easy to see that we need to find the level of dividend payment that will make the amount of total sources equal to the amount of total uses. A dividend payment of $25,000 keeps the statement balanced:

Harlow Corporation 1995 Sources and Uses Statement

Sources		Uses	
Depreciation	$0	Dividends	$25,000
Net income	$75,000	New assets	$50,000
Total Sources	$75,000	Total Uses	$75,000

Step 3: Next we use the 1995 sources and uses statement to form the year-end 1995 balance sheet. We recognize that assets rose by $50,000 and that equity (retained earnings) rose by the quantity: net income less dividends.

Harlow Corporation 12/31/95

Assets	Equity
$1,050,000	$1,050,000

Final Solution: We find that, given an income of $75,000, Harlow can meet its cash needs for expansion ($50,000) and still have money available for a $25,000 dividend. ◄┘

Problem 2 Using the financial projections in problem 1 above, forecast the sources and uses statements for Harlow Corporation for 1996 and 1997.

Solution to Problem 2
Financial statements for 1996 and 1997 are determined by repeating the same procedure used above. However, rather than using 1994 as the starting year, we use 1995 (the solutions to problem 1) as the starting point.

Step 1: The sources and uses statement is begun using the same format as above and by filling in the values that we already know:

Harlow Corporation 1996 Sources and Uses Statement

Sources		Uses	
Depreciation	$0	Dividends	?
Net income	$100,000	New assets	$50,000
Total Sources	$100,000	Total Uses	?

Notice that the net income figure for 1996 was used. It will be obvious upon reflection that a dividend payment of $50,000 keeps the statement balanced:

Harlow Corporation 1996 Sources and Uses Statement

Sources		Uses	
Depreciation	$0	Dividends	$ 50,000
Net income	$100,000	New assets	$ 50,000
Total Sources	$100,000	Total Uses	$100,000

Step 2: Next we use the 1996 sources and uses statement to form the year-end 1996 balance sheet. We know that assets rose by $50,000 and that equity (retained earnings) rose by the quantity: net income less dividends. We add these values to the 1995 balance sheet that was projected in question 1:

Harlow Corporation 12/31/96

Assets	Equity
$1,100,000	$1,100,000

Step 3: The next (1997) sources and uses statement is found using the same approach as above and by filling in the 1997 values that we already know:

Harlow Corporation 1997 Sources and Uses Statement

Sources		Uses	
Depreciation	$0	Dividends	$ 75,000
Net income	$125,000	New assets	$ 50,000
Total Sources	$125,000	Total Uses	$125,000

Notice that the $75,000 figure was inserted directly into our first draft in order to streamline the analysis

Step 4: Next we use the 1997 sources and uses statement to form the year-end 1997 balance sheet. We know that assets rose by $50,000 and that equity (retained earnings) rose by the quantity: net income less dividends. We add these values to the 1996 balance sheet that was projected in step 2:

Harlow Corporation 12/31/97

Assets	Equity
$1,150,000	$1,150,000

Final Solution: We find that, given incomes of $100,000 and $125,000 over the next two years, Harlow can meet its cash needs for expansion ($50,000) and still have money available for a $50,000 dividend in 1996 and a $75,000 dividend in 1997. ⏎

REVIEW QUESTIONS

1. Provide a one-sentence definition of financial analysis.
2. List the three general aspects of the firm that financial analysts investigate.
3. Why do modernists prefer to use market prices when analyzing the firm?
4. Why do traditionalists prefer to use accounting numbers when analyzing the firm?
5. Describe a situation in which a modernist might advocate using accounting numbers.
6. How do current assets or liabilities differ from fixed assets or liabilities?
7. Explain in one or two sentences what the balance sheet is measuring.
8. Explain in one or two sentences what the income statement is measuring.
9. In its simplest form, what is a financial ratio?
10. Define ratio analysis.
11. List one common ratio in each of the following areas: (1) debt usage, (2) liquidity, (3) profitability, and (4) efficiency. State briefly what each of these ratios is measuring.
12. What type of information is conveyed in the sources and uses statement?
13. Provide a one-sentence definition of corporate financial planning.
14. What is the "slack" variable, and how is it used in the financial planning model?

PROBLEMS

1. An office party on New Year's Eve overflowed into the accounting department of your corporation, causing ink to be spilled onto a balance sheet. The accountants are furious—especially since they are never invited to the parties. Can you help them by supplying the missing numbers?

The Balance Sheet for Problem #1
(in thousands of dollars)

Assets	1994	1993	Change
Cash and securities	$ 512	$ 453	$ _____
Accounts receivable	1,325	_____	+ 104
Inventory	$ _____	$ 8,386	$ _____
Total Current Assets	$ _____	$ _____	$ +300
Equipment	$ _____	$ 33,929	$ +8,010
Less accumulated depreciation	12,657	_____	+1,362
Net equipment	$ _____	$ _____	$ _____
Buildings	$ 95,129	$ _____	$ 0
Less accumulated depreciation	_____	51,237	+2,251
Net buildings	$ _____	$ _____	$ _____
Land	$ 73,012	$ _____	$ 0
Fixed Assets	$ _____	$ _____	$ _____
Total Assets	$ _____	$ _____	$ _____
Liabilities and Equity			
Accounts payable	$ _____	$ 1,423	$ + 76
Bank loans	3,664	$ _____	− 32
Debt due within year	$ 1,483	$ 1,327	$ _____
Total Current Liabilities	$ _____	$ _____	$ _____
Total Long-Term Debt	$ _____	$ _____	$ _____
Common stock ($.10 Par)	$ 1,500	$ 1,500	$ _____
Paid-in-surplus	$ 45,546	_____	0
Retained earnings	$ _____	$ _____	$ _____
Total Equity	$ 103,323	$ 102,876	$ _____
Total Liability and Equity	$ _____	$ _____	$ _____

2. Net working capital is defined as current assets less current liabilities.
   a. Determine the net working capital for Points of Light Corporation for each year given in Table 16.4.
   b. What would happen to net working capital in the last year if Points of Lights Corporation used $100,000 of cash to pay off $100,000 of bank loans?
   c. What would happen to net working capital in the last year if Points of Light Corporation used $100,000 of cash to buy inventory?
   d. Finally, what would happen to net working capital in the last

year if Points of Light Corporation used $100,000 of cash to buy a building?

3. Worn Out Equipment, Inc., has the following year-end balance sheet values for its depreciable assets:

Equipment	$478,213	Buildings	$8,648,382
Accumulated Depreciation	265,111	Accumulated Depreciation	2,424,171
Net Equipment	$213,102	Net Buildings	$6,224,211

   a. Determine the values for equipment, accumulated depreciation on equipment, and net equipment at the end of the next year if, until that time, the firm does not buy or sell any equipment but expenses another $52,099 of depreciation.
   b. Determine the values for buildings, accumulated depreciation on buildings, and net buildings at the end of the next year if, during the next year, the firm buys a new building for $1,500,000 and takes total depreciation (including the new building) of $404,764.

4. The Painted Post Corp. has the following year-end balance sheet values for its buildings and equipment:

Equipment and Buildings	$83,324,958
Accumulated Depreciation	23,114,145
Net Equipment and Buildings	60,210,813

Determine the values for each account at the end of the next year if, during the next year, the firm buys $12,000,000 of equipment, depreciates all buildings and equipment by $6,545,000, and sells an old building that it had purchased for $10,000,000 but which had an accumulated depreciation of $6,423,382.

5. Preemptive Rights, Inc., has the following values on its balance sheet:

	1994	1993
Common Stock ($1 Par)	$ 2,564,000	$ 2,400,000
Paid in Surplus of Par	8,439,000	8,000,000
Retained Earnings	$15,435,000	$14,328,000

   a. How many shares of common stock did the firm have in each year?
   b. How many shares of stock did the firm issue during 1994?
   c. How much money was raised above the $1 par value for these new shares?
   d. What must have been the selling price of each share of the new stock on average?

e. If the firm paid $500,000 in dividends during 1994, what was its net income?

6. Thieves have broken into your computer system and have stolen key numbers from your firm's income statement. Can you replace them?

Income Statement for Problem 6

	1994	1993
Sales	$2,658,000	$ 2,435,000
Costs of goods sold	_____	967,000
Selling and general expenses	867,000	831,000
Earnings before interest and taxes	$ 768,000	$ _____
Interest on debt	_____	200,000
Earnings before taxes	$ 558,000	$ _____
Taxes	_____	175,000
Net income	$ 335,000	_____

7. Referring to problem 6, during 1994 the firm paid $100,000 in dividends. The 1993 year-end retained earnings were $2,500,000. What would be the retained earnings on the firm's balance sheet statements in 1994?

8. Using the financial statements in Table 16.12 (see page 534), fill in the following debt ratios:

	1994	1993
a. The Debt Ratio	_____	_____
b. The Debt-to-Equity Ratio	_____	_____
c. The Equity Multiplier	_____	_____

9. Using the financial statements in Table 16.12, fill in the following liquidity ratios:

	1994	1993
a. The Cash Ratio	_____	_____
b. The Quick Ratio	_____	_____
c. The Current Ratio	_____	_____

10. Using the financial statements in Table 16.12, fill in the following profitability and efficiency ratios for 1994:

a. Net Return on Sales = _____ .
b. Net Return on Assets = _____ .
c. Net Return on Equity = _____ .
d. Net Profit Margin = _____ .
e. Inventory Turnover = _____ .
f. Receivables Turnover = _____ .
g. Average Collection Period = _____ .

11. Use the retained earnings figures and the net income in Table 16.12 to compute the dividends paid in 1994. What percentage of net income was this dividend?

TABLE 16.12
Balance Sheet for Problems 8–14 (in thousands of dollars)

	1994	1993
Assets		
Cash and Securities	$ 512	$ 453
Accounts receivable	1,325	1,215
Inventory	9,001	8,386
Total Current Assets	$ 10,838	$10,054
Fixed Assets	90,001	88,785
Total Assets	$100,839	$98,839
Liabilities and Equity		
Accounts payable	$ 1,301	$ 1,223
Bank loans	3,664	3,550
Debt due within year	1,483	1,327
Total Current Liabilities	$ 6,448	$ 6,100
Total Long-Term Debt	$ 39,100	39,000
Common stock ($.10 Par)	$ 2,000	$ 2,000
Paid-in-surplus	25,500	25,500
Retained earnings	27,791	26,239
Total Liability and Equity	$100,839	$98,839

Income Statement for Problems 8–14 (in thousands)

	1994	1993
Sales	$35,000	$34,000
Cost of goods sold	10,000	9,600
Depreciation	2,100	2,090
Selling and general expenses	12,450	12,500
Earnings before interest and taxes	$ 10,450	$ 9,810
Interest on debt	5,000	5,490
Earnings before taxes	$ 5,450	$ 4,320
Taxes	2,100	1,700
Net income	$ 3,350	$ 2,620

12. Find the changes between years for each account in the balance sheets in Table 16.12 and use those changes to construct a sources and uses of cash statement using the following format:

Sources	Uses
Net Income	Dividends
Depreciation $0	. . .
. . .	. . .
Total Sources	Total Uses

13. Condense the balance sheets in Table 16.12 by collapsing all current assets and current liabilities into a single figure entitled Net Working Capital. Then, use the condensed balance sheet to construct a sources and uses of funds statement using the same format as in problem 12.

14. Reformat the sources and uses statements in problems 12 and 13 in order to put the change in cash at the bottom of the sources and uses of cash statement and to put the change in net working capital at the bottom of the sources and uses of funds statement.

15. Chugging Along, Inc., is attempting to forecast its financial future and develop a financial plan. The firm's most recent income statement and balance sheet have been constructed. Highly condensed versions are shown below. For simplicity we are ignoring depreciation.

1994 Condensed Income Statement
Chugging Along, Inc. (in thousands of dollars)

Revenues	$ 100
Expenses	80
Net income	$ 20

12/31/94 Condensed Balance Sheet
Chugging Along, Inc. (in thousands of dollars)

Net working capital	$ 50
Fixed assets	150
Total Assets	$ 200
Long-term debt	$ 0
Equity	200
Total Debt and Equity	$ 200

The president of Chugging Along, Inc., is rather confident that revenues will grow by $10,000 per year. Expenses tend to run about 80% of revenues. Accordingly, it is rather straightforward to construct a forecast of next year's income statement:

1995 Forecasted Income Statement
Chugging Along, Inc. (in thousands of dollars)

Revenues	$ 110
Expenses	88
Net income	$ 22

You have been asked to compile a forecast of the balance sheet for the end of the next year. You are told that net working capital will need to expand by $5,000 but that fixed assets will not need to expand since there is already excess capacity. You are also told that the firm desires to grow without taking on new debt and that

any profits not needed to fund growth should be sent to the shareholders as a dividend. Begin by computing the sources and uses
of funds statement for 1995 using the given format. (Hint: All variables are determined except the dividend amount, which must be
set equal to the number that will allow the sources and uses to
balance.)

1995 Forecasted Sources and Uses of Funds Statement
Chugging Along, Inc.

Sources	
Net income	$ _____
Depreciation	0
(others?)	_____
Total Sources	$ _____
Uses	
Dividends	$ _____
(others?)	_____
Total uses	$ _____

16. Returning to Chugging Along, Inc., in problem 15, now use the
    forecasted sources and uses statement for 1995 to construct the
    firm's condensed balance sheet for the end of 1995. Use the same
    format as was used in the 1994 balance sheet.
17. Returning one last time to Chugging Along, Inc., the president
    asks you to forecast all three financial statements for 1996 using
    the same formats and forecasts as were used for 1995. In other
    words, revenues are expected to grow by another $10,000, net
    working capital is expected to grow by another $5,000, and so
    forth.
18. Johnny Checkpay has had his last bad day at work. Starting
    tomorrow, Johnny is putting his life savings into starting up his
    own company. The first thing he is going to do is put together a
    financial plan as part of the business plan he will take to the bank
    in an effort to obtain the financing which he needs. Johnny
    already knows the type of balance sheet he will need to get started:

Starting Condensed Balance Sheet, Checkpay, Inc.
(in thousands of dollars)

Net working capital	$ 100
Fixed assets	100
Total Assets	$ 200
Bank loan	$ 100
Equity	100
Total Debt and Equity	$ 200

Thus, Johnny knows that in order to obtain the net working capital and fixed assets he needs he will require a $100,000 bank loan

in addition to his life savings of $100,000. Johnny has also forecasted the income statements he expects for the first four years (we ignore depreciation and taxes):

Forecasted Condensed Income Statements,
Checkpay, Inc. (in thousand of dollars)

	Year 1	Year 2	Year 3	Year 4
Revenues	$100	$200	$300	$450
Expenses	170	230	300	360
Net Income	−70	−30	0	90

Johnny plans to go to the bank with a request for a $200,000 loan. He arrived at the amount by adding together the $100,000 immediate need for money to purchase assets as well as an additional $100,000 to cover the losses he expects to suffer in the first two years as the company gets going. Other than needing money to cover unexpected losses, can you think of anything that Johnny is forgetting?

19. Returning to Checkpay, Inc., in problem 18, Johnny returns from the bank very disappointed. It seems that the bank's analyst has questioned his financial plan. Upon questioning, Johnny had admitted that his plans for growth would require additional net working capital even though he proved that no additional fixed assets would be needed. Johnny forecasts that he will need to expand his net working capital by $20,000 per year to meet growth.

Construct a forecast of the first four years of sources and uses statements and the first four years of balance sheets. Use these statements to show Johnny how much of a bank loan he will ultimately need since it is new bank loans that must be used to meet capital needs. (In other words, the bank loan is the slack variable that will allow these financial statements to balance.) Ignore additional interest expense.

20. Returning to Checkpay, Inc., Johnny has discovered that his original projections of expenses were based upon only the first $100,000 of loans. Assuming that the interest rate is 10% and that Johnny is allowed to borrow more money as it is needed, how much will he have needed to borrow by the end of the third year to meet his growth goals and to pay the interest? You may assume that the interest on the bank loan is paid in the year following the loan and is based upon the previous year's ending balance of the loan. (Hint: This requires that each year's income statement be revised to add an interest expense (equal to 10% of the previous year's ending bank loan amount over $100,000) to the original expense projections. This will cause the equity account to become negative.) We have done the first statements to help get you started.

Sources and Uses Projection for Year 1
Checkpay, Inc.
(The bank loan amount was entered last so as to balance the statement.)

Sources	
Bank loan increase	90
Total Sources	90
Uses	
Net loss	70
Net working capital	20
Total Uses	90

Forecasted Condensed Balance Sheet, End of Year 1, Checkpay, Inc.

Net working capital	$ 120
Fixed assets	100
Total Assets	$ 220
Bank loan	$ 190
Equity	30
Total Debt and Equity	$ 220

Forecasted Income Statement, Year 2, Checkpay, Inc.

Revenues	200
Original expenses	230
Additional interest expense	9
Net income or loss	−39

21. Perform a rough financial analysis of the debt usage, liquidity, and profitability of Checkpay, Inc. How would you suggest that Johnny revise his plans in order to provide for a more reasonable financial future?

DISCUSSION QUESTIONS

1. The firm's accountant suggests that by taking less depreciation the firm will be able to increase its net income and therefore have sufficient earnings that the firm will not need to borrow money to fund expansion. You are asked to comment.

2. It is your decision on whether to extend a large amount of credit to Comic Adventures in order to fill a large order that they have placed with your firm. Your financial analysis of Comic Adventures, Inc., reveals that the firm's financial ratios have been improving and that they now meet or exceed all industry standards. However, the market price of both their debt and equity have fallen substantially in recent months. What would you do?

3. Why might an optimal financial ratio for one firm differ from the industry average financial ratio?
4. Why is depreciation listed as a source of cash or funds when it is an expense?
5. Why can a new firm's need for capital exceed the total of its projected losses and initial assets?
6. Which contains more information about the probability that a firm will be able to pay its debts: the price of one of its bonds or all of its current and past financial statements?

Chapter 17

Working Capital Management

Prerequisites: Chapters 1 through 6

Jan was in a bind. Tuition was due in four days and the penalty for late payment was $100. On top of tuition, the phone bill was due tomorrow or another late payment fee would be assessed. The money to pay the tuition was "locked" into a certificate of deposit (CD), which didn't come due for seven more days. If she withdrew the money from the bank she would have to pay a substantial interest penalty for early withdrawal.[1]

Despondent, Jan turned to the thing she had learned to trust: her corporate finance textbook. The pages fell open to the chapter on working capital management. Could the working capital management techniques of a major corporation apply to her personal financial decisions?

Suddenly, Jan saw hope. She could write the check for the tuition payment, take it to the bursar's office after banking hours, and then transfer the money from the CD to her checking account on the day that the CD matured. Perhaps the time period or "float" between when the check was written and when the money would be deducted from her checking account would be sufficient to enable the money to be transferred—especially since the time interval included a weekend.

Excited now, Jan continued to flip through the pages in hopes that the telephone bill problem could be solved as well. It was a little tougher, but she found a solution. As a start, Jan figured that she could pressure one of her roommates to pay back the money that she owed her, but that amount of money wouldn't be enough.

Jan was in charge of collecting rent from each of her roommates and turning it over to the landlord. Following the techniques of work-

---

1. Despite the bank's advertisements to the contrary, federal law does not require this penalty.

ing capital management, Jan offered one of her roommates (whom everyone not so affectionately called moneybags) a discount if she would pay her share of next month's rent in advance. Jan could pay the telephone bill using the rent money and then pay the rent money when the CD came due. The problem was solved, and she still had time to read a few extra chapters of her corporate finance textbook.

working capital management
The management of the firm's current assets and current liabilities.

The problems and solutions described above fall under the broad heading of **working capital management,** and the techniques apply to Jan's personal finances as well as to small and large corporations.

AN OVERVIEW OF WORKING CAPITAL MANAGEMENT

net working capital
The difference between current assets and current liabilities.

Working capital is defined as a firm's investments in current assets. A related concept is **net working capital,** defined as current assets minus current liabilities. Although it is possible to provide very detailed listings, the principal categories of working capital—often referred to as the components of working capital—are shown in Table 17.1. Working capital management refers to the specialized tools and strategies for making decisions with regard to these assets and liabilities.

The Three Tasks of Working Capital Management

The concepts underlying the problems and techniques of working capital management discussed in this chapter are remarkably familiar to most college students. Perhaps nowhere in finance is there such a similarity between corporate and personal finance. The three tasks or concepts underlying working capital management are:

1. Speeding up receipts of cash,
2. Delaying payments of cash, and
3. Investing excess cash.

Of course, implicit in each of these three tasks is the corporate objective to maximize shareholder wealth. Thus, they are to be per-

TABLE 17.1
Principal Categories of Working Capital

Current Assets	Current Liabilities
Cash	Accounts Payable
Marketable Securities	Bank Loans and Notes Payable
Accounts Receivable	Current Debt (due in one year)
Inventory	

formed in a manner that takes advantage of the time value of money in an optimal way. In other words, receipts should be speeded up, payments delayed, and cash invested if and only if the advantages outweigh the disadvantages.

The first part of this chapter discusses each of the components or categories of working capital individually in detail. Current assets will be presented first, followed by current liabilities.

The second part of the chapter will discuss overall working capital management techniques, such as the cash budget. This material will bring together concepts previously introduced for each component of working capital. If things appear complicated, remember that the tools in this chapter are familiar to each of us in everyday personal financial management.

CURRENT ASSET MANAGEMENT

We now discuss each type of current asset in detail, beginning with cash, the most liquid category, and ending with inventory, the least liquid category. Liquidity, the speed with which an asset can be converted into cash at a reasonable price, was discussed in Chapter 2.

Cash Management

cash management
The management of the firm's cash position. Cash management recognizes that, while cash is a necessary raw material, too much of it is wasteful.

Cash management plays perhaps the most important role in working capital management. Cash is a necessary asset for running a firm and must be held in sufficient quantity to meet demand. In this sense, cash is held in inventory just as are some other assets, such as the raw materials for production. The concept that drives cash management is that, while cash is necessary, too much of it is wasteful. In other words, the corporation's capital is a valuable commodity that could be put to work earning better rates of return elsewhere than it earns as cash—little or no interest in a bank's checking account. The goal of cash management is simply to minimize the total cost of providing cash liquidity to the firm.

Reviewing the EOQ Model for Cash Management. Chapter 2 included a brief introduction to the economic order quantity (EOQ) model, one of the simplest cash management models. The EOQ model determines the optimal amount of cash or any other inventory to order each time it is depleted.

In the EOQ model, cash is assumed to flow out at an even rate. There is a cost each time cash is replenished, called the order cost, and a cost to maintaining the cash inventory, called the storage cost. The optimal solution minimizes the total sum of these two costs over time.

FIGURE 17.1
The Flow of Cash in the EOQ Model

The EOQ model determines the optimal cash balance for the firm. The model assumes that the firm's cash is drawn down to zero and is immediately replenished up to the optimal level.

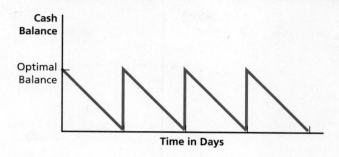

However, there is a serious problem with applying the EOQ model of Chapter 2 to cash management. The EOQ model ignores cash inflows and uncertainty, in that all movements of cash are assumed to be outflows and unchanged. This pattern is illustrated in Figure 17.1. Because the EOQ model ignores cash inflows, it is better suited for other types of management problems, such as traditional inventory management. We introduced the EOQ model as a cash management model in Chapter 2 because it lays a foundation upon which to build the model discussed next.

The Miller-Orr Model. This chapter will introduce an improved cash management model called the Miller-Orr model, which addresses some of the problems of EOQ. Of course, the Miller-Orr model does not address all of the complexities of managing the firm's cash position. In the Miller-Orr model, the cash balance is allowed to rise or fall randomly as the firm's operations either produce cash inflows or require cash outflows on a continuous basis, due to random events such as the timing of various transactions and bills.

Miller-Orr model

A cash management model that determines an upper and lower limit for the firm's cash balances. In the model, when the upper limit is reached, the cash manager invests the excess cash in a less liquid and more profitable asset. When the lower limit is reached the cash manager needs to replenish the cash balance by liquidating an asset or by borrowing.

The **Miller-Orr model** is similar to the EOQ in that the model determines when and how much to order: The upper limit and lower limit for cash balances are determined; when the model's upper limit is reached, the cash manager invests the excess cash in a less liquid and more profitable asset; when the lower limit is reached, the cash manager needs to replenish the cash balance by liquidating an asset or by borrowing.

When the upper or lower limit is reached, the model directs the cash manager to adjust to the optimal cash balance determined in the model. This optimal cash balance is located one-third of the distance from the lower limit toward the upper limit. These concepts are illustrated in Figure 17.2.

The lower limit in the Miller-Orr model is set by management and reflects their estimation of the lowest cash balance that should be held. The model generates the target cash balance that minimizes the

FIGURE 17.2
The Miller-Orr Cash Management Model

The Miller-Orr model allows the cash balance to build up and down. When the cash position hits the upper balance, securities are purchased and the cash balance is returned to the target level. When the cash position hits the lower balance, securities are turned into enough cash to bring the cash position to the target point.

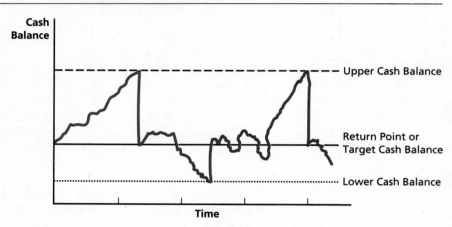

expected total costs of holding cash, shown in Figure 17.2 as the return point or target cash balance. Formula (17.1) determines the precise specification for the target cash balance according to the Miller-Orr model:

$$\text{Target Cash Balance} = \text{Lower Limit} + \left[\frac{3 * TCOST * \sigma^2}{4r} \right]^{1/3}. \quad (17.1)$$

This target cash balance requires estimation of the volatility of the cash flows given in the formula by the daily variance of cash flows (σ^2), estimation of the daily interest rate (r), and an estimate of the cost of returning the cash balance to its return point (*TCOST*). The variance and interest rate can also be expressed in annual terms.

Some calculators are unable to handle numbers as large as those that can result from Formula (17.1). In this case we suggest that Formula (17.1) be broken into the following parts:

$$\text{Target Cash Balance} = \text{Lower Limit} + \left[\frac{(3)^{1/3} * (TCOST)^{1/3} * (\sigma^2)^{1/3}}{(4r)^{1/3}} \right].$$

Given the target cash balance, the upper limit of cash is determined as:

$$\text{Upper Cash Limit} = [3 * \text{Target Cash Balance}] \qquad (17.2)$$
$$- [2 * \text{Lower Limit}].$$

Example 17.1 _____ For example, suppose that a firm sets the lower cash limit at $1,000, has an estimated daily variance of cash flows of $250, estimates its cost of returning to the target cash balance at $150, and assumes an annual interest rate of 10 percent so that the daily interest rate is .0274 percent. Using the Miller-Orr model, the target cash balance would be:

$$\text{Target Cash Balance} = \$1,000 + \left[\frac{3 * 150 * 250}{4 * .000274} \right]^{1/3}$$

$$= \$1,468.23,$$

and the upper limit on cash holdings would be:

$$\text{Upper Limit} = [3 * \$1,468.23] - [2 * \$1,000] = \$2,404.70.$$

Accordingly, the cash manager knows when and to what level to adjust the cash balance. ↵

Newer models have been developed that attempt to build on the Miller-Orr model by incorporating the predictability of some cash flows. Nevertheless, Miller-Orr provides a good starting point for the study and practice of cash management. All cash management models have in common the objective of finding the least-cost approach to providing a firm with an adequate cash balance to meet its liquidity needs.

Marketable Securities Management

We previously discussed the corporation's cash balances, such as their funds in checking accounts that earn no interest or a relatively low rate of interest. The second-most liquid category of assets for a corporation is marketable securities.

money market securities
Types of securities characterized by short-term maturity of one year or less and low risk of default. Examples of money market securities include U.S. Treasury bills, commercial paper, and certificates of deposit.

The marketable securities in which a corporation would typically invest are known as **money market securities.** The money market is not a physical place, such as the New York Stock Exchange, but simply refers to types of securities such as U.S. Treasury bills, repurchase agreements, commercial paper, certificates of deposit, money market mutual funds, and other short-term, relatively low-risk investments. An expanded discussion of marketable securities is included later in the chapter.

The advantage of marketable securities over cash is that they generally pay a higher rate of interest. The disadvantage is that they must be liquidated into cash in order to meet an expense, and the process of selling the security and receiving the cash usually takes one or two days.

The purpose of buying and holding marketable securities may be to provide funds to meet some expenses that are planned at future specific points in time or to meet unexpected expenses. Corporations occasionally hold large amounts of marketable securities "in waiting" as they search for major investment opportunities. When investing cash in marketable securities, it is important for the cash manager or treasurer to determine the probabilities of when the marketable securities might need to be liquidated to meet cash needs.

Example 17.2 —————— Consider Liberal Wines, Inc. (LW), a maker of traditional wines. LW receives somewhat regular cash inflows throughout the year. Unfortunately, many of LW's expenses are concentrated in the fall, when they pay local farmers for grapes and have enormous labor expenses for beginning production.

We would expect LW's liquidity to follow an annual cycle, with a peak balance of cash and marketable securities in the summer and minimum balances in the fall. Typically, we would expect LW to invest in marketable securities throughout the year and to liquidate these securities in the fall when the cash is needed. ◄┘

The Choice of Marketable Securities. Once it has been decided how much cash should be invested in marketable securities, the next issue is in which marketable securities should the firm invest. In selecting a marketable security a cash manager typically has three considerations—maturity, credit risk, and income taxes—which are discussed below.

1. *Maturity.* One of the most difficult decisions the cash manager faces is that involving the maturity of the marketable security. The advantage of investing in longer maturities is that they generally offer higher rates of return. The primary disadvantage of longer-term securities is that they fluctuate more in market price when interest rates change. In other words, longer-term securities have higher interest rate risk. Worse yet, if the security needs to be liquidated before it matures, the corporation might be forced to recognize a very low return or even a loss. These fluctuations in price and therefore in the return on longer-term marketable securities are usually disliked by cash managers and their bosses, such as the CFO and board of directors.

term structure of interest rates
The relationship between yield and time to maturity for similar-risk securities.

The relationship between interest rates and term to maturity is known as the **term structure of interest rates**. History reveals that the average returns of investing in longer-term money market securities are high relative to the small risks they pose. However, the realities of corporate politics often outweigh this theory of investment such that cash managers are notoriously conservative in bearing this risk of interest rate fluctuation.

2. *Credit Risk:* Credit risk is the potential for the issuer of the marketable security to default and be unable to pay back some or all of the investor's principal and interest.

In the United States, securities backed by the U.S. government are considered to be free of credit risk. There are enormous quantities of such securities available including U.S. Treasury bills and FDIC insured certificates of deposit.

Securities considered to be subject to credit risk include money market obligations of corporations (called commercial paper), uninsured certificates of deposit (uninsured because they exceed the $100,000 FDIC insurance limit), obligations of state and municipal governments, and banker's acceptances.

As we would expect, market interest rates adjust such that the securities with higher credit risk offer higher returns. Thus, the cash manager is faced with the dilemma that most higher returns in the money market are only available if credit risk is borne. Despite their conservative nature, cash managers frequently bear minor amounts of credit risk.

3. *Income Taxes:* The final major consideration for a cash manager is the effect of income taxes on marketable securities. Generally speaking, there are four levels of taxability:

   a. Fully taxable—including almost all securities backed by corporations and banks such as commercial paper, CDs, and money market mutual funds that buy them,

   b. Free of state income taxes—including direct obligations of the U.S. government,

   c. Partially excluded—including dividends from common stocks, which are substantially tax free and are usually held by cash managers through funds known as dividend capture funds, and

   d. Tax free—including interest from municipal and state obligations, which are free of federal income tax as well as totally tax free for residents of the municipality or state issuing the securities.

The rates of return offered by securities adjust to partially offset tax advantages. Thus, if everything else is equal, fully taxable securities pay the highest before-tax returns while tax-free securities pay the lowest returns.

Nevertheless, corporations in high tax brackets are well advised to consider seriously the last two categories. It is important to note, however, that the tax-advantaged securities tend to have higher levels of credit risk. Corporations in low tax brackets (which may be losing money) and nontaxed entities should invest only in the first two categories.

Summary of Marketable Securities

Marketable securities provide an excellent opportunity for a cash manager to invest excess cash for the purpose of producing higher returns while maintaining liquidity. However, there are no easy answers as to how a cash manager should decide among marketable securities, since prices in the money market will adjust such that all securities will be approximately equally desirable.

Market conditions and institutional features change. What is unlikely to change is that the decision will continue to involve maturity, credit risk, and taxability.

Accounts Receivable Management

Ch. 11

accounts receivable
Monies owed to a firm as a result of having sold its products to customers on credit.

Accounts receivable are the monies owed to a firm as a result of having sold its products to customers on credit. For example, consider the sales and collections on sales for a firm over the first half-year 1992:

Month	Sales	Collections on Sales
January	$2,000	$0
February	$2,000	$0
March	$2,000	$0
April	$2,000	$2,000 (From January)
May	$2,000	$0
June	$2,000	$2,000 (From February)

Over the first half of the year, sales are $12,000 but collections are only $4,000. Accounts receivable is $8,000.

There are three primary issues in the management of accounts receivable:

1. To whom to extend credit,
2. What should be the terms of the credit, and
3. What procedure should be used to collect the money.

We will discuss each of these issues separately.

To Whom to Extend Credit. As with any corporate decision, extending credit should be based upon a comparison of costs and benefits. In accounts receivable management, these costs and benefits are a little more complicated than one might initially think. The analysis must build in uncertainty, since we are uncertain of future payment, and we will handle this by computing the expected costs and expected benefits through payment probabilities.

The potential cost of extending credit is that the customer will not pay. Although there is a temptation to compute this cost as the full price of the product (the amount owed to the firm), it is almost always more appropriate to use the actual cost of the product, which is illustrated below.

The potential benefit of extending credit is not just the hope for profit on the one transaction, but rather the potential value of the customer for a long-term relationship.

Example 17.3 ——————— Assume that Deadbeats, Inc., has just placed an order for 1,200 of your firm's instant post holes. Your firm's selling price of post holes is $10 each, while the total cost is $5 each.

Based upon available information on Deadbeats, Inc., and your financial analysis, it is estimated that there is only a 30 percent chance that Deadbeats will pay. In the event that they are denied credit, you are sure that they will purchase post holes from your competitor. In the event that credit is extended, you would expect them to continue to do business with your firm. In fact, you would expect them to place a similar order each year.

Whether or not Deadbeats pays, the cost to your firm of having extended credit is the manufacturing cost of the product delivered, or $6,000 ($5 times 1,200 post holes), not the $12,000 listed price.

If Deadbeats pays and turns out to be a long-term customer, the benefit to your firm would be a profit of $6,000 per year. Applying the formula for a perpetuity from Chapter 5 and selecting 20 percent as a discount rate, we could roughly estimate the present value of this customer to be $30,000:

$$\text{Present Value of Deadbeat's Business} = \frac{\$6,000}{.20} = \$30,000.$$

The net present value of the decision to extend credit to Deadbeats, Inc., is found as the expected benefit of the sale minus the expected cost:

$$NPV = [\text{Probability of Payment} * \$30,000]$$

$$- [(1\text{-Probability of Payment}) * \$6,000].$$

Inserting the 30 percent probability of the customer paying produces a net benefit of $4,800:

$$NPV = [.3 * \$30,000] - [.7 * \$6,000] = \$4,800.$$

The analysis indicates that the credit should be extended. In fact, the probability of payment would have to drop to below 16.67 percent before the *NPV* of the credit extension decision to Deadbeats is negative. ◄┘

Perhaps this example explains why so many firms are willing to extend credit to consumers. As we have said, the potential loss to the firm is the cost of the product, not its price. Further, the potential benefit may include an ongoing relationship.[2]

We may generalize the formula for the *NPV* of a credit decision as:

$$NPV = [\text{Probability of Payment} * \text{Customer Value}] \\ - [(1 - \text{Probability of Payment}) * \text{Cost}]. \tag{17.3}$$

In the case of a one-time sale where no repeat business is anticipated, the customer value reduces to the profit for the one sale. In practice, however, the credit extension decision can become more complicated and often must be formalized into a policy that can be implemented consistently. Nevertheless, the decision should be based upon the general principles presented here.

Determining the Terms of the Accounts Receivable. Once the decision to grant credit has been made, the firm must establish the terms of the credit. These terms are called the terms of sale and give the buyer the time period for which, and the price at which, payment is due. While these terms of sale are usually discussed before the transaction is made, they are also listed on the firm's invoice—which is simply the bill for the order.

Example 17.4 ——————— Credit terms are often separated into two parts—the credit period, and the credit discount. Somewhat complex jargon that looks something like this is used:

2/10; net 30.

As shown, the terms of sale usually are presented as a string of numbers or words. In the example, the string needs to be broken up into pairs: The first pair is 2 and 10, and the second pair is net and 30.

The first item in each pair denotes the cost. The cost is listed as either a percentage discount or the word net, which

———————————
2. In the case of consumer purchases, the potential interest charges earned on the credit decision would need to be factored into the analysis.

means no discount. Thus the "2" in the above example indicates that the customer can receive a 2 percent discount, meaning that the seller will accept 98 percent of the billed price as payment in full.

The second number in each pair is the number of days for which the stated discount or net price will be available. In the above example, the 2 percent discount will be available only if the discounted price is paid within 10 days.

The second pair in the above example, net 30, offers alternate terms in the event that the buyer does not pay within the time period for the first payment option. Net 30 means that the customer must pay the full price within the 20 days following the initial discount period. If not paid by a total of 30 days, this bill will be considered overdue.

There are many terms that can be used to denote the terms of the discount and the terms of the credit sales without the discount. For example:

2/10; net 30; 18% over 30,

means that a 2 percent discount applies if the bill is paid within 10 days, that the net amount of credit is due in 30 days, and that annual interest of 18 percent will apply to any credit balance beyond 30 days. Also:

5/10–EOM; net 45,

means that a 5 percent discount applies if paid within 10 days of the end of the month (EOM), but that the net amount of credit is due within 45 days. ↵

As the examples show, most terms of sale offer the buyer an incentive to pay early. The advantage of including this incentive is that it increases the speed with which payments will be made and also may decrease the probability that collection efforts will be required or that payment will never be made.

As with all other financial decisions, a correct decision is made when all costs and benefits are included, using market prices and adjusted for time and risk. The issues involved with selecting a credit policy are too numerous to detail, but they are all based upon a common-sense application of the principles detailed throughout this text.

One key issue is the interest rate implied by the discount. For example, offering a 2 percent discount to accelerate payment by 20 days amounts to an annual time value of money of well over 36 percent. How this interest rate is computed is discussed in detail later in the section on accounts payable.

Accounts Receivable Collection Efforts.   Virtually anyone who has ever loaned money has learned the difficulty of collecting it. Collection of accounts receivable is an important process for a corporation and requires a well-designed and well-implemented policy.

factoring of accounts receivables
The selling of all or part of the firm's accounts receivables to another firm at an agreed-upon price. The buying firm is the factor and has developed an expertise in collection.

One technique is the **factoring of accounts receivables.** In a typical factoring arrangement, one firm will sell their accounts receivable(s) outright to another firm for an agreed-upon price. There is usually no recourse in such transactions, such that the buyer (also known as the factor) takes the loss if the purchaser of the goods does not ultimately pay for them. Obviously, the buyer of accounts receivables has developed an expertise in collections.

lock boxes
Collection locations spread geographically so as to reduce the amount of time required for checks mailed to the firm to be deposited and cleared. Typically the lock boxes are post office box addresses from which deposits go directly to a bank on the day of receipt.

Another technique to expedite the receipt of accounts receivable is to utilize **lock boxes.** Lock boxes are payment collection locations spread geographically so as to reduce the amount of time required for checks mailed to the firm to be deposited and cleared. Typically the lock boxes are post office box addresses from which deposits go directly to a bank on the day of receipt. The reduction of mailing time and check clearing time for the banks can produce significant savings when large sums of money are involved. Obviously, a challenging working capital management problem is the decision of how many lock boxes should be used and where they should be located.

Summary of Accounts Receivable

Accounts receivable are the monies owed to a firm as a result of having sold its products to customers on credit. The three primary issues in accounts receivable management are to whom to extend credit, the terms of the credit, and the procedure that should be used to collect the money. In most cases, these issues can be placed in the context of *NPV*, or the comparison of the present value of the benefits with the present value of the costs.

Inventory Management

The three primary types of inventory are raw materials, work in process, and finished goods, which are represented by the cumulated costs of items before, during, and after production, respectively. The benefit of an inventory is to assure that goods will be available as required. The primary costs of an inventory are the opportunity cost of the capital used to finance the inventory, ordering costs, and storage costs. Inventory management seeks to maximize the net benefit—the benefits minus costs—of the inventory. All benefits and costs should be measured using market prices adjusted for time and risk.

The EOQ model, introduced in Chapter 2 and reviewed earlier in this chapter, represents the foundation model for conventional inven-

just in time
A technique that seeks to maximize the net benefit of inventory through superior management, such as reducing inventory to near-zero levels.

tory management. In recent years, the concept of meeting demand on a continuous basis rather than having stockpiles of inventory has frequently been advocated. These inventory techniques, such as **just in time** inventory management, seek to maximize the net benefit through superior management.

Inventory management is an extremely important function within most businesses. The discipline is usually taught in business courses and labeled inventory control and management, production management, operations research, management science, or quantitative business.

CURRENT LIABILITY MANAGEMENT

We now detail the management of each of the current liabilities. Generally speaking, the categories will be discussed from most liquid to least liquid, as they are usually listed on a balance sheet.

Accounts Payable Management

accounts payables
Short-term liabilities that the firm has incurred as a result of buying products on credit from other corporations.

Accounts payables are short-term liabilities that the firm has incurred as a result of buying products on credit from other corporations. This is the other side of the transactions previously detailed under accounts receivable.

The accounts payable decision is rather straightforward. If a firm is offered several payment alternatives, the goal of accounts payable management is to select the payment alternative that maximizes shareholder wealth.

Using credit usually involves a cost that can be expressed as an interest rate. In theory, there is a benchmark interest rate which, if paid by a firm, would generate a zero net present value. The goal of accounts payable management is to accept an extension of credit whenever the interest rate implied by the credit is less than the benchmark rate, and to reject other extensions of credit.

Determining the Implied Interest Rate of an Accounts Payable.
As detailed in the subsection on accounts receivable, firms extend credit using a potentially complex jargon. However, using a time line and a financial calculator greatly simplifies the process.

Most extensions of credit can be reduced to the idea that there are one or more deadlines by which a particular amount of money must be paid or else the amount due will increase. Extensions of credit may be illustrated on a time line as follows. Each payment amount is listed above the last date that it will be accepted as payment in full. For example, if on March 1 a firm purchases $100,000 of products on the credit terms 2/10; net 30, the firm can pay $98,000 on March 11 or $100,000 on March 31:

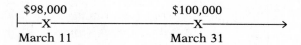

The decision to pay on the second date may now be viewed as the ability of the firm to borrow $98,000 and to repay the money in the form of $100,000 in 20 days. Note that 20 days can be turned into years by dividing by 365. The number of years is (approximately) 0.0548.

The interest rate may be determined using a financial calculator by entering $98,000 as *PV*, $100,000 as *FV*, and 0.0548 as the number of years and computing the interest rate. The answer is approximately 44.58 percent. Our analysis reveals that if the firm pays $100,000 on March 31, it has effectively borrowed money at an interest rate of 44.58 percent. This would certainly be larger than any benchmark and would therefore hurt shareholder wealth. The firm should not accept the extension of credit, and the account payable should be paid on March 11.

To summarize, the decision to accept credit is no different from other types of investment decisions. However, two mistakes are common in accounts payable analysis and must be avoided. First, the time period used to compute the interest rate should be the number of days between the two decision points, or 20 days in the above example. This is the true number of days for which the second payment option delays payment. Second, the base of the loan should not be the net amount of the loan ($100,000 in the example above) but should instead be the discounted amount of the loan ($98,000 in the example). Students should use a time line until these points are clear.

With only two potential payment dates, the problem is whether or not to defer the payment from the first date to the second date. A potential complexity is that there can be more than two potential payment dates such that there are several payment-deferral intervals, and since only one alternative can be accepted, they must be ranked. As discussed in Chapter 6, the net present value technique is often necessary to make ranking decisions.

Determining the benchmark interest rate is conceptually straightforward. The firm should use the interest rate that would be demanded in a competitive market in order to receive credit under similar conditions. For example, the interest rate on commercial paper of the firm or of similar firms would provide an approximate benchmark.

There are other issues involved in accounts payable management such as coordinating the timing of payments with other cash flows to assist the treasurer in maintaining the target level of liquidity for the firm. However, the biggest decision is selecting optimal payment options.

Bank Loan and Notes Payable Management

Firms often borrow money on a short-term basis to meet seasonal or other temporary cash needs. Financial management of these accounts involves attaining arrangements that permit overall firm liquidity at a minimum cost.

compensating balances
A requirement of banks that a percentage of the loan be kept in a non-interest-bearing account as long as the loan is outstanding.

Years ago, this subject was made complex by arrangements known as **compensating balances,** whereby banks required that a percentage of the loan be kept in a non-interest-bearing account over the life of the loan. Compensating balances increased the cost of the loan. However, this practice has become rare in recent years. Today, management of bank loans and other short-term credit involves choosing a lending institution with competitive loan rates, competitive fees, and the services most desired by the firm.

Commercial Paper

commercial paper
A short-term unsecured promissory note issued directly by the firm.

A short-term borrowing alternative that has become quite popular is the issuance of **commercial paper,** a short-term, unsecured promissory note issued directly by the firm. Because these notes are unsecured (there is no physical collateral backing the loan), the commercial paper market is usually confined to large, well-known, financially sound firms.

Issuing corporations view commercial paper as a cost-effective substitute for bank loans and other borrowing alternatives. Investors in commercial paper include insurance companies, pension funds, money market mutual funds, and other corporations.

Current Debt Management

Portions of long-term debt issues that become due within one year are listed as a current liability under a heading such as current payments on long-term debt. The payments may be required because the debt is maturing or because of regular debt repayment requirements, known as sinking fund provisions, under the terms of the debt contract. Working capital management involves planning how these obligations will be met.

WORKING CAPITAL MANAGEMENT TOOLS

The issues involved in each category of working capital were previously detailed. However, working capital management also requires the tools of managing the combined accounts. The most important aspect of this overall liquidity management is forecasting—budgeting or planning the firm's cash needs—which the following sections discuss.

The Cash Budget

cash budget
A schedule of anticipated cash inflows and outflows over a short time into the future, such as several months or quarters.

The **cash budget** is nothing more than a schedule of anticipated cash inflows and outflows over a short time into the future, such as several months or quarters. Table 17.2 illustrates a simplified format for a cash budget, from the beginning cash balance to the ending cash balance. Because the cash flows from operations change from quarter to quarter, the firm's cash balance will also change.

The key issue in cash budgeting is developing the best plan that will keep the cash balance within the range of allowable cash balances throughout the year. As was detailed in the subsection on cash management, most firms set an allowable range for their cash balance, which provides a trade-off between cash becoming too low and too high.

The purpose of the cash budgeting process is to forecast which transactions will be needed to maintain the firm's target cash balance in an optimal manner. There is a priority of what will be done if the cash balance begins to go outside its range. A simplified example would be:

Locations for Excess Cash	*Source for Cash*
Invest first $100,000 in money market mutual funds selected internally.	First $150,000 of borrowing through line of credit with bank.
	Next $100,000 using unsecured bank loan.
Additional cash placed in marketable securities with outside money manager.	Additional funds using notes.

When the firm's cash balance falls to the lower limit, it meets cash needs by liquidating some or all of its marketable securities. After marketable securities have been liquidated, the firm begins to borrow using the sources as listed above. In the opposite case, in which the cash balance reaches the upper limit, the firm would first pay off bor-

TABLE 17.2
Operational Cash Flows for a Cash Budget (numbers in thousands)

| | 1993 | | | | 1994 |
	Q1	Q2	Q3	Q4	Q1
Beginning Cash Balance	——	——	——	——	——
Cash inflows from operations	$740	$600	$250	$600	$760
Cash outflows from operations	($600)	($610)	($650)	($310)	($610)
Net cash flow from operations	$140	($ 10)	($400)	$290	$150
Ending Cash Balance	——	——	——	——	——

rowed funds (starting with the last funds borrowed, which would be the most expensive) before it switched to purchasing marketable securities.

Although at times the process may appear complex, the cash budgeting process is conceptually quite simple. As stated often, the manager attempts to keep the firm's liquidity within the range that maximizes shareholder wealth.

Example 17.5 ——————— The first step in setting up the cash budget is to work through the cash balances from the projections of net cash flows from operations that would occur if no other working capital decisions are made. This is shown in Table 17.3. Notice that the

TABLE 17.3
A First Pass at a Cash Balance (no borrowing or lending) (numbers in thousands)

| | 1993 | | | | 1994 |
	Q1	Q2	Q3	Q4	Q1
Beginning Cash Balance	$ 50[a]	$190	$180	($220)	$ 70
Cash inflows from operations	$740	$600	$250	$600	$760
Cash outflows from operations	($600)	($610)	($650)	($310)	($610)
Net cash flow from operations	$140	($ 10)	($400)	$290	$150
Ending Cash Balance	$190	$180	($220)	$ 70	$220

[a]The amount $50 was not part of the model but was supplied outside of the model.

initial cash balance of $50 in the first quarter of 1993 begins the process that ends in the first quarter of 1993 with a cash balance of $220.

In the example, the firm is planning for a seasonal cash flow pattern in which the firm's ending cash balance would start at $190, would fall to a low of −$220, and would rise to a high of $220. The seasonal pattern of cash flow that produces this variation is illustrated in Figure 17.3.

Clearly the seasonality is causing a range of cash balances that is unacceptable. Remember, the key to managing the cash budget is to adhere to a target range for the cash balance per quarter. For example, suppose the firm sets a range of $0 to $100 for its cash balance. Table 17.3 indicates that the firm must borrow cash during part of the year, and invest excess cash during other parts of the year to keep the cash balance within its target range. Table 17.4 illustrates the borrowing and investing that the cash budget indicates would need to occur during the year to stay within the target. Notice that money was borrowed and invested according to the priority previously listed.

For example, in the first quarter of 1993, the cash buildup of $190 allows for $100 to stay in the cash balance as well as for the excess of $90 to be placed in the money market mutual fund (MMMF). However, the third quarter of 1993 indicates that cash has fallen below zero to ($310), a full $310 below the lower target range of $0. In order to adhere to the cash target, the firm needs to (1) liquidate the $90 placed in the MMMF, (2) borrow $150 from its bank line, and (3) borrow $70 in the

FIGURE 17.3
A Seasonal Pattern of Ending Cash Balances

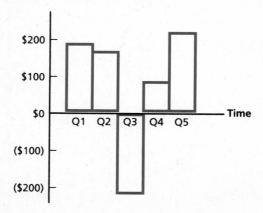

TABLE 17.4
The Completed Cash Budget (numbers in thousands)

| | 1993 | | | | 1994 |
	Q1	Q2	Q3	Q4	Q1
Beginning Cash	$ 50	$100	$ 90	$ 0	$ 70
Cash inflows from operations	$740	$600	$250	$600	$760
Cash outflows from operations	($600)	($610)	($650)	($310)	($610)
Net cash flow from operations	$140	($ 10)	($400)	$290	$150
Cash Buildup	$190	$ 90	($310)	$290	$220
To MMMF	$ 90	$ 0	($ 90)[a]	$ 0	$100
To securities	$ 0	$ 0	$ 0	$ 0	$ 20
From bank line	$ 0	$ 0	$150	($150)[b]	$ 0
From unsecured loan	$ 0	$ 0	$ 70	($ 70)[c]	$ 0
Ending Cash Balance	$100	$ 90	$ 0	$ 70	$100

[a] Negative $ 90 refers to selling off $90 of MMMFs to meet liquidity needs.
[b] Negative $150 refers to the payment of the bank line from the cash buildup.
[c] Negative $ 70 refers to the payment of the loan from the cash buildup.

form of an unsecured bank loan. In the fourth quarter of 1993, the cash buildup of $290 is used to pay off both the bank line of credit and the unsecured bank loan. Finally, in the first quarter of 1994, the cash buildup of $220 allows $100 to be placed again into the MMMF and $20 to be placed into securities, leaving an ending cash balance at the upper end of the target, or at $100. ↵

In actual practice, borrowing to maintain a minimum cash balance and investing of excess cash affects the cash flows in the same period as well as in the next period. This is because the interest income and interest expense are calculated based upon the balances either in the same period or in the previous period. A sophisticated cash budgeting model will include these cash flows based upon the balance in the same period.

The goal of the cash budgeting process is to develop a forecast and plan for borrowing and investing cash. In particular, the cash budget can signal to the manager when the firm needs to seek long-term financing to meet working capital needs, which enables the manager to make necessary arrangements and to monitor the firm's liquidity condition relative to a plan.

TABLE 17.5
Sales Forecasts (numbers in thousands)

	Jan 93	Feb 93	Mar 93	Apr 93	May 93	Jun 93
Sales Forecast	$50	$60	$70	$90	$80	$60

Cash Forecasting

A cash budget will only be as good as the cash flow forecasts used to create it. Perhaps the most critical input is the forecast of cash revenues from sales.

Growing firms and those with highly variable cash revenues struggle with the lag between payment of the costs of production and the receipt of revenues from sales.

A classic cash forecasting task is to convert a forecast of monthly sales into a forecast of monthly cash inflows, using the firm's collection experience. For example, a firm that extends credit terms such as 2/10; net 30 may find that 30 percent of its sales are collected in the first month, 50 percent in the second month, and 15 percent in the third month, and that 5 percent are never collected. To illustrate, consider the sales forecasts in Table 17.5. The cash inflows can be forecasted by applying the percentages above, as shown in Table 17.6.

The bottom line is then input into the cash budget. Similar cash schedules can be produced for other cash flows, such as the costs of manufacturing, by incorporating the delay between when a firm orders its materials and when it must pay for them.

TABLE 17.6
Cash Forecasts from Sales (numbers in thousands)

	Jan 93	Feb 93	Mar 93	Apr 93	May 93	Jun 93
Sales Forecast	$50	$60	$70	$90	$80	$60
Collections from Cash Sales (30%)	$15	$18	$21	$27	$24	$18
Collections from Last Month (50%)	$60[a]	$25	$30	$35	$45	$40
Collections from Two Months Ago (15%)	$21[b]	$18[a]	$ 7.5	$ 9	$10.5	$13.5
Total Collections	$96	$61	$58.5	$71	$79.5	$71.5

[a]Sales in December 1992 were $120.
[b]Sales in November 1992 were $140.

SUMMARY

☐ Net working capital is defined as current assets minus current liabilities. The three primary forces that emerge from working capital management are the desire to maximize shareholder wealth by accelerating cash inflows, delaying cash outflows, and maintaining an optimal level of liquidity.

☐ A liquid firm is one with sufficient cash to pay its bills. However, too much liquidity has certain costs, known as opportunity costs. In the case of working capital management, it may be optimal to maintain a low level of liquidity, which causes occasional problems but which minimizes opportunity costs.

☐ Examples of liquidity management include maintaining optimal levels of cash and optimal levels of inventory.

☐ Cash budgeting requires the scheduling of anticipated cash inflows and outflows over a short time into the future, such as several months or quarters. Cash budgeting is complicated by the fact that sales and cash collections from sales often do not occur in the same time period.

☐ Optimal management of working capital requires the decision maker to incorporate all advantages and disadvantages adjusted for time and risk.

DEMONSTRATION PROBLEMS

Problem 1   Abbey Corporation has set a minimum cash balance of $1,000. The daily variance of cash flows is $1,000,000, the transaction cost of adjusting the cash balance is $1,000, and the interest rate is 15%. Use the Miller-Orr model to find the target cash balance and upper cash balance.

Solution to Problem 1
The target cash balance is found by inserting the given figures into Formula (17.1). The upper cash balance is then found by inserting into Formula (17.2).

Step 1: The primary problem with applying Formula (17.1) can be that some calculators will not handle such large numbers. We use the next formula in the text in order to avoid this problem:

Target Cash Balance = Lower Limit

$$+ [3^{1/3} * TCOST^{1/3} * (\sigma^2)^{1/3}/(4r)^{1/3}].$$

Substituting $1,000 for the lower limit, $1,000 for *TCOST*, $1,000,000 for σ^2, and 15% for r gives:

Target Cash Balance = $1,000 + [1.442 * 10 * 100 /.8434].

Each of the figures can be raised to the 1/3 power by using the y^x key and setting $x = .33333$. Solving the above produces:

Target Cash Balance = $2,709.94.

Step 2: This is the target cash balance that the firm should adjust to each time it reaches the upper or lower limit. The upper cash balance limit is found as follows using Formula (17.2):

Upper Limit = [3 * Target Cash Balance] − [2 * Lower Limit]

Upper Limit = $6,129.81.

Final Solution: The firm should replenish its cash balance to $2,710 whenever the balance falls below $1,000 and should invest the excess cash above $2,710 whenever the cash balance exceeds $6,129.81. ↵

Problem 2   Woodelves Corporation invests excess cash—defined as cash in excess of $500,000—in Treasury bills. Woodelves also keeps its cash balance at or above $100,000 by borrowing money through a bank loan. Woodelves does not use the Miller-Orr model, but simply keeps its cash balance within these boundaries. Of course, before Woodelves Corporation uses a bank loan it makes sure that it has liquidated its Treasury bills. Similarly, before Woodelves Corporation buys Treasury bills it makes sure that its bank loan is paid off. Woodelves Corporation now (December 31) has a cash balance of $250,000. Woodelves Corporation is experiencing dramatic growth. Unfortunately, this creates immediate expenses, but revenues won't be received for several months. During the next six months, Woodelves expects the following net cash flows:

Jan	Feb	Mar	Apr	May	Jun
−$75,000	−$125,000	−$150,000	$−200,000	+$300,000	+$700,000

Woodelves now owns $200,000 of Treasury bills and has completely paid off its bank loan. Construct a cash budget in order to help the treasurer of Woodelves make plans for managing the firm's cash.

Solution to Problem 2

Notice that if our cash balance were allowed to "wander" in response to the cash flows without limits, the hypothetical balances would be:

Hypothetical End-of-Month Cash Balances

Dec	Jan	Feb	Mar	Apr	May	Jun
$250,000	+$175,000	+$50,000	−$100,000	$−300,000	+$0	+$700,000

These figures were found by starting with the given end-of-December cash balance of $250,000 and then adding in cash inflows (positive numbers) and subtracting out cash outflows (negative numbers).

The problem with the above "solution" is that the firm does not want the cash balance to drop below $100,000 or to rise above $500,000. This cash budget determines the combinations of bank loans and Treasury bills that will be used to keep the cash balance within its bounds.

Step 1: Design a cash budget using a format such as Table 17.4 and the specific features for the firm:

Cash Budget for Woodelves Corporation

Month	Jan	Feb	Mar	Apr	May	Jun
Starting cash	+$250,000					
Net cash flow	−$ 75,000	−$125,000	−$150,000	$−200,000	+$300,000	+$700,000
Cash buildup						
To T-bills						
To bank loan						
From T-bills						
From bank loan						
Ending cash balance						

This allows excess cash to be used to repay the bank loan or to buy Treasury bills. Cash deficiencies can be met by liquidating Treasury bills or by borrowing money.

Step 2: We now work through each month using the figures and procedures given in the problem. For example, January's $75,000 cash need can be met without lowering the firm's cash balance below the $100,000 lower limit. The cash balance falls by $75,000, from $250,000 to $175,000, in order to meet the $75,000 cash outflow. However, in February the firm expects an outflow of $125,000, which would lower the cash balance below its target. The cash balance can be restored to its minimum value of $100,000 by liquidating $50,000 of the $200,000 of Treasury bills that are owned. Thus, the cash budget should now look like this:

Cash Budget for Woodelves Corporation

Month	Jan	Feb	Mar	Apr	May	Jun
Starting cash	+$250,000	$175,000				
Net cash flow	−$ 75,000	−$125,000	−$150,000	$−200,000	+$300,000	+$700,000
Cash buildup	+$175,000	$ 50,000				
To T-bills	$0	$0				
To bank loan	$0	$0				
From T-bills	$0	$ 50,000				
From bank loan	$0	$0				
Ending cash balance	$175,000	$100,000				

Step 3: As the expected cash outflows continue, the Treasury bills are completely liquidated and the firm begins to borrow cash through its bank loan. Completed though the end of April, the cash budget should look like this:

Cash Budget for Woodelves Corporation

Month	Jan	Feb	Mar	Apr	May	Jun
Starting cash	+$250,000	$175,000	$100,000	$100,000		
Net cash flow	−$ 75,000	−$125,000	−$150,000	−$200,000	+$300,000	+$700,000
Cash buildup	+$175,000	$ 50,000	−$ 50,000	−$100,000		
To T-billls	$0	$0	$0	$0		
To bank loan	$0	$0	$0	$0		
From T-bills	$0	$ 50,000	$150,000	$0		
From bank loan	$0	$0	$0	$200,000		
Ending cash balance	$175,000	$100,000	$100,000	$100,000		

The Treasury bills were completely sold off in March, and in April the firm needed to borrow $200,000 to meet its minimum cash balance. These calculations come from the same sense of logic and priorities that guide our daily cash decisions in our personal-finance lives.

Step 4: Finally, in the last two months the firm's operations are bringing in more cash than is being spent. The result is that the firm first replenishes its cash balance to its maximum ($500,000), then repays the bank loan and begins buying Treasury bills as shown in our final budget:

Cash Budget for Woodelves Corporation

Month	Jan	Feb	Mar	Apr	May	Jun
Starting cash	+$250,000	$175,000	$100,000	$100,000	+$100,000	$400,000
Net cash flow	−$ 75,000	−$125,000	−$150,000	−$200,000	+$300,000	+$700,000
Cash buildup	+$175,000	$ 50,000	−$ 50,000	−$100,000	+$400,000	$1,100,000
To T-bills	$0	$0	$0	$0	$0	$400,000
To bank loan	$0	$0	$0	$0	$0	$200,000
From T-bills	$0	$ 50,000	$150,000	$0	$0	$0
From bank loan	$0	$0	$0	$200,000	$0	$0
Ending cash balance	$175,000	$100,000	$100,000	$100,000	$400,000	$500,000

Final Solution: The firm meets cash drains by liquidating its Treasury bills and then borrowing money. When money starts coming in, the firm pays off the bank loan and begins buying Treasury bills again. At all times the actual cash budget is kept within the desired range. ↵

REVIEW QUESTIONS

1. Provide a one-sentence definition of net working capital.
2. What are the three tasks or concepts that underlie working capital management?
3. Rank a typical firm's current assets from the most to the least liquid.
4. Describe, in a few sentences, the goal of cash management.
5. In nonstatistical nontechnical terms, explain how the Miller-Orr model differs from the EOQ model.
6. What is the money market? List at least two securities that trade in the money market.
7. In selecting the appropriate marketable security, which three qualities should the cash manager consider?
8. Define the "term structure of interest rates."
9. What is credit risk? Do U.S. Treasury bills contain credit risk? Do certificates of deposits or commercial paper contain credit risk? Explain.
10. What are the costs and benefits of extending credit in the form of an accounts receivable?
11. In accounts receivable management, explain the term "3/15; net 45."
12. What are lock boxes and how can they be used in managing accounts receivable?
13. What is accounts payable, and what is the goal of accounts payable management?
14. What is a cash budget, and what is the purpose of such a budget?

PROBLEMS

1. Caton Corporation's management has decided that the firm's minimum cash balance should be $50,000. A financial analyst has applied the Miller-Orr model and has determined that the firm's target cash balance should be $75,000.
   a. What would the firm's upper limit cash balance be?
   b. If the cash balance began to exceed the upper limit, what would the firm do and what would be the new cash balance?
   c. If the cash balance began to fall below the lower limit, what would the firm do and what would be the new cash balance?

2. Carder Corporation's management has determined that their minimum cash balance should be $10,000. The daily variance of the cash flows is $50,000, the daily interest rate is 0.0003, and the transaction cost of returning to the target cash balance is $500. Using the Miller-Orr model, determine:
   a. The target cash balance, and
   b. The upper limit.
3. Return to Carder Corporation from problem 2. Interest rates have risen to a daily rate of 0.0004. Find the new target cash balance and upper limit for the firm, assuming that all other variables remain the same.
4. Like many other models in finance, the Miller-Orr model produces an answer and requires the inputting of several other variables. Fill in the missing value, treating each line as a separate problem.

	Lower Limit	Transaction Cost	Daily Variance	Daily Interest Rate	Target Cash Balance
a.	$50,000	$100	$100,000	0.0003	_____
b.	$75,000	$100	$100,000	0.0003	_____
c.	$50,000	$800	$200,000	0.0004	_____
d.	$50,000	$600	$400,000	0.0005	_____

5. Suppose that one-year CDs (certificates of deposit) now offer 8% interest and two-year CDs now offer 9% interest (both compounded annually or expressed as effective annual interest rates).
   a. How much would $10,000 grow in two years if invested in the two-year CD?
   b. How much would $10,000 grow to in one year if invested in the one-year CD?
   c. Suppose that a cash manager invested $10,000 in a one-year CD and then took the proceeds at the end of that year (the answer to 5(b)) and reinvested the money in another one-year CD for a total of a two-year investment. What interest rate would the new one-year CD have to offer after the end of the first year such that the cash manager would end up with the same amount of money at the end of the second year as compared with the answer in 5(a)?
6. Unlucky Louie is a cash manager who invests in relatively long-term bonds in an effort to earn extra interest on his firm's working capital. Using the tools of Chapter 5, find the present value (i.e., market price) of a $10,000 zero coupon bond under the following circumstances.
   a. The bond's cash flow is due in one year, and annually compounded interest rates are 8%.
   b. The bond's cash flow is due in two years, and annually compounded interest rates are 8%.

    c. The bond's cash flow is due in one year, and annually compounded interest rates are 9%.

    d. The bond's cash flow is due in two years, and annually compounded interest rates are 9%.

7. Returning to Unlucky Louie in problem 6, suppose that he buys the one-year bond when interest rates are 8% and that interest rates immediately rise by 1% to 9%. In percentage terms, how much did his investment decline in value?

8. Returning again to Unlucky Louie in problems 6 and 7, suppose that he bought the two-year bond when interest rates were 8% and that interest rates immediately rose by 1% to 9%. In percentage terms, how much did this two-year investment decline in value?

9. Returning once again to Unlucky Louie in problems 6 through 8, there is a general rule in finance that when interest rates climb by 1% the price of zero coupon bonds falls by a percentage slightly smaller than their maturity. Verify that this is true by computing how much Unlucky would have lost as a percentage of the original purchase prices if he had bought one-half-year, three-year, and five-year zero coupon bonds just before the interest rates rose from 8% to 9%.

10. Unlucky Louie has decided to try his cash management skills in other areas of investments. Louie notices that one-year U.S. Treasury bills offer an annualized yield of 8% at the same time that an alternative one-year investment offers a return of 10% (assume annual compounding).

    a. By how much would $100,000 grow in one year if invested in the U.S. Treasury bill?

    b. By how much would $100,000 grow in one year if invested in the alternative that offers a 10% return?

    c. Assume that the U.S. Treasury bill cannot default but that the alternative investment has a 97% chance of paying fully and a 3% chance of paying nothing. What is the expected cash flow from investing $100,000 in the alternative investment?

    d. What would be the expected cash flow from a third one-year investment of $100,000 that offers a 90% chance of a 15% return, a 5% chance of paying back only 50 cents on each dollar invested, and a 5% chance of returning nothing?

11. Elkland Corporation is in a 34% federal income tax bracket and is comparing the after-tax yields between a municipal money market mutual fund offering 6% and a U.S. government money market mutual fund offering 3% more before tax. The municipal fund's 6% return is both a before-tax return and an after-tax return, since the returns from this fund are free of both federal and state income taxes. However, the U.S. government fund is taxable for federal income tax purposes (but not for state tax purposes).

   a. Compute the after-tax returns for the U.S government bond fund if its pretax return is 9%. Ignoring all other consideration such as risk, which investment offers the higher after-tax return?

   b. Assume that interest rates rise such that the municipal fund offers 12% while the U.S. government fund offers 15%. Now which fund would you prefer on the basis of after-tax returns alone?

12. Hornby Corporation is in a 34% federal income tax bracket and a 6% state income tax bracket. Ignoring interactions such as the ability to deduct some taxes in computing other taxes, compute the after-tax returns for each of the following alternatives.

   a. A totally tax-free municipal fund that offers 7%.

   b. A U.S. government fund that is federally taxable but tax-free at the state level and which offers 10% before taxes.

   c. A corporate fund that is fully taxable at both levels and offers 11% before taxes.

13. As a financial analyst at Presho, Inc., you are asked to determine whether credit should be extended to Fly By Nights, Inc. They have ordered $50,000 of products, which have a cost to your firm of $30,000. Based upon your analysis of Fly By Nights, Inc., credit history, you estimate that the probability of being paid is 50%. You do not expect them ever to order products from your firm again since you have been told that they have a one-time need for your products. Based upon expected cash flows, what is your decision?

14. Returning to Fly By Nights, Inc., a further analysis reveals that if Fly By Nights can remain in business for the next year, they will surely order and surely pay for $500,000 of similar products with similar costs in one year if and only if you will help them through this year. Based upon expected cash flows only, what is your decision?

15. Compute the annual interest rate implied by the following credit terms:

   a. 2/15; net 30.

   b. 2/30; net 60.

   c. 2/10—EOM; net 90 (purchased on the 10th of the month).

   d. 2/10—EOM; net 90 (purchased on the 31st of the month).

16. Winterfest Ski Corporation has seasonal net cash flows from operations that are projected as follows:

	1994	1995	1996
First quarter	+150,000	+160,000	+170,000
Second quarter	−120,000	−190,000	−100,000
Third quarter	− 10,000	− 15,000	− 20,000
Fourth quarter	+ 10,000	+110,000	+120,000

The cash management policy at Winterfest Ski Corporation is as follows:

a. A minimum cash balance of $50,000 should be kept and money should be borrowed using a line of credit at the bank if needed to maintain this balance.

b. Cash in excess of $100,000 should be invested in marketable securities.

c. No more than $100,000 should be invested in marketable securities. When this limit has been reached, the excess cash should be sent to the shareholders as a dividend.

The firm's cash balance is currently $100,000, and there is no investment in marketable securities and no loan outstanding to the bank. Use the following format to project the firm's cash balances, loan balances, marketable securities balances, and dividends. We have finished the first quarter and begun the second quarter for you. You may ignore interest paid on the loan or received on the investments.

	Year and Quarter	
	1994–1	*1994–2*
Beginning Cash	$100,000 (1)	$100,000
+ Operating cash inflow	150,000 (1)	0
+ New bank loan	0 (2)	
+ Market securities sold	0 (2)	
Available Cash	250,000 (3)	
− Operating cash outflow	0 (1)	120,000
− Loan repayment	0 (1)	0
− Market securities bought	100,000 (3)	0
− Dividends	50,000 (3)	
Cash Uses	150,000 (3)	
Ending Cash	100,000 (2)	

Notes:

(1) These figures were directly or indirectly given.

(2) These figures became clear when it was realized that there would be excess cash.

(3) These figures were deduced through the need to balance the statement and the priorities set forth in the firm's policy.

17. Return to Winterfest Ski Corporation in problem 16, repeat the exercise under the assumption that the firm will receive 2% interest each quarter on the funds kept in marketable securities and will pay 3% interest each quarter on the bank line of credit. How-

ever, these interest payments and receipts will not occur until the quarter that follows and will be based upon the balance at the end of the previous quarter. Use the following format, which we have partially completed.

	Year and Quarter		1994–3 Through 1996–4
	1994–1	1994–2	
Beginning Cash	$100,000 (1)	$100,000	
+ Operating cash inflow	150,000 (1)	0	
+ New bank loan	0 (2)		
+ Market securities sold	0 (2)		
+ Interest on previous securities	0 (1)	2,000	
Available Cash	250,000 (3)		
– Operating cash outflow	0 (1)	120,000	
– Loan repayment	0 (1)	0	
– Market securities bought	100,000 (3)	0	
– Interest on previous loan	0 (1)	0	
– Dividends	50,000 (3)		
Cash Uses	150,000 (3)		
Ending Cash	100,000 (2)		

Notes:
(1) These figures were directly or indirectly given.
(2) These figures became clear when it was realized that there would be excess cash.
(3) These figures were deduced through the need to balance the statement and the priorities set forth in the firm's policy.

18. What problems would be introduced if we returned to Winterfest Ski Corporation and assumed that the interest receipts and payments would occur in the quarter in which the funds were invested and borrowed?

19. Lagged Loot, Inc., collects 35% of all sales in the month of the sale, 45% in the second month, and 15% in the third month; 5% is never collected. Lagged Loot had sales of $154,000 in both October and November and $186,000 in December. It is now December 31, and the following sales projections have been given to you:

Jan	Feb	Mar	Apr	May	Jun
$200,000	$180,000	$170,000	$200,000	$200,000	$200,000

Compute the expected cash flows from sales for each of the first six months of the year.

20. Manweg's Grocery Store collects 100% of all sales in the month of the sale. However, most of the expenses it incurs are paid for on a delayed basis. Manweg's pays 50% of its bills in the month in which they are received, 45% in the second month, and 5% in the third month, and its expenses are 95% of sales. Manweg's is projecting cash flow for the first six months of the year. It is now December 31 and the following past sales and sales projections have been given to you:

Nov	Dec	Jan	Feb
$550,000	$650,000	$400,000	$400,000

Mar	Apr	May	Jun
$400,000	$400,000	$575,000	$600,000

Compute the expected cash flows from both sales and expense and net them for each of the first six months of the year.

21. Returning to Manweg's Grocery Store, the firm had a cash balance of $50,000 on December 31. Manweg's hopes to be able to buy $100,000 of equipment on April 30 using cash but does not want its cash balance to fall below $25,000.

   a. Will the firm be able to buy the equipment?

   b. How would your answer change if the firm received 1% interest on its cash balance each month (added to the cash balance on the first of each month based upon the ending balance of the previous month) and received a delay in the payment on the equipment purchase until June 1?

DISCUSSION QUESTIONS

1. What are the costs and benefits of having liquidity and why is there a theoretical optimal level of liquidity?
2. What are the reasons that a firm's cash flow would be cyclical?
3. Why would a firm buy very short-term securities in its cash management department while buying very long-term securities in its pension management?
4. Isn't a corporation shirking its responsibilities to pay taxes when it buys municipal securities that are free of income taxes?
5. If a firm extends small amounts of credit to all prospective customers in order to build relationships and learn about credit worthiness, what types of customers will it attract?

6. Optimal inventory management means never having to say that you are sorry that you are out of something. Please comment.
7. It is often said that cash budgets should be projected only weeks or months into the future. Please comment.
8. Referring to the Miller-Orr model: Wouldn't a target cash balance halfway between the lower and upper limits minimize the number of times the firm would incur the expense of adjusting its cash balance? Why isn't the midway point used in the Miller-Orr model?

International Finance

Wally World Amusement Parks, Inc., had earned a reputation for providing high-quality amusement entertainment in the United States, through the operation of five parks in highly competitive markets near major cities. While competing theme parks have moved recently into choice European and Asian locations, Wally World has been slow to react. The management at Wally World was at one time studying the possibility of opening a major park somewhere outside the United States. Possible locations that were considered included South America or Eastern Europe.

The dollar amount of investment required to open a first-class operation was a staggering $1 billion. This amount of money, however, was not far from the cost of a new theme park in the United States. What most concerned Wally World's management wasn't the amount of investment, but the international aspects of the venture. How could they plan for construction costs in a country that had a different currency? What types of risks would Wally World face due to fluctuations in currency values once the park began operating? What if the government of the country collapsed or decided to nationalize foreign assets? What types of regulations and liability exposures would they face outside the United States?

These questions had no easy answers, and operating within the borders of the United States had allowed the firm to avoid issues of international operations. But management was concerned whether Wally World could continue to be a world-class competitor without foreign expansion.

After months of careful study, management decided to take the safe course, to abandon plans for an international park, and to focus on an entirely domestic operation. This decision proved costly, as it soon became clear that the firm lost market share in the amusement park industry. Wally World's stock price fell to a new low at a time when their competitors were doing well.

Finally, the decision to go international was imposed on Wally World when a multinational firm bought them out. Wally World's top management team was replaced by a new set of managers who announced a goal of expanding Wally World's operations throughout the world.

AN OVERVIEW OF INTERNATIONAL FINANCE

This chapter examines corporate financial decisions in a multinational context. Multinational operations are quite common in corporations today. For example, in 1989, 40 percent of Coca-Cola's sales came from its domestic operations, while 60 percent of sales were earned in its international divisions.

How does international finance differ from domestic finance? The answer is not very much. In fact, most of the principles of modern corporate finance remain unchanged whether they are being applied to decision making inside the United States, outside the United States, or between the United States and another nation.

However, the decision to operate outside the domestic market does introduce some new and unique issues, such as handling different currencies. As we shall see, the fact that nations have different currencies is the primary issue in international corporate financial management.

We begin our development of international corporate finance by studying foreign currency exchange for immediate transactions, which are simpler in that there is no passage of time and little risk. Next the passage of time and risk will be introduced to foreign currency exchange. The final sections of the chapter discuss political risk and practical considerations.

THE ECONOMICS OF MULTIPLE CURRENCIES

Corporate decision making through *NPV* requires the discounting of all relevant costs and benefits using market values. In domestic situations, total revenues are determined by multiplying the number of units sold by the market price—measured in the decision maker's own currency. For example, a U.S. farmer harvesting 25,000 bushels of grain will compute total grain revenues by multiplying the amount of grain by its dollar price per bushel:

$$\text{Value of Grain} = \text{Bushels of Grain} \times \text{Price per Bushel}$$
$$\$100,000 \quad = \quad 25,000 \quad \times \quad \$4.$$

Next we examine how the value of goods and services in one currency can be converted into another currency.

The Foreign Exchange Market

foreign exchange market
A market where currencies of one country are exchanged into currencies of another. The foreign exchange market is a network of dealers linked by telephones and computers.

Currencies of one country are exchanged into currencies of another in the **foreign exchange market**, which is not a centralized location but rather a network of dealers linked by telephones and computers. Major holders and traders of currency include large money-center banks who exchange directly through the foreign exchange markets. Smaller users of currency, such as small businesses and tourists, exchange indirectly through smaller financial intermediaries such as community banks and local exchange offices.

The price at which currencies are traded is usually determined by the forces of supply and demand. A decreasing number of countries attempt to control their economies by making it illegal to trade their currency at any exchange rate other than the official exchange rate set by the government. Usually these governments set exchange rates that reflect a much higher value to their currency than would occur in a free market. In cases such as these, it is common for **black markets** to arise that trade the currency at exchange rates driven by supply and demand. The price of the currency on these markets is often much lower. For example, black market currency values might be 20 percent of the values set by the official exchange rate.

black market
A market consisting of the illicit buying and selling of goods and services in violation of legal controls.

Exchange Rates

When a firm's product or service is located in a foreign country, the computation of the market value of the resource must be determined in two steps. First, the product or service must be valued in foreign currency using the price of the resource in the local currencies.

$$\text{Foreign Currency Value} = \text{Number of Units} \qquad (18.1)$$
$$* \text{ Foreign Price per Unit.}$$

Next, the foreign currency value must be translated into the equivalent domestic currency value, the currency of the decision maker. This is is accomplished by multiplying the foreign currency value by the exchange rate between the foreign and domestic currencies:

$$\text{Domestic Currency Value} = \text{Foreign Currency Value} * \text{Exchange Rate.}$$

Example 18.1 ——————— Consider a U.S. truck manufacturer with international operations in Great Britain. If the division in Great Britain produces 1,000 small trucks at a cost of £5,100 (5,100 pounds), the foreign currency cost per truck would be:

$$\text{Cost of Trucks in Foreign Currency} = 1{,}000 * £5{,}100$$

$$= £5{,}100{,}000,$$

where £ is the symbol for British pounds. The cost in dollars would be determined by exchanging the foreign currency into the domestic currency. In this case, the transaction requires turning British pounds into U.S. dollars. If the exchange rate between British pounds and U.S. dollars is 1 pound = $1.5205, the total cost in dollars of producing trucks in Great Britain would be:

$$\text{Cost of Trucks in Domestic Currency} = £5{,}100{,}000 * \$1.5205$$

$$= \$7{,}754{,}550.$$

Thus, a cost of 5.1 million pounds is equivalent to a cost of approximately 7.7 million dollars. ↵

foreign exchange rate
The rate at which one currency can be traded for another.

Most nations have their own currency, and most currencies can be traded in the foreign exchange market. The rate at which one currency can be traded for another is called the **foreign exchange rate**. An exchange rate is the price of one currency in terms of another, and exchange rates can be expressed in terms of either currency. Figure 18.1 illustrates foreign exchange rates as listed in the *Wall Street Journal* as of Monday, June 7, 1993, and Friday, June 4, 1993, the previous trading day.

In the above example, on Monday, June 7, 1993, $1.5205 in U.S. dollars could be exchanged into one British pound. But as Figure 18.1 illustrates, we could also express the relationship between pounds and dollars by saying that one U.S. dollar was worth approximately 0.6577 British pounds. This is found by taking the inverse of 1.5205. Similar calculations can be made from the other 50 or so currencies listed in Figure 18.1. For instance, on June 7, 1993, $0.009322 in U.S. dollars could be exchanged into 1 Japanese yen, and one U.S. dollar was worth approximately 107.27 yen.

As shown in Figure 18.1, exchange rates can change through time. On Friday, June 4, 1993, it would have taken $1.5085 to purchase one British pound, $0.0120 less than the next day. Because more dollars are required to purchase pounds on Monday than on Friday, we say that the dollar weakened against the pound. The same was true for the Japanese yen. On Friday, June 4, 1993, $0.009268 would have purchased one Japanese yen, a change of $0.00054 from the subsequent trading day. Because more dollars are required to purchase yen on Monday than on Friday, we say that the dollar weakened against the yen.

FIGURE 18.1
Foreign Exchange Rates

Country	U.S. $ equiv. Mon.	U.S. $ equiv. Fri.	Currency per U.S. $ Mon.	Currency per U.S. $ Fri.
Argentina (Peso)	1.01	1.01	.99	.99
Australia (Dollar)	.6720	.6757	1.4881	1.4799
Austria (Schilling)	.08758	.08726	11.42	11.46
Bahrain (Dinar)	2.6522	2.6522	.3771	.3771
Belgium (Franc)	.02999	.02991	33.34	33.44
Brazil (Cruzeiro)	.0000235	.0000238	42583.02	42039.01
Britain (Pound)	1.5205	1.5085	.6577	.6629
30-Day Forward	1.5170	1.5051	.6592	.6644
90-Day Forward	1.5106	1.4988	.6620	.6672
180-Day Forward	1.5029	1.4917	.6654	.6704
Canada (Dollar)	.7803	.7819	1.2815	1.2790
30-Day Forward	.7794	.7808	1.2831	1.2807
90-Day Forward	.7771	.7786	1.2869	1.2844
180-Day Forward	.7734	.7749	1.2930	1.2905
Czech. Rep. (Koruna)				
Commercial rate	.0357526	.0357526	27.9700	27.9700
Chile (Peso)	.002545	.002545	392.86	392.99
China (Renminbi)	.174856	.174856	5.7190	5.7190
Colombia (Peso)	.001512	.001512	661.30	661.30
Denmark (Krone)	.1610	.1607	6.2103	6.2238
Ecuador (Sucre)				
Floating rate	.000540	.000535	1851.03	1870.03
Finland (Markka)	.18259	.18225	5.4766	5.4870
France (Franc)	.18310	.18253	5.4615	5.4785
30-Day Forward	.18241	.18182	5.4822	5.4998
90-Day Forward	.18118	.18060	5.5193	5.5370
180-Day Forward	.17974	.17915	5.5637	5.5820
Germany (Mark)	.6167	.6148	1.6215	1.6265
30-Day Forward	.6144	.6125	1.6277	1.6327
90-Day Forward	.6101	.6083	1.6390	1.6439
180-Day Forward	.6053	.6034	1.6521	1.6572
Greece (Drachma)	.004527	.004512	220.90	221.65
Hong Kong (Dollar) ..	.12940	.12942	7.7278	7.7265
Hungary (Forint)	.0116171	.0116131	86.0800	86.1100
India (Rupee)	.03213	.03211	31.12	31.14
Indonesia (Rupiah)	.0004810	.0004811	2079.00	2078.53
Ireland (Punt)	1.5026	1.4981	.6655	.6675
Israel (Shekel)	.3636	.3753	2.7500	2.6643
Italy (Lira)	.0006747	.0006764	1482.05	1478.50
Japan (Yen)	.009322	.009268	107.27	107.90
30-Day Forward	.009322	.009268	107.27	107.90
90-Day Forward	.009326	.009268	107.23	107.90
180-Day Forward	.009334	.009279	107.13	107.77
Jordan (Dinar)	1.4874	1.4984	.6723	.6674
Kuwait (Dinar)	3.3278	3.3267	.3005	.3006
Lebanon (Pound)	.000577	.000577	1733.00	1733.00
Malaysia (Ringgit)	.3914	.3912	2.5550	2.5560
Malta (Lira)	2.6954	2.7248	.3710	.3670
Mexico (Peso)				
Floating rate	.3200000	.3197953	3.1250	3.1270
Netherland (Guilder) ..	.5497	.5480	1.8191	1.8248
New Zealand (Dollar) .	.5358	.5379	1.8664	1.8591
Norway (Krone)	.1456	.1450	6.8675	6.8955
Pakistan (Rupee)	.0372	.0373	26.85	26.81
Peru (New Sol)	.5180	.5180	1.93	1.93
Philippines (Peso)	.03745	.03752	26.70	26.65
Poland (Zloty)	.00006101	.00006166	16392.02	16219.00
Portugal (Escudo)	.006481	.006404	154.29	156.14
Saudi Arabia (Riyal) ..	.26702	.26702	3.7450	3.7450
Singapore (Dollar)	.6215	.6192	1.6090	1.6150
Slovak Rep. (Koruna) .	.0357526	.0357526	27.9700	27.9700
South Africa (Rand)				
Commercial rate	.3136	.3138	3.1883	3.1868
Financial rate	.2176	.2170	4.5950	4.6075
South Korea (Won) ..	.0012441	.0012442	803.80	803.70
Spain (Peseta)	.008035	.007877	124.45	126.95
Sweden (Krona)	.1375	.1367	7.2708	7.3152
Switzerland (Franc) ...	.6873	.6838	1.4550	1.4625
30-Day Forward	.6861	.6826	1.4575	1.4649
90-Day Forward	.6841	.6806	1.4618	1.4693
180-Day Forward	.6820	.6788	1.4663	1.4732
Taiwan (Dollar)	.038226	.038685	26.16	25.85
Thailand (Baht)	.03973	.03981	25.17	25.12
Turkey (Lira)	.0000985	.0001004	10154.01	9956.00
United Arab (Dirham)	.2723	.2723	3.6725	3.6725
Uruguay (New Peso)				
Financial	.250312	.251256	4.00	3.98
Venezuela (Bolivar)				
Floating rate	.01137	.01151	87.95	86.88

Source: *The Wall Street Journal,* June 8, 1993, Section 3.

To summarize, transacting in a foreign currency is as simple as shopping for groceries. Just like apples, foreign currencies have prices that allow traders to express their value and transact in the currency of their choice. Foreign exchange rates allow one currency to be turned into another. Note that foreign exchange rates allow the value of goods in one country to be easily compared with the value of goods in another country. The comparison of goods between countries using exchange rates is next discussed in detail.

The Spot Market for Foreign Exchange

spot market
A market in which exchange takes place immediately.

In the previous discussion, the currency in one country was exchanged immediately into the currency of another country. Accordingly, the foreign exchange was obtained through the spot market. A **spot market** is nothing more than a market where exchange takes place immediately.[1]

Most students are familiar with trading in spot markets. A large majority of transactions in which we engage result in a nearly immediate exchange. For example, a consumer goes to the store and exchanges money for groceries. The store receives the money immediately and the consumer receives the groceries immediately—making this a spot transaction in a spot market.

Alternatively, someone may sign an agreement in which the exchange won't take place until some point in the future: for instance, a contract for lawn care service that will be performed and paid for at points in the future. Later in the chapter we will discuss other markets in which transactions agreed to today do not take place until weeks, months, or even years into the future.

Perfect Markets and the Law of One Price

The foreign exchange market allows participants to convert a given currency, such as U.S. currency, into the currency of virtually all other major countries and vice versa. Accordingly, foreign exchange markets allow people to purchase goods from throughout the world by starting with a single currency, such as U.S. dollars. This subsection will discuss the impact we would expect currency transactions to have on relative values throughout the world.

Chapter 2 introduced the economic principle called the law of one price, which states that, in a perfect market, competition will drive the price of two identical assets to be equal. Because there are no trading costs in perfect markets, anything other than equal prices would

---

1. In the case of the spot market for foreign exchange, the process actually takes about two days.

quickly vanish through the actions of people buying the underpriced asset and selling the overpriced asset.

For example, let's consider gold. Let's assume that the price at which U.S. dollars can be exchanged for an ounce of gold is approximately $400. But how much would we expect the price of gold to be in other currencies? Given perfect markets (i.e., markets with no trading costs), the value of gold would be equal regardless of the currency in which its value is expressed.

Example 18.2 —————— Suppose that, in U.S. markets, gold trades at $400 per ounce and French francs trade at $0.20. By taking the inverse of the exchange rate, we can calculate that five French francs are worth one U.S. dollar.

According to the law of one price, we can determine the price of gold in Paris in terms of French francs. Given that an ounce of gold in U.S. dollars costs $400, we can apply the law of one price by multiplying the price of gold in U.S. dollars by the price of U.S. dollars in terms of francs:

$$
\begin{array}{ccc}
\text{French Franc} & \text{Price of Gold} & \text{Price of Dollars} \\
\text{Price of Gold} = & \text{in U.S. Dollars} \times & \text{in French Francs} \\
2000 \quad = & \$400 & \times \text{ (5 Francs per Dollar).}
\end{array}
$$

Thus, the law of one price permits us to specify the Paris price of gold at 2000 francs. Conversely, if we observed first that the price of gold in Paris was 2000 francs and that the price of a franc in terms of U.S. dollars was $0.20, we could apply the law of one price to find the price of gold in terms of U.S. dollars:

$$
\begin{array}{ccc}
\text{U.S. Dollar} & \text{Price of Gold} & \text{Price of Francs} \\
\text{Cost of Gold} = & \text{in French Francs} \times & \text{in U.S. Dollars} \\
\$400 \quad = & 2000 & \times \quad \$0.20. \quad \hookleftarrow
\end{array}
$$

The Law of One Price and Arbitrage Opportunities. In the example above the price of gold was exactly the same whether the buyer used U.S. dollars or French francs. Why would we expect the prices to be equal? The answer is that if they were substantially different there would be an **arbitrage** opportunity—an opportunity to make profits with very little risk.

arbitrage
An opportunity to make profits with very little risk.

What would happen if the law of one price failed to hold? For example, suppose that the price of gold in U.S. dollars is $400, that the exchange rate between dollars and francs is $0.20 = 1 franc, and that an ounce of gold could be purchased in France for 1950 francs. In this case, the dollar price of gold in Paris is $390:

$$\$390 = 1{,}950 \text{ Francs} * \$0.20.$$

Given perfect markets, how could an individual take advantage of such a situation? The individual could earn an arbitrage profit by engaging in these three transactions: (1) trading $390 dollars for 1950 francs on the foreign exchange markets, (2) buying an ounce of gold in Paris for the 1950 francs, and (3) selling the gold in the U.S. for $400 per ounce, leaving a riskless profit of $10 per ounce.

In a similar fashion, an arbitrage profit can be made if the price of gold in U.S. dollars is $400, if the exchange rate between dollars and francs is $0.20 = 1 franc, and an ounce of gold in France costs 2,050 francs. In this case, the dollar price of gold in Paris is $410:

$$\$410 = 2{,}050 \text{ Francs} * \$0.20.$$

Given perfect markets, the individual could earn an arbitrage profit by engaging in these three transactions: (1) buying an ounce of gold in the U.S. for $400, (2) selling the gold in Paris for 2,050 francs, and (3) exchanging the 2,050 francs for $410, leaving a riskless profit of $10 per ounce.

Unfortunately, such easy profits do not exist in the real world. In the first arbitrage situation, the holder of the gold would not be willing to sell the gold for 1,950 francs if more money could be made by selling gold elsewhere and converting one currency into the currency of choice using the foreign exchange market. Also, the buyer of the gold would not pay $400 if it could be purchased elsewhere for a cost in terms of U.S. dollars of $390. The tiny differences in prices that do exist in the real world are only big enough to pay for the time and expenses of being an arbitrager—unless you're one of the best in the world. In perfect markets, the law of one price will hold even with multiple currencies.

> ⌛ In perfect markets the law of one price will hold even if multiple currencies are involved.

In other words, for those assets traded in perfect or near-perfect markets, the prices of identical assets being traded in different currencies will be equal to each other if they are converted into a common currency using foreign market exchange rates.

Imperfect Markets and the Law of One Price

Would we expect the prices of all goods in different countries selling for different currencies to reflect the law of one price, using market exchange rates? The answer is no! Most goods do not sell in perfect or near-perfect markets. How closely prices behave to the law of one price depends upon the type of good and the trading costs—in other words, the lack of perfection in the markets.

For widely traded, highly similar assets, such as precious metals and oil, we would expect prices to obey (approximately) the law of one price. This is because well-developed markets exist for the trading of such assets such that they can be transported around the world easily at relatively low costs.

However, for less often traded goods, dissimilar goods, or goods that are not easily transportable, we could expect price differences such that the law of one price fails to hold. For example, we would expect tropical fruit, a rare product in some northern countries, to sell for a higher price in Canada than in Brazil, when converted to a common currency. In other words, the U.S. dollar cost of tropical fruit in Canada is likely to be greater than the U.S. dollar cost of tropical fruit in Brazil. Even more so, we would expect the price of services such as manual labor, haircuts, and medical care to differ between countries since they are even less able to be transported.

In theory, perfect markets would be expected to produce identical prices. For assets that trade in near-perfect markets, the law of one price will approximately hold. For assets that do not trade in perfect markets, such as perishable foods and services, prices can differ when converted into a common currency.

Purchasing Power Parity

We have learned that virtually any currency can be used to buy any good. This is accomplished by simply exchanging currencies in the foreign exchange market. We next ask whether overall prices in one country must equal overall prices in another country. Said differently, do different currencies have equal purchasing power?

purchasing power of a currency

The value of a currency in purchasing goods directly, without first being exchanged into another currency.

For the purposes of this discussion, the **purchasing power of a currency** refers to the value of the currency in purchasing goods directly—without first being exchanged into another currency. Thus, purchasing power refers to the overall cost level of those goods that are offered for direct sale in the given currency. For example, the purchasing power of the French franc would refer to the amount of goods that could be used to purchase goods directly (mostly in France) without having to convert the francs into another currency.

Obviously, high purchasing power allows the holder to purchase more goods than does low purchasing power. The degree of purchasing power can be assessed through the following question: If $1000 is converted into French francs and is used to buy goods in Paris, how many goods could be purchased relative to what the U.S. dollars would have purchased in New York City?

One answer to this question is that, in perfect markets, spending the $1000 in the U.S. would be roughly equivalent to converting the

$1000 into francs and spending the money in Paris. Although France may have some goods that are relatively inexpensive, such as fine wine, and some that are relatively expensive, such as land, supply and demand pressures would force France to have the same overall purchasing power as the U.S. for a given level of wealth.

According to this argument, a U.S. dollar will have the same overall purchasing power in the United States as it does when converted to the local currency and spent in Paris, Japan, or Mexico. The argument that all currencies must have the same overall purchasing power is known as the **purchasing power parity** theorem. Proponents of this theorem argue that, if one currency had a higher overall purchasing power, competition would force its exchange rates up until it had the same purchasing power as all other currencies.

Clear thinking reveals that the notion of purchasing power parity can never hold exactly in imperfect markets. As we have said, some goods are not easily transportable and thus cannot have equal purchasing power around the globe—tropical fruit being one such example. Even more important, there is no such thing as an overall cost level that can be compared between countries. Can every country offer the same beauty, climate, medical care, safety, or culture? We are sure you agree the answer is no.

What we do know is that goods in near-perfect markets will sell at near-equal prices throughout the world, and that goods in imperfect markets can vary in price depending upon imperfections in the markets in which they trade.

purchasing power parity
A theory stating that the purchasing power of a currency in one country will have the same power when converted to another currency and spent in another country.

MULTIPLE CURRENCIES AND THE PASSAGE OF TIME

The previous section focused on the economics of multiple currencies in the absence of both time and risk. The purpose of this section is to introduce to the discussion the passage of time. Although we will mention risk occasionally in this section, a formal analysis of risk will occur later.

Example 18.3 —————— Consider Melissa's Fashions, Inc., a firm specializing in the importing and exporting of clothes. Melissa's Fashions is headquartered in the U.S., and has recently arranged to import a line of clothing from France to be sold domestically. The firm has agreed to purchase the clothing for 5,000,000 French francs, and to sell it to a U.S. retailer for $1,000,000.

At the time the arrangement is made, the exchange rate between dollars and francs is $0.18 = 1 franc. Given this exchange rate, Melissa's Fashions will make a profit on the transaction of $100,000:

$$\text{Profit} = \$1,000,000 - (5,000,000 \text{ Francs} * \$0.18)$$

$$= \$100,000.$$

While this appears to be a good arrangement for the firm, one potential problem is that all payments will occur in 60 days—and the exchange rate between dollars and francs might change. If the exchange rate should rise to $0.21 = 1 franc, Melissa's Fashions would have a loss of $50,000:

$$\text{Loss} = \$1,000,000 - (5,000,000 \text{ Francs} * \$0.21)$$

$$= -\$50,000.$$

What would happen if the exchange rate fell to $0.16 = 1 franc? The answer is that there would be a profit of $200,000:

$$\text{Profit} = \$1,000,000 - (5,000,000 \text{ Francs} * \$0.16)$$

$$= \$200,000. \qquad \hookleftarrow$$

Thus, when a transaction with multiple currencies occurs at a distant point in the future, it can be viewed as exposing the firm to foreign exchange risk, which is the fluctuations in profit and loss caused by fluctuations in the foreign exchange rate.

Forward Contracts

There is an interesting security known as a forward contract that solves the potential problem of foreign exchange risk quickly and easily and greatly simplifies the discussion of multiple currencies through time. Simply put, a **forward contract** allows someone to exchange future units of one currency for future units of another currency at a price agreed upon today. In other words, while spot market foreign exchange rates allow people to trade currencies today, forward foreign exchange markets allow people to agree today to trade currencies at some point in the future.

For example, Melissa's Fashions could enter a forward contract that would lock in the French franc exchange rate to be used in 60 days. The firm could perhaps use the forward market to buy 5,000,000 francs in 60 days for $0.18 each such that the dollar price of the franc exchange is $900,000. Because the firm will receive $1,000,000 in 60 days, the clothing transaction will net the firm a sure $100,000 profit.

forward contract
A contract allowing the exchange of future units of one currency for future units of another currency at an agreed-upon price today.

TABLE 18.1
Using Forward Contracts to Eliminate Foreign Exchange Risk

TODAY

Agree to buy clothing for 5,000,000 francs payable in 60 days.	Agree to sell clothing for $1,000,000 to be received in 60 days.

SPOT EXCHANGE RATE: $0.18 = 1 Franc
PROFIT IF TRANSACTED TODAY = $1,000,000 − (5,000,000 ∗ $0.18) = $100,000

Problem: All payments to occur in 60 days. Spot exchange rate in 60 days is uncertain.

Solution: Enter the forward foreign exchange market. Agree to buy francs in 60 days for $900,000 in the forward markets. Forward transaction locks in a profit of $100,000.

Since all of Melissa's Fashions revenues and expenses would now be locked in relative to U.S. dollars, the firm would be protected from fluctuations in the foreign exchange rates. These transactions are summarized in Table 18.1.

Thus, in situations where future revenues and/or expenses are known and are expressed in foreign currencies, a firm can usually eliminate foreign exchange risk by locking in exchange rates using forward contracts.

Futures Contracts

futures contract
A contract similar to a forward contract that allows participants to make agreements today to exchange currencies in the future.

There is another type of contract, called a **futures contract,** which is very closely related to a forward contract. In fact, futures contracts and forward contracts are so similar that many people view them as the same concept. Both contracts allow the participants to make agreements today to exchange currencies in the future. Window 18.1 discusses both of these contracts and their differences in detail.

Forward and futures contracts provide a simple and clear solution to the problem of major multiple currencies when there is a significant passage of time between the date of the agreement and the date of payment. The decision maker can use forward or future exchange rate contracts to convert the future prices into a common currency.

For example, let's return to Melissa's Fashions and consider a typical futures contract arrangement. Suppose the firm had agreed to import and sell clothing over the course of one year in four shipments corresponding to the four seasons. The firm agrees to accept four

Window 18.1

Forward Contracts and Futures Contracts

The basic features of the forward and futures contracts are the same—both allow for prices in the future to be locked in today. There are, however, important differences between these contracts. This window presents a brief discussion of these differences.

1. Forward contracts are agreements between individuals; therefore the terms of the contracts can be tailored to suit the needs of the individuals. Futures contracts trade on organized exchanges (backed by clearinghouses) and the exchanges set the specific terms, such as the size of each contract and the time of expiration.

For example, suppose that Melissa's Fashions, Inc., trades with a Mexican clothing manufacturer and takes on Mexican peso foreign currency risk that spans three and one-half months. A forward market arrangement would allow the firm to lock in a rate of Mexican peso exchange in exactly three and one-half months. In contrast, the choices available in the organized futures markets might not include a three-and-one-half-month contract for Mexican pesos. In this case, if Melissa's Fashions were to use futures contracts, the firm would need to find the contract that comes closest to the foreign currency risk it is trying to remove.

2. In futures contracts, the organized exchange guarantees the agreements of both parties, while no such guarantees exist in forward contracts. If Melissa's Fashions enters a forward contract to eliminate foreign exchange risk, the firm has accepted the risk that the other party will fail to convert the currency as promised. While forward contracts can be tailor-made to eliminate foreign currency risk through time, these contracts introduce another type of risk known as default risk. Because the clearinghouse guarantees that all futures participants will honor their agreements, no such default risk is introduced with futures contracts.

3. Futures contracts require a daily "settling-up" process, while forward contracts settle up only at maturity. The daily settling-up process works as follows: At the end of each day's trading, the clearinghouse calculates the profit or loss of each position as if these positions were to end. Settling-up provides a financial safeguard to ensure that futures traders will live up to their promises. Because forward contracts are promises between individuals, there is no settling-up process.

quarterly shipments of clothes from France at a cost of 5,000,000 francs and will deliver these shipments to retailers in the U.S. for $1,000,000 each. The first exchange of funds will take place in two months, the next in five months, the third in eight months, and the final in eleven months. How would Melissa's Fashions be able to accept such a business arrangement given the uncertainty regarding future exchange rates between francs and dollars?

The answer is found by using futures prices to "lock in" a foreign exchange rate for turning francs into dollars. For example, Table 18.2 provides a set of futures prices for French franc foreign exchange in two months, five months, eight months, and eleven months. These prices show a stable dollar relative to French francs. According to this set of futures prices, Melissa's Fashions can use the futures market to lock in an exchange rate at each of the four trading dates, guaranteeing a profit of $100,000 in each transaction.

Of course, the futures price of French franc foreign exchange need not be constant through time. For instance, Table 18.3 shows a set of futures prices whereby the dollar strengthens against the franc (it takes fewer and fewer dollars to purchase francs). Using these futures prices to remove foreign exchange risk, Melissa's Fashions locks in a different profit in each of the four transactions. Because the price of French francs in dollars declines through time, futures market transactions will guarantee a profit of $100,000 in two months, $150,000 in five months, $200,000 in eight months, and $250,000 in eleven months.

TABLE 18.2

Melissa's Fashions, Inc.:
Using Futures to Remove Foreign Exchange Risk

Maturity	Futures Exchange Rate
2 months	0.18
5 months	0.18
8 months	0.18
11 months	0.18

The Clothing Transaction

1. Firm agrees to pay 5,000,000 francs for clothing.
2. Firm has an agreement to sell the clothing for $1,000,000.
3. Firm locks in the rate of foreign exchange today for future transactions.

Profit in 2 months: $1,000,000 − (5,000,000 ∗ 0.18) = $100,000
Profit in 5 months: $1,000,000 − (5,000,000 ∗ 0.18) = $100,000
Profit in 8 months: $1,000,000 − (5,000,000 ∗ 0.18) = $100,000
Profit in 11 months: $1,000,000 − (5,000,000 ∗ 0.18) = $100,000

TABLE 18.3
Melissa's Fashions, Inc.:
Using Futures to Remove Foreign Exchange Risk

Maturity	Futures Exchange Rate
2 months	0.18
5 months	0.17
8 months	0.16
11 months	0.15

The Clothing Transaction

1. Firm agrees to pay 5,000,000 francs for clothing.
2. Firm has an agreement to sell the clothing for $1,000,000.
3. Firm locks in the rate of foreign exchange today for future transactions.

Profit in 2 months: $1,000,000 − (5,000,000 * 0.18) = $100,000
Profit in 5 months: $1,000,000 − (5,000,000 * 0.17) = $150,000
Profit in 8 months: $1,000,000 − (5,000,000 * 0.16) = $200,000
Profit in 11 months: $1,000,000 − (5,000,000 * 0.15) = $250,000

Finally, Table 18.4 shows another possible set of futures prices whereby the dollar weakens against the franc through time (it takes more and more dollars to purchase francs). Because the price of French francs in dollars declines through time, futures market transactions will guarantee a profit of $100,000 in two months, $50,000 in five months, $0 in eight months, and −$50,000 in 11 months.

TABLE 18.4
Melissa's Fashions, Inc.:
Using Futures to Remove Foreign Exchange Risk

Maturity	Futures Exchange Rate
2 months	0.18
5 months	0.19
8 months	0.20
11 months	0.21

The Clothing Transaction

1. Firm agrees to pay 5,000,000 francs for clothing.
2. Firm has an agreement to sell the clothing for $1,000,000.
3. Firm locks in the rate of foreign exchange today for future transactions.

Profit in 2 months: $1,000,000 − (5,000,000 * 0.18) = $100,000
Profit in 5 months: $1,000,000 − (5,000,000 * 0.19) = $ 50,000
Profit in 8 months: $1,000,000 − (5,000,000 * 0.20) = $ 0
Profit in 11 months: $1,000,000 − (5,000,000 * 0.21) = −$ 50,000

Tables 18.2 through 18.4 demonstrate that foreign exchange risk related to timing can be removed by using futures contracts to convert the currencies into fixed dollar costs. If future exchange rates reflect a stable dollar relative to francs, profits will remain constant. If future exchange rates reflect a strengthening dollar relative to francs, profits will increase through time in our example. If future exchange rates reflect a weakening dollar relative to francs, profits will decrease through time. Melissa's Fashions can use the prices in the futures markets to determine whether or not to arrange for the clothing shipment.

Forward and Futures Contracts as a Double-Edged Sword

As demonstrated above, different foreign currencies do not present major difficulties in the absence of risk, since forward and futures markets allow firms to lock in today the rate of foreign exchange in the future. However, in practice, there may be two problems with using forwards and futures.

The first problem is commitment. Forward and futures contracts commit their participants to an exchange even if the need to exchange currency vanishes. For example, suppose that after Melissa's Fashions enters into futures contracts, the French clothing manufacturer or the American retailer goes out of business. Because the clothes will not be delivered, there is no longer a need for foreign exchange. However, Melissa's Fashions is committed to buy 5,000,000 francs each quarter for a year as a result of the futures contracts.

The second problem is regret. Let's look at Table 18.2, where Melissa's Fashions uses futures contracts to lock in foreign exchange at a price of $0.18. How would top management and the shareholders react if during the next year the dollar strengthens against the franc such that the spot exchange rate of French francs for dollars drops to $0.15? The answer is not very well, as the firm would have had higher profits ($250,000 to be exact) if the futures contracts were not used. This is demonstrated in Table 18.5.

Table 18.5 illustrates that the futures contract is a commitment to pay $0.18 per franc even though the spot market price is $0.15. Remember, the purpose of the futures contract was to eliminate or hedge away the risk of currency fluctuations.[2] Of course, had the dollar strengthened against the franc such that the spot market price of a franc were $0.20, the profit on the clothing transaction in the

---

2. Even worse, sometimes these contracts will produce separate accounting "losses," which will cause some uninformed people to think that the manager is speculating in the futures markets.

TABLE 18.5
The Potential for Regret When Using Forward or Futures Contracts

Problem—Foreign Exchange Risk

Firm will receive clothes and will pay 5,000,000 francs in 60 days.
Firm will sell clothes for $1,000,000 in 60 days.

Solution: Use the futures market to lock in a profit. Enter a two-month futures contract to "buy" 5,000,000 francs for $0.18 each. Use the 5,000,000 francs to pay for the clothes at a cost of $900,000.

Result of Using the Futures Transaction: Receive clothes for $1,000,000 at a guaranteed cost of $900,000. Profit is locked in at $100,000.

Potential Regret: Suppose the dollar price for francs in 60 days falls such that francs can be purchased for $0.15 each. In the absence of a forward agreement, the cost in dollars of receiving the clothes is:

$$5,000,000 * 0.15 = \$750,000,$$

such that profit would have been:

$$\$1,000,000 - \$750,000 = \$250,000.$$

The futures agreement results in profits $150,000 below what they would have been in the absence of holding futures contracts.

absence of the futures contract would have been completely wiped out.

Options on Foreign Currency Risk to the Rescue

Fortunately, foreign exchange options allow users to avoid or lessen the problems just discussed. A foreign exchange option allows its holder the option to exchange a given amount of one currency for another without the obligation to do so. These options follow most of the same concepts and principles detailed in Chapter 9 (the core chapter on options).

Example 18.4 _____ Melissa's Fashions, Inc., could use options on French francs in order to protect itself from foreign exchange risk. The option would allow Melissa's Fashions to exchange U.S. dollars for 5,000,000 French francs at or near each of the four quarterly transaction dates. Each option would specify the amount of currency to be exchanged, the rate of exchange, and the time period. If the clothing deal fell through or if the dollar price per franc fell in value, Melissa's Fashions could walk away from its option to exchange francs for dollars by letting the option expire. On the other hand, if the dollar price per franc went up in value, Melissa's Fashions would be protected since they had locked in a purchase price for the francs required to purchase the clothing.

Of course, there are no free lunches in the real world. As shown in Chapter 9, the buyer of an option must pay a price, called a premium, for the privilege of owning the option. The person who sells or writes the option will demand this premium as a compensation for offering the option. ↵

In the highly efficient markets of foreign exchange it cannot be said that options, futures, or forwards will allow anyone to earn abnormal profits consistently. These markets simply allow their users to eliminate or hedge away the risks inherent in contracting while using multiple currencies.

Interest Rates and the Law of One Price

interest rate parity
A theory stating that risk-free bonds of various currencies must offer the same return when "translated" into a common currency using forward contracts.

In the near-perfect markets of foreign exchange and government bonds, the law of one price forces a relationship between international interest rates and exchange rates known as interest rate parity. The concept of interest rate parity is similar to purchasing power parity. **Interest rate parity** states that risk-free bonds of various currencies must offer the same return when "translated" into a common currency using forward contracts.

For example, consider two government-guaranteed zero coupon bonds with identical maturities of one year but issued by different countries. To simplify the analysis, let's assume that each bond is risk-free. Government bonds of the United States and England might provide somewhat realistic examples.

We know that an American investor can earn a risk-free return in U.S. dollars by simply purchasing a U.S. government bond. The investor pays U.S. dollars today for the bond and receives U.S. dollars in the future. If the interest rate on this U.S. government bond is 10 percent, the investor can invest $100 and receive a guaranteed payment of $110 in one year.

Is it possible for the American investor to use the British bond and foreign exchange markets to create an equivalent risk-free investment with a guaranteed return of U.S. dollars? The answer is yes, by following three steps: (1) convert dollars to pounds using the spot foreign exchange market, (2) buy the British bond using the pounds, and (3) enter into a forward foreign exchange contract, which allows the conversion of pounds received from the British bond into dollars in one year when the bond matures. The forward contract must be established at the same time that the bond is purchased so that the investor's future exchange rate can be locked in. These two equivalent alternatives are pictured on a time line in Figure 18.2.

FIGURE 18.2
Creating an Equivalent Risk-Free Investment

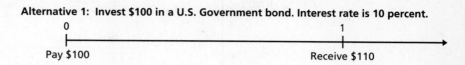

Alternative 1: Invest $100 in a U.S. Government bond. Interest rate is 10 percent.

Pay $100

Receive $110

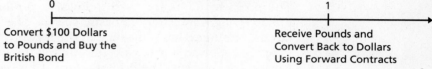

Alternative 2: Invest $100 in a British Government bond. Use the foreign exchange markets to exchange pounds for dollars.

Convert $100 Dollars
to Pounds and Buy the
British Bond

Receive Pounds and
Convert Back to Dollars
Using Forward Contracts

There are an infinite number of combinations of exchange rates and interest rates that would permit the British bond to pay the same return in U.S. dollars as the U.S. bond. For example, if the current spot exchange rate allows 0.8 British pounds to be exchanged for each U.S. dollar, if the forward exchange rate will allow 0.816 British pounds to be exchanged for each dollar in one year, and if the British bond pays 12.2 percent interest, then the payoff of a $100 investment in the British bond is equivalent to the payoff of a $100 investment in the U.S. government bond. This payoff is shown in the following transactions:

1. Convert $100 using 0.8 exchange rate into 80 pounds,
2. Invest 80 pounds at 12.2 percent bond return,
3. Receive 89.76 pounds at British bond maturity, and
4. Convert 89.76 pounds, using a forward exchange rate, of 0.816 into $110.

Notice that the British bond investment returns the same dollar amount as the U.S. bond investment. Even though the British bond earns a higher interest rate (12.2 percent versus 10 percent), the higher return is offset when converting dollars back into pounds.

The Interest Rate Parity Theorem. The relationship between interest rates and exchange rates described above can be generalized into the interest rate parity theorem:

$$\frac{\text{The Ratio Between}}{\text{Interest Rates}} = \frac{\text{The Ratio Between Forward and}}{\text{Spot Foreign Exchange Rates}}$$

$$\frac{(1 + \text{Domestic Yield})}{(1 + \text{Foreign Yield})} = \frac{\text{Spot Exchange Rate}}{\text{Forward Exchange Rate}}$$

(18.2)

The interest rate parity theorem states that international interest rate differences will be equal to differences between current and forward exchange rates.[3] In the previous example of British bonds and U.S. bonds, the interest rate parity theorem is:

$$\frac{(1.100)}{(1.122)} = \frac{0.800}{0.816}.$$

Summary of the Forward, Futures, and Options Markets

The problem of future cash inflows or outflows denominated in a major foreign currency[4] is easily solved. The firm can either sell in advance an undesired currency in the forward market or can prepare in advance for an outflow by contracting to purchase the currency in the forward market. The prices of forward foreign exchange contracts are determined by relative interest rates between the currencies.

Some corporations may wish to handle foreign exchange problems by purchasing options that allow the holder to exchange between currencies if exchange rates move against them but which allow the option holder to transact in the spot market if exchange rates move in a favorable direction.

MULTIPLE CURRENCIES WITH TIME AND RISK

Given our focus on corporate finance, and given that corporations are owned by shareholders, the most important question is how shareholders perceive the risk of transacting in foreign markets with different currencies. For instance, how does a shareholder of a major computer firm view the risks of commitments to sell major equipment at prices fixed in a foreign currency? In this section we formally discuss foreign exchange risks.

---

3. Some people think of the forward exchange rates as "guesses" of subsequent spot rates. In other words, they think that, because the forward exchange rate in the above example was 0.816, it must be true that market participants are estimating that the spot exchange rate is expected to rise to 0.816 during the next year. The viewpoint that forward prices are forecasts of subsequent spot prices has become so popular that it has even received a name: *the expectations theory of forward rates*. However, this "theory" ignores risk and is therefore fundamentally flawed. It is, at best, a crude approximation when dealing with forward contracts that contain risk.

4. Currencies of some smaller countries are not widely traded and can introduce a significant problem. Fortunately, the size of these transactions is relatively small, and often the corporations in these countries are accustomed to contracting using major currencies.

A Review of the Theory of Risk

Chapters 7 and 8 discussed the theory of risk in detail. To review, the most important lesson of these chapters is that there are two types of risk—systematic risk and diversifiable risk. Systematic risk is that variation in an asset's return that is correlated with the performance of the overall economy. Diversifiable risk is all other variation.

The ability to eliminate diversifiable risk through diversification leads to the conclusion that little or no added return should be demanded for bearing diversifiable risk. However, systematic risk is what ultimately flows through to shareholders and exposes them to the concern that they will have too little wealth if there is a general economic downturn. Only systematic risk requires a reward.

Another term for systematic risk is market risk, since it is the variation in return that is correlated with the entire economy or stock market. Market risk is measured by beta, and beta is used in an equation known as the capital asset pricing model in order to estimate a required rate of return.

The International Capital Asset Pricing Model

In Chapters 7 and 8 the overall performance of the economy was viewed as the performance of the stock market as captured by the S&P 500 stock portfolio or perhaps the overall U.S. economy. However, in theory, the market should comprise all assets. This includes stocks, bonds, real estate, automobiles, clothing, and so forth. Further, the market should include all of the wealth of the world—the international market portfolio—not just the wealth in the United States.

For the purposes of this chapter, market risk will be defined relative to the entire world economy. Thus, an asset will have systematic risk only to the extent that the performance of the asset is correlated with the overall world economy. All other risk will be considered as diversifiable risk. The required return on such an asset can be determined through **the international capital asset pricing model**.

the international capital asset pricing model
An asset valuation model built on the theory that an asset will have systematic risk only to the extent that the performance of the asset is correlated with the overall world economy. All other risk will be considered as diversifiable risk.

The notion that we should view the capital asset pricing model (CAPM) in an international context, with the market defined as the global portfolio, should be evident. The model itself would predict that investors would seek diversification and would therefore invest internationally. In fact, the more unrealistic view of the capital asset pricing model is to apply the model only to the economy of a single country such as the United States.

Systematic Risk and Multiple Currencies

The key question in a formal analysis of international systematic risk is whether or not systematic risk increases when contracting with or operating in foreign countries, as compared with otherwise similar domestic situations. For example, if a U.S. firm contracts to buy products from or sell products to a foreign firm, does it affect the systematic risk of the firm whether the transaction is fixed in terms of dollars or in a foreign currency?

The traditional view of international transactions is that they expose a firm to the fluctuations or risk inherent in foreign currencies. Thus, the decision of a firm to trade or operate internationally is often focused on the resulting exposure of the firm to foreign exchange risk.

Remember, however, that any contract using a foreign currency can be transformed into a fixed dollar arrangement by buying and selling through the forward market. This is illustrated below:

$$\begin{matrix} \text{Contract Fixed in} \\ \text{Foreign Currency} \end{matrix} + \begin{matrix} \text{Forward} \\ \text{Contracts} \end{matrix} = \begin{matrix} \text{Contract Fixed} \\ \text{in Domestic Currency} \end{matrix}$$

Thus, the decision of a firm to enter into international transactions in foreign currencies can be viewed as being economically similar to the decision to buy and sell forward contracts on foreign exchange rates.

Do contracts fixed in U.S. dollars have different levels of systematic risk relative to the world economy than do contracts fixed in yen, francs, pounds, lira, and so forth? Do forward contracts between two currencies have a positive beta?

The evidence from international markets tends to indicate that international transactions do not increase the systematic risk of a corporation. Accordingly, firms considering projects with international aspects should not require a higher rate of return when discounting cash flows for decision-making purposes.

In fact, international operations and trade tend to decrease the total risk to a firm by diversifying away some of the risk of the firm's domestic economy. Thus, a multinational corporation tends to be more diversified than an entirely domestic corporation because the multinational firm is less sensitive to the economic performance of a single country.

It is clear that a portfolio of international securities offers an investor enhanced diversification. Moreover, using a myriad of available mutual funds, shareholders of corporations are easily able to diversify across investments in various countries into a global portfolio. Since investors can accomplish this at little or no cost for themselves, it is not the job of domestic corporations to diversify into international transactions on behalf of their shareholders simply for the sake of diversification.

POLITICAL RISK

We have just discussed the systematic risk and diversification of international transactions, focusing on the extent to which the returns of assets from various countries differed in terms of systematic risk and the amount of diversification that they offered.

political risk
The risk that actions by a foreign government will have a negative impact on a firm's wealth.

This section discusses a very different analysis of risk: political risk. **Political risk** is the risk that actions by a foreign government will have a negative impact on a firm's wealth. An example of political risk is the danger that an operation in a foreign country will be nationalized, or seized by the existing government or by a new government through a coup d'etat.

Overview of Political Risk

Financial analysis in major developed nations takes for granted individuals' right to private property and their general protection from seizure by the government. Nationalization is the process whereby certain private property is seized by a government for the "good of the people," with little or no compensation to the original owner. To the citizens and governments of poor nations, the concept has a certain appeal—especially where a high percentage of the wealth in the nation is owned by an especially small percentage of the people or by the shareholders of foreign corporations.

However, nationalization is not the only form of political risk. Increased taxes or regulations can also harm shareholder wealth. In fact, nationalization can be viewed as a more complete form of taxation revision in which the tax rate is raised to 100 percent!

It is important to distinguish between high tax rates and uncertain tax rates. There is no problem in making a decision regarding investment in an environment of high tax rates, as long as the rates are stable. The investor simply takes taxes into account when estimating future cash flows. However, political risk is the risk that the tax rates will rise dramatically or that nationalization will occur after the investment is made. From the perspective of the country that hosts foreign assets, there is an obvious temptation to want to confiscate foreign wealth. Therefore, countries with political stability and a clearly defined process for legislating taxes have less political risk regardless of the level of their taxes.

Political Risk and Investment Decisions

As with all other potential expenses, the expected consequences of political risk must be incorporated into the estimation of a project's cash flows whenever the risk is viewed as being nontrivial. The higher the political risk and therefore the higher the probability of an adverse change in taxation, the lower should be the estimated cash inflows. Obviously, the greater the political risk, the less desirable the investment.

The degree of political risk depends in part upon the type of asset located in the host country. Assets that are of little value to the host country run a lower risk of being seized. Accordingly, a foreign operation that depends upon the parent company would have less political risk than a relatively autonomous operation. An example of a foreign asset carrying little political risk would be a foreign marketing office that depends on the sales office of the parent company. An example of a foreign asset carrying high political risk would be a low-technology manufacturing operation that can operate independently from the parent.

Innovative Financial Arrangements

Most political risk occurs from the incentives of governments to seize assets, and innovative financing arrangements can reduce political risk by reducing this incentive. The key is to ensure, directly or indirectly, that as large as possible a percentage of any losses due to seizure will be borne by the host country itself.

For example, political risk is reduced if the host country provides a portion of the project's financing. If such financing is provided, it may be useful to have a clause stating that, in the event of nationalization, any debts to the citizens of the host country would be forgiven. This clause is especially helpful when the parties providing the financing have some influence on the government.

PRACTICAL CONSIDERATIONS OF INTERNATIONAL FINANCIAL MANAGEMENT

As we have said, engaging in international trade is not as simple as engaging in domestic trade. We briefly review two issues that are directly or indirectly related to international finance. (There are a host of other issues such as shipping, marketing, and management that are important but outside the scope of this text.)

Receiving Goods

The decision to extend credit to a foreign customer is more risky than the decision to extend credit to a domestic customer, due to difficulty in obtaining information regarding the customer and difficulty in collection.

banker's acceptances and **irrevocable letters of credit**
Financial instruments often used to facilitate international trade. The banker's acceptance and letter of credit represents a guarantee of payment by the importer to the exporter.

Banker's acceptances and **irrevocable letters of credit** are often used for international trade. In both situations, payment of the bill is guaranteed by a bank. It is the responsibility of the buyer to arrange for one of these forms of guarantee.

Payment for Goods

The decision to purchase goods from a foreign operation is the opposite side of the previous transaction. If the foreign seller does not extend credit, the domestic buyer can arrange for either a banker's acceptance or an irrevocable letter of credit. Of course, it is important to ensure that payment will not be made until satisfactory receipt of the goods has occurred.

SUMMARY

☐ The primary financial problem that occurs in international finance is multiple currencies. In international transactions, the costs and benefits of a decision can be expressed in more than one currency or in a currency other than the currency of the shareholders. Proper decision making can be accomplished by converting all the costs and benefits into a common currency, adjusted for time and risk.

☐ Foreign exchange markets provide the opportunity to trade between currencies. In order to convert a current cost or current benefit into a desired currency, the decision maker multiplies the foreign currency by the spot rate of exchange between the currencies.

☐ The prices in various currencies of any good traded in a well-functioning market should be approximately equal when converted into a common currency using market exchange rates. This is an extension of the law of one price, which is a natural result of competition. However, goods that are dissimilar, expensive to transport, and otherwise trade in highly imperfect markets can have substantially different prices in different places.

☐ Purchasing power parity states that all currencies have approximately equal overall purchasing power when converted using market exchange rates. Overall purchasing power refers to the ability to purchase a common spectrum of goods for an ordinary lifestyle. Thus, the theory of purchasing power parity states that the law of one price will hold for overall purchasing. However, since so many goods are traded in highly imperfect markets, there is no reason to believe that purchasing power parity will hold.

☐ Financial managers can convert future costs and benefits into a desired currency using the forward or futures markets for foreign exchange. Forward and futures contracts allow the corporation to agree today and negotiate a price today for a transaction that will not be completed until some predetermined point in the future, such as a certain number of months hence.

☐ The law of one price can be applied to government bonds in various currencies since the bonds trade in rather well-functioning markets. This is also expressed as the interest rate parity theorem, which states that the ratios between interest rates across currencies will be determined simultaneously with the ratios between spot and forward exchange rates.

☐ When future benefits and costs are uncertain, currency differentials become more difficult to resolve. Foreign exchange options give the holder of the option the opportunity to exchange at predetermined prices—but not the obligation. Thus, the risk of currency differentials can be controlled at a cost.

☐ The international capital asset pricing model views the systematic risk of an asset as being determined by the correlation of the asset's return with the world economy. Within this model, currency differentials do not introduce substantial systematic risk and therefore corporations do not need to be overly concerned about currency differentials. The model predicts that shareholders do not need to be protected against the risks of fluctuations in the value of various currencies, since this risk is largely diversifiable and can be completely resolved by the shareholder without the help of the corporation.

☐ Political risk is the danger that the host country will seize, nationalize, confiscate, or heavily tax the benefits of a firm's foreign operation. This risk can be reduced through innovative financing arrangements that reduce the host country's benefit in such actions. An example would include the financing of foreign operations using money from the host country.

☐ International business involves a myriad of practical financial issues, of which the major ones are arranging receipt of payment for goods delivered to a foreign customer and arranging payment for goods received from a foreign supplier.

DEMONSTRATION PROBLEMS

Problem 1   Overland Corporation anticipates receiving 10,000,000 British pounds in exactly three months. The current value of a British pound in American dollars is $1.80. The corporation is considering the following alternatives:
a. Lock in an exchange rate for the pounds using a forward contract or a futures contract with an exchange rate of $1.80,
b. Lock in a potential exchange rate for the pounds using a foreign exchange option that would allow the 10,000,000 pounds to be converted into American dollars at an exchange rate of $1.80, or

c. Do nothing and accept the foreign exchange risk.
Compute the ultimate American dollar value of the 10,000,000 British pounds to Overland Corporation using each of the three strategies. Examine three scenarios in which the value of the pound drops to $1.50, rises to $2.10, and stays at $1.80 at the end of the three months. Ignore the costs of purchasing the foreign exchange option.

Solution to Problem 1

Step 1: The first strategy locks in a guaranteed value for British pounds to Overland Corporation of $1.80. Thus, whether the British pounds rise in value, fall in value, or stay at the same value, Overland will convert the pounds to American dollars at the locked-in exchange rate of $1.80. Thus, in three months the firm would receive $18,000,000.

Step 2: The second strategy has Overland purchase a foreign exchange option that will be used by the firm only in the event that the British pounds fall in value:

Scenario 1: Pound drops to $1.50
Result: Firm uses option to convert pounds to dollars at $1.80 and therefore receives $18,000,000.

Scenario 2: Pound stays at $1.80
Result: It makes no difference whether or not the firm uses the option, since either way Overland can convert pounds to dollars at $1.80 and therefore receive $18,000,000.

Scenario 3: Pound rises to $2.10
Result: Firm doesn't use option but rather converts pounds to dollars at $2.10 and therefore receives $21,000,000.

Step 3: The third strategy has Overland do nothing to protect itself. Therefore the firm will receive value based in American dollars, which depends upon whatever the market exchange rate is in three months.

Scenario 1: Pound drops to $1.50
Result: Firm converts pounds to dollars at $1.50 and therefore receives $15,000,000.

Scenario 2: Pound stays at $1.80.
Result: Firm converts pounds to dollars at $1.80 and therefore receives $18,000,000.

Scenario 3: Pound rises to $2.10
Result: Firm converts pounds to dollars at $2.10 and therefore receives $21,000,000.

Final Solution: The final position viewed in American dollars is:

	Outcome		
	Scenario 1 *($1.50)*	*Scenario 2* *($1.80)*	*Scenario 3* *($2.10)*
Strategy (a) (Futures)	$18,000,000	$18,000,000	$18,000,000
Strategy (b) (Option)	$18,000,000	$18,000,000	$21,000,000
Strategy (c) (Nothing)	$15,000,000	$18,000,000	$21,000,000

Notice that futures (or forwards) contracts eliminate the risk if the foreign currency is received. However, remember that if the deal falls through the firm may end up with an unhedged futures contract loss. Under the option, the firm would not lose money if the deal fell through and it has the chance of benefiting from favorable movements. However, options can be expensive. Finally, doing "nothing" exposes the firm (or perhaps its shareholders) to the risk of fluctuations in the value of British pounds. ↵

Problem 2   The short-term (three-month), risk-free interest rate in the U.S. is 3% on a particular day. The German short-term, risk-free interest rate in German marks is 9%. The current spot foreign exchange rate is that each mark is worth $0.65 and therefore that each dollar is worth 1.53846 German marks. Find the forward exchange rate for three months from today using interest rate parity theory.

Solution to Problem 2
The solution can be found by inserting the three known values into the interest rate parity equation, Formula (18.2), and solving for the unknown fourth variable. The primary complexity is figuring out whether to use the foreign exchange rate expressed in the domestic currency or the foreign currency. In our form of the formula it is necessary to express both the spot exchange rate and the forward exchange rate in the foreign currency (i.e., in our example use 1.53846 German marks per American dollar).

Step 1: Write down Formula (18.2):

$$\frac{(1 + \text{Domestic Yield})}{(1 + \text{Foreign Yield})} = \frac{\text{Spot Exchange Rate}}{\text{Forward Exchange Rate}}.$$

Step 2: Enter 3% as the domestic yield, 9% as the foreign yield, and 1.53846 as the spot foreign exchange rate:

1.03 / 1.09 = $1.53846 / (Forward Exchange Rate).

Step 3: Arrange the equation to place the unknown variable on the left side:

Forward Exchange Rate = 1.53846 * (1.09/1.03).

Step 4: Solve for the forward rate:

Forward Exchange Rate = 1.628.

Step 5: Convert the exchange rate to American dollars, if desired, by taking its inverse: $0.6142.

Final Solution: The forward foreign exchange rate is $0.6142, expressed as American dollars per German mark, or 1.628, expressed as German marks per American dollar. Thus, the higher foreign interest rate is fully offset by a decline in the German mark in the futures market relative to the spot market. ↵

REVIEW QUESTIONS

1. What is traded in the foreign exchange market?
2. Describe a "black market," and explain how it comes about.
3. Explain how an exchange rate can be used to transform one currency into another currency.
4. Explain the relevance of the law of one price in foreign exchange transactions.
5. Would we generally expect the prices of all world goods to obey the law of one price? Why or why not?
6. What is purchasing power parity, and what are its implications?
7. Explain how forward or futures contracts can eliminate foreign exchange risk through time.
8. List and explain briefly two potential problems associated with using forward or futures contracts to remove foreign exchange risk.
9. Explain how options on foreign exchange can be used to avoid the two problems with forward or futures contracts in review question 8. Why would a firm ever use forward or futures contracts if options exist?
10. What is interest rate parity and what are its implications?
11. Discuss systematic risk in the context of an international market portfolio.
12. Provide an example of political risk.
13. What is "nationalization" and how does it relate to political risk?

14. Describe how innovative financing can reduce political risk.
15. How do letters of credit facilitate international trade?

PROBLEMS

1. P & T Corporation is a specialty firm with a worldwide reputation for providing protection to egos. They are considering the import of equipment which costs 120,000 German marks and performs the same as a domestic model which costs $80,000.
   a. Which alternative has lower cost if the exchange rate is such that each German mark is worth $0.60?
   b. Which would be cheaper if the exchange rate were $0.70 per German mark?
   c. What would the exchange rate have to be expressed as a dollar cost per German mark in order to make the alternatives have equal cost?
   d. What would be the equivalent exchange rate from part (c) above that would express U.S. dollars in terms of German marks?
2. Use the exchange rates given in Figure 18.1 to convert the following values into U.S. dollars using the Monday columns.
   a. 140,000 Canadian dollars into U.S. dollars
   b. 340,000 German marks into U.S. dollars
   c. 804,000 Japanese yen into U.S. dollars
   d. 145,000 Swiss francs into U.S. dollars
3. Use the exchange rates given in Figure 18.1 to convert the following values from U.S. dollars into the listed currency, using the Monday columns.
   a. $123,000 into Canadian dollars
   b. $150,000 into German marks
   c. $ 8,000 into Japanese yen
   d. $456,000 into Swiss francs
4. If the price of an ounce of gold were $1000, use the exchange rates listed for Monday in Figure 18.1 to find the price of gold in the following currencies. Assume perfect markets.
   a. Australian dollars
   b. British pounds
   c. French francs
   d. Mexican pesos
   e. South African rands
5. Suppose that the price of gold in U.S. dollars is $1000, that the exchange rate between Australian dollars and U.S. dollars is $0.75 = 1 Australian dollar, and that an ounce of gold can be purchased in Australia for 1300 Australian dollars. Show how an investor can earn an arbitrage profit in this situation.

6. Matthew's Sports Importing Emporium Incorporated (Mat's) is considering signing contracts that will obligate the firm to purchase 100,000 German marks' worth of electronic timekeeping equipment at the end of each calendar quarter for the next two years. Mat's is also signing a contract with a major university system that will purchase this equipment from Mat's at a price of $75,000 (U.S.) per quarter.
   a. What would be Mat's profit or loss each quarter if the exchange rate is $0.60 per German mark throughout the life of the contract?
   b. What would be Mat's profit or loss if the value of the German mark rose by $0.05 per quarter starting at $0.65 in the first quarter and ending at $1.00 in the eighth quarter?
7. Returning to Mat's in problem 6, suppose that futures markets offer the following prices for German marks at the following times to delivery:

Quarters in Future	Futures Price of German Mark
1,2,3	$0.65
4,5,6	$0.75
7,8	$0.80

   a. Compute and aggregate the profit or loss for each quarter if Mat's buys the necessary German marks through the futures market.
   b. Would your answer change if the price of each futures contract fell by $0.05 before Mat's entered any contracts? Please detail.
8. Returning to problems 6 and 7, suppose that Mat's entered the futures contracts given in the table in problem 7 and that the price of German marks immediately fell to $0.60 for all contracts and stayed there for the next two years.
   a. What aggregate profit or loss would Mat's have for the eight quarters if Mat's entered the contracts using the prices from the table in problem 7?
   b. What aggregate profit or loss would Mat's have for the eight quarters if Mat's did not use futures contracts but instead used the actual spot rates that occurred ($0.60)?
   c. Viewed at the end of the eight quarters, if Mat's entered into the futures contracts as discussed above, what aggregate profit or loss was caused by this effort to protect itself from currency fluctuations?
9. Drunken Sailor Oil Corporation is negotiating the purchase of 1,000,000 barrels of oil to be delivered and paid for in exactly one year. Drunken Sailor Oil Corporation is willing to pay $25 per barrel, since they can sell the oil in advance to oil refineries. Unfor-

tunately, for political reasons, the oil exporter wants the contract expressed in French francs.

   a. What price per barrel of oil expressed in French francs is equivalent to $25 if the French franc exchange rate is $0.25?

   b. If the contract is signed at a price of 110 French francs per barrel and the oil corporation does not use futures contracts, in terms of U.S. dollars how much will it pay for the 1,000,000 barrels of oil if the exchange rate per French franc rises to $0.30?

   c. If the oil corporation buys the French francs in the futures markets for $0.26, how much will the oil cost in U.S. dollars (if the price of the oil was 110 francs)?

10. Returning to Drunken Sailor Oil Corporation in problem 9:

   a. If the oil corporation locks in an exchange rate of $0.26 per French franc but the exchange rate falls to $0.20 at the end of the year, how much money will the firm have lost due to its decision to use futures contracts?

   b. If the oil corporation locks in an exchange rate of $0.16 per French franc and the exchange rate rises to $0.25 at the end of the year, how much money will the firm have gained due to its decision to use futures contracts?

11. Returning to problems 6 through 8, how could Mat's have used options contracts to hedge against adverse currency fluctuations? Please give specific times and amounts.

12. Returning to Drunken Sailor Oil Corporation in problems 9 and 10, the firm's treasury department has suggested the purchase of an option that would enable the firm to exchange $24,750,000 U.S. dollars into 110,000,000 French francs at the end of the year. The option would cost the firm $2,000,000.

   a. What is the exercise or striking price (exchange rate) for this option expressed as U.S. dollars per French franc?

   b. Including the cost of the option, what would be the total cost of the oil in U.S. dollars if, at the end of the year, the exchange rate were $0.16 per French franc?

   c. Including the cost of the option, what would be the total cost of the oil in U.S. dollars if, at the end of the year, the exchange rate were $0.23 per French franc?

   d. Including the cost of the option, what would be the total cost of the oil in U.S. dollars if, at the end of the year, the exchange rate were $0.26 per French franc?

   e. Including the cost of the option, how much money would the option have saved the firm if, at the end of the year, the exchange rate were $0.27 per French franc?

13. Gret Wayneski can earn 6% interest in Canada or 8% interest at a U.S. bank. Both rates are risk-free. The current values of a Canadian dollar and U.S. dollar are equal. What would the one-year

forward price of a Canadian dollar be in terms of U.S. dollars if markets were perfect?

14. Returning to Gret Wayneski in problem 13, what would the one-year forward price of a Canadian dollar be in terms of U.S. dollars if markets were perfect and if the interest rates were reversed (i.e., the Canadian interest rate were 8% and the U.S. interest rate were 6%)?

15. Using the interest rate parity theorem, fill in the missing values.

	Domestic Yield	Foreign Yield	Spot Exchange Rate	Forward Exchange Rate
a.	10%	15%	$0.50	____
b.	18%	12%	____	$0.25
c.	15%	____	$0.20	$0.21
d.	____	10%	$0.44	$0.40

16. The U.S. risk-free interest rate is 8%, and a portfolio that reflects the world economy has an expected return in U.S. dollars of 18%. The U.S. stock market has an expected return of 24%.
    a. Using the international capital asset pricing model, should a U.S. firm's beta be computed against the world economy portfolio or the U.S. economy portfolio?
    b. If Project Trunk, located in the U.S., has an "international" beta of 0.5, what required rate of return should be used (expressed as a percentage rate of U.S. dollars)?
    c. Assume that Project Trunk has a beta with the domestic economy of 0.8 and find the required rate of return according to the domestic CAPM (expressed as a percentage rate of U.S. dollars).

17. The British risk-free interest rate is 0% and a portfolio that reflects the world economy has an expected return in British pounds of 10%. The British stock market has an expected return of 7%.
    a. According to the international capital asset pricing model, should a British firm's beta be computed against the world economy portfolio or the British economy portfolio?
    b. If a British project (named Project Boot) has an "international" beta of 0.5, what required rate of return should be used (expressed as a percentage rate of British pounds)?
    c. Assume that Project Boot has a "domestic" beta of 1.5 and find the required rate of return according to the domestic CAPM (expressed as a percentage rate of British pounds).

18. Referring to problems 16 and 17, for simplicity assume that the British pound and U.S. dollar now trade on a par basis (i.e., the exchange rate is 1.0).
    a. What would be the one-year forward exchange rate using the

risk-free interest rates in problems 16 and 17 and the interest rate parity theorem? Express the exchange rate as the number of U.S. dollars required to purchase one British pound.

b. Express your answer to (a) as a percentage change relative to the starting exchange rate ($1.00).

19. Use the forward exchange rate found in problem 18(a) and the percentage change in 18(b) in answering the following questions:
    a. Use the change in the forward exchange rate to convert the required rate of return in U.S. dollars from problem 16(b) into a required rate of return in British pounds by subtracting 18(b) from the answer to 16(b).
    b. Compare your answer in 19(a) with your answer in 17(b) and discuss.
    c. Use the forward exchange rate to convert the required rate of return in U.S. dollars from problem 16(c) into a required rate of return in British pounds by subtracting 18(b) from the answer in 16(c).
    d. Compare your answer in 19(c) with your answer in 17(c) and discuss.

20. Based upon your answers to problems 16 through 19, compare the international capital asset pricing model with domestic capital asset pricing models. It may help your analysis to assume that Projects Trunk and Boot are identical except that Project Trunk is located in the U.S. and Project Boot is located in England. Which model appears to be correct? What is the source of the difference?

DISCUSSION QUESTIONS

1. Do the issues presented in this chapter on international finance change the underlying principles and concepts of modern corporate finance?

2. Some Americans receiving pensions move to less developed countries in search of a higher standard of living. Does this refute the purchasing power parity theorem?

3. Firm Hops and Firm Barley both trade extensively with foreign countries. Firm Hops has a policy of using the futures market to lock in profits in U.S. dollars, while Firm Barley has a policy not to use futures markets and to accept the risk of foreign exchange. As a shareholder, how would you evaluate the decision to invest in Firm Hops as compared to Firm Barley?

4. Return to Firm Hops and Firm Barley in question 3. Recall that firm Hops uses the futures market to eliminate foreign exchange risk while firm Barley does not. As a manager, how would you analyze the decision to accept a job with Firm Hops as compared to Firm Barley?

5. Scoundrel Savings and Loan invested in assets that paid out cash in foreign currencies and borrowed money using certificates of deposits that promised U.S. dollars. Scoundrel's manager, I. M. Leavin, claims to have hedged this foreign currency risk by exchanging the foreign currencies for U.S. dollars in the futures markets. However, in the first year, the futures contract lost tens of millions of dollars while the firm's other operations only made a few million dollars of profit, according to the financial statements. Is there any explanation other than that I. M. Leavin mismanaged the firm?

6. Plastico, Inc., produces plastic exchanges used in common assembly processes. The market for these exchanges in the U.S. has dried up. However, the firm has an opportunity to produce and sell their product in a foreign country that recently moved from a "planned" economy to a "market" economy. What types of added risk would the firm face if they begin operations in the foreign country? What can they do to lessen such risks?

7. The European Community (EC) has discussed combining many different currencies into a single currency. What would be the advantages and disadvantages of such a move?

Chapter 19

Mergers and Other Reorganizations

Prerequisites: Chapters 1 through 12

Merger activity in the U.S. reached a heightened pace in the second half of the decade of the 1980s. During those years, countless financial headlines cited stories of mergers that were changing the face of American business. But of the over 4000 acquisitions that took place in 1988, none captured more attention than the takeover of RJR Nabisco, Inc., the food and tobacco conglomerate, by Kohlberg, Kravis, and Roberts (KKR). What made this takeover unique was the fact that RJR Nabisco was one of the largest Fortune 500 industrial companies, with annual sales over $10 billion. The takeover of a company as large as RJR Nabisco, inconceivable at one time, was now a reality.

The story of RJR's takeover was fascinating. RJR's chief executive officer (CEO), F. Ross Johnson, had a key role in the ultimate sale of the company. RJR was doing well under Mr. Johnson's direction, and his success as a CEO allowed him to build a close relationship with the board of directors. In fact, this close relationship with the board led Johnson to make a critical mistake. Johnson announced a plan to lead a group of investors to take over the company. The specifics of the plan—known as a leveraged buyout (LBO)—would raise the vast sums of money needed to accomplish the buyout by issuing debt.

There were two major problems with Johnson's LBO plan. First, it was disclosed that the LBO would have made Mr. Johnson and other top managers at RJR Nabisco exorbitantly wealthy. Second, and more important, it became known that the LBO would require RJR Nabisco to scale down by selling off a major part of its existing business.

The Johnson-led LBO plan attracted other groups of investors to consider the takeover of RJR Nabisco. In cases such as these, the board of directors has the responsibility to consider all reasonable bids, and to select the bid that is in the best interest of the shareholders. The bidding process for RJR resembled that of an auction, with one group, say KKR, announcing a bid, and another group outbidding them. Of course, the higher the bid, the better off were RJR Nabisco's shareholders, as they would receive a higher price for their shares. The rounds of bids for the takeover of RJR Nabisco are summarized in the table below.

Price per Share Bid to Take Over RJR Nabisco, Inc.
Pre-Bidding Price per Share = $56

Group	Round 1	Round 2	Round 3	Round 4	Round 5
F. Ross Johnson	$ 75	$100	$101	$108	$112
KKR	$ 90	$ 94	$106	$108	$109
First Boston	****	$105	DROPPED OUT		

First Boston, which entered the bidding process in Round 2, was the first to drop out. The board of directors at RJR Nabisco concluded, at the end of Round 2, that the two remaining bids were substantially equivalent, and that other factors would be used to determine which bid to accept.

Here KKR held the advantage. KKR announced that, as winners, they would keep the main part of the company together, would allow current shareholders the opportunity to retain partial ownership of the firm, and would agree to provide protection for the firm's employees. F. Ross Johnson's group was asked to do the same but refused. In the end, KKR was declared the winner and took control by paying to the shareholders $109 per share for stock that weeks earlier traded for $56 per share. F. Ross Johnson, the man who had landed the top spot at RJR only the year before, was replaced as CEO.

This chapter discusses mergers and other forms of corporate reorganizations. The traditional view of mergers is contrasted with the modernist view. While traditionalists tend to focus on the effect of mergers on competition and on society, modernists focus on mergers as vehicles to change the control of the firm's assets. Other types of reorganizations, such as divestitures and liquidations, are also discussed.

CORPORATE REORGANIZATIONS AND THE MARKET FOR CORPORATE CONTROL

market for corporate control
The study of corporate reorganizations, defined as a change in the control of one or more of the firm's major assets.

merger
The combination of two firms into a single firm.

Corporate reorganizations is a general term that includes mergers, divestitures, and liquidations. The study of corporate reorganizations is also known as the study of the **market for corporate control,** defined for the purposes of this chapter as a change in the control of one or more of the firm's major assets. Perhaps the most common type of corporate control change is the **merger,** or the combination of two firms into a single firm.

Corporate mergers seem to occur in waves or in periods of high activity. Figure 19.1 illustrates this tendency for periods of high and low merger activity.

FIGURE 19.1
A History of Merger Activity

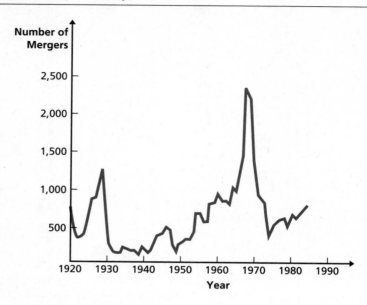

divestiture

The removal of part of the firm's current operations. The removal can be accomplished by the sale of assets to another firm, the setting up of a separate corporation to control the sold assets, or the liquidation of the assets.

Table 19.1 reports merger and divestiture activity annually from 1980 to 1989. A **divestiture** is the removal of part of the firm's current operations. The removal can be accomplished by the sale of assets to another firm, the setting up of a separate corporation to control the sold assets, or the liquidation of the assets. Divestitures will be discussed in detail later in the chapter.

From just under $33 billion in 1980, merger activity experienced a sevenfold increase to over $230 billion in 1989. The value of merger transactions in the 1980s totaled over $1.3 trillion. Divestiture activity experienced a twelvefold increase between 1980 and 1989, growing from slightly over $5 billion to just under $61 billion. With the recent volume of merger experience as background, we next discuss mergers in the context of corporate finance.

Mergers and Corporate Finance

In many ways, the decision to reorganize a corporation is no different from other investment and financing decisions. In a nutshell, corporate reorganizations should be evaluated by comparing the present value of benefits with the present value of costs.

Why, then, do we discuss mergers in a separate chapter? For one, mergers generate a great deal of media coverage and public-policy

TABLE 19.1
Corporate Reorganization Activity in the 1980s

Year	Merger Activity Value in Billions	Divestiture Activity Value in Billions
1980	$ 32.8	$ 5.1
1981	$ 69.5	$ 10.2
1982	$ 60.7	$ 8.4
1983	$ 52.7	$ 12.9
1984	$126.1	$ 30.6
1985	$146.0	$ 43.5
1986	$205.8	$ 72.4
1987	$178.3	$ 57.7
1988	$236.4	$ 83.2
1989	$231.4	$ 60.8

debate. Governmental leaders, members of the media, and business leaders appear to be captivated by mergers and other corporate reorganizations.

Further, many people view corporate reorganizations as events that can have major impacts on individual firms and on the economy in general. For instance, mergers can result in the closing of a plant or in the general reduction in a firm's workforce. Perhaps people believe that they should try to understand these events in order to try to influence them. In addition, finance scholars are especially interested in corporate reorganizations, since they offer the equivalent of a laboratory in which to test our understanding of finance.

Whatever the reason, students of finance need to be introduced to the issues surrounding corporate reorganizations and to the special vocabulary that serves these issues.

Friendly Versus Hostile Mergers

Mergers can be friendly agreements between the board of directors representing the acquiring company and the board of directors representing the target company. In contrast to friendly agreements, boards may not agree to be combined and a hostile fight for control may ensue. In such a case, the acquiring company attempts to gain control of the target firm without the approval of the target's board of directors.

Friendly Mergers. In a friendly merger, the management of the two firms agree in principle to be combined into one firm. Friendly mergers usually result from a consensus that the two firms are worth more together than the sum of the two firms held separately. This is called

synergy. By merging, the combined firm benefits from the synergy of the merger.

In the case of a friendly merger, the two boards will issue a statement outlining the terms of the agreement and ask for stockholder approval. If the stockholders of the target firm agree to be acquired, they will sign over the ownership rights of those shares to the acquiring firm. In return for their shares, the shareholders of the target firm will usually either receive cash or the common stock of the acquiring firm.

Unfriendly or Hostile Mergers. In an unfriendly or hostile takeover, the acquiring firm makes an offer to buy stock directly from the shareholders of the target firm. Sometimes these offers occur after friendly overtures have been rebuffed.

In the context of a hostile merger, the offer to buy stock is called a **tender offer.** The objective of the tender offer is to persuade the shareholders of the target company to "tender" enough shares to the acquiring firm to enable it to take control of the company. Chances for success are greatly improved when the acquiring firm sets the price of the tender offer well above the current market price of the target firm's shares. The control of the firm is transferred when the acquiring firm accumulates enough stock to vote in a new board of directors and set a new direction for the target firm.

Target firm management may resist a hostile takeover, due at least partly to the fact that the change in control will likely result in a replacement of current management with a new management team. The resistance to takeovers can come in many forms, ranging from a recommendation to the shareholders not to tender their shares, to antitakeover measures. **Antitakeover measures** are enacted in order to make it more difficult for a firm to be merged with another firm. Window 19.1 lists and discusses the most common antitakeover measures.

The next section reviews the more traditional approach to mergers, to be followed by some modernist perspectives.

THE TRADITIONAL VIEW OF CORPORATE REORGANIZATIONS

Most early analysis of mergers focused on the potential impact of merger activity in reducing competition and therefore harming the public good. Traditionally, merger analysis attempted to explain why firms were being combined, and what impact the merger would have on the competitive forces of the industry.

Window 19.1

Common Antitakeover Measures

1. Poison Pills: Acts of target management whose purpose is to make the target firm less appealing to the acquiring firm. An example of a poison pill is the right given to the target's shareholders to buy more stock in the target firm at a bargain price. The right to buy these shares is usually contingent on the target firm losing control.

2. Golden Parachutes: Compensation to the top management of the target firm in the event that the target firm loses control. This compensation package can be of large magnitude, and is usually viewed as an attempt to make the target firm less susceptible to being taken over.

3. Scorched Earth Strategy: The sale of a profitable division or other prized assets in the target firm in order to make it less appealing to the acquiring firm.

4. Targeted Repurchases: The purchase of the shares of the target firm from the acquiring firm at a premium price. A condition of the purchase is that the potential acquirer leave the target firm intact. Targeted repurchases are also known as *greenmail*.

5. Changes in the Corporate Charter: The corporate charter contains the laws that govern the firm, and includes provisions that govern the transfer of control. The corporate charter can be changed so that a large majority, say 80 percent, of the shareholders must approve the merger. This type of change is known as a *super majority provision*. Because it is difficult for any group to acquire such a large percent of approval, takeovers become less likely to occur.

6. Staggered Board: The classification of the board of directors into groups such that only one group is reelected each year. The acquiring firm can therefore not quickly control the board of the target even after obtaining a majority of the shares.

Types of Mergers

vertical mergers
Mergers between firms in related industries but at different points in the production and distribution process.

One way to study the impact of mergers is to categorize the relationship between the two firms being merged. **Vertical mergers** are mergers between firms in related industries but at different points in the production and distribution process. For example, if a paper manufacturer merges with a publisher, the combined firm would span a larger portion of the entire process of producing printed material. These mergers were popular in the early part of this century.

In contrast, **horizontal mergers** are mergers between two firms in the same industry. The merger of two automobile manufacturers would be an example of a horizontal merger. Finally, **conglomerate mergers** are mergers between firms in unrelated industries that result in larger and more diversified firms. Conglomerate mergers were especially popular in the 1960s.

horizontal mergers
Mergers between two firms in the same industry.

conglomerate mergers
Mergers between firms in unrelated industries.

Classifying mergers in this way focuses on the tendency of horizontal and vertical mergers to reduce competition and therefore to harm the public good. For example, if a firm becomes the only firm within an industry, it is said to be a monopoly and may be able to raise prices and profits at the expense of consumers. An industry comprised of a small number of firms is said to be an oligopoly. Oligopolies can also lessen competition and may harm consumers.

Merger Law

Given that mergers have the potential to reduce competition and harm the public good, people have acted through government in an attempt to discourage such activity. Under the goal of promoting the public good, laws have been enacted to curtail mergers that would significantly and adversely affect competition. For example, a merger that would combine the top producers in an industry such that the combined firm would control over 50 percent of the market would not be allowed under such law. Window 19.2 details the legislation in the United States directed at merger activity that has the potential to reduce competition.

Government's role in regulating merger activity changes as administrations (i.e., as presidents) change. For example, some argue that the Reagan Administration (1981–1989) viewed antitrust laws as a drain on the economy, and allowed most mergers to take place without government interference. Perhaps this partially explains why mergers move in waves, as was shown in Figure 19.1.

The Medium of Exchange in a Merger

There are numerous ways to finance a merger. The acquiring firm may purchase the shares of the acquired firm using cash. The cash may be raised from a new issue of securities by the acquiring firm or, in the case of small acquisitions, may be raised from working capital.

The acquisition is often accomplished by offering securities in the merged firm in exchange for the shares of the acquired firm. Perhaps the most simple exchange of securities occurs when the shareholders of the acquired firm simply exchange their shares for new shares of common stock in the acquiring firm. A ratio of exchange is set such

Window 19.2

Mergers and Antitrust Laws

A series of laws have been enacted in the U.S. to ensure that mergers do not act to "restrain trade" or monopolize activity in the market. Such laws are known as *antitrust laws.* The first antitrust law dates back to the Sherman Act of 1890, and others include the Federal Trade Commission Act of 1914 and the Clayton Act of 1914. The Clayton Act forbids the acquisition of assets that could potentially result in a significant decrease in competition, such as in creating a monopoly. Because the Clayton Act focuses on the potential for competition to be lessened, it has become the act that is most cited regarding questions of competition as a result of a merger. Under the Clayton Act, enforcement officials must show only that the probable effect of the merger will be to reduce competition.

Antitrust laws are enforced by the Justice Department's Antitrust Division. A civil suit brought by the Justice Department against an anticompetitive merger, if successful, will result in divestment. A criminal suit will result in more severe punishment. In most cases, the Justice Department will meet with firms considering a merger and will provide an opinion regarding whether legal action is likely to ensue.

A second antitrust enforcement body is the Federal Trade Commission. As a regulatory agency, its decisions are binding but can be appealed through the courts. The FTC will usually conduct investigations concerning potential mergers, and, like the Justice Department, will issue its opinion indicating the likely response to a proposed merger.

Finally, Securities and Exchange Commission (SEC) regulations attempt to promote competition through disclosure to the public of all information pertaining to the likelihood of a merger. For example, the SEC requires any investor accumulating five or more percent of another firm's common stock to disclose such information by filing a form. Other filing rules of the SEC provide additional information regarding the potential for a merger.

that shareholders of the acquired firm will receive a stated dollar amount of shares in the merged firm.

Sometimes the shares of the acquired firm may be financed through a blend of cash and securities.[1] Often the package of securi-

---

1. For example, the takeover of RJR Nabisco by KKR for $109 per share was financed through the following package: $81 per share in cash, convertible bonds valued at $10 per share, and preferred shares valued at $18 per share.

ties includes bonds or preferred stocks in addition to cash or common stock.

Motivations for Mergers—The Traditionalist View

According to traditionalists, mergers can be motivated by factors related to anticompetition, synergy, and tax shields. After discussing these factors, we offer two irrational motivations for mergers.

Anticompetitive Reasons to Merge.   One reason to merge is to reduce competition and therefore reap the financial benefits of being in a less competitive industry. The typical example of this type of merger is the acquisition by one of the leading firms in an industry of one of its largest competitors. Examples include the automotive industry and the airline industry.

As discussed in Window 19.2, antitrust laws in the United States and other nations are designed to control horizontal mergers that reduce the competitive forces in the industry. It is usually argued that firms of significant size can control the market such that prices are higher and service levels are lower than would be expected in competitive markets. However, enforcement of these laws is less than 100 percent effective, and reduced competition is a potential motivation for mergers that cannot be dismissed entirely.

Synergistic Motivations for Mergers.   Clearly the most important justification for a merger is synergy, which refers to the potential for the combination of two objects to be worth more than the sum of the parts. The synergy is usually expected to result from economies of scale, whereby average costs are lower in large firms than in smaller firms. Economies of scale can result from the use of more advanced or specialized equipment, from the fact that a large plant can purchase raw materials in larger quantities with larger discounts, or from the ability to operate a large plant more efficiently.

For example, a retail store or manufacturer may find that certain expenses rise more slowly at higher and higher levels of sales. Thus, it can be argued that a merger allows the combined firms to reach a higher level of production, become more cost efficient, and therefore be more valuable to the shareholders. In terms of finance, synergy therefore refers to the potential for the value of two merged firms to be greater than the sum of their values as individual firms.

It is also argued that synergy makes the firms' combined operations more efficient by eliminating certain expenses that are shared by the combined firms. For example, if two firms being merged both have a sales force, numerous regional sales offices, and several manufacturing facilities, it might be possible to consolidate certain overlapping facilities.

Unused Tax Shields.   Unused tax shields provide still another motivation for mergers. Federal income tax laws limit the ability of a firm to take advantage of losses for tax purposes unless the firm has offsetting profits elsewhere. A merger can provide a method of allowing one firm to use its losses to offset the profits and potential tax liabilities of another. Thus, again, the value of the combination of the firms would be greater than the combination of their individual values. This special type of synergy would in fact be due to a transfer of wealth from the government through reduced aggregate taxes.

Irrational Motivations for Mergers.   The three motivating forces we just discussed are rational in that they provide a valid explanation of the sources of the gains from the merger. For example, it is rational to believe that tax laws are constructed in a manner in which some corporate actions can be more advantageous than others.

However, mergers are sometimes attributed to factors that must be considered irrational, since they cannot provide a convincing explanation of the derivation of gains. Two examples of irrational reasons for mergers are (1) diversification and (2) earnings-per-share bootstrapping.

When Sears launched a corporate strategy in the early 1980s to acquire financial service firms, it was argued that the principal motivation behind such moves was in diversifying the firm's operations. The argument was that insurance, real estate, and brokerage services would diversify the firm's earnings away from its retail operation. It was further argued that diversification would increase the value of the firm. Why, then, is diversification an irrational motivation for a merger?

The problem with diversification is that it is far more cost effective for shareholders to diversify their own portfolios by owning shares in several firms. For example, if Sears' shareholders desired to diversify into real estate, then they could have purchased shares in a real estate firm directly without the expenses of acquiring Coldwell Banker. In other words, the shareholders could have easily accomplished the benefits of diversification on their own.

Another irrational motivation for a merger is an attempt to use the merger to boost a firm's accounting earnings. For example, a firm with stagnant profits might attempt to acquire another with high earnings in the hope that the combined firm will have a higher earnings per share and therefore a higher market value to the stock.

This explanation implies that financial analysts are concerned with accounting numbers in such a simplistic fashion that they would place a higher value on the combined firms than they did in pricing the firms separately. The earnings-per-share explanation implies that shareholders will benefit, but there is no solid explanation concerning the source of their added value.

In summary, diversification and accounting games are highly questionable motivations for merger. True economic gains from mergers are more likely to result from cost reductions and other operational synergies.

Legal and Tax Aspects of Mergers

The antitrust legislation discussed in Window 19.2 is designed to discourage or prevent certain mergers from occurring, and it can become a tricky part of the mechanics of mergers.

For example, in the case of hostile takeovers, the management of a target firm may attempt to block the merger. Public announcements by target firm management often indicate that the desire to avoid a merger is attributable to potential effect of the merger on the employees, the community, or even the long-run health of the corporation itself. Perhaps a more realistic explanation of managerial resistance is concern for their own careers.

Management can use antitrust legislation as a shield against hostile mergers by engaging in a business that is closely regulated. For example, a large manufacturing concern, such as a major producer of copying machines, may acquire a closely regulated firm, such as an insurance business, so that government approval will be required for the combined firm to be acquired. The management can then enlist the aid of politicians who serve the corporation's community to prevent a hostile takeover.

Shifting to taxes, there are two levels of tax concerns in relation to mergers: corporate income taxes and personal income taxes. As we have discussed, corporate income tax laws serve as a potential motivation for mergers since losses of one firm can be used to offset taxable profits of another firm when they merge.

Alternatively, highly progressive income tax structures can discourage mergers, since larger firms tend to have higher profits, which are taxed at higher rates in a progressive tax system. However, as shown in Chapter 3, the top U.S. corporate tax rate is reached at such a low level of income that most U.S. corporations pay tax at the same rate.

There are also personal income tax implications to mergers. When a firm is acquired, it is possible that the acquired (target) firm's shareholders will have to pay personal income taxes on the proceeds from selling their shares. Structuring the deal such that the merger does not cause a taxable exchange is a frequent solution to this potential tax liability.

THE MODERNIST VIEW OF MERGERS

Modernists view mergers not as attempts to gain efficiency, but as battles for the control of the corporation's assets. While efficiency gains fall in the category of rational motivations, the same efficiencies can be gained without the expenses associated with mergers. For instance, economies of scale can be achieved through the formation of joint ventures.

Joint ventures are similar to mergers in that resources are combined, but they differ in that they achieve this combination through a partnership arrangement rather than through a legal combination of the acquiring and target firm. Further, joint ventures do not result in complete changes in managerial control.

joint ventures
The combination of resources through a partnership arrangement rather than through a legal combination of the acquiring and target firm.

Recent years have spawned a variety of joint ventures. Examples include the partnership between Toyota and General Motors, in which an idle GM plant in California was set up to produce Toyota cars, and the agreement between American Motors and the Peking Automobile Factory to produce Jeep-brand automobiles. Firms can also cooperate through licensing arrangements, as did IBM and Apple Computer, who found that both sides benefit by allowing their computers to use similar software.

Since most of the advantages of merger activity could be accomplished with joint ventures, which would avoid the cost of mergers, modernists look to reasons beyond efficiency to explain mergers. Modernists believe that mergers can be explained by (1) managers attempting to advance their careers, and (2) shareholders attempting to gain from replacement of an inefficient management team.

Mergers Motivated by Managers

In a perfect world, it might be expected that managers would perform their jobs exactly as directed by shareholders. In other words, managers would maximize shareholder wealth and in so doing would benefit by being regarded as excellent performers. However, in the real world it is difficult for shareholders of a widely held public corporation to understand fully the performance of their managers, to reward their managers in proportion to their performance, or to select new managers based upon their past performance.

Accordingly, as a practical matter, corporate managers of widely held corporations have an incentive—and are often permitted—to seek objectives significantly different from shareholder wealth maximization. This subject is studied in conjunction with agency theory and has been discussed at various points in the earlier chapters of the book. It is important to remember, for this discussion, that managers of a widely held corporation may be viewed as having been entrusted with the assets of a major firm, which they will often operate so as to benefit themselves even at the cost of harming the shareholders they serve.

There is an obvious motivation for managers to want "their" firm to acquire other firms. Because the management team of the acquiring firm usually manages the target firm, the merger serves as a type of promotion as job responsibilities are enlarged. Managers of merged firms often enjoy higher compensation, greater prestige, greater power, and the satisfaction of moving up the corporate ladder.

On the other side of the merger transaction, the management teams of target firms usually lose prestige and power in the battle for control. If the merger was hostile, the acquired managers can at best usually hope for a golden parachute that will provide financial benefits but will not provide traditional career advancement. If the merger was friendly, there is a greater chance that target firm managers will remain in their jobs or be offered an especially good compensation package or golden parachute.

In the battle for corporate control, managers of widely held firms battle to be the acquirer and to avoid being the acquired firm. Often a management team recognizes that a company's acquisition is inevitable and begins looking for the best deal. The mergers that result often are friendly takeovers in which the management teams divide up the spoils of the merger. In other words, the economic benefits are often shared by the acquiring and acquired management teams, and not necessarily by the shareholders of the respective firms.

Mergers Motivated by Owners

Some mergers are motivated by an attempt by the shareholders of a closely held firm to acquire the assets of a widely held firm. The motivation for the merger is to gain control of the inefficiently operated firm (the target firm) from its shareholders so that the inefficient management team can be replaced. The acquiring firm hopes to buy the firm at a price that has become depressed, to replace the inefficient management team, and make other changes such that the benefits of the merger will exceed the cost.

leveraged buyout
The buyout of a target firm financed with money raised through the issuance of large amounts of debt. The proceeds from the debt issue are used to purchase the target firm's common stock, whereby the target firm is no longer a publicly held corporation but becomes a privately held firm.

The Levered Buyout by Outsiders.   In the opening of this chapter we discussed a situation in which a small group of investors, represented by the firm Kohlberg, Kravis, and Roberts, sought and eventually won control of RJR Nabisco, one of the largest Fortune 500 firms. How were they able to accomplish such a task? The answer is that they raised a large amount of money by issuing new debt, using the proceeds from the debt issue to buy RJR Nabisco's common stock. The stock was then retired, making RJR Nabisco no longer a publicly held corporation but now privately held. Because "going private" is accomplished through the use of debt, such a transaction has become known as a **leveraged buyout** (an LBO).

Financial leverage was discussed in Chapter 10 as a way to manipulate risk through the use of debt. In a sense, LBOs are extremely risky transactions because the new private firm must generate enough cash flow to pay significant amounts of debt interest payments. Of course, if the private firm is managed efficiently and effectively, the leverage works to the advantage of the new shareholders, inasmuch as the residual cash flow that remains gets shared by a small group.

The LBO will also create additional tax shields that originate from the interest paid on the new debt. As shown by Modigliani and Miller and discussed in Chapter 11, tax shields have the potential of increasing firm value. Recall, however, that the tax benefits enjoyed by debt at the corporate level can potentially be offset or even eliminated at the personal tax level. Therefore, whether or not tax shields provide an incentive for LBO transactions depends, at least partly, on this unresolved debate regarding tax shields and their effect on firm value.

Finally, many people question whether LBOs have been a success, a difficult question to answer for at least two reasons. First, part of the success of the LBO depends on factors outside of management's control. LBOs tend to be successful in a growing economy, but they tend not to be successful in recessionary economies. Second, it is difficult to assess the health of the private firm, given that its stock price can no longer be observed.

The Levered Buyout by Insiders. Management teams that are operating inefficiently sometimes recognize that, with the proper incentives, they could manage the firm in a manner that would significantly increase its value. The managers are willing to make these extremely difficult changes only if they can be the primary beneficiaries of the enhanced value. In an effort to exploit these opportunities, the managers can attempt to perform an LBO on their own firm.

The basic characteristics of the insider-initiated LBO are the same as those initiated by outsiders. The management-led team raises large amounts of money through new debt, and uses the proceeds from the debt to purchase the firm's publicly traded shares. The success of the insider-led LBO depends on the ability of the management team to use the incentives of the LBO to increase firm value.

Mergers and Changes in Shareholder Wealth

Numerous empirical studies have been performed that attempt to determine how shareholders have been affected by mergers. These studies shed light on the modernists' view of mergers motivated by owners. This subsection summarizes some of the empirical evidence.

Target Firm Shareholders. Most studies that examine the merger's effect on shareholders agree that target firm shareholders gain when

TABLE 19.2
The Effect of Merger Announcements on Target Firm Shareholders

	Abnormal Stock Price Returns Around Merger Announcements (target shareholders)
Tender Offer (unfriendly)	39%
Merger (friendly)	27%

Source: "The Market For Corporate Control: A Review of the Evidence," in Peter Dodd, *The Revolution in Corporate Finance,* ed. Joel Stern and Donald Chew (New York: Basil Blackwell). Reprinted by permission of Blackwell Publishers.

the merger is announced. The gain is largest when the merger involves an unfriendly attempt by the acquirer to gain control, but is also large for friendly mergers. These results are summarized in Table 19.2

The percentages listed in Table 19.2 represent "abnormal" returns earned by the shareholders. Abnormal returns are measured as the actual return minus the expected return. In other words, abnormal returns are those returns earned above and beyond what was reasonable to expect given the risk of the firm. The extremely large abnormal returns in Table 19.2 make it quite clear that the shareholders of the target firm benefit upon the announcement of the merger.

Do the abnormal returns shown in Table 19.2 prove that mergers are motivated by attempts to remove managers of poorly run firms? Maybe. But this conclusion assumes that these abnormal returns derive from the expectation that the acquiring group will improve upon the operation of the target firm.

Another explanation of the results in Table 19.2 is that the abnormal returns are wealth transfers from another group. For instance, perhaps the gain to the shareholders of the target firm comes not from improved performance expected after the merger but from the pockets of the acquiring firm shareholders. This could occur if the acquiring firm pays too much for the right to control the assets of the target firm, which we examine next.

Acquiring Firm Shareholders. Most merger studies show that gains to shareholders of acquiring firms are not nearly as large as gains to target shareholders. In fact, many studies show that acquiring firm shareholders do not gain at all at the time of the merger announcement. These results are shown in Table 19.3.

According to Table 19.3, the shareholders of the acquiring firms receive small negative abnormal returns at the time of the merger announcement. The abnormal returns are, however, so small that they can be considered to be zero in a statistical sense.

TABLE 19.3
The Effect of Merger Announcements on Acquiring Firm Shareholders

	Abnormal Stock Price Returns Around Merger Announcements (acquiring shareholders)
Tender Offer (unfriendly)	−1%
Merger (friendly)	−1%

Source: "The Market For Corporate Control: A Review of the Evidence," in Peter Dodd, *The Revolution in Corporate Finance,* ed. Joel Stern and Donald Chew (New York: Basil Blackwell). Reprinted by permission of Blackwell Publishers.

Looking at the results of both Table 19.2 and 19.3, mergers appear on net to be value enhancing. On average, mergers increase the value to the shareholders of target firms while not significantly reducing the value to the shareholders of acquiring firms. This supports the modernist view that mergers are a technique to remove inefficient managers from control.

Do Tables 19.2 and 19.3 Tell the Entire Story?

Although the combined results in Tables 19.2 and 19.3 suggest that mergers are value enhancing, it is possible that the gain in value comes not from the removal of target firm managers but from other groups. For instance, it's possible that the gains to target shareholders come from the bondholders of the target firm, or from the federal government in the form of tax shields. Finally, the gains could also be transfers from other groups, such as employee unions—if the merger will break a lucrative union contract—from pension holders, or even from plaintiffs in a pending lawsuit.

Some empirical studies have examined these issues and have been unable to develop support for a specific source of the value transfer. Thus, although the issue has not been completely resolved, the modernist viewpoint has survived a great deal of empirical scrutiny.

The Ethics of Corporate Takeovers

Modernists view corporate reorganizations in general and merger activity in particular as inevitable activities within a free market. These battles occur so that assets can be put to their best use. Winning corporate control is one method by which shareholders replace inefficient management and take advantage of synergistic opportunities.

There are, however, several groups that attempt to enter the battle and disrupt this process. These other groups, known as stakeholders, argue that they are affected by, and therefore have a stake in, the outcome of the battle for control. Since the shareholders have direct legal ownership of the corporations, these stakeholders attempt to use government to interfere with the rights of shareholders to control their own company.

Management, labor unions, local citizens, and local politicians attempt to use government control to block corporate reorganizations that they perceive have undesirable consequences. A good example of this is the antitakeover law passed in 1990 in the state of Pennsylvania, which created penalties on firms that attempted to take over a Pennsylvania-based company. Research estimates that Pennsylvania Senate Bill 1310 caused a large loss to shareholders of Pennsylvania firms. Thus, the long-term consequences of government control have been shown time and time again to be detrimental to society.

Entrenched and inefficient management, as well as the board of directors, will often utilize the resources of the firm in an attempt to prevent these reorganizations under the rallying cry that the reorganization is bad for the firm's long-term future. However, managers and directors have fiduciary responsibilities requiring them to make decisions that benefit the people who have hired them—the shareholders. Accordingly, corporate reorganization battles are increasingly being fought in courtrooms and through government legislation.

The modernist view is that government interference in the battle for corporate control weakens the economy and reduces the competitiveness of the country in the global marketplace.

A Modernist's Fairy Tale

Once upon a time, there was a highly regarded manufacturer of food products nestled in Pennsylvania. The company had been run for years by the family that had established the firm in 1914 as Stoltzfus's Foods and had worked hard to maintain the quality and efficiency that were the hallmark of its reputation.

In the early 1960s, the firm went public and changed its name to Good Old Boys, Inc. (GOB, Inc.). In other words, the family sold the vast majority of its ownership through a public offering of common stock. GOB, Inc., became a widely held public corporation with thousands of shareholders. The family stepped down from managing the firm and was replaced by a new management team of highly educated professionals.

In 1964, GOB, Inc., was rich with cash from the continued success of its food products, which enjoyed a tremendous reputation and an extremely loyal following during its 50-year history. Starting in 1964, and continuing though the late 1960s and 1970s, the firm gobbled up other firms in a frenzy of highly priced acquisitions under the guidance of its new management team.

Unfortunately, the market price of the common stock of GOB, Inc., performed rather dismally during and after its enormous merger activity. Financial analysts complained that the company was poorly managed; however, management generally did not feel it needed to respond to financial analysts or even shareholders, for that matter. Management cited costly and cumbersome union contracts and dynamic global factors as reasons for past problems, but it offered optimistic assessments of the long-term effects of its latest strategic changes.

Some shareholders noticed that, each year, certain unprofitable divisions were sold to enable the purchase or development of new and more promising divisions. However, it appeared that each new division ended up as one of the unprofitable divisions that later needed to be sold.

Shareholders of GOB, Inc., expressed displeasure with the stock's performance at the annual shareholder's meetings, but they were unable to effect changes. Shareholders who attempted to pass resolutions in opposition to the managers' decisions were strongly rebuffed by management, which utilized its ability to make virtually unlimited mailings of its viewpoint to its shareholders.

GOB's management defended its enormous salaries, citing the size of the firm and the salaries of managers of other similarly sized firms. Management complained that financial markets, driven by financial institutions, were attempting to pressure the firm into shortsighted decisions that would destroy the firm's long-run health.

Finally, in 1988, a small consulting firm, backed with millions of dollars of capital obtained from high-risk debt issues, launched a bid to acquire the firm. Management fought diligently to save the firm and had enlisted the help of state and federal politicians to block the right of GOB's shareholders to sell it. In fact, Pennsylvania had even passed a law restricting the rights of shareholders to sell their firms.

In the end, top managers were promised spectacular financial packages if they would stop fighting the merger—and they finally approved, stating publicly that it was inevitable and that the agreement would minimize the negative impact of the merger on the communities involved. The politicians even seemed to approve of the final merger agreement—especially those raising campaign funds.

In retrospect, the change in corporate control saved the firm. The successful product lines were retained, and those product lines that had no competitive advantage were spun off or sold outright. Although the firm that survived was much smaller and operated with a far smaller labor force, it seemed obvious that the alternative to the smaller, better managed firm was no firm at all. With the new owner/

managers in charge, it seemed as though everyone would live happily ever after.

DIVESTITURES AND LIQUIDATIONS

Although we emphasize mergers in this chapter, other forms of corporate reorganizations include divestitures and liquidations. A divestiture is defined as the sale of assets from a firm, and thus can be considered the antithesis of a merger. A firm may divest itself of an asset by selling it directly or by spinning the asset off as a separate corporation. For example, a bank, utility, or other highly regulated corporation may find it advantageous to remove the nonregulated portion of the business from the highly regulated parent corporation. The shares in the newly formed corporation can be sold by the parent firm or sent directly to its shareholders in the form of a dividend.

Divestitures can also result from the perception that a certain segment of a corporation's business no longer fits. This is especially true for firms that have gone through a conglomerate merger strategy and found, in hindsight, that certain divisions have not been adding to the value of the firm but have been instead detracting from firm value. This type of divestiture may also lead to a management buyout, whereby the managers of the sold division purchase the division themselves, and reorganize the division as its own firm.

A liquidation will occur if the assets which the firm chooses to divest are worth more dead than alive. In a liquidation, the firm sells some or all of its assets and distributes the cash to the firm's claimants. In a voluntary liquidation, the cash usually goes to the shareholders. If the firm liquidates assets as part of bankruptcy proceedings, the cash usually goes to the bondholders and other creditors. In the latter case, the rules concerning how the assets are to be liquidated come under the general heading of bankruptcy, and were discussed in Window 10.2 on bankruptcy.

SUMMARY

☐ Mergers are one type of corporate reorganization. Other types of corporate reorganization include divestitures, liquidations, and bankruptcy.

☐ Throughout modern economic history, mergers have tended to occur in waves and have been the subject of public policy debate and legislation. Merger waves have tended to be differentiated by types of mergers such as vertical, horizontal, and conglomerate.

☐ Mergers also differ by whether the acquired management approves of the merger (a friendly merger) or fights the merger (a hostile takeover). The financing of the mergers also differs.

☐ In the mid-to-late 1980s there was a wave of merger activity financed by the use of large amounts of debt. These mergers included leveraged buyouts, in which the money used to buy the shares of the publicly traded corporation comes from newly issued debt.

☐ There are several important motivations for mergers, including the replacement of inefficient management and the synergies of combining assets and operations. There are also several motivations offered for mergers that fail to survive deductive scrutiny. Among these questionable motivations for mergers are diversification and manipulation of accounting data.

☐ Perhaps the clearest understanding of mergers results from the application of agency theory. Within this modernist view, mergers are viewed as battles for corporate control: Managers are assumed to have interests that differ from the shareholders. Many mergers can be viewed as the acquisition of an inefficiently operated firm, with entrenched management and widely dispersed shareholders, by a more closely held corporation. The evidence on mergers and the effects on shareholder wealth supports this view. Other mergers can be viewed as the acquisition of one widely held firm by another widely held firm, without regard to the effect on shareholder wealth.

DEMONSTRATION PROBLEMS

Problem 1 A foreign airline has offered to acquire a major U.S. airline at a huge premium relative to the price at which the airline's stock is currently trading. Discuss this potential merger from the "traditionalist" viewpoint.

Solution to Problem 1
There might be several factors that would motivate such a merger, but first we must consider the potential impact on the air traveler in particular and the nation's economy in general.

If the U.S. airline and the foreign airline now serve similar markets, this merger might reduce competition and cause higher air fares. However, even if the airlines have complementary markets, the U.S. could suffer from having more and more of its airline industry owned and controlled by foreign corporations. Thus, the merger plans need to be modified or scrapped entirely if the interests of consumers or the nation as a whole could be seriously and adversely affected.

Next, let's examine the merger from an investor's perspective. We need to examine why the merger has been proposed and what the potential benefits and costs are to the firms involved. For example, the merger might be very healthy for each of the companies if it would permit easier connecting schedules, shared ticketing and maintenance facilities, and so forth. These "synergies" are operational, since they improve the performance ability of the firm's operations and offer cost savings.

From a financial perspective, the merger might provide the U.S. airline with better access to financing from European sources (or vice versa) and might bolster the airline's dismal income statement and balance sheet. The merger would also make sense if it allowed the U.S. corporation to take advantage of the tax losses that are now going unused. Finally, it might make sense from a diversification perspective, since the merged firms would be less vulnerable to huge losses from regional problems, such as reduced air travel or increased competition.

In summary, there can be real advantages to allowing firms to merge when the obvious benefits of such mergers can be passed on to society in general or at least won't harm society. However, when mergers create monopolistic power groups (or oligopolies), it is necessary for government to intervene and ensure through legislation that competition will continue. ↵

Problem 2 Now discuss this potential merger from a "modernist" perspective.

Solution to Problem 2
It is not necessary to worry about the long-run impact of this merger on the air traveler or the overall United States. As long as governments stay out of it, competition will eventually provide air travelers with the services they desire at a price consistent with providing the services. Time and time again, it is shown that government control and interference hurts the economy in the long run rather than helping it. We should allow free competition and trade regardless, since it is the shareholders' firm and it is up to them if they want to sell it.

What is interesting about this merger is the motives of the people. Why is the management of the foreign airline anxious to buy that particular domestic carrier? What are the motivations of the managers and shareholders of the U.S. airline facing acquisition?

The idea of cost-saving operational synergies or better financial capabilities is just a "smoke screen." The firms can form joint ventures without the merger in order to exploit operational synergies—many firms have already formed such "partnerships." In terms of financial statements, Wall Street investors are not easily fooled by simply combining them. Whatever the airlines can accomplish as merged firms can be accomplished as independent firms.

Why have the managers of the foreign airline sought control of another firm? If their shareholders desired ownership of the U.S. airline, they were free to purchase shares in the airline by themselves, and they could have done so at a price much lower than the merger costs. Perhaps the managers are building their egos (and their salaries) by trying to create an "empire." Or perhaps the managers of the foreign airline realize how incompetent these American managers are, and they know that by purchasing the airline they can dramatically improve its performance.

It's clear that the shareholders of the U.S. airline can simply "vote" with their shares. No doubt, the shareholders are anxious to sell their shares to the foreign airline and reap the tremendous gain.

Perhaps the most telling indication is the response of the management of the U.S. airline to the proposal. If these managers fight the merger, then regardless of what they say it seems clear that they are the incompetent managers who are worried more about their careers than the shareholders that hired them. If the American managers support the merger (at the best possible price), it seems clear that it is the foreign firm whose managers have motives that are suspect. ↵

REVIEW QUESTIONS

1. What is the difference between a merger and a divestiture?
2. A firm that makes computers merges with a firm that designs computer software. Is this a vertical, horizontal, or conglomerate merger?
3. What is the purpose of antitrust legislation?
4. Are all mergers friendly agreements? Explain.
5. What is synergy, and how does synergy relate to mergers?
6. What is a tender offer, and how is it used as a merger strategy?
7. List and describe at least three antitakeover measures.
8. Explain how unused tax shields can provide a motivation for mergers.
9. Why is diversification considered an irrational motivation for mergers?
10. How does a joint venture differ from a merger?
11. Use agency costs to explain the modernist view of mergers as motivated by managers.
12. What is a levered buyout (an LBO)?
13. Do shareholders of target firms gain at the time of the merger announcement? How about shareholders of acquiring firms? Why?

DISCUSSION QUESTIONS

1. Chapter 2 introduced the law of conservation of value, which states that the market value of a combination of assets must be equal to the sum of the market values of all the assets held in isolation. Given this law, how can we explain merger activities?

2. Antitrust legislation is designed to promote market competitiveness. Assume that you work for the Justice Department and are given the responsibility of deciding whether or not a particular merger should take place. What criteria would you use to determine the effect of the merger on competition?

3. Synergy was discussed as a rational or valid reason to merge. Make a list of industries that you believe would be prime candidates for "synergy-related" mergers. Now make a list of industries that you believe would not be good candidates for "synergy-related" mergers. Explain.

4. A manager was quoted as saying, "Our company's recent LBO has really changed things around here. We seem to be 'watching our pennies' like never before." Why would an LBO result in a firm's having to "watch its pennies"? Is this good or bad? Explain.

5. The Chairman of the Federal Reserve went before a congressional committee to argue that allowing banks to diversify out of their traditional lines of business by merging with other types of financial service firms (insurance, real estate, investment banking) would result in a less risky banking industry. Would this be a valid reason for bank mergers? Why or why not?

6. In 1990, the state of Pennsylvania passed an act that essentially insulated corporations headquartered in Pennsylvania from being taken over. Who is the winner as a result of such legislation? Who is the loser?

Index

FROM THE LIBRARY OF

Blair P Dwyer

PARADISE WON

PARADISE WON
The Struggle for South Moresby

Elizabeth E. May

Canadian Cataloguing in Publication Data
May, Elizabeth
    Paradise won : the struggle for South Moresby

ISBN 0-7710-5772-5

1. National parks and reserves - British Columbia - Queen
Charlotte Islands. 2. Nature conservation - British Columbia
- Queen Charlotte Islands. 3. Nature conservation - British
Columbia - Queen Charlotte Islands - Citizen participation.
4. Wilderness areas - British Columbia - Queen Charlotte
Islands. 5. Forests and forestry - British Columbia - Queen
Charlotte Islands. I. Title.

QH77.C3M39 1990   333.78'4'0971112   C90-093321-6

Map by John Broadhead
Designed by Annabelle Stanley
Printed and bound in Canada

McClelland & Stewart Inc.
The Canadian Publishers
481 University Avenue
Toronto, Ontario
M5G 2E9

To John Fraser
and the Conspiracy to Save the Planet

CONTENTS

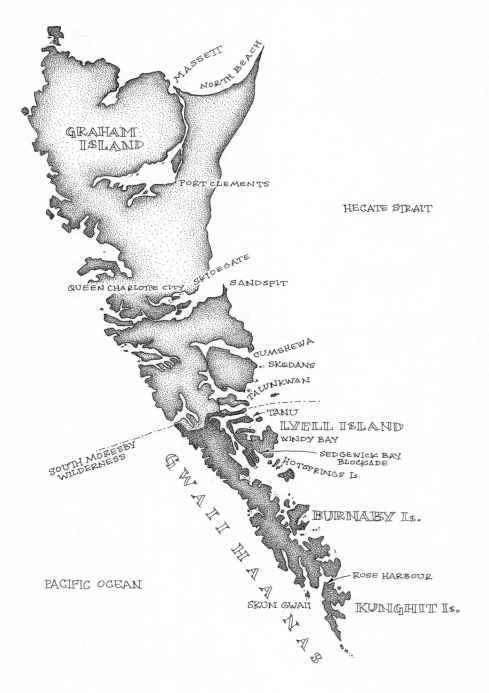

HAIDA GWAII
QUEEN CHARLOTTE ISLANDS

MASSETT

NORTH BEACH

GRAHAM ISLAND

PORT CLEMENTS

HECATE STRAIT

SKIDEGATE

QUEEN CHARLOTTE CITY

SANDSPIT

CUMSHEWA

SKEDANS

TALUNKWAN

TANU

LYELL ISLAND

WINDY BAY

SEDGEWICK BAY
BLOCKADE

HOTSPRINGS Is.

SOUTH MORESBY
WILDERNESS

GWAII HAANAS

BURNABY Is.

ROSE HARBOUR

PACIFIC OCEAN

KUNGHIT Is.

SKUN GWAII

ACKNOWLEDGEMENTS

Paradise won is a true story, as much as any story can be true. It is objective, as much as I can be objective about something I worked for, prayed for, and wept for. I am not a reporter; I am a story teller, writing from my own perspective – not that of the Haida Nation, nor of any of the other crusaders who struggled so long and so hard to save South Moresby. I dedicate my story to them – the many people who appear in these pages and all those others, not named, without whom the chains saws would still be at work in South Moresby.

There are many people I must thank, especially those who suffered through long and repeated interviews, as I attempted to find out what had happened all those years ago and to sort out fact from faulty memory: J.B., Huck, Guujaaw, Paul and Adriane, David and Tara, Colleen, Jeff, Vicky and Patrick, Kevin, Gregg, Miles, Bristol, Cameron Young, Keith Moore, Barry Olsen, Sharon Chow, Sue Stephenson, Dan McAskill, Bryan Williams, Murray Rankin, Brian Smith, Jamie Alley, John Fraser, Jim Fulton, Terry Collins, Ada Yovanovitch, Ethel Jones, Al Whitney, Pat Armstrong, and Charles Caccia. Thank you all for so generously giving me your time and for reminiscing about the history of the struggle.

My parents, John and Stephanie, and my brother Geoffrey and his wife, Rebecca-Lynne, read my early drafts and acted as my loving critics. Thank you so much. Thanks also to my uncle, Tom Middleton, who has always been my role model as a writer. Thanks to Glen Davis for his eagle-eyed perusal of the manuscript. I also want to thank Dinah Forbes, my editor, who helped me figure out how to tell the same story in half the number of pages I first wrote, and whose pencil magically transformed the manuscript into a book. For donating their work, I must thank John Broadhead, who drew the beautiful map on page viii, and Jeff Gibbs and Richard Krieger for their photographs. Love and thanks, too, to Farley Mowat for encouraging me to write this book and for contributing a wonderful foreword minimizing my weight. And last, thanks to Doug and Tim, without whom this book would have been finished a lot sooner.

FOREWORD

UNTIL 1986, ALONG WITH A FEW THOUSAND OTHER Canadians, I followed the South Moresby story in the media, wondering would there be a park? Would British Columbia and the federal government ever agree whether there should be logging in these pristine forests? Would the Haida be allowed to keep this exquisite part of their island home free of the sounds of chain saws? Then in July 1986, my interest in South Moresby took on a distinctly personal flavour. Someone I knew from Cape Breton environmental crusades had become embroiled in the thick of negotiations over South Moresby by accepting a job as senior policy adviser to Tom McMillan, the federal minister of the environment.

At thirty-five, Elizabeth May is a little slip of a thing (as her kind used to be described), imbued with an air of beguiling innocence. But she talks a blue streak and is as effervescent and bouncy as the proverbial cat on a hot tin roof. She is as vivid and as vital as an electric storm. The first time she exploded into the quiet of my Cape Breton retreat, I felt as if a typhoon had caught me in its swirl. I have aged considerably since then – but Elizabeth has not. She gives the impression of being a kind of female Peter Pan, never to lose her youthful exuberance or her insatiable curiosity. But the impression that she is an ephemeral spirit is misleading. She is a crusader, born and bred; and the cause to which she has committed herself, mind, body, and spirit, is the struggle to save the living world from destruction by her own species.

Her commitment is no recent phenomenon. As a child she was seized by the certainty that mankind was devilishly *un*kind to the rest of animate creation, whether those creatures were luna moths being zapped by electric bug killers, or great whales being destroyed by bombs exploded in their bellies. Her mother, Stephanie (who is also of the crusading breed), told me that even in early childhood Elizabeth possessed an absolute awareness that human beings were ruining the natural world, and that they could not be permitted (for their own good, as well as the world's good) to continue doing so. "She didn't argue. She just knew she was right; and she just knew she could and must help change things around. She wasn't grim or fanatical about it. She had the sunny optimism of absolute conviction. And nothing could persuade her otherwise."

To this day nothing has, and I doubt very much if anything ever will.

Elizabeth May is a crusader, but not of the stereotyped variety. She does not engage the enemy with weapons of shining steel, or of cutting intellect. Instead, she relies on love, compassion, the powers born of subjective feelings and an inner faith. She is of the primaeval tradition, which has recently been identified as the Gaia movement, whose central tenet is that all life is of one flesh, indivisible and mutually supportive. According to the Gaia concept the apparent differences between the multitudinous varieties of living beings do not isolate them as separate entities, but rather link them together as component parts of a single, world-girdling and living fabric.

Born in the U.S.A., Elizabeth was eighteen when she and her family came to Canada in 1973 and bought a decrepit restaurant on the west coast of Cape Breton

Island. It did not sustain them, *they* sustained it, with the result that for almost a decade Elizabeth had to forego her plans to become an environmental lawyer, while she cooked and washed dishes instead. But she never lost touch with her Gaia concerns, and she read so extensively on her own that she eventually knew as much about environmental problems as many a tenured professor.

"Elizabeth trained herself," her mother told me, "like some medieaval knight preparing for a quest."

The challenge came in 1975 when Swedish-owned Nova Scotia Forest Industries, with the support of the Nova Scotia government, began preparations to spray pesticides over much of Cape Breton Island to combat an outbreak of spruce budworm. It was a unilateral decision. The people of Cape Breton were not consulted, nor were they warned of the risks to life and health. However, Elizabeth May had apprised herself of these, and so she rode out from the Schooner Restaurant in Margaree Harbour to sound the tocsin. She became the prime mover in rousing such a ground swell of grassroots resistance to the spray program that eventually the government withdrew its support and the pulp companies found themselves defeated.

By 1979 the budworm epidemic was dying down of its own accord, and Elizabeth at long last was able to begin university. But a few years later another major environmental threat surfaced in Nova Scotia. The forest industries had concluded that they could expand future production by resorting to a massive aerial spraying of herbicides, which would kill most forest vegetation except profitable softwoods such as spruce and balsam. Compliant with industry as usual, the government departments concerned quietly approved a request for permits – this time to spray from aircraft a mixture of 2,4-D and 2,4,5-T, the active ingredients in the infamous Agent Orange used by the U.S. military to defoliate much of Vietnam, causing uncounted cases of cancer amongst the Vietnamese.

Proponents of the herbicide program had learned a lesson from their defeat over the use of pesticides. The new plan was announced only two weeks before the planes were due to take to the air. Doubtless the industry and the government were convinced that nothing could be done to interfere with their plans at such short notice. But Elizabeth dropped everything and rode out to rally the troops. She did so to such effect that ten days later she and her allies had obtained a temporary injunction to halt the spraying.

The battle that followed was ferocious. With three major pulp companies and the provincial government arrayed against them, Elizabeth and her allies struggled mightily for two years. But the struggle was, as writer June Callwood said at the time, between David and Goliath. . . only it was Goliath who had the sling.

And this time Goliath won.

In order to pay her share of the legal and other costs involved, Elizabeth had to sell her car and her family had to sell a one-hundred-acre farm they owned near Baddeck. The Mays shrugged it off. "We would have sold the restaurant too if that would have helped Elizabeth win," Stephanie May remembers.

Elizabeth duly graduated from law school and moved on from Nova Scotia to broader battlefields. She became instrumental in organizing the Canadian Environmental Defence Fund, which provides legal assistance to groups all over Canada fighting to preserve and protect the natural world. She was determined that when next the environmental David faced the industrial Goliath, the weapons would be more equal.

Then in August 1986, she was asked by Tom McMillan, minister of the environment in the federal government, to become his senior adviser on environmental matters. She held this enormously influential post until June 1988. Before her resignation (on a matter of principle to which she alludes in this book), she had been instrumental in implementing plans for several new national parks; had worked on the Ozone Protocol, and on vital reforms to the federal Environmental Assessment Act. She had also channelled more than a million dollars of government funds to assist the environmental movement all across Canada.

In the autumn of 1988, Elizabeth organized a nation-wide publicity campaign in an (unsuccessful) attempt to force the three major Canadian political parties to promise more than lip service to environmental problems. She has spent the past year deeply embroiled in the campaign to save what remains of the world's rain forests while also serving as the unpaid executive director of Cultural Survival (Canada), which works with indigenous people to save both them and their natural environment. In one way or another she remains actively involved with almost every other major environmental issue as one of the most effective defenders of the living, breathing earth that we possess.

Now she has begun to give rein to a talent which may dwarf the many others she possesses. As this book attests, Elizabeth May is a born story teller in the grand tradition. It may well be that she will achieve her greatest successes in defence of life upon this outraged planet as a writer, whose clarity, honesty, and conviction brook no denials.

Farley Mowat
January 1990

INTRODUCTION

IT WAS SUNDAY, JULY 12, 1987 – THE MORNING AFTER THE big Haida feast in Skidegate. Most of the customers at the Helm Café in nearby Queen Charlotte City were weary celebrants. It was a measure of the power and magic of the feast that so much of its mood could linger over the gleaming formica and bacon grease of the small, nondescript café.

Tom McMillan, federal minister of the environment, took his last bite of french toast and congealing syrup, and polished it off with a glass of milk. I sipped my coffee and surveyed the old Haida men, Parks bureaucrats, elated environmentalists, and reporters gathered around their separate tables savouring the memories of the previous night's celebration – translucent images of hereditary chiefs in their traditional costumes of feathers, fur, and masks, of young Haida paddlers dancing newly created steps, cheering their own accomplishment, and of Tom McMillan's cake that proclaimed, in green icing, South Moresby National Park. I had been working for Tom for almost a year, and that celebration of the arrival of *Loo Taas,* which coincided with the saving of South Moresby, of the end of logging within the area, was the culmination of everything that I had worked and prayed for. In the café were good friends gained in the effort to protect South Moresby: John Broadhead (J.B.), who had put the last decade or so into the cause; Vicky Husband, who had been working non-stop for the last six years of her life; Kevin McNamee, who worked for a Toronto-based parks group. He had been in the thick of it for several years as well.

We were in a mood to count our blessings – and our friends. "You know," Vicky said, "we could never have done this without John Fraser. If it wasn't for John, the whole thing could never have happened."

"When you consider how close we came to losing, over and over again," I added, still feeling a sense of unreality. "I mean, it really was a miracle. And each time it was nearly lost, someone – Dalton Camp or Mazankowski – just kept it alive." After all this time, it was hard to believe the battle was really won.

And so we went around the table, marvelling at all the people who in one way or another had helped to save the day. Paramount in our thoughts were the dedication and sacrifice of the Haida, especially the seventy-two men and women who had faced arrest on the logging road of Lyell Island. Then Tom said something that reminded me how perceptive he could be. "You know," he began, "not only was the effort of each person absolutely indispensable, but each person contributed something that only he was capable of contributing. Only David Suzuki could have brought South Moresby to public attention the way he did through The Nature of Things and through his own reputation. And only Jim Fulton, as MP for the area, could have known so much of the local scene and been so committed to saving it. And ultimately, no one but the Prime Minister could have gotten Vander Zalm's attention. You know, I really believe that the effort of each person, no matter how small, even those people who wrote a single letter, was indispensable and each was unique."

"It's such an incredible story," Vicky said. "I'm trying to talk Sam [her friend Cameron Young] into writing a book about it."

I found myself saying without thinking, "No, I'm going to write the book." Tom pushed back from the table. "Oh," he said teasingly, "I know the kind of book Elizabeth would write. We'd all just be pawns, moved about as if the whole campaign to save South Moresby were part of some sort of giant cosmic divine plan."

J.B. smiled in his cryptic, Mona-Lisa way, and said, "Exactly."

|1|

THE EAGLE

A LONE KAYAKER DIPPED HIS PADDLE INTO THE WATER, breaking the pink-orange reflection of the morning sky on the sea, scattering the sunrise into a hundred rippled waves. He had not seen another human being in days. Paddling through small channels and across large stretches of almost open sea, he had camped on the sites of ancient Haida villages, where the decaying totem poles stood guard while he slept. Once he thought he saw an Indian warrior among the mortuary poles. But he had soon realized that it was either a ghost or his imagination, or a bit of both. It's like that when you are alone.

As he pulled around the east side of a large island, the tide turned against him. A small bay beckoned, and looked worth exploring. He pulled his collapsible kayak onto the beach and almost immediately he was in deep forest. He crossed a shallow creek, crystal clear and gurgling, and clambered up the far bank to the mossy forest floor. The sun's rays pierced the dark and heavy branches of the ancient cedar and spruce, casting a dappled glow on the blanket of mosses, lichens, and ferns. It was intoxicating. This forest had power. Its trees stretched so high their tops could not be seen. Their trunks seemed as wide as houses, and their lower branches were festooned with hanging gardens of ferns and dripping moss.

The cry of an eagle broke the stillness. Thrushes called, and occasionally he could hear the chattering of a raven. He had been many places and seen many things, but nothing more beautiful than this.

Back on the beach he searched for dry driftwood to make a fire so he could cook that universal frybread, bannock. And then he saw it. Right beside him, an arm's length away, was a dead bald eagle. Carefully he extended the wings, for rigor mortis had not yet set in. Outstretched they spanned some seven feet. It had no wounds, no marks. Even in death, the eagle was magnificent.

"This should be preserved," he thought. "It should go in a museum." He took out his knife and cleaned the eagle, emptying the body cavity and then reverently refilling it with dry sphagnum moss. Folding its wings, he tied the eagle together and carried it to his kayak. He placed it gently in the stern, cradled among his gear.

Now he could hear the eagle's mate, screaming in grief from a tree-top. It was time to leave, and the tide was right. Pushing out into the bay, leaving behind those magnificent trees, he sang a song he knew from long ago – an Indian song. It seemed to fit. He asked the eagle, singing its lament from the forest canopy, to give his small craft its wings. As the kayak pulled out of the bay a southwest breeze came up, and he raised the sail to catch it. He had drawn on his sail the face of an eagle, copied from one on an old pole he had seen at an abandoned village. He moved fast, paddling into the long June evening, until at dusk he came within sight of the point of land on the northern island he had fixed as his destination.

There was a Haida man on that point who saw some sort of movement on the water. It looked like an eagle skimming the surface of the sea, its wings glinting silver in the sunlight. And, when it came closer, it showed the face of an eagle. It was like nothing he had ever seen on earth. He could not be sure that it was of this earth. He stayed still and watched and waited.

The young man pulled his kayak out of the water and prepared to make camp, and the Haida man watched him until their eyes met. "Ah," thought the young man, so unaccustomed was he to speech after days alone. "I should show this man my eagle. Maybe he could take it to a local museum." He went to the stern of the kayak and carefully lifted up the eagle. Holding it before him like an offering, he approached the older man. The silence was broken.

"Why do you bring me this eagle?" the Haida man asked.

"Because there are so few of them left," came the answer.

HUCKLEBERRY

THOM HENLEY WAS ONE OF NINE CHILDREN FROM A GOOD Catholic family and was raised in Lansing, Michigan, within sight of the giant Oldsmobile factory where his dad was a foreman. As a small boy Thom discovered wilderness, if only in his imagination. Less than a block from the factory there was a vacant lot on which grew a dozen trees and a thick tangle of underbrush. To Thom it was a jungle, and he was its only inhabitant.

In many ways he had a typical childhood in a 1950s' ideal nuclear family. But a boy who faces death twice has not had a completely uneventful time of it. At the age of seven, he contracted polio and lay in a hospital bed, paralysed for six months. And at fifteen, he was striken with spinal meningitis and fell into a three-day death-like coma. When he recovered, he was changed, more serious than kids his own age. Still, to outer appearances, he was a normal teenager – nervous on dates, unaware that the girls thought he was a dreamboat. A good student, Thom went to the local university after graduating from high school.

By 1968, it was clear that the United States was fighting the least popular war in its history. Record numbers of protesters were gathering in front of the White House and on the streets of New York, Los Angeles, and every major city. There was never any possibility in Thom's mind that he would fight in Vietnam. In 1970, aged twenty-one, holding honours, he left university in protest against the war and against the class discrimination that permitted him a student deferment but drafted thousands of black, Hispanic, and working-class white kids. He was promptly drafted.

Before his induction notice showed up, he decided to explore the mountains of Alaska. He had not intended to be a draft-dodger, but in Alaska he quickly discovered that he was wanted for interstate flight to avoid prosecution. Penalities mounted, and he ended up living underground for several years. When he felt the FBI closing in on him, he stowed away on a ferry to Vancouver, and the safe haven called Canada.

Like most Americans, Thom believed Canada was a country where moderation and tolerance reigned, where war resisters were welcomed and the Prime Minister spoke sagely and critically of the U.S. adventure in Vietnam. But Thom had chosen a bad day to arrive in Canada. It was the day the War Measures Act was declared by Prime Minister Trudeau. Thom was walking through Stanley Park when an RCMP officer on horseback charged him. The horse knocked him to the ground and the officer clubbed him before riding on. Reality seemed to be coming unglued.

He found shelter and friends in Vancouver at a safe house for draft resisters. On their advice he moved to the long sandy beaches of the west coast of Vancouver Island and built a cabin amid the red-dotted huckleberry bushes. He was known thereafter as Huckleberry, Huck for short. He returned to Alaska for a year, working at odd jobs, logging on Prince of Wales Island until his natural wanderlust took hold again. He embarked on an ambitious kayak trip, from Alaska to the Amazon and back. He got as far as Honduras, when sick and tired, weak with dysentery and flat broke, he turned back to kayak to what he now considered home – Alaska.

In June 1973, Huck found himself on the dock in Prince Rupert, British Columbia. The barge for the Queen Charlotte Islands was to leave in an hour. Other kayakers were on the wharf, and they extolled the virtues and little-known wonders of the Charlottes. "You should come," they urged. "You'll never get another chance like this." Reasoning that inspiration flows in the same direction as impulse, he bought passage, loaded bag and baggage, and endured a rough ride over the Hecate Strait to the northernmost settlement on the Charlotte's northern island, the small Haida town of Massett.

Huck arrived in the pitch-darkness. Hoping to find shelter, he walked toward a small collection of buildings where someone might still be awake. Abruptly he was confronted by a drunken man who stood in his path and said, "Get out of here." If Huck had had any money for the return fare to Prince Rupert, he would have left the Charlottes forever at that moment. But he had spent his last money on the crossing, and until he found work somewhere, he was stuck. Weary and depressed, he fell into a fitful sleep on the beach.

The next morning he walked into Old Massett, and almost immediately the same man who had threatened him the night before emerged from a small wood-frame house. Seeming to have no recollection of the previous evening, the young man (for by daylight Huck could see that he was young, and also not as large as he had been the night before) said, "My mother has been expecting you. She is preparing a special lunch in your honour." Huck demurred, "I'm sorry. I think you've mistaken me for someone else." But the man would not take no for an answer.

It turned out to be a feast. In the tradition of the Haida, for whom wealth and social status are derived from the hospitality and generosity shown to others,

Huck was offered every delicacy of the Charlottes' lands and waters. Octopus, halibut, scallops, and abalone; pickled herring roe on seaweed; venison and potatoes; salmon and dried crunchy seaweed; sea urchin roe, and the favoured small fish of the Haida – greasy oolichans in their pungent oil. All this and more was piled on the table before him. Conversation was thin, as the old lady spoke little English and Huck spoke no Haida at all.

Despite being greeted like the prodigal son, Huck was a long way from liking the Queen Charlotte Islands known by the Haida as Haida Gwaii (Hi-da-Gwy). Massett seemed small and depressing in the way of so many dreary mining towns in Alaska. While the long stretch of its beach was beautiful, so were many more places he had visited up and down the west coast. It was not until he had hitch-hiked and kayaked to the southern island of Moresby that he began to appreciate the islands.

As he paddled along, the sweet smell of spruce and cedar forest caught his nostrils. Snow-capped mountains rose up in the interior, and along the shore, sea-birds flocked and sea-lions sunned themselves on their rocky out-croppings. Eagles, with the skill of magicians, pulled quicksilver fish out of the dark water. Paddling close to land, Huck examined the rocks speckled with bright pink lichens and purple algae and adorned with reddish, orange, and blue starfish. When the tide fell, the starfish lost their hold on the rocks and lowered themselves, tentacle by tentacle, back into the sea.

As the sun set on the longest day of the year, he pulled into Cumshewa Inlet – Haida for "riches at the head of the waters." Securing his kayak on a small island in the inlet's mouth, Huck watched the sun sink behind the mountains of Moresby Island, turning the green rain forest into gold.

On the summer solstice of 1973, Huckleberry fell in love with the Queen Charlotte Islands. And if he fell in love with them, did they, like Isak Dinesen's Ngong Hills, fall a little in love with him?

GUUJAAW

In 1956 VINCENT MASSEY, CANADA'S GOVERNOR GENERAL, paid an official visit to the village of Massett on the northern coast of Haida Gwaii. Residents and dignitaries, local business people and town councillors, formed a receiving line. As the official representative of Her Majesty the Queen shook hands with the properly respectful queue, a small boy stepped forward. A dark-skinned, black-haired Haida child, with big brown eyes, he looked about three years old. The Governor General smiled down at him, and extended his hand. The little boy refused, clasping his hands tightly behind his back. Although he has no memory of it, some claim he looked up and asked, "Whose land do you think you're standing on?"

The Governor General's answer is nowhere recorded, but for the impudence of this and many other questions, the little boy was given the Haida name of Ghigndiging, variously translated as Questioning One or The One Who Questions The Answers He's Given. His Anglo name was Gary Edenshaw, but as an adult, he would be known as Guujaaw (Gooj-ow).

His question to the Governor General was a good one. The history of the Queen Charlotte Islands, as European explorers called them, does not contain a single decisive victory over the Haida nor a single treaty to provide a conclusive answer.

For thousands of years, the Haida had lived on the islands they called Haida Gwaii, Islands of the People.

Their remembered history extends back past two floods, each covering the earth, cleansing creation, and giving humankind a fresh start. After the first flood, the Raven sought out land, prying humans out of hiding in their clamshell. By the nineteenth century, an estimated ten thousand people lived on Haida Gwaii – one of the highest densities of hunter-gatherer people anywhere in the world. Several hundred villages dotted the archipelago, each fitting into an intricate social fabric of clans and conquest.

The lands and waters of the islands were rich. Food was abundant, and shelter was provided by the cedar tree, which both served and reigned over the Haida people. Huge longhouses shielded extended families of thirty or forty people from the driving rains and ferocious winds of winter. The wealth of the seas and forests ensured a certain amount of leisure time and allowed the development of sophisticated art forms. Highly skilled artisans carved or painted complex patterns onto totem poles, mortuary poles, canoes, longhouse doorways, bent cedar boxes – indeed, the surface of every utilitarian object of Haida life was adorned.

Their society was organized into two large family groups, or phratries, of Ravens and Eagles. Marriage between members of the same phratry was forbidden. Eagles must marry Ravens, Ravens could only marry Eagles. Within these phratries, the Haida were divided into clans of family groups, each of which possessed its own crest. The all-important line of inheritance was matrilineal, the mother's phratry determining descent. The sons of chiefs knew that they would likely never rise to their fathers' rank, and the chief looked to his oldest sister's son to assume the duties of leadership.

By the end of the eighteenth century, Spanish explorers had "discovered" Haida Gwaii and the riches of its shores. British ships and Yankee traders followed, lured by the money to be made from sea-otter pelts.

Hundreds of vessels plied the waters of Haida Gwaii. Captain George Dixon, after a particularly profitable trading voyage, named the archipelago after his ship and his queen – Queen Charlotte.

Many Haida view this period as the zenith of their artistry. The spectacular poles of the village of Tanu, now found in museums across Canada, were carved with the iron tools gained in trade with the Europeans. Their canoes and longhouses became even more embellished and their clothing more ornate. For the most part, the Haida were left alone. European interest in the islands was for trade, not conquest or settlement. By the mid 1800s, the vigorous sea-otter trade virtually ceased – the sea otters were all but gone. In the nineteenth century some whites began to settle on the islands of Haida Gwaii. First came the trading posts, then missionaries, followed by gold miners, trappers, hunters, and whalers. Contact with Europeans brought more than iron tools to Haida Gwaii. It brought smallpox. The first serious outbreak was at Skincuttle, when Haida trading canoes returned from Victoria with some crew members dead or dying. In 1862, a trader brought a dying European to Ninstints – infecting the whole village. Other stories persist among the Haida that smallpox was deliberately introduced by white traders. Whole villages were literally annihilated in the summer of 1872. Village medicine men, the shamen, were impotent in the face of new, introduced illness. Their magic failed them. Their faith, their culture, their beliefs, and their sense of pride and purpose in the world, all were shaken. They wondered how they had offended the spirits that guided their lives.

There were vaccines in Victoria, but there is no record of any attempt to distribute them to the Haida. Well-intentioned Europeans offered only missionary zeal. God was punishing the Haida for their heathen ways. Accepting Christ as their saviour was the only way to restore their world.

According to Haida oral tradition, a chief in one of the southern villages moved into his sweat-lodge in search of a vision. He asked a raven to fly all over the islands to find the other survivors. No one could believe the vision: All of the villages were gone. There was too little time to bury the dead, and no one was left alive to carve mortuary poles for them. The powerful ceremonial trappings of death were ignored as the dead were piled together in mass graves. The Haida Nation fell from a population of many thousands to several hundred in the period of a few years – the worst of it in a few weeks. Where there had once been several hundred villages, now the bereaved and bewildered survivors gathered in only two – in Massett and in Skidegate on northern Graham Island.

Their social fabric was in tatters, but the basic threads were preserved. Even though no Haida lived in the abandoned villages, the descendants of those places maintained the hereditary chain of title to chieftainship. The system of government and of social status continued, despite the banning of its central ceremony, the potlatch. But while all other trappings of being Haida were subsumed under the pressures to learn English, never to speak Haida, and to dress as the colonizers dressed, the Haida's maintained their bond to Haida Gwaii.

For young Guujaaw, there was no doubt about whose land it was. It was Haida land. He grew up with a sense of pride. Unlike Indian kids growing up in cities, keenly aware of their minority status, Haida kids didn't feel oppressed. Rather, they ruled the roost at school. Guujaaw grew up under the tutelage of his mother's brother, Percy Williams – Uncle Kulga. He listened in awe to his father, his uncle, and their friends as they told stories of bravery, of supernatural beings, of daring exploits of the past. These legends lived on.

He spent summers with his mother's grandmother. When he was a boy of six, she was over a hundred years old. She had long white hair and a tattoo of a grizzly bear on her chest. When the children visited, she would dress them in blankets and old head-dresses from a trunk, teaching them Haida songs and laughing at their childhood imitations of warriors.

The influence of his family, and his inheritance of Haida legend and belief, made Guujaaw fiercely proud and independent. He loved overnight camping outings with his friends, especially when they went to the old forest beside a peat island that jiggled when they walked on it. When it was logged, Guujaaw realized that something was amiss. It didn't seem right that anyone should be allowed to take a whole forest for himself. And the hurt of losing his forest was aggravated by the sting that a stranger had done so on Haida land.

Uncle Kulga taught Guujaaw how to spear abalone. He learned how to hunt ducks and geese, to track deer, to fish for salmon, to catch prawns, to collect sea urchins. He visited the ancestral village sites of Skedans and Tanu, and stared in awe at the remains of the longhouses, overgrown with moss, visible only to those who know what they are seeing.

He enjoyed working the trapline with his uncle, from the south end of Lyell Island to below Burnaby Island. Life was just fine for a young Haida man in his early twenties. But then came the disquieting news that a timber company had applied for a licence to log Burnaby, a beautiful and heavily forested island to the south of Lyell Island. The company, Rayonier Canada (B.C.) Ltd, a subsidiary of one of the largest corporations in the world, IT&T, had been logging on Talunkwan

Island, adjacent to the northern portion of Moresby.

Travelling by boat with his uncle, Guujaaw had seen firsthand the devastation of Talunkwan. It was even worse than the destruction of his boyhood campsite. Steep slopes had been clear-cut, leaving behind a moonscape. Salmon streams were fouled, and eagle nests were downed. The scars of logging grew worse over time, as the slopes slid away in landslides after each heavy rain. Now this same company wanted to log Burnaby Island, using the same contractor. In October 1974 Rayonier proposed its new five-year logging plan to the provincial government, and no one seemed inclined to oppose it. It was not as if no one had ever logged on those islands before. A relatively small area, some four hundred hectares, of the southern parts of Moresby and its sister islands had been selectively logged in the 1930s.

Guujaaw was alarmed by the Rayonier proposal. He had learned a lot about logging from his father, Lee Edenshaw, who was himself a logger. His father had been shocked when the company yarded gravel from the Yakoun River, spreading out the river bed across the road and leaving salmon eggs to be devoured by flocks of sea-gulls. He knew the difference between selective logging and clear-cutting in an area of steep slopes and unstable soils. Not every tree should be logged. Years before, Guujaaw and others had successfully intervened when the Massett Band Council had proposed logging around one of the old village sites. But fighting a big company like Rayonier was going to be a lot tougher than convincing the Massett Band Council. If the logging of Burnaby Island was to be stopped, he needed a larger strategy.

One night Guujaaw headed to a party thrown by Trudy Carson, who lived in a little house along the Tlell River. He enjoyed himself and, as usual, was the life of the party. Despite the good time, the Rayonier proposal was weighing on his mind. As the evening wound down, most of the guests elected to stay at the house, crashing on the front porch in a bundled row of blankets and sleeping bags. Guujaaw couldn't sleep. He tossed and turned, fretting about the logging plans for Burnaby. Finally he spoke aloud into the darkness, "Anyone awake?" he asked. And from somewhere down the porch, Huckleberry answered.

ISLANDS
PROTECTION

Huck had not stayed long in one place since he first kayaked through the waters of Haida Gwaii. He had paddled around many of the islands and had built a cabin at Lepas Bay on the northern tip. But he had returned to Alaska in 1973, realizing the precariousness of living as a squatter in a country where he had no status.

He was at Trudy's party a year later because Canada's immigration policy changed in 1974. Landed immigrant status was now made available to anyone who had lived the requisite amount of time in Canada and who applied from outside the country. As he fulfilled both requirements, Huck was relieved and elated. He returned to his cabin in the Charlottes in the spring of 1974. Lying on the porch that night, watching the moon, Huck was thinking about the proposal to log Burnaby Island when Guujaaw asked, "What are you thinking about?" Huck answered that he was just thinking about the threat to Burnaby. "So was I," said Guujaaw.

It was around three in the morning when Guujaaw and Huck got up. They had met briefly before, still Huck extended his hand. But nothing in the last twenty years had changed Guujaaw's mind on the subject of handshakes with white men. They went into the kitchen, lit a lamp, spread out a map of the islands, and began to plan strategically. If they were going to fight the logging, they had better be prepared to fight to save all the islands in the southern third of the archipelago. Both Huck and Guujaaw had been impressed with a huge virgin stand of old-growth forest on the east coast of Lyell Island, a place called Windy Bay on the map. It would make no sense, they reasoned, to save Burnaby Island at the expense of such forests. They tried to decide where to draw the line demarcating the forests to be saved. The key, they realized, was to draw it far enough south that there would be several years' worth of cutting rights left to the north of it (thus buying time for the fight to preserve the southern portion of the archipelago), and far enough north to preserve the maximum amount of unspoiled area.

When the rest of the guests woke up, Huck and Guujaaw presented them with the Southern Moresby Wilderness Proposal, a petition to save the area from logging, and a new organization, the Islands Protection Committee. They had drawn the line from the height of land of the Tangil Peninsula, west along natural contours to just south of the old iron mine at Tasu on the west coast. The name, Islands Protection Committee, had been in Guujaaw's mind for some time. It was a rough translation of the Haida word Kangaliag Waii. Years earlier, he had written, "There is a need on these islands of ours for an organization, and that organization should be called 'Islands Protection'."

When they drew the line on the map they drew it along existing demarcations drawn by the province, on top of an existing boundary between two cutting blocks. This meant that the proposal would start showing up on government maps. The line existed. It would just start being re-identified as the wilderness proposal.

Guujaaw and Huck recruited the rest of the party's guests to help type, copy, and circulate petitions, then headed back to Massett to plan what they thought would be a straightforward campaign. They reasoned that their chances of success were fairly high. The premier of British Columbia, Dave Barrett, presided over the first social-democratic government in North America. The New Democrats, they thought, would be sympathetic.

The first step would be to gain the backing of the Skidegate Band Council, which was responsible for the southern portion of Haida Gwaii. Through his uncle, Percy Williams, who was chief councillor at Skidegate, Guujaaw knew that a representative of Rayonier was due to make a presentation to the Band Council within the week. Although the meeting would primarily be for council members, the public could attend to learn more about the proposal. Guujaaw went to see his uncle to try to persuade him of the need for a different perspective at the meeting, one that would stress the ancestral and spiritual significance of the lands in question.

Percy Williams looked at the line Guujaaw and Huck had drawn on the map and saw that the huge wilderness proposal encompassed nearly fifteen hundred square kilometres of land, much of it covered in valuable timber. Percy, among other things, was a logger, and while he valued the economic activity the forest companies brought to the islands, he knew that clear-cut logging had choked many streams with silt and mud. He could imagine how quickly the life of the intertidal narrows would be fouled if Burnaby were to suffer the same fate as Talunkwan. He had some understanding of Guujaaw's passionate concern, but thought that maybe there was room for compromise. He knew that Rayonier had held the tree farm licence, known as TFL 24, since 1958, and that it wouldn't just give up and go away. His uncle said patiently, "You're asking for too much." "It is not enough," Guujaaw replied.

On a cool October day in the fall of 1974, Guujaaw
and Huck attended the meeting in Skidegate and
listened to the Rayonier representatives give their
presentation, stressing the employment and economic
opportunities of logging Burnaby Island. Huck had a
sinking feeling that the Islands Protection Committee
was out-gunned from the start. Then Percy Williams
took the floor to moderate an open discussion between
the company and the Haida Council. He looked out
across the hall, filled with friends and neighbours.
There was not a face he did not know.

"I want to tell you a story about something that
happened to me a year or so ago," he began, and he
told of a strange encounter he had had with a young
man who was carried over the water in a craft that
looked like an eagle and who had offered him a dead
eagle. The crowd in the hall was hushed. Among the
Haida, stories about eagles are not taken lightly.

"So I said to the man, 'Why do you bring me this
eagle?' and he said, 'Because there are so few of them
left.' Now I can tell you my first impression was that this
was some kind of a sign. It made me stop and think.
When I'm out on the water down around Burnaby
Island, well, it isn't anything to see twenty eagles in a
day, to see three in the same tree. But I realized what
this young man said was true. Most places in the world,
there aren't many eagles left. I realized that what we
have here is special and that, if we don't take care of it,
there won't be any place like it left in the world." Percy
Williams paused and looked over to his nephew and
the young man sitting with him, "Now I'd like to ask
that young man who brought me that eagle to speak."

Huck was the young man who had found the eagle
on the beach at Windy Bay. He had not seen Percy
Williams since, and now he was introduced to the
Haida Nation on the strength of a vision.

Huck and Guujaaw went to the front of the hall and proceeded to throw some very tough questions at the representatives of Rayonier. They asked what road-building techniques Rayonier planned to use. Rayonier's people were not sure. They asked what they planned to do about steep slopes, and if the company would provide any guarantee that it wouldn't cause landslides as it had on Talunkwan. They grilled and peppered the ill-prepared company flacks with question after question, for which they had no answer. The company men were embarrassed. This was supposed to be an easy snow job on a bunch of Indians.

The meeting was a triumph for Guujaaw and Huck, and a major set-back for Rayonier. The Skidegate Band Council went on record opposing Rayonier's plans for Burnaby. And an honest-to-goodness, broad-based community group was born.

Nathan Young, hereditary chief of Tanu, the old Haida village just north of Lyell, expressed his strong support of the wilderness proposal. The petition became the subject of much coverage in the *Queen Charlotte Islands Observer*. And worried representatives of Rayonier met again with the Skidegate Band Council, but this time with the official participation of the Islands Protection Committee, the provincial Forest Service, and the federal Department of Fisheries.

At Percy Williams's invitation, Premier Dave Barrett came to Skidegate to meet with the Haida. Percy made the case for preserving Burnaby Island, and Barrett was persuaded. They accepted his word that Burnaby would not be logged.

In December 1974, the minister of lands, forests, and water resources, Bob Williams, announced a five-year moratorium on logging on Burnaby Island, fulfilling the Premier's personal pledge. Rayonier withdrew its application to log cutting block four within its tree farm licence, but simultaneously applied for a cutting permit for Lyell Island, squarely within the boundaries of the wilderness proposal.

On a drizzly February day in 1975, Huck, Trudy Carson, and Viola Wood, who wrote social notes for the Charlottes' newspaper, delivered petitions with the names of five hundred island residents to the parliament building in Victoria. They had hopes of being allowed to meet the Premier, so it was with some disappointment they learned that they were to see their own MLA, Graham Lea, instead. Lea was minister of highways, but in his T-shirt he didn't look the part. He leaned back in his chair, propping his stocking feet up on his desk. "Petitions?" he glowered. "Here's what they mean to us," gesturing to the waste basket. "Sure," he continued, acting the role of a worldly wise politician who would give these starry-eyed dreamers a dose of reality, "we'd like to put a barrier around the whole province. But the guys need jobs. And logging provides jobs. Simple as that."

In April 1975, the province granted Rayonier a licence to log Lyell Island. As a sop to the environmentalists, Barrett promised that the Environment and Land Use Committee Secretariat (ELUCS), a technical committee serving ministers from environment and resource portfolios, would take a serious look at the wilderness proposal. A pattern was set against which Huck and Guujaaw would fight for the next twelve years: government reviews, studies, special commissions, and advisory committees debating the fate of the wilderness proposal while logging within it continued. Guujaaw knew enough of what they were in for to tell Huck, "This is war."

|5|

J.B.

John broadhead first came to massett in the
Charlottes in the fall of 1973 to spend the winter fly-
fishing and print-making. Aged twenty-four, he had left
a full scholarship in science to begin a professional career as an artist and graphic designer. One thing he did
not plan to be was a full-time environmentalist.

In 1974, he moved back to Vancouver to work with
the National Film Board. When he returned to Massett
the following spring, he found that a character named
Huckleberry was living in his chicken coop. The first
thing that struck him about his new tenant was Huck's
sense of aesthetics. Chicken coop renovation had never
before reached such heights – stained wood, coral walls,
and a sound system that had been run underground
from the main stereo inside the house. The other thing
that struck him about Huck was his Tom Sawyer-like
qualities. Like the original Huck's alter ego, this one
could con just about anyone into doing whatever he
wanted and have the person thanking him for the privilege. But however much he liked Huck, John
Broadhead (J.B.) was not interested in getting involved
in this wilderness crusade.

J.B. was in a minority. The fight for the Southern
Moresby Wilderness Proposal had taken over the lives
of many of the people he knew. The IPC had recruited
far and wide. When Huck had learned that B.C. Hydro
planned to cut a power corridor through the forest

at Tlell River, he had issued a call to arms. After a visit from Guujaaw, Dan Bowditch, the local head of Hydro's operations, had come to see Huck. The power lines went in with a minimum of damage, and Dan and his wife, Ursel, had become mainstays of the IPC. But despite all the organizing going on around him, J.B. remained detached.

One day Huck came in to see him, bringing a pile of papers and drawings. He explained that this was the raw material for the third edition of the IPC magazine, *About Time for an Island*. "I was just wondering," Huck said. "Do you have any ideas for how this might look better?" J.B. surveyed the dog-eared mess of scribbled notes, typed essays, pen-and-ink drawings, and short stories. "Yes," he said, with a half smile. "It's not too hard to think of ways that this could look better," and he volunteered to help.

J.B. was still not yet an activist. Schooled since his boyhood to believe in wise resource management, he saw no reason to criticize logging methods. The forests were in good hands. But when he went back to his favourite fishing holes, to streams that had glistened with trout and salmon just a year before, he found them radically altered. He saw mud slides, caved-in banks, silty flood waters, and no matter how attractive his fly-fishing lure, the trout did not respond. All around him there was new logging activity. He was angry, as only someone who feels betrayed can be. Forestry in British Columbia was not being done right. He began to put in much longer hours with the IPC magazine.

In the spring of 1976, a much-improved magazine was published. The name of the publication changed to *All Alone Stone*, after the tiny island of the same name in Juan Perez Sound in the heart of the wilderness proposal area. The magazine confronted forest management practices in British Columbia, and warned that the fundamental principle of sustained-yield forestry was being replaced by forest technocrats with the new and dangerous buzzwords, "intensive silviculture" and "multiple use" – quickly revised by J.B. to "multiple abuse." The Islands Protection Committee was not alone in raising these issues. Across British Columbia, there was a new wave of concern about silvicultural practices.

This was not the first time that the public had shown an interest in the province's forestry policies. Back in 1943, provincial foresters had convinced the government of the day of the need for radical reforms to forest policy. The province's chief forester, C.D. Orchard, had warned, "We have nothing like the timber resources we once thought we had...Our most valuable areas are being overcut...Our production...must of necessity fall off sharply during the next few decades if prompt measures are not taken to forestall it." In response to these concerns, the Premier had employed the favourite tactic of a politician with a tough choice to make. He had appointed a Royal Commission. The Commission had recommended the creation of management units to guarantee "sustained yield." But if the concept of forest management licences, later to become tree farm licences, had ever ensured sustainable forestry, it was clear by the early 1970s that this was no longer the case. No longer content to wait the hundred and fifty years between harvests assumed in traditional sustained-yield practice, the timber companies had argued that new technology allowed them to grow trees faster and cut them sooner. Since the early 1950s, clear-cutting had increased dramatically as a proportion of the total area harvested. The total area logged annually was also going up. Vast areas were not replanted and failed to regenerate naturally.

In 1974, public pressure had led to yet another Royal Commission. The Pearse Royal Commission on Timber Rights and Forest Policy provided a lightning rod for environmentalists. Groups from across the province prepared detailed briefs documenting the over-cutting of the provincial forests. Huck, Guujaaw, J.B., and the growing numbers of IPC volunteers pored through the documents and found scientific and technical arguments to support the evidence of their own eyes: Poor logging practices were wiping out fish habitat, causing massive erosion, and threatening the future of any long-term forest industry. They discovered that the licence to log Lyell Island had been granted in violation of the Forest Service's own guidelines, which forbade the cutting of slopes in excess of 65 per cent. They were more determined than ever to oppose the logging of Lyell.

The provincial election campaign had come and gone. Dave Barrett and the New Democrats had been replaced by the ultra-conservative Social Credit Party of Bill Bennett. The IPC remained optimistic that government would eventually listen. It greeted the news that the Socred government would allow the ELUCS review of the wilderness proposal promised by Barrett without cynicism, even though logging of Lyell Island was due to begin within the year.

The IPC learned only later that the new minister of forests, Tom Waterland, had written a reassuring letter to Rayonier in June 1976: "The present government believes in honouring contracts, thus there will be no wholesale withdrawals of land from TFL 24. The ELUCS study will proceed and it will cover the southern portion of Moresby Island, including TFL 24, as originally planned. It is an overview study only, which will catalogue the important and unique features of the area and make recommendations for the future." In other words, it would not interfere with logging.

PAUL

IN 1976, A NEW GROWTH INDUSTRY STARTED ON THE Charlottes – the Study Industry took hold. Over the course of the year, no fewer than eight different studies were conducted by various branches of federal and provincial governments relating to the Southern Moresby Wilderness Proposal. The Islands Protection Committee took almost every sign of interest from any government agency as a good sign. The exception was the interest of the Royal Canadian Mounted Police.

The Islands Protection leaders had become the subject of police investigation. The RCMP viewed the committee as a hotbed of political radicalism. In the winter of 1975, Huck's entire food supply, sacks of grains and flour, had been ripped open during a police search for illegal weapons. As well, some IPC members had noticed clicking sounds on their telephones, and suspected that their lines were being tapped.

One day in the winter of 1976, Guujaaw was working in the IPC office in Dan and Ursel Bowditch's basement, when there was a knock on the door. Guujaaw opened it to a complete stranger – a young man, tall and burly with long blond hair, a beard, and slightly mismatched clothes, as if buttons had been sewn on to avoid the button holes. Guujaaw thought he must be the police infiltrator the committee had been half-expecting.

The stranger grinned and said, "Hi. I've been looking all over for the Islands Protection Committee office. I've come up from Victoria and I want to work with you." He extended his hand, which Guujaaw refused, saying, "I don't know who you are. How do I know you're not a cop?"

Paul George was stunned. A cop? Why would anyone think he was a cop? In his whole life such a case of mistaken identity had never before occurred. A native of Minnesota, Paul had emigrated to Canada in 1967 with his wife and three children. In 1974, he was hired by the provincial Department of Education to prepare a grade eleven biology correspondence course. For the next two years he did little else but work on the manuscript, researching interesting biological systems within the province, which might draw students more closely into the subject. He came across a PhD thesis on small mammals endemic to the Queen Charlotte Islands written in the early 1960s by Dr Bristol Foster. On the Charlottes, Bristol had observed kinds of plants and animals found nowhere else on earth. He postulated that somehow these varieties had evolved in isolation on the Queen Charlotte Islands, changing only in response to local conditions. The Charlottes were a giant laboratory for the study of the evolutionary process. Bristol had dubbed the Queen Charlotte Islands the "Canadian Galapagos."

Biologists initially maintained that the islands must have been missed by the blanket of ice that covered most of British Columbia ten thousand years ago. Geologists countered that the glaciers must have also covered the Charlottes. Biologists then proposed the "refugia" theory, which posited that, while ice covered much of the area, small pockets, or refugia, remained ice-free. Within those enclaves of biological life, unique species survived and evolved. Support for the theory came from the observations of biologists and also from analysis of bogs and core samples, which contained pollen and other signs of life from ten thousand years ago. These studies suggested that a complete climax forest was thriving in areas of the Charlottes when the glaciers should have been retreating leaving nothing but scarred, bare rock in their wakes.

Paul was captivated by these theories about the Queen Charlotte Islands. The world's largest black bear, the now-extinct, but unique Dawson's caribou, river otter, pine marten, Haida ermine, deer mice, shrews, stickleback fish – all had evolved through isolation into forms unknown elsewhere in the world. He searched for good illustrations to use in his book, but there seemed to be scant information about the Canadian Galapagos. Then he came across the January 1976 edition of *Nature Canada*, containing an article about the controversy on the Charlottes. Paul was delighted to find there was an organization fighting to preserve the area. He started to think of writing a book that documented the unique fauna of the Charlottes. As a first step, he tracked down Bristol Foster, who was working in Victoria as director of the Provincial Ecological Reserves Unit. Paul was immediately impressed. Bristol was not a typical bureaucrat.

Born in Toronto in 1932, Bristol had been an avid naturalist and bird-watcher since childhood. In his mid-twenties, having completed a master's degree from the University of Toronto, he headed off with a boyhood friend on a trek around the world, through Africa, Asia, and Australia. Robert Bateman and Bristol made most of their trip by Land Rover, seeking out the remote places where wildlife could be seen, nearly undisturbed by man. Bateman's observations were shared with the world when he became one of

Canada's most loved artists. When he returned, Bristol started his PhD at the University of British Columbia, studying the native mammals of the Queen Charlotte Islands. By 1974 he was part of the provincial bureaucracy of British Columbia. As head of the new Ecological Reserves Unit, he had been following the controversy over logging in the Charlottes. He sympathized with the Islands Protection Committee, but he was convinced that it did not have a prayer.

Now an earnest Paul George sat in his office and laid before him grandiose plans for a major illustrated work to be sold in aid of the conservation battle. Bristol encouraged Paul to produce a book about the ecological wealth of the Queen Charlottes. That was all Paul needed to hear. He set off from Victoria almost immediately, heading to Massett and to Guujaaw's sceptical reaction.

After hearing Paul's plans, Guujaaw told him, "We didn't send for you. We don't know you. And we don't need you." If there was to be a book, the committee would do it itself. Paul was not easily dissuaded. For one thing, he could see the enormous odds the preservation movement was up against. His first visit to the Charlottes coincided with the first All Islands Symposium, at which the Southern Moresby Wilderness Proposal was the key issue. Community support was high, but the preliminary report from the province's Environmental and Land Use Committee Secretariat was devastating. It recommended continued logging with some small conservation measures. Paul felt that the Islands Protection Committee needed him, whether it liked it or not.

Back in Victoria, Paul recruited his friend and neighbour Richard Krieger, who had the ideal combination of photographic skill and independent means. Paul and Richard spent nearly a year planning their dream project – to spend an entire summer photographing the wilderness proposal area.

In June 1977, Paul George and Richard Krieger arrived in Haida Gwaii with piles of sophisticated photographic equipment – a Hasselblad camera, huge telephoto lenses, tripods, tape recorders, and microphones. They dubbed themselves the Galapagos Book Collaborators and immediately made a splash in the *Queen Charlotte Islands Observer*. They made it known that they had arrived to produce the definitive work. They visited with foresters working for Rayonier and they interviewed members of the IPC, but they spent most of their time in the wilderness area. Guujaaw agreed to be their guide. Richard had brought an inflatable boat with an outboard motor, and the three of them loaded it with equipment, and headed down the west side of the archipelago.

By June 21, they had reached the southern island of Skungwai, known on the charts as Anthony Island. The area had been nominated for World Heritage status by UNESCO. Richard took roll after roll of photographs of the remnants of the village of Ninstints – of the mounds of moss-shrouded roof beams where the longhouses once stood, of the ghostly mortuary poles of killer whales, ravens, eagles, and beavers looking out to sea, with huge impassive, impenetrable eyes. Later they hiked inland, with Guujaaw and Paul acting as African porters, calling out "Bwana" to Richard as they struggled with the weight of his delicate gear. They saw the alpine meadows of the interior and viewed from their heights the scattered emerald islands below. They photographed the rich intertidal sea life of Burnaby Narrows, locally known as the sushi bar, and the huge trees of Windy Bay. Richard snapped eagles in their nests, bears turning over rocks on the shore at dusk, tufted puffins diving for fish off Kunghit Island, sealions on their craggy rookeries, tiny deer foraging among the poles of abandoned villages, and rare thrushes in the cedar. They shot roll after roll of film of existing clear-cuts, of eagles' nests lying amid the rubble after crashing from their lofty perch, of bare hillsides eroding into the sea, and of the loggers at work, men with monstrous chain saws doing a hard job well, felling the ancient giants.

By the end of the summer, the Galapagos Book Collaborators had assembled the most comprehensive series of colour photographs ever taken of Haida Gwaii. They decided not to wait for a book to put the images to work. Paul and Richard organized a slide show and Paul laboured over maps to calculate a few basic statistics that were not part of the IPC repertoire. He counted a total of 138 islands within the wilderness proposal, accounting for an astonishing 1,700 miles of coastline.

In the fall of 1977, Guujaaw, Huck, and the Galapagos Book Collaborators took their show on the road to Massett and Queen Charlotte City, as well as to the logging camps of Sewell Inlet and Powrivco Bay on Lyell Island, where the loggers jeered the idea of preserving the area.

The slide show sparked direct dialogue between the environmentalists and the loggers, but it was not the first or the last occasion for a clash of views. That spring, the Forest Service had established the Queen Charlotte Islands Public Advisory Committee. Ostensibly the Public Advisory Commitee (PAC) was created to encourage public participation in Forest Service policies, but its meetings quickly degenerated into shouting matches. It was becoming clear from the public meetings that sentiment toward the wilderness proposal was divided on the islands. The residents of Massett, Queen Charlotte City, Port Clements, and Skidegate, while not unanimously in favour of the wilderness proposal, were in favour of some measure of preservation. But across the water from Skidegate,

Sandspit, the only permanent community on Moresby Island, was beginning to feel itself isolated as the centre of support for logging all of TFL 24. It was the smallest of the islands' communities – just 250 people – but it was the headquarters of Rayonier for the area, as well as the base for Frank Beban Logging.

Frank Beban was easily the most popular guy in town. He ran the local helicopter charter, the only motel and lounge in town, as well as his logging business, which employed some seventy men down on Lyell. But for all the studies and meetings and bally-hoo about the wilderness proposal, Frank was not about to get spooked. The executives of Rayonier had received assurances from government, verging on guarantees, that the TFL would be renewed without any reductions to accommodate the environmentalists. Frank and members of his crew went along to PAC meetings with Rayonier, feeling pretty sure that government would never take "a bunch of hippies" seriously.

During this period, despite the priority attached to the wilderness proposal, the IPC had its volunteer hands full with other issues. The government was proposing to allow a super-tanker port on the west coast of British Columbia opposite Haida Gwaii at Kitimat. More or less the same people who formed the IPC shifted gears to oppose the proposal at the federal West Coast Oil Port Inquiry. To raise money for their participation in the federal inquiry, J.B. teamed up with a local Haida artist with a wicked sense of humour, Mike Nicholl. They put together the first of the islands' conservationist comic books, *Tales of Raven – No Tankers, T'anks.*

The committee gathered its energies together again for the second annual All Islands Symposium in November 1977. Following up on a resolution passed at the Public Advisory Committee, where it had even been supported by the Rayonier representative, the All

Islands Symposium called for public hearings prior to the renewal of tree farm licences. The two-day event was well attended by federal and provincial government representatives, by industry, and by the growing coalition of Haida, non-native residents, and environmentalists. But logging continued, and the trees of Windy Bay were next. Paul learned that biologists had long been aware that the area from Windy Bay to Dodge Point contained the largest known ancient murrelet colony in British Columbia, an estimated sixty thousand pairs of birds. In Victoria for the winter, Paul went back to see Bristol Foster to ask for his help.

Bristol had been asked to intercede on the wilderness proposal before. Huck had come in to see him, asking for the whole southern Moresby area to be set aside. Bristol had explained the procedures to Huck, as he now explained them to Paul. If a proposal for ecological reserve status was accepted for review, there could be no logging or road building until such time as the Ecological Reserves Unit completed their evaluation. But the mandate of the unit was fairly narrow. An area the size of the entire wilderness proposal could never be considered an ecological reserve. However, something a lot smaller, with the right characteristics as a research and teaching area, might very well be considered. "Bingo," thought Paul. He and Richard got the appropriate forms and made their case for protecting Windy Bay and the ancient murrelets of Dodge Point through the special status of a provincial ecological reserve. The Ecological Reserve Unit accepted the proposal for review, thus freezing any logging permits for Windy Bay.

Later, that following spring, Paul George encountered a slightly drunk and very angry Frank Beban in the lounge of his motel. Beban boomed at him accusingly, "Your ecological reserve proposal is just a clever ploy to stop logging!" Slightly drunk himself, Paul grinned back, "Of course it is, and it's working!"

REDISCOVERY

WHEN HUCK, PAUL GEORGE, AND RICHARD KREIGER SAT around a camp-fire on the beach at Windy Bay in the summer of 1978, they had reason to feel disheartened. The battle to save the southern portion of Haida Gwaii had begun four years before, but Lyell Island was still being logged. Despite public meetings, provincial inquiries, petitions, and symposia, the IPC had few accomplishments to its credit. The federal West Coast Oil Port Inquiry had been aborted and it looked as if the Kitimat proposal was defeated. But the protection of the southern Moresby wilderness was as elusive as ever.

Huck particularly felt a sense of impending loss – not only loss of the enormous trees around him, but loss of a culture. Huck had been adopted by a woman in Massett. His Haida mother, Mary Swanson, was of the Eagle clan, and Huck had been absorbing Haida ways like a sponge. This land and this people were so much a part of him, he could not imagine a time when he had not shared this life. The Haida's love and respect for the wilderness had to be communicated to others. Something in him boiled up, and sitting alone on a log on a beach, he began feverishly to write a proposal for a youth camp on Haida Gwaii. The camp, to be called Rediscovery, would aim to connect children and teenagers, Haida and non-Haida, with the spiritual value of wilderness. The camp counsellors would include young people and Haida elders who could tell the children stories and myths they had learned from their parents. It could take place out at Lepas Bay, using Huck's cabin as a first shelter, and it could include a kayak trip down into the wilderness proposal area. All he needed now was the funding to organize it and make it available to every child on the islands. It was not until Huck stood up, after over an hour of non-stop writing, that he looked around the beach and realized that he had been sitting on the same spot where he had found the eagle four years before.

Back on Graham Island, he went to Port Clements to see Jim Fulton, the local probation officer with responsibility for all of the Charlottes. Jim Fulton was young, gregarious, and distinctly non-bureacratic in his approach. Jim read over Huck's proposal. "It's absolutely perfect," Jim enthused. "It's exactly what is needed for these kids." Within weeks, Jim had arranged three years' funding for the camp through the correctional service.

Rediscovery, while not part of any campaign to save wilderness, played a part in the increased awareness of Haida culture among non-Haida. It coincided with the rise in pride the Haida had already started to experience. Claude Davidson was teaching Haida children the old dance steps, and Wanagan, the self-appointed guardian of Ninstints Village, was teaching them about the old poles. Rediscovery was immediately supported by Haida elders and by young activists like Guujaaw and Mike Nicholl. The program was a success in developing new, creative approaches to wilderness education. It was so popular that soon children begged to be accepted. They learned ceremonies, and a favourite camp activity was recreating a day in the life of an old Haida village. For these and other festivities, Rediscovery needed costumes. Huck wrote to the Provincial Museum and requested any old furs or animals the museum didn't need, for conversion to cloaks, dance masks, and head-dresses. In one shipment a beautiful bald eagle arrived. Huck stared at its identification tag in disbelief. It read, "Donated by Percy Williams, Skidegate, 1973."

One of the key figures in the renaissance of Haida culture was a man who had never seen Haida Gwaii until his twenty-third year. Bill Reid was born of a Haida mother and a Scottish-German father in 1920. His grandmother had been a native of Tanu, belonging to the Raven phratry and the Wolf clan. When smallpox nearly wiped out her village, she had moved north with the survivors from other communities. Widowed, she had remarried, and Bill's mother, Sophie Gladstone, was born. Sophie left Skidegate when she married an American from Detroit, William Ronald Reid.

As a young man, Bill was not self-conscious of his Haida-ness, but his mother's background fascinated him. In 1943, he travelled to the Haida Gwaii for the first time. The beach that had once been lined with magnificent poles – house poles, mortuary poles, potlatch poles – all telling their family's story, was now lined only with the small frame houses of a typical Indian reserve. Still, Bill felt at home on those remote islands, in a way he had not felt before. It would be years before he returned, but the islands had touched him.

He lived in Toronto, working as a broadcaster for CBC Radio. At first his fascination with jewelry-making was just a hobby. But gradually it became a passion, as he laboured over bits of gold and silver in his basement, rediscovering the stylized art forms of the Northwest Coast Indians. He began to be known as a Haida artist, and that connection drew him back to Haida Gwaii.

In 1955, Bill Reid was part of a team put together by the B.C. Provincial Museum to travel to the abandoned Haida villages on the southern portion of the

archipelago. In what must have been a painful decision, Bill Reid, anthropologist Wilson Duff, and the
museum team removed the remaining standing poles.

This trip to rescue poles took Bill to his grandmother's village of Tanu, reputed to have created the
zenith of Haida carving. The team's second trip in
1957 took them to the village of Ninstints on the
southern island of Skungwai. Eleven poles were taken
down, one sixteen metres high, and each weighing
several tons. The mortuary poles could not be
removed as they were standing graves, containing
human remains. The few remaining memorial poles
were judged to be beyond restoration. No one could
guess that, within thirty years, these poles would
promote Ninstints' designation as a World Heritage
Site by the United Nations.

By 1958 Bill Reid was busy restoring and replicating
the poles for museums. He first carved poles as part of
that effort, working with the Kwakiutl carver, Mungo
Martin. From that experience, Bill Reid was pulled
inexorably into the art of carving. With Kwakiutl artist
Doug Crammer, Reid built two longhouses and seven
new poles for the University of British Columbia
Museum of Anthropology.

In 1978, Bill Reid was back in Skidegate working on
a pole that would have greater significance than
anything put into a museum. Reid had said at the time
that he felt as though he had made his reputation on
the bones of his ancestors. Now he was carving a pole
for his children to be raised at the front of a new
longhouse, the new quarters for the Skidegate Band
Council. It would be the first pole in nearly a hundred
years to grace the beach at Skidegate.

The day Guujaaw visited the master carver to talk to
him about the wilderness proposal, Bill was hard at
work and his hands barely slowed as Guujaaw laid the
issue before him. Bill wished him well, but didn't want

to get involved with a lot of publicity or speech-making. He'd leave that to the politicians. As Guujaaw prepared to leave, he said, "I'd be interested in helping you carve." Reid looked up from his work, and said, "Good. Here you are." He handed Guujaaw a mallet and chisel, and gesturing to the pole said, "Do the other side." Guujaaw became Bill Reid's apprentice, living in a small bus by the carving shed.

On the day of the raising of the Dogfish Pole at Skidegate in 1978, the longhouse was surrounded with men and women in red and black button blankets. Hereditary chiefs wore the head-dresses of their clans. A wolf-skin cloak, with the wolf's mouth wide and teeth bared, bobbed among the crowd, staring down the placid face of a Haida moon head-dress. Children ran everywhere in wide-eyed excitement. Dogs raced in a crazed frenzy up and down the beach. Guujaaw drummed, and joined the elders in singing the traditional Haida songs, with their pulsating chants. The people of the village gathered to raise the pole, carved from a single cedar. It told the story of the village and its supernatural guardians – Grizzly Bear, Raven, and Killer Whale had all had their adventures with the peoples of the islands. Of his creation, Reid said, "They were already there. They were under the wood just waiting to be let out."

Two hundred men and women, straining at four ropes, levered the huge pole into place. Fewer people could have raised it, but everyone wanted to lend strength to the effort. It was a day of enormous joy and pride in Skidegate.

TAKING THE MINISTER
TO COURT

IN THE FALL OF 1977, THE QUEEN CHARLOTTE ISLANDS
Public Advisory Committee recommended that public
hearings be held into the renewal of Rayonier's tree
farm licence. The unprecedented unanimity of the
committee, which was, after all, established by the
Forest Service to advise it, led a good number of people
to expect that there would be public hearings. That expectation grew when the All Islands Symposium endorsed the idea. No one from the Forest Service
quelled the expectation. Meanwhile, Rayonier submitted its five-year logging plan to the Forest Service for
review. It dropped the controversial planned logging of
Windy Bay, and proposed instead extensive clear-cutting of Gate Creek to the south of Windy Bay, also on
Lyell Island. This plan was still contingent on the renewal of TFL 24.

Against this backdrop, came a forest controversy that
became known as the Shoot-out at Riley Creek. Riley
Creek was one of several small creeks running into
Rennell Sound on the west coast of Graham Island.
Because of the likelihood of landslides damaging an
important salmon stream, the federal Department
of Fisheries ordered that logging in the area not be allowed. The timber company, Q.C. Timber, a wholly
owned subsidiary of the giant Japanese corporation C.
Itoh, ignored the order. The conflict escalated until the
Mounties were called in to arrest the loggers. The company

sent in reinforcements. Helicopters arrived with more fallers to replace those who had been arrested. It was a battle. The timber industry in British Columbia wanted a showdown in order to prove that the federal Fisheries Act could not be used to interfere with logging operations. At the war operations room for Q.C. Timber in Rennell Sound, MacMillan Bloedel's lawyer was giving the orders. Between March 19 and 23, 1978, fifteen men were flown into Riley Creek to continue logging in defiance of the federal Fisheries order. The Mounties arrested the reinforcements, and they laid charges against the company and Q.C. Timber's logging supervisor.

This highly publicized round of arrests generated a lot of controversy outside the Charlottes. Jack Munro, head of the province's International Woodworkers of America, decried the arrest of honest fellows just trying to do a day's work. The Premier and the provincial forests minister angrily denounced the federal government for attempting to dictate forest policy to the province. The forest companies howled that they were not criminals; they were just bringing prosperity to British Columbians. In the midst of the performance of righteous indignation, all the charges were dropped, stayed by the provincial attorney general. But the lessons of the Shoot-out at Riley Creek were not lost on the Public Advisory Committee. It was getting harder to trust the industry or even the government, which was supposed to regulate it.

During that fall, heavy rains caused massive landslides along Riley Creek. The largest was two thousand feet long, two hundred feet wide, and five feet deep. On hearing of the slides, Forest Minister Tom Waterland suggested they were caused by deer browsing in the undergrowth, which prompted one local wit to quip that he was going to get an elephant gun and get one of them deer. Haida fisherman Charles Bellis tried to lay his own charges for the Riley Creek devastation. But when he got to court, they found their charges had been stayed by the provincial attorney general. Environment Minister Stephen Rogers eventually confirmed that logging had caused the slides at Riley Creek.

More or less at the same time as the escalation of the Riley Creek dispute, the issue of the renewal of TFL's was at the forefront of everyone's mind. When the new Forest Act was finally presented for first reading in May 1978, the Public Advisory Committee pushed for public hearings. No need to worry, said the Forest Service representatives who attended PAC meetings, there will be lots of time for public input before third reading, which would not take place until November. Huck and Guujaaw flew down to Victoria in May to focus attention on the act, which provided for virtually automatic renewals of tree farm licences and which scrapped the notion of "sustained yield." Sustained yield units were to be renamed "timber supply areas." Huck and Guujaaw picketed in front of the Parliament Buildings in Victoria. On the local television news that night they were dubbed "a small delegation with a big cause."

Despite assurances to the contrary, the Forest Act was rushed through second and third reading in the month of June. In November the federal MP for the area, Liberal Iona Campagnolo, and MLA Graham Lea joined the call for public hearings on the renewal of TFL 24.

Through the fall, Huck, Guujaaw, and Paul strategized about how best to force public hearings. Gradually, the idea of taking the minister to court over the TFL renewal began to take hold. Rayonier's contract for TFL 24 had been the first ever term lease in the province, and was thus the first to come up for renewal. Challenging its renewal would have tremendous precedent-setting value. What's more, the renewal was for another period of twenty-five years.

Guujaaw sought out Andrew Thompson, the Vancouver lawyer who had headed up the aborted

Kitimat Oil Port Inquiry. Thompson remained a sympathetic adviser, but recommended that they consult Garth Evans. In order for it to be recognized by the court, Garth advised the Islands Protection Committee to become incorporated. In doing so, it lost one of its founders. Guujaaw was adamantly against the idea of incorporation, and while he remained critically involved in all aspects of saving the wilderness, he never considered himself part of the newly named Islands Protection Society.

In February 1979 the hereditary chief of Tanu, Nathan Young, Guujaaw, seeking standing as a hunter-gatherer, Glen Naylor (a non-Haida with a registered trapline), and the Islands Protection Society took the forestry minister to court. They petitioned for an order that the minister had a duty to act fairly, and that public hearings should be held prior to renewal of Rayonier's licence. Extensive affidavits were filed, setting out the history of their dealings with the Forest Service and the reasons for their concern. Paul George was heavily involved in the case, documenting over-cutting by Rayonier on its TFL in his own affidavit. The government lawyers never challenged any of the petitioners' evidence.

The legal action was supported by the Skidegate Band Council, the Public Advisory Committee, and the Graham Island Advisory Planning Commission, as well as by many residents of the islands who threw themselves into the task of community fundraising. Before the legal case was over they would rack up $30,000 in legal fees and expenses. But that prospect did nothing to dampen their pride in holding the single most successful benefit dance ever in Haida Gwaii, bringing in a record $2,300.

Their court action did not force public hearings, but it did result in important precedents. Chief Nathan Young and Guujaaw were granted standing, as was Glen Naylor. Only the Islands Protection Society was denied the right to challenge the minister. The judge ruled that while the minister had a duty to act fairly in the renewal of the TFL, the minister had not made the decision to renew. The deadline for renewal was May 1, 1979, and so the petitioners now expected fair treatment from the minister. They sent off registered letters to the Forest Service renewing their request for access to government files relevant to the minister's decision. The letters were ignored. The court case also generated the first significant provincial press coverage of the controversy.

Events were quickly overtaking the court case and the TFL renewal. A provincial election had been called. And, after four years of study, the final report of the Environment and Land Use Committee Secretariat, the one promised by Premier Barrett and the former government, was released immediately after the court case. For all the time taken in preparation, the Islands Protection Society found it riddled with inaccuracies. But more disturbing was the final recommendation that the government set up yet another study team to examine "multiple use" options for logging the wilderness proposal area. Of course, logging of Lyell Island would continue as the options were studied.

With less than two weeks until the deadline for renewal of Rayonier's licence, the petitioners reluctantly decided to return to court, or at least their lawyer pleaded reluctance. For Guujaaw and Paul, this was the chance of a lifetime to force the Forest Service to open its files. Citing the unanswered requests for information and the court's finding that the minister had a duty to act fairly, they petitioned the court on April 19 for an order that the minister release the information. Their hearing date was set for April 30.

On April 26, just as the provincial election campaign moved into high gear, their lawyer was contacted by the government counsel. The Forest Service, he claimed, had simply forgotten to answer their letters. Paul and

Guujaaw were invited to Victoria to meet with the Forest Service. Although they wanted no part in negotiating terms for the licence renewal, they took advantage of the opportunity. They were met by a phalanx of two government lawyers, two deputy ministers, and a dozen other forestry officials. The government asked them to drop the second petition to avoid embarrassing a government two weeks away from an election. Paul and Guujaaw countered with detailed amendments to the TFL renewal, and intense negotiations began. During the course of the next few days, several small but significant changes were negotiated to the TFL renewal. The most significant part of their meeting, however, was the admission by government representatives that TFL holders were no longer required to practise sustained-yield management.

When the hearing date arrived, the deputy minister of forests, Mike Apsey, swore out an affidavit that the minister had acted fairly, had consulted and had even made changes based on input from the petitioners. The petition was dismissed. The next day, Tom Waterland renewed Rayonier's tree farm licence for a twenty-five-year term. The new licence did not contain any of the negotiated amendments. They applied to the Supreme Court without success. The court held that it was a provincial matter over which it had no competence.

Back on Haida Gwaii, the Public Advisory Committee was paying for its support of the court action. Biickert, the Forest Service district manager, made it clear to the PAC chairman that the minister wanted to disband the committee. The only way to prove that the committee reflected legitimate public concern would be if the Southern Moresby Wilderness Proposal was voted down. Bit by bit, over the summer and into the fall, the industry began to pack the advisory committee meetings. By September 1979, the pro-logging forces were a majority. Led by Frank Beban, the pro-forestry group put forward a resolution that the PAC would support any and all decisions made by the Forest Service. It passed narrowly, amid cheers and shouts of derision. With a taste for irony, Paul George took the floor and moved that since everybody was now happy with the Forest Service, there was no need for further public input and therefore, boomed Paul, "I move that the Queen Charlotte Islands Public Advisory Committee be disbanded!" Guujaaw seconded the motion and, before the pro-logging forces realized what was happening, it was passed. Skidegate Chief Tom Greene would later comment, "After twenty years as an Indian politician, my experience is that once the public is consulted by bureaucrats, the decision has already been made."

Public advice to the Forest Service had come to an end. But a new species of public consultation study group, the South Moresby Resource Planning Team, was just beginning.

OF MATHEMATICS AND MURRELETS

PUBLICITY OVER THE COURT ACTIONS HAD SENT THE message far and wide that the pristine forests of southern Moresby were endangered. Conservation groups from around the country began to endorse the Island Protection Society's wilderness proposal and to support its efforts. There were invitations to give slide shows and to speak at meetings in Victoria and Vancouver. International attention was beginning to focus on the islands. The UNESCO nomination of Ninstints as a World Heritage Site was the first sign. And then the Pacific Seabird Group, representing biologists from thirty-nine countries, unanimously urged that the area be protected. Through its own efforts, aided by federal government grants, IPS had hired biologists to conduct wildlife surveys, proving that over a quarter of all the nesting sea birds on the British Columbia coast nested within the wilderness proposal area, including almost half of the endangered Peale's peregrine falcon population. They knew that the largest rookeries for sea-lions in the Canadian Pacific were found along the rocky outcroppings of the southern archipelago. And they confirmed that the area boasted one of the highest densities of nesting bald eagles in North America.

When Huck and Guujaaw had drawn the line, they knew instinctively that the area was special. Now, they could prove it by objective scientific standards. They were being taken seriously by federal members of Parliament, including their own MP Iona Campagnolo, by international scientific bodies, and by the national media. And while they were still ignored by the recently re-elected government of Bill Bennett, the Islands Protection Society began to take itself more seriously, as well.

A more strategic approach was required. For some time, Paul had been arguing with the IPS founders that merely wanting to stop all logging was not enough. They needed to promote an alternative. Paul was impatient with Huck, Guujaaw, and other IPS supporters who were unwilling to adopt the idea of national park status for the area.

The study by Parks Canada that led to the nomination of Ninstints for World Heritage Site designation had indicated the potential of the whole southern Moresby area for national park status. With that sort of appraisal, Paul argued that pushing for a national park would be the best alternative for the area. Besides, the economic value of tourism could help offset the losses to the local economy from an end to the logging. Huck and Guujaaw objected to any alternative that would compromise Haida interests in the land. A movement for political union of the Haida was growing, as was the support for Haida land rights to all of the islands. Law professor Murray Rankin gave Paul a copy of the National Parks Act and pointed out that the act allowed for national park reserves, specifically to avoid compromising native land claims. Paul in turn argued the point with J.B. and Huck. Their opposition softened. Gradually, without ever admitting that park status was their goal, the Islands Protection Society at least ceased to argue against a park. The Haida simply maintained their position that the logging must be stopped, the lands must remain intact.

Meanwhile, Paul and Richard Krieger were learning the value of public relations. They had produced a black and white poster of one of Richard's photographs. It was of one of the giant trees from the forest along Windy Bay creek. Using the current tourism slogan of the B.C. government, "Super, Natural British Columbia," the poster was captioned "Supernatural Windy Bay – Let it be." Rather than continue with the unwieldy name Southern Moresby Wilderness Proposal, the poster referred simply to South Moresby.

In June 1979, the South Moresby Planning Team was set up by the provincial government to represent all the key groups with interests in the South Moresby issue. Its members represented the Skidegate Band Council, the Islands Protection Society, Rayonier, the Queen Charlotte Islands Museum Society, the Forest Service, the Ministry of the Environment, the Ministry of Mines, the Ecological Reserves Unit, the federal Department of Fisheries, and the public. The team's mandate was impressive. It was "a decision-making team, with substantial authority delegated from the Forest Service and other agencies." But as IPS representatives were quick to point out, the terms of reference for the team precluded a recommendation for the preservation of the entire wilderness proposal.

For the entire life span of the planning team a debate raged among the members of the Islands Protection Society. Should they participate in a farce and thereby lend it credibility, or should they boycott the entire charade and risk losing the opportunity to influence the process? The first of the IPS representatives were Dan Bowditch and Paul George. Guujaaw and Wanagan participated throughout as the Haida delegates. Rayonier was represented by its local forester, Bill Dumont. Public input was provided by Mary Morris, a tour operator, and by Jack Miller, a local scaler working for the timber companies. Jack Miller was, despite his profession, or maybe because of it, critical of forest company policies. He worked for years with IPS to try to bring accountability to forestry practices in the Charlottes. And he paid for his dedication by being blacklisted from hiring by the big companies. The team was chaired, after an initial scuffle in which a Forest Service representative was ousted from the chair, by the local museum curator, Nick Gessler.

During his year on the planning team, Paul George grew increasingly frustrated. When a planning team member representing the B.C.-Yukon Chamber of Mines staked a claim on Windy Bay the day before the team was to deliberate Windy Bay's future, Paul exploded to J.B., "This entire planning process is nothing but a machiavellian technique designed to divert our attention from the real issues!" He resigned, moved to Vancouver, and started the Western Canada Wilderness Committee, or WC Squared as it is known to its friends. He left Haida Gwaii but he remained an integral part of the fight to save it.

Huck took Paul's place as representative for IPS, but he did not last nearly as long. It came to the attention of the planning team that Frank Beban was logging in an area on the east side of Lyell Island called Gogit Passage without benefit of a cutting permit from the minister of forests. Trespass logging. Huck was incensed. He phoned the Forest Service and informed them of this gross violation of the Forest Act. He was reassured by the Forest Service representative: "There's no need to be concerned. The district manager had verbally approved the cutting, and has just back-dated the permit to when the logging started."

Huck exploded to J.B., "This whole process is a farce!" "Yes," said J.B. "But you knew that." Sitting in the background at planning team meetings, listening to the mathematical arguments, the computer jargon and pseudo-professional gamesmanship, J.B. had become interested in the games that were being played. He thought he might be quite good at them. Over the objections of nearly everyone associated with IPS, who wanted to boycott the planning team, J.B. joined the team as the IPS representative. He was right. He was good at these games.

There was another important change in the players at the table. While Bill Dumont remained a fixture, his corporate affiliation changed. In the fall of 1980, Western Forest Products, an amalgamation of three existing B.C. firms, B.C. Forest Products, Doman Industries, and Whonnock Industries, purchased Rayonier's assets – and "bought" Rayonier's timber rights for one dollar.

Between 1980 and 1981 there was a slump in the fortunes of the forest industry. In an effort to help the industry maintain profitability, disguised as concern for jobs, the British Columbia Forest Service adopted a new principle. In true Orwellian form, it was called "sympathetic administration." It meant that the forest industry would no longer be held to the "rigorous" standards imposed on it during the times that Riley Creek and Talunkwan were logged. Part of sympathetic administration were the new buzzwords "relaxed utilization of the over-mature," which allowed levels of waste in clear-cutting that violated Forest Service regulations. The theory was that someday, when times got better, the forest companies would come back and retrieve the timber they had left to rot. Utilization became extremely relaxed, and the administration was very sympathetic.

Meanwhile, in the planning team meetings, J.B. was studying the rationalizations for over-cutting. He was quite a contrast to Paul and Huck. He wasn't pugnacious or difficult. He smiled when Bill Dumont said, "Boy! Wish you'd been here from the beginning. At last we've got someone reasonable." J.B. did not mind taking his time. He viewed the team meetings as an opportunity to get a good look at industry's foundation, while deciding which stones to pull out.

Western Forest Products' calculation of the value of the timber resource provided J.B.'s first lesson in the mathematical intricacies of inflating the value of trees. The company claimed the estimated end-product value of timber from the South Moresby area to be almost $31.4 million per year and pegged the employment value at between $200 and $300 million. It took J.B. a while, but he finally thought he had figured out how it had wangled the figures. He was euphoric as he explained to Huck how the game was played by WFP's managers. First, they measured the volume of scaled logs sitting in the water within a boom. Then they divided the total payroll by the base hourly wage rate to get a number for how many man-hours it took to get the logs there. From that they developed a ratio of how many man-hours went into each cubic metre of product, which they applied to the original volume of logs they had cut back on the hillsides. But, by excluding all the wood left behind through relaxed utilization, and ignoring all the overtime pay in the payroll, they wildly exaggerated the amount of labour for logs they actually removed from the site.

Once they had established the man-hours-to-product ratio, they multiplied it by how many man-hours were currently employed. To inflate the end figure, they used the monthly payroll, including those paid wages considerably in excess of the basic wage rate in the forests. Loggers with seniority, or those being paid overtime, might earn up to three hundred dollars a day. But the WFP calculation divided the basic wage rate of $14 an hour into the entire monthly payroll.

From that small sample of wood, excluding waste, compounded with an artificially skewed number of man-hours, they produced a productivity index. The productivity index was then multiplied out over thirty years of their annual allowable cut. And somehow, Bill Dumont could say with a straight face that the labour value of South Moresby was $200 million, not counting spin-offs and indirect employment. J.B. stopped for breath. Huck was reeling. "How do they think they can get away with that?" Huck asked. And J.B. said smiling, "Because they always do. That's how it's done."

In planning team meetings, J.B. would take out his calculator as he followed along with Bill Dumont's presentation, and the Forest Service computer program. It was called the Multiple Use Sustained Yield Calculator, but they just called it "music." Every now and then, J.B. would look up from his scribblings and quietly interject. Just like the time he said, "Mr Chairman, by my calculations, based on the mathematical model before us, it will take seven hundred men twenty years to log Windy Bay." And Gessler, barely containing his laughter, would repeat the calculation and agree. Dumont or his assistant, Ron Bronstein, would protest, "These calculations were done by qualified economists using accepted economic analytical techniques." At which point, no one, other than the WFP reps, could refrain from laughing out loud.

Guujaaw, who served on the planning team for its entire duration, exercised his scrutiny over details like boundaries and road building plans. He focussed on semantics and subtle issues, like why logging areas were coloured green on planning team maps, while wilderness was coloured red.

The process was becoming bearable. Guujaaw didn't mind going out for an occasional beer with the WFP boys. And Dumont seemed to almost enjoy his company, when after drinking and laughing and arguing into the night, they gave up, realizing the impossibility of either one convincing the other. On one field trip the rest of the group left in search of the rare Peale's peregrine falcon as Guujaaw and Dumont lay hungover on the beach at Hot Springs. With expert ornithologists at the lead, the study team saw only murrelets, failing to catch even a glimpse of the elusive falcon. Meanwhile, Guujaaw and Dumont were awakened by the piercing screech of a rare falcon overhead. Dumont cursed it from within his sleeping bag. But the timber companies were getting impatient with all the talk about rare birds, and especially those little ancient murrelets, which had, thanks to the Ecological Reserve Unit, stymied logging in Windy Bay. MacMillan Bloedel held a square-mile timber licence for Dodge Point, adjacent to Windy Bay, and home to record-setting murrelet populations. In exasperation, one of their executives asked, "How much is a damn murrelet worth anyway? We'll buy them!"

Now that J.B. had figured out from the forest company how to calculate the value of anything, he decided to try to answer their question.

At first blush, it would seem an impossible task. The ancient murrelet is not easily converted to mathematical rendering. J.B.'s first move was to recruit Huck to work on the calculations with him. It was the birth of their consulting business, Broadhead, Henley & Associates. It never made either of them rich, but it did open up new lines of endeavour.

They decided to mimic as closely as possible the approach of Western Forest Products in its calculations. In order to perform an assessment of the economic value of the ancient murrelet colony at Dodge Point, they took a typical pair of murrelets. To maintain the parallel with industrial accounting, they optimized the birds' productivity by eliminating the effects of predators and they converted the murrelet population into a commercial farming operation. They would create an industrial murrelet farm.

They were sure of high levels of productivity of murrelets, but there was no immediate market for them. Perhaps murrelet pot pies would catch on, they mused. But the obvious choice, heading to where the real money lay, was in using murrelets as food for rare falcons. Saudi Arabian sheiks would pay up to $20,000 for a single falcon. So the commercial murrelet breeding fantasy was expanded to raise falcons for export. Allowing for the value and demand for murrelets and falcons to rise exponentially with their populations over the forest industry's rotation period of eighty years, to allow for a level playing field with the competing timber industry, J.B. and Huck concluded that the value of the ancient murrelet colony to the economy of British Columbia was $3.2 billion.

"Sorry," J.B. told the forest company representatives, "but you can't afford to buy the ancient murrelets."

WFP's Ron Bronstein was incensed. Dramatically throwing his pencil down, rolling his eyes, he said, "Mr Chairman, let's get serious or what!"

"Exactly my point, Mr Chairman," said J.B. To which the chair observed that the economic calculations of murrelets and timber all seemed to bear a direct correlation to the value of rubber in Malaysia.

But for all the fun and games of the planning team process, J.B. was learning some important things and was becoming more and more obsessed with saving South Moresby and bringing some semblance of accountability to forestry. He frequently travelled to Victoria in this period to lobby politicians, meet reporters, do research, and show slides.

One day, flying back to Haida Gwaii, he looked out the plane window. It was a clear day, and he could see the three little villages below, Sandspit, Queen Charlotte City, and Skidegate. And in a moment of broadened perception, he knew that no decision would be made in this place. "The impetus is here," he thought. "But the decisions will be made in Victoria and Ottawa." J.B. realized that he must move to Victoria and carry on the fight from there.

THE NATURE OF THINGS

IT WAS AN ODD TIME TO DECIDE TO MOVE. J.B. HAD AL-most finished building a house on the shore of North Beach, outside Massett. But the decision he had made on the plane – that he needed to be near the people, re-sources, photographers, politicians, and reporters whose influence could save the islands – made more sense to him by the minute.

Before he left, he persuaded Huckleberry to move to Victoria, as well. The two of them had a clear vision of what needed to be done in order to save South Moresby. They wanted to introduce as many Canadians as possi-ble to the splendours of the area – to acquaint millions of people with the breathtaking vistas, the miraculous intertidal worlds, the breaching whales, and the fallen totem poles of the wilderness proposal. He wanted the most beautiful colour images of Haida Gwaii and the most evocative text possible to grace the coffee tables of influential Canadians from Victoria to Halifax. It was not the same book that Paul and the Galapagos Group had had in mind. But it was to be a book – Broadhead, Henley & Associates' finest endeavour.

The Galapagos Book Collaborators passed over the project to J.B. and Huck at the Kettle of Fish restaurant in Vancouver. Paul George felt the personal sacrifice of treating the group to dinner was well worth it when one of his guests, Bill Reid, agreed to write a chapter for the book. J.B. and Huck also had the generous support of many photographers who offered their work free of charge.

In 1982, J.B.'s wife, Maureen, moved down to Vancouver Island to find a house for Islands Protection, Victoria branch. J.B. left his nearly perfect little house by the beach, packed his art supplies and print-maker and his elderly cat, and headed for Victoria. Huck followed. Both of them made fairly regular trips back to Haida Gwaii. J.B. continued with the Planning Team, which was to meet for another two years. Huck returned to work with Rediscovery as well as to maintain a hand in IPS affairs. But the reins of IPS itself were handed over to those who remained on the islands – environmentalist-logger Jack Miller, another American expatriate and dogged IPS volunteer, Tom Schneider, and a recently immigrated medical doctor from France, Josette Weir.

The level of islands-based activism continued unabated after the departure of two of its key protagonists. Guujaaw was becoming more and more involved in Haida politics, and Haida politics was becoming more involved in wilderness preservation. In 1981, the Haida formally registered the hereditary boundaries of Haida Gwaii with the United Nations, objecting to the Law of the Sea Convention, which allowed Canada a 200-mile jurisdiction that conflicted with Haida territories. A copy of their objection was sent to Canada. The Haida refused to accept that anything about their assertion of title was a "claim" ("It is Canada which claims Haida land," said Guujaaw.), but the federal government always referred to the boundaries of First Nations as "land claims." The Haida based theirs not only on their ancestral occupation, but also on a moral responsibility to protect their lands from the abuse condoned and practised by the government and by lease-holding companies.

Huck and J.B. were by now the closest of friends. Together they had survived the rigours of keeping IPS afloat, of policy disagreements over the planning team, and of launching the first private funding for Rediscovery. When they applied for foundation funding for Rediscovery, they realized that they brought out the Madison Avenue in each other. J.B. made an imitation bent-cedar box with a Haida design on top as the envelope for their proposal. They got the funding. Now they set about the task of interesting a publisher in the South Moresby book project. They decided on Vancouver-based Douglas & McIntyre, a strong regional publishing house able to distribute the book across the country. They prepared a proposal, complete with stunning photos, and placed it in an envelope made as a black and red Haida button blanket. Right down to its abalone shell fastenings, it was a small masterpiece. They asked for permission to show their slides to the publishers. Permission was granted, and in new suits and sporting new haircuts, Huck and J.B. found themselves before the editorial board of Douglas & McIntyre. They showed their best slides to the board, talked their best line, and walked out of the room with a contract.

J.B. and Huck were not the only ones who wanted to get South Moresby into the living rooms of the nation. The new member of Parliament for Skeena, elected in 1979, wanted to get the South Moresby battle on television. Jim Fulton, the same Jim Fulton who had given Rediscovery its first boost, had moved from probation officer for Port Clements to the New Democratic caucus of the House of Commons. Saving South Moresby was not just one of the things he wanted to accomplish in Ottawa. It was the thing he most wanted to accomplish. Despite the strong economic clout of the logging industry in his riding, he was prepared to take on the forest companies.

Now that he was in Parliament, Jim Fulton saw his job as helping the less fortunate, pursuing social justice for minority groups, especially for the native people who made up a third of his riding's population, and protecting the environment. The loftiness of these goals was tempered by an irrepressible sense of humour and an endearing reluctance to take himself or anything else about Ottawa too seriously. In 1980, he introduced a private members bill, parallel to one being introduced in the B.C. legislature by MLA Graham Lea, to facilitate the creation of a national park for South Moresby, but like nearly all such bills, it died on the order paper. The federal Liberal government had little interest in the environment. As critic for Forestry and the Environment, Jim became friends with his Tory counterpart, the Progressive Conservative environment critic. Tory and NDP members are supposed to mix like oil and water, but to Jim's delight, this guy, a nice young fellow from Prince Edward Island, seemed to be a real environmentalist. Tom McMillan and Jim Fulton would get together for beers and share their grievances about the lack of government action. And Jim found himself asking McMillan more than once if he was really sure that he was a Tory.

Fulton maintained close contact with the Haida, and Paul George kept him up to date on the wilderness wars of British Columbia. The Western Canada Wilderness Committee had completed a four-month-long survey of the attitude of federal members to conservation. Paul was thrilled to report that of those who responded, most members of all parties said they wanted to protect South Moresby, including former prime minister Joe Clark and a lot of Liberal back-benchers, if not cabinet members. Neither Jim nor Paul was surprised by the strong support Paul discovered from the member for Vancouver South, John Fraser. Fraser had been minister of environment briefly during the nine-month reign of the Clark government in 1979, making his mark in identifying acid rain as an urgent priority. But his environmental bent had been known long before that. Fraser offered Paul George his support.

Despite the potential of all-party support for the wilderness proposal, Fulton was frustrated by the handicap of being on the Opposition benches of the House of Commons. In 1982 he phoned his friend Dr David Suzuki, host of the CBC show The Nature of Things. "Suzook!" Jim bellowed. "You've just gotta do a show on South Moresby." David Suzuki didn't like being told that he'd "gotta" do anything. But Jim was very persuasive and David asked his researchers and producers to take a look at this South Moresby thing. Nancy Archibald, the producer, had already received a call about South Moresby. Bristol Foster, nearing the end of his rope, attending planning team meetings while Lyell Island was shaved of its trees, had phoned Nancy, "How about doing a show on Windy Bay?" Nancy and Jim Murray, David's CBC boss and best friend, had a look and decided there was at least a half-hour's worth of television in the controversy.

When David Suzuki headed out to the Charlottes, he was just doing another in a series of television programs aimed at increasing the public's awareness of science. A brilliant geneticist, he was the perfect choice for a broadcast medium. He spoke in non-perplexing language, and was able to decode the jargon of each discipline into everyday language. He was good-looking and hip, bearded and blue-denimed. His presence on television was both familiar and authoritative. Jim Fulton was right to believe that if David Suzuki told Canadians about South Moresby, Canadians would listen.

The David Suzuki who flew into the Queen Charlotte Islands had no intention of getting involved in the campaign to save South Moresby. He had never been a champion of Indian rights and he was leery of environmental activists who seemed constantly to demand his help. The interviews arranged by Nancy and Jim included a representative of Western Forest Products, a Haida Indian, an environmentalist, and a couple of bureaucrats involved in the planning team. It wasn't until he was back in Toronto, reviewing footage for editing, that he realized that his way of thinking had been profoundly affected.

The interview that caused the change was with Guujaaw. Guujaaw was now nearly thirty. Bearded, with his long hair pulled back and braided, he looked tough. Suzuki had probed Guujaaw to try to understand why the Haida cared about the area. David had thought that the reasons were tied to the historic connection, the fact of ancestral occupation. And those were the answers he thought he had taped, until back in Toronto in the studio, watching it for perhaps the third time, he heard what Guujaaw had been saying: "Our people have determined that Windy Bay and other areas must be left in their natural condition so that we can keep our identity and pass it on to following generations. The forests, those oceans are what keep us as Haida people today." David had interjected with the open-ended half-question, "So if they're logged off?" And Guujaaw answered, "If they're logged off, we'll probably end up the same as everyone else, I guess." David hit the rewind button and played that last bit again, "If they're logged off, *we'll probably end up the same as everyone else.*"

The trip to Haida Gwaii converted David Suzuki into one of South Moresby's most fervent supporters, and it also made him think differently about the relationship of human beings to nature. He learned from Guujaaw that wilderness was more than an environmental concern. It was a question of identity. The giant western red cedar tree was not just something used by the Haida; it defined the Haida. This first important contact with the continent's indigenous people would take David and his wife, Tara, deeply into the lives of Northwest Coast Indians, and eventually to become advocates for indigenous people world-wide.

THE RED NECK NEWS

THE SUPPORTERS OF SOUTH MORESBY REJOICED WHEN they saw David's program, but the pro-logging forces in Sandspit were anything but pleased. The Nature of Things and its rhapsodic prose about the forests they earned a living from logging made their blood boil. The footage of the world's biggest black bear caused them to agitate as if the world had been subject to a giant hoax. "That bastard Suzuki took the film of that bear right in back of Frank's place in Sandspit. They never saw a bear south of here." And as for the much-vaunted "spiritual kinship" between the Haida and the wilderness, Frank Beban and the boys at the bar jeered. They had worked with Haida loggers and had never noticed anything particularly "spiritual" in the way they felled a tree.

Frank Beban's crews had been steadily logging on Lyell Island since the approval of the cutting permit in 1975. Gate Creek had been almost totally clear-cut, as had the northern slopes of the island. Lyell, the largest of the islands within the South Moresby area, had a significant economic value to Western Forest Products. And once the existing cutting permits, based on WFP's 1978 five-year harvesting plan, were exhausted, Frank and WFP expected to move into the Windy Bay area.

In planning team meetings, Bill Dumont was making a case for what the industry called Option B. This would allow logging of the entire upper watershed of Windy Bay, or approximately 70 per cent of the proposed ecological reserve. Industry argued that protecting the big trees at the base of the watershed, near the mouth of the creek, was enough. Environmentalists countered that, by logging the upper watershed, the integrity of the eco-system would be destroyed. The creek would be unfit as salmon habitat. The winds, which were strong enough to give the bay its name, would increase and result in blow-downs at the periphery, soil stability would be compromised, and erosion would increase.

Frank Beban was not particularly adept at public relations. But he did think something had to be done to stir up troops to fight the environmentalist threat. And for that job he recruited a very strange bird named R.L. Smith.

In 1982, Smith had been involved in a controversy over whether or not the B.C. Ferry service would be extended to the Charlottes, replacing the barge from Prince Rupert. Islands Protection wanted to have public involvement in the decision, and this was interpreted by Smith as another case of environmentalists being against everything. He decided to take them on in the self-proclaimed *Red Neck News*. It was to be only a short-term adventure, something to give Sandspit residents more of a voice in the ferry dispute. But Frank Beban saw in the *Red Neck News* the vehicle to mobilize the logging community and, with any luck, to intimidate any South Moresby supporters within Sandspit itself. Beban approached Smith to ask him to continue publication of the mimeo-sheet with the anonymous financial support of Beban Logging.

Smith was glad to help. He enjoyed baiting South Moresby supporters, attacking them as "draft-dodgers, hippies, dope-smokers, and dizzy flakes who don't care about our jobs." He accused them of having exploited the issue for their own financial gain, charging that they drew big fat salaries while trying to put decent guys out of work. Smith promised his readers that "you can expect me to do whatever has to be done. I will threaten, intimidate, browbeat, cajole and suck. It's quite true that my nose will grow to tremendous proportions over South Moresby." Still, he warned, "Don't believe what you read in the *Red Neck News*. It's just entertainment."

The *Red Neck News* gained an eager audience on the Charlottes, and also on the mainland. Readers delighted in the artless cartoons, such as the one showing environmentalists with "Save South Moresby" signs kicking a blind man and robbing from his tin cup. Every issue carried letters from the paper's fans who reported how pleased they were finally to read the truth about all this environmental stuff. Letters of support came in from Socred politicians, from Progressive Conservative MPs, and from resource industry representatives from around the country.

Huck and J.B. were miles away, establishing themselves in Victoria. J.B. made something of a living through his art, painting watercolours for record album covers. But most of their time was devoted to the all-consuming issue. They made frequent trips to Vancouver to see their publishers, to visit Guujaaw, who was working under Bill Reid's guidance on a major carving for the University of B.C. Museum of Anthropology, *Raven Discovering Mankind in a Clamshell,* and to visit the headquarters of Western Canada Wilderness Committee in Paul George's apartment, now a Mecca for activists from around the province. The champion of the campaign to save the Valhalla Mountains in the Kootenays from logging, a young firebrand named Colleen McCrory, stayed there whenever she was in Vancouver. And like all the wilderness workers who used Paul's apartment as an office-cum-hostel, Colleen took an interest in other issues, such as South Moresby, while in the midst of her own crusade.

J.B. and Huck had but a single focus. Shortly after moving to Victoria they heard about a woman who was making a film on Ninstints. Vicky Husband had been to

Haida Gwaii several times, filming, seeking the assistance of the Skidegate Band Council and its young band manager, Miles Richardson. The challenge of making a half-hour movie about a dozen deteriorating poles did not daunt her. Vicky Husband was a woman possessed of an indomitable spirit, relentless drive, and an intrepid heart.

As J.B. and Huck worked on their book, Vicky offered advice and editorial comment. More than anyone else who had come along in the cause of South Moresby, Vicky was to provide something indispensable to Huck and J.B.'s work. She had what they lacked, a tenacity that insisted there be no slacking off, no opportunity wasted. It was not that J.B. and Huck were lazy. But they had been at the business of saving South Moresby for years, and sometimes they needed a strong reminder, like a mother calling over the noise of the television, "Have you done your homework?"

In Victoria, J.B., Huck, and Vicky became the core of a network that encompassed the IPS volunteers on the Charlottes, the Vancouver activists, and supporters across the province. J.B. and Huck missed no one in their search for supporters. If they were refused a meeting with a minister, they'd explain the whole wilderness proposal to his secretary. Soon the secretaries of the parliament buildings made sure J.B. and Huck knew how many letters for and against the wilderness proposal were arriving, and they always had a cup of coffee for the good-looking duo who haunted the halls.

Once, when the two of them were on their way to meet with the environment minister, Stephen Rogers, they stopped in to see their MLA, Graham Lea, the former highways minister who had sneered at their petitions eight years before. Cocky as ever, he started to lecture them on the futility of lobbying Socred ministers. "You guys are wasting your time on this government. The sooner we get rid of them and get back in the

NDP, the better." Warming to his subject, he began to explain reality to J.B. and Huck, "You see boys, there's two kinds of people in this world –" J.B. interrupted with a remark that summed up the attitude of the South Moresby advocates. "Yes, Graham, those that think there are two kinds of people, and those who know better."

COLLEEN

COLLEEN MCCRORY COULD NOT QUITE BELIEVE THAT ALL the things that had happened could really have happened. She looked out the window of the big Air Canada jet, flying back to British Columbia from her first-ever trip to the Maritimes in February 1984. After twelve years of work, eight of which had totally consumed her, the Valhalla Mountain range was finally protected as a Class A Provincial Park. It was almost too good to be true. And, even more incredible, she thought, were the accolades that had just been heaped upon her in Prince Edward Island, where she had been given the Governor General's Conservation Award. Now and then she was tempted to pinch herself.

Colleen had never been to the Queen Charlotte Islands. In fact, she lived over a thousand miles from them. But she had, nevertheless, fallen in love with South Moresby. She had seen the slide show the IPS had toured across the province and had kept up with the issue through Paul George and the fairly regular irregular mailings from WC Squared. She even had some of the materials with her, colour pictures of the park proposal – for by inches, Paul George had finally succeeded in convincing the South Moresby movement to pursue national park status.

Colleen's flight included a stopover in Ottawa. It suddenly seemed clear to her that the reason for her award and her trip was to put her in a position to lobby for

South Moresby. She determined to get an appointment with the federal minister of the environment, and talk him into saving South Moresby.

Arriving in Ottawa, Colleen headed straight for Parliament Hill. It was her first time in Canada's capital, but she allowed no time for sightseeing. Carrying her suitcases, she made her way to Jim Fulton's office. She didn't know him well, but announced that she had come to meet the environment minister and persuade him to save South Moresby.

Charles Caccia, Liberal member for the Toronto riding of Davenport, had been made environment minister in August 1983. Environmentalists across the country could hardly believe it. Prime Minister Trudeau had finally appointed someone who actually cared about the subject. The previous Liberal environment ministers just did time until the next promotion came along, but Charles Caccia was a committed, die-hard, passionate environmental advocate.

Born in Milan, Italy, Caccia had studied forestry at the University of Vienna. Studying forestry in Canada is not likely to lead to environmentalism as Canadian forestry schools tend to concentrate on how to maximize economic efficiency in producing the species desired by the industry. Foresters like to say that modern silviculture is just like agriculture: You plant a crop, spray it, harvest it. The fact that this approach results in monocultures of even-aged trees, vulnerable to insects and disease, with a simplified eco-system that drastically reduces species diversity, is not an important consideration. But studying forestry in Europe is a different matter. The saying goes that in North America, foresters think in decades; in Europe, foresters think in centuries. Of course, both time frames out-distance politicians, who think in four-year mandates, gearing their life's work to the next election.

The ability to think in centuries made Charles Caccia, in the Canadian context, an unusual forester. It made him an even more unusual politician. Colleen was sure that if she could talk to him, she could interest him in South Moresby. The problem was getting to see him. At the end of the day, she had made no progress. She had missed her plane to British Columbia, and had nowhere to stay. But she was determined to remain in Ottawa until she saw Caccia. The only person she knew in Ottawa was the member for her riding. She had helped canvas for Lyle Kristiansen, New Democratic candidate for Parliament, so she phoned to ask if she could stay with him. There was no answer. In desperation, she persuaded one of the security guards in the Confederation Building, where she had been using Fulton's office, to drive her to Kristiansen's home somewhere in the suburbs of Ottawa. When her MP returned home, he found one of his constituents asleep on the couch, let in by his children.

The next day, Colleen was back at Fulton's office trying by phone to talk her way into a meeting with Charles Caccia. By afternoon, she had nearly given up. Jim Fulton offered to take the direct approach. During Question Period, he passed Caccia a note asking if he would meet with a B.C. environmentalist concerning South Moresby.

Late that night Colleen met with a very tired minister of the environment in his office at Centre Block. Colleen put it to Caccia that saving South Moresby was simply the most important wilderness battle in Canada. She showed him pictures and told him about the unique endemic plants and animals, the eagles' nesting densities, the eleven species of whales, the thousand-year-old trees.

When she paused for breath, Caccia asked, "How much will a park cost?" Colleen didn't really know. She had not been involved with South Moresby long enough or in sufficient detail to be able to do other than take a wild guess. Which is what she did. Calculating fast, trying to come up with a reasonable figure to compensate Western Forest Products, she hardly missed a beat before answering, "Twenty million dollars."

She was thunderstruck when Caccia said, "Then we should be able to do this. By tomorrow morning can you get me a detailed map of the proposed national park area and a breakdown on the cost of establishing the park?" Colleen had no map, no cost breakdown, so she said, "Yes. Of course."

That night she phoned John Broadhead. He told her to contact John Carruthers, the Parks Service planner who had written the original Parks Canada appraisal of South Moresby's potential. He also filled Colleen in on the final report of the South Moresby Resource Planning Team. It had recently been released and was a disappointing document for nearly everyone. For one thing, it read like washing-machine instructions. Only four options were presented for consideration by the provincial cabinet, from Option 1, which would permit logging and mining over almost the entire area, with small enclaves of "core recreation areas," to Option 4, which proposed the largest area of preservation, but would allow continued logging on Lyell Island of everything but Windy Bay. The report provided a frame of reference for federal government action.

Colleen was most nervous about her next question. "John, I told Caccia it would cost about twenty million. Is that okay?" "Yeah," J.B. responded, "that's pretty close to what we've calculated, depending on how much of the area is national and how much is provincial park. That should just about cover it."

Colleen heaved a sigh of relief as she hung up and redialled to reach Carruthers. He agreed to meet her at

Caccia's office in the morning with maps and further briefing notes.

The effort to engage the federal government in the creation of a national park at South Moresby began with Colleen's Ottawa visit. A flurry of correspondence followed. Colleen sent further refinements of compensation estimates to Caccia's office. J.B. prepared the first detailed analysis of the value of tree farm licences, timber licences, and unamortized facilities, which might form the basis of cash compensation to the major forestry companies. The estimates remained in the $20 to $23 million range.

By the middle of March 1984, Caccia's office and Parks bureaucrats had made their first move in what would resemble a three-year chess match – a test of nerves and negotiating gambits between Ottawa and Victoria. Federal interest in a national park in South Moresby was signalled through a letter to Tony Brummet, B.C.'s minister of lands, parks, and housing. Caccia's letter focussed on the recently released report of the South Moresby Resource Planning Team. Not surprisingly, Caccia recommended that the provincial government pursue maximum preservation through Option 4. The federal proposal consisted of a mixed pattern of provincial and national park throughout the wilderness proposal. A map attached to Caccia's letter sketched out a national terrestrial park, as well as a national marine park encompassing the southernmost part of the area. The national park would comprise most of the small islands and waters in Juan Perez Sound, including Burnaby Island and areas of Moresby itself, north of Burnaby. The federal government proposed provincial park, Class A status for the rest: Lyell, Tanu, Richardson, and a large chunk of Moresby. Caccia wrote, "The heritage values of the South Moresby area are of both national and international significance, and

should therefore be protected for all time." The letter to
Brummet was a private communication, but Caccia's
closing line warned that the province could ignore the
federal offer only at its peril: "I would like to make my
proposal known within a couple of weeks if you have no
objection or other advice."

In late May, Caccia's office issued a press release,
"Protection Proposed for South Moresby Area." By making his letter to Brummet public, Charles Caccia turned
up the heat on the provincial government while increasing the credibility of the activists who had been fighting
for the previous ten years to save the area. Negotiations
began between the two levels of government – if only
half-heartedly. Tony Brummet remarked that Caccia's
offer "only complicates the decision." Brummet and the
Environment and Land Use Committee ministers had
been planning to visit the wilderness area prior to making any decision on the planning team's four options.
The trip was postponed, as was the cabinet's decision on
South Moresby. As a federal election was likely before
the fall, the provincial government probably recognized
that the chances of its having to deal with Caccia after
the election were slim.

Colleen McCrory realized the same thing. Charles
Caccia was too good to last. After nearly sixteen years of
Liberal government, Trudeau had allowed an environmentalist to be minister of the environment only for less
than a year. But if the players were going to change,
Colleen was going to be ready. As Colleen saw it, the
nailing down of national political parties was straightforward; it was all a matter of whom you knew. The ques-
tionnaire Paul George had conducted a few years before
made it clear several Tories would support South
Moresby, including former prime minister Joe Clark.
But the most sympathetic Tory was John Fraser. Colleen
phoned Tom Schneider and Jack Miller in the
Charlottes and counselled them to get Fraser's commit-

ment before the election call that the Tories would be on-side.

Fraser didn't need any persuading. He set up meetings in Ottawa during the month of May for Jack and Tom with the current Tory environment critic, Dr Gary Gurbin, and started his own arm-twisting within the party. On June 29, 1984, two letters were sent by Gary Gurbin, one to Tom at IPS, the other to the provincial government of Bill Bennett. Both letters confirmed that, if elected, the Progressive Conservative Party led by Brian Mulroney would support the establishment of a park at South Moresby.

That same day, the five ministers of the B.C. cabinet's Environment and Land Use Committee finally toured South Moresby. It was their first and last visit as a committee, and it was a disaster. The misty isles were at their mistiest. A helicopter tour of the area was cancelled, as little could be seen through the fog. Then they attempted a one-day tour by boat, to see the wilderness at close range. In driving rains and rocking seas, the ministers stayed in the ship's lounge, watching the chandelier sway disquietingly. They had plenty to drink and good food on board, even if it was hard to hold it down. The boat put them ashore only twice, first at the old whaling station at Rose Harbour within the wilderness proposal area, and later at Talunkwan Island, north of the park proposal and already heavily logged. Every suspicion they had that no one but crazed hippies would find such a desolate place attractive was confirmed. The idea that South Moresby could ever attract tourists was loony.

Their comments in the guest log summed up the day. Tony Brummet's was pleasant: "Great trip and great service!" Stephen Rogers's comment was non-committal: "A whole new look at the Queen Charlotte Islands. Good time." But the minister of forests, Tom Waterland, left this chilling pun: "A clear cut issue. A GREAT FOREST RESOURCE."

ISLANDS
AT THE EDGE

THROUGHOUT THE WINTER OF 1983-1984 J.B. HAD EN-
tertained the occasional thought of placing his hands
around Huck's throat. This little vision had served to
cheer him as he laboured over the editing of the South
Moresby book and the growing demands of the escalating controversy. Huck had taken a trip to Africa at what
J.B. considered a critical moment. To Huck, every moment was critical, but after ten years of struggle he had
acquired a certain amount of perspective.

Preoccupied with the book, J.B. increasingly came to
rely on the nearly full-time coordination provided by
Vicky Husband, the editing assistance of the former editor of the provincial Forestry Department's *Forest Talk*,
Cameron Young, and on Sharon Chow, the staff person
for the Sierra Club of Western Canada, which had an office next door to IPS. Endorsements and letters of support were flooding in as the profile of the issue rose.
Former U.S. president Jimmy Carter went steelhead
fishing in the Charlottes in 1984 and wrote a plea for
their protection to the Prime Minister and to Bill
Bennett. Colleen's effort to recruit labour unions to the
cause, off-setting the opposition of the International
Woodworkers of America's Canadian head, Jack Munro,
was successful in lining up the Pulp, Paper and
Woodworkers of Canada, Local 4, and the Canadian
Smelter and Allied Workers Union, among others. J.B.
felt sure that the release of the book would bring the

issue to even greater public attention and gain an international following as well.

The book was taking shape beautifully. Its title had become *Islands at the Edge,* and Bill Reid had contributed a chapter, which read in part, "These shining islands may be the signposts that point the way to a renewed harmonious relationship with this, the only world we're ever going to have."

Huck returned in the early summer in time to help J.B. with the final massive edit and lay-out. For this operation, they relocated temporarily to Vancouver to be near their publisher. Lying on the grass of a small park in the hot sun, they sorted through slide sheets and wrote captions. The book was released in November 1984, and all copies were sold before the end of the month.

September had brought a landslide victory for Brian Mulroney at the polls. The new prime minister may not have realized that his government was already committed to creating a park in the Queen Charlotte Islands. It soon became clear that, in any event, his choice for minister of the environment didn't have a clue.

Suzanne Blais-Grenier was a first-time member of Parliament, swept in with the Tory tide. With a string of degrees in sociology and economics, she was an attractive prospect for a cabinet position. Mulroney was keen to appoint as many women and francophones to key positions as possible, and Blais-Grenier was both.

Unfortunately, she had no background in environmental issues and saw her job as a peripheral portfolio. To succeed to a more important position she would have to please her political masters, and in the early days of the Mulroney government, the task-master was Deputy Prime Minister Erik Nielsen. Nielsen was convinced there was fat to be trimmed in the civil service, so Blais-Grenier decided to deliver him some substantial budget cuts. Unfortunately, the Department of the

Environment's budget had been one of the previous government's leanest.

The deputy minister, Jacques Guerin, who was in favour of the department acting as an environmental advocate, found it almost impossible to communicate with the new minister. Soon the halls of the department were full of gossip as the staff spread horror stories of near warfare between the minister's office and the department. They took no delight in the rumours. Morale fell, and people worried that Jacques Guerin might not survive.

Blais-Grenier fixed her attention on the Canadian Wildlife Service as the ideal candidate for a budgetary cut. Guerin cautioned her strongly against any such move, warning that the Wildlife Service was one of the most visible and popular parts of the department. Cutting the jobs of biologists who study and protect Canada's ducks, deer, and other wildlife was unthinkable – like nuking Bambi. But the more fervently her deputy argued against these cuts, the more adamant the minister became. Blais-Grenier, or Suzie Two-Names as she had been renamed by the departmental staff, was convinced that whatever Guerin recommended would be disastrous. She was sure his goal was to encourage her to make mistakes that would cost the Mulroney government.

When the cuts were announced, one-third of the department's wildlife biologists were fired. Public outrage was heard from coast to coast, and the minister was deluged with letters of protest from the most successful spontaneous campaign in the country's environmental history. Some departmental observers hoped that perhaps, now, Blais-Grenier would listen to her deputy's advice. But, if anything, their relationship deteriorated. It seemed she was convinced Guerin had deliberately encouraged her not to cut the Wildlife Service, knowing that she would choose to do the opposite.

During this chaos in Environment Canada, Colleen McCrory arrived in January 1985 to follow up on the Conservative commitment to a park at South Moresby. She also planned to use the trip to create the National Committee to Save South Moresby, signing up the growing roster of prominent Canadians who were championing the area.

Her hero, John Fraser, was now minister of fisheries, and he readily reaffirmed the government's interest in saving South Moresby. In a media interview following his meeting with Colleen, Fraser was unequivocal, "I couldn't care less if it's a national park or a provincial park or anything else. I'd just like to see a park."

Colleen was also thrilled with the continuing support from Charles Caccia, now environment critic for the Opposition. Using Caccia's office as a base, she burned up the phone lines to get a national committee off the ground. She lined up Robert Bateman, David Suzuki, nature photographer Freeman Patterson, and, of course, Jim Fulton and Charles Caccia. Colleen persuaded the conservation director of the Canadian Nature Federation, Gregg Sheehy, to act as chair, and she dragooned the executive director of the National and Provincial Parks Association of Canada, Kevin McNamee, into devoting far more of his resources to the cause. She tried in vain to reach two more high-profile Canadians, best-selling authors Pierre Berton and Farley Mowat. She had managed to get their telephone numbers, but they were both out of town. Charles Caccia tried reaching them as well, but finally suggested to the determined Colleen that she had enough well-known and respected board members already. "No," said Colleen, "I just know they'd support this, if I can reach them. I need Farley Mowat and Pierre Berton."

Taking a break from the frantic phoning and lobbying, Colleen took Caccia up on his invitation to attend Question Period – that free-for-all session that tries the endurance of members and provides a stage for every repressed ham in the House of Commons. While she was in the gallery watching the antics, a page slipped in and handed her a note. It was from Caccia, and it said "Look over to the opposite gallery." She looked up. Across the House, in a visitors' box facing her own, sat Pierre Berton and Farley Mowat, together. In no time flat, Colleen had traded boxes and Berton and Mowat had joined the roster of supporters of the National Committee to Save South Moresby.

After several days in Ottawa, Colleen finally received word that Blais-Grenier would meet with her. By luck, Diane Pachal of the Alberta Wilderness Society was in town, and joined Colleen for the first direct plea to the minister. Suzanne Blais-Grenier was attractive and charming. She greeted both women warmly and listened with interest and animation to the pitch for the Charlottes' park. Then, with what appeared to be a spontaneous spark, the minister made an unusual proposal. She confirmed that the federal government was interested in a park, and suggested that the total cost might be around $6 million.

Colleen was about to dispute this low figure with her when the minister explained her position. The federal government would be prepared to put $2 million into the deal, the province would have to contribute another $2 million, and the environmentalists would have to raise the last $2 million. Not to be accused of making an impossible proposition, the minister offered an initial $400,000 to get the fundraising campaign underway. Colleen and Diane did not know what to say. The minister was beaming, sure that she had found an innovative solution to the problem, at minimal federal expense. The meeting was over. Colleen and Diane stammered a few thank-yous and left.

Colleen went straight to Fulton's office. Jim had no trouble assessing the pros and cons of the Blais-Grenier scheme. "It's absolutely nuts! The land is public land. It would mean we'd never get another park in Canada unless groups were prepared to spend years fundraising." Colleen wasn't sure, "What will she do if we say no?" Jim Fulton was adamant, "We can't get involved in anything like this. It's a dangerous precedent, and besides, $2 million from the federal government is not nearly large enough a commitment to get the B.C. government even to open negotiations."

Relieved, Colleen alerted the troops of the newly formed national committee. Kevin McNamee from the Parks Association was stunned. He knew that national parks policy takes years to change. This was a completely new policy direction, and it looked as though the minister had made it up on the spot. The irony was that 1985 was being billed by the Parks Service as a major promotional year. It had been one hundred years since Sir John A. Macdonald created the country's first national park at Banff Springs. The Parks Service was gearing up for a major conference on the future of the parks system, to take place in Banff in September. Meanwhile, at the helm of the department, the minister had set herself on a collision course with the conservation community: first, the cuts to the Wildlife Service; second, her $6-million cost-sharing scheme for South Moresby; and third, an off-hand remark that there was no reason why mining and logging should not be allowed within Canada's national parks.

It seemed as if there was crisis on all fronts. An environmental assessment panel was to hold hearings on the prospect of west coast oil exploration. The Islands Protection Society was busily contacting experts to appear in support of a moratorium on off-shore drilling. The logging of Lyell Island was continuing. And now their best hope, the federal minister of the environment, had become a source of anger and embarrassment.

Still, the growing network of South Moresby supporters remained optimistic. They always thought they saw another ray of hope on the horizon.

NETWORKING

IN MARCH 1985, BEBAN'S CREW, CLEAR-CUTTING FOR Western Forest Products, caused a major landslide within the wilderness proposal. Landrick Creek, a rich salmon habitat facing Juan Perez Sound, was in the heart of what Parks Canada had sketched out for a marine park, and now it was choking in mud and a thirty-foot-high dam of debris.

On March 26, Colleen McCrory and a delegation from WC Squared went to Victoria to meet the new provincial environment minister, Austin Pelton. Pelton assured them he was in favour of creating park status for at least some of the area. But that, of course, he was just one man in cabinet, and could not commit the whole government. But he did say he would meet with his federal counterpart to pursue the matter.

In what was the first face-to-face meeting between the federal and provincial environment ministers to discuss the fate of South Moresby, Austin Pelton and Suzanne Blais-Grenier took a few minutes out from a May 1985 session of the Canadian Council of Resource and Environment Ministers. An emergency meeting had been pulled together in Montreal to discuss polychlorinated byphenols – PCBs. A highway spill on the Trans-Canada Highway near Kenora, Ontario, had forced the ministers to beat their chests about the need to manage toxic chemicals in Canada. All of the politicians at the meeting were aware that, for the first time, an environmental issue appeared to have affected an election. The Ontario government of Frank Miller had gone down to defeat, including the environment minister whose famous last words had been, "The only health risk from PCBs would be to any rats licking the stuff off the road." The lesson was sinking in. The environment had political salience.

Austin Pelton wanted to pursue Caccia's proposal for South Moresby, but Blais-Grenier had disassociated herself from Caccia's position. She put it to Pelton that the cost-sharing scheme was as far as federal interest would go. If the province would cough up $2 million, and environmentalists raised an equal amount, then the feds would ante-up. But not a minute before, and not a dollar more.

That summer, Austin Pelton went to Haida Gwaii. Standing in a tidal pool in Burnaby Narrows, with his light summer trousers rolled up, the sun shone down as he reached into the icy waters to fish out clams and mussels. From that moment on Pelton felt a deep concern for the area.

Meanwhile, Colleen McCrory and Vicky Husband were on their way to Ottawa for their first joint lobbying effort. By now, Colleen was an old hand at it and she was eager to show Vicky the ropes. Both women had been selected as delegates to the annual meeting of the Canadian Environment Network held at the Katimavik Centre, outside Ottawa.

Over the three days of the network meetings, Colleen and Vicky won over environmentalists from around the country. South Moresby already had the support of the nation's parks and conservation groups, but the Canadian environmental movement has several focuses. Without gatherings such as the annual network meeting, it was unlikely that activists overwhelmed with their own priorities – pesticides, acid rain, nuclear waste, toxic chemicals, uranium mining, hydro dams – would have found the time or inclination to learn about the country's most high-profile wilderness struggle. Most environmentalists were too busy to watch The Nature of Things, even if they owned televisions.

The first night's meeting was scheduled to end with a plenary of the hundred or so delegates. Vicky was determined to show her slides on South Moresby. No, said the organizers, there's not time in the program. A social hour had been planned back at the dining area, and no one wanted to be subjected to another presentation.

As the chair of the evening plenary announced that the meeting was adjourned, Vicky popped out of her seat and announced loud and clear that now there would be a slide presentation on South Moresby. The organizer looked daggers at Vicky and Colleen as they took over, setting up the screen and projector, dimming the house lights, and announcing the show.

For the next forty minutes they held the audience in the palm of their hand. Activists from all over the country from Newfoundland and the Yukon to Toronto and Thunder Bay were transfixed by the same images that had captured Colleen years before. Closing with a magnificent slide of an eagle, Vicky slowed in her running commentary. There was a hush in the room. Then, from the back, a voice in the dark cracked, "It's beautiful. You know, it's almost as nice as Cape Breton." There were groans and laughs and the familiar voice of Norm Rubin, the other congenital joker of the environment network, said scoldingly, "Elizabeth, *really!*"

This is where I come in. Not that I played an important role at this stage. I didn't. I had come through two years of legal action against a Swedish pulp and paper company in Nova Scotia, which had been attempting to spray the herbicides 2,4-D and 2,4,5-T on forests in Cape Breton. We lost our case, and even though it had been over for more than a year, our defeat was still painful.

On the Monday the Honourable Suzie B-G was scheduled to attend the network meeting. By this time

nearly every group in attendance had supported a resolution to save the South Moresby wilderness. They
joined with approximately five hundred thousand other
Canadians – the members of all the organizations that
had already endorsed the proposal. The ragtag assemblage of activists, lawyers, farmers, latter-day hippies,
and trade-unionists had put on its Sunday best for the
minister. Two-and-a-half hours late, she arrived to meet
with the country's leading environmentalists. One by
one the regional caucuses met with Blais-Grenier for abbreviated fifteen-minute sessions. Each region had
agreed to press South Moresby so that she would realize
that the issue was not merely the concern of British
Columbians. Some caucuses even volunteered that
parks proposed within their areas take a back seat to
South Moresby. Blais-Grenier smiled. "Ah, yes," she said,
"I am very concerned that we do something for South
Moresby."

Before leaving Ottawa, Colleen visited John Fraser.
Colleen had phoned Fraser to set up the meeting from
the store she ran in the Kootenays. For years, the
Valhalla Trading Post had served as the hub for the frenetic environmental activity in Colleen's home town.
She supported herself with the marginal income from
the store, supplemented with a Sears catalogue operation. With Fraser on the line, her call button from Sears
had lit up, "Just a second," she had said, "I've got to put
you on hold." Fraser had been stunned. "Colleen, I'm a
very busy man." She had responded, "I know, and I'm a
busy woman." When Colleen met with him in Ottawa,
Fraser was very upset about the damage Blais-Grenier
was doing both to the environment and to the party's
environmental record. He promised Colleen that he
would do whatever he could as fisheries minister to stop
the logging.

The women gave slide shows several more times
while they were in Ottawa. Charles Caccia arranged for
them to show it to interested MPs and their staffs, and

Vicky ran the slides in the living room of her friends Derek and Joan Burney. They made personal visits to MPs from B.C., sympathetic or not. They distributed a recent *Equinox* article on the issue, "Paradise in Peril," and gave copies of *Islands at the Edge* to the most promising and influential members.

After a whirlwind of persuasion in Ottawa, Vicky and Colleen stopped off in Toronto where they made the rounds of the *Globe and Mail,* the *Toronto Star,* and the CBC. They worked well together and liked each other tremendously. Soon Vicky and Colleen would become as recognizable a duo lobbying in Ottawa as Huck and J.B. had become in Victoria.

In June, Percy Williams and Maurice Strong, a prominent Liberal from the Trudeau era who had chaired the 1972 Stockholm Conference on the Environment, sponsored a $100-a-plate salmon barbecue at the longhouse at the University of British Columbia Museum of Anthropology to raise funds for saving South Moresby. Many of Bill Reid's more recent pieces were displayed inside, including the piece Guujaaw had helped carve, *Raven Discovering Man in a Clamshell.*

By now Guujaaw had become an accomplished craftsman. He had constructed a longhouse at the old Haida village of Kiusta. At the potlatch for the dedication of the house, he had been given the great gift of his new Haida name, Guujaaw , meaning drum. It symbolized his role as a singer, his leadership in bringing many young people back to their culture, and his penchant for marching to a different drum.

Despite the recent successes in organizing support, one member of the National Committee to Save South Moresby held little hope that the area could be saved. Bristol Foster had resigned his post as director of the Ecological Reserves Unit a year before. The Bennett government had been steadily cutting back funding to the unit and Foster was being pressured to stop commenting on wilderness issues in public. Finally, Bristol resigned in disgust. And now, a year later, he saw no reason to expect that the provincial government would ever protect the southern portion of the magnificent Charlottes archipelago unless he could focus public awareness on the issue. The newspaper headlined Foster's latest comments: "Fight to Save South Moresby Lost, Says Ex-Parks Director." But while his head told him the cause was lost, he told friends his big toe still told him South Moresby would be saved.

MILES

THROUGHOUT THE SUMMER OF 1985, THE SOUTH Moresby issue was building to a boil. Austin Pelton's willingness to consider a park did nothing to help the federal position, now split between an intransigent environment minister and an impassioned fisheries minister.

On the Charlottes, R.L.Smith was cranking up the decibel levels on the rhetoric. He had finally found an environmentalist who not only rose to his bait, but was wounded by it. Smith targeted Colleen McCrory. He devoted whole issues of the *Red Neck News* to attacks on Colleen and the Valhalla Wilderness Society. He accused them of terrorism and of arson. And he went so far as to blanket all householders in the Valhalla area in his broadside assaults on Colleen and her friends. For the first time in twelve years of working on environmental issues in the area, Colleen experienced hostility from people in New Denver. Some members of her group were physically assaulted. A rock flew through Colleen's window in the night, and eventually the boycott of her store, sparked by R.L. Smith's attacks, put her out of business.

Colleen was not the only one Smith subjected to personal attacks. He also targeted the new president of the Council of the Haida Nation, Miles Richardson. Miles was one of a new breed of highly educated Indian political leaders, with a degree in economics from the

University of Victoria. His father, Miles Richardson Sr., was hereditary chief of Tanu. His mother's grandfather, Gedanst, had been an important person within the Haida Nation and would have been chief of Skidegate Village, except that shortly after the smallpox epidemic, Gedanst had become the first Haida to convert to Christianity. He made the decision that he could no longer be chief.

Miles went to university to excel in the Canadian world, but he did not abandon the Haida one. In the summers he worked in the forests, logging for MacMillan Bloedel, or worked in commercial fishing operations, seining for herring. Miles was aware of the conflict over the future of the southern islands. Guujaaw had spoken to him about it one day when they met on the seiner on which Miles was working, and he had offered Guujaaw his help.

Miles's mentor was Percy Gladstone, a former Haida bomber pilot who had pioneered the idea of Haida political unity. Percy had even offered to pay Miles to read books on Indian politics. He drew him into the current debates and negotiations, and made sure that Miles attended conventions and other gatherings as an alternate delegate.

Miles planned to be a businessman, but gradually the dream of justice for native people took hold. After completing university he became manager of the Skidegate Band Council, where his only involvement in the South Moresby issue was to ensure that the Haida were properly represented in the planning team meetings. Miles accepted that the Haida Nation had decided years before that there would be no logging south of the line drawn by Huck and Guujaaw. But the frustration of years of participating in good faith in futile consultations and participation exercises was growing throughout the Haida. When Miles was elected vice-president of the Council of the Haida Nation in 1984, serving alongside

President Percy Williams, he knew that stopping the logging on Lyell Island had to be one of his top priorities. The following year, in August 1985, he was elected president.

Within months of becoming the political leader of the Haida Nation, Miles met respectively with Austin Pelton and John Fraser. Moreover, he persuaded both the ministers to meet with him on Haida Gwaii, touring the wilderness proposal. The meeting with Pelton brought the first tangible result since Percy Williams's plea to Dave Barrett eleven years before. Austin Pelton agreed to block any new logging permits for Lyell Island until the provincial cabinet's Environment and Land Use Committee could reach a decision on the whole wilderness proposal. Pelton promised to convene the committee in Skidegate in early September and sealed his commitment with a handshake. One week later, Guujaaw escorted John Fraser on a tour of the proposed park. Fraser was deeply impressed. Following the tour, Fraser met with Miles Richardson, after which he made a public commitment to protect Lyell Island, using the full force of the Fisheries Act, if need be. "My job is to look after those streams. Anyone who thinks logging won't damage [them] is whistling in the wind...Once you get logging in some of those areas, you've got a real problem." Fraser had been flown low over the landslide at Landrick Creek. It made the case loud and clear that clear-cutting destroyed salmon habitat. Fraser told reporters that he would prefer not to have to resort to the sanctions in the powerful Fisheries Act to prevent clear-cutting near streams, but added, "Nobody should think I won't use it, because I will."

Miles Richardson was pleased with Pelton's commitment and with Fraser's unequivocal support, but J.B. had a deep sense of foreboding. He had represented the Islands Protection Society during Fraser's visit. He had liked Fraser, and Fraser had enjoyed his company.

But when Fraser's comments hit the newspapers, he was worried. He remembered the Shoot-out at Riley Creek. Even if the minister was prepared to use the Fisheries Act to prosecute forestry companies, would he be able to do so? J.B. realized that Fraser had gone out on a limb, one that could be sawn off. Within the month, Fraser was gone from cabinet.

On September 23, John Fraser was forced to resign over what became known as the Tainted Tuna Scandal, in a scenario manipulated by the deputy prime minister, Erik Nielsen. During their days in Opposition, Fraser often disagreed with the member for the Yukon. In the year since the Tories had come to power, Fraser had voted with the Opposition against the testing of American Cruise Missiles over Canadian territory. That the two men did not like each other much was no secret. They essentially represented opposite ends of the political spectrum found within the Conservative Party – Fraser on the left, Nielsen on the right. The tuna scandal brought their incompatibility to a head. Nielsen was more than pleased to see Fraser out of the way.

J.B. did not know any of the inside scuttle-butt. All he knew was that the campaign to save South Moresby had just lost its strongest ally in cabinet.

Pelton's commitment that logging permits would be denied until a final solution was reached infuriated the pro-logging community of Sandspit. It did not matter to Beban or his employees that they had already cut their quota for the year. Under departmental regulations, they could over-cut one year as long as the cut averaged out over a period of years. Beban wanted to get as much cut now as possible, and especially in areas that might end up as parkland. If the trees were not harvested now, next year or the year after might be too late.

R.L.Smith fanned the flames by accusing the environmentalists of making their living from the "Environment Industry" and of putting loggers out of work. He attacked David Suzuki, Robert Bateman, and Farley Mowat for reaping personal gain from their "supposedly...charitable activities" with the National Committee to Save South Moresby. But there was only so much the *Red Neck News* could do. Then Smith was given help from a relative newcomer to the area named Pat Armstrong, whom the *Red Neck News* had described as "an ex-squatter living right here in Sandspit." Pat Armstrong was a draft-dodger and ex-hippie, who now bitterly opposed the values and politics of the hippie movement of the 1960s. He had never espoused their values, he had only lived their life-style. He and his wife had moved to the Queen Charlotte Islands in 1982, where they had become friends of the logging community. He learned the Sandspit perspective on the wilderness issues and on the people trying to save South Moresby. He heard all the local gossip about Haida shooting whales, about activists living off government grants, about the Haida really wanting to log the island themselves. Toward the end of the planning team process, Pat decided to become involved. He saw the whole campaign to preserve South Moresby as a giant hoax, as deliberate deception. The environmentalists were not merely wrong. They were making it up. They were lying.

Pat started talking with the community leaders who would be the nucleus of a new group: Frank Beban; R.L. Smith; Duane Gould, owner of a local garage, justice of the peace, and chairman of the school board; and Mavis Warren, a widow who had worked for Frank Beban at the motel for years. Pat saw the tactical error in allowing the forest company executives to make the case against the park. What was needed, he told his neighbours, was a local citizen's group to give the pro-logging forces a sympathetic face.

In the late summer of 1985, three hundred and fifty people gathered in the Lion's Hall in Sandspit for the inaugural meeting of Moresby Island Concerned

Citizens. Pat was in Kansas City for the first meeting, but he was elected chairman all the same. Frank Beban would have covered expenses for the new group, but Pat had the political savvy to realize that it would be far better to raise money through community events and dances, the way the Islands Protection Society always had.

Meanwhile, back in Ottawa, Suzanne Blais-Grenier had succeeded in destroying her deputy minister's will. Guerin requested to be transfered to another department. A few days later, word leaked out of a planned cabinet shuffle. As news of Blais-Grenier's imminent departure spread within the department, there were mixed feelings: relief that her reign was over, and bitterness at the irony that Guerin was leaving as well. One enterprising bureaucrat ordered a limited edition of T-shirts to be sold surreptitiously to raise money for the deputy's farewell gift. On the front were emblazened the words, "I survived Suzie B.-G.!" with a cartoon of the minister at the controls of a bulldozer, a squashed beaver under the blade. On the back was another political cartoon of a bear holding a newspaper with the headline "Blais-Grenier out of Environment Canada" and addressing an assemblage of rabbits, beavers, raccoons, and a moose: "You get the cake. You get the balloons. You get the whistles. I'll get the bubbly." The shirts sold like hot-cakes.

The new minister, who had entered the cabinet with Blais-Grenier the previous fall, was receiving a promotion. Tom McMillan loved the idea of being environment minister. Unlike his previous portfolio of tourism, the environment was a full-fledged ministry, and in the early 1980s, he had been environment critic. He felt sure he would be popular in his new position and that he could make up for all the awful things Blais-Grenier had done both to the cause of the environment and to the Tories' record.

Within days of being sworn in as environment minister, Tom McMillan was burning the midnight oil, wading through the voluminous briefing books prepared by his bureaucrats to familiarize him with the department. They were each the size of a Toronto telephone directory, and were written in the thoroughly sanitized prose perfected by the civil service. Bleary eyed, Tom McMillan wondered how such a fascinating subject could have been made so boring. A good deal of his briefing materials dealt with issues he had never associated with the environment – the costs of snow clearance in Banff, the new computers required for the Atmospheric Environment Service, the structural reorganization of the department in the never-ending task of cutting "person-years." He grit his teeth. Perhaps the purpose of the exercise was to so overwhelm a new minister that he or she would gladly leave most matters to the discretion of senior bureaucrats.

Then he turned to a page on the proposed National Park for South Moresby. He had never heard of the Canadian Galapagos, and he could hardly believe that the magical place described in this lyrical briefing note really existed. He marked the page, and made a mental note to pursue the matter with the assistant deputy minister for parks, Al Davidson. And then he turned the page and started reading about the structural problems of the Trent-Severn Waterway.

|16|

HIJACKING
THE BANFF ASSEMBLY

THROUGHOUT THE SUMMER OF 1985, THE FEVERISH
pitch of activity of the far flung South Moresby crusaders grew even more intense. In New Denver, Colleen
McCrory wrote To Do lists with as many as sixty-eight
different things to be done, including at the top, "Hug
my kids!" In Victoria, Vicky Husband's life was being
consumed by the South Moresby crisis and she had
started calling South Moresby "the black hole." The
phone in her home outside Victoria never stopped ringing, prompting her partner, Patrick Pothier, to answer,
"You have reached the offices of Save the World. She's
not home." The pressures on John Broadhead and his
wife were becoming unbearable. He was unable to work
on anything but South Moresby, a field in which employers are few and far between. The strain would eventually cause his marriage to fall apart.

Toward the end of August, someone phoned Vicky
and said, "You've got to go to this Banff conference."
Vicky had not been aware of the upcoming Canadian
Assembly on National Parks and Protected Areas. It was
to be Parks Canada's major showpiece for its centennial
celebrations. For nearly two years, committees and sub-
committees had met to organize the conference.
Conservation and parks groups had been consulted,
discussion papers had been drafted and themes identified, and the title, "Heritage for Tomorrow" agreed
upon. Now that Blais-Grenier was gone, there was a

sudden upsurge in interest among conservationists.

Vicky immediately saw the point in going. The new minister would be there. Vicky was sure McMillan would be an improvement over Blais-Grenier, and there was no point in missing an opportunity to recruit him in the first days of his new position. The British Columbia delegation to the conference was still being organized. Vicky started phoning.

Colleen McCrory agreed to join Vicky at the conference. She phoned her neighbour and Valhalla comrade-in-arms, Grant Copeland, to recruit him to promote the saving of the Stikine. Grant was dubious: "Colleen, is this going to be one of those things where you end up cramming six or seven people into the same motel room?" Colleen solemnly swore that if Grant would agree to drive to Banff with her, she wouldn't offer space in their shared room to anyone else.

Paul George was eager to go. He prepared stacks of materials from the Western Canada Wilderness Committee on all their key issues: South Moresby, the Stikine, Meares Island, and the Stein. Patrick Pothier had taken a photograph of a burned-over clear-cut, logged by B.C. Forest Products near Tofino on Vancouver Island. It was a horrific picture of mud, deep scars in the earth, charred remains of trunks, and patches of snow amid the trash wood. J.B. had taken one look at it and said, "I have the perfect quote to go with it on a poster." It was from Shakespeare's *Julius Caesar*: "O pardon me, thou bleeding piece of earth, that I am meek and gentle with these butchers." Hundreds of posters were readied for the conference.

Vicky was determined that Huck should come to speak at the assembly. Huck, as usual, was completely broke. In desperation, Vicky paid his airfare, and she found a ride for herself.

As the conference attendees arrived, several feet of snow fell on Banff. It didn't really surprise Grant

Copeland when sixteen people ended up in his motel room. Colleen could only giggle, "I promised we wouldn't have six or seven! So we've got sixteen!"

The British Columbia crew lost no time in hanging a huge Save South Moresby banner over the major entrance to the conference hall. No one at this conference was going to be allowed to forget South Moresby for an instant. The British Columbians were not alone in pressing South Moresby. Gregg Sheehy from the Canadian Nature Federation and chair of the National Committee to Save South Moresby was also at the assembly, as was Kevin McNamee of the National and Provincial Parks Association of Canada. The South Moresby delegation had achieved critical mass, and nothing could stop it.

For three days, Vicky and Colleen worked constantly. Other members of the South Moresby contingent at least made a show of following the conference plan, attending workshops, and listening to presentations on other issues. Colleen and Vicky knew that they didn't have time. Vicky interrupted workshops to announce special, unscheduled slide shows on the Queen Charlotte Islands' wilderness, and she would haul Huck out of whatever session he was attending to provide the accompanying lecture. Vicky knew people thought she was pushy, and she didn't care.

On evening of the second day, the Save South Moresby committee was able to hold one of its first truly national meetings. Gregg Sheehy reported that he was working on placing a full-page advertisement in the *Globe and Mail*. He had also met the previous week with McMillan's chief of staff, Les McElroy, who had assured him that it was extremely unlikely that McMillan would want the public to raise funds for a park. Moreover, McMillan had already said in a *Globe and Mail* interview, that his "knee-jerk reaction" favoured creating a national park for South Moresby. Things looked promising on the federal front.

Colleen's report on the situation in British Columbia was less optimistic. Pelton's commitment had been to hold up logging permits until a decision could be reached by the Environment and Land Use Committee. But the September 21, 1985, deadline for the decision was looming. Huck reported that the Haida Nation had made an unequivocal commitment to block any logging that occurred after September 25.

By the morning of the last day, Vicky, Colleen, Paul, and Huck knew they had done their work well. The whole conference was buzzing about South Moresby. There was an unstoppable ground swell that the Banff Assembly should break the rules made for the conference and move a resolution that the area be saved. The conference organizers didn't know how to handle it. The closing plenary would take place with each workshop reporting back to the whole, then the minister was to make the closing address. They could not allow the session to degenerate into debates over resolutions. They decided to let the South Moresby group say a few words at the end of the other workshop reports, but there would be no resolutions.

Predictably, the workshop reports each ran over their fifteen-minute allotment. The South Moresby and Stikine groups were told that they had a total of five minutes to present both issues. Grant Copeland started by reading a resolution on the Stikine River. He then asked Colleen to present the case for South Moresby. Colleen had never before addressed such a large gathering, or been under so much pressure. Nearly three hundred faces looked up at her as she nervously began. "We bring before the Canadian Assembly a sense of urgency because we have a crisis with the South Moresby area of British Columbia. People have worked for over twelve years to have this area preserved..." Colleen and Grant knew they were out of time. The moderator gestured for them to leave the podium. Colleen took a deep breath and said, "I would now like to ask Thom Henley to speak about South Moresby."

Huck rose to sustained applause. The organizers began to sense that they were no longer running the conference. The South Moresby activists had hijacked it. Huck came to the microphone, and said, "I guess I have thirty seconds to tell you about South Moresby." Then, ignoring an officious man with a watch, he plunged into an emotional, brilliant, and brief address. With tears in his eyes and a catch in his throat, he told the audience, "I feel that the forests, the sea-birds, the eagles, the falcons, the sea-lions and the whales – all the life forms on South Moresby – need to be recognized and represented here today…" Vicky was sitting in the hall, having previously arranged for the South Moresby activists to be evenly sprinkled throughout the audience to spark applause. She was watching Huck with one eye and the other was scanning the crowd for any sign of the new minister.

Huck was just hitting his stride when Vicky saw Tom McMillan come in and take a seat at the back. The conference planners had arranged the closing session so that the minister would not be subjected to any of the tedious workshop reports. No one had expected there to be a riveting speech in progress when he made his entrance.

"Meanwhile, the area continues to be logged," Huck continued, blind to the notes that read, Your time is up! "It is being logged today as I stand here speaking to you. We would ask that this assembly come forward with a very strong recommendation that, as a way of celebrating the National Parks Centennial, we actually do something truly significant." Grant took the microphone and read out the resolution that the entire South Moresby wilderness area be made into a national park reserve with an adjacent marine park reserve. The organizer reclaimed the podium to explain that no resolutions were allowed, but the audience thought differently. The standing ovation was thunderous and prolonged. No one, least of all McMillan, could doubt that South Moresby had the unanimous support of the nation's parks and conservation community.

McMillan watched all this from the rear of the hall. He was about to give his first major speech as environment minister. He realized he had a tough act to follow. His prepared text had highlighted the important news that negotiations for a new national park reserve in the Arctic, on Ellesmere Island, were near completion. Ordinarily, such an announcement would have sent this crowd into delerium. But as McMillan quickly read over his speech, he realized it was not enough. He found an appropriate spot in the text, and wrote in the words, "Working with British Columbians to protect the terrestrial and marine treasures of South Moresby is a top priority for me." The South Moresby guerrillas had done their work. Not only had they captured the assembly, they had captured the minister as well.

Afterwards, in Grant's crowded motel room, Paul suggested the South Moresby crew use a Haida tactic, and give McMillan a thank-you gift. McMillan would still be in Banff the next day for a closing reception at the Banff Springs Hotel, and Colleen and Huck had been invited for a private meeting with him. Inspiration struck Colleen, "We've got to get a big cake made, saying Thank You Tom McMillan and smuggle it into the final reception to give to him!" The group pooled the proceeds from selling posters and books to pay for a big cake, and Paul and his wife, Adriane, headed out to find a bakery in Banff that would bake a cake overnight.

Finally, they managed to arrange the group, the cake, the minister, and a large crowd to be together at one time. Colleen beamed as she presented the cake to McMillan in front of the whole assembly. In bright green icing, decorated with trees, it proclaimed Thank

You Tom McMillan! South Moresby National Park! McMillan was thrilled. For the moment, he was the darling of the environmental movement. As Colleen offered him a knife to cut the cake, Tom brushed it away with a gallant wave of his hand. He didn't need to score any more points with the activists present, but he said, "It wouldn't be right to enjoy our celebration of South Moresby Park, until it *is* a park! Put this cake in the freezer, and we'll share it when South Moresby is saved!"

In Which the Fight Is Nearly Won

BACK IN OTTAWA, TOM MCMILLAN WASTED NO TIME IN arranging a trip to the Queen Charlotte Islands. On October 9, one month after the Banff Assembly, he arrived in Sandspit. It was one of those glorious warm autumn days on Haida Gwaii that makes you wonder why anyone would live anywhere else. The minister's first order of business was to make a five-hour helicopter tour of the area. His guides were Huck for IPS, Guujaaw for the Haida Nation, and Duane Gould for the oppositional Moresby Island Concerned Citizens. The helicopter was equipped with earphones and mikes so communication was possible over the roar of the blades, but with Duane Gould and Huck competing to point out healthy regeneration and logging scars, McMillan was getting cross fire in stereo.

Their first stop within the wilderness proposal area was Windy Bay. McMillan followed Huck and Guujaaw, and a television crew or two brought up the rear, as this was basically as much a ministerial photo opportunity as it was a fact-finding mission. Tom McMillan was truly overwhelmed. He had expected beauty, but he had never seen trees so large, or moss so deep, or hanging ferns and new seedlings all growing in such undisciplined profusion.

Once the camera crews were gone, the unlikely group continued its tour, flying further south to Hot Springs Island. Even with Duane Gould along, grumbling about the whole idea of creating a park, the group was starting to have fun. Tom was impressed by Guujaaw's and Huck's knowledge of natural history. He loved the experience of seeing the forest through Guujaaw's eyes. On Hot Springs Island, Guujaaw told them that the traditional Haida way was to go naked into the natural healing waters. Standing on the rim of the rocky pool, the idea was hard to resist. McMillan and Huck compromised by wearing their underwear, but Guujaaw jumped in *au naturel*. It was glorious, sitting in the naturally warm water, looking out over the rocks to Juan Perez Sound. McMillan, former tourism minister, was well aware that the entire Canadian parks system had started in order to protect the hot springs at Banff. Tourists and hot springs go together like *Anne of Green Gables* and Prince Edward Island. McMillan started to picture real possiblities for the area as a tourist destination, creating economic activity that could offset the loss of jobs from logging.

Later, as McMillan stepped onto the tarmac at the Sandspit airport, an angry mob closed in on him, waving placards that read, We Want to Work! and B.C.'s Number One Industry: Forestry. The new minister was pushed; picket signs waved perilously close to his head, and more than by any physical violence, he was scorched by a burning hatred he had never encountered before. McMillan had not realized the effect his press statements would have on the men who wanted to log those woods. Members of the Sandspit committee had read the story of Tom McMillan's triumphant maiden speech in Banff. They were livid. No new logging permits had been issued since Pelton's announcement, and the logging crew on Lyell Island had dropped from eighty men to fifty-three. Logging continued under existing permits, but unless new permits were issued fast there would only be another week's work. Tom McMillan's commitment to make the area a park had made them apoplectic. They raged at the man they saw as hoping to make his political future at the expense of their livelihoods.

Bob Long was the son of a prominent Socred, president of the Queen Charlotte Islands Chamber of Commerce, soda pop salesman, and politically ambitious. He put it to the minister that the area could support logging and a park. McMillan stood his ground. "You can't have logging in a park," he retorted. "Either you have a park or you don't." But McMillan stopped short of committing himself to saving the entire area. As he explained to reporters, there would be some preservation, but "the question is: how much, and where, and, I suppose, how much will it cost?"

McMillan had a far more cordial meeting with representatives from the Council of the Haida Nation. He felt an almost immediate personal rapport with Miles Richardson, who made it clear to him that the area is Haida land, and that the Haida were not interested in a national park, except to the extent it helped stop the logging. McMillan would never forget the critical role the Haida would have to play in any strategy he might adopt.

The national television news that night carried pictures of the handsome young minister stepping out from his helicopter and drawing in his breath at the magnificence of the forest. For many Canadians those images would cement in their minds the idea of Tom McMillan as a serious environmentalist.

Tom McMillan left Haida Gwaii more committed than ever to South Moresby. He headed down to Vancouver to capitalize on his recent visit by doing the requisite interviews. He expected to have a fairly easy ride. After all, he was, as he would often comment, on the side of the angels. But his first interview the next day was with the irreverent and irascible broadcaster Jack Webster. What McMillan did not know was that Webster was a die-hard logging advocate who had been exerting strong behind-the-scenes pressure on Bill Bennett to allow logging on Lyell Island to resume. Later it was revealed that Webster was a shareholder in WFP's pulp partnership venture that depended on Lyell Island's trees for its mills.

As McMillan waited to be introduced, the show opened with a video in fast forward of his arrival in Windy Bay the day before. McMillan came out of the helicopter like a Keystone Kop. Then the tape was reversed, and he scurried backwards into the helicopter. Now forwards. Then backwards. Over and over, while Webster announced, "The minister doesn't know where he's going on this issue." Tom McMillan kept his composure. Then Webster taunted, "I heard you were skinny-dipping yesterday with a bunch of hippies." Tom smiled and said, "Well, Jack, I wore my shorts, so I wouldn't call that skinny-dipping, would you?"

Over and over, McMillan argued for saving a national wilderness treasure. Webster responded by calling the environmentalists "selfish" and unconcerned with the fate of the loggers. Tom was effective, but whether or not he knew it, he was infuriating British Columbia politicians. His tone was slightly too superior for their tastes. And even if he had not said, "we must save British Columbia from its own stupidity," he had come close to it. Austin Pelton, who essentially agreed with McMillan, was annoyed. McMillan was stealing the show. And other than give press interviews, he had done nothing concrete – there was no new federal proposal for the province's consideration.

Expectations were running high that a joint announcement on the fate of the islands would be made during McMillan's visit. The British Columbia cabinet had met while he had been touring the islands, and comments from senior provincial bureaucrats seemed to suggest that a park, of some size, was currently

favoured. A number of members of Bennett's cabinet
were softening in their opposition to a park, among
them Tourism Minister Tony Brummett. With an election looming sometime in the coming months for the
Socred Government, the time was right to put the whole
South Moresby controversy behind them. Public opinion in the province seemed to be decidedly in favour of
the creation of a South Moresby park. The *Vancouver
Sun* had taken an editorial position in support of maximum preservation, accurately summing up the state of
affairs: "If the debate in Cabinet has come down to
stand-off between Mr. Pelton and a few development-
minded ministers, the premier is going to have to take
the lead and nudge it in the right direction."

Pelton left a meeting with Bennett and Norman
Spector, the Premier's right-hand man, convinced that
the Premier would do just that. He was sure that
Bennett would announce within days that the South
Moresby area, with the exception of parts of Lyell
Island, would be saved as federal and provincial park.
But it was not to be.

What Norm Spector and the Premier had realized
was that the issue required handling. They were not yet
ready to make a decision that would anger the forest industry, the loggers, or such senior members of cabinet
as Forests Minister Tom Waterland. Something really
clever would be required to ease the pressure, while allowing logging to continue. They found the solution in
a well-intentioned, even courageous letter from twenty
prominent British Columbians, urging the Premier to
save South Moresby. The letter had been the brainchild
of a respected Vancouver lawyer, Bryan Williams.
Williams had been moved to exert whatever influence
he might have over Bennett after a sailing tour of the
area with guide Al Whitney.

Within a week of receiving the letter Bennett phoned
Bryan Williams, suggesting that he might need

Williams's help. A week or so later, Williams was in Bridgeport, Connecticut, in the middle of a case. Norm Spector tracked him down to explain the shape of the assistance the Premier would require of Williams. Bennett and Spector had come up with an entirely new gambit – a Special Advisory Committee on Wilderness Preservation. Williams was being asked to chair it. To his surprise it would not just examine the South Moresby conflict, but study and provide recommendations on twenty-three different controversial areas, from the Stein Valley in southwestern B.C. to the grizzly bear valley of the Khutzeymateen in the northern interior. The committee was to have a firm deadline of no later than February 15, 1986. Four months to study twenty-three areas.

Williams was in a quandry. He knew that any such committee would be attacked as wholly inadequate to the task, but it was an almost irresistible challenge. Chairing a high-profile advisory committee with an impossible mandate and an unreasonably short time-frame had, in its own way, a perverse appeal for a lawyer. What Williams did not immediately realize was that the creation of the Wilderness Advisory Committee would be announced simultaneously with the issuance of new logging permits for Lyell Island.

Meanwhile, media speculation that the area was on the verge of salvation was at an all-time high. John Broadhead was quoted as saying, "I think that at long last, we've won." The national profile of the issue had never been higher. David Suzuki's special on South Moresby had been the most popular segment in the history of The Nature of Things and had been repeatedly rebroadcast by public demand. And on the eve of a major environment and forestry conference sponsored by the Ontario Sierra Club, the Globe and Mail ran a full-page advertisement appealing for the preservation of South Moresby. It was the work of the Canadian

Nature Federation's Gregg Sheehy and was published with a substantial price concession from the newspaper itself. The following evening, Huck and Bill Reid jointly accepted the B.C. Booksellers' Choice Book of the Year Award for *Islands at the Edge*. The South Moresby wilderness crusade had become respectable. John Turner, former prime minister and leader of the federal Liberal Party, had joined the legions of politicians on all sides of the House of Commons in Ottawa in calling for the preservation of the islands. Tom McMillan's trip to British Columbia and Austin Pelton's words of support combined to create an aura of pending euphoria. The victory was at hand.

No one, not even Austin Pelton, was prepared for the announcement he was forced to make on October 18. Pelton put the best face he could on what must have been a heartbreaking setback. He told reporters that, while he was "personally persuaded" that "South Moresby is an area that must be preserved to the greatest extent possible...there is a need to balance the concern for wilderness preservation with the jobs of those whose livelihoods are dependent [on logging]." Pelton announced the creation of the Wilderness Advisory Committee. Pelton's press release was issued at four on a Friday afternoon. Vicky Husband just happened to wander into Pelton's office as the Wilderness Advisory Committee was being announced. The committee was clearly dominated by forest and mining interests; none of its members represented environmental or native groups. Of the six panel members working with chairman Bryan Williams, two were academics, the third was a senior executive of Cominco Mining, the fourth was a vice-president of the International Woodworkers of America, the fifth, the only woman, was a lawyer and executive officer of Carrier Lumber in Prince George, and the sixth was a well-known and powerful forestry professor, Les Reed, widely reputed to favour economic interests over wilderness preservation.

The same day that Pelton made this announcement, Tom Waterland granted new logging permits for the south side of Lyell Island.

Vicky was deeply shocked. She phoned activists in Vancouver and Victoria, reading the entire press release long distance over and over, and set in motion a chain reaction of outrage. J.B. phoned Huck from Toronto. Colleen phoned Vicky from New Denver. Huck phoned Miles in Prince Rupert. One word was on everyone's lips: Betrayal. After eleven years of battle, after the four-year Environment and Land Use Committee study, the Public Advisory Committee charade, the four-year South Moresby Planning Team exercise, and on the verge of a final decision, yet another committee had been created, one that would be used to justify logging in the study area. As well, there would be twenty-two other areas all thrown into the pot for a decision within four months.

The Saturday papers from Toronto to Victoria carried news of the reaction of the Haida and environmentalists. The Haida immediately announced that they would not participate. Colleen attacked the committee as an "absolute outrage" and "a total sell-out." Vicky predicted the decision would spell a crisis for the islands. Huck called it a "total betrayal" of the Haida people, recalling that Austin Pelton had been to the islands twice, once accompanied by three cabinet colleagues, each time promising the Haida that there would be no further logging within the wilderness proposal area until a final solution was reached. Tom McMillan expressed disappointment, saying, "I personally prefer preserving as much as possible of the relevant islands." The federal minister of Indian affairs and northern development, David Crombie, who happened to be in Vancouver, spoke strongly in favour of the native interests: "All three political parties support the idea of a park...I see the stewardship of the Haida people with respect to that park as a significant priority."

When he heard the news, John Broadhead was attending the Woodshock Conference in Toronto, organized by the Sierra Club. Saturday was the closing day of the Club's attempt to build trust between environmentalists, the government, and the forest industry. Charles Caccia had pulled no punches in his closing address, suggesting that it was time to consider placing the forest industry under public control: "I've seen what happens in B.C., where, thanks to the pursuit of profit, the industry is getting away with murder."

The conference organizers had winced. The meeting's theme of cooperation and consultation was straining at the edges. But the mood of conciliation was still sufficiently strong that the conference appeared to welcome Pelton's initiative of the advisory committee. John Broadhead was to be allowed a few minutes to speak on the subject of this important new development at the very end of the proceedings. The chairman, Tony Whittingham, cautioned him to keep his remarks in context – to be positive. Then Whittingham called on the recent winner of the B.C. Book of the Year Award to present a few closing remarks, "to talk to us about the new B.C. Wilderness Advisory Committee and highlight the opportunties for government and industry and environmentalists and natives to build new bridges of understanding."

J.B. realized that his message could not build bridges; it could only burn them. He looked out at the delegates, some four hundred representatives of environmental groups, governments, and forest companies. He held his emotions in check, but inside he was seething. "I take heart from the people and the good intentions of the Woodshock Conference, but if the industry, the government, environmentalists, and native people are to get together and talk to each other, before the process can succeed there has to be trust, respect, believability, credibility." Tony Whittingham leaned over to J.B., whispering desperately, "Don't, John. Please." J.B. did not stop. He reviewed the series of study groups and planning teams. He explained that the new Wilderness Advisory Committee had been used to end the moratorium on the logging of the south side of Lyell Island, violating the trust implicit in Pelton's handshake agreement with the elders at Skidegate.

"So now the government and industry are saying that we have to log this area – that it is critical to the economic survival of British Columbia. But I know from the Forest Resource Report that the area of land not satisfactorily restocked in British Columbia is four million hectares, and that it is growing every year by an area twice the size of South Moresby. I know that two South Moresbys are going ignored, wasted, every year. And you're telling me that we cannot afford to save South Moresby. You're not making sense."

Men in blue suits squirmed in their seats. Quite a few environmentalists looked distraught. These words were not the up-beat send-off they had expected. This was the reality that three days of discussion had tried to avoid. Tony Whittingham broke in again in a last-ditch plea, "John, you're breaking the balloon. You're bringing them down!"

Meanwhile, Miles Richardson wasted no time in making the Haida position public and absolutely clear. "The Haida people have made a decision that there is to be no further logging in that area. We fully intend to uphold that." Adding weight to the pledge, Miles added, "We are mobilizing our people to place them on Lyell Island to stop logging." Miles, with Skidegate Chief Tom Greene and band manager Willard Wilson, flew to Vancouver to meet with David Crombie. They were impressed with him and his sincere sympathy with the Indians' concern to protect their homeland. The next day, they went straight on to Victoria to see Austin Pelton. Pelton looked at the young president of the

Council of the Haida Nation and apologetically explained, "I didn't have the authority to promise that there would be no more logging permits."

Miles could see it all. Pelton had been overruled by the rest of cabinet. For a man of honour to be forced to break his word was a brutal blow. As they left his office and headed down the corridors of Victoria's parliament building, Miles turned and looked back. There, in his office door, were Pelton and a young aide. The word "betrayal" did not come to mind. Miles felt no anger toward Pelton. He thought that Pelton looked like a broken man.

18

THE HAIDA
BLOCKADE

THERE WAS NO TIME TO WASTE. THE GOVERNMENT HAD broken its word. Logging was resuming despite the fact that Beban had already logged his annual quota. Logging was resuming even while the "blue-chip" committee was deciding the area's fate. Logging was resuming even though the federal minister of Indian affairs was willing to resolve the Haida land claim, even though the federal environment minister had offered compensation to create a park. The Haida decided to do whatever it took to stop the logging on Lyell.

The forest company representatives knew that the Haida would not take the new permits lying down. Beban requested RCMP support as he began to increase the workforce at the Powrivco Bay logging camp on Lyell Island. The Queen Charlotte Islands manager for Western Forest Products, Harvey Hurd, admitted to reporters, "I'd be crazy to tell you I'm not expecting something." The debate over strategy preoccupied the Haida leadership and their environmental supporters. Prominent Canadians were volunteering to come forward to join the Haida in blocking the logging roads.

Bill Reid told the press, "I'll go when I'm recruited," and non-Haida supporters, such as David Suzuki and Robert Bateman, were reported to be willing to face arrest, if necessary.

Fishing boats loaded with cargoes of young men and building supplies were dispatched to Sedgewick Bay on the south side of Lyell to prepare an encampment. Two camphouses were built and cook-stoves and water barrels were installed. Each new boat brought shipments of food and other supplies to sustain the Haida in what promised to be a lengthy seige.

Back in Vancouver, Bryan Williams was trying to save the credibility of the committee he had agreed to chair. He desperately wanted a strong environmentalist to join, and he knew who was needed. He pressured the government to appoint Ken Farquarson, whom he had met during the battle to save the Skagit River Valley. Williams realized that the committee's credibility was seriously eroded by the decision to allow logging on Lyell Island during its deliberations. He pleaded with the Premier's office for an extended moratorium on forest operations within the wilderness proposal. He was successful in only one of these pleas. Farquarson joined the committee, but logging continued on Lyell Island.

By October 30, Haida men and women had taken up their positions, standing on the road between Frank Beban's camp and the new cutting blocks. As Guujaaw drummed, Chief Dempsey Collison of Skidegate stepped forward, his arms extended, his button blanket flapping in the breeze. The logging trucks rounded the bend in the road and stopped dead. The human barricade was successful. No trucks dared pass, and Beban's operations were shut down for the day.

A new wave of activity hit Haida Gwaii. By rented helicopter and chartered airplane, news crews from all over the province arrived. Political columnist Marjorie Nichols quipped that, "More reporters [were] hunkered down...at Sandspit...than were in the press gallery in Victoria." Miles Richardson told the assembled news media, "We are staying here. We cannot stand by and have all this land alienated from us."

Charles Caccia publicly supported the use of civil disobedience to end the logging, while both Austin Pelton and Tom McMillan ducked reporters. Within the week Western Forest Products' lawyers were in court seeking an injunction against Haida occupation of the logging road. Having created the climate for confrontation, Tom Waterland commented, "I don't know what is happening there, but I hope it will be solved through rational discussion instead of confrontation." As for the issue of native land claims, Waterland added, "Every time someone makes a claim to an area of land, we can't go and turn history back or the forest industry would be dead."

For a few days in November, the scene of conflict moved from the muddy roads above Sedgewick Bay to the law courts of Vancouver. For several days, a small skirmish was played out between the lawyers for the forest company, the judge, and the Haida. The Haida appeared without a lawyer to oppose WFP's application for an injunction. Dressed in full Haida regalia, Miles Richardson requested a three-month adjournment in order to prepare the Haida case. The judge, His Lordship Harry MacKay, gave him two and a half hours in which to find a lawyer. Some of the province's best lawyers offered their services *pro bono*. But the Haida decided not to be represented by counsel. When Miles returned two days in a row without a lawyer, the judge pleaded with him to retain proper legal representation. Miles explained that the Haida Nation had decided the issue was too important to be addressed by lawyers. Instead, Miles asked for leave to present the Haida evidence as oral testimony, rather than in the written affidavit form customary in such matters. The request was justified, he argued, because the Haida tradition is an oral one. Further, he explained to the judge, when a Haida rose to speak in public it would not be countenanced that he spoke anything but the truth. Judge MacKay agreed and also allowed Miles's requests for translation so that testimony could be given in Haida, and for a swearing-in without use of the Bible. As the Haida could not accept the loss of sovereignty implied in addressing the judge as "Your Worship" or "Your Lordship," they called him "Kilslii" – a Haida word denoting the greatest respect that can be bestowed on a chief. For two days, a parade of blanketed Haida elders, chiefs, and young people took the stand to provide the most moving and articulate testimony Judge MacKay had ever heard.

Diane Brown, a beautiful young Haida woman with long dark brown hair and a steady gaze, told the court, "We were put on the islands as caretakers of this land...Without that land I very much fear for the Haida Nation...I don't want my children to inherit a land of stumps." Miles's father, Miles Richardson Sr., wearing the traditional dress of an hereditary chief, spoke of his life as a Haida and a logger: "The continuity of our way of life is more important than anything. Future generations will depend on the area for subsistence, and that is more important than short-term logging of old-growth trees."

As the witnesses spoke, the Haida filling the courtroom held hands, some quietly weeping. Lavina Lightbone, a white-haired woman with a will of steel, sang a Haida song from the witness box. She nearly broke down as she told MacKay, "It's a terrible thing...to see a nation die, to see rivers die. It's humiliating to sit here and shed tears, but the devastation put upon us has to come to an end."

The testimony was having its effect both on the court in Vancouver and on the court of public opinion and the politicians who respond to its changes of mood. Every night the Haida's cause was the leading news item on television, and it was the stuff of daily headlines across the province. From Ottawa, Tom McMillan tried to intercede to avert further confrontation, offering to join with the province to buy out Western Forest

Products' timber rights. McMillan estimated that the timber values in question were about $12 million, a figure ridiculed by WFP's president, Roger Manning. Manning reframed the issue of compensation to include not only the company's logging rights but its operations at two pulp mills he claimed relied on Lyell Island for their supply of raw material. "That [$12 million] won't even pay our fuel bills for a year...I just can't believe that figure."

Tom Waterland was no more receptive to McMillan's offer, snapping that Ottawa "should keep its nose out of a matter that isn't any of their business." Even Pelton was unable to respond positively, saying that the matter "is in the hands of a committee that was set up to deal with it."

In an effort to avert further clashes on Lyell Island, church leaders met with B.C. Attorney General Brian Smith to plead for talks with the Haida on the land-ownership issue. But Smith discouraged any hope of negotiation: "It would be a breach of our trust, as representatives of the people of British Columbia, if we even held out the slimmest hope...that we were going to negotiate any land claims on an aboriginal title basis."

A political solution was not possible. The B.C. government was intransigent. It would not open land-claim negotiations. It would not halt logging. It would not consider the federal offer to negotiate compensation for the forest industry. With its head firmly in the sand, it would wait out the crisis: wait for the whole problem to go away; wait for the Haida to be hauled away by the long arm of the law; wait for Beban to finish logging Lyell Island; wait for the next provincial election.

On November 9, 1985, Judge MacKay told a packed and emotionally drained courtroom that he was constrained by the law that he was sworn to uphold to grant Western Forest Products its injunction, making it illegal for the Haida to obstruct the logging road. The only choice now, if the protest was to continue, was to break Canadian law. Anyone blocking the road would have to be prepared to go to jail. No one wanted to be arrested, but the Haida were determined to stop the logging and to preserve their land.

In the early morning of November 14, heavy winds buffeted a small helicopter as it waited outside the Skidegate Band Council office. Most of the young Haida who were prepared to make their stand on Lyell Island had already moved into the area they called Gwaii Haanas, Haida for Place of Wonder and Beauty, but re-inforcements were preparing to come in by chopper: Diane Brown, the young woman who had impressed Judge MacKay with her eloquence, was joined by her Eagle mother, Ada Yovanovitch; by Ada's uncle, a hered-itary chief in his eighties, Watson Price; by Ethel Jones, an elder from Massett; and by Ethel's older cousin, Adolphus Marks. Ethel and Ada had spent much of the night in prayer, seeking guidance for the action they were prepared to take.

It was still dark when the elders clambered into the helicopter and strapped themselves in for the journey over the turbulent waters of Haida Gwaii. An hour's flight took them to Sedgewick Bay, where they were greeted by Guujaaw, by the other Haida youth, buoyed by the arrival of their elders, and by the RCMP. The Mounties had sent Haida members of the force down to Lyell, and at the sight of the elders, they embraced them before heading off to Beban's camp to get further in-structions. This was an unexpected development. Arresting young men was one thing, but no one wanted to arrest elderly women.

The elders were brought coffee and sandwiches as Ada, Ethel, Watson, and Adolphus kept their vigil in the middle of the logging road. Later that day, at the cook-house at the Haida base, the local chief of the Mounties paid them a call. Harry Wallace had been a friend of Ada's husband, a Yugoslavian logger who had died years before, and was still a friend of the family's. He was solicitous, but firm. "If any of you are found blocking the road, you'll be served with court papers. And if you ignore them, you know what will happen." "Yes," said Ethel, "but this is our fight and we have to do it." "You know we'd have to arrest you. You'll have to go to jail," said Wallace. Ada tried to cheer him up. "As long as I have a lot of fancy work to keep me busy, I don't care."

Up on the road, a human barricade of young Haida warriors was being given the same message. They had painted their faces red and had smeared them with black charcoal indicating that they were prepared to make any sacrifice. They shook rattles made with the shells of the islands, while Guujaaw drummed. The Mounties stepped forward and served each of them with a copy of the writ. When the loggers' yellow trucks pulled up, the line parted and allowed them through. Miles explained to reporters that they had permitted the trucks to pass out of respect for Judge MacKay, whom they still called Kilslii. But the press was advised not to leave the area yet.

Back at the camp, late into the night of November 14, discussion and debate raged over how many and exactly who should face arrest. As usual in Haida meetings, these issues were not put to a vote, and the endless round of discussions wore on in search of consensus. Miles, Guujaaw, and the hereditary chiefs had to be persuaded, much against their will, that they were too valuable strategically and would be the first targets for arrest. Then Ada and Ethel put forward their argument that the elders should be the first to be arrested. The whole country would see the humiliation of the nation of Canada arresting the elders of the Haida Nation. They saw it as a way to shame the government for its refusal to discuss the issue, forcing old men and women onto the logging road. The younger Haida disagreed. In an emotional round, everyone in the room had a chance to express his views. Nearly all of them pleaded with their elders not to go alone, not to be taken off to makeshift jails somewhere in Beban's camp, but they were adamant.

Very early on Saturday, November 15, the only non-Haida member of the group went from bunk to bunk, quietly waking the others. Vancouver New Democrat MP Svend Robinson had been invited to join the Sedgewick Bay camp during a chance encounter with Miles the week before. Other non-native supporters had stayed away, honouring the Haida leadership's decision to discourage non-Haida participation for fear it would muddy the waters.

As Ada got dressed, Diane came running in. She had been walking along a little stream and had heard the Raven above. She was sure its chattering was a good omen.

Ada, Ethel, and Watson struggled up the path to the logging road wearing their button blankets over their warm clothes, Adolphus having had to return to Skidegate. Ada and Ethel stood quietly for a while, saying their prayers together and dismissing intruding reporters: "This is our devotion time." They took their places on the benches that blocked the road and waited for whatever was to come. The young people formed a line down each side of the road. Holding cedar branches, they sang and chanted in Haida.

The logging trucks pulled up and stopped in front of the elders. Frank Beban came forward, "You're blocking the road. You're breaking the law." Television cameras crowded in on the burly logger, and microphones pointed into his face, while sound crews ducked to keep the illusion of direct confrontation for the evening news. The Haida young people and elders stayed calm and stared out as impassive as totem carvings – unblinking in

the face of the mass media, the Mounties, and the loggers. Frank Beban continued, "Will you please stand
aside and let us go to work?" No one responded. Harry
Wallace and the other officers began serving writs on
the Haida. Ethel felt a piece of paper being tucked between her folded arms but kept concentrating on maintaining her dignity, on not speaking, on not weeping.
The paper fell into the mud and she never knew what it
said.

Once the writs were served, Frank Beban demanded
again, "Will you please step aside and let us go to work?"
The elders stared straight ahead, and a few moments
later Beban turned away to find the police. The reporters pressed in for comment from the Haida. They
wanted anger. This was a confrontation, after all, and
they wanted a good ten-second clip for the evening
news: Hostile logger confronts militant Haida. "Aren't
you angry?" one reporter demanded of the impassive
Ethel. "No," she answered slowly. "We're not angry. We
just don't like the loggers destroying our land."

The Mounties moved forward to make their arrests,
but backed off and waited politely while Ethel prayed
aloud in Haida. Ada then called for the singing of a
hymn, and led the roadside congregation in "How
Great Thou Art." As the elders moved to the police cars
and vans, shipped in from Graham Island to haul away
the protesters, she turned to address the young people
who would be left behind. "We have to go now," she said.
"So whatever you do, do it with peace and dignity." She
opened the Bible she had had on her lap and read
aloud from the second letter of Paul to Timothy: "For I
am already on the point of being sacrificed; the time of
my departure has come. I have fought the good fight, I
have finished the course. I have kept the faith." For one
young officer the moment was too painful. Alan Wilson
was Haida, from Massett, and he was Ethel's nephew –
the son of her "sister" Gracie, for while Grace was not re-

lated by birth, the community referred to the close friends as sisters. Tears rolled down his cheeks as he prepared to arrest his aunt. She whispered, "You don't have to lay a hand on me. Just put your arm out and let me put my arm through yours. It won't look so bad. Just like we're going for a walk." Unable to speak, Alan followed Ethel's instructions. The protestors on the sidelines drummed and sang, and the procession of Haida elders and Mounties, some in tears, moved to the vans that would take them to the waiting helicopter. They were greeted upon their arrival in Sandspit by dozens of friends and supporters, all Haida, all wearing their finest ceremonial clothes. The three elders were taken to a makeshift jail, where they were fingerprinted and photographed.

Duane Gould, leader of the Moresby Island Concerned Citizens, was also a justice of the peace. He had known Ada and her late husband for years. He hardly looked up at her as he asked, "Your name?" She answered, "Jaadsaankinlhan." She did not tell Gould that it meant Woman of High State Looking Up. Duane Gould tried to write it down and gave up part way. Ethel submitted to finger-printing saying, "For me to be doing this is a disgrace to you people. What did I do wrong for you to do this to me?"

At the same time, in Victoria, a rally of several hundred protesters gathered in front of the parliament buildings to hear the news of the arrests and speeches from Bill Reid, Bristol Foster, and the leader of the Salish Nation, Tom Sampson. It was pouring rain, but the determined crowd stayed to the end, listening to native prayers and Haida songs. Forrest DeWitt, a Tlingit chief from Alaska, offered the closing prayer for peace between native and non-native. Eighty-two years old, he was the most distinguished of the elders at the Victoria rally. His wife, Grace, Ethel Jones's "sister," did not know as she stood on the steps of the parliament building that her son had just arrested Ethel. She was concerned about her husband, who had insisted on coming to Victoria against the advice of his doctor.

After the rally, some fifty people made their way to Huck's house. The small living room was jam-packed when the six o'clock news came on. There was stunned silence as the Haida saw Alan leading Ethel away. Hands reached out to comfort Grace DeWitt, "Don't worry, Nonny Grace. He had to do that." But Grace and Huck were more worried about Forrest, who was shaking with feverish chills. Huck decided to phone the hospital, but the old man made him hang up the phone. "I just want to get to Vancouver tonight," he insisted.

In Queen Charlotte City, Ada was dressing for a potlatch that had been planned to inaugurate the hereditary chief of Skedans, an ancient Haida village on an island north of Lyell. Now the potlatch would be an opportunity for the Haida to share the emotions and experience of the day's traumatic events. After the fingerprinting, all three elders had been released pending their trial, set for January. Boatloads of the others on the blockade were on their way back from Lyell to join in Saturday night's feast. Ada watched the television coverage of the arrests and of the support rally in Victoria. She saw her old friend Grace and heard part of Forrest's prayer. An hour later, as she was on her way out the door, the phone rang with news from Victoria. Forrest had died of a heart attack on the ferry to Vancouver.

Over four hundred people came to the potlatch in Skidegate. Svend Robinson came over to Ada and hugged her. "I'm sorry to tell you that we broke our promise to you to behave with dignity, Ada," he said. "We all cried." "Oh, my dear boy," said Ada, embracing him. If not at that moment, soon thereafter she resolved to adopt Svend Robinson in the Haida tradition as her own son.

The potlatch lasted late into the evening with speeches from Ada and Ethel and Watson, and tributes to their courage from the assembled Haida Nation. There would be no blockade the next day. But the loggers did not observe the Sabbath. During the Haida's day of rest, the logging continued.

19

CONFLICTS
AND CARAVANS

FOR THE NEXT THREE WEEKS THE ARRESTS CONTINUED, and so did the intense interest of the national news media. Scenes of the Haida blocking the road and of Frank Beban and the police asking them to stand aside were becoming standard fare on television. People who had never before heard of South Moresby had now heard of Lyell Island. Pressure built on federal politicians, who appeared increasingly helpless, to intercede and end the dispute.

Western Forest Products' lawyers returned to court twice in those weeks. First they attempted, unsuccessfully, to obtain a court order to require the RCMP to enforce the injunction more vigorously. Next they obtained citations against seventeen people for contempt of court because they were supporting the blockade from the sidelines. This group included Guujaaw, who would not deny *his* contempt, and Svend Robinson, who had stood, wrapped in a button blanket, on the side of the road.

By November 25, ten days after the first arrests, nearly fifty Haida had been arrested and a further seventeen had been charged with contempt. Demonstrations continued in front of the B.C. legislature, and plywood silhouettes of Haida figures, made by Patrick Pothier, appeared on the lawn of the parliament building.

In Ottawa, Jim Fulton was arguing the Haida cause with David Crombie, pointing out the unfairness of the departmental policy that restricted land-claim negotiations to a maximum of six at one time. This comprehensive claims policy had created an endless queue and had institutionalized paralysis. Crombie surprised Fulton by making an unprecedented offer – to develop a "special process," outside the normal policy, to negotiate the Haida claim. When Miles Richardson phoned him later, Crombie volunteered to fly out to B.C. to get negotiations underway, if the provincial government would agree.

Meanwhile, Opposition leader John Turner, a former member of the board of MacMillan Bloedel, was using Question Period to demand federal intervention in the controversy. He directed his question to the Prime Minister, charging that Haida lands were being "despoiled" and asking that Mulroney move to protect "this priceless national treasure." For days Mulroney had resisted the pressure to respond in the House to the escalating crisis on the Queen Charlotte Islands. Tom McMillan had fielded Opposition questions, reiterating the interest of the federal government in preserving the area and lamenting its impotence in the face of provincial obduracy. But the issue was not going away. Bill Bennett was expected in Ottawa on November 26 for discussions in advance of the next First Ministers' Conference. Finally, Brian Mulroney could avoid questions no longer. In answer to a question from NDP leader Ed Broadbent, he vowed to raise the matter with Bennett, calling South Moresby a "troubling situation," and repeating expressions of interest from his two relevant ministers, Crombie and McMillan.

The climate seemed to be warming toward compromise, but Bennett's arrival quickly chilled the air. After meeting with Mulroney, he called a press conference and rejected any notion of federal mediation in the conflict. He was unyielding. The primary consideration, he explained, was "that we...not interrupt the forest licence."

Bennett's intractable position was nearly incomprehensible, but political observers began to suspect a strategy of galling cynicism. With a provincial election possible in early spring, many began to speculate that Bill Bennett was deliberately inflaming the stand-off at Lyell Island in order to exploit anti-Indian sentiment in the election campaign. Editorial comment in the *Globe and Mail* was direct, saying that Bennett's behaviour "lends credence to Opposition charges that he is laying the foundation for a mean-spirited anti-Indian campaign in the next election, widely expected next spring."

Court dates came and went. Contributions and pledges of financial support poured into the Haida Nation from across the country. American folk music legend Pete Seeger held a benefit concert, raising $30,000 toward the Haida's legal costs, and Bruce Cockburn donated $35,000 from a Vancouver concert. Church groups, human rights organizations, and concerned environmentalists sent donations. The Anglican Church, without success, attempted to gain status in the trials as a friend of the court in support of the Haida. Rev Peter Hamel of the Anglican Church, bird-watcher and naturalist, had a long history of commitment to conservation and native justice issues. He spent more and more time working with the Haida Nation. "This is a human rights issue," he said. The former moderator of the United Church, Bob Smith, visited the Charlottes and explained his presence by saying that God exerts a "preferential option" and sides with the poor and oppressed.

By the end of November, seventy-two Haida had been arrested for blocking the road. Over two hundred thousand dollars had been spent to maintain the police force on the island and to transport the protesters. The cost to the Haida had been far greater. Days upon days had been spent in court hearings, but the issue was no closer to resolution. B.C. Attorney General Brian Smith maintained that he could not meet with representatives of the Haida Nation as long as the blockades were in place and the matter was before the courts. When they heard this excuse, the Haida suspended their blockade. Still Smith refused to meet with them. Instead, the provincial government unsuccessfully sought an extraordinary injunction, prohibiting the Haida from going anywhere near Lyell Island, including its coastal waters. This clear infringement of civil liberties led to protests from the legal community. A public opinion poll conducted by the *Vancouver Sun* should have given Bennett pause. It demonstrated that 60 per cent of British Columbians favoured opening land claim talks with the Haida. Tom Waterland dismissed the poll as "uninformed opinion."

Finally, on December 10, Smith agreed to meet with representatives from the Council of the Haida Nation: Tom Greene, Lavina Lightbone, Guujaaw, and Miles. After more than two hours of intense discussion, Miles left to tell waiting reporters that the meeting had accomplished little. Smith admitted that he had been impressed by the passion of the Haida and the breadth of their arguments, and he told the press that he would ask cabinet to reconsider logging Lyell, but he held out little hope of opening discussions to resolve the land claim.

In Victoria, J.B. had spent the past few weeks poring over court affidavits from the 1978 legal challenge to the renewal of the tree farm licence, as well as figures submitted by Western Forest Products to the Planning Team. He was certain that the climate for confrontation had been artificially fuelled by WFP's claim of economic disaster if Lyell were not logged. The Islands Protection Society held a press conference in Victoria to challenge WFP's claim. J.B. supported his charges using the company's own figures. Far from supplying 20 per cent of the mills' requirements as WFP claimed, J.B. showed that the South Moresby portion of the TFL provided only 6 per cent. Moreover, one of the forest companies in the WFP conglomerate, Whonnock Industries, was actually exporting logs to Asia, significantly undermining any suggestion that local supplies were tight. As for WFP president Roger Manning's claim that the South Moresby timber was worth $45 million annually, J.B. told reporters, "this is the most bizarre of all WFP's claims. [It] works out to a value of over $250 per cubic metre of wood, when court affidavits from Beban clearly show a value to him of $26 per cubic metre."

Reporters seemed surprised by these figures and especially by the news that Beban had already completed his 1985 quota and had been preparing for the normal seasonal shut-down when the new permits were allowed. No one from the media had questioned the loggers' arguments. From a press angle, the pathos of unemployed loggers had been the perfect counterpoint to the tremendous appeal of Haida elders clutching their Bibles on the logging road. Even the press outside Canada found it an irrestible story. The *National Geographic* was preparing an article, and stories had already appeared in English, Indian, German, and Dutch newspapers. The South Moresby crew saw the possibility of forming international alliances.

A coalition of U.S. groups had already formed to support the Canadian crusade to save South Moresby. They nominated South Moresby for listing as one of the world's most threatened natural areas by the International Union for the Conservation of Nature, based in Geneva. In mid-December, they met with Canada's ambassador to the United States, Allan Gotlieb. Representatives of some of the largest and most respected conservation groups in the world, from the National Parks and Conservation Association to the Audubon Society and the Sierra Club, hinted to Gotlieb that Vancouver's Expo 86 might be made a target for international action. Paul Pritchard, president of the NPCA, told Canadian reporters, "The coalition is urging visitors to see both sides of B.C. if they visit Expo 86...[including] the unparalled destruction of South Moresby."

As Christmas approached, the seething controversy on Lyell Island appeared to be waning. Beban's crews would be stopping work through the holidays, and were not expected to resume until later in January. Huck and J.B. decided to head east during the respite to do a little media work and fundraising. Monte Hummel, executive director of Canada's World Wildlife Fund, arranged for them to show their South Moresby slides in the Toronto office of Adam Zimmerman, president of MacMillan Bloedel. Hummel had gathered a small group of influential and well-heeled businessmen for the presentation. Zimmerman himself appeared to lose interest sometime during Huck's description of the endemic species of the Canadian Galapagos, and left to attend a Christmas party. But the remaining corporate and monied Torontonians were impressed. One of them was so moved he donated enough money to keep J.B. and Huck in groceries for the next two years. For while there were many things that Huck and J.B. did well, taking care of their basic financial needs was not among them. All royalties from *Islands at the Edge* went to the Islands Protection Society, while they lived from hand to mouth. Somehow this was apparent to Glen Davis, a supporter of the World Wildlife Fund, who nearly adopted J.B. and Huck.

In Ottawa, Huck, J.B., and Gregg Sheehy organized a small rally on Parliament Hill. Before leaving town, Huck, putting on his Tom Sawyer hat, outlined for Gregg a grandiose scheme for a national train caravan in March 1986 – a whistle-stop tour from Newfoundland to Vancouver, gathering support with rallies in each town along the way. Huck wasn't discouraged when

Gregg protested there was not enough time to organize it properly, saying, "Well, sleep on it. I'm sure we could do it."

In B.C. Bryan Williams was valiantly trying to save the credibility of the Wilderness Advisory Committee when he read an item in the business section of the *Vancouver Sun* stating that Western Pulp, a company in which he had invested in 1982, was a partnership of which Western Forests Products was a part. He realized that this conflict of interest could sink both the WAC and his own reputation for personal integrity. He immediately instructed his lawyer and his investment broker to place his debenture in Western Pulp in a blind trust.

A few weeks later, in mid-January 1986, the CBC revealed that the man who had personally granted logging permits to WFP since its inception – Tom Waterland – held a $20,000 investment in Western Pulp. Then Glen Bohn of the *Vancouver Sun* discovered that Stephen Rogers had a $100,000 holding in the same company. As energy minister, Rogers determined the rates pulp mills paid for electricity. He and Waterland both sat on the the cabinet's Environment and Land Use Committee. Editorials across the province were quick to demand the resignation of both ministers.

When Glen Bohn phoned Williams, he was prepared for the inevitable question and Williams calmly explained that he had placed his shares in a blind trust. Bohn had a good story in any event. If Williams had been smart enough to realize his conflict of interest when he was only a temporary adviser to government, why hadn't the two ministers had the sense to do the same thing?

The media and the public were scandalized and, eventually, Premier Bennett called for Tom Waterland's resignation. The man who had described South Moresby as "a clear-cut decision" was finally (albeit briefly) out of the cabinet. In firing only Waterland, Bennett drew a curious distinction between the two ministers, explaining that Rogers did not have a conflict of interest as he did not have direct ministerial responsibility for forestry. The explanation didn't wash, and a few weeks later, Rogers did step down for a short time.

With the scandal dominating the headlines, the province announced that there would be a moratorium on new logging permits for Lyell Island until the WAC reported back. Beban's crews could continue logging the south side of Lyell Island under the permits Waterland had issued in November. When this was announced in the first week of February 1986, logging crews had nearly completed the over-cutting they had begun in November. Once again, Beban raised the alarm that men would have to be laid off if the moratorium remained in force.

Meanwhile, WAC members fanned out in an attempt to see all twenty-three areas for which they had to issue recommendations. They could not all visit each site, but at least one member of the committee reached every contested wilderness area, if only to hover over it by helicopter. It was rapidly becoming clear that, of all the diverse areas under their consideration, only South Moresby and the Stein Valley were truly contentious within the committee.

Committee members had pledged to keep their internal debates and potential compromises confidential, but there were several leaks. Colleen saw a consultant's report to the committee indicating that a sixty-kilometre logging corridor would be recommended within the Moresby wilderness. She blasted Williams in the press saying that the WAC was "moving toward a complete sell-out of the South Moresby preservation area." Williams was quick to deny it. More disturbing to committee members were nearly verbatim accounts of their meetings, repeated in a way that suggested the pro-logging side was winning within the committee. Only one of their own members could leak such information, but that person was never identified.

The WAC report was expected in early March, and preparations were moving into high gear for the great national train caravan, which Huck had proposed to Gregg Sheehy. It had to arrive in Vancouver before the report was published. Gregg Sheehy had suppressed his doubts and had agreed to organize it, even before J.B. and Huck had left Ottawa before Christmas. The caravan would begin in St John's, Newfoundland, on March 5, 1986, and would arrive in Vancouver ten days later. The trip would be punctuated with five overnight stops: Halifax, Montreal, Toronto, Winnipeg, and Vancouver. The Canadian Nature Federation office in Ottawa was the nerve centre, working with volunteer regional co-ordinators across the country. Huck, J.B., and others organized the Regina to Vancouver route, with Pat Stephenson, a native coordinator, working out of Victoria. Gregg Sheehy had never before taken on such a daunting organizational nightmare. It was a Big Plan fraught with risk. If it failed, it would fail publicly and miserably.

In Sandspit, Pat Armstrong saw possibilities for the caravan as well. If Thom Henley was going to go cross-country spinning his magic about the misty isles, Pat was determined to dog his every step to present the other side of the story. The forest industry contributed money toward the costs of two counter-caravan campaigners, but Pat made sure they were also backed by community money raised in two dances on the islands. The Moresby Island Concerned Citizens Committee selected Bob Long and Pat to follow the caravan. They flew from city to city, while the caravan chugged along on Via Rail. With the time they saved in transit, Bob and Pat held press conferences, visited other forest industry representatives, and lobbied politicians.

By the time Huck and Gregg got to St John's for the start of the tour, Pat and Bob had already done much to undermine their credibility. Thanks to the anti-sealing protests of the 1970s, environmentalists were not popular in Newfoundland. Bob and Pat met with the Canadian Sealers' Association to ask for their support, arguing that the South Moresby crusaders were out to get the working man, just like the save-the-seals softies had been. But the advance work by the Chain Saw Twins, as they were called by the caravaners, had the unintentional side-effect of increasing press interest in the issue. The possibility of confrontation between the two sides attracted more reporters and increased their audience. At the St John's public meeting the night before the start of the caravan, Huck and Gregg yielded the floor to give Bob and Pat equal time. By the end of the meeting, it was clear that the environmentalists had won the argument. Sealers stood in line to buy buttons and to sign petitions to save South Moresby.

In North Sydney, Cape Breton, after the overnight ferry crossing from Newfoundland, Huck and Gregg were thrilled when twenty supporters boarded their train, including seventeen young Micmac Indians from the Eskasoni Reserve who drummed and sang on the long ride to Halifax. Sue Stephenson, Atlantic Region coordinator for the caravan, boarded in Moncton, carrying a woollen blanket to which she planned to stitch patches made by supporters across the country. The patchwork blanket would be given to the Haida at the end of the trip. There was a strong contingent of cheering Acadians on the platform as the train pulled out of Moncton, and Huck began to believe that his crazy idea might actually work. Sometime after midnight, when Huck was awakened by a commotion outside his window, he saw that the caravan *was* succeeding in mobilizing new support. The train had stopped at the tiny station of Fredericton Junction, and Huck was amazed to see a stalwart band of some thirty-five people standing knee-deep in the snow and waving placards and balloons at one in the morning.

In Montreal, a rally had been organized at a local church – the first Quebec event to raise awareness of South Moresby. The next morning the caravan members faced an unexpected blow. They owed $800 for the use of the church, an unforeseen expense they had no way of paying. As they boarded the train in Montreal, an elderly woman came forward. She pressed a cheque into Sue's hand, saying, "Thank you. This gives me hope." Sue's eyes welled with tears as she saw the amount, $1,000.

Bob Long and Pat Armstrong continued to garner press coverage in every city they visited. They had skipped Montreal and had flown on to Ottawa in order to lobby members of Parliament and the cabinet. Their staunchest supporters were the members of the Progressive Conservative caucus from B.C., who organized a breakfast meeting for the Chain Saw Twins. Bob Long and Pat Armstrong were in their element. Bob railed against the hippy draft-dodgers who were trying to put Frank Beban out of work. They urged the caucus to pressure Tom McMillan and David Crombie to back off. This was B.C.'s business, they argued, and if the federal Tories understood where their support lay, they would stop championing NDP causes.

John Fraser sat quietly through most of the session. He was in what he would later refer to with an ironic twinkle as "disgrace." He was no longer a minister, but he was respected in the House of Commons, and not without clout, even now. As he cleared his throat, his colleagues shifted nervously in their chairs. Fraser's views on South Moresby were well known and the other caucus members had hoped that he would not disturb an otherwise harmonious breakfast.

Fraser narrowed his gaze on Bob Long and asked, "Two or three generations from now, where will anyone be able to see a thousand-year-old tree on the B.C. coast?" Bob Long pooh-poohed the issue, "That's not the point – " Fraser persisted, "Where is there a single thousand-year-old tree, except for in existing parks, that is not already part of a tree farm licence?" Bob and Pat were stumped.

Canadian Nature Federation supporters had planned a rally at the Ottawa train station to greet the arrival of the growing number of caravaners. Inside the station almost two hundred people waited for the train and for Tom McMillan, who was due to welcome the South Moresby stalwarts and to speak at the rally. As the train pulled up to the station, bleary-eyed caravaners poured out to the cheers of the waiting throng. A huge kite in the form of an eagle was paraded through the station to the accompaniment of bagpipes. Charles Caccia spoke to the crowd about the wide non-partisan support for the cause. The train was due to leave for Toronto in fifteen minutes when Tom McMillan showed up with several harried aides trailing behind. He put on a caravan hat and said that he favoured saving "as much of South Moresby as possible, including Lyell Island."

Caccia boarded the train for the ride to Toronto, plying the weary travellers with juice and cookies. Sue Stephenson sewed a new patch on the blanket. Other caravaners walked through the cars, selling buttons, putting up balloons, and gathering signatures on the petition. The mood on board became festive and contagious. Conductors and other passengers caught it. At each stop, supporters brought dozens more completed petitions.

In Toronto, Pat Armstrong and Bob Long were waiting at Union Station for the train to arrive, but the

Chain Saw Twins were about to be totally upstaged. Throughout the trip they had made the claim that they were the only real residents of the Charlottes on the caravan. As they held court with the press in a corner of the station, they heard a familiar and commanding voice. Ada Yovanovitch, Haida elder, road blockader, and definitely a resident of Haida Gwaii, was joining the caravan together with Ethel Jones, Watson Price, Guujaaw, and Ethel's sister, Grace.

The organizers of the Toronto event scheduled for later that evening were extremely anxious. Rev Peter Hamel had reserved the largest church in Toronto, St Paul's, which could hold three thousand people. Kevin McNamee had lined up entertainers and speakers, including Pierre Berton and the Most Reverend Edward Scott. Meanwhile, another organizing committee led by a Massett resident and community organizer, David Phillips, had planned an event at the Diamond Club to follow the church event, featuring performances from the Nylons, the Canadian Aces, and other popular bands. The Diamond Club organizers and the St Paul's Church coordinators had nearly come to blows in the frantic weeks leading up to the Caravan night. Kevin had argued with David that the two events would split the audience. David was certain that the Diamond Club event would be a hit. "We have to synchromesh!" he pleaded with Kevin. "We have to make it happen." Kevin was despondent. He had no idea if anyone, much less several thousand people, would show up at the church. It was a miserable night, pouring rain and bleak. But shortly before seven-thirty, people began to pour into the church. By the time Pierre Berton arrived, there were at least seventeen hundred people, where a few minutes before there had been no one. Each one of them had had to pass by the Chain Saw Twins, lobbying on the church steps.

The high point of the evening was the arrival of the Haida elders. Wearing the traditional black and red flannel of the Haida, Ada, Ethel, Watson, and Grace walked slowly to the altar. Most of the people in the church had seen them on the evening news being led away to police vans. Seeing them in the flesh, their dignity and stoicism evident, caused an unexpected wave of emotion. The entire audience spontaneously rose to its feet. Much to their amusement, the elders were introduced as "criminals" to cheers and prolonged applause.

When Pierre Berton spoke, he called the clear-cut logging of South Moresby "an act of vandalism, a national disgrace." Miles Richardson was the first guest since the Pope to speak from St Paul's pulpit. He spoke with his characteristic eloquence, and David Crombie joined this roster of powerful speakers, preaching to the converted.

It seemed that nothing could top the enormous success of that event, but the Diamond Club benefit was still to come. The contrast between the two events was startling. On the club's dance floor, young women and men with spiked hair and safety-pin earrings danced to deafening music. Beer was served from a garbage can to a full and noisy crowd. Amid all this stood the Haida elders, staring in disbelief at the throngs of young Torontonians gyrating in a smoky bar. Kevin was concerned that they might be offended. As he put his arm around Ada, she started to cry. "Oh, Kevin," she blurted out, "I had no idea people this far away cared."

To the bizarre crowd of punks and freaks, Miles was introduced as though he were a rock star. Bob Rae, provincial leader of the NDP, played the piano, and the comedians from the Second City improvisational company performed. The event was an enormous success. Both events had been triumphs, and had drawn entirely different audiences. The church and the rock'n'roll bar had synchromeshed.

On the train from Toronto, the major topic of conversation among the caravaners was the Wilderness Advisory Committee, whose report had just been released. Its South Moresby recommendation was an attempt at compromise, protecting most of the wilderness proposal but allowing continued logging. On Lyell Island, only a thin buffer of trees would be protected along the coast of Darwin Sound. On the Windy Bay watershed, the committee recommended a 675-hectare ecological reserve be established, but not protected as part of a national park. The string of islands at the north of the wilderness proposal area - Richardson, Tanu, and Kunga – would be logged.

The compromise pleased no one. Environmentalists assailed it, and forest industry executives claimed it would cost the province millions in lost revenues while creating higher unemployment. Colleen led the charge against the committee for its failure to protect Lyell. But in a rare spirit of something akin to compromise, Colleen did express gratitude that, at least, the committee had recommended national park status for most of the area.

The WAC recommendations caused a dilemma for the South Moresby supporters. Ninety per cent protection was better than nothing. But the whole campaign had arisen in large part thanks to the spectacular beauty of Windy Bay, which would be heavily logged under the WAC plan. Moreover, as long as logging on Lyell continued, so would confrontations with the Haida. The WAC recommendations were clearly unacceptable to the Save South Moresby campaigners. Even Bob Long, still following along behind the caravaners, ridiculed the recommendations. In a remark that delighted even his strongest adversaries, he said that the committee had opted for "the sailboat option – setting aside corridors so that guys sailing their sailboats can be happy with not having to see any type of industrial development in South Moresby. Landscape logging is not going to work."

As Bob Waldon, the organizer of the Winnipeg caravan event, said, "Sharing South Moresby with the logging

industry is like sharing your horse with a glue factory."
Waldon had put together a rally at Hotel Fort Garry,
where four hundred people watched Cree and Métis
dancers and heard songs from the Haida caravan members. In Regina, a crowd of well-wishers maintained
their candlelight vigil for South Moresby until the 3 a.m.
train rolled in at dawn.

As the train crossed the mountains into British
Columbia, spirits soared. The caravaners were headed
for the largest rally yet, in the place where it was most
needed. They had twenty-seven thousand more names
on petitions than they had when they had left St John's.
Thousands of people had participated in the cross-
country string of rallies, vigils and concerts. But
Vancouver would have to be the biggest and the best.
WC Squared stalwarts Paul George and Ken Lay had
worked for weeks to ensure that the rally would be a success. As the train rolled on through the night, Guujaaw
kept a group of passengers awake teaching them the
song he had sung on the logging road at Lyell, the
Coming into the House song.

The train was due into Vancouver at 1 p.m., on
March 15. Over two thousand people jammed into the
terminal to celebrate its arrival. Huck and Gregg unfurled the eagle banner and walked into the station,
leading the hundred or so people who had joined the
caravan. With Guujaaw drumming, the neophyte
singers formed a solid chorus behind the eagle. They
were joined by singers inside the station led by Mike
Nicholl and other Haida who had come down from
Haida Gwaii for the rally. To everyone's great delight,
the two choruses discovered they were both singing the
Coming into the House song – in unison. Welcoming
speeches were made by Robert Bateman and Bristol
Foster, while Salish Indians danced in greeting.
Thousands of people then poured out from the station
to march down Georgia Street to the Canada Place

Pavilion for the rally. Later that evening there would be a benefit concert with Long John Baldry and Doug and the Slugs. As the street filled with the jubilant marchers, above the train station in downtown Vancouver, a lone bald eagle circled.

20

FATE
OF THE EARTH

IN THE SPRING OF 1986, BRITISH COLUMBIANS PREPARED
to welcome the world to their extravagant showpiece,
Expo 86. Premier Bill Bennett could not be accused of
underestimating the fair's significance when he declared that it was "certainly the most important event of
the century for British Columbians." With international
attention fixed on Expo, the South Moresby crusaders
made sure that the wilderness islands were not over-
shadowed.

On April 31, the Prince of Wales officially opened
Expo, accompanied by his wife. But even the tightly
controlled protocol of a royal tour could not keep
South Moresby out of the headlines. As soldiers stood at
attention outside the parliament buildings and the
army band, replete in freshly starched uniforms and
pith helmets, played the royal anthem, overhead an airplane circled. Trailing behind the plane was a banner
for all to see, proclaiming, GOD SAVE THE QUEEN
CHARLOTTE ISLANDS. Late that night, Prince Charles
spoke at a dinner and said that B.C. should save South
Moresby.

Another visit of the world community to Vancouver
was expected in spring 1986. The World Commission
on Environment and Development, chaired by
Norway's prime minister, Gro Harlem Brundtland, had
been set up by the United Nations to address the critical
global issues of environmental degradation, population

pressures, poverty, and militarism. It was coming to Vancouver to hold one of a series of public hearings in Canada. It had already held meetings in places as diverse as Jakarta, Oslo, and São Paulo, where a full gamut of interest groups – peasant farmers, politicians, and industrialists – had presented their concerns.

The meetings in Vancouver were scheduled for the end of May, following sessions in Halifax, Quebec City, Ottawa, Toronto, and Edmonton. Canada's representative on the commission was a long-time South Moresby supporter, Maurice Strong, who was proud of the quality and calibre of presentations they had heard across Canada. But then they got to B.C. There, while promoting tourism to Expo with native dance and art, the provincial government decided not to allow any native presentations to the commission. Miles Richardson had contacted the Vancouver coordinators of the commission's hearing with a request to speak. It had been denied. Maurice Strong was appalled and arranged for a separate meeting with the Haida. After the official hearing in Vancouver, a delegation headed to Skidegate for meetings with Miles Richardson and other Haida representatives. The visit had an indelible impact on the commissioners. Emil Salim, the minister of environment from Indonesia, was shocked. He later asked a Canadian friend, "If Canada cannot save an area like South Moresby, what hope is there for the rest of the world?"

Although Emil Salim's comment was spoken only to one friend, it reverberated: If we can't save this one little place, what hope is there?

Within days of the Brundtland Commission's Canadian tour, Tom McMillan launched the first ever high-profile, million-buck Environment Week. It was a disaster. Caught with a sudden influx of money and no plans for how to spend it, the departmental organizers spent it badly. Over six hundred and fifty thousand dollars went to produce a rock video on an environment

theme, featuring Tom McMillan singing with the
Edmonton Oilers. Another eighty thousand dollars or
so was spent on hot-air balloons that had to be cancelled
after one nearly broke loose on Parliament Hill.
McMillan's honeymoon with environmentalists appeared to be over. The South Moresby group was still
giving him the benefit of the doubt, but other environmentalists across the country felt that the time for pa-
tience was over.

After the opening of Expo 86, Bill Bennett surprised
political observers by announcing his resignation. The
press had been prepared for an election call in British
Columbia. Now they also had a Social Credit leadership
race to keep them busy reading political tea leaves.

South Moresby receded from the headlines. On May
20, the provincial cabinet had decided to accept the recommendations of the Wilderness Advisory Committee
"in principle." They had made a vague commitment to
discussions with the federal government to create a national park at South Moresby, but nothing was moving
very fast in those negotiations.

In late June, senior federal bureaucrats met in
Vancouver for what they thought would be the first genuine bargaining session with their provincial counterparts. Instead, the provincial officials explained that
formal negotiations for the creation of a national park
in the Charlottes could not begin until two events occurred. First, the British Columbia cabinet had to approve their negotiating position, and second, the
province demanded that Ottawa clear away the seven-
teen-year-old debt for the Pacific Rim National Park.
This was Canada's first west coast national park, encompassing the long white beaches of west Vancouver
Island. Protracted negotiations had finally resolved to
expand the park to include a contested area of forest
called the Nitinat Triangle. But the $24 million payment

Bald Eagle at Windy Bay, Lyell Island.

Lone kayaker surveys the clear-cut slopes of Lyell Island.

Richard Krieger

Huck (Thom Henley) crouches on the stump of an eagle's nest tree. Lyell Island, 1978

Richard Krieger

Guujaaw between decaying mortuary poles at Ninstints, 1978.

Richard Krieger

Huck, Guujaaw, and Paul George on the shore at Gwaii Haanas.

Islands at the Edge, with J.B. (John Broadhead) and Huck looking every bit its proud authors.

The RCMP read the injunction order prior to arresting the Haida elders in 1985. Seated, l. to r., Ethel Jones, Ada Yovanovitch, Watson Price, Adolphus Marks. Standing behind Watson Price: Diane Brown and Svend Robinson.

The Haida
demonstrate
in front of the
Vancouver law
courts, following
their sentencing
in December 1985.

Huck leads the
caravan parade
in Vancouver,
March 15, 1986.
Centre; Mike
Nicholl, drum-
ming, next to
Miles Richardson,
president of the
Council of the
Haida Nation.

Caravan rally
in Vancouver.
Foreground, l. to r.,
Ada Yovanovitch,
Ethel Watson,
and Guujaaw,
drumming.

Miles Richardson
dancing at the
Sedgewick Bay
bunkhouse,
March 1987.

Jeff Gibbs

Jeff Gibbs

Guujaaw drum-
ming as the
RCMP join in the
dance during
the dedication of
the Windy Bay
longhouse.

Bill Reid (front)
in *Loo Taas*
in Vancouver
Harbour before
its voyage to
Haida Gwaii.

Martin Roland

The South Moresby agreement is signed in Victoria, July 1, 1987. L. to r., Tom McMillan, Brian Mulroney, Bill Vander Zalm, Bruce Strachan.

Celebrating in the aisle of the P.M.'s back-up plane. Clockwise from bottom l., Bristol Foster, Elizabeth May, David Suzuki, Sharon Chow, Al Whitney, Peter McAllister, Kevin McNamee.

Skidegate band chief, Tom Greene, presenting Jim Fulton with a blanket from the Haida, July 1987.

Tom McMillan cuts the cake he ordered to replace the one "squashed by a bear in Banff." L. to r., Vicky Husband, Tom, Miles, Huck.

Celebrations at Windy Bay. L. to r., Gregg Sheehy, Colleen McCrory, Vicky Husband.

More celebrations. L. to r., Huck, Jeff Gibbs, Kevin McNamee, Vicky Husband, John Faser, J.B., Colleen McCrory, Tara Cullis, Elizabeth May, David Suzuki, Gregg Sheehy, Terry Husband.

in compensation to the province had not been paid by Ottawa.

Within a week of the first South Moresby negotiations, the B.C. government approved five new cutting blocks on Lyell Island and logging resumed on July 9. To reaffirm the sovereignty of the Haida Nation over the area, Guujaaw, Miles, and seven other Haida renounced their Canadian citizenship. "As Canadians your courts ruled that we have no rights to protect our land," said Miles. Despite a province-wide strike by members of the International Woodworkers of America, Frank Beban was able to start logging by working out a sweetheart deal with the union.

Meanwhile most attention in B.C. was focussed on the Socred leadership race, not on South Moresby. The leadership convention was set for the first week of August at Whistler and competition for Bennett's post was keen. The early odds-on favourite was the flamboyant extrovert, devout Roman Catholic, and Dutch immigrant William Vander Zalm. With a toothpaste smile and an infectious enthusiasm for people and politics, Vander Zalm seemed to herald an era of optimism. In the late 1960s he had hoped to capture the leadership of the provincial Liberal Party. In that distant time, Vander Zalm had courted the support of Vancouver lawyer Bryan Williams, the man who later chaired the Wilderness Advisory Committee. During his speech at a Liberal rally in Penticton, Vander Zalm had suggested that criminals should be whipped. Williams had been concerned. "Bill," he cautioned, "you really shouldn't joke about a thing like that." Vander Zalm was nonplussed, "I wasn't joking." "Then you're in the wrong party," said Williams. Within a few years, Vander Zalm had become an avid member of the Social Credit Party.

He had been minister of social services in the Bennett government, but for the last few years had been out of provincial politics. In August 1986, Bill Vander

Zalm became premier of B.C. and all that was required for the official anointment was the political mandate of a successful election campaign.

An equally significant change in government took place at the federal level with hardly a whimper. Deputy Prime Minister Erik Nielsen resigned in June and Mulroney appointed as his new senior lieutenant a former car salesman from Alberta. Don Mazankowski had distinguished himself in the transportation portfolio, and Maz, as he was known, would run the government for the remainder of the Tories' first mandate and into the second. The difference in the Mulroney government between Nielsen's guidance and Mazankowski's was nearly as distinct as if an election and change of parties had taken place. Mazankowski cleaned the Prime Minister's Office, bringing in seasoned professionals to replace the small circle of old friends who had dominated decision-making in the first part of the Mulroney mandate.

In the first week of June 1986, activists from around the world came to Ottawa for the Fate of the Earth conference. The organizers wanted to ensure that the plight of the Haida be given prominence among all the other international issues. On the night of the first public plenary session, the hall at the Ottawa Congress Centre was full to capacity to hear Nobel Prize winner Dr George Wald, folk singer and activist Pete Seeger, movie actress Margot Kidder, Marion Dewar, Ottawa's mayor, and Guujaaw. George Wald addressed the crippling problem of Third World debt, identifying it as a cause of environmental disasters and human suffering around the world. Margot Kidder talked about the need for activists to join political parties and work within the system. But for all the celebrities and fanfare, for all the movie-star glitter, Guujaaw stole the show.

When Guujaaw rose to speak, without warning, he opened with a long, compelling war song in Haida. He sang a cappella, for he was even without his drum. Some quick-witted lighting technician instantly killed the house lights and put a baby spotlight on the long-haired Haida. When the song was over, he had the audience in the palm of his hand. He spoke of the history of the Haida Nation when his people roamed the seas and were masters of the coast, when food was plentiful within the waters of Gwaii Haanas. He told of the deaths of thousands of Haida, felled by white man's diseases. He talked of the Haida's long search to regain their culture and traditions. "We are trying to rebuild our numbers," he told the transfixed crowd. "Us young fellas do all we can." And then he laughed, and hundreds of people roared with him. He went on to describe the fight for Lyell Island, and he won over the whole conference to the cause.

The day after the conference ended, Tom McMillan attended the annual meeting of the Canadian Environmental Network. It was the network's first meeting since the Katimavik session with Suzanne Blais-Grenier. McMillan felt he could win over the audience of sceptical activists with a little coup all his own. He knew he needed better relations with people in the conservation and environmental community. Meetings were sporadic and follow-up inconsistent. He often did not know until it was too late that some well-intentioned press release would mean hell to pay from his environmental constituency. He decided that what he needed was a real live honest-to-God environmentalist working right in his own office. In late May, he arranged a meeting with someone he had already described in a national radio interview as a new member of his staff – me!

When McMillan called, I had no idea what he wanted to talk to me about. I had known him slightly since his time as environment critic, largely because one of my friends from Dalhousie Law School had worked as an aide to McMillan on and off. It seemed that every other time I was flying from Halifax, where I lived and practised law, I bumped into Rob Burnett and Tom McMillan at the airport. I had talked to Tom about tourism when he was tourism minister, because my family had had the misfortune of going into the tourism business in Cape Breton.

In 1973, my family had left behind an affluent life in Connecticut to open a restaurant on the Cabot Trail. Largely because of my mother's political activism against nuclear weapons testing in the atmosphere, and later against the war in Vietnam, I had grown up with the idea that all of us have to do whatever we can to stop unconscionable actions. It was my grandmother's motto that seemed to run my mother's and my reaction to problems: "Thought without constructive action is demoralizing."

When we moved to Cape Breton it seemed unlikely that I would ever be an activist again. I was too busy trying to keep the family business afloat. I couldn't afford to return to university, and spent nine years cooking and waitressing. But I did get involved when there were environmental threats, joining with neighbours to oppose chemical spraying of our forests, first against the use of insecticides to kill budworms, and then in a costly, unsuccessful, devastating court battle to prevent the use of herbicides to kill hardwoods. During the court case against 2,4-D and 2,4,5-T, I had somehow managed to finish law school, having returned to university as a mature student in 1980. By 1983 I was working in a downtown Halifax law firm, recuperating from the pain of losing the two-year herbicide case. I was just beginning to feel like my old self again when I got a job offer in Ottawa – a chance to work full time for good causes without having to worry about how the clients could pay. So I moved to become associate general council to the

Public Interest Advocacy Centre. The move to Ottawa roughly coincided with Tom McMillan's becoming environment minister, an appointment I wholeheartedly supported. It also coincided with the Fate of the Earth Conference, to which I was elected co-chair. When McMillan's office called to ask if I was available for a meeting, I thought that it might have to do with the conference. The last thing in the world I expected when I finally met him in the boarding lounge of the government hangar at the Ottawa airport, was to hear that he wanted me to come work for him, to be something like an in-house environmental lobbyist.

I explained that I could not possibly think of taking another job. He had to dash for his plane, but urged me to think about it. I did. Indeed, I could think of nothing else. I phoned friends in the movement for advice and, of course, my family. With only one exception, everyone urged me to give it a try, but to be very cautious and to brace myself for the accusation that I had sold out. When I next met with him, a week or so later, I had my questions thought through.

We met in his office in Les Terraces de les Chaudières in Hull, overlooking the hills of Quebec and the Chaudière Falls on the Ottawa River. I didn't realize that he had already virtually announced my appointment during a CBC Radio interview. He would have agreed, I think, to almost anything to get me to join his staff. Everytime I suggested that there were things I would no longer be able to do, he would counter, "Oh, no. You could still do that." Whether it was completing the Ontario bar admission course or serving on the boards of environmental groups, of which I was on a half a dozen, McMillan denied that anything would have to change if I agreed to be his adviser on environmental issues. He even dismissed my suggestion that I would have to stop speaking in public about environmental issues, saying, "As long as you make it clear that you don't represent the government of Canada when you speak, I

want you to stay involved in the environmental groups. I
want you to be my ambassador to the movement, and
the movement's ambassador to me."

I said, "Tom, I don't know how to say this, because I
like you, and I think you've been doing a good job as
minister, but" – and here I took a deep breath (how do
you ask someone if you can trust them without sounding
as though you don't?) – "the thing is I'd have to be really
involved in decisions." "Of course, you would be," he
said earnestly. "You'd be in every discussion on every environmental decision." It was getting harder than I had
thought to say no.

I tried a more direct approach. "I couldn't be used as
window-dressing – not that I'm saying you'd do that. It's
just that you have to be very careful hiring a person like
me," I continued, taking one last deep breath, "because
I'm the kind of person who'd quit on principle and that
would be worse than if you'd never hired me at all."

McMillan leaned foward, and said gravely, "It's precisely because you're the kind of person who'd resign
on principle that I want you to advise me on issues."

I had warned him. There was no reason to say no, unless I was more afraid of the loss of face in being called a
sell-out than I was interested in seeing if I could make a
difference from the inside. I found myself saying yes.

In retrospect, I realize that I should have asked such
questions as "Will I still be able to do my laundry?" or "Is
it okay with you if I buy groceries?" But I did not know
that then, and I had run out of objections.

On June 9, 1986, I turned thirty-two, and Tom
McMillan announced to assembled environmentalists
from around the country that I was their ambassador.
Only some of them thought this was good news.

I showed up for my first day of work on August 1 to
the top floor of the tallest high-rise tower in Hull,
Quebec. Things were slow in the summer of 1986. The

House was in its summer recess and ministers' offices had relaxed from the frenetic pace of winter to a nearly comotose state. McMillan was in P.E.I. for the summer, mingling with his constituents on the island's beaches. Just what an adviser was supposed to do with no one to advise was not clear to me or to anyone else on staff. The acting chief of staff was welcoming and friendly when I presented myself for duty. But it was clear he had no idea what my job was. There was no written job description and no precedent for the position I'd been recruited to fill. I finally latched onto the deputy minister's executive assistant on the other side of our floor. The line down the middle of the twenty-eighth floor of les Terraces de les Chaudières separates the minister's "exempt" or political staff from the department and the non-partisan, but intensely political, ranks of the civil service. Crossing this line between the never-never land of the political staff and the domain of the career bureaucracy would prove to be valuable. Most ministerial staffers stay out of the civil service turf. If a chat with a bureaucrat is necessary, the political aide sends a message to the relevant assistant deputy minister and a reluctant official is summoned to the minister's office to meet with a member of his staff.

In the doldrums of August, the only life on our floor was on the deputy's side of the office. While no one in the department had any idea what my job was either, they were prepared to provide information, briefing notes, and ideas about what I might be interested in. McMillan's entire staff was composed of four special assistants, a speech writer, and the chief of staff. None of them was interested in environmental issues and no one followed up on ministerial policy commitments, such as promised national parks or new toxic chemical legislation. Instead, the staff functioned reactively. Criticism from environmental groups was automatically perceived as a bad thing, and environmentalists were considered trouble. The staff seemed to see their job as keeping people away from the minister – especially those pesky environmentalists.

My sense that McMillan's staff was not sympathetic to environmentalists was confirmed by a call from Colleen McCrory. We had been friends since we had first met at the Katimavik meeting of the Canadian Environmental Network the previous year. Colleen outlined months of unreturned telephone calls and fruitless attempts to get a meeting with McMillan. "He said he wanted to meet with us on South Moresby in June, but I can't get anyone in his office to call back. It costs a fortune to call from B.C. just to get the run-around in Ottawa. Thank God you're in there, Elizabeth." I told Colleen I'd find out what was happening on South Moresby as soon as possible, and arrange a meeting with McMillan.

But before I got a chance to start work on South Moresby, I was presented with the challenge of resolving an impasse over the creation of a national park on Ellesmere Island in the Arctic. Kevin McNamee from the National and Provincial Parks Association of Canada had written a letter to the editor of the *Globe and Mail,* which was published on my second day at work. It began, "Canadians should stop giving federal Environment Minister Thomas McMillan standing ovations every time he promises us a national park." The letter went on to detail McMillan's promise for South Moresby, for Ontario's Bruce Peninsula, and for the park on Ellesmere Island. This was the park Tom McMillan had promised to the Banff Assembly in September 1985. McNamee charged, "It is almost one year later and the agreement sits unsigned, a victim of political gamesmanship...I hope that the Minister's welcome commitment to South Moresby exceeds his commitment to completing Ellesmere. It's time to stop promising and start delivering."

McMillan, interviewed later that day from Charlottetown, called McNamee's charges "bull," and went on to blame the Tungavik Federation of Nunavut for "playing politics and holding the park hostage." I didn't know whether McMillan's answer was his own natural response, or whether someone in the department had suggested a defensive position. By the time I saw the interview, I had already pursued my natural inclination. I'd picked up the phone as soon as I got to the office and called Kevin McNamee in Toronto. He seemed to know chapter and verse how a national park on Ellesmere Island, once a forgone conclusion, was slipping away. "The whole thing has been messed up from day one. The Territories' government hasn't heard from McMillan's office in months about scheduling the signing."

I thanked him and promised to keep him posted as I tried to get the park back on track. In retrospect, it was quite wonderful that no one was around to try to indoctrinate me in the etiquette of ministers' staffs. I called people I thought had the best information. I called Kevin for help without worrying whether it would make the government look good. I ignored hierarchy; it saved a lot of time. I phoned the Ellesmere Park planner, Murray McComb, down in the bowels of the building. He had nearly given up. All his entreaties for action had stalled somewhere between his office and the deputy's. He could hardly believe it when I said I wanted his help to get the park deal signed before winter. He was ecstatic.

The bureaucracy had braced itself for my arrival, expecting a cross between Bernadette Devlin and Patty Hearst. Within no time, however, those who wanted to accomplish something, whether in parks or in control of toxic chemicals or acid rain, realized that I wanted to help. Word spread through the department that I was interested in parks. On August 15, I got a call from the South Moresby park planner. "My name's Barry Olsen, and I was just wondering if you'd like a briefing on South Moresby?" Within ten minutes, a good-looking,

sandy-haired fellow in his late thirties was sitting opposite me in my tiny office.

Barry Olsen was the bureaucrat who had written the
lyrical briefing note that had enraptured McMillan a
year before. He had been working on Moresby for years
and was as committed to saving it as any of the activists.
But while meeting with me, he maintained his civil-ser-
vice bearing and presented the professional view of a
dispassionate parks planner. He outlined the progress,
and the lack of it, in the negotiations with the province.
"What I'm really worried about," he explained, "is that
the minister said in a radio interview out in B.C. a few
weeks ago that he would be going to British Columbia
soon for a meeting with his provincial counterpart. But
no one from the minister's office has phoned anyone in
B.C.'s government. It will be embarrassing when the
press follows up on it."

We obviously had to get McMillan out to the West
Coast as soon as possible. I took two pages of notes and
scribbled all over the copies of letters and memos that
detailed the current state of affairs. Barry showed me
the difference between the WAC boundaries and the
original wilderness proposal boundaries, upon which
both the Haida and the environmentalists would insist.

I stared at the map. I didn't know much about the
South Moresby issue. I'd never even seen a detailed map
of the various boundary options, but I did know how determined Colleen and Vicky could be, and I remembered Guujaaw's speech at the Fate of the Earth
conference, and the arrests of the Haida the previous
November on the logging roads of Lyell Island. I may
not have known much, but I did know that a park without Lyell Island would result in outrage from the people
who had fought to save South Moresby.

During my first month on the job, I drew up a tenta-
tive agenda of fall events. I had unofficially declared
September to be Parks Month. We had to get to the
Arctic to create the Ellesmere National Park; we had to

get to Victoria to meet Austin Pelton and provide a firm commitment that the Pacific Rim debt would be paid off so that South Moresby negotiations could begin in earnest; and, to round things off, we could release a long-awaited Marine Parks policy in Toronto at the end of the month.

McMillan returned in late August, looking tanned after a summer of constituency work. He seemed worried that I had actually been in the office so much. "I hope you weren't here just in case I phoned?" he asked. "No," I said. "I really found quite a lot to do." He looked baffled. For the next two years, I really don't think he ever understood what it was I did when I was not completely consumed by his personal requests.

I had asked Gerry Fitzsimmons, the deputy minister's executive assistant, if Ellesmere and South Moresby could be put on the agenda at the deputy minister's briefing, the only formal meeting to review issues and divine ministerial attitudes. The new deputy had joined the department at roughly the same time as McMillan had assumed the portfolio. In keeping with Mulroney's aggressive promotion of women and francophones, Genevieve Ste Marie was both. Fortunately her executive assistant had had experience working with Jacques Guerin. But Ste Marie's inexperience, for this was her first deputy ministerial assignment, would be a handicap for McMillan. The senior bureaucrat of the national Parks Service was also a recent appointment. Jim Collinson had become assistant deputy minister earlier that year, coming from a background in Treasury Board and Indian Affairs. All of us gathered in the boardroom for the briefing.

Collinson set out for McMillan where the Ellesmere issue lay. I added my information on Kevin's concerns and stressed the Territories' desire that the agreement be signed in the North. We would not have much time, as by the end of September the weather would deteriorate. To my surprise, Tom looked over to me and said,

"All right, Elizabeth. I want you to look over every aspect of the Ellesmere issue. I want you to personally attend to every detail. Call the minister's office in the Territories and pick a date." He paused for emphasis, "You understand? I do not want you to delegate a thing."

I was surprised, but pleased. McMillan had previously cautioned me as a non-Tory member of his staff not to call other minister's offices. It was always a little murky as to when I could be seen as a member of McMillan's staff and when I should be invisible. But the Ellesmere experience set the pattern for my role. First I would advise that a course be taken, and once McMillan was persuaded, I would be responsible for steering it.

A National Park Reserve was created on Ellesmere Island on September 20, 1986. We were joined on our trip north by Kevin McNamee, who witnessed the agreement on behalf of the people of Canada. And, thanks to a call from a friend who was an Arctic scientist, we managed to establish the North's first National Wildlife Area at Polar Bear Pass on the same trip. I was beginning to feel giddy. Nothing had ever seemed as easy as making wonderful things happen from the minister's office.

It was a shame that Jim Collinson and I would not see eye to eye on South Moresby. We certainly had a good foundation for working together after Ellesmere. As we flew back to Edmonton from Resolute, I presented him with a birthday cake I had ordered from Ottawa. The other passengers – media, government dignitaries, and civil servants – played along in surprising him and singing a boisterous version of "Happy Birthday!" We were all feeling close and in good spirits when we landed in Edmonton, and Tom, Rob Burnett, and I got off the plane on which we'd spent nearly thirty hours to catch a commercial flight to Vancouver and our first negotiating session on South Moresby.

21

THE MIRACLE OPTION

TOM MCMILLAN HAD MORE THAN ONE REASON TO HEAD for British Columbia after establishing his first national park. Monday, September 22, was officially Prince Edward Island Day at Expo. *Anne of Green Gables* would be performed, and a roster of Island dignitaries would be on hand for the festivities. The Environment Canada British Columbia office went all out for the minister's visit. They rented limousines – long, white monsters that Tom complained made him feel like a pimp.

The meeting with Auston Pelton was almost entirely a formality. Our two offices had agreed in advance on a joint press release to announce the beginning of serious negotiations to create a national park at South Moresby. The major obstacle to those negotiations, the outstanding debt for the Pacific Rim National Park, was to be removed. Jim Collinson had hoped that the minister would seek "new money" to pay off the $25 million, plus interest, owed for the last seventeen years by the federal government to British Columbia. But Tom McMillan's opinion was that "you can only go to the well so often." Having just obtained $5 million to fund Ellesmere Island National Park for its first few years, Tom was loath to return to cabinet, hat in hand. He instructed Collinson to find the money within the basic Parks' budget, even if it meant that maintenance of existing parks would suffer.

McMillan and Pelton greeted each other as old friends before they closeted themselves away for a private chat. Later they called in their staffs for a final review of the press release. It was all terribly cordial and civilized. For the moment, the federal and provincial government were prepared to agree to disagree. British Columbia was willing to negotiate a national park at South Moresby based on the boundaries proposed by the Wilderness Advisory Committee. McMillan countered that the federal government wanted to have a much larger area for the park, including a marine park. The starting negotiating positions were far apart, but the key news was that discussions to close the gap were finally beginning in earnest. I phoned Colleen and Vicky to let them know the content of the news release, while Tom made an important phone call to Miles Richardson. McMillan wanted the Haida to be kept fully informed of developments.

Election fever was heating up across British Columbia. Later that week, Bill Vander Zalm flew up to the Charlottes in a surprise pre-campaign swing, showing up to go fishing and mingle with the folks without so much as an aide or a press attaché in sight. The prospective Socred candidates for the riding wooed their new provincial leader, but Bob Long, half of the Chain Saw Twins, had the inside track. His father had been a deputy minister in the Bennett government and had worked for Vander Zalm in his leadership bid. As he was one of the leaders of the pro-logging lobby in Sandspit, Bob Long's candidacy was seen as a test of the loggers' political strength. The *Red Neck News* urged its readers to "Vote Long – Save our Jobs!"

While Vander Zalm campaigned with a pledge to end the confrontational style of the Socred government, the Haida were preparing for another round of blockades. Quietly, avoiding press attention, they transported materials to Lyell Island to build a longhouse on the shores of Windy Bay. Frank Beban's crews began cutting new logging roads to the blocks on the south-facing slopes of Lyell, looking out toward Hot Springs Island.

Western Forest Products submitted their new five-year logging plan to the provincial Forest Service. The most effective access-to-information process in Canada, well-timed leaks, allowed the maps and cut plans to make it to my office in Ottawa, as well as to J.B. and Huck. By 1990, the clear-cutting would reach well into the Windy Bay watershed. It was clear that the next battleground would be Windy Bay – the place that had inspired the campaign twelve years before. The British Columbia government wrote to the Haida warning that the building of any structure on Lyell was illegal, then promptly began some construction of its own – temporary holding cells at Beban's camp. The transportation of the arrested Haida blockaders had put too large a dent in the provincial treasury. This time temporary jails would be ready on site.

On October 22, 1986, the people of British Columbia elected a new government, or at least they gave Bill Vander Zalm a political mandate. In the course of the campaign, he had dodged South Moresby as an issue, except to suggest that logging Lyell Island would be necessary as the trees were "diseased." Colleen McCrory had managed to elicit this response at an all-candidates meeting in Nelson, just before she had been shouted down. In the Charlottes, Bob Long lost to the NDP candidate, Dan Miller. R.L.Smith's repeated endorsements in the *Red Neck News* had not been sufficient to sway the body politic.

Vander Zalm's first cabinet shuffle removed Austin Pelton as environment minister and handed the portfolio over to Stephen Rogers, the former energy minister with the troublesome $100,000 investment in Western Pulp. That investment had forced a brief cabinet resignation for Rogers, allowing him to enter the environment portfolio with a clean slate. Jack Kempf became minister of forests. With a reputation as a maverick within cabinet, he was known as Wolfman Jack. The loss of Pelton was seen as a bad sign for the future of South Moresby. Even though he had been unable to stop logging or to preserve the area, the Haida and environmentalists had felt that his heart was in the right place. Stephen Rogers was another matter altogether. Within days of his appointment, rumours circulated that the cabinet had decided to reconsider its approval in principle of the WAC recommendations. Some observers feared that the whole negotiating process would go off the rails. These fears were justified in December when the B.C. government announced that Western Forest Products' five-year plan had been approved, with the caveat that any logging of Windy Bay would require a further cabinet-level decision. But WFP's whole five-year plan was premised on the logging of Windy Bay.

In negotiating sessions throughout October and November, provincial officials insisted that most of Windy Bay would have to be logged. The federal position was less clear. Parks Canada's internal map indicated protection for a few more areas – strips of trees along the shoreline of Lyell, Richardson, Tanu, and Kunga, to shield tourists from any view of clear-cuts – and showed Windy Bay as a proposed provincial ecological reserve.

I did not realize until it was nearly too late that federal negotiators had conceded in the very first session in early October that the WAC boundaries were acceptable "in principle" for a national park. Parks Canada's position was that the federal government was interested in "possible modifications" to the WAC line. It was like a house buyer holding tough with a vendor saying, "You want $200,000 for this house, and eventually I'll be prepared to pay that. But for now, I'd like to see if you'll sell it to me for less."

During these negotiations, I was distracted by a myriad of other issues, assuming that South Moresby was in hand. Briefing notes from the department did not reveal that our negotiators had given away the store on day one. I learned that from Vicky Husband and Colleen McCrory. I couldn't believe it and asked to see copies of the minutes of the negotiating sessions, instead of the sanitized summaries in briefing notes. There it was in black and white. Colleen and Vicky were right. We had given up Windy Bay. I asked Tom if he realized this had happened. He denied it and promised we would make it clear that we wanted much more than the WAC compromise position. But as I railed to sympathetic friends in the Parks Service about Collinson's acceptance of the WAC boundaries, word came back to me that he had had McMillan's approval before he took that position. I had no way of knowing for sure if this was true. All I knew was that we had to reverse the position.

Ever since Stephen Rogers' appointment as environment minister, we had been planning a negotiating session between him and McMillan. The issue of boundaries could no longer be left to the vague platitudes of ministerial press scrums. I was convinced that we had to spell out what we were prepared to have logged and what we would fight to include in a national park. In private, Tom had agreed that we needed a thorough briefing to review the whole situation, but time was at a premium. Through November and December both he and I were swamped with drafting new legislation on toxic chemicals, amendments to the National Parks Act, the reform of federal environmental assessment, federal-provincial acid-rain agreements, not to mention the normal daily crises.

But Colleen kept phoning, and Mike Nicholl, now executive director of the Council of the Haida Nation, gave me cryptic messages about imminent Haida blockades. Vicky called several times a week, each time with the same message: "Elizabeth, you've got to make Tom understand that accepting the WAC boundaries would be the worst thing he could do. We'd feel totally betrayed by the federal government. Nothing would have been solved, and arrests would go on." I tried to reassure her that I would give the message to Tom, but I had misgivings myself. "Vicky, what if we lose the whole thing? I mean isn't ninety per cent of it better than nothing?"

"Not if it means logging Windy Bay. Windy Bay is critical to the whole proposal. It's the heart of the entire wilderness area. If the federal government caves in and accepts a national park on the WAC boundaries, it will make it that much harder for the Haida and the rest of us to protect Windy Bay. National public opinion may think the issue has been resolved." Vicky was very persuasive. "Look, Elizabeth, tell Tom we'll defend him if he takes a stand for Lyell Island and negotiations fail. But," she added, "we will not defend him if he gives away Windy Bay."

One night one of the province's most sympathetic bureaucrats dropped by Huck's house when Vicky and other South Moresby supporters were there. He pleaded with them to compromise on the boundaries. Vicky could stand it no longer. She leaped from her chair and stunned even her friends by the vehemence in her voice, "No! We've compromised enough already. Lyell Island has been logged almost every day for the last ten years. Every tree lost was a compromise. No more. We are going to save the whole thing, including Windy Bay. That's how it's going to be." And shaking with anger, she left the room.

Her conviction persuaded me that somehow they'd save the whole thing – as long as we didn't sabotage them. I didn't know how they'd do it, but I knew that they would. By early January 1987, I was determined that Tom McMillan had to meet Stephen Rogers before it was too late and make it clear that a park without Windy Bay was no park at all.

Then I learned the British Columbia press had unearthed yet another scandal. Once again, Stephen

Rogers was involved. This time, it was the inclusion in his financial disclosure form of his interest – more than 30 per cent – in Forest Investments Ltd, a holding company with investments in MacMillan Bloedel and its parent company, Noranda Mines. As MacMillan Bloedel had a timber licence covering part of South Moresby, including portions of Lyell Island, Rogers had a clear conflict of interest. The New Democratic opposition was quick to demand his resignation, but Vander Zalm defended his minister, reasoning that what was good for MacBlo was good for the province. "Obviously, we want the value of shares to increase, and we want the values of industries to increase. The only thing is we don't want people making decisions for personal gain."

Rogers did not resign and I started the long process of finding a convenient time for both ministers to meet. The first available date was not until mid-February.

Following the approval of Western Forest Products' five-year plan, the national media increasingly pressed Tom McMillan about South Moresby. Conservation spokesmen had urged that the federal government withhold federal equalization payments to British Columbia, bringing the full weight of federal government authority to bear. Tom rejected the suggestion, saying that any such federal-provincial war was antithetical to the principles of cooperation that typify Canada. But then he went on to suggest to reporters that he did not have much support in cabinet. The eyes of his cabinet colleagues, he said, "glaze over" when parks are discussed. He painted himself as the lone environmentalist in a sea of red-necks.

Reaction to his comments was swift. In British Columbia it was read as an admission of defeat. The provincial government said it welcomed McMillan's conciliatory remarks, but environmentalists were outraged. In private, cabinet ministers asked him why he had assumed he had little support when he hadn't yet raised the subject. Some of the reaction surprised him.

Almost in awe of his cabinet colleagues, Tom had not believed they were interested in the environment. "You know, Elizabeth," he told me in wonder, "after caucus today, Barbara McDougall came up to me and said, 'I hope you know that I support you on South Moresby.' How about that? Barbara McDougall!" And he was left musing over the support he didn't know he had. Over the next few weeks, other cabinet ministers – Flora MacDonald, Joe Clark, and Pat Carney, among others – took the time to tell him that they could be counted among South Moresby's supporters.

British Columbia's recent actions had strained federal-provincial harmony. The federal government had collected an estimated $375 million through a 15 per cent lumber export tax, earmarked for forest worker retraining and silviculture projects. But, Kempf, B.C.'s new minister of forests, announced that the money would be placed in the general revenue fund to offset some of the provincial debt. Forty million seedlings, costing $30 million, were ready to be planted in nurseries around the province. With the money gone, the program was cancelled, and so were the seedlings. Pat Carney, the formidable minister of trade and a member of the federal Tory B.C. caucus, was indignant, "Every British Columbia member of Parliament knows that our forests are a silvicultural slum."

As the February negotiation session with Rogers approached, I was having a hard time placing South Moresby on the agenda of the weekly ministerial briefing sessions. Week after week, the South Moresby item slipped off the bottom of an overcrowded agenda, and I grew increasingly nervous. Then, a happy combination of events allowed me to force the issue. The meeting with Stephen Rogers had been scheduled for February 18. Jim Murray, executive producer of The Nature of Things, had requested an interview with McMillan for early February for a further special on Windy Bay, and the Canadian Nature Federation had invited him to the

film première of a documentary on the Save South
Moresby Caravan on February 10. We could no longer
afford to wait until the eve of the meeting with Rogers
to sort out our position on boundaries. The CBC interview would be broadcast after McMillan's meeting with
Rogers. Whatever he said in the interview would have to
be consistent with what he said to Rogers and to the
Canadian Nature Federation crowd at the film première. I was finally able to put South Moresby first on
the agenda for a ministerial briefing.

It became clear in the preliminary strategy meetings
that the Parks Service and the Policy branches of
Environment Canada were not going to agree. The
Parks officials saw the goal as the creation of a national
park in the Queen Charlotte Islands at the least possible
cost. The policy group saw the goal as meeting public
expectations that the Haida's homeland and a spectacular wilderness would be protected. These goals were not
entirely convergent.

After fruitless attempts to arrive at a consensus I met
with Gerry Fitzsimmons (who had moved from being
executive assistant to the deputy to head up the federal-
provincial relations branch of the policy group), to
hammer out an analysis to present at the next briefing
session. In all our discussions, bureaucrats and officials
had demanded to know what good I thought it could
possibly do to hold out for more. What could possibly
persuade the British Columbia government to halt logging and create a park beyond the WAC boundaries?
There was only one honest answer: "a miracle." So,
identifying the issue as "What result for South Moresby
equals a success for the Minister of the Environment
and the Federal Government?" Gerry and I outlined
four options:

"(1) *Miracle Option* – Minister convinces B.C. to halt
logging to preserve status quo during negotiations.

"(2) *High Road/Mobilize Option* – Minister stands firm
in public and in private for more of Lyell Island (i.e.,

Windy Bay, South Slopes).

"(3) *Mobilize Support/High Road/Confront Option* –
Minister stands firm with ultimatum to B.C.: Either include Lyell or forget the whole thing.

"(4) *Capitulate Option* – Minister accepts WAC boundaries. Gets park, loses public."

The ministerial briefing session was a little like the
shoot-out at the O.K. Corral. Down one side of the table
sat an array of senior officials. The minister, as always,
sat at the head of the table, and to his right were members of his personal staff. I was seated in my now-usual
place – first in from the chief of staff. The meeting was
tense from the start.

Jim Collinson, who knew I would not accept the WAC
boundaries, did his level best to convince McMillan that
they were as good as we were going to get from the B.C.
government. He argued that there was nothing particularly special or significant about Windy Bay from a Parks
point of view. "Every single species found there, every
natural feature, can be found in other parts of the area
within the WAC boundaries." He suggested that the
Haida would likely log Lyell Island, if they ever got control. "The environmentalists are just being used by the
Haida." This argument would be used two ways over the
next few months. Sometimes it was argued that the environmentalists were the dupes of those tricky Indians.
Other times, it was put that the environmentalists were
manipulating the gullible Haida.

I countered with our memo, supported by a number
of soon-to-be chastised bureaucrats from the Policy
branch, and described what I thought would be the result of a decision to create a park on the WAC boundaries. "The confrontation will get worse," I began. "The
Haida have already built a longhouse at Windy Bay and
they're prepared for a long siege. And this time, every
Haida is prepared to get arrested. And when there are
no more Haida to face arrest, David Suzuki and his wife
and his father have said they'll get arrested. And, of

course, Bill Reid, and Maurice Strong, and dozens of environmentalists – probably entertainers like Bruce Cockburn. It would go on for weeks, and the federal government would be seen to be on the wrong side of the issue. We will have given away the one bargaining lever we had, creating a national park. Everyone will accuse us of betrayal."

Back and forth we went. I could see hostility flash in the eyes of the deputy minister and the assistant deputy minister for Parks. I had learned enough of the ways of political staff and bureaucrats to know that you were never supposed to disagree in front of the minister, as the minister was never to be put in the position of making an actual choice. The "choice" was narrowed to a range of three options, and everyone, including the minister, knew he was supposed to pick the middle one. But as much as I regretted the blows to egos and careers that might take place, I knew I had no choice. If the minister was not prepared to take a chance, to try saying just once to B.C., "It's Lyell Island or nothing," then we would never know what might have been possible.

I moderated my argument. "All I'm suggesting, Mr Minister, is that it's too early to cave in to the WAC boundaries, and that we should hold the line that we want as much of Lyell Island as possible – what you've said all along."

Tom sat silent for a moment. Then he took a breath and assumed control of the meeting. "My instinct on this is that we have to be on the side of the angels." I breathed a sigh of relief. Tom continued, "When I meet with Stephen Rogers, I'll make it clear that there are certain minimum features to a national park and that protecting as much of Lyell as possible is necessary if we are to have a park."

I looked over apologetically at Jim, but inwardly I cheered. Then Tom turned to me, "And Elizabeth," he said sternly, "you better make sure that the Colleens and Vickies of this world stand by me on this."

22

THE ELEMENT
OF SURPRISE

DURING THE CABINET SHUFFLE OF JULY 1986, THE HAIDA
had lost their staunchest supporter; David Crombie was
moved to become secretary of state for multiculturalism
– a move intended to give the popular Crombie a portfolio with a greater profile in his native Toronto. He was
replaced by Bill McKnight, a Saskatchewan member
with no experience and little interest in native rights
and land claims.

If anyone was more surprised by Mulroney's decision
than the country's native leaders, it was McKnight himself. Bill McKnight was direct, stubborn, and on the
right wing of the party. He immediately distanced himself from some of the policy directions of his predeces-
sor. Any thought of dumping the comprehensive claims
policy was abandoned, as was Crombie's commitment to
a "special process" to deal with the Haida land claim.
But this issue was a thorn in the side of Indian Affairs.
While McKnight was not prepared to deal with the land
claim, neither did he want to see arrests of the Haida –
that was a political tinderbox no one wanted to see ignit-
ed. In that regard, McMillan had the support of his
House of Commons benchmate, Bill McKnight. If the
Haida issue could be resolved by the environment minister, it was one less headache for McKnight, at least
from a public-relations standpoint.

Miles Richardson had been upset by remarks
McMillan had made to the press earlier that he could

not use "heavy handed" tactics to save South Moresby, but Miles knew that McMillan was still the best hope and the strongest ally the Haida now had in cabinet. I stayed in touch nearly daily with Mike Nicholl. As the logging moved onto the south slopes, even Parks officials became concerned this would compromise the park. I kept hoping a blockade of some kind was imminent.

Again and again, Mike would tell me that the Haida were about to move on Lyell. We knew that the RCMP were ready to move, but were the Haida actually going to risk arrest again? I wasn't the only one wondering. Activists throughout British Columbia were calling the offices of the Council of the Haida Nation, offering help, asking to be allowed to join the blockade. But Miles was biding his time, waiting for the moment when there was no choice but to hold the line.

On the evening of February 10, 1987, the Canadian Nature Federation held its gala South Moresby Caravan film première in the ballroom of the Château Laurier in Ottawa. Tom and I arrived late, finding our seats in the darkened room as the film was underway. It was quite good, considering its shoe-string budget. Tom was impressed, whispering, "That's Lorne Green narrating this, isn't it?" The song at the end of the film was donated by Bruce Cockburn and, again, Tom was impressed. A panel discussion followed, including master canoeist and film-maker Bill Mason and Parks' own Barry Olsen among the speakers. The emcee recognized the VIPs in the audience, among them Charles Caccia and Tom McMillan. McMillan was asked to make a few remarks. Tom whispered to me, "What should I say?" I smiled encouragingly, "Just speak from the heart."

I had grown to trust Tom's instincts. I knew that in a room full of supporters, he would say the right thing. His speech was the best I had ever heard him give. It was brief, and in contrast to his much-laboured-over written speeches, he was not pedantic or overly clever in his turn of phrase. He spoke clearly about the magnificence of the area and of his commitment to save it. And he went one step further than he ever had gone in public before by saying that the national park must include Windy Bay. The audience of several hundred applauded loudly.

With our trip to British Columbia less than a week away, South Moresby began to dominate our daily agenda as it had never done before. Tom had a meeting with Bill McKnight to keep him informed and to solicit his agreement that the Haida be kept fully involved in park negotiations. Based on meetings I had had with McKnight's political staff, it seemed reasonable that we could tap into some money for tourism development from the Native Economic Development Fund. Tom and McKnight discussed the possibility of pooling resources to get more money into the kitty for a park deal. McKnight agreed, provided nothing we did could be viewed as settling the Haida land claim.

The other major item for the meeting with Stephen Rogers on February 18 was the Pacific Rim Agreement. The two ministers would finally be signing the legal document creating the park, which had been established seventeen years before. Tom wanted to have cash in hand, for dramatic effect. He told Collinson, "I want a cheque with me for eight million dollars to the province. And I don't want them to know about it. I want to be able to produce it at the proper moment at the press conference." Then he lowered his voice, "But if I don't like the way things are going, I'll just keep it in my breast pocket and bring it back to Ottawa. It may just help with the South Moresby negotiations." Jim agreed, and for the next week he jumped through innumerable hoops with Treasury Board to get permission to draw a cheque for $8 million. Orders went down the line that no mention of the cheque should be made in the joint federal-provincial press release.

We flew to Vancouver in the government's Challenger jet, a comfortable eight-seater with such good acoustics that it was possible to hold useful meetings in mid-air. Jim Collinson was grinning from ear to ear as he passed the cheque to each of us. "I don't know, Jim," I smiled. "With a small plane and eight million, why don't we just go to Tahiti?" Despite his resentment of my forcing changes to our position on the boundaries, Jim and I were still managing to get along fairly well. And the flight to Vancouver was made in high spirits.

Those good spirits crashed the next morning. We held an early briefing session with the regional officers of Environment Canada before the 8:30 a.m. meeting with Forests Minister Jack Kempf. In the briefing session we were given a draft of the joint federal-provincial press release. We were outraged. After all the insistence on total secrecy about the cheque, there it was in the press release. McMillan was seething, "Does this mean that the province knows I have a cheque for eight million?" Nervous officials looked everywhere but at the minister. The bravest of them summoned the courage to mumble, "Yes, minister."

"I see," said Tom. "Well, I don't know how this happened. But I guess we've lost the element of surprise. And I'm not pleased." That last part was a huge understatement.

The meeting with Kempf was brief and inconclusive, as he left the real discussion to be conducted by Stephen Rogers. As Kempf left, the next round of meetings began, one I had been looking forward to. I had set up a session with Vicky Husband and a coalition of B.C. wilderness groups: Sharon Chow came from the Sierra Club of Western Canada, John Mikus and Al Whitney came from the wilderness tourism groups, and there were also representatives from the B.C. Wildlife Federation and local affiliates of the Nature Federation.

Tom McMillan needed to go through the South Moresby strategy with this inner circle before facing Rogers. Al Whitney spread out a large map on the table, around which a dozen of us were seated. He pointed to where logging was happening at that moment – slopes McMillan had seen in the fall of 1985 on Lyell that were being clear-cut. Vicky stressed that Windy Bay was the heart of the wilderness proposal. Tom reviewed his strategy with them, asking, "If I risk it all to save Windy Bay, will you back me up?" Vicky, Sharon, and Al spoke for the rest: "Absolutely."

The meeting restored Tom's good spirits. After some hugs with old friends, we headed off for Tom's meeting with Stephen Rogers. The press conference was scheduled for 2 p.m. and we thought that the ministers would have a short private chat and then invite their staffs to join them for substantive negotiations. As it was, Stephen Rogers, a burly mustachioed man, took the more diminutive, dapper McMillan straight into his office for nearly two hours of conversation. Vicky, John Broadhead, and other environmentalists waited in the hallway, along with reporters, for the beginning of the press conference. A room away I nervously paced and wondered aloud, if quietly, "What the hell is going on in there?"

Inside, Tom McMillan was wondering if Stephen Rogers could possibly be the environment minister. Afterwards, he told me that he had never heard such a string of epithets against environmentalists in his life. "The whole South Moresby thing was started by a bunch of hippy draft-dodgers, you know." Tom said that he hadn't known that. "Bunch of tree-huggers..." Rogers went on in a virtually non-stop diatribe against the people Tom looked to as his strongest supporters. Tom finally did tell Rogers that he could not accept a park on the basis of the WAC boundaries, that a national park had a requirement for certain minimum features, and that if Lyell Island was clear-cut, too much would be lost to justify a national park. Rogers didn't seem overly concerned. If there was no park at all, it would be just fine with him. Eventually, they agreed to go out and face the press, knowing the difference in their views would come to light.

After the formality of the official signing of the Pacific Rim Agreement and the presentation of the $8 million cheque, the ministers agreed to answer questions. Tom reviewed the progress of his talks, first with Pelton, and now with Rogers. He explained that Pelton had favoured a park based on the WAC boundaries, but that the federal government had assumed that this was merely a starting point for negotiations. "Unfortunately, there has not been any movement on British Columbia's part," Tom said. "We do not see eye to eye on the boundaries question. For our part, if there's going to be a national park, it must go beyond the WAC boundaries to include a marine park and a substantial part of Lyell Island."

The "if" in Tom's answer had caused reporters' pens to stop in mid-scribble. Then someone asked, "Are you saying that the boundary issue jeopardizes the creation of a national park?" To which Stephen Rogers and Tom McMillan simultaneously answered, "Yes."

This was news the press had not expected. Tom McMillan had seemed so anxious for a park that the idea that he might actually walk away from negotiations over the issue of boundaries had not occurred to anyone. "Look," Tom said, warming to his position, "There is no interest on our part in cutting a quick and dirty deal for the sake of saying we have a national park. It must meet certain minimum park values." He went on to argue for a logging moratorium during negotiations, as more and more land would be "foreclosed" from national park status as it was logged.

Newspapers across British Columbia picked up the

significance of his position. The *Vancouver Sun* headline the next day read, "South Moresby Park Threatened – Ottawa, B.C. can't resolve logging." Its editorial called on the B.C. cabinet to reconsider its position, especially in light of the federal government's commitment to pay off its Pacific Rim debt and compensate B.C. for South Moresby. Straight from the press conference, Tom had gone to Jack Webster's studio for an interview. He held his ground well against Webster's aggressive questions, denying that he was trying to force the park down any-one's throat. "Look, Jack," he spoke soothingly, "if we create a national park at South Moresby it will be be-cause the people of British Columbia want a national park at South Moresby."

The ball was now in the federal government's court. Tom had promised Stephen Rogers that the federal gov-ernment would put the specifics of its proposal on paper so that Rogers could take it to cabinet. I knew this meant another round of difficult sessions with Parks of-ficials. So far, even Tom's bold step of insisting on more of Lyell Island had been devoid of specifics. Drawing the federal government line at anything less than the full wilderness proposal would be painful and difficult. But, as much as I wanted the whole area to be protected, I knew that was impossible. I just held firm to the idea of saving Windy Bay. Meanwhile, Vicky was as good as her word, telling reporters, "We're happy the federal gov-ernment realizes a national park is not a national park without Lyell Island. A logging road is being built into Lyell right now. Hopefully, there'll be some eleventh-hour agreement." She could not have known how close she was to predicting the precise moment the issue would be resolved.

23

Chain Saw
Concerto

Sᴏᴜᴛʜ ᴍᴏʀᴇsʙʏ ʜᴀᴅ ᴛᴏ ᴛᴀᴋᴇ ᴀ ʙᴀᴄᴋ sᴇᴀᴛ ᴛᴏ ᴏᴛʜᴇʀ issues for the rest of February. We were trying to conclude acid-rain agreements with reluctant provincial governments in New Brunswick and Nova Scotia and we were arranging signing ceremonies with Prince Edward Island, Newfoundland, Ontario, Quebec, and Manitoba. The idea was to have the Canadian acid-rain control program in place before the Mulroney's next summit with Ronald Reagan in April. The draft environmental protection legislation required fairly constant review, and, as always, dozens of other issues kept leaping to the fore, demanding resolution.

One afternoon in early March, Kevin McNamee phoned. We had stayed in fairly close contact since the trip to Ellesmere and he was devoting a much larger portion of his time to South Moresby. "Elizabeth, I just wanted to check with you about a telegram we'd like to send to Mulroney," he began. "Do you think it would be helpful if we asked him to raise South Moresby in his meeting with Vander Zalm?" I felt stupid. "What meeting with Vander Zalm?" Then I learned that they were to have a meeting to discuss federal-provincial concerns on March 5 in Ottawa. I told Kevin that a telegram sounded like a great idea, and then I hung up to figure out what the ministerial equivalent of a telegram would be. It turned out that the federal-provincial branch of the Privy Council Office – the civil service equivalent of a deputy minister's office to the Prime Minister – was working on a briefing note on South Moresby for the upcoming meeting. In one of the less noticed political shifts, Premier Bennett's whiz kid, Norm Spector, had left British Columbia after Vander Zalm took the helm to become director of federal-provincial relations in the Privy Council Office. (I was now sufficiently Ottawa-ized that the alphabet-soup note on Spector heading up FPRO in PCO did not faze me.) Briefing notes to Mulroney on the significance of the WAC boundaries would be vetted by the man who had orchestrated the WAC in the first place.

I called one of Spector's assistants and found she already had a draft memo based on a briefing with Parks officials. It said in part: "The federal position on Windy Bay is that it should be completely protected (not just 10% of it) as an important ecological site, but it is not park material," and "The federal Minister of the Environment is prepared to see future logging on Lyell Island and is not pressing to include Windy Bay in the park designation." These contradictory statements reflected the current schizophrenia between the minister's position and the Parks officials' preference. Until we could finalize the letter to Rogers such confusion was, I supposed, inevitable. The Privy Council staff was prepared to amend its memo and we traded drafts for the next few days. Mulroney's information would now be in accord with McMillan's stated position that more of Lyell Island, including Windy Bay, should be protected. Mulroney would also be briefed to suggest that a preliminary estimate of the cost of a South Moresby national park for the federal government could be as much as $39 million over ten years. Barry Olsen had, through his own channels, found out about the Privy Council briefing notes. He'd rushed over to help draft them, using the latest estimates from the Parks socio-economic branch – figures that even McMillan had not seen yet. The notes were in good shape, but no one was sure that the Prime Minister would use them. No one knew if he would raise the issue, if Vander Zalm did not.

The day before the meeting between Mulroney and Vander Zalm, I had a chance to ask Tom about it. "Do you think it would help if you called the Prime Minister and talked to him about South Moresby before tomorrow morning?" I asked. Tom thought it over. He looked confounded at the prospect. "Lookit, Elizabeth. Call my brother Charlie. Tell him I'm just too busy to call myself and apologize for me. But ask him if he thinks it would be appropriate for me to phone the Prime Minister, and, if so, how we would go about it."

I had never met Dr Charles McMillan, Tom's twin brother and a member of the staff at PMO, and it seemed strange that Tom wanted me to make the call. But I did as I was told, and if Charlie McMillan thought my request was odd, he didn't betray it. "Just have Tom call the PMO switchboard between nine and ten tonight, and they'll put him through to the Prime Minister's residence." It seemed straightforward enough.

That evening, I went over to Tom's suite on Parliament Hill to tell him the upshot of my conversation with Charlie. Tom was anxious. "Are you sure the Prime Minister expects my call?" I wasn't sure, but Charlie had been reassuring, so I said, "Yup. Charlie said to call. It's no problem."

Tom fidgeted, and then looked up at me from behind his desk. It was one of those moments when the arrogance of power vanished and he reminded me, more than anything else, of a small boy. "Elizabeth, I've never called the Prime Minister at home before. I mean, I *see* him all the time, but I don't know…What would I say?" I tried to sound confident and matter of fact. Tom would be doing the Prime Minister a service by drawing the issue to his attention. The negotiations were at an impasse. If Mulroney could nudge them along by letting Vander Zalm know that the government was fully behind the minister of the environment, he would be helping immeasurably in getting the negotiations moving. What's more, maybe he could push for a moratorium on logging while the negotiations were underway.

Tom pulled himself together. "O.K., I'll do it." Then he hesitated, "Do you really know how to place a call to the Prime Minister at home?"

"Yup," I smiled. "It's easy." And then I slipped out to ask Tom's superb secretary, Gillian, to call the PMO switchboard, hoping desperately that it was as straightforward as I had led Tom to believe. After a few anxious moments, waiting with Tom in his office, Gillian buzzed him to put the call through. Tom had totally regained his composure. "Hello, Brian," he said, sounding self-assured. "I'm sorry to be calling you at home. Is this a bad time?"

On the contrary, Mulroney was prepared to have a fairly lengthy chat with his environment minister. "Well, look, Brian, the reason I'm calling is about the South Moresby national park issue. I don't know how familiar you are with it, but..." And here Mulroney must have interjected. "Oh," said Tom, "that's wonderful. Yes, it would be very helpful if you raised the matter with Premier Vander Zalm." And then Tom launched into his spiel, "Brian, South Moresby has a salience well beyond its specifics. It has achieved a symbolic importance to people across Canada that rivals acid rain as one of Canadians' major environmental concerns. As a matter of fact, I receive more letters urging the saving of South Moresby than on any other issue."

The conversation continued for a few more minutes with Mulroney doing most of the talking. Tom ended by stressing that the negotiations were stalled and that, ideally, we needed a moratorium on logging areas we wanted within a national park. Tom hung up and looked

over to me, euphoric. "He knew all about it!" he enthused. "He said he planned to raise it with Vander Zalm
tomorrow and that he really appreciated my call!"

In British Columbia, Vicky and Huck were organizing yet another demonstration. The B.C. legislature was
scheduled to open March 9 for the first time since the
fall election victory of the Socreds. Huck asked Patrick
Pothier, Vicky's musician partner, if he could play "God
Save the Queen" on a chain saw at the rally. Patrick
thought it unlikely, but for the next few days, he experimented with different saws, without chains to avoid accident, at different pitches.

The day of the rally, over two hundred and fifty people gathered in front of the parliament buildings to
protest a grab-bag of issues – the resumption of uranium
mining, native land claims, the threat of logging to the
Stein Valley, and assaults on Strathcona Provincial Park
– but mostly to demand the preservation of South
Moresby. Bill Reid spoke eloquently of the importance
of saving the Haida's homeland. Then, just as artist
Robert Bateman prepared to speak, a flock of great
blue herons, some seventy-five of them, flew overhead.
Bateman excitedly proclaimed it must be a sign.
Bristol Foster described the protesters' effort, in his
speech to the rally, as "trying sweet reason on the
provincial government."

Vander Zalm arrived to wait on the steps of the parliament building for the lieutenant-governor, steadfastly
ignoring the chants of "Open Government!" and the
beating of the Indian drums, but not the singing of "O
Canada," which forced him to stay at attention or risk
showing disrespect for the national anthem.

Finally, Patrick came forward, baton in hand. "Over
the years," he said, "composers have been inspired by
the sounds of the natural environment. Now, the sounds
of the Charlottes have inspired this new piece." Then he

conducted his small orchestra, five "musicians" with chain saws, in an unrecognizable rendition of "God Save the Queen." The air was full of oil smoke and the roar of the chain saw concerto, but Bill Vander Zalm remained impassive and unsmiling. To loud boos, he and the lieutenant-governor made their way into the B.C. legislature, flanked by officers in red serge and ceremonial hats, their chests glistening with medals.

The lieutenant-governor delivered the speech from the throne, the Vander Zalm agenda for the government. No one was particularly surprised that it called for funding "to reduce the high rate of abortions," or the appointment of "a private sector task force to work on the privitization of Crown corporations." But there were murmers of surprise at the commitment to "attempt to expedite the federal-provincial negotiations for the establishment of a national park on South Moresby in the Queen Charlottes" and for a bilateral agreement with Ottawa to develop "the enormous tourism potential this area offers."

The throne speech was faxed to our offices in Ottawa and I read the relevant paragraph over the phone to Tom. "It must have been the talk the Prime Minister had with Vander Zalm that prompted this, don't you think?" Tom agreed. Mulroney had told him that his chat with the Premier about South Moresby seemed to go very well. Maybe this was really progress.

The Parks officials thought it was. The next day we finally dispatched our written proposal to the British Columbia government. In the last three weeks, both ministers with whom McMillan had met in Vancouver had been replaced. Stephen Rogers had been shuffled to another portfolio, and Jack Kempf had been forced to resign over allegations of improper handling of his personal finances. We were back to square one in our negotiations.

*

McMillan's letter to the new minister of environment, Bruce Strachan, was the result of weeks of haggling. The proposal stressed that with "small adjustments" to the WAC boundary "South Moresby's potential can be realized to its fullest extent." Two full paragraphs emphasized the need to preserve Windy Bay: "This area is the largest remaining unlogged watershed in South Moresby, with trees more than one thousand years old, the area's most important salmon stream, and considerable evidence of the Haida culture. And yet your government has accepted in principle the WAC's recommendation that most of it be logged, leaving only a small strip of ecological reserve. Already largely surrounded by clear-cuts, Windy Bay itself is to be logged, beginning this year, according to the forest company's five-year plan." But the federal position fell short of insisting Windy Bay be included in the park boundaries. The Parks Service would simply not agree with us as it might cost millions more in compensation to Western Forest Products. The strongest language I managed to use was that we would be prepared to include Windy Bay in the national park as an alternative to the provincial ecological reserve proposal.

Attached to McMillan's letter was a lengthy proposal, which set out the specifics of the boundaries of the terrestrial and marine park, and a map. We could use weasel words in a letter, but we could not fudge our position on a map. I argued that as we were shading in those areas we wanted, if Windy Bay were not also shaded in, we would be giving the go-ahead to logging. The legend to the maps Barry showed me described three boundaries: (1) the proposed national marine park, (2) B.C.'s boundary proposal, and (3) Environment Canada's proposed additions. These last were shown not by a line, but by dots over the areas we wished to add. I looked at Barry, "We've got to dot Windy Bay."

He gave me one of those here-we-go-again looks.

"Elizabeth, we're not insisting it be added. The text of the letter makes it clear that we think it should be protected."

I launched my favourite weapon, a line I'd been using for weeks to achieve improvements in the letter: "But if the map was ever made public, and Windy Bay isn't included, then everybody will say we've abandoned it and betrayed them."

Barry sighed. "They won't like it downstairs, but I'll get two maps done – one with Windy Bay dotted, and one without – and you'll have to get the minister to decide which one we send."

When I showed Tom both versions of the map, he didn't hesitate, tapping his finger down on the one including Windy Bay. "Send this one." And with that, he signed the letter to Bruce Strachan and phoned to welcome him to the portfolio and alert him that the long-awaited federal proposal was on its way.

While we seemed, at long last, to be making progress with the B.C. government, an unexpected source of opposition was mobilizing closer to home. The B.C. caucus of the federal Progressive Conservative Party was getting heat from the forest industry back in its ridings. Mulroney's intervention in support of McMillan's tree-hugging crusade had not been appreciated. As luck would have it for the strongest pro-logging voices, they were the only ones who attended their next caucus meeting. They dispatched a strong letter to McMillan, with a copy to Mulroney, which claimed to be the "unanimous position" of the B.C. caucus and endorsed the boundaries proposed by WFP. That boundary would allow logging not only on Lyell, but also on Burnaby and on the other heavily forested areas of the proposal. In McMillan's office, we referred to it as "the park without trees" proposal.

I thought the letter was a problem. Under Tom's instructions, I had ignored the B.C. caucus. Tom had asked me to keep Jim Fulton, the NDP member for the area, posted, and Jim and I were quickly becoming friends. But no one in Tom's office was dealing with the back-benchers from B.C.

"Tom," I asked. "Don't you think you ought to meet with them? Doesn't the Prime Minister hate it when his ministers ignore the caucus?" This was a repeated and dreaded problem for ministers. Angering caucus was a nearly cardinal sin. As a result, most ministers' offices, and certainly the non-francophone offices, had a special assistant whose full-time job was catering exclusively to the Quebec caucus. But for some reason we weren't dealing at all with the British Columbia back-benchers. I suggested that if Tom didn't want to deal with them, I would. Tom laughed, "You're the last person I'd let meet with them. They'd probably think you're a Communist or something. They probably think *I'm* a Communist. Just ignore them."

But that was easier said than done. I was terribly worried about the threat of a back-bencher revolt against the park, and there was no one I could turn to. Then a few days later Vicky called to say that the caucus's letter had made it to B.C. First the industry had it, then people in Sandspit, and now the environmentalists knew all about it, too.

"Elizabeth," said Vicky, "this could be serious." "Yeah, I know, but I don't know where to turn," I replied. Vicky did. "Call John Fraser," she said. "He'll know what to do. As Speaker, he can't take public positions, but he is interested. He's from B.C. after all, and he's been involved in environmental issues forever." There did not seem to be any reason not to. I phoned his office and was given an appointment for the next day.

I wasn't sure that John Fraser would remember me from the days I lobbied him when he was environment minister, so I was pleased when, dressed in his Speaker's costume, he greeted me as an old friend. Fraser sat down and gave me his full attention, "Well, what can I do for you?"

I cleared my throat and started, "It may not be right for me to be here. But I just didn't know where else to turn. I'm worried about the B.C. caucus and South Moresby." Fraser frowned. "Yes, I know. I've got a copy of this so-called unanimous position right here." Then he proceeded to explain what he could and could not do as Speaker. It was clear that I'd done the right thing by coming. In fact, Fraser couldn't understand why I had taken so long to ask for his help. "After all," he explained, "all three parties at the federal level have taken positions in favour of saving South Moresby. It's not a controversial issue within the House of Commons. And while I can't go around making speeches, I can and should keep members on all sides of the House informed and serve their wishes."

I felt a little foolish and very grateful. Before I left, he gave me a run-down of which members of the B.C. caucus were in favour of saving South Moresby. I was pleased that the list was so long: Bob Wenman, Mary Collins, Vince Dantzer, Pat Crofton, and, of course, Pat Carney. There were others who were on the fence. It was hardly a unanimous WFP team. Fraser encouraged me to get Tom to phone them and to keep the caucus involved.

That evening I caught up with Tom. I said, as if it were the most natural thing in the world, "I saw John Fraser today." "You did?" Tom was taken aback. "I didn't know you knew him that well." "No," I said. "Neither did I."

From that day forward, John Fraser played an indispensable role in the federal strategy for saving South Moresby.

24

THE LOGGERS' FEAST

IN EARLY JANUARY, JOHN BROADHEAD HAD FELT THE power centre of B.C. shift. And so he had moved from Victoria to Vancouver, the city where he'd grown up, to push South Moresby into the mainstream of B.C.'s establishment. In late February, he took a break and flew east. In Ottawa he stayed with his old friend Barry Olsen and his wife. Over dinner Barry said, "I've got to get you to meet the minister's adviser. She's calling the shots in that office these days."

The next day, Barry brought John Broadhead up to meet me. I'd spoken by phone with J.B. often before, but my primary contacts had remained Vicky and Colleen. I was used to the intensity they, and others, brought to South Moresby strategy sessions, but J.B. blithely ignored the troubling details of negotiations. Instead he sketched out grandiose schemes to reintroduce sea otters to Haida Gwaii, to persuade major Canadian musicians to play benefit concerts, to invite British royalty to the islands. He was spellbinding. I liked him immediately.

Back in Vancouver, J.B. continued efforts to establish his new organization, Earthlife Canada Foundation, and to expand his contacts in the mainstream business community.

It was unlikely that a high school student would provide the key to open the door to Vancouver society, and when Jeff Gibbs started haunting the offices of Earthlife it was not immediately apparent that this tall, lanky red-head would prove useful to anyone.

Jeff was an alumnus of an innovative five-month education program, B.C. Quest. Like Rediscovery, Quest sought to motivate kids by exposing them to a wilderness adventure. The program was so successful that its veterans maintained contacts as ExQuesters and organized many environmental activities. In 1982, the ExQuesters had circulated a petition to the B.C. government to save Windy Bay, which eighteen thousand people had signed.

The kids' interest in South Moresby had been sparked by one of the Quest teachers, Tom Ellison, who took a few students on a summer tour of Haida Gwaii on his sailboat. Jeff had been on the trip and had become a dedicated Moresby activist. Although he was only in grade eleven at the time, Jeff had done much of the work to organize the Vancouver caravan rally. He had also done his share of envelope-stuffing and newsletter-distribution for the Western Canada Wilderness Committee. But he still looked so young it was hard for J.B. to take him seriously.

Jeff asked J.B. if he would be willing to come speak at his school. J.B. knew a thing or two about Prince of Wales High School. For one thing, it was in the Shaughnessy area, a community reputed to have more doctors, lawyers, judges, and chief executive officers per square inch than any other community in Canada. It was fertile ground for the work he wanted to do. J.B. gladly accepted Jeff's invitation and gave several talks at Prince of Wales. Then one of the ExQuesters' parents asked him to show his South Moresby slides to some friends. One evening led to another, and J.B. found his support base of wealthy well-connected people. From the living rooms of Shaughnessy, through the spring and early summer of 1987, John raised close to sixty thousand dollars for South Moresby.

Jeff, in the meantime, helped to organize a march from Robson Square to the headquarters of Western Forest Products in downtown Vancouver in mid-March. Working with the Sierra Club and other groups, he got five hundred people out to hear speeches from Bill Reid, Thom Henley, David Suzuki, Vicky Husband, and Haida artist Robert Davidson. At nineteen years old, Jeff Gibbs acted as emcee, and the media had a new angle for their South Moresby story, The Youth Crusade. But Jeff was not content to stay in Vancouver and organize rallies. He was insistent that a group of high school students should go to Lyell Island and join the next Haida blockade. The previous fall, he had been at Windy Bay to help with construction of the new longhouse, on the site of a long-abandoned Haida village. He told Miles that he wanted to come back for the next action. According to the rumour mill, another confrontation was imminent as the chain saws chewed their way down the shore of Faraday Passage and the southern belly of Lyell.

Jeff called everyone he thought he could persuade to join the blockade, even though J.B. had cautioned him that the Haida were not yet prepared to welcome any non-Haida particpation. Jeff wasn't discouraged. He talked to Bill Reid about his plans. Reid liked the idea and started calling the ExQuesters the "Youth Brigade." "I'd like to join your Youth Brigade," he told Jeff cheerily. Bill Reid and a number of other Haida had staged the last, little-noted blockade on Lyell the previous October. None of them had been arrested, but Reid was prepared for a longer siege and arrests the next time. Reid's affliction with Parkinson's disease was slowing him down more than he'd ever want to admit. Sixty-seven years old, he quite fancied the Youth Brigade.

Finally Jeff got confirmation that there would be a Haida blockade on Lyell on a long weekend in March. The Youth Brigade members prepared to leave, even though they didn't know if they would be allowed to come. It was touch and go all one long Thursday afternoon, until Guujaaw called to invite them as the only non-Haida for the next Lyell logging blockade. While they were on their way to Lyell Island, they received word of a totally unexpected development. On March 20, the British Columbia government announced a moratorium on the issuance of new logging permits for South Moresby.

Vicky, Colleen, J.B., and Huck scrambled to figure out the significance of the moratorium. Newspapers headlined, "Logging on Lyell to Halt," but reports from the island indicated that Beban's crews were still working in double and triple shifts. Vicky got hold of the press release from Strachan's office. The acting forests minister, John Savage, was quoted as saying that the suspension of new permits was to ensure that "we do not compromise any option that may give rise to the successful conclusion of negotiations for a national park in the area." B.C. claimed the moratorium was a response to McMillan's proposal.

Loggers were livid. Frank Beban's partner, Bill Verchere, blasted the provincial government for not consulting them. Once again, newspapers were full of stories of pending lay-offs – doom and gloom for the forest industry. In Ottawa, I was elated by the news until I learned from Vicky that Beban's crews had three to four months' logging left on Lyell under existing permits. I reported to Tom that logging was continuing on Lyell Island, and I told him that Bruce Strachan wanted to speak with him by phone.

I sat in Tom's office as he listened to Strachan's assessment of negotiations. It sounded encouraging. Strachan was clearly floating a few trial balloons: maybe we could work out a timber trade somewhere else; maybe we could get Fisheries to relax objections to logging on another area in order to trade for more of Lyell.

There was a flexible tone to the conversation. Tom thanked Strachan for the gesture of good faith in deferring the granting of new permits and the commitment of the B.C. government as reflected in the throne speech, then he hung up the receiver and said, "It looks really good, Elizabeth. Our bureaucrats meet again this week and I think we're getting close." So much had happened in the two weeks since Mulroney had met with Vander Zalm that I couldn't help but think that the PM's much-vaunted friendship with the Premier was paying off.

On board a fishing boat that plied its way through the waters off Lyell Island were Jeff Gibbs and the rest of the Youth Brigade. They had been joined by Guujaaw and fifteen other Haida of all ages. Guujaaw sang and taught the young Vancouverites warrior dances. Once on Lyell, they headed for Sedgewick Bay, where the November 1985 blockade had been staged. Ever since, the Haida had kept the Sedgewick Bay longhouse in a state of readiness. Ada Yovanovitch had been with her daughter to take inventory on the food stored there (enough for a month-long siege), occasioning her Mountie friend, Harry Wallace, to issue a cautionary word. Now, everyone was back in earnest. About fifty Haida were already there, including Miles Richardson, his younger brother, Colin, Ada, Ethel Jones, and several hereditary chiefs. The teenagers from Vancouver were introduced and greeted warmly. Many of the Haida had seen coverage of the rally in Vancouver the week before, and had heard of the high school students who had pulled it off. Jeff grinned and blushed. He looked closer to sixteen than nineteen. They sang Haida songs and the young people danced, Haida and non-Haida alike, pounding their feet on the rough floor of the longhouse. There was a swell of emotion and joy. They knew that the RCMP expected a blockade.

Everyone on the Powrivco Bay side at Beban's camp knew that they were there. The makeshift jails were ready for the Haida at the other end of the logging road. Through the evening various options were debated. Jeff listened and wondered what was the right thing to do.

The next morning, everyone was awake before dawn. The elders and the chiefs dressed in their ceremonial finery. The young people put button blankets over their down vests and carried chairs for the elders up to the logging road. They put charcoal on their faces and carried cedar branches as they had sixteen months before. Skidegate Chief Tom Greene, a big man with a generous heart, stood on the road between Nonny Ethel and Ada's daughter, Diane Brown. The Youth Brigade and the rest of the Haida took their places along each side of the road. As the sun came up, Guujaaw drummed and everyone sang. The stage was set exactly as it had been the last time. The only difference was that no network camera crews were present. The Haida had decided that this was not to be a media event.

The first truck arrived and the logging foreman stepped out of the cab and ambled toward the blockade of three in the centre of the road. He tried to sound relaxed. "How are you doing today?" he asked no one in particular. Ethel Jones stepped forward to deliver the message that had been agreed upon the night before: "We'd like to invite you and your men and all your families to a big feast we're preparing for you today."

His face showed his disbelief. Of all the possible consequences of another Haida blockade, an invitation to a feast was the least probable. Too taken aback to think of another response, he said, "Yeah. We'll be there. Thanks." And with that the elders and Diane left the road, and everyone went back to camp to start preparing the feast.

The idea of a feast for the loggers had been planned in Skidegate. Only the kids from Vancouver had thought they were there to block the road. To Jeff, the idea had seemed to have come out of nowhere the night before. They had so much food stored up, and after the moratorium announcement, a blockade just didn't make much sense. Jeff had been surprised to learn that the communities of Haida and loggers were not as far apart as he had believed. Genuine concern had been expressed for the loggers' feelings over possible lay-offs in June and the decision made to heal the wounds between their communities.

All day long they prepared the feast. The men went fishing for more fresh delicacies, and the women barbecued octopus, abalone, prawns, scallops, halibut, cod, salmon, deer, gaaw, and baked bread and cakes.

Toward evening the loggers and their families started to arrive, all wearing their "Beban Logging" work jackets and looking slightly nervous. Once grace had been said and the food passed among them the divisions blurred, and they all started to enjoy themselves. Miles made a short speech explaining that the Haida Nation was not against working people, but had taken a stand against further logging of Lyell. The feast, he told them, was to show the Haida's respect for the people in the camp and to bid them farewell. The foreman spoke, too, thanking their hosts for the feast. "We feel caught in the middle," he said. "It's company policy, and we just want it all resolved one way or another."

25

GOOD FAITH BARGAINING

WITHIN A WEEK OF THE MORATORIUM BEING AN-
nounced, the B.C. government "clarified" the scope of
the suspension of permits. The clarification completely
erased any notion of a meaningful halt to logging, or
even of a meaningful pause. The moratorium would be
in effect for only six weeks, less time than the already-ap-
proved cut blocks would take to log. A further restric-
tion was that it would apply only to those areas the
federal government had expressed an interest in including within the national park. As the federal proposal was
not yet public, this left people wondering just which
areas would be off-limits to loggers. When asked, Tom's
new press secretary, Terry Collins, a former *Toronto Sun*
reporter, declined to make our map public, fuelling further speculation in the B.C. press. Jim Fulton called to
tell me that logging was going on in double shifts, and
that the scars were clearly visible from Juan Perez
Sound.

My network of South Moresby contacts was growing
exponentially. Well-placed Tories in the House and
Senate had plugged me into a network of former aides
to Vander Zalm and current moles within the Socred
political staff. I was getting a fuller picture by the day.

Whatever Strachan might want to do, it was clear that
almost the entire cabinet was against any proposal for a
park, except perhaps for the "park without trees" proposal from Western Forest Products. A mole in Victoria

confirmed that the impetus to resolve South Moresby had been the Mulroney breakfast with Vander Zalm in early March. The so-called moratorium had been announced in good faith; the "clarification" was the result of intense heat from the forest industry, and not just from those companies immediately affected. Other companies backed WFP and MacMillan Bloedel. They viewed South Moresby the way Dean Rusk had viewed South Vietnam – it might cause a domino effect. If we were going to get a deal, we had to get it while the momentum was with us. But word was that we were already losing momentum. The more time that went by, reducing the impact of Mulroney's words to Vander Zalm, the harder it would be to get a deal. We knew that the six-week moratorium, while having no relevance to logging, was a real psychological deadline for the B.C. government. If we didn't have a deal by the end of April, we could pretty well forget the whole thing.

We hammered out draft memoranda to cabinet suggesting a Regional Economic Development Agreement for the Charlottes, enlisting as many federal departments as possible: Regional Economic Expansion; Tourism; Fisheries and Oceans; Indian Affairs and Northern Development; Energy, Mines and Resources; the Canadian Forest Service. Anyone and everyone with possible jurisdiction and a little money to spend was recruited. The Parks Service had forestry consultants frantically number-crunching, developing estimates of the value of the forestry resource for which we would have to offer compensation on a fifty-fifty basis with the province. Tourism consultants worked out the likely employment that could be generated by a national park versus that lost to logging. They estimated that a park on South Moresby would generate in the first ten years 70,000 visitor-days a year and provide 3,700 person-years of employment – more than the current number of logging person-years.

As our negotiating team headed out to Victoria for another round of talks, Bill Reid announced that he would discontinue work on a major piece of sculpture commissioned for the new Canadian embassy in Washington, D.C. Reid had been working on the massive *Spirit Canoe* for nearly two years. He explained. "I couldn't live with it anymore, using the Haida symbols to advertise a government – and I mean all levels of government, provincial as well as federal – that we felt was not cooperating with us in what I consider to be very minimal, legitimate requests." Earlier that week, the First Ministers' Conference on Aboriginal Rights had ended in failure. Press coverage suggested that the western premiers had been the least cooperative in resolving the status of aborignal rights under the constitution. Tim Harper somewhat exaggerated the impact of Reid's gesture when he wrote in the *Toronto Star*, "In one fell swoop, Reid's action may have been at least as effective as a logging road blockade in bringing the plight of the Haida to the attention of B.C. and the country as a whole."

That same week, David Suzuki's third program on South Moresby was aired. Suzuki's clip of Tom McMillan focussed on the minister's plea for the public to make its voice heard, to push governments to save Windy Bay. In his closing editorial comment, Suzuki called McMillan's plea a "cop-out," arguing that the public had already expressed its support for South Moresby through thousands of letters and petitions. He challenged politicians to show some leadership. The program inspired hundreds of people to write McMillan and Mulroney demanding they save Windy Bay. We had never before received so much mail. I imagined that Strachan and Vander Zalm's offices were getting at least an equal amount.

Federal officials had a productive negotiating meeting in Vancouver and returned to brief McMillan. Tom had a dinner meeting scheduled with New Brunswick Premier Richard Hatfield to persuade him to honour his commitment to an acid-rain accord. They were to meet rather late at the Château Laurier, so Jim Collinson and our West Coast regional head, Kirk Dawson, and I met with McMillan in the lounge area between the hotel lobby and dining room. I kept one eye peeled for Hatfield while our senior bureaucrats layed out the state of negotiations.

"We've made a lot of progress," Jim explained in a hushed tone. We were sitting on comfy chairs with our heads lowered, trying to catch every word and keep our conversation private. "They've agreed to go beyond the WAC boundaries, to include the south slopes of Lyell and portions of Richardson, Kunga, and Tanu islands." This sounded good. I crossed my fingers that the next words would be that Windy Bay, or most of it, would be saved as well. Jim continued, "But we're not going to get Windy Bay. The value of the timber on that watershed is maybe five to ten years' more logging. It would cost tens of millions of dollars in compensation. They'll preserve the lower watershed as a provincial ecological reserve, but they'll clear-cut the rest. After logging, we could probably get a deal to have it added to the park." Tom looked a little sick at the prospect. "Well, Mr Minister, after a few years, it should green up. Eventually, there'll be trees on it again."

My mouth was dry. I looked at Kirk. He had shared my perspective in pushing for more of Lyell. He worked for the Weather Service and was not contaminated with what I now thought of as "Parks culture." We were friends and I trusted him. He read my mind. "We won't get anymore than this," he said soberly. "All my contacts in the provincial bureaucracy say its this or nothing."

"What about helicopter logging of the upper watershed of Windy Bay?" I could hardly believe I was asking the question, but taking the trees out selectively might preserve the lower watershed from landslides, stream siltation, and erosion. "I don't think they'd be interested," Jim said, "but, I could ask."

"Well," Tom said, " I guess that's as good as we'll get." And then to me, "Elizabeth, you'll have to get Colleen and Vicky and the others to understand." I nodded numbly. Hatfield came into the room flanked by aides, and Tom left to shift gears to acid rain. I talked longer with Kirk and Jim, getting more details and feeling an immeasurable weight of sadness. Then I went home, tired and discouraged. I had given up on Windy Bay. No miracles had arrived. And time had just run out.

But the next morning, I felt differently. Strachan and McMillan had a negotiating session scheduled for April 8. Maybe Mulroney could have a word with Vander Zalm. We couldn't give up. I phoned Barry Olsen to tell him we had to think of how we could make one last try for Windy Bay. Barry was surprised, "I'd heard you'd given up and accepted the latest B.C. position. The word going around is that you're prepared to compromise." I suddenly realized that it wasn't just the minister to whom people looked for signals. How I felt and what I said was being analysed throughout the department. I decided to be more careful in allowing my moods to show.

I called Kirk Dawson and told him I wasn't prepared to give up on Windy Bay. He sounded pleased and surprised. I called Jim Collinson. He wasn't pleased, just surprised. Hoping I had squelched the rumour of my surrender, I headed for our morning briefing session with Tom. I told him I thought we owed ourselves one last try, but Tom didn't see any point in persisting. Once again he asked me to break the news to Vicky and Colleen and the others.

Suddenly I realized how we could summon the strength for another run at Windy Bay. "Maybe if you met with them Tom, you could explain things. I know I couldn't do it by phone." Tom brightened, "Yes, that's a good idea. I need to meet with them and lay the whole situation out for them and see what they recommend. Maybe there's something we've missed." He then gave me instructions to get Vicky, Colleen, J.B., Huck, and Gregg Sheehy to a meeting in Ottawa. "Fly them in. Do you think they'll come?" Tom asked.

I was sure of it.

The next morning, Tom and I showed up at the parliamentary restaurant's private dining room for a breakfast meeting with the B.C. caucus, Frank Beban, and a Western Forest Products representative, Hank Hansen. I'd never seen Beban before, except on television, but I couldn't help but like him. He reminded me of Fred Flintstone, big and beefy. He tried every argument against a park. No one would ever go there. "Can you imagine driving your Winnebago with the kids and then finding out there's no road to this national park?" He had brought photographs of trees planted ten years ago, forty years ago; trees on areas clear-cut thirty years ago. "See? It greens up just fine." It was a long breakfast. As we left and got out of earshot, Tom smiled. "I've never heard so many versions of 'If you've seen one tree, you've seen them all'!"

The next day, Vicky, Colleen, and the others were to meet with McMillan. "The others" was becoming quite a crowd. Colleen had called, "Paul George has got to be there, Elizabeth. I know you don't know him, but he played a major role." I tried to dissaude her, knowing that the more they were, the less effective they would be.

Vicky called, "Good news. David Suzuki is coming." I didn't think that was good news. "Vicky, Tom didn't like the way he was treated on the last Nature of Things. Why bring Suzuki into it?" Vicky wouldn't budge. "He's got to be there. You said yourself, this meeting is our last chance."

Colleen called back. "Peter Hamel's got to be there." "Who's Peter Hamel?" I felt exasperated. "He's with the Anglican Church and he's worked for years on this. Trust me."

They all rolled into town the night of April 6. I met with them the next morning in Jim Fulton's office: Colleen, Vicky, J.B., Gregg Sheehy, Huck, whom I'd only met briefly at the caravan rally in Ottawa, and three people I had never met before: David Suzuki, Paul George, bear-like and unkempt, and Peter Hamel, as dapper as Paul was dishevelled. For a few minutes there was a wonderful confusion of hugs and introductions, then we got serious.

"We don't have much time before your meeting with Tom, so I thought I'd tell you what we're facing at tomorrow's meeting with Strachan," I said. I unfurled our map, and as we all crowded around Jim's coffee table, I started outlining which areas would be in the park, and which ones wouldn't.

Paul George was furious. "Why would you give away half of Richardson Island and parts of the others? This is awful!" Colleen wasn't pleased either, "You mean the federal government has already given up on most of Lyell?"

I knew this would happen. I wanted to be sure that they had a chance to vent their anger *before* seeing Tom. I could take being yelled at a lot better than he could. I tried to explain how difficult it had been to get any movement past the WAC boundaries. Fulton said knowingly, "Yeah, but if your negotiators hadn't agreed to the WAC boundaries from the beginning, you wouldn't be in this mess."

Gradually, everyone blew off enough steam to focus on the strategy of persuading Tom to hold out for Windy Bay. I tried to prepare them for the worst. "We may not be able to get anything more," I said. "And if we walk away now, we won't have been bargaining in good faith."

Vicky was supportive, "Don't worry, Elizabeth. If you can't do it, you can't do it. We'll still save Windy Bay – our own way."

We made our way, minus Fulton, down to Tom's office. Jim spoke on the phone immediately with Tom to persuade him of the need for a bold new bargaining ploy. "Fire your negotiators! Send in a new team and start over."

Soon we were all squeezed into Tom's powder-blue office, and Tom started the ball rolling by reiterating that this was an "off the record" session. They all nodded. He then briefly summarized the progress of the negotiations, succinctly highlighting our few victories: the so-called moratorium, movement beyond the WAC boundaries, and the federal government's willingness to more than triple the first figure that Tom had mentioned for the park deal. In a year, it had moved from $12 million to $39 million – a far cry from Blais-Grenier's offer of $2 million. Tom explained that the latest thinking was that we would allow some logging to continue on Lyell to serve as a necessary bridge between a logging and a tourism economy. But he also stressed that he was open to hearing their views, especially on the fate of Windy Bay. With that, he turned the meeting over to Huck.

Huck had been chosen to act as chair of the group, and he called on each in turn to make his or her best pitch. David Suzuki spoke first. He was passionate and direct. "Preserving this area is a measure of leadership. You'll be a hero if you save it. Windy Bay is non-negotiable. Logging and the protection of Windy Bay are mutually exclusive. If Windy Bay is touched, all hell will break loose!"

Paul George pointed out that Windy Bay represented only five days' logging out of the annual provincial yield, and he plugged a videotape into Tom's VCR to show him the latest devastation. It was hard to watch. "All this happened in the last six weeks," said Paul, as the camera panned across slopes of tree stumps.

Peter Hamel spoke of the Haida's interests and of the full support of a coalition of churches for the resolution of the Haida land claim. Gregg Sheehy pointed out new public opinion polls in B.C. that supported South Moresby. Vicky mentioned her contacts with B.C. politicians who were increasingly sympathetic to a park.

J.B. was very effective. "Your 'Lyell Island or nothing' gambit was a brilliant move." Tom glowed. "You've made Moresby a political liability for the Socreds." Then he outlined the possibilities for a "corporate-source solution" – a timber trade with MacMillan Bloedel, or a private acquisition through the Nature Conservancy, a group that puts private money into purchasing endangered areas. He told Tom that the *National Geographic* would have a feature article on South Moresby in its July edition. "It has a direct circulation of fourteen million people. Any story on a possible tourism destination results in an average of a hundred thousand immediate inquiries. Tourism for the park is an increasingly attractive proposition."

Tom was impressed. "I can't make any promises. I don't know what will happen when I get to Victoria tomorrow. But you have my word that I'll do my best to push for Windy Bay."

Vicky spoke for the group. "No matter what happens, Tom, we want you to know that we appreciate what you've done. You've moved this thing farther than anyone else. Even if it all falls through and we have to block the logging roads on Windy Bay, we'll always be grateful to you for what you've tried to do."

Late that evening, Tom, Jim Collinson, Terry Collins, and I flew to Vancouver. We had an insanely busy schedule for the next day, visiting Fort Langley, Vancouver, Victoria, Prince George, Fort St James, and Prince George again, arriving in Edmonton that night. We were scheduled to be in Victoria for the meeting with Strachan for only two and a half hours.

It was already spring in Victoria and the weather was lovely. Despite the tension of not knowing how we would fare in these critical negotiations, I felt optimistic. Flanked by a handful of bureaucrats, we walked through the marble corridors of the parliament buildings. Tom left Jim, our regional head, Kirk Dawson, and me to sip coffee and wait while he met privately with Strachan. Exactly twenty-two minutes later, Tom emerged looking grim. "Is your meeting over already?" I asked. Tom spoke under his breath with an intensity that alarmed me, "We've got to get out of here."

A reporter from Canadian Press ran to catch up with Tom as he strode toward the exit. "Any progress, Mr McMillan?" "Mr Strachan has presented us with an entirely new proposal and it would be premature to comment on it."

We made it to the car, with Tom looking like he had been dropped on his head. "You'll never believe it," he said. And he proceeded to describe, in painful detail, his meeting with Strachan.

As soon as Tom had sat down with him, Strachan had said that he had a new proposal and had indicated several maps propped on an easel. The first showed the WAC boundaries, and on the second, the additional areas Parks Canada wanted included had been highlighted with a florescent orange marker. No surprises so far. Then Strachan had unveiled the third map, "B.C. Revision to Canada's National Park Proposal." It was a sea of orange. All of Lyell, all of Richardson, Tanu, Kunga, everything from the height of land of the Tangil Peninsula south had been highlighted.

Tom had been amazed, wondering if Strachan had somehow confused his maps. It was too good to be the whole proposal. Then Strachan had dropped the other shoe: The B.C. government would put in a maximum of

$8 million toward the costs of compensating the holders
of tree farm and timber licences; the federal government would be responsible for all negotiations with the
forest industry and other third-party interests, would assume responsibility for all the lands in question, and
would ensure that the current workforce on Lyell would
be employed logging timber in the area for ten years.

That was not all. Other conditions included a small-
craft dock and a wharf for Sandspit, a boat launch for
Moresby Camp, $20 million to be spent on capital im-
provements over the next ten years, and – unbelievably
– ten annual payments of $10-million each from the fed-
eral government into "the Queen Charlotte Islands
Forest Ecology Benefit Trust." In other words, a $100
million goody to the province. Tom's head had been
reeling. He had held his emotions in check, telling
Strachan that he would need time to review this new
proposal with his cabinet colleagues. That was when
Strachan had dropped his final bombshell: We had until
April 21 to respond.

There was a moment's silence in the car as we tried to
grasp the full horror of what Tom had just told us. Jim
Collinson was the first to speak. He was appalled. "We
just spoke to their negotiators yesterday. No one said
anything about a new proposal." "Well," said Tom, without a trace of irony, "maybe they wanted the element of
surprise."

I flipped through the proposal Strachan had handed
to Tom in a cheap Duo-Tang file, looking at the maps,
reading the conditions, frantically trying to sort out the
good from the bad, the loony from the possible. Rather
lamely I asked, "Is there any way we can accept their
boundaries and then work from there, one item at a
time?" "No," said Tom. "I rather had the impression that
this was a package deal. Take it or leave it."

The car wasn't moving. We had asked to be driven
back to the restaurant where we had eaten lunch before

the meeting. Now we were just sitting there in the parking lot, in shock. "Well, it's a trap," I said, pointing out the obvious. "They want to be able to say to the public, 'Look, we offered the federal government the whole thing and they didn't want it. They weren't prepared to pay for it.'"

"Yes, but who would think we should have accepted a park with logging in it for ten years?" asked Tom in exasperation. "It totally violates the National Parks Act. It's just totally nuts."

I reread the proposal. "You know," I ventured hopefully, "it's not entirely clear that they want logging to be maintained within the national park. It says 'timber supply from within the area,' but maybe that is the whole Queen Charlottes area."

"I didn't get that impression from Strachan," said Tom, "but maybe you're right. Jim, could you nose around and see what clarifications you can get from the officials you know here?"

Collinson readily agreed. Kirk Dawson speculated, "Maybe you were just supposed to throw up your hands and call it quits right then?" "I thought about it," said Tom glumly.

There was nothing more to be said. Kirk and Jim left to do some sleuthing and Tom, Terry, and I headed for the airport. We were scheduled to fly to remote Fort St James to inspect an historic church MP Lorne McCuish wanted federal money to repair. I did not mind the thought of getting to a church at all.

26

PARALYSIS

THE PHONE JANGLED, WAKING ME FROM A DEEP SLEEP. IT was pitch dark and I was somewhere unfamiliar. I had no idea where.

"Elizabeth. Sorry to wake you. It's Jim Collinson," said the voice over the phone.

"Jim? What time is it?" I asked. I remembered where I was: a hotel room in Edmonton.

"About two-thirty in the morning your time, I think. But I just finished meeting with B.C.'s deputy minister, Vince Collins. We went out for a few beers, and I thought you'd want to know right away what I found out about their latest proposal," he explained. "It's not great news," Jim continued. "They definitely want us to maintain ten years' worth of logging at current rates from within the national park boundaries. They just want to hand the federal government all their headaches – the whole package. Hand the land over to us, while insisting we keep up ten years' worth of logging," Jim explained.

"That is so absolutely nuts. Do they really think that we'll even consider that? Or is this just a stunt to get us to walk away?" I asked.

"I don't know," Jim said. "But I noticed something about that map that we missed this afternoon. Their new boundary is not the entire original wilderness proposal. They've cut off the little triangle of water at the top right corner that contains those three tiny islands, Limestone, Reef, and Skedans. There's no trees to speak of there, just Haida artifacts and a sea-lion rookery. But B.C. thinks they might have some interesting underwater oil and gas possibilities. The point is, if they weren't serious about these boundaries, if they weren't prepared to have a park along these lines, if it was just a trick, why bother to leave out those three little islands?"

I saw his point. It made me hopeful. Maybe we could hang onto the new boundaries after all. Jim went on to fill me in on what he'd learned about the evolution of B.C.'s crazy new position. Their senior negotiator, Vince Collins, had met twice with the Premier in the last few days, but the new position had been developed at a cabinet meeting just about an hour before Strachan's meeting with McMillan. The florescent orange could hardly have been dry.

"Vince Collins told me that when we met last week, he honestly thought that the negotiations would proceed in the direction we were going," Jim explained. "Now he says the whole thing's political. He can't negotiate anything." Jim went on to outline the recent frustrations that cumulatively had made the chip on B.C.'s shoulder grow to the size of a boulder. Recent announcements of economic assistance to General Motors in Ontario and to the oil and gas industry in Alberta had increased the perennial cries of "B.C. never gets it's fair share!" On top of that, Vander Zalm felt that he had been unfairly singled out by federal aides as a cause of the failure of the recent constitutional talks on aboriginal rights. In short, federal-provincial relations had soured, and South Moresby was the nearest target for retaliation. "Besides," Jim added, "the way they see it, maybe South Moresby is a chance to get some really significant dollars, so they're linking all kinds of other economic initiatives to a park deal."

For the next few days, no matter how often Tom and I reviewed the B.C. proposal, we could not figure out what our next move should be. The more we examined it the less sense it made. On the one hand, B.C. was demanding a $100-million trust fund to compensate the province for what it claimed would be a net loss of $30 million a year as a result of the cessation of logging. On the other hand, we were supposed to guarantee that logging would not stop. "It's diabolical," I said to Tom. He and Strachan had agreed not to reveal their new proposal to anyone. Vicky, Colleen, and J.B. phoned to see how the session in Victoria had gone, but all I could tell them was that B.C.'s new proposal was "very bizarre, totally new, and totally weird." When they expressed their frustration at being kept in the dark after being brought in for the last-minute strategy meeting, all I could say was "Trust me. We haven't given anything away. We're back to square one."

Tom was as appalled as I was by the audacity of the provincial move. The April 21 deadline was less than two weeks away, and Parliament's Easter recess fell within those two weeks. Even if we had been prepared to accept the provincial offer, there was no way we could have put it through cabinet in the time allowed.

Our manoeuvrability was further limited by instructions from the PMO not to annoy British Columbia before the constitutional talks on April 30, or before the first meeting of the new Pacific Council of Ministers, established to provide a forum for resolution of federal-B.C. irritants. I wondered if it was just coincidence that the deadline was the same day as that first meeting between federal ministers Pat Carney and Don Mazankowski and such provincial representatives as Stephen Rogers. I worried that the park might get tangled in the give and take of federal-provincial relations: You get an ice-breaker, we get South Moresby.

In the meantime, we faced a serious problem within our own shop. Jim Collinson saw the B.C. proposal as an opportunity to resurrect his recommendation that we accept the WAC boundaries. I couldn't believe that Jim was serious. The boundaries were the only good thing about B.C.'s proposal. But Jim was insistent, and we went back to arguing over whether Windy Bay was special, and over whether the Haida were being used by environmentalists or vice versa. Jim finally countered with a lengthy memo in which he argued that the position being advanced by the Haida and the environmentalists (and, by implication, me) was that we insist on Windy Bay or nothing. This was premised, he explained, on the following "highly questionable" assumptions:

"(1) There is a good chance B.C. will agree to including Windy Bay on a basis acceptable to Canada;

"(2) Funds will be made available by Cabinet to pay the increased compensation;

"(3) After a break down of negotiations, public pressure will build on B.C. and the province will change its position before Windy Bay is logged;

"(4) If B.C. does not agree to include Windy Bay and, as a result, the park negotiations break down, the federal position will receive public support in both the short and long term."

I had to agree with Jim that those were the assumptions, and I couldn't disagree with his view that they were highly unlikely. But they were just barely possible. I held to my recommendation that we buy time and try to come up with a way to accept the boundaries and deal with B.C.'s other demands one at a time. Tom agreed with me.

On April 15, Tom wrote to Strachan asking for an extension of the moratorium, which was due to expire on April 30. Tom suggested that in order to review B.C.'s proposal and prepare a formal response, he would need until late May. We got past the April 21 deadline on the basis of a verbal okay relayed through official channels, but on April 24 we received Strachan's written reply. The letter opened expressing regret that Canada would need until late May in order to respond: "This issue is already one of long standing, and further delay will only serve to heighten anxiety and uncertainty." I had a feeling this letter was written for more than one audience. In a tone of generosity in the face of severe provocation, the letter went on to say: "Nevertheless, the province is prepared to give Canada this additional opportunity to formulate a reply."

But from sweet acquiescence, the letter took one of the Kafkaesque turns we were accustomed to in negotiations with B.C. In order to maintain the moratorium, the federal government had to agree that new logging permits be issued on Lyell, almost immediately. Worse yet, Strachan wanted McMillan to choose which of three possible sites would get clear-cut: Windy Bay, Gate Creek, or the southern slopes of Lyell Island. Tom looked horror-struck. "I'm not going to *approve* logging on Lyell Island, on Windy Bay, for God's sake! What kind of a time extension is this?"

Obviously, Windy Bay and the southern slopes were the areas of Lyell we most wanted in the park. Gate Creek, on the other hand, was not as sensitive from a national park standpoint, but as Strachan hinted in his letter, "It is likely that your assistance will be required to secure Federal Fisheries approval." Jim Collinson confirmed that Gate Creek was an important salmon-spawning stream. Fisheries had already determined that logging there would destroy salmon habitat.

"Great," said Tom bitterly, "As environment minister, I'm supposed to lean on Tom Siddon, the federal fisheries minister, to get him to overrule his officials to allow clear-cutting along a salmon stream. And, if I *don't* agree to new logging permits being issued, then the moratorium will be over. They'll break off negotiation and they'll log. That's it, isn't it?" He shook his head in disgust. "That's about it, Mr Minister," Jim agreed.

Tom grimaced. "Well, Jim, tell them we need some time to review it. I'll have a chat with Siddon, just to let him know about this. But I sure as hell am not going to suggest he approve logging a salmon stream!"

One evening soon after, J.B. called me at my house, late. He had just been talking to a local CBC reporter. "She said that when she was talking to Strachan today, she got the impression that there'd be an announcement of a park soon. But when she pressed for details about a national park, he was evasive, as though it might be a provincial park instead."

"Oh God, J.B., that's it!" I suddenly saw the B.C. plan as clearly as if I saw it laid out before me. "They'll wait till we've given up, or they'll throw us another ultimatum which we can't meet, and then they'll announce that the federal government didn't want a park, so they've gone ahead and protected the area themselves. They'll announce it like it's great news for the environment. Hallelujah! But it'll be a park on the WAC boundaries." I reconsidered, " No, it'll be worse. It'll probably be the Western Forest Product boundaries. The federal government will look like the bad guys, and they probably figure by the time the public figures out the difference between a provincial park and a national park, they will be too confused to get angry. Oh God! That's exactly what they'll do." Somehow knowing what B.C. had planned was empowering. I no longer felt totally victimized by the cat-and-mouse game. But neither did I know what we should do to outsmart them. I realized that, in this little drama, the federal government was playing the part of the mouse.

Through late April, we tried to develop a compromise position, somehow taking British Columbia's concerns into account. Parks officials proposed the idea of offering a period of four to five years of logging. They suggested that we not play with boundaries, just stick to the phrasing of B.C.'s offer. How many years' worth of logging could be maintained on Lyell? We knew that the Haida would object. We knew that environmentalists would be outraged. But we had to come up with some response, and I agreed with Tom that this one was better than falling back on the WAC boundaries. Besides, I had a growing conviction that this was an exercise in futility. We would go through the motions until the moment when B.C. would proclaim the game over, fold up their board, and take it home. A comment Bruce Strachan made to a reporter confirmed my intuition. On April 30, he was quoted as saying the logging moratorium "will remain in place until the negotiations fail."

On May 1, Tom dispatched a lengthy letter to Strachan outlining our problems with his offer of April 8. He pointed out those little technicalities that Strachan may have missed: that logging in a national park would violate the National Parks Act and that it seemed inconsistent to demand a $100-million fund to compensate for the loss of logging, while insisting that logging continue. But to show some movement in B.C.'s direction, and as a gesture of good faith, we floated the trial balloon of four to five years' more logging.

We didn't have to wait long for it to be shot down. On May 6 a letter from Strachan came in over the fax machine a little after 6:30 p.m. It was an ultimatum. No date was mentioned, but the letter read like a final notice. "Given the public sentiments of support for a national park; given your public and private statements of interest on behalf of the Government of Canada; and given British Columbia's generous offer to relinquish its beneficial economic interests in the area, I would have expected much more movement in your position. Furthermore, I find it disturbing that in spite of lengthy discussions with your B.C. Caucus, you have not taken the substance of our most recent offer to your Cabinet colleagues. As matters stand now, the prospects for settlement appear elusive…"

The ultimatum was thinly veiled and short. Strachan concluded by saying that unless Tom McMillan concurred with the granting of new cutting permits somewhere on Lyell Island, negotiations would be at an end. "The time has arrived," Strachan wrote, "in which we must conclude a deal, or reluctantly, we must conclude that a satisfactory settlement is not possible."

After arranging for Tom to phone Strachan as soon as possible, I waited to find out from Tom what had transpired. There wasn't much to hear. We had a few more days to respond. But probably not beyond May 11.

We were almost out of time, and we had to develop a strategy. The Parks officials proposed a range of options, including the inevitable suggestion that we try accepting the WAC boundaries. But one course they suggested was surprisingly close to my own view – that we find the best way to end negotiations, disclose the positions of both governments, and hope that public opinion could force British Columbia back to the bargaining table.

"Before we do anything irrevocable," Tom said, "I want to be sure we've consulted with all the key players. That means the Haida, environmentalists, Jim Fulton, the B.C. caucus, and, of course, cabinet. I want everyone onside before we do whatever it is we have to do."

I pointed out that Tom was already scheduled to meet with the annual gathering of the Canadian Environmental Network on Monday. "Vicky and Colleen and Kevin are all going to be there anyway," I added.

"Great," said Tom, "but get John Broadhead and Thom Henley there, too, and Gregg Sheehy, and see if Miles Richardson can come to Ottawa." I phoned Vancouver immediately. J.B. agreed to come on Saturday night. But Huck and Miles were busy on the home front, so we arranged for them to speak to Tom by phone. Tom headed back to Charlottetown for the weekend, and I kept my fingers crossed that a strategy session on Monday, May 11, would not be too late.

Vicky and Colleen arrived Friday, and I joined them, spending most of the weekend out at the Katimavik

Centre where the Canadian Environmental Network had met two years before with Blais-Grenier.

By Sunday, the core group was assembled – J.B., Colleen, Vicky, and Kevin. We sat down on the grass outside the main chapel at Katimavik. The sun beat down as I set out the state of the negotiations. "Don't let on to Tom that I've told you," I said, "but I know he's going to tell you the whole thing tomorrow anyway and this proposal is so weird that it takes a couple of days to be able to think clearly about anything after hearing it." I told them the secret I had been keeping for over a month. They were shocked. I reviewed the various options that Tom was now considering, explaining that he was leaning toward issuing a press release, breaking off negotiations and laying out the B.C. position. Everyone quickly agreed that that seemed to be the best strategy and that we should issue it as soon as possible, preferably the next day.

"I don't know," said J.B. "It would be better if the press release did not end the negotiations." He suggested a new twist, "*Before* either side admits the negotiations are over, Tom should issue a release urging B.C. to stay at the negotiating table and spelling out the positions of both governments."

"That's brilliant," I said. "That way we haven't signalled or precipitated the breakdown of talks. It might just put enough public pressure on B.C. to keep them talking." With a new strategy to propose to Tom, I was feeling almost optimistic.

Early the next morning, we all went to the airport to meet Tom's incoming flight from Prince Edward Island. Vicky had to leave on a morning plane to Toronto, so she spent a few private moments talking with Tom by the baggage carousel. The plan was for the rest of us to ride with Tom to the Katimavik Centre, holding our strategy meeting in the car.

Ministerial limousines are roomy and comfortable for four to five people, including the driver. There were seven of us: Paul Rowe (Tom's chauffeur), Terry Collins, Tom, Kevin, J.B., Colleen, and me. Terry was desperate not to miss the strategy session in the car, so he persuaded Paul to let him drive, so that there would be one less person. Paul's departure had the added bonus of extending the length of our moving meeting, for while there may not be a better press secretary than Terry, there are certainly better chauffeurs. He would become engrossed in the conversation in the back seat, and Tom would say, rather sharply, "Terry, are we going the right way?"

Tom was wedged in between J.B. and Kevin in the back seat, while Colleen was in the front with me. Tom wanted to go by his apartment on the way to the meeting in the Gatineau, to drop off his luggage and change into the casual attire appropriate for his meeting with a sampling of the country's environmental community. The ride from the airport to his apartment building was interminable. Tom told the story of his meeting with Strachan in excrutiating detail. Convinced that he held the tiny audience in the palm of his hand, he unburdened himself of the suspenseful tale of drama and intrigue, leaving out no recollection – however minute.

Once at Tom's building, he and Terry went inside with the luggage, and the rest of us broke into laughter from the suppressed frustration of listening to a story we already knew retold in painful detail. J.B. put it, "At this rate, he'll get to the part where Strachan unveils the last map, just as we drive into the Katimavik Centre. Is there any way we can speed this up?"

Tom helped us out by taking a long time getting changed. He took his clothes seriously, even his jeans looked tailor-made. When he got back to the car, much to the relief of our volunteer strategists, I told him,

"Tom, I hope you don't mind, but since we're running a little late, I've brought everyone up to date on what's been going on."

He didn't mind, and the South Moresby crew demonstrated superb thespian skills, acting out shock and sympathy as if they had just heard the latest loopy curve in negotiations for the first time. "So," said Tom, finally getting to the purpose of our meeting, "Now that you know where we stand, what do you recommend?"

J.B. spoke first. He stressed that B.C. should not be allowed to spring the trap they had so obviously set for the federal government. "You have to pre-empt their strategy," he urged coolly. "And the only way to do that is to make B.C.'s negotiating position public, *before* they break off talks and announce a provincial park instead."

Tom liked the idea. "That's much better than being seen as spoilers who have left the bargaining table, no matter what the provocation. I like it." Kevin and Colleen added bits of recent intelligence from their grapevine of contacts. "The only way to go now", said Colleen, "is for you to stake out the federal government's position and let the public judge B.C.'s position for what it is – blackmail."

It had already been a long day for McMillan. He had risen early, an hour's time difference to the east, had crowded in a car for a long drive and a very intense strategy session, and he now faced a hundred or so activists, each with a pressing concern. The discussion went well. On a range of issues, from the proposed expansion of the Sunshine Village ski resort in Banff, to measures to protect the ozone layer, to the proposed Rafferty-Alameda dams in Saskatchewan, Tom pledged to put environmental concerns first and foremost. South Moresby was next on the agenda. Colleen spoke passionately about the current crisis, only obliquely referring to very difficult negotiations. She called on groups from around the country to support Tom McMillan, even if the situation appeared to worsen. Her remarks were met with sustained applause.

Tom thanked her, and then did something I had not expected and could hardly believe. He asked the gathering of over a hundred people to keep in confidence what he was about to tell them. Tom filled them in on the whole of B.C.'s proposal – the expanded boundaries, the logging in the park for ten years, the outlandish dollar figures, the whole thing. "Obviously," Tom said, "there is no way we can authorize logging in a national park. On that count alone, a deal is not possible." The crowd was stunned. Support for the minister and for South Moresby soared that morning as activists from around the country realized what the odds against preserving South Moresby really were.

We left Katimavik to return to a full agenda in Ottawa. The principal task for the day was the drafting of the press release along the lines we had agreed upon in the limo meeting. It was written, edited by Tom, and then rewritten. It was crafted to such an exquisite degree that each word served a purpose and packed a strategic punch.

Tom phoned Miles Richardson to discuss the strategy with him. A meeting was scheduled with the B.C. caucus for the next morning and a copy of the draft release was sent to Deputy Prime Minister Don Mazankowski and Senator Lowell Murray, Mulroney's minister for federal-provincial relations.

We dated the release for the next day, May 12, and alerted our communications staff to distribute it as soon as we had approval from Maz and from Lowell Murray. Later that evening, Tom and I made our way over to a reception hosted by John Fraser in honour of the Canadian Environmental Network's tenth anniversary. We arrived late and missed the speeches by Fraser, Charles Caccia, Jim Fulton, and the NDP environment critic, Bill Blaikie. Tom spoke briefly and then mingled with the guests. Wine flowed and canapés were served. It may have looked like a cocktail party, but it sounded like a council of war. Liz Calder, a good friend from my Cape Breton anti-spray campaigns, circulated, lining up support for her plan to charter a plane from Nova Scotia and load it with people prepared to get arrested on the Charlottes. People from all over the country were planning to put their own fights on hold in order to mobilize support for South Moresby.

Kevin and J.B. left the sumptuous committee room used for the reception and wandered out into the corridors in search of a washroom. John opened a likely looking door and found himself looking into the House of Commons. It was the entrance used by the Speaker, which lies behind his large chair. They ventured in feeling like little boys in a place they knew they shouldn't be. J.B. spotted a desk on the right. "That's where Mulroney sits! Shouldn't we leave him a note or something?" He grinned mischievously. They opened J.B.'s briefcase to look for a likely item. "This should do nicely," said J.B., removing a political cartoon that had recently appeared in the *Vancouver Sun* about Bill Reid's refusal to complete his sculpture for the Canadian Embassy. It featured Reid carving what looked like the beginning of a hand, giving the finger. Canadian Embassy staff in the corner of the drawing provided the caption: "I don't think I like the way this thing is taking shape." They left it inside Mulroney's desk as an offering, an inside joke, a reminder.

J.B. was staying at my house, and when I got home around midnight from the last re-draftings of the press release, I was pleased to find he was still awake. Together we reviewed the draft. "This should do the trick," he said smiling. And then he told me about what I had missed at the Speaker's reception. "You should have heard Fraser's speech," said J.B. "He said that we were all part of the conspiracy to save the planet."

27

THE CONSPIRACY

Tuesday morning, May 12. Tom's secretary, Gillian, and I fussed in Tom's outer office, setting out coffee, juice, tea and milk, muffins and butter for the B.C. caucus. Die-hard pro-loggers Lorne McCuish, Fred King, and Lorne Greenaway were there; chairman Ted Schellenberg, whose fence-sitting tilted decidedly toward the forest industry camp; and park supporters Pat Crofton, Mary Collins, and John Fraser balanced things out.

Ted Schellenberg brought along a recent clipping from a paper in his riding, the *Alberni Valley Times,* in which B.C. Tourism Minister Bill Reid was quoted as saying that logging, mining, fishing, and tourism would operate side by side in the province's recreational areas, and "South Moresby will be the place we'll prove it." It was passed around to groans, amid the muffins and butter.

Tom called the session to order, explaining that the federal government that day would be forced to admit that the negotiations had stalled, and that, under the tense circumstances, he wanted caucus to be fully aware of the status of those talks to date. Then he spelled out Strachan's offer of April 8 and the recent series of counter-proposals and ultimatums.

I hadn't expected caucus to be as horrified by B.C.'s gambit as we were. Even the staunchest pro-loggers were aghast when they heard what B.C. had been proposing.

With each new condition, they recoiled. Lorne McCuish, champion of Moresby Island Concerned Citizens, was blunt in his assessment. He doubted very much whether Bruce Strachan could be responsible for such a scheme: "I'll bet anything Stephen Rogers is behind it. Rogers and Strachan are doing a Bergen and McCarthy routine!"

MPs with contacts in Vander Zalm's office said he'd been under tremendous pressure from the major forest companies ever since the throne speech. All the caucus members, even those who had never supported Tom McMillan before, supported his proposed strategy now. They admitted that they had thought the federal government was being greedy in wanting more of Lyell Island, but it was nothing compared to the avarice of the B.C. proposal. Pat Crofton minced no words, "You'd better make the federal government's position bloody public and soon." Mary Collins agreed, and suggested that maybe Mazankowski should call Vander Zalm. John Fraser had excused himself early to head back to the House and to avoid any partisan discussion. His only advice had been that the federal government had to be prepared to pay a fair price.

Tom was pleased with the advice from caucus, but we both felt that there was no time to waste in getting our position released. Chances were not insignificant that someone in caucus, maybe not among those present, would tip our hand to the province. We had our usual Tuesday morning briefing session with the deputy minister and had to focus on an agenda of other issues, but our attention was never far removed from the imminent release of the minister's statement on South Moresby. It had taken on the characteristics and language of a military manoeuvre, a "pre-emptive first strike."

The day wore on, but still we did not have approval to release it. With a First Ministers' Conference on the constitution scheduled for the first week of June, all ministers were under direct orders not to rock any provincial boats. Planning a "pre-emptive first strike" was thought to fall outside the realm of friendly relations. Tom went to a cabinet committee meeting, hoping to catch Maz and Lowell Murray. Terry and I waited in the outer chamber. It was getting on toward early evening, and still Tom had not surfaced to give us the "all clear." I had just stepped into one of the cabinet lobby phone booths when, through the leaded glass doors, I saw Tom emerge with a man I recognized as Mulroney's old buddy from St Francis Xavier University, Lowell Murray. As Murray turned on his heels, Terry and I rushed over to Tom. He was in a black mood. "We can't release this," he said.

"Why not?" I objected. "Don't they realize –" Tom cut me off with a peremptory tone. "There's nothing more to be said. The constitutional talks in June take precedence over everything else just now, and this would be seen as unnecessarily provoking British Columbia."

"So, we just have to wait like sitting ducks for B.C. to blow us out of the water?" Terry asked in exasperation.

"I do not want to hear anything more from either of you," Tom said, as though to disobedient children. "That's all there is to it." He turned away from us and headed back into the cabinet room. I thought I might start to cry right there. Terry didn't look dry-eyed either. "What are we going to do now?" I asked. He shook his head, "I dunno. Nothing we can do."

Later that evening, Mazankowski asked Tom to come into his office for a chat. Nothing concentrates the mind like an upcoming execution, unless it's a particularly well-written press release demonstrating the way in which an event will unfold. In the case of Tom's South Moresby statement, it succinctly brought home the reality of an impending disaster. The breakdown of negotiations would not be good for federal-provincial relations either. Mazankowski decided to try to mediate. Maz and

Tom put through a call to Bill Vander Zalm. The deputy prime minister told the Premier that he understood that negotiations between their respective environment ministers seemed to have fallen apart. He expressed concern that the two governments not give up on such an important initiative. Vander Zalm agreed. He had given up his belief that Mulroney had any real interest in South Moresby, but now that he was talking to the deputy prime minister, maybe there was still hope. They spoke in generalities for a while about the importance both governments attached to striking a deal, and then Tom spoke to Vander Zalm, extolling the virtues of the Charlottes as a tourism destination. With the province's own tourism minister saying that the islands were too remote and rainy for anyone to go there, Tom felt that their commercial viability could use a little selling. When Vander Zalm expressed doubts about their proximity to tourist markets, Tom waxed eloquent. As a former tourism minister, he knew all the stock phrases. "Tourism is a highly segmented market," he told the premier of the "Super, Natural" province. "Times have changed since the days when Mom and Pop and the kids and the dog piled into their station wagon and drove to their holiday destination. Now people will pay top dollars for a wilderness tourism experience. The more remote the better. Tourism is now the number one industry for the Yukon, and surely its weather is as problematic and its location as remote as the Queen Charlotte Islands."

Tom knew he was on a roll. The Premier was interested. "But how would people get there?" he asked. "Well," Tom said, exuding confidence, "cruise ships take people right past the Charlottes all the time to tour Alaska. I'm sure they could include a national park in the Charlottes in their itinerary. And, of course, people can fly in and then join a charter. There are already a dozen or so operators offering kayak excursions or sailboat charters. Even without promotion, tourism in the area is growing exponentially."

Vander Zalm seized on the idea of cruise ships. "Could we get cruise ships to the Charlottes?" he asked. "Certainly," said Tom. "We already have some inquiries from some companies and after the July issue of *National Geographic*, we could be swamped." Tom felt that he had succeeded in getting Vander Zalm really excited about a national park for the first time, throwing around a lot of his favourite phrases – evocations like "world class." Visions of the Love Boat stopping in at Sandspit. Now we were talking. It wasn't just a park for some tree-huggers that would be nice to do as a favour for the Prime Minister. This was a hot prospect.

Mazankowski got back on the line with Vander Zalm to see if the two of them couldn't sort things out and agree on a new process of negotiations. Vander Zalm asked if the two governments had made any progress, "Do we agree on anything?"

Mazankowski, holding the phone to his ear, turned and repeated the question to Tom. Tom thought fast. "Yes," he said. "Tell him we agree to their position on boundaries in their April 8th offer." Maz did. And Vander Zalm said that that was, at least, a start. We agree on boundaries and we'll take the rest from there. Vander Zalm and Mazankowski agreed that from here on in, they would handle the talks themselves. The negotiations had been booted up from the environment ministers to Canada's deputy prime minister and B.C's Premier. But, Vander Zalm cautioned, they couldn't take forever. If they hadn't made substantial progress in a few days, then it might not be possible to conclude an agreement.

From his phone conversation with McMillan and Mazankowski, Vander Zalm went straight to the press gallery to fill in the fourth estate on the latest development, telling reporters that Ottawa had a few more days, or else the province would "go it alone." "I'm not threatening," he said. "I'm not putting out an ultimatum, except I'm saying there has to be a deadline."

Late-breaking stories were keeping the Victoria press gallery hopping. After the Premier's surprise press scrum, a Canadian Press reporter and a Southam reporter both got hold of fairly complete versions of the province's April 8 offer from different sources. Now they had the whole story. They knew why the negotiations had broken down earlier in the day. They knew that B.C. had been insisting on a $100-million trust fund, $40 to 50 million in other goodies, and ten years' more logging inside the park. The next morning's papers carried news of both developments: Vander Zalm's chat with Mazankowski and the details of B.C.'s April 8 offer.

I was ecstatic. Until I saw the headlines, I had been in the depths of despair. Now I could hardly believe it. Mazankowski hadn't thrown us to the slings and arrows of outrageous British Columbia. He had stepped in and saved the day. Tom was keen to tell me all about the spectacular about-face in our fortunes.

Things were moving along as a result of the public exposure of British Columbia's bargaining ploy. Reporters in B.C. couldn't find their usual press contacts as Vicky, Colleen, and J.B. were still on their way back west. But Jeff Gibbs gave a great interview, setting out clearly why the environmentalists felt that the federal government was being set up and how important it was for people to support the federal position. Jim Fulton characterized the province's last offer as "an insane, bizarre proposal." By my count, two of Jim Collinson's assumptions of what was most unlikely to happen had just come to pass: B.C. had agreed to a park, including all of Lyell Island, and the public was rallying behind the federal position.

Midday, I got a call from a reporter in the Victoria press gallery. Vander Zalm and Strachan had just announced that they had dropped their demand for ten years' more logging in the park. "There would be a phase-out of logging" with a park deal, Strachan had explained. "There would be no more cutting permits." Vander Zalm had told reporters that he expected to speak with Mazankowski again that day. "I'm pretty sure there's going to be a park," he said smiling.

In Ottawa, Question Period was sprinkled with more questions on South Moresby than at any time since the Haida blockade. Tom's answers reflected the giddy optimism of negotiations that were progressing hour by hour. In the afternoon, I sat in Tom's office while he took a phone call from Bruce Strachan. Strachan reported that they were taking an idea to cabinet. It would be based on their April offer, but they'd find logging somewhere else. Furthermore, he told Tom that they would "take over the Frank Beban problem" and remove the cap on their $8-million contribution. B.C.'s new proposal was due the next day, May 14. When Tom hung up, he looked euphoric. "I think we've got a deal, Elizabeth." Neither of us could quite believe it.

With developments occurring by the minute, I spent most of the day on the telephone, keeping John Fraser, Jim Fulton, Miles Richardson, and Vicky, or J.B., or whomever I could reach, up to date. I had to call Pat Carney's staff and Maz's office and reporters and far-flung contacts. My secretary, Karen, was juggling four or five phone lines, all flashing away on hold with people who either wanted to tell me what had just happened, or to find out. Time flew and I had completely forgotten about my dinner meeting with Kevin McNamee and the author of the task-force report on New Park Establishment, Arlin Hackman, when Kevin showed up to fetch me.

I was just going out the door, when Tom's legislative assistant, Marc Grenier, came rushing up. He looked stressed, as he often did. "We've got an Opposition motion for tomorrow. They just now sent it over to us!" This was always bad news. There are a scant twenty-five opposition days on the parliamentary calendar, divided between the opposition parties. An opposition day meant that the minister responsible for the subject of the debate had to speak and also had to line up other government members to speak in support. In simple terms, it meant that the minister's staff would spend all night arranging speakers and writing speeches for the minister and the other government speakers prepared to debate. Marc handed me the motion, "It's from Jim Fulton and it's on South Moresby," and then he smiled. It turned out that Jim had received permission from his own caucus to use one of its precious opposition days for South Moresby with only minutes to spare before the filing deadline. He had drafted the motion hurriedly, but it lost nothing because of haste. It was a brilliant move.

"That's fantastic!" I told Marc. "We'll have a whole day in the House to campaign for South Moresby. This is great! Yay Jim!"

Kevin watched in amusement as the office seemed to erupt in happy chaos. He turned to Marc, who was still grinning. "The government isn't supposed to like opposition motions, is it?" Marc laughed, "Not usually, no."

Marc and I quickly got down to business, reviewing the best possible candidates to join the debate on Jim's motion. "Try to get Bill McKnight." It turned out that McKnight had a major press conference in the morning. The fact that he made it to join the debate was one of the best things he did as minister of Indian affairs.

I reported for duty on the second floor of our building to work with Barry Olsen and Jim Shearon of the Parks' communications branch. Each of us was to write one speech, focussing on a different aspect of the issue. The minister's could be the most wide-ranging and lyrical. McKnight's would, of course, focus on the Haida interest, and the third, for an as yet unnamed B.C. member, would deal with the economic benefits of expanded tourism in the Charlottes. I reached Tom by phone and he gave me a blow-by-blow outline of the speech he wanted to give the next day. It already sounded great. Jim Shearon plunked me down in front of a computer. I had never used a computer to write on before, but it seemed idiot-proof and in no time, I was typing away, lost in the mood of *Islands at the Edge.* I'd never been to Haida Gwaii, so in order to describe the places I knew Tom had seen, I studied the book's various images and let the words pour out.

Late that night, as I waited for the speech to print out, I looked at the big Parks Canada map on the wall. All the national parks were shown in green. I picked up a green magic marker and started colouring in the bottom third of the Queen Charlotte Islands archipelago. "What are you doing?" asked Barry. "Protecting South Moresby," I said.

I got home late, around 2 a.m. There was no sign of Kevin, who was staying at my house, though I was grateful for his note that my poor dog had been walked. I collapsed on my bed, holding onto my copy of *Islands at the Edge.*

Tom liked my draft the next morning and made a few changes, strengthening it here and there, and adding a line about his personal impressions of the islands: "Despite advance descriptions from people who had visited the islands before me...I was singularly unprepared for the magnificence...the awe-inspiring forest canopies, the bubbling hot springs, the teeming wildlife, the wide-open spaces, the pristine stillness, the sheer beauty of an unspoiled world...I feel a special kinship to those remote misty isles."

The motion that had inspired such lofty prose and had launched such a frantic whirl of activity was itself fairly prosaic:

"Pursuant to Standing Order 82 (12), moved that this House calls on the Government of British Columbia to cooperate in setting aside the South Moresby area of the Queen Charlotte Islands as a National Park Reserve; and,

"Further, that the federal government provide such compensation to those interests affected by such National Park Reserve; and,

"Further, that the House confirms its intention to ensure the continued participation of the Haida people in matters affecting South Moresby."

As an opposition motion for debate, Fulton's motion could not be put to a vote. It was a debating exercise, nothing more. Ordinarily, such motions stir little excitement, other than for the few MPs who directly participate. Not only do they interest the media hardly at all, neither do they draw much of a crowd in the House. The minimum number of members on all sides of the House are forced to attend to maintain a quorum. Something on the order of a dozen souls catch up on correspondence, while another honourable member delivers a fine parliamentary oratory into the echoing void. Only proceedings in the Senate attract less interest, and that's because they're not televised.

Because of the unexciting nature of the morning session of Parliament, the Speaker of the House, having ceremoniously paraded through the outer halls of Centre Block to the chair wearing his three-cornered hat and flanked by the golden mace of office, usually slips out the exit behind his chair with a good deal less pomp. The Speaker returns to his chambers for the avalanche of parliamentary business that awaits him every day, between refereeing rounds at Question Period.

But on the morning of May 14, John Fraser showed no inclination to leave his position, presiding over the resolution pursuant to Standing Order 82 (12). Jim Fulton was the first to speak to his own motion. He set a standard of brilliant and evocative eloquence that was maintained, but not surpassed, throughout the day-long debate. Speaker after speaker departed from the usual rancour of the House to employ words rarely heard in parliamentary debate. As Vince Dantzer, Tory member for Okanagan, who carried the B.C. Tory banner in the debate, said toward the end of the day's proceedings, "This is more like a love-in than a debate."

From his opening remarks, Jim Fulton stressed the non-partisan nature of his motion. He recounted a conversation he had had years before with a Haida elder. "What he said to me sunk in my heart and will be with me for as long as I live. He said, 'Jim, if a Haida went down on a skidder to a large graveyard in Vancouver and drove around with the blade down and pushed all of the headstones into a big pile, what do you think the white people in Vancouver would do?' He said, 'That is how I feel about the logging on Lyell Island. That is how I feel about what is going on in South Moresby.'"

Fulton spoke longer than his allotted time, but John Fraser showed no sign of impatience. Some might find a friendship between a dyed-in-the-wool Tory and a zealous New Democrat to be an unlikely match, but Jim Fulton and John Fraser were friends of long-standing, bound together by a shared love of the natural environment. Fulton was the only person I knew who called the Speaker "Fraze," and Fraser spoke with affection of Jim's "impish quality." The previous fall, when the first-time election of a Speaker on a free vote was being discussed by members of Parliament, Fulton and Fraser happened to share a flight back to Vancouver from Ottawa. As they sat together, Jim wedging his substantial form into the airplane seat by the window, he tried to persuade Fraser to let his name stand for Speaker. "C'mon, Fraze. You'd be great. The House really needs you," Jim had urged.

Fraser had tried to discourage the notion, "I don't think you'd really like it." With a twinkle, Fraser had recalled the time that Jim had smuggled a dead salmon, concealed down one trouser leg, into the chamber, and had dropped it on Mulroney's desk during Question Period. "If I'd been in the chair when you brought in that dead fish, I wouldn't have recognized you for six months!" Now, as one of the most important issues in the lives of both men was hanging in the balance, each counted himself fortunate that the other was there.

Brian Tobin, a fiesty Newfoundland member, rose to speak on behalf of the leader of the official Opposition. John Turner was out of town, but fortunately his support for saving South Moresby had been recorded on several previous occasions in Hansard.

As Tom and I prepared for his address, our B.C. office faxed us the latest Vancouver press. The tabloid-style *Province* heralded "Moresby Wins! B.C. expects pact today on national park." Strachan was quoted as saying that he hoped to conclude talks within the day. Vander Zalm was smiling again, "I like it. It is a great tourist destination." He told reporters that cruise ships were the solution to the problem of remoteness and that the federal government would build a cruise-ship facility in the park. Vicky phoned, "Has Tom really promised a cruise-ship dock? That would be a real ecological disaster!" I reassured her that Vander Zalm had just gotten a little over-enthusiastic.

I listened to Tom's speech from the gallery. It went well. "South Moresby is the litmus test of our values as a society. How much importance do we attach to the aesthetic, the intangible, even the spiritual values that South Moresby represents? Those qualities do not readily lend themselves to a cost-benefit analysis. That fact does not make them any the less compelling. Again, some of the strongest arguments for saving South Moresby are economic. But it is the other arguments that cry out for us to act: the ones that strike at the heart of what we stand for as a people, the ones that address whether we stand for anything beyond feeding and clothing and sheltering ourselves."

The spirit of unanimity was so rare and the values expressed so exemplary, that several members later could not remember another day such as this. It was intoxicating.

As McMillan answered friendly questions after his speech, Bill Blaikie rose to propose an unusual procedure. "Could the Minister indicate whether he would be willing to support a proposal at the end of the day to have this motion deemed to have been passed by the House?"

A non-votable motion converted into a unanimous vote? It would be parliamentary alchemy. Tom was quick to his feet, "Mr Speaker, I think that is an inspired suggestion." Brian Tobin, speaking for the official Opposition, was just as eager to support a unanimous resolution on a non-votable motion.

Fraser had not ruled when Blaikie rose on a point of order, "Given the unanimous views which have been expressed, could the House agree and have you put it on the record, with unanimous consent, that the motion we are debating at this point will be deemed to have been passed at the end of the day?"

Fraser knew that he had to be careful. The "unanimity" on all sides of the House did not include a few recalcitrant Tories from British Columbia. Tom McMillan looked at Fraser encouragingly. Fulton gave "Fraze" a hopeful grin. And in the gallery, I held my breath and crossed all my fingers, and prayed.

Fraser ruled judiciously. All the 'i's had to be dotted and the 't's crossed if the little network of conspirators was going to be able to pull this off. "The House has heard the suggestion of the Honourable Member for Winnipeg – Birds Hill, the comment from the Honourable Minister of the Environment and the comment from the Honourable Member for Humber – Port au Port – St Barbe." Bases covered, all three parties were on the record. The House is the master of its own proceedings, so where its will is clear no lack of precedent

should deter it. This was Fraser's logic as he ruled that
the procedure proposed was acceptable. "The record
will show that at the end of the debate, the House has
been unanimous in supporting the motion put forward
by the New Democratic Party. I take it that that is the
pleasure of the House?" Those present quickly agreed.

Fraser paused, "Honourable Members have heard
the motion. Is it agreed?"

I scanned the nearly empty benches. There was no
sign of anyone who would oppose the motion. I wondered where Benno Freisen and Gerry St Germain,
strong pro-logging members who had been on the floor
moments before, had disappeared to. They could appear
at any moment, but as it turned out they were busy, just a
few feet away in the government lobby, trying to browbeat
Vince Dantzer into not speaking for the motion.

Back in the chamber, waiting for the objection everyone hoped would not be made, Fraser let his last "Is it
agreed?" hang in the air like an auctioneer's gavel. All
present shouted "Agreed!" and the Speaker ruled "That
will be appropriately recorded." This was the finest moment of Fraser's noble Conspiracy to Save the Planet.
Tom and Fulton may not have actually let out a cheer,
but it seemed that the House erupted in an exclamation
of exultation. The Speaker adjourned proceedings until
after lunch, and Tom McMillan and John Fraser and Jim
Fulton and Bill Blaikie and Brian Tobin and Nelson Riis
shook hands and hugged and generally acted in ways
unrecognizable to those who see them only in Question
Period.

In Queen Charlotte City, Miles and Guujaaw were
watching the proceedings via satellite. The concerns of
the Haida Nation had never before dominated a full day
of proceedings in the Parliament of Canada. Every call
for wilderness preservation in the course of the debate
was matched by a demand that the interests of the
Haida Nation be respected. They stayed close to the set

through addresses from Bill McKnight, Ian Waddell, and Charles Caccia, for whom the approaching reality of a South Moresby deal was a dream come true.

Back in the Hill office, Tom and I were still congratulating each other for a major coup and an incredible morning, when the phone rang. Mazankowski was calling to see what the dickens was going on. He had received some irate calls from members of the B.C. caucus, and he wanted to know just what the hell McMillan thought he was up to. Tom calmed Maz, "Everyone present agreed, and I thought it would strengthen our hand in the negotiations with British Columbia." Mazankowski was appeased, but still carried out the obligatory call to the Speaker. Fraser showed equal sang-froid. Nothing unusual had transpired, although it was true that no one could recall another time in parliamentary history when a non-votable motion from an opposition party had been deemed to have been passed unanimously before the debate was half over.

The next day, Jim Fulton told the press that Miles Richardson said, "The Great Spirit hovered over the House of Commons briefly yesterday."

28

ENVIRONMENT
WEEK

DURING THE MAY 14 DEBATE, JIM FULTON HAD LEFT THE
floor to take a phone call in the opposition lobby. A
deep baritone voice had said, "Hello, Jim, this is Brian
Mulroney." Jim knew a prankster when he heard one, so
he had laughed. "Yeah, sure. Quit bullshittin' me. Who
is this really?"

To which a startled Prime Minister had insisted, "Jim,
this is Brian Mulroney."

Jim's jaw had dropped. It turned out that Mulroney
had just wanted to ask him how he thought things were
going, both the debate and the negotiations. The two
men had chatted for a while, and Jim had hung up, in-
credulous. We spoke by phone later in the day. "Geez,
Elizabeth," Jim said. "I couldn't believe it. The Prime
Minister has never called me before. I think he's really
worried about South Moresby."

By the next morning, we had B.C.'s revised proposal.
It did not go as far or make as many concessions as
Strachan had done in his last phone call to Tom. But it
was a quantum leap from where we had been just four
days before. It was essentially the April 8 offer, without
the demand for ten years' more logging. All the other
terms and conditions remained. The total package,
after including the federal government's direct costs,
would be close to $200 million. The deadline for our re-
sponse was the following Friday, May 22.

We were getting close enough to think about defrosting

the famous cake. The *Vancouver Sun* headlined, "Moresby deal said close to wire." Tom left for the weekend, asking me to arrange calls for him to Miles Richardson and B.C. caucus chairman Ted Schellenberg, and, of course, any calls from the deputy prime minister or Strachan. The momentum was strong, and we assumed that talks would continue through the long weekend.

People around the country were stretching the limits of their creativity to figure out what they could do to help. Monte Hummel of the World Wildlife Fund had excellent contacts and a strong commitment to South Moresby. It struck him that an appeal to Vander Zalm's Dutch roots might not hurt. One of the founders of the World Wildlife Fund was Prince Bernhard of the Netherlands. Monte contacted Soesdijk Palace, to suggest that a telegram from His Royal Highness might prove helpful with a certain Dutch premier in Canada. Prince Bernhard telegraphed Bill Vander Zalm with an eloquent appeal to save South Moresby, part of the world heritage. He closed saying, "I would be proud to have one of my countrymen associated with this conservation achievement."

Monte phoned me to read the telegram. I was impressed. "Let me know if you ever feel that we need a telegram from Prince Philip. I can always get in touch with Buckingham Palace." I told him I would keep that in mind. Prince Philip was president of World Wildlife International and was widely known for his personal interest in environmental issues.

Monte's was not the only effort to marshal international support. The Jacques Cousteau Society sent an urgent telex to the B.C. government, as did the National Parks and Conservation Association and the Audubon Society from the U.S.A. Staff from the National Parks and Conservation Association started phoning me almost daily to see how we were doing in the negotiations and to ask what more they could do to help.

In some ways it was wonderful to have the brunt of negotiating with British Columbia managed from a different office. I kept in touch with Maz's staff on a daily basis, and Parks Canada officals had been virtually seconded to Maz's office for technical back-up. In other ways it was a disadvantage. For one thing, despite briefings between offices, I was much less in the information flow. And, for that matter, so was Tom. Jim Collinson kept developments very close to his vest. He was under no obligation to brief me, but it did seem strange that, from time to time, developments occurred that Collinson did not inform McMillan about, either.

But, as always, Tom and I had plenty of other concerns to keep us occupied. He had decided to put negotiations for a grasslands national park in Saskatchewan into high gear, meeting with their minister responsible for water rights just days before flying west for Environment Week. We still hoped we might get the whole matter resolved in time for an announcement during the early June visit of the Duke of Edinburgh, coinciding with Environment Week. We would use Prince Philip's visit shamelessly to get as much money for wildlife habitat protection programs as was humanly possible.

As late May turned into June, it seemed that Mazankowski was prepared to counter B.C.'s offer with significantly more dollars than our last $39-million bid. For months, Maz had been presiding over one of the worst-kept secrets in Ottawa – the Western Diversification Fund. Nothing had been announced, but departments were already forming a queue in front of the Western Diversification trough. It was rumoured to be around one billion dollars. With policy reserves for the cabinet committees bone-dry, a one-billion-dollar fund was an oasis in a desert of fiscal restraint. Environment Canada was already drafting applications to the non-existent fund for money to implement prairie wetland habitat restoration and "Centres of Excellence" for wildlife toxicology. As Maz had responsibility for the fund and was also carrying the South Moresby negotiations, it wasn't hard for people to guess where additional bucks for a South Moresby deal might come from.

South Moresby now faced a new obstacle. Jealous supplicants to the imaginary fund began to make noises about South Moresby getting "their" project monies. Even our own deputy, Genevieve Ste Marie, worried that South Moresby might get "our" duck money. Our application for restoration of prairie wetland had been submitted a few weeks before. What if it were decided that Environment Canada couldn't get a park and ducks? If the deputy minister of the Parks Service was worried about South Moresby grabbing the potential goodies in the giant Western Diversification Fund cookie jar, B.C. caucus members were apoplectic. Eventually they would convince British Columbia to insist in the negotiations that the money not come from Western Diversification. Which pocket the federal government dug into to give the money to B.C. should have not concerned B.C. at all, but it was on its way to becoming a bone of contention.

On June 2, Vander Zalm came to Ottawa for what are now known as the Meech Lake constitutional talks. McMillan arranged to see Vander Zalm briefly before the first ministers closeted themselves away for the Meech Lake lock-up. They slipped away in search of a private place to chat. Tom looked for a likely spot, opened a door, and found himself alone with the Premier in a laundry room. Vander Zalm was clearly sold on a park. He was excited about it and told Tom that he felt confident that he and Maz could make progress on the deal during his Ottawa visit. Tom was thrilled. The momentum was with us, and, Tom assured me, the agreement on boundaries was holding firm.

The next day, we took off for Regina, Saskatchewan, and Environment Week festivities. As well as attending

events arranged for Prince Philip, Tom was also scheduled
to speak to the annual meeting of the Canadian Nature
Federation being held in Saskatoon. Thom Henley and
John Broadhead were being awarded the prestigious
Pimlott Conservation Prize for outstanding work in the
cause of conservation. For the next two days, Huck, J.B.,
Tom, and I travelled across southern Saskatchewan to
wildlife events starring His Royal Highness.

Before we left Ottawa, I had asked Monte Hummel,
the ringmaster for the royal three-ring circus, if there
would be any problem orchestrating a brief audience
with Prince Philip for J.B. and Huck. He had agreed that
the benefits to the cause made it worth an effort. So at
the first morning's opening press conference, I had J.B.
and Huck positioned as instructed by Monte in a spot by
which Prince Philip would pass. Monte would introduce
them. I had a photographer ready. Monte and Prince
Philip walked right by them, Monte looking preoccupied. He apologized later – "running late for Canada
A.M." We planned a second attempt at the afternoon's
ceremonial opening of World Wildlife Fund's project to
restore the endangered burrowing owl population.
"Have them there," Monte assured me, "and I'll make
sure they are introduced."

The afternoon's event took place at a farm about a
forty-minute drive outside of Regina. Grant Fahlman
had been one of the first Prairie farmers to enrol in
Operation Burrowing Owl, agreeing to leave a portion
of his fields out of production, sparing the use of chemical insecticides, so that the rare underground owls had
a chance to survive. As we crossed the hot fields of
Saskatchewan, J.B. retreated to the shadow of the
Fahlman barn to work on the carving of a traditional
Haida pipe. Huck, wearing his going-to-lobby suit,
looked for all the world like a ministerial aide. Tom enjoyed his company, as did I, and Huck played the part of
the minister's official photographer to the hilt. All
around the periphery of the protected habitat in the

blazing sun, held back behind sturdy ropes, were several thousand conservationists, monarchists, and country-fair lovers. The first portion of the program was the introduction of the burrowing owls to McMillan and Prince Philip. Lorne Scott, head of the Saskatchewan Wildlife Federation, had rigged one of their nests in advance, so that all he had to do was lift a piece of plywood in order to expose the tiny, naked, ugly, and squawking baby birds to the blinding sun. As the baby owls were passed around – one to the Prince, one to McMillan, another to a local dignitary – I wondered how many more endangered birds would bite the dust because of our efforts to save them. (I checked later. All the baby owls had survived – a credit to their endurance.) Prince Philip toured the perimeter of the field, showing the baby owl to the crowd of adoring fans who had come to see a real live prince, not a threatened species. His Royal Highness is a dedicated conservationist and a good educator. He made sure that no one missed the point of the exercise. And he scolded the media for focussing their cameras on him instead of on the burrowing owl.

Tom McMillan handed his owl back to Lorne Scott, but I noticed that he didn't seem comfortable. I was part way across the field when I noticed that Tom was holding his hand at a rather odd angle from his body. I wandered over to where he was, realizing the cause of his discomforture – a yellow glop in the palm of his hand. Appropriate, I thought, for an environment minister to be shat upon by an endangered species. They so rarely get the chance. I ever so discretely handed Tom a serviette from my purse. Without a word, he wiped his palm, and with equal inconspicuous ease, handed the dirty napkin back to me.

Huck clicked away with a highly professional flare, as Tom joined Prince Philip for the walkabout. As I obediently followed behind, I said, "Tom, you know, if you got the chance, it would really mean a lot to me to meet Prince Philip."

Tom looked surprised, and in an apologetic tone, said, "Oh, I'm sorry. I thought you'd met." I suppressed the desire to ask, "*When?* The last time I had tea at Buckingham Palace?"

Immediately, Tom spoke up, "Excuse me, Your Royal Highness?" Prince Philip turned to face us. He may have said, "Yes?" or his regal bearing may have just conveyed it. Tom began, very graciously, "I'd like to present to you a member of my personal staff. This is Elizabeth May, and she –" At this point, I could tell Tom was warming up to say something really nice about me. Maybe to tell His Royal Highness that I was an environmentalist in my own right, and not just a well-dressed flunkie. But before Tom could say whatever it was he was planning to say, Prince Philip cut him off, extended his hand to me and said, "Yes, I know. She provides you with Kleenexes." I laughed, amazed that anyone, least of all the centre of attention, had noticed our very surreptitious exchange. If Prince Philip were a bird, he would definitely be a raptor. He has sharp enough eyes.

Although I had received my introduction to royalty, Monte decided that the Fahlman farm was not a good place to introduce Huck and J.B. "Bring them tonight to the dinner. They can meet there."

The Ducks Unlimited-World Wildlife Fund gala and art auction was a $500-per-head event. I already had my ticket, paid for by the department. Tom, of course, would be sitting at the head table. Premier Devine would be there, as well as countless Prairie politicians and dignitaries, and bigwigs from Toronto, like Adam Zimmerman and Doug Bassett. Another two tickets at $500 a shot might not faze most of the guests, but as I paid for J.B.'s and Huck's tickets out of my own pocket, I decided that these two new brothers of mine were turning into an expensive proposition. Still, in all my time in McMillan's office, I had never had so much fun. It was almost like being off-duty. Tom was in great cheer, and word from Ottawa continued to be encouraging about the prospects for quick resolution of the thirteen-year crusade. We were dizzy with happiness.

That afternoon, I had a phone call in my hotel room from Michael Keating, environmental reporter for the *Globe and Mail.* "What's this about an agreement in principle?" he asked. Then he told me that, as soon as Vander Zalm returned to B.C. soil, or at least the tarmac of the Victoria airport, he had told the waiting reporters that he had struck "an agreement in principle" with Mazankowski, and that he expected federal bureaucrats to come out to B.C. early the following week to sort out the details. I reported all this to Tom, and we checked with Ottawa. It seemed that Vander Zalm was, true to his nature, being a little over-enthusiatic. Talks had gone well, but Ottawa was still drafting the proposal. We should have worried about Vander Zalm's exaggerated sense of progress, or about the federal caution. But since both sides professed that a deal was close, we took all news as good news.

The formal dinner was memorable, but once again, J.B. and Huck did not meet Prince Philip. So the next morning, I rented a car to convey me, J.B., and Huck to the hundredth anniversary party for the first wildlife sanctuary in North America – Last Mountain Lake. McMillan and Terry Collins were travelling by helicopter with Prince Philip to the event, and as there had been only room for one staff member, I was glad to opt out and accept ground transportation.

We got to the lake on schedule and joined the thousands who had already assembled to catch a glimpse of His Royal Highness. Tom was there to declare officially Last Mountain Lake a National Wildlife Area. I was able to find two seats for J.B. and Huck in the front row of the VIP section behind the rope barriers. As Prince Philip prepared to leave, he was taken down the front row of dignitaries. There was no way for Prince Philip to miss them now. Monte introduced our two conservation heroes, heaping praise upon them for their dedication and their national award. They presented Prince Philip with a copy of *Islands at the Edge* and a recently published book, a handsome volume on the life and art of Bill Reid. Tom McMillan stood next to Monte, beaming as J.B. and Huck had their picture snapped with Prince Philip. As Monte passed me to get on his helicopter, he stopped to give me a congratulatory hug. "Let me know if Moresby needs a telegram from Buckingham Palace." Again I told him I wouldn't forget.

Back in Ottawa on Monday everything seemed to be going well. Jim reported that the final touches were being put on a package Mazankowski hoped to send to Vander Zalm. Mulroney was in Venice for an economic summit, Environment Week not yet being the stuff of prime ministerial agendas.

Tuesday was my birthday and the anniversary of Tom's announcement to the Canadian Environmental Network that I would join his staff. It did not seem possible that it had happened only a year before. Nor did it seem likely that I was only one year older on this birthday. It felt like ten. That afternoon my birthday cheer was dampened by a call from Canadian Press reporter Daphne Brougham in Victoria. "Something's gone wrong. Vander Zalm is complaining that B.C. was expecting a senior federal negotiating team out here yesterday, and no one showed. It sounds serious," said Daphne, relating both facts and intuition.

I called Jim Collinson and reported the news. "Oh, they just got it all wrong," he assured me. "We never said that we were sending anyone out on Monday. We'll send a team out after they've looked at our proposal, but we haven't sent it to them yet. There'd be no point in flying out now."

I called Mazankowski's staff. "Maybe we ought to dispatch some senior people right away so Vander Zalm won't feel slighted." They didn't agree. They took Jim's line, there was no reason to panic. The team would go out when it had something to talk about.

But I took Daphne's warning seriously. I was convinced that the success of negotiations depended entirely on Vander Zalm. The B.C. cabinet was nearly unanimously against a national park at South Moresby. Rogers and Strachan must have been livid when Vander Zalm had agreed to the enlarged boundaries and then, the next day, had decided to abandon the demand for ten years' worth of logging. Instead of the federal government being hoist with its own petard, Ottawa had been handed a chance at success. Rogers and others would be quick to rally cabinet support for a much smaller provincial park the moment that momentum flagged in the Mazankowski round of talks. If Vander Zalm lost heart, we were sunk.

On June 10, it nearly all fell apart. In mid-afternoon Tom received a phone call from Maz's office. His staff expected B.C. to break off talks that afternoon and were not planning anything to keep them on track. We scrambled. Jim Collinson rushed to Tom's office. He brought the latest federal offer, which had been faxed to British Columbia that morning. I was shocked that Tom had not seen the offer before it had been sent. We read it quickly. The bottom line was that the federal government was offering a $106-million package for South Moresby. Tom was amazed that so much money had been promised. In his nearly two years as minister, he had never seen so much money committed to a single environmental project. "Why would they break off talks just when we are offering so much?" I asked no one in particular. Tom suggested that I call Strachan's assistant, Nan Selkirk, to see what I could find out. She didn't know anything about the faxed offer from Mazankowski. The B.C. cabinet was meeting as we spoke. I asked her to check: Was it possible the offer had gone astray? Tom looked at me with a steady gaze. "Call John Fraser. See if there's anything he can do through his contacts in British Columbia."

I got on the phone with the Speaker's principal secretary, Stephen Ash. "We don't know what's going on, or why they're angry, but we may lose the whole thing any minute," I told him. "Okay," said Ash. "Leave it with me."

An hour or so later he called back. Fraser's best contact within the B.C. cabinet was Attorney General Brian Smith. They had been friends since the days of their first law practices and involvement with the Young Conservatives, twenty-five years before. Over the last few months, Fraser had applied so much pressure on his old friend to support South Moresby that he feared jeopardizing their relationship. But it turned out that Smith was not in the cabinet meeting in Victoria. He was, in those fateful hours, in Vancouver, attempting to obtain a writ to squash trade-union protests against Vander Zalm's latest labour legislation, Bill 19. Without Smith in cabinet, we realized that Vander Zalm would have virtually no support for a park, for while Smith was not a champion of South Moresby, he was at least aware of the larger political and national dimensions of the issue.

Ash had also called David Poole, Vander Zalm's right-hand man. Ash had pointed out that breaking off talks of such personal interest to Mulroney when he was in Venice would be a personal slight. Vander Zalm then tried to telephone Mulroney in Venice, but was unable to reach him. It now appeared that British Columbia would give us a few more days, at least until the Prime Minister was back in Canada.

Tom and I sat in his Parliament Hill office through the tense afternoon, reviewing the letter dispatched that morning to Vander Zalm. The offer, on the whole, was fantastic – a package beyond our wildest dreams. The federal government was offering $50 million over ten

years for a Queen Charlotte Islands Regional
Development Fund. We were offering to forgo our usual
fifty-fifty cost-sharing ratio for buying out timber interests. We would match B.C.'s $8-million contribution
with 23 million federal dollars. We had upped the estimates of what it would cost Parks Canada to establish
and operate the park. Capital development costs had
been raised to $20 million over ten years, and opera-
tions had gone up to $12 million. This $32-million portion of the $106 million was money that B.C. would
never see. It was essentially a windfall for the Parks
Service; enough money to really run a park. It looked
great. But as I studied the letter, I became alarmed
about a few little wrinkles. They would not be apparent
to the media or the public or most observers, but I noticed them and wondered why we had risked annoying
Vander Zalm with what might appear, in the multi-mil-
lion dollar context, to be nickel-and-diming him. I
pointed them out to Tom. We were insisting that if the
total forest compensation costs exceeded $31 million
(their eight plus our twenty-three), B.C. would be expected to continue to contribute to forest compensation on the established 75:25 ratio. "They've stuck to
their $8-million cap pretty hard," I argued. "Why bother
insisting on this when every independent assessment
we've got estimates the compensation costs at well below
$31 million?"

Jim explained, "We want to ensure that they're on
the hook for more. If they're not, they may deliberately
encourage the forest companies to go for an unreasonable amount." I could see Jim's point, but I also wondered if this was what Vander Zalm meant when he
complained to the press about federal officials gum-
ming up the works. But more serious was the explanation that if the compensation costs exceeded $31
million, the federal government would find its share by
deducting it from the promised $50-million fund. I

knew B.C. would not like this condition at all. I wondered if this was what Vander Zalm meant by our "backing off." If we promised $50 million one week, and then suggested that we would be taking money from that pocket to fill another, he could interpret that as reneging on the earlier commitment. Jim argued that this was another way we had to ensure that B.C. would use its clout with the forest industry to keep the costs reasonable. But we had suggested that an independent arbiter determine those costs. If B.C. would agree to binding arbitration on compensation costs, and we reasonably expected them to be within the $31-million package, why risk losing the whole deal over these irritants?

Tom agreed with me, saying that if he'd seen the letter first, he would have modified or removed these small twists. "But," he continued, "on the whole the offer is so fair and so generous, that I'm sure now that the province has given us a few more days, cooler heads will prevail and they'll take it seriously." After all, $106 million over ten years was an unprecedented offer to a province in the course of negotiations to create a national park.

That evening was the Speaker's annual garden party. Waiting in the queue for the very short receiving line consisting of the Speaker and his wife, Cate, I looked out at the sea of smart hats and clever dresses. As I shook hands with Fraser, he regarded me gravely, "Did we keep things on track today?"

"Yes. Barely," I answered. "Thank you, as always, more than I can say." He nodded briskly, and turned to the next guest. As I sipped wine and downed a few baby shrimp, I saw a red-faced Gerry St Germain, looming over Stephen Ash, jabbing his chest with an angry finger. I didn't need to ask what they were discussing.

Back on Haida Gwaii, organizing was underway for the potlatch for the longhouse at Windy Bay. It was the first Haida structure on the mossy banks of Windy Bay Creek built in the last hundred years. The front of the house, in traditional Haida style, offered a minimal point of entry, as protection from wild weather and enemy raiding parties. A small oval was the only "door" facing out to sea. All around the oval was a painting in red and black of three Watchmen. One Watchman stared out from the centre of the wall, while on either side two more in profile provided the perfect symmetry of the Haida art form. The Looking Around and Blinking House was a masterpiece.

Built as a deterrent to logging and for cultural inspiration, the time had come to consecrate the longhouse with a Haida potlatch. On the weekend of June 12, close to a hundred Haida and non-Haida supporters came by boat and seaplane to the shores of Windy Bay. Invited by the Haida Nation, the Mounties were distinguished guests at the feast. Wearing their traditional red serge, the yellow pinstripe down the trouser legs, spurs shining, they came to stand at either side of the longhouse, framing the scene in black and red. The feast was tinged with an expectant glow; everyone hoping, believing, that the house would never need to be put to the purpose for which it was built – a base for the next blockade.

Over the weekend, I reviewed the June 10 letter over and over, analysing it and wondering if we shouldn't make an adjustment or two without waiting for B.C.'s response. I spoke with my contacts out on the West Coast. Kirk Dawson had been nosing about. His information was not encouraging. "We can expect a twenty-four-hour ultimatum from them tomorrow," he told me, confirming that Vander Zalm believed he had been jerked around. I called my few spies within the B.C. government. Everyone sounded pessimistic. The word in Victoria was that federal officials were "screwing things up." A deal was no longer likely.

I called Tom at home in Charlottetown to tell him what I'd learned. "With the Prime Minister back in Canada, we've lost the only reason that Vander Zalm delayed pulling the plug. They don't like our offer. What's worse is that they think we're playing games with them. And, frankly, I don't blame them. We shouldn't be mucking about, threatening to take money away that we've already committed." I told Tom that I thought he should try to reach Mazankowski over the weekend. "The good news is that in all the griping from B.C., nobody is criticizing you, or Maz, or the PM. It's federal bureaucrats who are getting the heat. So whether it's deserved or not, let's use it to advantage. Call Vander Zalm and tell him that the bureaucrats have been pulled from the negotiating team. Have Maz take it over personally again, using his staff, or PMO staff – or maybe offer more money. I'm afraid if we don't do anything, by Monday it could be too late."

Tom heard me out. "Okay, Elizabeth. This is what I want you to do. Write up your analysis and include a couple of scenarios for fiddling with our offer. Put in all the numbers of the costs of different permutations you think might work. Have it ready for me on Monday morning. I'm sure that won't be too late."

29

THE WEEK OF
JUNE 15, 1987

MONDAY MORNING, I SENT MY TWO-PAGE MEMO TO TOM in Charlottetown. He was taking the day to travel to Montreal with his wife, Kathy, and would not be in until Tuesday morning. The memo argued that from British Columbia's perspective we had gone back on our word, by conditionally reducing the $50-million fund. Moreover, in absolute dollars, an offer we had made to British Columbia some months ago – a fifty-fifty split on forest compensation costs up to the WAC boundary, with the federal government paying 100 per cent for anything beyond them – would actually be no different from B.C.'s current position of an $8-million cap on its contribution.

I spoke to Tom and he promised to give Maz a call. All day I was anxious, wondering when B.C. would lower the boom. But the day passed without incident. Maz's staff said they didn't expect to hear from B.C. that day. Jim Collinson felt that, while things weren't as good as they had been a week or so before, nothing momentous was likely to occur.

Like thousands of other Canadians, at 10 p.m. that evening I was watching the CBC national television news, relaxing, distractedly filling in my room-mate, Heather, on the day's events. My attention was suddenly riveted to the television when the now-familiar graphic used for items about South Moresby appeared over Knowlton Nash's left shoulder. "There will be no national park at South Moresby in British Columbia's Queen Charlotte Islands. Negotiations between B.C. and the federal government have broken off. B.C. will create a provincial park in the area instead. The provincial cabinet will meet next week to determine the boundaries of the new park."

Knowlton Nash kept on talking – other stories, other news. I didn't hear a word he said. I just stared straight ahead. It did not sink in. How could Knowlton Nash, the embodiment of authority, have said those words? Heather looked over at me, "Are you all right?" I wasn't sure. I felt as though I was underwater, not quite in the room, not quite hearing. Coming to the surface, I said, "Yeah, I'm okay."

I started breathing again. Thinking, figuring out what should be done. "I know this sounds crazy," I said, "but I think it's got to be some kind of mistake. I mean, it could be true, but it just doesn't feel true."

I reached for the phone. If anyone should know if negotiations had broken down, it would be Jim Collinson. He answered, sounding cordial and relaxed. He was not among the thousands of Canadians watching The National. "Jim, they just announced that the negotiations are over. That there'll be no national park." Jim was shocked. He promised to make some phone calls to find out what had happened.

I hung up and decided to check with CBC in Vancouver for more details. No, they said, they knew nothing about it. They didn't even know how the story had got to Toronto. I called Terry Collins. He didn't know about the story either, but promised to track down Tom Van Dusen, Mazankowski's press secretary, to find out if he had any more information.

I called half a dozen other people and, within the hour, the story had gelled. Vicky had spoken to reporters at the press gallery in Victoria. She called me to report that sometime after 6 p.m. (B.C. time), Vander Zalm and Strachan had made a joint announcement. In

Victoria, major policy statements were often made by the Premier rather casually. Bruce Strachan had joined him for this announcement. CBC Victoria had filed it straight to Toronto to get it on the 10 p.m. national news in central Canada. It was no mistake. But it didn't feel true.

Tom McMillan still didn't know. For the first time in the year I had been working for him, he was taking the night entirely off. He and Kathy were staying overnight in Montreal. Whenever he returned to his hotel, among the pile of messages would be one from me: "B.C.'s broken off talks. Don't worry. Call me in the morning."

Meanwhile Terry Collins was arguing with his counterparts in the office of the deputy prime minister. Van Dusen had confirmed that at a little after 6 p.m. (Ottawa time), more than four hours ago, Mazankowski had spoken with Vander Zalm. They agreed that they could not strike a deal. The gap in dollars was just too wide. As far as Maz's people were concerned that was the end of the matter. Case closed. Terry pleaded with Van Dusen to allow McMillan to say that the federal government's offer was still on the table. "Let's leave a crack in the door open for further negotiations if B.C. reconsiders," Terry urged Maz's press secretary. Van Dusen was persuaded, but a change in our final position and media line had to be cleared with people higher up. Terry called Jamie Burns, Mazankowski's chief of staff, and begged him to let us keep hope alive. Burns agreed.

Terry then called me to fill me in on Mazankowski's last telephone conversation with B.C. He told me that our official press line was that our generous offer of $106 million was still on the table, if only B.C. would reconsider. But he didn't tell me that he alone had been responsible for changing that line from an obituary to a reprieve.

While I was going through my own non-stop telephone alert, Terry was doing a substantial amount of sandbagging to save South Moresby. At midnight, he got dressed and headed over to his office in Hull. He managed to reach Tom in the hotel in Montreal and get his "go-ahead" for a little late-night undercover work. Terry photocopied Mazankowski's letter to Vander Zalm of June 10 and drove it over to the night desk at Canadian Press. He hand-delivered it to a friend, someone he could trust not to divulge the source. Terry figured that if the morning news was that B.C. had rejected the federal government's offer, the public ought to know precisely what was being refused.

I stayed on the phone alerting the troops, calling as many key people as possible, and putting in place some sort of strategy for the next day. I woke up Jim Fulton and his wife, Elizabeth, who did not seem wholly happy to hear from me at 11:30 p.m. Jim had seen the news and had made a lot of his own inquiries. He was relieved to hear that the offer was still on the table. As it got later I switched to making calls only to B.C., where the time change gave me half a chance of doing another day's work before I went to sleep. I reached Colleen and Vicky. Huck was unavailable, as he was working flat out somewhere on the B.C. coast on an expedition of the Haida war canoe, *Loo Taas*. I felt a twinge of exasperation – a canoe expedition at a time like this! John Broadhead was in a great mood, having just arrived home from a party. He could not believe the news, cheerily insisting that I must be kidding.

I needed to reach Miles Richardson. The Haida reaction to B.C.'s announcement would be critical. We all knew what a provincial park for South Moresby would mean. Regardless of the precise boundaries, we could be sure that it would not include Lyell Island. Logging on Lyell would resume within days of the permits being issued, probably in Windy Bay. The Haida had made it very clear that any resumption of logging on Lyell would be met with direct confrontation and blockades. I wanted to let Miles know that the federal government was not going to give up. But I couldn't reach him at any of the half-dozen places I usually tried.

Heather brought me wine between calls, and generally marvelled that I was not, in any visible way, falling apart. When the wine was all gone, around 1 a.m., we rummaged through the kitchen shelves to see what remained to be drunk. My numbness was a protective condition at this point. I didn't want it to wear off. We found white rum, canned pineapples, and coconut milk. About two years before I had bought the ingredients for pina coladas, but had never gotten around to making them. The only missing ingredient was ice. I kept dialling through the sticky Ottawa night, forcing down the appalling sweetness of warm pina colada slush.

Just before 3 a.m., nearly midnight B.C. time, I reached Miles. He hadn't heard the news. He agreed that we would all stress that the issue was not over, and he confirmed that the Haida Nation would obstruct any further logging on Lyell. Miles was my last call. Exhausted, I fell into bed and turned myself off for the night.

I hadn't managed to get dressed and out of the house the next morning before Tom McMillan called. He was on the car phone on his way back from Montreal. The line cracked, cutting in and out as I tried to piece together for him the events of the night before. Tom sounded shaky. We had been so close to a deal and now everything had gone to hell. He peppered me with questions. How had Miles reacted? Did Fulton think there was still a chance? What were Colleen and Vicky and J.B. going to do?

I told Tom that I was quite sure that it really was not over. After all, why else would Vander Zalm have set the following week's cabinet meeting for the decision on boundaries? The British Columbia cabinet knew the boundaries the logging companies would want and the majority of cabinet members would support them. I was convinced that the only reason for the delay before the issuance of logging permits was to give the federal government one last chance. Vander Zalm had just taken the ultimate gamble. He'd given us nine days to save the deal. "Okay, Elizabeth. This is what I want when I get back to Ottawa. I want a brief, crisp statement for Question Period. Have you got a pen?" and he proceeded to dictate the statement that he would deliver virtually verbatim later that day. I promised to meet him with the draft statement at the House of Commons by midmorning. He was on the roster for mandatory attendance at the morning session – House Duty.

I hung up and rushed to the office. Tom tried to concentrate on correspondence as the limo streaked back toward Ottawa. One letter in the pile seemed worth taking some time over. It was a routine response to Thom Henley, prepared, as almost every ministerial response is, by the department. Tom was unusual, insisting on at least seeing every letter before it went out, and on signing all of them himself. Most ministers have a machine for that. Tom updated the now sadly irrelevant response to a letter Huck had sent in March: "P.S. Thom, As I write this in a car headed for Ottawa from Montreal, the talks with B.C. on South Moresby have just broken down. I refuse to believe, though, that the cause is permanently lost, it depends on whether public opinion can be mobilized. It could be the movement's finest hour or its worst, depending on whether people will/can/want to rise to the occasion – Tom."

The *Globe and Mail* ran a front page story that day, "No National Park for South Moresby." Vander Zalm was quoted as saying that he was relieved that it was all over and that the loggers could now get back to work. "We have to protect the loggers and protect not only those jobs for today, but jobs for the future. We're certainly not going to hold up operations."

I drafted Tom's statement, ending with Yogi Berra's words, "It ain't over till it's over." Karen, my secretary, finished typing it, and I grabbed a taxi from the department's offices in Hull, Quebec, across the Ottawa River to the Parliament Buildings. But all the while anger about the little twists that had been inserted into Mazankowski's June 10 letter to Vander Zalm was coming to the surface. I had a growing suspicion that the negotiations had gone off the rails either through deliberate sabotage or unintentional stupidity on the part of our own bureaucrats. Had we purposely thrown the fight by crafting a letter that would look good to the press and public, but would contain enough sneaky little irritants to convince Vander Zalm that the federal government was not playing straight with him? The fact that the letter from Mazankowski to Vander Zalm had not been shown to Tom McMillan before it was sent did not lessen my paranoia.

I needed a hug. Tom and I had been through a lot on this issue and I knew he cared desperately about it. I was sure that he felt as stunned by the developments as I did, and I looked forward to seeing him for a few minutes in the government lobby, the long comfortable lounge found behind the curtains and doorways on the government side of the House. But when Tom came out in response to my note, he was brusque. Whatever he was feeling, he didn't want to share it. He didn't want to talk. And he never was the sort of person who could comfortably hug anyone.

I wandered down the hall of Centre Block, past the marble and granite bas reliefs of Indians and beavers, the carved columns and wrought-iron lanterns, down the empty marble halls. I had not planned to try to see the Speaker of the House, but I found my feet taking me to his door.

My numbness was wearing off, and I thought I might start to cry any minute. Fraser's principal secretary, Stephen Ash, met me in the foyer and ushered me into his own office. "I know the Speaker will want to talk to you. He's been very upset about all this." He left to see if

Fraser could join us. I sat on the edge of the sofa, biting my lower lip, feeling shaky and hoping I could keep it together to ask the Speaker what he thought I should do now.

Fraser had been in a meeting in his office, but excusing himself, he broke away and came in with Stephen Ash. He sat down saying, "It was good of you to come. What happened? I thought we'd bought enough time to keep the thing on the tracks."

I had spoken with him just yesterday, but so much had changed since then. I went straight to the theory I had found too disturbing to mention to anyone besides McMillan. "I think our own bureaucrats put in conditions that they knew, or should have known, would make B.C. balk. The business about the 75:25 split for any logging compensation costs above the $31 million. And then the idea that any additional compensation costs for the federal government would be deducted from the $50–million Regional Economic Development Fund. Those terms wouldn't attract any interest from the press, but B.C. could see them as the feds reneging on the talks we had last week. I'm really afraid that the June 10 letter may have been designed to make the federal government look good, but with enough twists to make talks fall apart. You know how much the B.C. caucus doesn't want the South Moresby deal funded out of the Western Diversification Fund? Well, with this offer, they can look good, not have to spend the money, and use it on other initiatives the caucus wants."

I told Fraser that I didn't think it was Mazankowski's idea, or that he even knew about it. But that I thought it was very strange that the letter Mazankowski sent was drafted by Environment Canada's senior Parks bureaucrats, without ever checking the draft or the details with McMillan. I stopped, looked out the window, and tried to keep my emotions in check.

Fraser sighed and sank back in his chair. "Oh God," he said, not as a curse but a prayer. He closed his eyes and held his face in his hands. He looked so awfully tired. Shaking it off, he became businesslike. "Look dear, you've got to go see Dalton Camp and tell him exactly what you've told us."

I was speechless. Dalton Camp, the legend, the power-broker, the man who, in terms of political geology, is a mountain who watches grains of prime ministerial sand blow away. He's not someone you actually meet. Even Tom spoke of him in awestruck tones, once taking days to decide it would be possible to call him for help when New Brunswick reneged on its acid-rain commitments. I stammered, "I don't think he'd agree to see me. I mean I'm only ministerial staff –"

Fraser cut me off. "Of course he'll see you. He's a friend of mine. He's got to get into this. He's got to make sure that the Prime Minister is getting the full picture, and from what you're saying, he's not likely to get it from the bureaucrats. And the only person who can save this now is the Prime Minister." He stopped again and sighed. "Damn," he said, summing up the sadness and anger and heartbreak we were feeling. "Damn."

Stephen Ash and the Speaker and I pulled ourselves together. "Okay," I agreed. "I'll call Mr Camp as soon as I get back to my office." I still needed a hug. I got two.

In British Columbia, the South Moresby troops were mobilizing. In the small mining town of New Denver in the Kootenays, Colleen had set her alarm for 5 a.m. While her kids slept, she used the time-zone advantage to phone her press contacts in Toronto. "This is war," she declared, determined that, before Windy Bay could be scarred by logging, she would do whatever she had to do. She decided to phone every community in British Columbia to get at least one person in each area to start a phone-in campaign to Vander Zalm. The Victoria government telephone lines had to be jammed with pleas to return to the bargaining table, to accept the federal offer. On her own phone, with no one to help pay for the calls, Colleen started systematically waking people up across the province.

J.B. headed for the Earthlife Canada office in Vancouver early that morning. Walking from Bill Reid's house, where he had been living for months, toward Granville Ferry, he decided that what was needed was a full-page advertisement in the *[* In his office, he poured himself a cup of coffee and sat at his desk. He started composing at his computer, "South Moresby – For Your Children's Children. An Appeal to Premier William Vander Zalm."

Across town, at the unofficial offices of the Western Canada Wilderness Committee in Paul George's apartment, volunteers and staff started work on a protest rally. Ken Lay, one of WC Squared's most stalwart staffers, was debating the pros and cons of different locations. Should the rally be in downtown Vancouver at Robson Square? Or in Victoria in front of the Parliament Buildings? The main object was to get Vander Zalm's attention, and, of course, to get good press coverage. It would have to be on the weekend to get maximum numbers of people. And it would have to be this weekend, before next Wednesday's deadline, to have any effect at all. Then it hit him: Vander Zalm's own backyard, just behind the Sleeping Beauty castle at Fantasy Gardens. Vander Zalm's home is in his amusement park, complete with fairy-tale and Biblical characters, in what was supposed to have been a protected greenbelt outside Vancouver. (He once said, "When I think of how Fantasy Gardens all came together, I know there must be a higher authority at work.") Fantasy Gardens was the perfect choice for a Saturday rally.

In Victoria, Vicky phoned the media, calling contacts across the country, giving interviews, and raising money. And people were calling her, such prominent people as the chancellor of the University of British Columbia,

offering help, asking what they should do to save South
Moresby. Across British Columbia and throughout
much of Canada, the alarm had rung out. The message
was simple: Drop everything and do whatever you can to
save South Moresby.

But the two people who had started all this thirteen
years before, the two people who had started calling the
southern third of the Queen Charlottes archipelago
"South Moresby," who had invented the South Moresby
Wilderness Proposal, who had drawn the line across the
height of land from Tangil Peninsula to the west coast of
Moresby Island – Huck and Guujaaw – were almost un-
affected by the news. Huck was totally absorbed with
preparations for the return of the Haida war canoe, *Loo
Taas* (*Wave Eater*) from Vancouver to its home on Haida
Gwaii. Guujaaw was at a sun dance in Alberta. Two
weeks of abstinence were followed by four days of fasting
and dancing in a traditional ritual of purification. He
had been involved with the carving of *Loo Taas* from its
design stage.

Bill Reid had supervised the carving of *Loo Taas* from
a single seven-hundred-year-old cedar log almost two
years before. Reid had long wanted to revive the art of
full-scale expedition canoe building. With Expo planning to display exotic vessels of the world, Reid saw his
opportunity to find the necessary support for such a
massive undertaking. He persuaded the Bank of British
Columbia to sponsor the project, and set to work in
September 1985. For the Haida Nation, *Loo Taas* was not
a gimmick. Tourist appeal was the furthest thing from
Reid's mind when he built the canoe. To Reid, it represented a new threshold in the revival of Haida culture
and identity. Unlike the magnificent totem poles he had
carved, a canoe was dynamic. A totem pole stood guard.
A canoe could fly. The skills revived with the creation
of a Haida war canoe extended beyond its carving to

include its mastery – paddling and navigating through the rough waters of the Hecate Strait. A Haida canoe represented the Haida Nation, in motion.

It was fifty feet long and weighed 1,500 pounds. On its bow was carved and painted the face of Killer Whale to give it strength and speed in the ocean waves. The Haida carved it using the techniques of their ancestors who had used stone adzes to create their canoes and poles. Cedar, that perfect wood that clothed, cradled, sheltered, and defined the Haida, was shaped, as if by magic, into a canoe. Young Haida, who had never before seen it done, steamed the cedar log. No living Haida had ever seen it done. Not even Reid knew how to estimate the effects of the steaming by which his ancestors increased the beam of their canoes by as much as a third. Before the carving, he had experimented with a model at one-fifth scale in fibreglass, which he had compressed back into the confines of a log shape. It buckled, producing a humped back. And so that is what Reid instructed them to carve – a funny-looking vessel with straight sides and a bulging back. When it had had its interior hollowed out, the steaming process began. Outside the carving shed, on a bluff at the east end of Skidegate Village, they poured water into the canoe and then placed loads of hot rocks into the water. Steam was everywhere, and as Reid later wrote, "Murphy suspended his Law, and after only two hours the boat fell almost of its own volition into its intended shape."

Once finished, the Haida canoe was a thing of intense beauty, a work of art. But it was also a powerful and expert ocean-faring craft. Young Haida men found that the craft was so exquisitely balanced that they could walk along her gunwales and land in the sea only if they lost their own balance. Huck and Reid hoped that an expedition could be arranged to paddle *Loo Taas* to Expo in Vancouver, but in the end, they ran out of time. And the great Haida war canoe was, rather ignominiously, brought by barge to Vancouver.

Once the fair was over, Bill Reid approached the Bank of British Columbia and requested the return of *Loo Taas* to its home on Haida Gwaii. The Bank officials were unyielding. They told Reid that because they had commissioned *Loo Taas*, it belonged to them and they would display it in the foyer of their new building. *Loo Taas*, that mighty war canoe, vessel of national spirit and magic, had become a corporate asset. But then the Bank of British Columbia faltered, and was bought out by the Bank of Hong Kong. It had little use for a fifty-foot Haida war canoe. When approached by Reid, the management agreed with his proposal that *Loo Taas* should be returned to Haida Gwaii, where it belonged, to be used as a living craft, plying the waters of those bountiful seas. News of the liberation of *Loo Taas* rekindled plans for its ocean voyage home. The first Haida war canoe in one hundred years was going to make the first such voyage up the B.C. coast in as many years.

Bill Reid and the Skidegate Band Council had asked Huck to work on the expedition. On Tuesday, June 16, Huck was too overwhelmed with the details and logistics of the *Loo Taas* expedition to be diverted by the latest set-back in his thirteen-year campaign on Haida Gwaii.

That night, back in Ottawa, I went to see McMillan. We were both feeling a little stronger, and Tom was in much better spirits than when I had seen him in the House that morning. He had handled Question Period brilliantly that day. John Turner, leader of the official Opposition, had opened the day's volley of charge and counter-charge with a question on South Moresby. Turner framed and directed his question to the Prime Minister. He asked, "Does the Prime Minister stand by the first promise made by his minister of the environment? And will there indeed be a national park at South Moresby?" But Mulroney did not rise to answer the question. As is customary in the House, when the Prime Minister chooses not to answer a question, all it takes is a nod in the direction of the appropriate minister, and they are on their feet in a flash. In this case, Mulroney gave Tom the nod, and Tom rose to make the statement we had worked out that morning. Turner persisted, "Initially, when the minister was sworn in to the portfolio...he promised a fruitful result...The minister has failed." He went on to urge that the Prime Minister persuade the Premier of British Columbia to return to the negotiations.

Tom's answer was better than any other I had heard him give. The usual bombast and hyperbole were gone. His voice cracked at one point, and friends hearing it later told me it had sounded like he might break down. "Mr Speaker, if the South Moresby file turns out to be a failure, it will not be a failure only of this minister of the environment. It will be a failure not only of this government, but of all of Canada. As I pointed out on the floor of the House of Commons on a previous occasion, whether or not we can screw up the courage and the will to save this magnificent wilderness treasure will be the litmus test of our values as a civilized country." He finished by saying, "I urge the leader of the Opposition, his party, and every member of this House to use all our resources to bring wisdom to bear on this very important international question." To which, according to Hansard, some honourable members said, "Hear, hear!" The next questions were also for Tom. He finally said, "It isn't over until it is over," cleaning up Yogi Berra's grammar.

Regardless of the fate of South Moresby, Tom McMillan, politician, had had a good day. His issue had dominated Question Period. In scrums outside the House he had answered a throng of reporters. He knew he had handled it well. And that fact alone had boosted his spirits.

He was standing in back of his desk as I entered his office that evening, sorting papers, reviewing correspondence. He looked up as I came in. "I thought I'd better let you in on something Fraser and I are cooking up," I said. Part of me was afraid that Tom would disapprove of my going to see Dalton Camp. Tom generally wanted to keep my visible involvement in his office away from powerful Tories. And few were as powerful as Dalton Camp. I tried for a cheery, light-hearted approach. "We're thinking of finding a way to get more money into the pot, and get the Prime Minister involved." "How are you going to do that?" Tom asked. "I'm going to see Dalton Camp tomorrow."

Tom looked surprised, "You've got an appointment?" "Yup," I tried to sound unintimidated by the prospect. Tom gave me a look I'd seen a few times before, as though he was seeing me for the first time. He became serious again. Refocussing, he said, "Yes, of course. Good luck."

Wednesday, June 17. Two days since the negotiations had broken off, we had only one week to get them restarted. I had a 10 a.m. meeting with Dalton Camp on the second floor of the Langevin Block. I put on my best suit, armed myself with a synopsis of events in the negotiations covering the highlights from last September to this week, and copies of all key documents – offers and counter-offers. And I went in to see the power-broker. Someone in whom I had placed all our hopes. Our last chance.

Camp was affable, cordial, and far less intimidating than people with half his clout. His eyes twinkled, and his face betrayed a nearly constant sense of humour. It was hard to guess his age. While he looked to be in his mid-sixties, I knew he had to be older. After all, he'd managed to oust a prime minister of his own party nearly thirty years before. He smiled, and gestured to a chair in front of his desk. "Sit down and tell us what all this is about." I liked him immediately.

A bright young man was also present. Camp's aide, Andy Stark, was to take notes, probe for more information, and provide whatever follow-up the meeting would require. I had rehearsed everything I would say in my mind. I plunged in, walking them through the chronology of the negotiations, and offering several views of the reason for the breakdown. I stressed that the hard part was over. The issues surrounding the boundary were what was really impossible. Negotiating money issues, in comparison, was easy. I argued that Vander Zalm really wanted the Prime Minister to intervene. Why else would he have given us this week? Camp leaned back in his chair. "What would you say were the potential down-sides of getting the Prime Minister involved?"

"Before I speculate on disadvantages, let me just say what the advantages are. Thousands of Canadians, maybe millions, want South Moresby to be saved. Public opinion polls in B.C. say the majority of people in that province want it to be saved. It's been featured on CBC's The Nature of Things, in *Saturday Night* magazine, and virtually all major news and information programs on television and radio. All the major newspapers in Canada have had editorials over the last two days urging B.C. to reconsider. It's been covered in the international press. And this week, the latest *National Geographic* will be out with a feature article on the area and the current controversy.

"On Monday," I continued, "when B.C. broke off talks and said there would be no national park, they set the stage for the Prime Minister to accomplish the impossible. To create a national park when no less an authority than Knowlton Nash had told Canadians that all hope was lost. You couldn't write a movie script with more drama. I mean, it's better than the last scene in *The Natural* or *The Verdict* or *High Noon*. The Prime Minister can ride in and stop the logging and save South Moresby." I sketched out a few ways we could revise our offer to make it more acceptable to B.C. – removing those little irritants that I felt had contributed to the collapse of talks.

"Well, you've sold me," Camp said. I was reeling as we turned our attention to how we would engage Mulroney's interest in this. We started discussing possible approaches, deadlines and contacts. I asked, "Is the PM scheduled to be in British Columbia any time soon?" Dalton Camp reached for a file folder with the Prime Minister's draft travel itinerary for the next few weeks. "Yes, at the moment he's supposed to be in B.C. touring Vancouver beaches and other summer festivals on Saturday, July 11th."

I got chills. At that moment, I *knew* South Moresby would be saved. "That's perfect," I said. "That's the day the Haida war canoe, *Loo Taas*, reaches Skidegate."

"The *what?*" asked Dalton, not understanding why I was so excited.

"It's a traditional Haida war canoe. It leaves from Vancouver on Sunday to paddle up the coast to the Charlottes. They've already got a big feast planned. Neither Mulroney nor Vander Zalm are going to want to even be in the province that day if South Moresby isn't saved. But if it is" – in my mind's eye, I could see the most glorious of celebrations: Haida hereditary chiefs lined up on the shore to welcome Vander Zalm and Mulroney, arriving by war canoe – "maybe the Prime Minister and Vander Zalm could be there, to celebrate the return of *Loo Taas* and the saving of the area. It would be incredible."

Our hour nearly expired, we wrapped up the meeting with our assignments made, putting the wheels in motion to get the Prime Minister to save the deal. I left the Langevin Block, crossed Wellington Street, and headed up the great green lawn in front of the Parliament Buildings. The lawn was already scattered with tourists, clicking pictures in front of the Peace Tower, posing in front of the eternal flame. I was hurrying along to see Fraser and Ash and report to them on a successful meeting. I may have been walking, but I don't recall if my feet touched the ground.

Back in Hull at my own office I started returning the dozens of phone messages piled up on my desk. People from all across the country were calling, offering encouragement, asking how they could help, reporting back on phone conversations with the Premier's office in B.C. I realized that an impending mail strike, or threats of one, was a tremendous boon to the effort; everyone was using the phone. No one wanted to risk having a protest letter stranded by Canada Post. And the one-week deadline ensured that anyone who was concerned was acting now. Sara Jennings phoned to say that she would try to get her brother Peter to broadcast the South Moresby crisis on the ABC World News. Socred supporters of Vander Zalm called from B.C. to ask what they could do to help. Even friends of Bill and Lilly Vander Zalm phoned with offers of support. One such woman told me, "I saw them the other night at a party, and I told Bill, 'If you start logging Lyell Island, you'll have to arrest me too!'"

It was time to pull out all the stops. I remembered Monte Hummel's offer. If there was ever a time we needed a telegram from Buckingham Palace, it was now. For that matter, if I had had any access to Mother Teresa or the Pope, I would not have hesitated to appeal to them for help. As it was, I phoned Monte Hummel in Toronto. "Monte, do you remember your offer about Prince Philip? Well, now's the time."

Monte was thrown for a loop. "Look, Elizabeth," he answered testily, "I can't just ring up Buckingham Palace and ask H.R.H. to dispatch a telegram. These things take time." I reminded him that this had not been my idea. "Don't worry about it. I promised to let you know when things got desperate. And they don't get any more desperate than this." Somewhat sheepishly, he replied, "Oh yeah. Right. Well, I'll see what I can do."

A little after 2 p.m., Andy Stark from Camp's office called, "Are you watching Question Period? Quick. Turn it on!" I hung up and rushed to the set in McMillan's office.

Jim Fulton was speaking. "As I'm sure the Prime Minister is aware, more Canadians have written to the

Prime Minister and his cabinet colleagues on this issue than on any other environmental issue in the history of Canada. The minister of the environment has done his best. The deputy prime minister has done his best. This Parliament has unanimously expressed itself as wanting that area set aside as a national park reserve. I'd like to ask the Prime Minister, knowing that one week from today the British Columbia cabinet is going to make their final decision, if he would contact Premier Vander Zalm and express to him one more time, that from co-operation comes cooperation in this nation, and on this issue he should understand that very well."

Tom told me later that he looked over to the Prime Minister to register his willingness to grab the hot potato. He waited for the nod, but Mulroney's gesture said no, he would answer the question himself.

"I've met with Premier Vander Zalm in the past on this issue and on other matters that affect B.C." Mulroney digressed to praise the Premier's role in developing the Meech Lake accord. But he didn't dodge the question. He continued, "I think this environmental question in British Columbia has national implications. I have spoken with the Premier. I shall do so again. I shall use every lever to persuade the Premier of British Columbia that this is not only in the interest of British Columbia. This is an intitiative on behalf of all Canadians that ought to be upheld and defended."

I gasped. How did Camp do it so fast? It was a miracle. I rushed back to my own office where the phone was ringing. It was Andy. Before I could say anything, Andy asked, "Did you get to him?"

"No. You mean you didn't either?"

"No, not that I know of. I don't think Mr Camp has spoken with him yet. If you didn't brief him, and we didn't brief him, who did?" Andy was genuinely puzzled.

"Maybe he just knew. Maybe Mila watches The Nature of Things. Maybe his kids told him. I don't know. I'm just so happy. He just breathed life into a corpse."

"Well," said Andy, not wishing to join me in speculating about the environmental attitudes of the Mulroney clan, "at least we've got his attention. The next step is to have a thorough briefing package for him to review before he calls the Premier. The Federal-Provincial Relations Office will prepare one, and I'm sure your bureaucrats will have input, but Mr Camp wants to give the Prime Minister his own analysis, and he wants you to write it."

"When does he want it?" I felt the increasing pressure. A sudden realization of my role in all this. An almost physical awareness of extra weight, not necessarily on my shoulders. More like deep-water diving: extra weight everywhere.

"He wants it ten minutes ago. So, listen. This is how the Prime Minister likes memos. Put all the key points on the first page or so. In point form. They don't have to be in whole sentences. It's better if they're not. Just really concise. He calls them bullets." Andy continued to lay out for me the form and style of the memorandum. I took notes and tried to remember to keep breathing. I hung up and went out to my secretary.

"Karen, try to hold all my calls, unless it's Andy Stark or Dalton Camp or John Fraser or the minister or Miles Richardson, or anyone else really important. And I'm afraid I'm going to have to ask you to do an awful lot of typing, awfully fast." I went back to my office, locked my door, pulled out my files, and started making silver bullets.

Brian Smith was not at all pleased. For months, his old friend John Fraser had been trying to talk him into taking on the South Moresby cause as his own. It was not that Smith was immune to the Haida Gwaii magic. He had travelled through the Charlottes, first as education minister, and then as part of his leadership bid in 1986. He had seen something of the magnificence of South Moresby, travelling back by helicopter on a spectacularly

beautiful evening. Smith realized that it should be preserved, but on the other hand, he sympathized with the
pro-logging contingent. Pro-loggers in the B.C. cabinet
bitterly resented being made the object of international
pressure. They hated the fact that Jacques Cousteau and
the *National Geographic* were trying to tell them what to
do. Brian Smith travelled regularly to Ottawa and visited
the B.C. caucus. Just like the members of the B.C. cabinet, Gerry St Germain and the staunch anti-environ-
mental federal Tories despised those "tree-huggers and
draft-dodgers" who were making such a fuss about a lot
of good logs. The caucus didn't like McMillan's style
and they did not much like McMillan either. They
sensed that he thought he was better than they were.

Brian Smith had a better sense than most other
provincial politicians in British Columbia of the political currents surging around South Moresby. The
Queen Charlotte Islands have the highest-energy coastline in Canada. Its political currents were no less
strong. And as the deal fell apart on June 15, Smith
could feel the Vander Zalm government getting caught
in the undertow.

Editorials from around the country were attacking
the B.C. government. The *Globe and Mail* headlined its
editorial, "A park for ransom." The *Toronto Star* characterized B.C.'s tactics as "bad faith bargaining." "Sleazy
political ransom" was what the *Ottawa Citizen* editorial
writers called it. And this time, despite Vander Zalm's
petulant statement that he would not let a bunch of
"Easterners" tell B.C. what to do, the criticism was hardly
restricted to egghead types from Toronto. The
Edmonton Journal accused British Columbia's government of "myopic greed." Even on the west side of the
Rockies, that great natural, cultural, physical, and psy-
chic barrier that separates British Columbia from the
rest of Canada, editorial passions were running high.
The *Victoria Times-Colonist* even-handedly argued that

fault might lie on both sides, but urged "the moral responsibility of both governments [is] to return to the bargaining table and keep talking – without spurious deadlines and ultimatums." The *Vancouver Province* ridiculed the idea of a smaller provincial park, heading its editorial, "Moresby Must Be Big National Park." The *Vancouver Sun* editorial was harder to ignore. Headlined "Put Moresby Above Crass Interest," it concluded, "The [Vander Zalm government] should be ashamed of itself. People are laughing again. With tears in their eyes."

South Moresby was turning into a poltical nightmare. And it could only get worse. When new logging permits were issued, it would be naïve not to expect a long, protracted confrontation on the logging roads of Lyell Island. The public spotlight would remain on South Moresby, and neither government – provincial or federal – would look good.

This was what Brian Smith realized that his colleagues did not. This could no longer be dissmissed as hippy draft-dodgers trying to save trees. This was something that both the Prime Minister and the Premier of British Columbia wanted to accomplish being scuttled by pressure from the provincial cabinet and their like-minded buddies in the federal B.C. caucus. Smith agreed with Fraser that someone had to knock some sense into anti-park forces. But it would not be easy.

The momentum of events decreased the likelihood of resuming negotiations, almost by the minute. The vast majority of the B.C. cabinet was ecstatic that the deal had fallen through. Now they would not have to face the ire of the province's forest industry. The lobbying pressure from Western Forest Products, MacMillan Bloedel, and Frank Beban Logging, backed by every forest company in the province, had been intense. The whole Socred membership in the Charlottes was against the park. Stephen Rogers had led the efforts to block any preservation, and Strachan had carried out his plans.

Out of the whole provincial government caucus, only
Brian Smith, Kim Campbell, and former environment
minister Tony Brummet supported Vander Zalm in his
desire to cinch a national park deal with the feds. At
some cabinet meetings, the Premier had been the only
member supporting a park. And now Vander Zalm felt
hard done by – tricked and jerked around by federal
bureaucrats, abandoned by his friend the Prime
Minister.

As for the federal Tory caucus, many of the back-
benchers were as pleased as punch that the deal had fall-
en through. And while it was unclear exactly how active
a role they had played in the alienation of affections between Victoria and Ottawa, it was probable that members of the caucus had planted the bug in Victoria's ear
to oppose funding from the Western Diversification
Fund. That money was meant for economic development, not caving in to a bunch of eco-freaks. And if you
were to take a poll on the member of B.C. caucus most
likely to scuttle a park deal, the smart money would be
on Gerry St Germain, member for Mission – Port
Moody.

Gerry St Germain was Métis, born in St Boniface,
Manitoba. Bill McKnight, as Indian affairs minister, enjoyed drawing attention to this, calling St Germain, "my
native brother." He had nothing in common with
McMillan. He disliked his appearance, his style, and his
politics. St Germain saw the issue in black and white.
Support for the park came from people who would
never vote Tory. Wilderness freaks were a bunch of tree-
hugging New Democrats. How the federal government,
right up to and including the Prime Minister, could be
prepared to sink $106 million into an NDP riding was
beyond St Germain. The politics of it made no sense.
McMillan knew intuitively that he wanted to be on the
side of the angels. St Germain's instincts told him the
angels were on the wrong side.

It took a phone call from Brian Smith to put it force-fully to St Germain that their respective leaders had staked a significant amount of political capital on a deal. And that it wasn't altogether bright to sabotage their efforts. Smith's call neutralized the fifth column within the federal ranks.

As the week wore on and the countdown to British Columbia's do-or-die deadline approached, the public pressure steadily mounted. The Prime Minister's promise to call Vander Zalm and to use whatever personal and private charms of persuasion he could work on the eccentric premier had rekindled hope across the country.

Even Tom McMillan seemed to think we might yet win the fight. He had not expected Mulroney's commitment any more than I had, and he was clearly buoyed when answering questions in the scrum following Question Period. "He's very persuasive, the Prime Minister is, and one of his many strengths is his ability to move people from firm positions." Tom told reporters he would "bet money" that Mulroney would get a deal. On one point, I couldn't have agreed more with Tom. He was quoted as saying, "Any intervention by the Prime Minister will have to be immediate to have any effect...Obviously, time is of the essence."

Meanwhile, the B.C. tone was softening, if only slightly. Environment Minister Bruce Strachan said in a radio interview that the door was still open to negotiations. But Strachan also threw out a new red herring – that the negotiations had broken down because of the federal government's refusal to resort to an independent determination of the economic value of the forest area to be included in a national park. An independent audit had been suggested in our last offer, and we were baffled over whether Strachan and, more importantly,

Vander Zalm believed that this non-issue was, in fact, controversial.

The airwaves were full of condemnation of B.C. as Strachan tried to keep the provincial flag high. On CBC Radio's national show As It Happens he argued that while South Moresby did contain many unique species, they weren't "that unique." Besides, he told another interviewer, "the only endangered species on South Moresby are the loggers." Colleen McCrory blasted B.C. on the same program, saying "Vander Zalm is holding a gun to the heads of the people of Canada." Cartoonists picked up on the blackmail theme. The *Globe and Mail* ran a sketch of B.C.'s Premier holding a gun against a tree, saying, "Give me $200 million, or the tree gets it!" Another depicted a letter from Vander Zalm to Mulroney made from pasted letters cut out from magazines, a cartoon ransom note: "Put $200 million in a brown paper bag…"

By Friday, Mulroney still had not called Vander Zalm. We had finished work on the memo to the Prime Minister. McMillan had mentioned to him in the House privately that it was really urgent that he call the Premier soon, preferably before the weekend. We were nervous about the delay from a Wednesday promise to "use every lever" to no action three days later. Even more worrying was the attitude of some of Mazankowski's staff: "This is perfect. We get all the credit for a super-generous offer. And we won't ever have to spend the money." I could almost see the fiscal vultures circling over the South Moresby carcass. There would be factories and pulp mills, oil wells and theme parks all lining up at the Western Diversification trough.

Terry and I kept trying to point out to the bright young men of the deputy prime minister's office that as soon as the Haida started being arrested on Lyell Island, along with Bill Reid, Robert Bateman, Maurice Strong,

David Suzuki's family, and other prominent Canadians, the federal government would cease "looking good." Through this whole period, Terry was the only other member of McMillan's small staff who kept pulling for the park, working with me, trying to keep on top of the latest rumours from the press secretaries attached to the PMO and Mazankowski's office. We were both getting increasingly anxious about what the "real" strategy was.

We were not the only ones. I spoke to Fraser at least once a day, and he speculated, "It may be the most brilliant strategy in the world to let them stew in their own juice for a while, but it's dangerous to wait too long." I kept in touch with Dalton Camp's office. Messages back through Andy Stark were reassuring, "Don't bother having Tom try to phone the Prime Minister again. Matters are being taken care of here." I trusted that Camp was capable of miracles. But still I worried.

Jim Fulton was another several-times-a-day phone fix. We both agreed that the best way to conclude negotiations successfully would be to take them totally out of the hands of bureaucrats. And we both knew who, in an ideal world, we would want to handle the bargaining process, if it ever resumed.

In March, in one of those coincidences that make you question the notion of randomness in the universe, the Prime Minister had chosen a new chief of staff. Instead of appointing one of his old university chums, Mulroney surprised those media-watchers who thought him incapable of surrounding himself with anyone but old cronies. He went to the ranks of the civil service and appointed a man with a distinguished record in the diplomatic corps, a career bureaucrat with External Affairs, who also happened to be a Tory. The Prime Minister's chief of staff, arguably the second most powerful person in Ottawa, was now Derek Burney. Joan and Derek Burney were the Ottawa friends with whom Vicky had stayed.

Jim Fulton and I were convinced that the only way to get the talks going again was to boot them up one more notch in Ottawa's power hierarchy. Mazankowski had accomplished a great deal since he took the file over after talks broke down in May. Now, the only way to save things was to have the negotiations handled directly by the Prime Minister's Office.

On a glorious sunny June Saturday in Vancouver, Tara Cullis was indoors on the phone. The Kitsilano beach was in sight, just past her back garden fence. The sky was a sparkling blue, rivalling the harbour and its dancing waves, which reflected the sunlight in brilliant flashes of white light. Tara didn't notice. For days she'd been attached to her phone trying to arrange anything and everything to push British Columbia back to the bargaining table.

The weekend was the perfect time to get thousands of people involved. But they weren't watching television or reading the papers. They were on the beach. So Tara decided that she should hire an airplane with a banner to fly over the beaches and alert the masses. Her husband, David Suzuki, was thousands of miles away, taping a Nature of Things segment in the Soviet Union. He was going slowly crazy, knowing South Moresby's fate was hanging by a thread, and he was stuck in Siberia.

Between calls to arrange the plane and try to solicit some contributions toward its cost, Tara and her friend Mary Jane were organizing a flotilla of boats to see *Loo Taas* out of Vancouver Harbour, Mrs Miniver style. Mary Jane was in the military and knew some higher-ups in the Coast Guard. A Coast Guard escort would be a powerful gesture as the Haida war canoe left False Creek and headed for the open seas. So Tara stayed on the phone, lining up boats and planes.

South of Vancouver, at Fantasy Gardens, a good-sized crowd had gathered to protest Vander Zalm's decision to reject a national park for South Moresby. Always the gracious host, he'd come out of his castle to chat directly with the demonstrators. Amid flashes of hostility, Vander Zalm just kept on smiling a big white grin that said "Fantastic," even when he didn't.

Huck was weary to the point of delerium. He had not stopped in days from the endless rounds of organizing paddlers, their supplies, their transportation to Vancouver, their lodging en route, the press kits, the photographers. The problems seemed insurmountable. Some of the young Haida men and women had never paddled before. Some experienced paddlers had come down with flu. Practice in the actual craft had been perfunctory, and today was the beginning of a voyage that would take them seventeen days, over six hundred miles.

The whole crew felt that the return of *Loo Taas* to Haida Gwaii would be a turning point in the fate of South Moresby. The termination of negotiations had given the expedition new impetus. Miles announced that, if need be, *Loo Taas* would be diverted to Lyell Island in case cutting operations had resumed there. *Loo Taas* was not a replica of a Haida war canoe; it was a war canoe. The threat of logging had resurrected the craft in the spirit of its ancestors.

A crowd gathered around False Creek, off English Bay, waiting for a sight no one had witnessed in a century. The young male and female paddlers applied oil to their arms and legs, anointing themselves for the voyage and protecting their skin from the sea spray. They wore the traditional Haida button cloaks bearing their clan emblems – Raven, Bear, Wolf, Beaver, and Eagle. To protect their heads from the hot sun, they wore broad conical hats, painted with red and black designs – Seaweed, Moon, Dogfish. Each paddle was also adorned with the animal spirits that represented the families and clans of the Haida Nation. And *Loo Taas* itself, with its white killer whale teeth glistening in the sun, looked ready to eat any wave that came its way.

The press had turned out in full force. Miles Richardson told them, "What is at stake is our survival as a nation. We can't survive in a land of stumps."

As the Haida youth paddled *Loo Taas* out into the bay, Robert Davidson drummed and sang Haida songs of war and coming home again. All around them was a flotilla of kayaks and pleasure craft. It provided a way for even the staunchest Socred to demonstrate support for the park, as Herb Capozzi, former owner of the B.C. Lions, drove his motorboat amid the kayaks. As if spontaneously, the fire hoses of the Coast Guard's red and white vessel sent a fountain of water heavenward. The crescendo of water, like an explosion of liquid fireworks, caught the imagination of every onlooker and a huge cheer went up. To the Haida Nation it symbolized an official recognition by the Canadian government of another sovereign nation.

Tara looked up from the wonderful scene to see an airplane flying by. Behind it trailed a banner, "SAVE S. MORESBY – PH.VDZ – 387-1715."

By the next day, so many people had phoned the Victoria office buildings that its phone system and the back-up went down. B.C. Tel had no explanation. It had never happened before. So people switched to sending telegrams.

J.B. phoned me that day to say that his advertisement was all set for the next day's *Vancouver Sun*. We were running out of time, but that was the earliest they could run it. It would cost $15,000, but raising the money had not been a problem. Monte Hummel called to say the telegram from Prince Philip would be dispatched soon to Vander Zalm. Dozens of people were calling me, leaving tidbits of information, good ideas, and questions. The major one was: Has the Prime Minister called Vander Zalm yet? To which the answer was no.

I had called Andy first thing in the morning and then the Prime Minister's Office, just to be sure. I had been hoping and praying all weekend that Mulroney was on the phone to the Premier. I wished desperately that on Monday morning, when I came in to work, there would be good news. But there was none. And in this case, no news was definitely not good news.

When the reporters showed up for work in Victoria, around noon Ottawa time, I got firsthand reports of how things looked from a B.C. perspective. According to one member of the press gallery, it had become their standing joke – "Has Brian called yet?" Every time they saw the Premier, they'd call out the question, and he'd laugh a little and say, "Well, he's got my number. I don't know what the problem is." Worse yet, it had come to the point that the press and the Premier doubted that the Prime Minister would ever call. And the cabinet meeting was the day after tomorrow.

If it was a strategic decision to make Vander Zalm desperate, it seemed to be working. He said to reporters that he was willing to fly to Ottawa the next day, if Ottawa came forward with a new proposal. All the Prime Minister had to do was call, the Premier said, and "I'll delay issuing logging permits. If I had my druthers, I would like to see a federal park."

As the day wore on, I restrained a nearly hysterical fear that we were going to lose South Moresby. The momentum was disappearing from the Prime Minister's promise. Maybe the school of thought that we could "look good" and keep the money was holding sway. Maybe the Prime Minister was just too busy with the capital punishment debate on which he would speak that night. Maybe he just didn't realize that a call on Tuesday to meet a Wednesday deadline might be too late.

A little after 5 p.m., I went over to Tom's Parliament Hill office. He was in his shirtsleeves, preferring an open window to the whirr of an air conditioner even in the humid misery of an Ottawa summer. Tom looked up from his desk, expectantly, as though maybe there might be some good news.

"Tom," I began with a sigh, "I am worried that if Mulroney doesn't make that call tonight, it will be too late. If it's Tuesday and all the pro-logging boys are ready to roll for a Wednesday meeting, they'll probably have told Western Forest Products where their next permits will be, and where the new provincial park boundaries will be located. They'll have maps ready for the press, and it will be too late to turn things around. It reminds me of a story my father told me about why the Germans invaded France in the First World War. They realized at the last minute that it would be a tactical advantage to attack Russia, but the generals said, 'We can't. All the trains are pointing west, and there's no way to turn them around.'"

Tom looked defeated. "I know. Don't you think I know that? But, what do you want me to do? I've spoken to the Prime Minister and he tells me that he will make that call. I will not call him again," he added sternly.

"I don't know," I struggled to come up with an idea that Tom would not reject. "Maybe if you wrote him a short personal note, in your own handwriting, just letting him know that Vander Zalm says all he has to do is call – he doesn't even have to offer anything new – all he has to do is call and they won't issue logging permits. I could make sure it gets hand-delivered."

"You can do that?" asked Tom skeptically. "Sure. I'll deliver it myself tonight right after he finishes his capital punishment speech," I promised, not knowing if I could pull it off, but trying to sound convincing.

Tom brightened. He liked writing letters, and he wrote good ones. He took out his personal stationery and his blue fountain pen, and started, "Dear Brian…"

With the letter in hand, I headed over to the House, to see if I could find a way into the government lobby.

Only one member of a minister's staff has a pass to the lobby, and it was permanently designated for the Question Period assistant. On my way out the door, I bumped into Terry and told him where I was headed. He offered to come with me, being more likely to reach Mulroney. Terry had been on Mulroney's campaign plane when he was with the *Toronto Sun* in 1984. He had even written nice things about the future prime minister.

At the guarded doors into the House and the lobbies, I looked for any MP who might bend the rules to escort us in. Bob Wenman, one of the strongest of the park supporters in the B.C. caucus, was on his way out. He obliged, but I think he extracted a promise from me of money for further renovations to historic Fort Langley in return.

Our timing was perfect. Brian Mulroney had just finished giving one of his finest parliamentary addresses, one in defence of the abolition of capital punishment. He was being greeted and congratulated by a handful of MPs half-way up the room. He was heading toward us. Terry gave me a signal to melt into the background as he walked toward a small knot of well-wishers. I saw Terry make eye contact, and Mulroney came over, hand outstretched. Terry handed him the note, and I could see him adding a few earnest words of his own. Mulroney took the envelope, placed it in his breast pocket and patted it reassuringly. *Sotto voce*, he said to Terry, "We'll let them sweat a little." Then he moved on, smiling at me even as I tried to be invisible.

I went to sleep that night not knowing how long Mulroney would let Vander Zalm sweat. I set my alarm for the CBC Radio news at 7 a.m. the following morning. That evening, sometime after 9 p.m., Ottawa time, Mulroney called Vander Zalm. On June 23, I woke up to the news that the negotiations had resumed to create a national park at South Moresby. We were back on track.

30

THE ELEVENTH HOUR

TUESDAY MORNING, RIDING THE ELEVATOR TO MY FLOOR, my fellow employees were jubilant. We hugged each other, as people departed for their floor in the different services of the department – atmospheric environment service, finances and administration, corporate planning, parks service – all the branches housed in Les Terraces shared in the cliff-hanger, Perils-of-Pauline atmosphere of the negotiations.

I bounced into my office to check the day's newspapers. All the major papers across the country carried the news of the twenty-minute phone call the night before. Mulroney's personal appeal had brought British Columbia back to the bargaining table. Vander Zalm had extended the deadline to conclude an agreement by one or two weeks.

Colleen was quoted as saying, "The eyes of all Canadians will be on Vander Zalm over the next few weeks." J.B. who had assiduously avoided accusing Vander Zalm of blackmail, focussed on the numbers being thrown around for the value of Lyell Island's logging industry. "The numbers the province has been using just don't add up at all. Timber on Lyell is worth about $17.5 million a year, not the billions of dollars the government is throwing around."

In a press backgrounder, J.B. pulled out an equation reminiscent of the murrelet study, "If [Forests Minister] Parker is right, then the whole B.C. logging industry is worth $370 billion a year – in which case we could solve all our problems by simply buying Ontario."

The *Vancouver Sun*'s front page headline was "Mulroney's Call on Park Re-opens Talks on Moresby," and inside on page five was the full-page advertisement: "South Moresby – For Your Children's Children." Nearly half the page was devoted to a large photograph of Windy Bay, a young man on a log looking into the verdant lushness – a self-portrait by Jeff Gibbs. It looked great and it was not too late. It was written as a direct appeal to Premier Vander Zalm:

"Dear Sir,

"There are about 180 places in the world that are worthy of international recognition as World Heritage Cultural or Natural Sites. Twelve places qualify on both counts. Only one of these is found in North America – South Moresby."

The *Vancouver Sun* advertisement asked people to make their views known to Vander Zalm. Across the bottom of the page appeared the phone, telex, and fax numbers for the Premier's office. But the advertisement had not attacked Vander Zalm. Graciously and diplomatically, it pointed out that Ottawa's last offer was $106 million: "It is a generous unprecedented offer, and you deserve full marks for very effective bargaining. It will be to your everlasting credit to accept that offer, to end the controversy and to invite the world to share our wilderness heritage – our national park."

Peter C. Newman, senior editor of *Maclean's*, had called J.B. to suggest another full-page advertisement. This one to feature signatures from leading business and professional people – an expanded public version of Bryan Williams's letter to Premier Bill Bennett two years before.

In Ottawa, by Tuesday mid-morning we were assembled in the departmental boardroom for the deputy's briefing with McMillan. We had an extremely hectic week ahead, even without South Moresby's roller-coaster ride. On Friday, June 26, the day we hoped we might have a deal closed with B.C., the new legislation, the Canadian Environmental Protection Act, would be tabled for first reading. Later that day, it became clear that Mulroney's chief of staff, Derek Burney, was running the negotiations, dealing with Vander Zalm's political right hand, David Poole. The Queen Charlotte Islands, in addition to having the most active coastline, the most earthquake-prone region in Canada, was also capable of shaking the political Richter scale. Tremors continued, whether they were aftershocks of the previous week's quake or precursors of new shakes to come, we could only guess. I kept in touch with former Vander Zalm aides who could help me read the indicators, as well as with my few contacts in the B.C. bureaucracy. More than checking for hard facts, I kept checking, long-distance, on the mood. As long as reporters and others reported that Vander Zalm was smiling, I felt that we'd be all right.

Meanwhile, support was pouring in from totally new sources. Margaret Atwood launched a fundraising campaign to save South Moresby. Arguing that the federal government should pay whatever it took to save South Moresby, she got the ball rolling by pledging $1,000 of her own money to the costs of the park and calling on others to do the same. By Wednesday, artists Robert Bateman, Toni Onley, and Jack Shadbolt had matched her offer through donated works of art.

The idea of putting more money into the pot seemed to be gaining momentum with the public. On the CBC national television show Midday, both Tom McMillan and John Broadhead defended the unprecedented generosity of the federal offer, while host Peter Downie argued that the public wouldn't mind seeing more money spent to save a nationally significant, unique wilderness. Tom McMillan talked about fiscal responsibility and the need not to hand B.C. "the keys to the treasury." Downie tapped into what thousands of Canadians were thinking. "I don't think the public would mind. I mean billions are spent on nuclear submarines and other things the public doesn't care half as much about as South Moresby."

John Fraser felt the same. Falling back on his legal training, he would rage impatiently to me, "I wish we could get people to understand that this is not about determining fair market value. This is about finding the price that will force a sale on an unwilling vendor."

I started checking to see whether the South Moresby offer really was the most expensive national park in history. I doubted it. The South Moresby negotiations were definitely the only time that a package of expenditures for a ten-year period had been costed out as part of the acquisition discussions. I knew that part of the deal for the Gros Morne National Park in Newfoundland had been a commitment from the federal government to build roads across Newfoundland to reach the park. There had been no monetary estimates tied to that commitment. But I had it confirmed by Parks officials that, over time, the costs of Gros Morne and its accompanying highways had come to $130 million – $24 million more than the South Moresby offer.

Meanwhile, as the negotiations laboured toward a solution, the Haida war canoe *Loo Taas* was working toward the same goal in its own way. Coming up the coast, *Wave Eater* and her crew had put into small native villages where they were welcomed and feasted. Dirt-poor communities had put on, and in some cases, sewn from scratch, ceremonial finery to greet the Haida war canoe and the expedition party. In one village, an elder told the proud young paddlers that the last time a Haida canoe had landed in their village, the crew had left only three people alive. The Haida kids had looked at their feet, not sure how to integrate this aspect of their culture into the critical process of exploring and retaining national pride. But by morning, they were back in the canoe, straining their weary muscles against the coastal waters, at one with the sea and the salt spray, paddling on to save Haida Gwaii.

By Friday afternoon, things were looking very good. Tom got a call to attend an afternoon meeting with Burney, Mazankowski, and Maz's chief of staff, Jamie Burns. Tom had a flight to catch to Charlottetown, so he went to the meeting planning to leave directly from there to the airport with Terry. That evening I was on the phone with Terry. "What happened?" I asked anxiously.

"It's not good," said Terry, in a matter-of-fact tone. "They want us to subsidize their ferry service."

"What! How did ferries get into this?" I was appalled. "I thought the big surprises were over. I thought we had a deal and all the fiddling would be over dollars."

"Well, it sounds like it was Stephen Rogers' idea. But the way it came up was that they figure more tourists to the Charlottes mean more of a strain on the ferry service. And, apparently, it's a long-standing gripe with B.C. that Newfoundland's ferry service is subsidized by the feds to the tune of $125 million a year, but B.C. only gets a $20-million ferry subsidy. They have an annual deficit of $9 million for the Charlottes' ferry service. So they're suggesting we should throw in another $9 million a year annually for ten years."

"Oh my God. Another $90 million, on top of our $106. That's back up to their original $200 million package! This is incredible. So where do we stand now?" I almost didn't want to hear.

"Well, we're still talking, but I don't think we'll get a deal this week," Terry answered resignedly.

I called Fraser with news of the latest set-back. He phoned me at home with confirmation that the B.C. ferry subsidies were raised at a cabinet meeting on

Wednesday. Most ferry routes in British Columbia were losing money. Even though Newfoundland's ferry subsidies had been part of the deal to get them into Confederation, B.C. felt that, once again, it was getting the short end of the stick. Still, as far as anyone knew, the talks were still moving along.

On Monday another wrinkle developed. This one struck me as a good and reasonable idea, as, at least, it was actually related to national parks. Parks Canada's regional office in Calgary was responsible for the parks within British Columbia. The latest proposal was to create a regional Parks Canada office in B.C. to administer the existing B.C. parks and report directly to Ottawa. Tom liked the notion, suggesting to Collinson that we should agree with a proposal to build up, over time, an autonomous Parks Canada office for the Pacific-Yukon Region. Moreover, Tom told Collinson that we should be able to fund such an office from within our existing budget. Collinson saw red and continued to advise the Privy Council Office bureaucrats who were providing back-up to Burney with the drafting of proposals that we were against any new Parks office in B.C., except for a small one that would report to Regional headquarters in Calgary.

We now had new variables in the endless recalculations of a package for British Columbia. In addition to all those other pieces – compensation, small-boat wharfs, regional economic development funds, park operations and maintenance – we had ferry subsidies and a new Parks Canada office to juggle. At least we were still talking.

I was still in my office late Monday night when I got a disturbing bulletin from British Columbia. The 6 p.m. TV news in B.C. had, for the first time, made the ferry subsidy issue public. It was a damaging story and I was livid. I called Terry and read him the transcript I had of the news item. "Terry, someone from the federal government leaked this. Listen: 'Ottawa sources say the B.C. government has introduced major new demands that could add at least $70 million to the $106 million the federal government has already offered...Ottawa officials say they're just about fed up dealing with Bill Vander Zalm and his government. Just when a deal seemed imminent, B.C. demanded that Ottawa pick up the annual $9-million deficit to operate the ferry between Prince Rupert and the Queen Charlottes.'"

Terry agreed it sounded bad. It was the kind of story designed to annoy Vander Zalm. But if the leak upset Vander Zalm, he didn't show it. He continued to express the hope that a deal would be struck. He went so far as to offer to fly to Ottawa to complete negotiations directly with the Prime Minister if that was what was required.

Tuesday, June 30, was the last day Parliament was in session before the summer recess. I was very nervous that, with Parliament adjourned and Question Period no longer available as a daily prod to the process of negotiations, we might lose momentum. My only hope was that between the last day of the House of Commons session and the total political languor of summer stood Mulroney's weekend visit to the beaches and picnics of British Columbia. But if we didn't have an agreement by the weekend of July 11...I feared the worst.

Stephen Ash called in early afternoon to let me know that Mulroney had just spoken to Vander Zalm again, about half an hour before. As the last session of Question Period commenced, Mulroney had reason to feel confident about progress. Jim Fulton rose in the House, directing a friendly and overly optimistic question to Mulroney. Rumours were rampant that Vander Zalm had already accepted the $106-million package, as long as the ferry subsidy issue was addressed and the Parks office opened in Vancouver. Jim prefaced his question by saying, "My question, and I would hope congratulations, is to the Prime Minister because it appears that the unanimous voice of Parliament has been heard out West."

Mulroney was self-assured and good-natured as he answered, "When the Honourable Member announced the settlement, I was wondering if he'd had a phone call that I hadn't, because while there's been a lot of work done and we have made some progress, there has been no settlement."

Jim tried again, "Just prior to Question Period...the Premier had, as is often the case in B.C., gone and held a press conference regarding this matter; that he has accepted the $106-million federal offer. And the only other two conditions that B.C. wishes to have met are totally achievable and reasonable."

Brian Mulroney tried again to dampen Jim's premature enthusiasm. "Not being a British Columbian, I didn't realize that successful negotiations depended upon catching the Premier's scrums." At which point, every member from B.C. on the other side of the House laughed and called out, "It does!" The members were in good spirits, like school children in the last class before summer vacation. Mulroney joined in the general conviviality, laughing, "Oh, it does? Well, that's probably why he's been so successful!" Mulroney confirmed that not only had he just spoken to Vander Zalm, he expected to speak with him again, soon.

Before leaving for what would be the bulk of the summer recess, Tom sat down with Jim Collinson and the deputy to review the on-going priorities. "Of course," he said, "I'll come back the minute any agreement is reached on South Moresby, and assuming that everything goes well, I'll fly right out for a signing in B.C. And Jim, have your people located that cake yet?" Jim smiled indulgently, "Don't worry, Mr Minister. It's in a freezer in Banff where you left it."

July 1, Canada Day, provided a break in the tension of the negotiations. While most Canadians celebrated with barbecued dinners, the *Loo Taas* expedition was being welcomed at Waglisha Village at Bella Bella. By now the paddlers had grown confident. The experience of cutting their way through the walls of water had made them strong. It was increasingly difficult to get them out of the canoe and replace them with fresh paddlers. No one wanted to spend time on the tug. With each stroke, Huck realized that *Loo Taas* and saving South Moresby were intrinsically linked.

Throughout the Canada Day holiday, calls continued between Derek Burney and David Poole. Finally, we seemed to have found a formula. But first thing the next morning, I was back in crisis-management mode. We were in big trouble with one of the caucuses. This time it was the Alberta Tory caucus. Vander Zalm had told the media about his plans to have the Calgary Parks office "moved" to Vancouver, and Albertans were up in arms. Calgary Mayor Ralph Klein accused Vander Zalm of extortion and I had to phone the federal members from the Calgary area to reassure them that, if an office were opened in British Columbia, it would not be at the expense of the existing office in Calgary. It looked less and less likely that either the Privy Council Office or Parks Canada would allow the federal negotiating position to include an honest-to-God regional office for B.C. Meanwhile, Burney's office ended the great tussle over Western Diversification monies, by indicating that funds for South Moresby would come from some other mysterious pocket.

Friday night John Fraser called me from his home. He had just spoken to Brian Smith and reported that things looked good. Through Saturday and Sunday, progress appeared to be made hourly. Sunday night, John Fraser called again. "Look dear," he said, "I don't think you're going to have to get arrested. Brian Smith just called and he went over a draft agreement with me. It sounded close to final. Things are looking very good."

It was hard to believe. We had been so close before and seen everything fall apart. I would not cheer, nor cancel my jail reservations, until I was one hundred per cent sure that we had a deal.

Still, I was feeling optimistic, bordering on giddy by Monday, July 6. Among all the other demands of the day, I checked in with the friendly spies of the B.C. government. No one expected an agreement for a few days. The ferry subsidy issue was still sticky and the question of the number of employees of the prospective B.C. Parks office was still disputed. Collinson's version corroborated what I had learned through unofficial channels. Close, but no cigar.

At around 4 p.m., I was in the small boardroom, meeting with officials from External Affairs and the Canadian Wildlife Service to discuss the planned signing of the Canada-U.S. Porcupine Caribou Agreement when my secretary, Karen Palmer, knocked and entered. As she handed me a note on a scrap of pink paper, she looked breathless and wide-eyed. I looked at the message form: "Dalton Camp. On hold for you. NOW!!"

I made quick apologies and literally ran down the hall to my office. I had not spoken directly with Dalton Camp since our meeting two weeks before. I tried to sound nonchalant as I picked up the receiver, "Hello, Mr Camp. How nice of you to call." He chuckled. "Congratulations." My heart stopped. "Congratulations on what?"

"You've got your park."

I could not believe it. "Are you sure?" I asked, knowing that this was a really dumb question. "Yes. Bruce Phillips will have it announced at 6 p.m. this evening." He continued in lowered tones, "It would be best if you told no one until then."

"Oh God! Really! Oh my dear Lord!" I suddenly feared becoming incoherent. I pulled myself together to think of rational questions. "But, I just talked with our ADM and he said there were still lots of unresolved issues. My sources in B.C. said the same."

"Well," Camp explained, "there were. But Burney and Poole just decided that since none of the outstanding issues were so critical as to make either side walk away from the deal, it would be better to end the agony and begin planning the formal signing ceremony. They'll sign it on Saturday when the PM is in B.C." I was almost speechless. Once it began to sink in that, at long last, we really had won, it dawned on me how extraordinarily kind it was of Dalton Camp to have phoned me. "Mr Camp, I just cannot thank you enough" – I may have gushed, as I was near tears – "for everything. For getting the negotiations back on track, and now for phoning me. It is so amazing and wonderful and sweet of you to have thought of me at all. And to call me personally like this. It's just unbelievable."

"Well, of course, I had to call you," he said with affection. "You were the spark."

I hung up, my mind slipping into delirium. Tom. I had to tell Tom. My hands trembled as I touch-toned Tom's home number in Prince Edward Island. He answered the phone himself. "Tom. It's Elizabeth." By this time, my voice started to break up on me. It's a genetic trait. My whole family is emotional. Our voices disintegrate into little gulp-like squeaks.

"Elizabeth? Is that you? Are you all right?" Tom sounded worried.

"Yeah, I'm fine. It's just that, Tom, we got it. We got the park!"

"I don't think so. I just spoke with the deputy and she said that there are still a few outstanding issues." Tom was reasonably sceptical.

"I'm absolutely sure. Dalton Camp just phoned me and he said that Bruce Phillips is releasing the news at 6 p.m. Ottawa time, but we should keep it quiet till then," I explained.

Now Tom was really shocked, "Dalton Camp called you? Why would Dalton Camp call you?"

I did not often, maybe never, blow my own horn to Tom, but I couldn't resist repeating the nicest compliment I had ever been paid. "He said I was the spark."

"He said that? And he's sure there's a deal?" Tom asked, bewildered.

"Uh-huh. The signing will be on Saturday," and I repeated to Tom all the details Camp had given me. "Tom. You've done a great job."

As Tom hung up, I knew he wouldn't really believe it until he heard it on the six o'clock news. I sat at my desk for a moment, my hand stuck on the phone receiver. Suddenly I remembered the Porcupine Caribou meeting. I went back into the boardroom and explained that something had come up. "Are you okay?" they asked. I realized that I was trying to sound normal while crying and giggling at the same time. "Yeah, I'm fine. You'll understand tomorrow, but I think I'd better call it a day."

Karen looked at me as I headed back to my office. "Can I get you something? Is everything all right?" I reassured her that I wasn't finally undergoing spontaneous human combustion, nor was I having a nervous breakdown, even if it looked that way. But I realized that if I was to keep such news to myself, I had better go home. Before leaving the office, I could not resist making another call. I phoned the Speaker's office. Amazingly, he was free to speak with me. "John, would you have any respect for someone who couldn't keep a secret Dalton Camp gave her for fifteen minutes?"

"I just got off the phone with him," laughed Fraser. "Congratulations!" I hung up. "I must go home," I thought to myself. But I picked up the receiver and punched the familiar number of Earthlife in Vancouver. "J.B. You've got to promise you won't tell anyone what

I'm about to tell you, at least for an hour and a half."

"Sure, Elizabeth." I could feel him grinning.

"We've won. We've got the park. The whole thing, right up to the height of land on the Tangil Peninsula." I was finally believing it myself.

"Really? For sure?"

"Yes. One hundred per cent for sure! But wait til 6 p.m. Ottawa time, before saying anything to anyone else, okay?" I asked foolishly, for no one who had just spent nearly the last decade of his life working on the issue could be expected to keep such news from the people who had spent thirteen years, or six years, or four years making the moment come to pass. J.B. agreed, laughing deliciously and with no intention of keeping the news to himself.

When he hung up from talking to me, he called Vicky and Miles Richardson and other key people, advising each of them to keep quiet until after Phillips' news release was over the wire. He took the bottle of champagne out of the fridge, where he had, as a gesture of optimism, confidence, and blind faith, placed it on ice some months before. As he unwound the wire from the cork, the phone rang. It was one of his friends within the B.C. bureaucracy calling to fill him in on the latest snag in the negotiations. News that, now that they were down to the fine strokes, the big boys had decided it was a done deal had not yet filtered down to either federal or provincial officials. J.B. listened without betraying the news that was threatening to explode within him. Reading his mind, the champagne spontaneously expelled its cork with a triumphant bang. The deep-throat at the other end asked, "What was that?" J.B. kept his composure, "Car backfire, I think."

I went home and paced and cried and stood up and sat down again and hugged my dog and trembled. At six o'clock, I turned on the television and the radio at once and tried to monitor both. It was not the lead item on the CBC World at Six. I tensed from head to toe. Maybe something had gone wrong again. And then, at nearly the end, "And this just in. The federal and British Columbia governments have reached an agreement to create a national park at South Moresby in the Queen Charlotte Islands."

I cheered and called Vicky and Colleen and Terry and Miles and everyone I thought should know. "If only I could reach Guujaaw and Huckleberry." I wished I knew how to contact them on the *Loo Taas* expedition. But for the time being, I surrendered to joy.

As news spread that a park agreement had finally been reached, the weary paddlers had completed their seventeenth day on the open waters. They were approaching the end of Banks Island and the protection it afforded. Within days, they would set out for the most arduous portion of their odyssey, the twenty-hour haul across the often violent waters of Hecate Strait. As they approached the village of Hartley Bay, they heard singing and so the paddlers began to sing a song of coming home. Huck heard the voices from the tug boat travelling in tandem. The songs of the Tsimshian of Hartley Bay mixed and mingled with the Haida over the water. The sun set and the sky was full of colour and voices. Huck thought, "This is the most beautiful part of the experience. I'll never forget this." This was peace.

That night, after the ceremonies of greeting and the hospitality of feasting, Huck and Guujaaw were in the home of the local chief where they and other Haida were billeted. They sipped their tea, as a television provided background noise. Suddenly Huck whirled around. Knowlton Nash was announcing that there would be a national park at South Moresby. Guujaaw and the others rushed to watch. "Details will be announced on Saturday when the Prime Minister and the Premier will sign the accord." Huck let out a cheer. Then his partner in the sublime appeared on the screen. J.B. was shown, briefly, a phone crooked against one ear, a yellow flower twirling in his fingers, an open bottle of champagne on his desk, as he sipped from a celebratory glass of the same. To Huck, it was one of those pictures worth a thousand words. J.B. was interviewed looking happy, but able to speak coherently about his reaction to sweet victory.

In Hartley Bay, someone said, "I don't know. I mean, how do we know that this is good news? Maybe it doesn't include Lyell Island."

Huck laughed. "Look, knowing how J.B. and Elizabeth get along, there's no way he'd be celebrating unless he knew. She must have called him. If he's drinking champagne, it means we have really won." He could barely believe it himself. "We have won it all. All of Lyell Island. All of Windy Bay. It will never be logged."

It was fitting that nearly thirteen years after the night they had met and drawn a line on a map, Huck and Guujaaw would be together to learn that their vision was now a reality. Neither of them had thought it would take more than a year or so to convince the powers that be of the wisdom of their proposal. Just save a little bit of raw wilderness. Save one tenth of one per cent of the annual allowable cut of British Columbia. Save an area with more rare endemic species than any other area of Canada. Save a place with record-breaking everything: waves, ancient murrelets, bald eagles, black bears, peregrine falcons, sea-lions, whales, earthquakes, skies, cedars, totem poles. Save something unique. Irreplaceable. Spectacular. Awe-inspiring. Save South Moresby.

That it took thirteen years, millions of dollars, the determination of the whole Haida Nation, the support of thousands of people, the personal involvement of the Prime Minister and the B.C. Premier, not to mention the crowned heads of Europe, is only a little more amazing than that it happened at all.

31

JUBILATION

L ATE MONDAY NIGHT, I FINALLY REACHED MIKE NICHOLL, executive director of the Council of the Haida Nation. I filled him in on the details I was allowed to divulge and shared his exuberance at the news. As I was preparing to hang up, he said, "Well, I guess I'll see you in Skidegate on Saturday." I wasn't sure what he meant. He reminded me, "The feast for *Loo Taas* on Saturday. You'll be coming, won't you?"

The next morning I lay in bed, contemplating heading for Haida Gwaii, when the phone rang. I was wanted at a meeting in half an hour with Derek Burney at the Langevin Block. I hurriedly dressed and rushed to be there. Waiting for Burney in the large boardroom outside the Prime Minister's personal suite of offices, I realized that I was in pretty heady company. Bruce Phillips, the former CTV reporter who was now the Prime Minister's communications director, was there. So was Marc Lortie, the PM's press secretary, and the senior Privy Council Office people who had worked over the last month as bureaucratic support to the deputy and to the PMO. The only other Environment Canada person present was Bruce Amos, at the moment the ranking Parks Canada representative.

The draft agreement was passed around for comment. We had done well in the last few weeks' negotiations. We had not increased our offer. It was still a $106-million package. Incredibly, we had persuaded

B.C. to increase their contribution. In addition to its $8-million share of forest compensation costs, B.C. had agreed to kick in a further $12 million to be matched by $12 million from within the federal $50-million economic development fund. The total of $24 million would be used as a "forest replacement fund." The payment schedule for the federal funds had been accelerated from ten years to eight, with a kick-start of $15 million in the first year from the regional development fund. As for the ferry subsidy problem, it had been solved by the federal government accepting, as a matter of principle, that British Columbia should not be stuck bearing the entire costs of any increased burden on the ferries created by the new national park. Ottawa also committed to talks with B.C. to discuss the whole ferry issue. The rest of the agreement fell out along the lines of Mazankowski's offer of June 10. As to what would happen if costs of compensating the industry surpassed our $31-million estimate, the agreement was silent.

The agreement would be put through the Cabinet Priorities and Planning Committee on Thursday, July 9, in time for the PM to sign the memorandum of agreement on Saturday.

Back on Haida Gwaii, word continued to spread to those few key people and activists who were out of touch with the modern mass media. Al and Irene Whitney were conducting a regular charter on *Darwin Sound II*. Their friend, Mary MacDonald, was along as the resident ornithologist for the trip and guests included the new *New York Times* Canadian bureau chief. The deck-hand was Bryan Williams's daughter, Shannon, joining the *Darwin Sound II* for the first time. On Tuesday, July 7, the ketch was making her way through the familiar, if treacherous, waters of Hecate Strait. Al was dealing with a fifteen-knot wind sailing out of the wilderness area, north of Lyell, when Mary, reaching her husband by VHF radio, cried out from below decks, "We got it! We got it!"

Across the waters at Sandspit, there was no rejoicing. R.L.Smith cranked out the latest *Red Neck News* carrying the grim news. "We gave it our best shot," reported an almost philosphical *Red Neck* editor, "but…a gullible public, by the thousands, misinformed by the media, brought tremendous pressure on our governments to end logging in South Moresby." R.L.Smith went on to predict a future when Haida land claims were finally resolved and the area returned to them. "We will all be looking forward to the screams of agony from our draft-dodger environmental friends when logging, initiated by our Haida friends and neighbours, returns once more to South Moresby." He closed with a cheery thought from a friend in Sandspit, "If you want to save a tree, kill a beaver."

Frank Beban was quoted as saying "I can't get mad at Bill Vander Zalm…He tried really hard to save our jobs, but when you're being blackmailed by the Prime Minister, it's pretty tough." Mulroney, known for a government "of lies and deceit" was held squarely to blame by the *Red Neck News.*

Moresby Island Concerned Citizens organized the wearing of black arm bands as a visible sign of mourning. But behind all the gnashing of teeth, Pat Armstrong and others began to strategize about how to get hold of that $50-million regional economic development fund.

Work in Ottawa continued at a frantic pace to nail down the final text and plan the signing ceremony. As the days slipped away, news leaked out that the first five years of funding for the South Moresby agreement was coming out of Western Diversification after all. I was surprised. "How did that happen?" I asked one of the behind-the-scenes types. "Poole blinked," was the answer.

One last detail eluded me. I wasn't getting a straight answer about Tom's cake. For months we had been told the cake was in a freezer in Banff. Now it appeared that no one knew where it was. Jim Collinson's executive assistant offered an explanation. "Well," he tried, rather bravely in the circumstances, "the minister could say that the cake was stored in one of the big freezers where they keep the road-kill and other big game from the park, and he could say that a big frozen bear fell on the cake and squashed it." He looked rather pleased with this eminently press-worthy version of events.

"Is that what happened?" I asked with what I hoped was a pained inflection. "It could have happened," he offered. "But, as far as you know, that's not what happened?" I pressed. He looked at his shoes, "Well, no. Not exactly."

Tom accepted the news of the lost cake with muttered incredulity and asked me to order a new cake made to look like the first one. No one really wanted to eat a cake that had been in the freezer for almost two years anyway. As for the original cake, for all we know, it is still in a freezer in Banff. For all we know, a bear fell on it.

Loo Taas had surpassed expectations. Far from having one last desperate paddle to reach Skidegate within twenty-one days, the crew members had come within shooting distance of their village a full day ahead of time. Time and tide may wait for no man, but the *Wave Eater* transversed those dimensions like an old friend. The crew decided to hold out in a nearby cove and make their dramatic homecoming arrival as scheduled.

At noon, hundreds of residents gathered on the shore of Skidegate Village. As *Loo Taas* came toward the shore, the village regained some of its tradition. Most of the people on shore wore button blankets. All the hereditary chiefs wore their family head-dresses. Young men and women beat their painted skin drums, wide and shallow like a small shield. Teenagers from recently established native dance groups practised their steps on shore. When *Loo Taas* came within view, a tremendous cheer erupted from the crowd. It seemed almost as loud as the cheer of the several thousand in Vancouver when Loo Taas had pulled out of False Creek three weeks before. Tara Cullis was there to join in both cheers. She clutched her two little girls as the canoe made its way home.

On the waters of Skidegate Bay, the paddlers heard the cheer. They changed the rhythm of their paddling, punctuating two powerful strokes by bringing the paddles up to a horizontal position and banging them against the gunwales. Stroke! Stroke! Bang! Bang! To the accompaniment of their own drum beats, they sang as they came into shore, paced by their coxswain, an Alaskan Haida who had measured out the metre of their strokes for days.

In the dazzling sun, Vicky, Colleen, and J.B. looked out at the sparkling, dancing waters and the war canoe that was bringing home their dream. Waiting on shore, Ada Yovanovitch stood with her daughter, Diane, and her old friend Ethel Jones. Their case had never gone to trial. No one had wanted to prosecute the elders for their "crime." Reporters mingled with the crowd, seeking the reaction of the Haida to the end of logging. Ethel smiled. "I'd do it again," she said of her experience blocking the logging road. "But I'm happy now that I won't have to."

The paddlers reached the beach, and leapt from the canoe to pull it up on shore with the strength and confidence borne of weeks of eating waves. The young men and women who had brought *Loo Taas* up the coast were immediately swallowed up in the arms of the villagers. Miles Richardson proclaimed, "*Loo Taas* is home!" Speeches poured forth. Bill Reid was cheered. Miles spoke of the victory, not only of *Loo Taas* and her crew, but of the decision to resolve the land-use controversy of South Moresby in favour of wilderness. Ahead lay the battle over ownership, but it was right to celebrate their victory in forcing two levels of government and the consciousness of their neighbour nation, Canada, to accept the spiritual value of places too sacred to despoil.

Hundreds of miles to the south, in an ornate ball-room, under elaborate crystal chandeliers, Brian Mulroney was quoting Miles Richardson: "The fate of the land parallels the fate of our culture." Just before the signing, the ministers had met privately in a beautiful drawing room overlooking the many intricate, formal flower beds of Government House, blooming in profusion. Pat Carney looked at the small group of her male colleagues – the political powers that be. "This is what you will be remembered for," she told them. "Announcements about ice breakers are a one-day wonder. But this matters. This is important. It is an achievement that will last, and it is something for which future generations will thank you."

After the signing, Vander Zalm hammed it up, describing his recipe for success. "When you mix several parts of Irish charm and Dutch stubbornness – pardon me, determination – and shake things up, good, positive things happen."

The reception afterward was a happy confusion. Paul George hugged me and admitted that he couldn't really believe it had finally happened. It had been a long time since Guujaaw had refused his handshake, since he had printed up the first Save South Moresby poster, since he had dreamed up the ecological reserve proposal that had halted logging on Windy Bay for the critical years of negotiations. Now he just stood there, a big bear of a man, grinning from ear to ear like a kid on Christmas morning. Bristol Foster agreed with Paul that he had never thought he would see the day. He shook his head in wonder, scanning the incongruous sight of this cluster of environmental warriors mingling with government officials and no less than the Prime Minister around a lavish spread of finger food, and, of course, champagne.

As the media availability session wound down, I started doing my mother-hen routine, rounding up the chicks for the flight to Skidegate. Everyone was chomping at the bit to get to the celebratory feast for the *Loo Taas* homecoming. But no commercial flights were available to reach the Sandspit airport before morning. My enterprising cohort at Environment Canada, Steve Gorman, had suggested we "borrow" the Prime Minister's back-up plane. I was amazed to realize that there was such a thing, travelling a discrete distance from the PM's entourage in case of mechanical failure. I was even more amazed when after one friendly phone call to the PMO, I was lent the plane for the afternoon. My passenger roster for Haida Gwaii was the fun group: Kevin McNamee, now a veteran of two park signing ceremonies, Gregg Sheehy, heading to South Moresby for the first time, Sharon Chow and Peter McAlister of the Sierra Club of Western Canada, Al Whitney, captain of *Darwin Sound II,* Bristol Foster, Gary Clarke from the Travel Industry Association of Canada, Jim Fulton, and David Suzuki, plus a few reporters, including Daphne Brougham from the Victoria press gallery. I had bought several bottles of champagne in Ottawa, of which I'd left two with Tom's plane, and laid two on for our trip. As soon as we were airborne, I suddenly felt free. I didn't have to worry about anyone's schedule or press releases, or whether the Prime Minister's pen had ink or whether the press kits had their French translation. I was off duty, and I could hug whom I wanted and cry in public and generally join the celebration as a full-fledged crazily happy person. We drank champagne and giggled. Everyone was indecently thrilled to be flying on the PM's plane. Our flight crew from the Department of National Defence must have had pause to consider if we were really an authorized government contingent.

As we approached the chain of islands, the pilot obligingly flew at 6,000 feet, so we could get a good look.

Peering out the windows of the government jet, I caught my first glimpse of what we had fought so hard to save. I was not disappointed. Even from the unnatural vantage point of 6,000 feet, it was beautiful, like a scattering of green velvet cushions. They looked soft and inviting. Al Whitney and Bristol Foster pointed out the well-known features, names I knew, places I felt I knew like the back of my hand. No one needed to tell me when we were over Lyell Island. The sight of great expanses of clear-cuts was the first sign of anything other than how God had made it. Someone once told me that when people destroy something man-made, we call it vandalism, but when people destroy something God made, we call it progress. I had never had a stronger sense of outrage, of disgust at an act of vandalism, than when I looked down from that plane and saw the scars on Lyell.

As we approached the Sandspit airport, we realized that we had missed the ferry over to Queen Charlotte City. There wouldn't be another ferry for an hour, and we would miss the beginning of the feast. By now my desire to see Vicky and Colleen and J.B. and Huck and Miles was to the point of obsession. Every minute I was not with them was intolerable. Al Whitney sensed the impatience of our group, and got on the plane radio to ask Irene to come fetch us on the *Darwin Sound II*. When we touched down in Sandspit, there was no sign of her. But there was a reception party, what might have been called a "neck-tie" party in an old Western movie. When David Suzuki stepped onto the tarmac, a small cluster of placard-waving protesters jeered menacingly. That week's *Red Neck News* would report on the airport scene, depicting David kicking a child in the head, as his "My Dad Was a Logger" sign went flying. I had been expecting some trouble in Sandspit, based on reports from everyone who had been there recently. In fact, I'd requested a discreet RCMP back-up as security for McMillan. It just had not occurred to me that our group would be harrassed as well. I was anxious not to spend a single minute more in Sandspit, but I felt stymied. I set off through the crowd of angry loggers, Al Whitney as my escort.

As I headed for the Sandspit Inn, I noticed what looked like a Coast Guard flight crew walking back toward the airport. It occurred to me that I could "borrow" the giant Sikorski helicopter on the runway after I remembered that it was there in order to convey Tom and the rest of his group quickly over to the feast. But as Tom was an hour or so behind us, according to our pilot, there was no risk of missing him if they could fly us over before his arrival. I explained all this to the genial pilot and navigator. The flight crew happily agreed, even volunteering to take us to Windy Bay in the morning. "It will be more fun than the last time," he said, explaining that we were borrowing the same helicopter that had served as paddy wagon, ferrying arrested Haida back from Lyell Island in 1985.

Our pilot knew just where to take us, and lowered his massive craft in the ball-field next to the community hall where the feast was in progress. The rotary blades chopped the air and stirred gusts of wind, overturning barbecues where salmon was roasting, kicking up dust and dry blades of grass. Our arrival attracted a crowd. I saw Miles Richardson running toward the helicopter, and I realized he would expect Tom to be with us. Although Tom was nowhere in sight, Miles was not completely disappointed. He greeted his old friends Jim Fulton and David Suzuki. He hugged me and asked, "Where's Tom?" I told him I hoped he'd be along in about an hour, and he decided reluctantly to start serving the food. They had been holding dinner for the minister with the world's worst reputation for punctuality.

Vicky rushed up, hugged me, and led me into the hall. It was jam-packed, full to overflowing. Every square inch of floor space seemed occupied, and above us, in

overhanging balconies, were more people. All around
were Haida paintings, and cedar boughs had been used
to adorn the frames of windows, doors, paintings, even
basketball hoops, for like most community halls, this
one served more than banquets. In the back of the hall
Guujaaw was drumming. The hereditary chiefs began
their solemn ceremonial entrance, as the drums beat
and the crowd cheered. I'd never seen anything like it.
Each elderly man walked forward wearing the symbols
of his lineage and of the spiritual connection to the natural world. All the chiefs were present. Ravens, eagles,
bears, and sharks danced in costume. Chief Skedans
wore a particularly beautiful full-face moon staring
placidly at the crowd from the front piece of his head-
dress. A black wolf's head bobbed above the others, and
the drums kept beating as the room exploded in joy. I
hadn't slept or eaten in what felt like days. Between jet
lag and exhaustion, my perceptions were stretched to
the edge of other realities. And in that moment of ecsta-
cy, the scene had the quality of another dimension, of
magic and myth, of having stepped into a Tolkein
Middle Earth world.

The din in the hall was nearly deafening. There was a
steady roar of drumming and chatter and laughter
while Haida and non-Haida women in button blankets
began to serve the feast. How they moved through the
packed room, I couldn't imagine. But they seemed to
glide unimpeded between the tables, depositing enormous platters of barbecued salmon and halibut, of octopus, turkey, abalone, gaaw, scallops. Suddenly, the whole
room trembled with the sound of the giant Sikorski helicopter overhead. "It's Tom!" I said to Vicky, and raced
to greet him.

Tom was hugged by everyone, and I hugged Terry
and Bruce Amos and Pat Thomson as though I hadn't
seen them in years. Tom seemed to be getting used to
being hugged I thought as I saw him work his way

through the emotional crowd. Miles brought him around to the front entrance of the hall, the door through which the hereditary chiefs had entered. From the head table, he was introduced, "The Honourable Tom McMillan, federal minister of the environment." Tom received a standing ovation, while the Haida drums beat to sustain the energy of the welcome, and people let out cheers and what sounded like war cries. He turned and waved, smiling to the crowd. And the cheering and applause went on, long and loud. I wondered if ever in his political career, he had ever had a welcome to touch this. When I asked him later, still somewhat dazed he said he had not. MPs Mary Collins and Bob Wenman were warmly received as well, as all the federal representatives joined the distinguished elders and honoured guests at the head table. Dancing began. A young man in Raven mask swirled through the open area in front of the chiefs, arms outstretched. Between dances, each of the hereditary chiefs spoke, some in Haida, some in English, some in both languages.

At around one in the morning, which I started to realize was four in the morning according to my internal clock, the traditional gift-giving began. Tea towels, mugs, cutlery, china, and Hudson Bay blankets were stacked up as high as they could be balanced on a table at the end of the hall. Bill Reid had lithographed prints of his Loo Taas design; there were images of that Haida craft swallowing the sea for every guest. Diane Brown served as emcee as each person was called forward to be presented with a blanket by Skidegate chief Tom Greene. Huck and J.B. were honoured for their role in stopping the logging, as were David Suzuki and Jim Fulton. After Tom McMillan received his blanket, he was asked to speak. He had brought the pen Mulroney had used to sign the agreement as a gift for Miles. And last, but not least, we had brought cake. Lots of cake. The departmental staff in Vancouver had ordered three huge cakes, each proclaiming, "South Moresby National Park" in green icing. He cut up the South Moresby cake, and served it to Miles, J.B., Huck, Vicky, and Colleen. It had been a long time since Colleen had had her cake brainwave in Banff. She grinned at me, "I still can't believe this is happening." Tom served cake to Haida elders and children, and somehow, like the loaves and fishes, there was still more cake.

When Miles rose to speak, it was late. But he spoke brilliantly. He thanked Tom for the pen, but explained that he couldn't use it until the larger battle was won, until the issue of Haida land rights was resolved.

Finally, as tired celebrants moved from the hall, plastic bags were handed out. I was baffled. "You take your food with you at a Haida feast," J.B. explained. "Nothing is wasted and nothing is left behind, or you have insulted your hosts." Vicky had already sprung into action. A group of us were planning to stay at Windy Bay the next night, and Vicky was stocking up on the world's most delicious food for our camping expedition.

The next morning, after breakfast at the Helm Café next to the ferry dock, we reconvened at the ball-field to load up our helicopters. A tall, red-headed kid introduced himself as Jeff Gibbs, and asked if I could give him and his collapsible kayak and a pile of gear a ride to Windy Bay. I told him that if there were a way, I'd squeeze him in – if you could consider it "squeezing" to fit the world's least inobtrusive young man and a mountain of gear into a helicopter. But Jeff has a lucky star. He got on the helicopter, as Miles, Vicky, and J.B. decided to travel later on their own. Terry loaded the media, I loaded the hitchhikers, and we headed south for Windy Bay.

I couldn't believe that I was finally there. It was so beautiful, as we hovered over it, like a green velvet goblet. I stumbled, trance-like from the helicopter, walking into my own dream. I had wished this place safe so often. I saw its forest through a mist, but one of my own tears, for the giant trees were bathed in bright sunshine. Jeff rushed forward to start giving a tour to Bob Wenman, pointing out the old foundations of the abandoned longhouses. We walked back to the largest tree, up along Windy Bay Creek, deep in the woods, where despite the brightness of the day, we were plunged into near night. Arms outstreched, a dozen of us tried to reach all the way around the base of the tree. We couldn't. I'd never known a tree could be so big.

We heard the sound of a float-plane and rushed back to find that Miles and Vicky and J.B. had arrived. Tom and Miles started to talk about how exactly the Haida would be involved in every phase of the park management and implementation. It was the commitment the federal government had made. They sat on a bench in front of the longhouse and spoke earnestly and candidly about their hopes for the future. Then Tom and the rest of his contingent headed back to complete their aerial survey of South Moresby. I had decided to stay put and soak up the forests we had saved.

By some miracle, we had been able to assemble in one of the least accessible places on this continent almost all the people with whom we wanted to be. Colleen arrived by small boat, bringing additional provisions. During previous trips to Haida Gwaii, bad weather had prevented her from getting to South Moresby. We cheered the arrival of one of those without whom South Moresby would have been lost. As she set foot on Windy Bay's shores for the first time, we both cried again. I never knew I had such a capacity to weep from joy. There was no end to my tears. I cried when Miles and Huck arrived with friends Reg Wesley, Patricia Kelly, and Charlene Aleck.

David Suzuki showed up with Tara Cullis and their kids, Severne and Sarika, and David's father, Carr Suzuki. The next day, John Fraser arrived by helicopter, just to see us for a few hours. I hadn't seen him since the phone call from Dalton Camp telling us that at long last we had won. We kept telling each other, and anyone within earshot, that it would not have been possible without the other. We walked up Windy Bay Creek, Colleen sinking herself into cushiony moss at the base of a tree and smiling. Some kayakers from Germany, who had stumbled across Windy Bay, expecting to find it deserted, took some wonderful pictures.

After such a long struggle, we could finally sit on the moss, and listen to the creek gurgle by, and know with the certainty of God that the sound of a chain saw would never disturb this stillness. Those of us who were relative newcomers to the crusade marvelled at how we had been accepted by the others. David Suzuki mentioned this one night as we sat around the dying embers of our campfire. He had been surprised, he said, by how little ego there seemed to be; by how readily he was made to feel a part of the family. I felt the same, and as Huck and Reg sang that night, and I watched the stars overhead, I thanked those lucky ones that had directed me to my new family, and had allowed me to be part of saving South Moresby.

32

UNFINISHED
BUSINESS

WITHIN TWO WEEKS OF THE FORMAL DECLARATION OF
the national park at South Moresby, Frank Beban had
closed down his camp, lined up his rows of yellow
trucks, and started to think about the advantages and
opportunities of increased tourism in the Charlottes.
After all, as the owner of the only hotel in Sandspit, as
well as a charter helicopter company, which was already
advertising "Sandspit – Gateway to South Moresby," he
was hardly insensitive to the economic potential of
tourism. And then, quite suddenly, he died.

Local adherents of the *Red Neck News* insisted that he
had died of a broken heart. They went so far as to accuse
Mulroney of being responsible for his death. At a large
public meeting of island residents soon thereafter,
Beban's old friend and adversary in his desire to log
Lyell Island put people straight on a thing or two. Ada
Yovanovitch brought her imposing presence to its full
height and dimension. "Frank was my friend," she told
them, "and he had a heart condition for years. And I
grieve for his loss. But if anyone is responsible, I tell you
it was not the people who wanted to stop the logging."
She turned to stare directly into the faces of those she
addressed, "When I saw everyone in Sandspit wearing
black arm bands, I thought, 'Oh no, whose death will
they bring on this community?' Symbols of death are
powerful. These islands have seen much death. You do
not play with death."

Back in Ottawa, I continued to work toward the completion of the South Moresby mission. We were negotiating a full federal-provincial agreement with British Columbia, fleshing out the four-page memorandum of understanding. We needed to confirm the Haida's full and meaningful participation in every aspect of park implementation and management. We needed to establish local liaison committees. We needed to get as much economic development underway as possible, to reassure those residents who had not wanted a park that in the long run the wilderness alternative would even be to their economic advantage.

I wouldn't have guessed that it would take a full year, six months longer than originally projected, to complete and sign the final legal agreement with British Columbia – that, fleshed out, those four pages would run to well over one hundred. I wouldn't have believed that the federal government would be so disorganized as to be unable to get the relevant departments and agencies to agree on a framework for a working relationship with the Haida Nation. Nor that simple promises to the people of Sandspit would be so hard to keep. And that, at the last minute, with only a few weeks before finalization of the area's national park status, the provincial government would give out permits for mineral exploration within the park. It was the stuff of nightmares.

In all the disappointments of the years since the memorandum of understanding was signed, there has remained one unalterable fact: The area will never be logged. But against that success – a success due to the perseverence and passion of a handful of environmentalists and of the Haida – stand many failures. Chief among them has been the failure to deal with the Haida Nation. It is fair to say that in no aspect of what was promised has delivery been without difficulties and delay.

We made some progress in the final agreement. At least the three little islands – Limestone, Reef, and

Skedans – would be protected as provincial wildlife areas. But, overall, the tying up of loose ends looked more like a contest with flypaper than with red tape. Everything stuck in the wrong places. Every commitment to the Haida Nation required Bill McKnight's approval. Literally hundreds of hours went into the preparation of letters from McMillan and McKnight to Miles Richardson. Bureaucrats from three departments, Indian Affairs and Northern Development, Environment Canada, and the Privy Council Office, laboured for weeks to produce a letter on which everyone could agree, only to have McKnight refuse to sign it, based on potential, and unspecified, revenue implications raised by bureaucrats working for the Western Diversification Fund, for which McKnight was the responsible minister.

By the winter of 1987-1988, we were finally negotiating with the Haida Nation. Of course, these talks had nothing to do with land claims. The comprehensive claims policy still dictated that only six claims be dealt with at a time. Of the sixteen British Columbia native land claims accepted for negotiation by the federal government, only the Nishga's claim was approved for active negotiations. Now that the logging controversy on Lyell Island was resolved, Indian Affairs officials estimated the Haida claim might come up for negotiation in another thirty-five years.

It took a long time to persuade the senior bureaucrats at Indian Affairs that South Moresby created opportunities for some innovative approaches to national park management. The negotiating team on Haida Gwaii, comprised of representatives of the Haida Nation and of Parks Canada, began to make real progress. The starting Haida position had been that they must have an equal say in all decisions affecting Gwaii Haanas. Ottawa's position was that the minister of environment had a statutory responsibility under the National Parks

Act to be the ultimate authority. Fine, said Guujaaw, but
the minister is not the ultimate authority over Haida
Gwaii. It was difficult to develop a framework for cooperation without touching on the more fundamental
question: "Whose land do you think you're standing
on?"

Still, by spring 1988, a workable statement of "Interim
Purpose and Objectives" had been reached. It was combined with an information and promotional booklet
about the backgound of the South Moresby – Gwaii
Haanas area, with details of the federal-provincial agreement and the Haida-Canada statement of objectives.

The booklet was beautiful. With a dramatic border of
black, the cover photograph of a fresh water lake, high
in the San Christoval mountains, offered a view of South
Moresby that was rarely featured. Inside, the text was
evocative and richly illustrated. With the booklet printed, a Haida-Canada purposes and objectives statement
completed, and the Canada-British Columbia agreement ready to sign, it seemed that, perhaps, we were finally back on track. But then British Columbia gave out
permits for mineral exploration in areas within the park
boundaries to Diamond Resources. Bill McKnight decided to hold up the federal-provincial agreement because of its revenue implications for the Western
Diversification Fund. And last, but certainly not least,
the federal Department of Justice became interested in
the interim statement of purposes and objectives.
Justice saw our beautiful little booklet, South Moresby –
Gwaii Haanas, and didn't like it one bit. The book contained ominous references to the "hereditary activities
of the Haida." There were dangerous suggestions that
the Haida considered the area to be "a vital part of their
spiritual and ancestral home." The booklet and its interim statement confirmed that both Canada and the
Haida recognized that the Haida Nation had lived on
the islands of Haida Gwaii for thousands of years, in

harmony with nature. What's worse, it suggested there might be some "right" to continue traditional activities. Justice lawyers said we could not risk saying such things. It might eventually compromise our land claims negotiations with the Haida.

I was totally disgusted when this latest roadblock was put in our way. Guujaaw had had to get every syllable approved by the elders and by the Council of the Haida Nation. This was not a simple matter of cancelling one publication; this risked undermining our whole relationship with the Haida. I suggested to Jim Collinson that the Department of Justice would like us to change the captions under the picture of the totem poles of Ninstints to read that those poles were carved by extraterrestrials.

The Department of Justice insisted that the booklets be shredded – every single one of them. Close to twenty thousand dollars' worth of printing, just shredded.

Environment Week 1988: Months later, Tom told me his theory that it was jinxed. There were no rock videos, no hot-air balloons, no budget to attract the watchful eye of the Auditor General. But neither was there the final South Moresby signing. And, sadly, behind the scenes, a deal was being put together that would lead to my resignation within days: damned dams.

I discovered that Tom McMillan had agreed to sign permits for the construction of two dams on the Souris River in Saskatchewan, without federal environmental assessment, without an agreement to protect the downstream province of Manitoba, all in order to get Saskatchewan to translate their statutes into French, with a grasslands national park thrown into the bargain. When I realized what Premier Devine had been able to barter for a national park, suddenly Stephen Rogers and company looked like a bunch of amateurs. I did not want to leave McMillan's office; there was so much unfinished business. But I realized my job had disappeared. If the Rafferty and Alameda dams could be approved as part of a political trade-off without any consultation with me, then, in reality, I no longer had the role of senior policy adviser to play. I resigned.

The federal-provincial agreement on South Moresby was finally signed in the second week of July 1988. I wasn't there. Neither was Tom McMillan; his staff had double-booked him, and he was committed to staying in Prince Edward Island for the day of the signing ceremony. Fisheries Minister Tom Siddon signed the agreement in his place, with Terry Huberts, B.C.'s new minister for Parks. There were no invited guests. If Tom couldn't be there, he wanted it very low-key. It was so anticlimactic, it was almost invisible.

Since that time, Guujaaw has continued to work away on a Canada-Haida agreement. Sometimes, it seems that real progress has been made. Occasionally, the Haida Nation issues a warning that the park will be closed to tourists unless the question of joint management is resolved. Last I heard, Guujaaw had finally negotiated a draft agreement with the federal government that overcame the major obstacles. But the chiefs and councillors of the Haida Nation were so tired of the process of reviewing approved drafts, only to have the federal government renege, that Guujaaw couldn't get them very excited about looking at the latest effort.

After I resigned, I headed for islands, for places that heal. Cape Breton Island offered the Atlantic's dancing waves and pilot whales, which looked over the boat's railings, making eye contact with me before lowering themselves back into the sea. And Haida Gwaii massaged my weary soul with sunrises and shooting stars, tufted puffins darting about like wind-up toys, sea-lions splashing into the ocean, and heavenly forests where there was nothing to be done but to sit, forced down by the overwhelming beauty of the place.

I worked with Huck and Jeff on a tour boat showing Gwaii Haanas to tourists, with Ada and Ethel on board as interpreters. The boat, *The Norsal,* was the same one the B.C. ministers had taken through storm and rain when Tom Waterland concluded that South Moresby was "a clear-cut issue." I was kitchen help, cooking breakfasts and trying to prepare dinner when the guests were kayaking or ashore with Huck, while the galley pitched and rolled in the Hecate Strait. The party from California called me "the girl," while I prepared abalone the way Miles had taught me the year before in Windy Bay. "What do you do when you're not cooking here?" asked one of the more inquisitive visitors.

It's a good idea not to let people who call you "girl" get away with it. "Until June, I was senior policy adviser to the federal minister of the environment, and I'm a lawyer, but I'm thinking of writing a book."

33

EPILOGUE

THE FIRELIGHT FLICKERED ACROSS FACES DECORATED with paint and glowing dark in the reflected light of the fire. Guujaaw warmed the skin of his drum against the flames. When the drum's surface had just the right tension, when it gave to his drumstick with the proper reverberating elasticity, then Guujaaw burned sage as an offering to the ancestors, lifted his drum, and began to sing. His song rose to a night sky and stars I could not recognize, for we were not below the heavens of Haida Gwaii.

The Haida music he made was a Strong Heart song for the warriors who sat in a large circle around him. They understood no Haida, neither did they understand English. His song was a gift to the Kaiapo warriors of the Xingu. We were in the Amazon Basin of Brazil, which is threatened with dams and flooding, with deforestation and burning, gold mining and mercury poisoning. The Kaiapo Indians of Brazil are threatened with extinction, as are the thousands – no, millions – of lifeforms whose home is the tropical forest.

In the fourteen years it took to save South Moresby, one quarter of the world's forests were logged. The tropical forest is devoured at a rate of 74,000 acres a day. Tropical rain forests cover only 7 per cent of the earth's surface, but contain half of all the species of plants and animals on this planet. And they are disappearing at a rate of 74,000 acres every day.

In Brazil, the forests are not even cut down for timber, but are burned just to get them out of the way. The smoke rises constantly in the dry season – one of those few human activities visible from orbiting satellites. The burning of tropical forests and deforestation around the world contributes approximately 20 per cent to climate warming, the so-called greenhouse effect. Deforestation around the globe threatens us all. Richard St Barbe Baker, known during his life as "the man of the trees," said, "We are skinning the planet alive." Yes, we are.

Medicine men from the plains of the United States told the Haida that saving South Moresby was essential to turn the tide of plantery destruction. If they could save Gwaii Haanas, their prophecies said, the whole world would go that way. But, if they couldn't save it, it would ripple back on the earth. But we don't have time to spend fourteen years saving every precious island of wilderness. We do not have fourteen years to save our earth island. We only have now.

Huck managed to travel deep into the jungles of Sarawak in Malaysia, to meet the embattled Penan people. Like the Haida, they have been blocking logging roads, trying to preserve their homeland. The forests of Sarawak on the island of Borneo are disappearing at the fastest rate in the world: three hectares every minute of every day, seven days a week, every day of the year. The forests of Malaysia are being chopped down to make cheap plywood, used once in construction – concrete forms, scaffolding – and then thrown away. Part of the forest goes to make disposable chopsticks. The forests of Southeast Asia are disappearing into the yawning maw of Japan.

The forests of Thailand are nearly all gone. The King declared a moratorium on logging when less than 17 per cent of his kingdom's forests remained. When Malaysia's forests are all gone, the loggers will finish off

Indonesia. The Philippines' forests have been felled. The rain forests of the Amazon are disappearing. Who will save them?

The least powerful people, the poorest, are those with the most to lose. Indigenous people around the world are in the frontline to save their homes, the forests: Paulinho Paiakan of the Kaiapo in Brazil, Harrison Ngo in Sarawak, Malaysia, Gary Potts in Temagami, Ontario. Threatened, too, are the people who live in harmony with the forests, such as the rubber tappers of Brazil, once led by Chico Mendes, whose memory fights on to protect the Amazon, even from his grave.

We went to the Amazon in February 1989 to support the indigenous people of Brazil, fighting to protect their home. Several of us were South Moresby veterans: David Suzuki and Tara Cullis, Jeff Gibbs, Guujaaw, and me. In March and April that year, I travelled through the rain forests of peninsular Malaysia with Vicky and with Huck, who has devoted an ever-increasing amount of his life to the preservation of tropical forests and to aid their peoples. Huck's parents came as well. And we rode the rapids of the Tembling River, garishly bright kingfishers daredevil diving from the river banks, giant hornbills flying overhead, and monkeys calling from the canopy.

The South Moresby crusaders stay together despite the miles separating us. Colleen is still waging wilderness campaigns from her battle station in New Denver. Paul George and the growing WC Squared gang mobilizing now for the preservation of tropical and temperate forests. Vicky still raises the alarm over the relentless destruction of Canada's old-growth forests – Carmanah Creek, Clayoquot Sound, the Khutzeymateen and the Stein valleys.

This story was about a small group of people who changed the minds of powerful men; who, against all odds, accomplished what seemed at times to be the impossible. It should inspire us. We need inspiration and courage. We have less time now in which to accomplish more. The planet's natural systems – atmosphere, ocean, biomass – are all under stress: They are tearing at the edges – a hole in the ozone layer, dead seals on Nordic coastlines, advancing deserts, and topsoil blown away by the ton to silt and clog the life of countless rivers. We have to change the way people, especially those in rich, industrialized countries such as Canada, do just about everything. We have to change the way we grow crops, the ways we waste energy, the way we rip at the planet never thinking of the cost, the consequences.

The earth is our home. Bill Reid wrote of South Moresby: "These shining islands may be the signposts that point the way to a renewed harmonious relationship with this, the only world we're ever going to have." That was what South Moresby was about. And if it made sense to preserve those fragile islands at the edge, then it makes sense to preserve the gentle planet on which they float, somewhere between ocean wave and brilliant sky. Earth is calling us home.

WHERE ARE THEY NOW?

*A guide for those interested in supporting the work of
the key crusaders of **Paradise Won**.*

In 1988 the Governor General's Conservation Award was presented jointly to **John Broadhead, Tom McMillan**, and **Miles Richardson** (who declined the award), for their work in preserving the forests and waters of South Moresby.

Tom McMillan lost his seat in the House of Commons in the 1988 federal election, and in 1989 he was appointed Canada's Consul General to Boston, Mass.

John Broadhead (J.B.) remains very active in various B.C. conservation issues through Earthlife Canada.
Earthlife Canada, Box 592, Queen Charlotte City, B.C., V0T 1S0.

Miles Richardson, as president, and **Guujaw** are the representatives of the Haida Nation in the continuing negotiations with the federal government over the terms of the final agreement on the South Moresby National Park Reserve.
Council of the Haida Nation, Box 589, Massett, Haida Gwaii, B.C., V0T 1M0.

Thom Henley (Huck) continues his work with Rediscovery and is author of the 1988 book, published by the Western Canada Wilderness Committee, *Rediscovery: Ancient Pathways, New Directions.* He is also involved in the effort to protect the rain forests of Brazil and Southeast Asia.
Rediscovery International, 343 Sylvia Street, Victoria, B.C., V8V 1C5.

In 1988 **Vicky Husband** won the prestigious United Nations Global 500 Award. She is now director of the Sierra Club of Western Canada. Vicky and **Sharon Chow** remain active, through the Sierra Club, in B.C.'s many environmental issues.
The Sierra Club of Western Canada, 314-620 View Street, Vancouver, B.C., V8W 1J6.

Paul George and **Adriane Carr** are both still working with WC Squared. Among its many activities, in 1989 the organization produced the book *Carmanah: Artistic Visions of an Ancient Rainforest.*

Western Canada Wilderness Committee, 1200 Hornby Street, Vancouver, B.C., V6Z 2E2.

Colleen McCrory, who won the Governor General's Conservation Award in 1984, was awarded, in 1990, *Equinox* magazine's first Citation for Environment Achievement. She and **Grant Copeland**, who produced a new B.C. wilderness map in 1988, are still both very active in B.C.'s environmental movement.

Valhalla Wilderness Society, Box 284, New Denver, B.C., V0G 1S0.

Gregg Sheehy has left the Canadian Nature Federation to become a private consultant in Ottawa, and **Kevin McNamee** has left the Canadian Parks and Wilderness Society to join the CNF as its protected areas coordinator.

Canadian Nature Federation, 453 Sussex Drive, Ottawa, Ont., K1N 6Z4.

Canadian Parks and Wilderness Society, 160 Bloor Street East, Toronto, Ont., M4W 1B9.

Margo Hearne heads up the Islands Protection Society, which continues its work on Haida Gwaii, challenging the use of pesticides and the proposed opening of a gold mine on the Yakoun River, and protecting the bird sanctuary near Massett.

Islands Protection Society, Box 557, Massett, B.C., V0T 1M0.

Monte Hummel, as president of World Wildlife Fund Canada, organized a campaign that raised $80,000 to help defray the expenses of the South Moresby crusaders. He now heads up the Endangered Spaces campaign, which is attempting to establish a network of protected areas in Canada by the year 2000, and was the editor of the 1989 book *Endangered Spaces.*

World Wildlife Fund Canada, 60 St. Clair Avenue East, Toronto, Ont., M4T 1N5.

Since 1989 **Elizabeth May** has been volunteer executive director of Cultural Survival (Canada), an organization set up to protect threatened tropical and temperate forests and their inhabitants around the world. In February 1990, she also became the Ottawa representative to the Sierra Club of Canada.

Cultural Survival (Canada), 1 Nicholas Street, Suite 420, Ottawa, Ont., K1N 7B7.

Sierra Club of Canada, 1 Nicholas Street, Suite 421, Ottawa, Ont., K1N 7B7.